In the Matter of Color

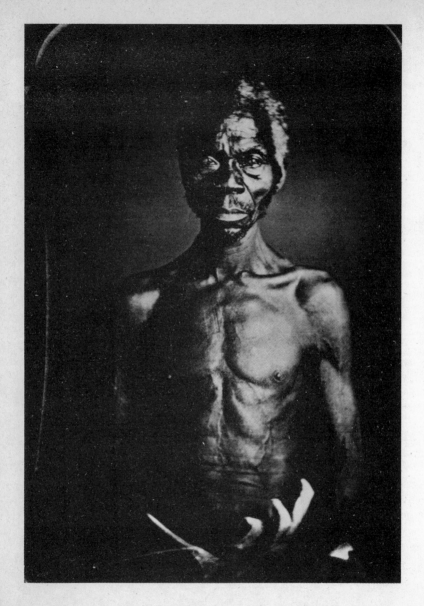

A daguerreotype of Renty, a "Congo" slave on B. F. Taylor's plantation, Columbia, South Carolina.

In the Matter of Color

RACE AND THE
AMERICAN LEGAL PROCESS

The Colonial Period

A. LEON HIGGINBOTHAM, JR.

OXFORD UNIVERSITY PRESS
Oxford   New York   Toronto   Melbourne

Oxford University Press
Oxford   London   Glasgow
New York   Toronto   Melbourne   Wellington
Nairobi   Dar es Salaam   Cape Town
Kuala Lumpur   Singapore   Jakarta   Hong Kong   Tokyo
Delhi   Bombay   Calcutta   Madras   Karachi

Copyright © 1978 by Oxford University Press, Inc.
First published by Oxford University Press, New York, 1978
First issued as an Oxford University Press paperback, 1980

Library of Congress Cataloging in Publication Data

Higginbotham, A. Leon, 1928-
   In the matter of color.
   Bibliography: p.
   Includes index.
   CONTENTS: [1]   The colonial period.
   1.   Afro-Americans–Legal status, laws, etc.–History.
I.   Title.
KF4757.H53   342'.73'087   76-51713
ISBN 0-19-502745-0 pbk. (v. 1)

printing, last digit: 10 9 8 7

Printed in the United States of America

To the memory of my mother,
Emma Lee Douglass Higginbotham

Peace between races is not to be secured by degrading one race and exalting another, by giving power to one race and withholding it from another; but by maintaining a state of equal justice between all classes.

—Frederick Douglass's reply to
President Andrew Johnson,
February 7, 1866

PREFACE

T HIS book has been "in the writing" for almost ten years. But if isolated personal incidents really do play the dramatic role in redirecting lives they often seem to have played, I have to go back for the book's very beginnings to a painful memory that comes out of my freshman year at college. Perhaps it was not the incident itself, but the "proper" legal basis upon which the personal affront was rationalized that may turn out to have been the seed out of which this work has slowly grown.

In 1944, I was a 16-year-old freshman at Purdue University— one of twelve black civilian students. If we wanted to live in West Lafayette, Indiana, where the university was located, solely because of our color the twelve of us at Purdue were forced to live in a crowded private house rather than, as did most of our white class-mates, in the university campus dormitories. We slept barracks-style in an unheated attic.

One night, as the temperature was close to zero, I felt that I could suffer the personal indignities and denigration no longer. The United States was more than two years into the Second World War, a war our government had promised would "make the world safe for democracy." Surely there was room enough in that world, I told myself that night, for twelve black students in a northern univer-sity in the United States to be given a small corner of the on-campus heated dormitories for their quarters. Perhaps all that was needed was for one of us to speak up, to make sure the administration knew exactly how a small group of its students had been treated by those charged with assigning student housing.

The next morning, I went to the office of Edward Charles Elliot, president of Purdue University, and asked to see him. I was given an appointment.

At the scheduled time I arrived at President Elliot's office, neatly (but not elegantly) dressed, shoes polished, fingernails clean, hair cut short. Why was it, I asked him, that blacks—and blacks alone—had been subjected to this special ignominy? Though there were larger issues I might have raised with the president of an American university (this was but ten years before *Brown* v. *Board of Education*) I had not come that morning to move mountains, only to get myself and eleven friends out of the cold. Forcefully, but nonetheless deferentially, I put forth my modest request: that the black students of Purdue be allowed to stay in some section of the state-owned dormitories; segregated, if necessary, but at least not humiliated.

Perhaps if President Elliot had talked with me sympathetically that morning, explaining his own impotence to change things but his willingness to take up the problem with those who could, I might not have felt as I did. Perhaps if he had communicated with some word or gesture, or even a sigh, that I had caused him to review his own commitment to things as they were, I might have felt I had won a small victory. But President Elliot, with directness and with no apparent qualms, answered, "Higginbotham, the law doesn't require us to let colored students in the dorm, and you either accept things as they are or leave the University immediately."

As I walked back to the house that afternoon, I reflected on the ambiguity of the day's events. I had heard, on that morning, an eloquent lecture on the history of the Declaration of Independence, and of the genius of the founding fathers. That afternoon I had been told that under the law the black civilian students at Purdue University could be treated differently from their 6,000 white classmates. Yet I knew that by nightfall hundreds of black soldiers would be injured, maimed, and some even killed on far flung battlefields to make the world safe for democracy. Almost like a mystical experience, a thousand thoughts raced through my mind as I walked across campus. I knew then I had been touched in a way I had never been touched before, and that one day I would have to return to the most disturbing element in this incident—how a legal system that proclaims "equal justice for all" could simultaneously deny even a semblance of dignity to a 16-year-old boy who had committed no wrong. Shortly thereafter, I left Purdue University and transferred to Antioch College. Ultimately, I chose the law as my vocation, and in 1952 I graduated from Yale Law School.

As I write this preface, I see an America still struggling with the problem of race; but I also see a nation that has made extraordinary progress since President Elliot told me to pack up and leave Purdue University if I would not accept that my having to sleep in an unheated attic was simply a matter of color.

As the idea for this work grew, I became intensely eager to acquaint myself with the part the legal process played, to learn the lessons of racial history, to ascertain to what extent the law itself had created the mores of racial repression. Did the law merely perpetuate old biases and prejudices? Or had it been an instrument first in establishing and only later in attacking injustices based on color? During my early years, I focused primarily on current events—what had happened last month, last year, or the last decade. As I was drawn deeper, I became aware that I would have to start at least as far back as the colonial period to understand the interrelationship of the law and color in America.

Today, America is finally at the point where it has the potential to resolve in a positive way so many of the problems of the past. If we dare ignore this opportunity, the alternative will be to drift into further polarization. The ultimate direction in which this nation moves may well depend on how it interprets the legacy—both to its black citizens and to its white—of centuries of slavery assured and guaranteed by the law.

On December 1, 1862, in the midst of our fierce civil war over this very issue, Abraham Lincoln in his Message to Congress said:

> Fellow citizens, we cannot escape history. We . . . will be remembered in spite of ourselves. No personal significance or insignificance can spare one or another of us. The fiery trial through which we pass will light us down in honor or dishonor to the latest generation . . . We . . . hold the power and bear the responsibility.

Perhaps this volume will help us better understand the history we cannot escape and cause us to assume the responsibility we owe to our future.

February 12, 1978
United States Court House
Independence Mall
Philadelphia, Pennsylvania

ACKNOWLEDGMENTS

IN this pursuit, I have been aided and inspired by hundreds through their writings, their concerns, their questions, and even the confusions and contradictions among scholars. It is impossible to pay tribute to all who have helped, and even more difficult to acknowledge the importance of so many individual contributions.

I have had the privilege of teaching at Yale University, at the University of Hawaii, at the University of Michigan Law School, and, for a period of years, at both the Graduate School and the Law School of the University of Pennsylvania. At each of these institutions, I have had the opportunity to probe the issues of race and law. Dr. Renée C. Fox and Dr. Marvin Wolfgang, respectively present and past Chairmen of the Department of Sociology at the University of Pennsylvania, have listened with patience, have responded with keen insight, and have always asked the critical questions forcing me to focus on the sociology of law. Deans Bernard Wolfman and Louis Pollak of the University of Pennsylvania Law School gave me the opportunity to teach students who seldom were satisfied with the conventional "answers." Dean Pollak read several chapters and, as is his custom, forced me to delineate issues more precisely. Professor Charles Davis, Chairman of the Department of Afro-American Studies at Yale University, reassured me throughout of the importance of the project. Dr. Mary Frances Berry, Professor of History and Law of the University of Colorado and presently on leave to serve as Assistant Secretary for Education with HEW, has synthesized the insights of both history and law. She would never let me proffer the answer that would satisfy only one of those disciplines.

Finally, in 1975, when I considered the first volume completed, the manuscript was submitted to Professor John Hope Franklin of the University of Chicago and Professor Benjamin Quarles of Morgan State University. Each read the manuscript with painstaking care. When they asked me why I had not focused on South Carolina and Georgia, and how I could justify waiting until the second volume to explain the uniqueness of Pennsylvania, I conceded, with difficulty, the soundness of their criticisms. I delayed the book another two years, as I researched thousands of additional cases, statutes, and original documents.

In many respects I have been exploring an era of 300 years duration; thus, a project of this magnitude could never have been finished by just one person even working full time over several years. Because of my judicial obligations, six persons have spent at various times at least one full year researching with me one aspect of the subject. They are David Rigney and Brenda Spears, now of the New York bar; Anne Whatley, now of the Pennsylvania bar; Michael Fitts, who took one year's leave from Yale Law School; Wendy Blank, who deferred entering law school for one year; and Nancy Fullam, who worked full time indefatigably even while going to college. All, after their "graduation," have kept in touch and have given to their successors the assurance that the project was worth the demanding effort. Over the years, there has been generated a rare, precious friendship and dedication, with them and others.

Special mention must be made of Vance Fort, Joanne Doddy, Linda Lee Walker, R. Merinda Davis, Denise Shaw, Charisse Lillie-Andrews, Vanessa Lawrence, Yolanda Pizarro, Sally Fullam, and Kathryn S. Lewis who worked during various summers. Law clerks Thomas Gannon, S.J., Edward Dennis, Robert Potamkin, James Manning, and Jason Shargel were continually looking over our shoulders, challenging even basic assumptions.

I know that the present volume does not reflect the scope of the research over the years, but I am hopeful future volumes will record the results of these efforts.

Four secretaries have also given their very best. With patience they came to accept the fact that the "last draft" would always be revised. They are Mrs. Essie M. Brock, Ms. Dorothea Lutz, Mrs. Dolores Lewis, and Mrs. Bettie C. Lee. During this long period

Dorothea Lutz became our resident librarian on all colonial matters, as well.

Many librarians have given to me that special care that makes scholars want to continue to explore. The sensitive staffs of the libraries of the University of Pennsylvania have displayed unlimited patience. Richard Sloane, Nancy Arnold, Paul Gay, and Jeanne Williams of the Law School library tolerated my belatedness in returning books and found others we thought never existed. Special mention must be made also of Marlene McGuirl, Director of the American-British Law Division of the Library of Congress, and Daniel Boorstin, Librarian at the Library of Congress; Professor Carl Lamberg-Karlovsky, Director of the Peabody Museum of Archaeology and Ethnology at Harvard University; Dr. Michael R. Winston, Director, and Dr. Thomas C. Battle, Curator of .Manuscripts, Moorland-Spingarn Research Center, Howard University; and the Chester County Historical Society and Culver Pictures. George Beach worked intensely on the jacket design and even provided colonial era clippings from his extensive private library. Professor Robert Engs of the University of Pennsylvania, Gilbert Ware of Drexel University, John Blassingame of Yale University, and Philip Foner of Lincoln University were sounding boards and superb critics, and like all others in this field I have learned much from the many penetrating and thoughtful books and articles by professors Foner, Blassingame, and Ware. When my spirits were low, Chief Justice Earl Warren and the late Chief Judge William Hastie of the United States Court of Appeals for the Third Circuit kept noting their continued interest and urged me to finish the task. Without the generosity of two foundations the project would have floundered years ago. Both the Rockefeller Foundation and the William Penn Foundation gave support through grants made to the University of Pennsylvania for secretarial and research assistance. John and Chara Haas, as well as Victor Potamkin, were more than benefactors to the University; they also had faith that the task was worth it.

By their attention to detail, the staff at Oxford University Press has demonstrated to me why, for more than 500 years, Oxford has been a leader of excellence in its field. I am privileged to have had Susan Rabiner as my editor. She has that persistent skepticism of lawyers, believing that in their writing they often mask rather than clarify what they mean, and she had the ability to help me make the obscure more readable. With her dedication as a proficient copy editor, Ellen Royer painstakingly proofread and helped finalize the manuscript. I wish also to thank Bernice Colt for her excellent index.

Above all others, I must thank my family: Jeanne, my wife; my children Stephen, Karen and Kenneth; and my father A. L. Higginbotham, Sr., for their patience and tolerance of more than ten years as I retreated to probe matters two centuries old while neglecting their priorities, preferences, and needs of the day. My hope is that in some small way this book will provide a legacy for my children's generation that can partially justify my frequent absences. It pains me most that my mother, who believed in and heard so much about "the book," is not here to see it. Born in rural Virginia, where she faced daily the harshest of racial barriers, she developed nevertheless an amazing fortitude and confidence that the worst of the past could be overcome and that the future would be what we sought to make it.

SUMMARY OF CONTENTS

Preface   vii

Acknowledgements   xi

Part One: RACE AND THE AMERICAN LEGAL PROCESS

   1   Introduction   3

Part Two: THE BLACK EXPERIENCE IN COLONIAL AMERICA

   2   Virginia: The Leader   19

   3   Massachusetts: Slaves and the Pilgrims   61

   4   New York: From Half-Freedom to Slavery   100

   5   South Carolina: White Minority/Black Majority   151

   6   Georgia: From Antislavery to Slavery   216

   7   Pennsylvania: The Quaker and German Liberal Influence   267

Part Three: THE ENGLISH EXPERIENCE WITH SLAVERY

   8   The Setting   313

9   The Case of James Sommersett, A Negro   333

10   The Legacy of Sommersett   356

Part Four: THE REVOLUTION

11   The Declaration of Independence: A Self-Evident Truth
      or A Self-Evident Lie?   371

Epilogue: IN THE MATTER OF COLOR   390

Appendix: A Note on the Indentured Servant System   392

Bibliography   397

Notes   405

Index   481

Table of Cases   511

Creditor and Estate Rights in Slaves: Were Slaves Like Horses and Dogs or Like Real Estate?   50

  Rights of Servants   53

  Nonrights of Slaves and Blacks   55

Virginia: An Evaluation   58

3   Massachusetts: Slaves and the Pilgrims   61

Participation in the International Slave Trade   62

Enslavement as Punishment for Crime   66

  The Special Brand of Indian Enslavement   68

Black Slavery in New England   71

Changing Legal Concepts of Blacks   78

  Black Codes in Massachusetts   80

Movement for Abolition   82

Efforts to Enact a Constitution   89

Quock Walker: Did It Abolish Slavery in Massachusetts?   91

Massachusetts: An Evaluation   98

4   New York: From Half-Freedom to Slavery   100

The New Netherlands Experience   100

  The Dutch Settlers: Humane Masters?   100

  The Half-Freedom Status   105

  The Ordinances and Judicial Rulings of New Netherland   109

The Early New York Experience   114

  Statutory Recognition of Slavery Under English Rule   114

  Procedural Rights of Slaves and Blacks   123

  Blacks as Defendants   124

  The Relevance of Religion   126

  Manumission in New York   128

TABLE OF CONTENTS

Preface vii

Acknowledgements xi

Part One: RACE AND THE AMERICAN LEGAL
PROCESS

1 Introduction 3

Part Two: THE BLACK EXPERIENCE IN COLONIAL
AMERICA

2 Virginia: The Leader 19

The Beginning 20

The Early Cases 22

*The Fear of an Alliance Among White Indentured Servants,
Indians and Blacks* 26

The Special Treatment of Indians 31

*Codification of Prejudice: the Early Legislative
Experience* 32

*Christianity: Meaningful for Whites but Irrelevant
for Blacks* 36

*White Male Domination and Interracial Sexual
Relations* 40

Manumission and Emancipation 47

Slave Revolts and Legislative Reactions   131

*Revolutionary War and the Impetus Toward
Abolition*   135

Blacks in New York After the War   138

The Emancipation Statute   143

New York: An Evaluation   148

5   South Carolina: White Minority/Black Majority   151

Introduction   151

*The Decline of Indentured Servitude for Whites and the
Escalation of Slavery for Blacks*   154

White Bondage in Colonial South Carolina   154

Indian Slavery   160

*Black Slavery: "When I have Land, What shall I
doe with it?"*   162

The Early Colonial Period   162

*The Later Colonial Period: Predominance of a
Rice Economy*   165

Legislative Enforcement of Racial Slavery   167

Early Legislation, 1690-1739   169

Freehold vs. Chattel: Was There a Difference?   169

The Limitation of Slaves' Liberties   170

The pass system   171

Trading   172

Property held by slaves   173

Hiring out   174

Manumission   175

The Runaway Slave   176

Tensions in Dealing with Criminal Slaves   179

The magistrate's court   179

Criminal offenses and penalties 181

Detection of criminal offenses 183

*Compensation and incentives to enforce criminal
penalties* 184

Slave assaults 186

Protection of the Slave 187

*Legislative Efforts to Raise Revenue and Restrict the
Black Population* 190

Slave Resistance: The Stono Rebellion of 1739 192

The 1740 Code and Subsequent Slave Legislation 193

*The 1740 Slave Code: To Be Kept in Due
Subjection and Obedience* 193

The 1751 Slave Legislation 198

Christianity and Slavery 199

Free Blacks in Colonial South Carolina 201

Number and Origin of Free Blacks 201

Legal Status of Free Blacks 203

The Judicial System and Slavery 208

*General Conditions of Slaves During the Colonial
Period* 210

*The Practice of Dealing with Slaves as Chattel
Property* 211

The Court's Protection of White Servants 212

South Carolina: An Evaluation 214

6   Georgia: From Antislavery to Slavery   216

The Importance of Georgia 216

*Was Georgia Founded with Humanitarian Motives
Toward Blacks?* 216

*Origins of the Antislavery Law: The Georgia
Charter* 218

The Goals of Georgia 220

The 1735 Antislavery Law 222

*The Decision to Ban Slavery: A Process of
Amoral Decision-Making* 222

Provisions of the Antislavery Law 225

*Lackadaisical Enforcement of the 1735 Antislavery
Law* 227

*Judicial Antagonism to the Prohibition of Slavery:
A Study in Judicial Activism Against Blacks* 227

*Judicial Disregard of Explicit Provisions of the
1735 Law* 230

Slavery During the Antislavery Period 235

The Failure of the Indentured Servant System 236

The Growing Political Opposition to Slavery 241

The Burden of Competition 247

The Introduction of Slavery: The 1750 Slavery Law 248

Restraints of the 1750 Law 249

The Slave Codes of Georgia 252

The 1755 Slave Code 252

Protection of the Slave's Life Under the Code 253

Assaults on Slaves 255

Slaves as Defendants 256

Trial Procedures for Slaves 257

Patrol Systems 259

The 1765 and 1770 Slave Codes 262

Laws On the Hiring of Blacks 264

Georgia: An Evaluation 266

7 Pennsylvania: The Quaker and German Liberal
Influence 267

Introduction   267

   Slavery in Pre-1700 Pennsylvania   269

   Comparative Legal Status of 17th-Century White Servants and Blacks   277

   Statutory Restrictions on Blacks: The Post-1700 Era   280

   Judicial Policy Toward Blacks   288

     To Make "Slaves Examples of Terror to Others of their Complexion"   290

  Manumission of Slaves   292

   Legislative Abolition of Slavery   299

   Legislative Refinements of the 1780 Act   303

    The 1782 Act   303

    The 1788 Act   304

  Pennsylvania's Tolerance and Opposition to Slavery: An Evaluation   305

Part Three: THE ENGLISH EXPERIENCE WITH SLAVERY

8   The Setting   313

   The Economics of English Slavery   316

   The Developing English Case Law of Slavery   320

   The Influence of the Abolitionists   329

9   The Case of James Sommersett, A Negro   333

   Hargrave's Arguments in Behalf of Sommersett   336

   The Legal Precedents for and Against Slavery   338

   Mr. Dunning, Counsel for Stuart and Knowles   344

   Mr. Davy, Counsel for Sommersett   347

   Lord Mansfield: An Able and Independent Jurist   348

   The Decision-Making Process   351

The Significance and Impact of Sommersett   353

10   The Legacy of Sommersett   356

*The English Abolition of the International Slave Trade
and of Slavery*   363

Part Four: THE REVOLUTION

11   The Declaration of Independence: A Self-Evident Truth
or A Self-Evident Lie?   371

Roots of the Revolution   371

The White Colonists' Perception of Their Enslavement   375

*The Moral Antecedents for Challenging, in 1776,
the Continuance of Slavery*   377

*The Discarded July 2 Draft: A Futile Diatribe on the
International Slave Trade*   380

The Deleted Clause   380

*The Impact of the Declaration of Independence:
"The Tendency of a Principle to Expand Itself
to the Limit of its Logic"*   383

Epilogue: In the Matter of Color   390

Appendix: A Note on the Indentured Servant System   392

Bibliography   397

Notes   405

Index   481

Table of Cases   511

I

Race and the
American Legal Process

1

INTRODUCTION

"Why of all of the multitudinous groups of people in this country [do] you have to single out Negroes and give them this separate treatment."

> —Oral argument before the United States Supreme Court by Thurgood Marshall, then Chief Counsel for the Plaintiffs in Brown v. Board of Education.[1]

AT approximately 7:17 P.M., April 4, 1968, an assassin fired a shot mortally wounding Martin Luther King.[2] Late that evening I received a call from the President, Lyndon Johnson, who had appointed me four years earlier to the United States District Court, asking me to come to the White House early the next morning to discuss with others who were being called the national significance of Dr. King's death. Though the President acted quickly in collecting his counselors for a meeting the next morning, another section of the nation would not wait the night to express its own response to this national tragedy. Ten blocks from the White House, buildings in the largely black ghettoes of Washington, D.C. were already in flames.[3] As the painful night lingered on, news reports indicated that more and more people had taken to the streets, many striking out irrationally and in anger, in city after city, in response to the senseless death of the prophet of nonviolence.[4]

President Johnson opened the meeting at the White House the next morning with the question, "What can we do now?"

There were many thoughtful responses. Some talked of strengthening civil rights legislation, others spoke of further improving manpower programs, still others argued for additional condemnations of racism. The idea for appointing yet another presidential commission was also introduced. Although the discussion was calm and dispassionate, a deep sense of shared pain was apparent. Most of us present had known Dr. King intimately and had worked with him in the attempt to obliterate racism from American life.

As I listened and reflected on the various suggestions made from such thoughtful and well-meaning people, I kept thinking of the question Thurgood Marshall had asked the Supreme Court thirteen years earlier: "Why," he had asked, "of all the multitudinous groups of people in this country, do you have to single out Negroes and give them this separate treatment." That morning, sitting in the White House, I knew there was an indisputable nexus between the dark shadow of repression under which, historically, most American blacks have lived and the rioting occurring within ten blocks of the White House. Why, I thought to myself, in the land of the free and the home of the brave, had even brave blacks so often failed to get free? Why had that very legal process that had been devised to protect the rights of individuals against the will of the government and the whim of the majority been often employed so malevolently against blacks? What were the options that ought to have been exercised years ago, even centuries ago, to narrow those disparities in meted-out justice that had periodically—and had now once more—kindled black hatred and white fear?

In the company of the great lawyers present at the President's meeting—Supreme Court Associate Justice Thurgood Marshall and Attorney General Ramsey Clark—as well as the other notable government and public officials—Cabinet officer Robert C. Weaver, Civil Rights leaders Roy Wilkins, Whitney Young, Clarence Mitchell, Reverend Leon Sullivan, and Vice President Humphrey[5] —it was inevitable that I would ponder how the legal process had contributed to this malaise. For in 1968, in this nation's 192nd year, things could have been different.[6] If the legal process had been racially just, the nation in the 1960s would not have been torn asunder as it was by the unrelenting demands by blacks for dignity and equal justice under the law pulling against the stubborn resistance of those who had been conditioned to believe in the status quo as the ultimate expression of "liberty and justice for all."[7]

The institutionalized injustice of racial apartness had first brought Martin Luther King to the forefront and now, ultimately, had brought him to his death.

Particularly during this Bicentennial era, it is appropriate to assess the interrelationship of race and the American legal process.[8] This nation has just celebrated its 200th birthday in a most grandiose fashion. Conventions have been held in almost every town to reaffirm those "self-evident truths," and the oratory will continue to 1987, the 200th anniversary of the United States Constitution. As praise is heaped on the great leaders of yesterday, and as some laud 1776 as the Golden Era of liberty, it is often suggested that if only today's leaders had the integrity and character of Jefferson, Franklin, John Adams, Washington, and Madison, today's racial difficulties might be quickly resolved. Few have had the temerity to contradict this general but misdirected consensus, for it is bad bicentennial form to refer to the fact that many of America's founding fathers owned slaves and that most, either directly or indirectly, profited from the evil institution that enslaved black human beings only.

The bicentennial drum roll of revolutionary heroes and events, then, symbolizes one thing to white Americans but quite another to blacks. From a predominantly white perspective, the Declaration of Independence is viewed as former President Nixon described it: "the greatest achievement in the history of man. We are the beneficiaries of that achievement."[9] But who, until recently, did the "we" describe? Not black America. Frederick Douglass, a leading abolitionist who was born a slave, described Independence Day in 1852 from the perspective of blacks and slaves rather than whites and slaveholders:

> This Fourth of July is *yours,* not mine. You may rejoice, I must mourn. To drag a man in fetters to the grand illuminated temple of liberty, and call upon him to join you in joyous anthems, were inhuman mockery and sacriligious irony. . . . I say it with a sad sense of the disparity between us. I am not included within the pale of this glorious anniversary. . . . The blessings in which you, this day, rejoice, are not enjoyed in common. The rich inheritance of justice, liberty, prosperity

and independence, bequeathed by your fathers, is shared by you, not by me. The sunlight that brought light and healing to you, has brought stripes and death to me.[10]

Likewise, from a predominantly white perspective, the pledges of the Preamble to the Constitution honestly set out the largest principles for which the new American legal process would strive.

We the people . . . in order to form a more perfect union, establish justice, . . . promote the general welfare, and secure the blessings of liberty to ourselves and our posterity. . . .

From a black perspective, however, the Constitution's references to justice, welfare, and liberty were mocked by the treatment meted out daily to blacks from the seventeenth to nineteenth centuries through the courts, in legislative statutes, and in those provisions of the Constitution that sanctioned slavery for the majority of black Americans and allowed disparate treatment for those few blacks legally "free."

Further, whatever opening there might have been for one day peacefully redefining "We the people" to include, as it should have in the first place, black Americans, was abruptly closed with the 1857 U.S. Supreme Court decision *Dred Scott* v. *Sandford*. When asked if the phrase "We the people" included black people and whether blacks were embraced in the egalitarian language of the Declaration of Independence, Chief Justice Roger Taney, speaking for the majority, wrote:

[A]t the time of the Declaration of Independence, and when the Constitution of the United States was framed and adopted . . . [blacks] had no rights which the white man was bound to respect.[11]

In effect, Taney had not answered the question. Rather, he had gone back in time in an attempt to determine what the founding fathers had intended, and in so doing, had argued from the untenable position that the Constitution might never be any larger than the restrictive vision of eighteenth-century America.

Thus, for black Americans today—the children of all the hundreds of Kunta Kintes unjustly chained in bondage—the early failure of the nation's founders and their constitutional heirs to share the legacy of freedom with black Americans is at least one factor in America's perpetual racial tensions. Twenty years after the Civil War, over one hundred years after the Declaration of Independence, two hundred fifty years after the first black man set foot in America, in *Huckleberry Finn,* Mark Twain, in a parody of white attitudes, suggested that as late as 1884 many white Americans still failed to perceive blacks as human beings. He writes:

> "Good gracious. Anybody hurt?"
> "No'm. Killed a nigger."
> "Well, it's lucky because sometimes people do get hurt." . . .[12]

This book will treat from a legal standpoint this historically persistent failure of perception. What should have been on the minds of all in power during the seventeenth and eighteenth centuries was the question James Otis raised in his provocative paper of 1764:

> Does it follow that, tis right to enslave a man because he is black?[13]

Specifically, this book will document the vacillation of the courts, the state legislatures, and even honest public servants in trying to decide whether blacks were people, and if so, whether they were a species apart from white humans, the difference justifying separate and different treatment.

I am aware that an analysis of cases, statutes, and legal edicts does not tell the whole story as to why and how this sordid legal tradition managed to establish itself. Nevertheless, there is merit in abolitionist William Goodell's statement: "No people were ever yet found who were better than their laws, though many have been known to be worse."[14]

While I recognize that a view of slavery from the perspective of the law does not make a complete picture,[15] I join in the conclusions of Winthrop D. Jordan when writing on the Colonial period and C. Vann Woodward when writing on the Reconstruction period. Jordan has advised us:

> while statutes usually speak falsely as to actual behavior, they afford probably the best single means of ascertaining what a society thinks behavior ought to be; they sweep up the felt

necessities of the day and indirectly expound the social norm of the legislators.[16]

And C. Vann Woodward has stated:

> I am convinced that law has a special importance in the history of segregation, more importance than some sociologists would allow, and that the emphasis on legal history is justified.[17]

While I do not represent what I put forward here as a complete picture of the practices of the society, that canvas will never be painted unless someone first treats adequately the interrelationship of race and the American legal process.

Obviously, there were several factors that contributed to the inclination of the legal process to treat blacks so differently from all others. Many have written in great detail on some of these factors.[18] For instance, in so many legal decisions, there was the powerful presence of the economics of slavery. The key question for many a righteous and learned community leader was whether it was cheaper to have blacks as slaves or to have blacks as "free" labor. Or, possibly, instead of black slaves would it have been cheaper to have had white indentured servants or white free labor.

The issue of safety and the natural fear of slave revolts was also intertwined in the chain of legal judgments. While never reluctant to protect and maximize their property rights in the slaves, many judges and legislators were reluctant to recognize that slaves had, in their own right, any basic human rights. Many feared that any judicial protection of the slave would trigger further challenges to the legitimacy of the dehumanized status of blacks and slaves. Since the plantations were often in isolated settings and there was an ever threatening possibility that the slaves might rise up and slay their oppressors, any judge whose decision criticized racial injustice might be accused of weakening the master-slave system. For instance, in a famous North Carolina decision *State* v. *Mann*[19] involving the issue of whether or not it was a criminal offense to subject a slave woman to "a cruel and unreasonable battery," the court stated that a slave was to "labor upon a principle of natural duty," to disregard "his own personal happiness," and that the purpose of the legal system was to convince each slave that he had

no will of his own [and that he must surrender] his will in implicit obedience to that of another. Such obedience is the consequence only of uncontrolled authority over the body. There
is nothing else that can operate to produce the effect. The
power of the master must be absolute to render the submission of the slave perfect.[20]

The court emphasized that for the slave "there is no remedy,"
that "[w]e cannot allow the right of the master to be brought into
discussion in the courts of justice. The slave, to remain a slave, must
be made sensible that there is no appeal from his master; that his
power is in no instance usurped; but is conferred by the laws of man
at least, if not by the law of God." The court noted that this unlimited "dominion is essential to the value of slaves as property, and
to the security of the master, and the public tranquility."[21]

The control the court sought was the *total* submission of
blacks. It had incorporated into its law-made morality the psychological conceptions Frederick Douglass subsequently described:

Beat and cuff the slave, keep him hungry and spiritless, and
he will follow the chain of his master like a dog, but feed and
clothe him well, work him moderately and surround him with
physical comfort, and dreams of freedom will intrude. . . .
You may hurl a man so low beneath the level of his kind, that
he loses all just ideas of his natural position, but elevate him
a little, and the clear conception of rights rises to life and
power, and leads him onward.[22]

With only slightly less paranoia, white society feared that
slaves and free blacks would form an alliance with either indentured
servants or poor whites to topple the plantation aristocracy, which
exploited both blacks and poor whites. As the percentage of blacks,
slave or free, increased, the probability of successful rebellions and
revolts became greater. Thus, in examining degrees of repression
one can almost correlate a rise in the black population with an increased level of legal repression.

In terms of moral and religious issues, there was the underlying question of whether or not America had the right to treat differently and more malevolently people whose skins were darker.
From this perspective it became necessary to determine whether

blacks were part of the human family and whether, after they had adopted your "religion," they were then entitled to be treated as equals, or at least less harshly. In a nation "under God" the moral or religious rationale that justified or rejected the institution of slavery had to have been an important factor.[23] But what tortuous moral or religious rationale had to have been devised for a religious people to have tolerated treating black human beings more like horses or dogs than white human beings?[24]

Finally, there was always the issue of whether or not blacks were inherently inferior to whites.[25] If blacks could be perceived as inferior, basically uneducable and inherently venal, it might be intellectually less self-condemnatory to relegate them because of their "lower status" to a subordinate role—either for "their own good" or, as one judge had the audacity to express it, for the good of the total society, whites and blacks alike.[26]

Thus it was that even the man many Americans see as one of the major forces for liberty and equality, Thomas Jefferson, found blacks to be "inferior to whites in the endowments both of body and mind."[27] After comparing the characteristics of the three major races in America, white, black, and red, Jefferson concluded that although the condition of slavery imposed great misery on blacks, the inferiority of the black race was caused by more than mere environmental factors:

> The improvement of the blacks in body and mind, in the first instance of their mixture with the whites, has been observed by everyone, and proves that their inferiority is not the effect merely of their condition of life. . . . This unfortunate difference of color, and perhaps of faculty, is a powerful obstacle to the emancipation of these people.[28]

Yet even during the seventeenth and eighteenth centuries, there were voices that challenged the morality and legality of slavery. In our chapters on Pennsylvania and the Declaration of Independence we note the moral antecedents to the Declaration of Independence; as early as February, 1688 the Germantown Mennonites of Philadelphia had issued a proclamation against slavery, having found it inconsistent with Christian principles. In our chapter on the English experience we deal in detail with the *Sommersett* case as a contrast to the American counterpart sanctioning domestic slavery. In 1772, four years prior to our Declaration of Independence and fifteen years prior to the Constitution, Lord Mansfield, Chief Justice of the King's Bench, said that "the state of slavery is of such a nature that it is incapable of being introduced on any reasons moral or political, . . . It is so odious that nothing can be suffered to support it, but positive law." And with that statement, Lord Mansfield freed the slave, Sommersett, demonstrating that there was no universal view on slavery among the civilized nations of the world.

As we survey in this volume legislative and judicial doctrines, it will be difficult to isolate one and only one factor as the sole explanation for the legislated, adjudicated, and upheld racial deprivation that gained the official approval of the American legal establishment. As in most things, the causal factors were multifaceted. On some occasions the economic concerns seemed the dominating influence, while in other instances a moral or religious aspect appeared to be more significant. But however tightly woven into the history of their country is the legalization of black suppression, many Americans still find it too traumatic to study the true story of racism as it has existed under their "rule of law." For many, the primary conclusion of the National Commission on Civil Disorders is still too painful to hear:

> What white Americans have never fully understood—but what the Negro can never forget—is that white society is deeply implicated in the ghetto. White institutions created it, white institutions maintain it, and white society condones it.[29]

Since the language of the law shields one's consciousness from direct involvement with the stark plight of its victims, the human tragedy of the slavery system does not surface from the mere reading of cases, statutes, and constitutional provisions. Rather it takes a skeptical reading of most of the early cases and statutes to avoid having one's surprise and anger dulled by the casualness with which the legal process dealt with human beings who happened to be slaves. Generally neither the courts nor the legislatures seemed to have been any more sensitive about commercial transactions involving slaves than they were about sales of corn, lumber, horses, or dogs. This casualness is reflected in a perfectly legal and acceptable advertisement of that era:

> One hundred and twenty Negroes for sale—The subscriber has just arrived from Petersburg, Virginia, with one hundred and twenty likely young Negroes of both sexes and every description, which he offers for sale on the most reasonable terms. The lot now on hand consists of plough-boys, several likely and well-qualified house servants of both sexes, several women and children, small girls suitable for nurses, and *several small boys without their mothers.* Planters and traders are earnestly requested to give the subscriber a call previously to making purchases elsewhere, as he is enabled to sell as cheap or cheaper than can be sold by any other person in the trade.

> —Hamburg, South Carolina, Benjamin Davis[30]

The advertisement of Benjamin Davis was not unique; it was typical of thousands of advertisements posted in newspapers and bulletin boards throughout our land. In the *New Orleans Bee* an advertisement noted:

> Negroes for sale—a Negro woman, 24 years of age, and her two children, one eight and the other three years old. Said Negroes will be sold separately or together, as desired. The woman is a good seamstress. She will be sold low for cash, or exchange for groceries. For terms apply to Matthew Bliss and Company, 1 Front Levee.[31]

How could a legal system encourage and sanction such cruelty—cruelty that permitted the sale, as Benjamin Davis bragged, of "several small boys without their mothers"? Was there any justice in a legal process that permitted a mother, twenty-four years of age, to be sold in exchange for groceries and separated from her children, only eight and three years old? Looking past the commercial façade, one sees the advertisement as stating that American laws encouraged the destruction of black families and the selling of human beings. The only criterion was the demand of the marketplace.

In our chapters on Georgia and South Carolina, for example, we cite several statutes that offered rewards to bounty hunters bringing in the scalp and ears of runaway slaves. These statutes, subtly cast in the language of lawyers, can make one oblivious to the fact that the lives of human beings were involved. From one perspective, it appears that these two legislatures were merely defining penalties and granting rewards—just as they would do upon the recovery of an individual's lost property or as a reward for the slaying of a bear or wild coyote. Yet the scalps and the ears referred to in the Georgia and South Carolina statutes were *not* those of wild animals. They were not those of murderers or traitors. They were the scalps and ears of human beings, persons who had committed no crime other than that of seeking that same freedom the colonists declared to be the birthright of all whites.

As I reflect on these statutes, I think of my experiences as a youngster forty years ago viewing the local cowboy and Indian movies. The bad guys—the Indians, naturally—would occasionally scalp some white adult. Always as my friends and I left the movies, we were angry because of the cruelty the Indians had inflicted on those innocent pioneers, who were merely traveling over Indian land. Thus, it was a matter of astonishment to learn as an adult that the legislatures of Georgia, South Carolina and many of the other colonies actually legalized acts as inhumane as those dreamt up by movie producers. Perhaps the movies were fictionalized accounts representing Hollywood screenwriters' vivid imagination. But the colonial statutes were not bits of fiction; they were the reality of the colonial legal process, a process that rewarded those who were willing to scalp and cut off the ears of blacks who dared to seek freedom.

While we recognize today how inhumane and how immoral this legal process was, it seems that Americans would rather distort their history than face the extraordinary brutality to which these advertisements attest and the inadequacy of a system of laws that promoted and sanctioned such brutality.

The legal process has never been devoid of values, preferences, or policy positions. By the very nature of its pronouncements, when the legal process establishes a right of one particular person, group, or institution, it simultaneously imposes a restraint on those whose preferences impinge on the right established. Ultimately, the legal process has always acted as an expression of social control. Professor Vilhelm Aubert has argued that "beneath the veneer of consensus on legal principles, a struggle of interest is going on, and the law is seen as a weapon in the hands of those who possess the power to use it for their own ends."[32]

The mechanisms of control through judicial decisions and statutes span the sanctioning of slavery and the special limitations imposed on free blacks, to the prohibitions against interracial marriage and sexual activity, to the eliminating of the legal significance of blacks' "conversions to Christianity," to generally restricting any activities or aspirations of blacks that might threaten the groups in control. The law is usually perceived as a normative system, founded on a society's custom and convention.

Charles Warren, one of the most distinguished scholars on the history of the Supreme Court, observed:

> The Court is not an organism dissociated from the conditions and history of the times in which it exists. It does not formulate and deliver its opinions in a legal vacuum. Its Judges are not abstract and impersonal oracles, but are men whose views are necessarily, though by no conscious intent, affected by inheritance, education and environment and by the impact of history past and present. . . .[33]

Oliver Wendell Holmes shared this perception:

> The life of the law has not been logic: it has been experience. The felt necessities of the time, the prevalent moral and political theories, intuitions of public policy, avowed or unconscious, even the prejudices which judges share with their fellow-men, have had a good deal more to do than the syllogism in determining the rules by which men should be governed.[34]

In treating the first 200 years of black presence in America, this book will demonstrate how the entire legal apparatus was used by those with the power to do so to establish a solid legal tradition for the absolute enslavement of blacks. It will be an effort to look at this history primarily through the special focus of a legal lens, to examine the pathology of the law, its creation, its sanctioning, its tolerance, and its occasional eradication of the racist practices that caused one group of human beings to receive such special, harsh, and disparate treatment.

Though this book focuses on only six colonies—Virginia, Massachusetts, New York, South Carolina, Georgia, and Pennsylvania—I believe these six provide representative examples of the range of arguments and methods by which laws and judicial decisions specifically governing blacks developed, and by which slavery became entrenched in North American colonies. To be sure, historians can unerringly point to some differences within the colonies not studied here. Nevertheless, I am confident that these six are fair examples of the whole spectrum.

Some might suggest that when probing any pattern of man's inhumanity to man the proper place to start ought to be at the beginning of human history. Be that as it may, a special lesson lies in tracing and trying to understand exactly how the American legal process was able to set its conscience aside and, by pragmatic toadying to economic "needs," rationalize a regression of human rights for blacks. Most interesting will be to see if we can discover how it came to do so during the very period it was displaying such compassion, courage, and even genius in extending and reinforcing as never before the freedom of whites. We might then better understand what many blacks see so clearly—a direct lineage of contemptuous law from the wasteland centuries of slavery, through the hundred years of false equality since the Emancipation Proclamation, to the "confrontation street politics" of the sixties.

Having taught classes on race and the American legal process for several years to students of history and students of law, I can predict that many will find this book painful and that some, defensively, will ask: "Why hasn't he spent as much time on the positive aspects of the American colonial period—a period during which the rights of mankind may have been advanced more than during any other period in history of comparable length?"

My answer to this question is first, that the positive aspects of our colonial tradition have been examined and justly praised. In fact, it may very well be that it was particularly to avoid tarnishing the aura of egalitarianism surrounding the birth of our nation that the negative aspects of this period have been so long ignored. I further recognize that many enduring strengths in the American constitutional and legal process came out of this very colonial period I now criticize, and that it was these strengths that nineteenth-

and twentieth-century black Americans eventually relied upon in their legal struggle for their own liberty.

Second, that the history of the American colonial period is incomplete and dishonest without an examination of its dark side. I write not to encourage racial polarity, anger, or hatred, but instead to heighten our consciousness so that we, both blacks and whites, will understand how the law has contributed to perpetuating villainy on millions of Americans, solely because of their darker color.

In future years I plan to complete at least three additional volumes on the progress of racial justice from 1776 to 1964. These volumes will reveal how, through the legal process, racial injustice was further perpetuated and how, eventually, it was partially eradicated.

II

The Black Experience
in Colonial America

2

VIRGINIA
THE LEADER

A S the homeland of Thomas Jefferson, James Madison, George Washington, and Patrick Henry, Virginia justifiably claims that from the earliest years it singularly provided significant leadership for all the colonies. In many ways, relatively, it was a model of agricultural and economic success as one of the first colonies. It played a major role in precipitating the American Revolution and in shaping the destiny of the new nation after 1776. Yet, tragically, Virginia was also a leader in the gradual debasement of blacks through its ultimate institutionalization of slavery. It pioneered a legal process that assured blacks a uniquely degraded status—one in which the cruelties of slavery and pervasive racial injustice were guaranteed by its laws. Just as they emulated other aspects of Virginia's policies, many colonies would also follow Virginia's leadership in slavery law.

From 1619 to approximately 1660 there appears to have been no systematic effort in Virginia to define broadly the rights or nonrights of blacks. The decisions produced in the occasional judicial cases heard often failed to make clear whether they were simply based on a finding of the facts, of significance only to those involved in that particular litigation, or were they judicial announcements of binding legal principles that unmistakeably set precedents upon which the legal status of all blacks in the colony would be decided. The following pages first review the range of surviving decisions and demonstrate the difficulty in reaching definitive conclusions about the legal status of blacks in the early Virginia colonial era. Later we will see how the deprivations were solidified through the slave laws as Virginia completed the process of the debasement and dehumanization of blacks through a relatively rigid legal process. Finally, in the late eighteenth century it tried to restrain some of the cruelties while at the same time assuring the economic viability of a slavery system that inherently deprived blacks of basic human rights.

The Beginning

about the last of August, there came to Virginia a Dutchman of Warre that sold us twenty Negers.[1]

John Rolfe, Secretary and Recorder of the Virginia colony, made the above entry toward the end of August, 1619. It survives as the earliest known record dating the arrival of blacks at an American colony. These first "Negers," who arrived in Jamestown a year before the Pilgrims landed at Plymouth Rock, had not volunteered for the voyage. Unlike the hopeful Pilgrims, they had been brought to America unwillingly, captives, in fact, of Dutchmen who had apparently seized them from a Spanish ship to sell them to the labor-short colonists.

In 1619, when these first twenty blacks arrived in Jamestown, there was not as yet a statutory process to especially fix the legal standing of blacks. Although the American colonists seemed to have practiced from the very beginning the "same discrimination which white men had practiced against the Negro all along and before any statutes decreed it,"[2] these first blacks were not exposed to the systematic degradation to which later blacks would be subjected. Yet they were not free. Where did they stand? After centuries of investigation and discussion scholars are still unable to agree.

Paradoxically, it has been argued that the capture by the Dutch ship of the twenty blacks who arrived in Jamestown in 1619 was a "godsend" to these blacks. Their removal from the Spanish slave ship altered their permanent slave status under Spanish rule to "something indeterminate and transitory, which 'faded out' or merged automatically . . . into servitude analogous to that of the indentured white servants when they touched Virginia soil."[3] In fact, the status of these first blacks in America was made even more nebulous because of a fascinating mixture of Spanish and English law whereby a Spanish subject who had been christened or baptized was by that act enfranchised or set free under English law and admitted to the privileges of a free person. Since English law governed Virginia in 1619, and since most of the twenty blacks captured by the Spanish had been baptized by their captors, there was legal as well as moral force to the argument that they should be freed.

Although this enfranchisement doctrine was not reported in judicial opinions until the 1677 decisions of the Court of King's Bench in *Butts* v. *Penny*,[4] the concept seems to have been implicitly recognized as early as 1612. A black man, John Philip, was reportedly "baptized" in 1612 in England. As a result, in 1624 the General Court of Virginia ruled that "John Philip A negro, . . . was qualified as a free man and Christian to give testimony, because he had been 'Christened in England 12 years since.' "[5] There is, however, no surviving record of freedom suits instituted by blacks for the short period during which the colonists continued to recognize this special situation in English law.

As far back as 1896, for instance, Philip A. Bruce had asserted that the blacks brought to Virginia in 1619 came as slaves, whereas only six years later, J. C. Ballagh, in *A History of Slavery in Virginia,* contended that they were servants whose statutory enslavement did not begin until 1660.[6] More recently, John Hope Franklin has authoritatively stated, "there is no doubt that the earliest Negroes in Virginia occupied a position similar to that of the white servants in the colony,"[7] and on this same point, Mary and Oscar Handlin note that initially both blacks and whites in Virginia (and in the other colonies) were relatively unfree, that "almost everyone, including tenants and laborers, bore some sort of servile obligation," and that although many of these classes of individuals gradually gained their freedom before 1660, those both black and white who had not were identified and treated as servants rather than slaves.[8]

There is sufficient evidence, then, to consider at least the possibility that these first black Jamestown arrivals, as well as many of those blacks who followed them in the next few decades, were treated by the early Jamestown colonists more or less as additions to the already existing social class into which whites had often been pressed—that of indentured servant. Some scholars have argued that for at least half a century the status of blacks in America remained incompletely defined—socially somewhere at the bottom of the white servant class perhaps, but nowhere near chattel slaves.

Helen Catterall has suggested that an analysis of cases adjudicating the rights and nonrights of poor whites, blacks, and Indians reveals that in a relatively short period judicial recognition of the following strata, in order of social precedence, became apparent.

1. White indentured servants
2. White servants without indentures (of whom there were two classes, those who came voluntarily and those who came involuntarily)
3. Christian black servants
4. Indian servants
5. Mulatto servants (with black or Indian parentage)
6. Indian slaves
7. Black slaves[9]

Just how then did the legal process, haltingly at first and later without hesitation, help fix those social prejudices by which an individual's status was determined solely on the basis of race? For an answer we must look not only at those judicial decisions and legislative enactments setting out the rights and obligations of blacks and slaves in this early period but, as important, at the legislative and judicial restraints applied against whites, including those that first defined the rights and obligations of white indentured servants.*

The Early Cases

The Virginia colonial cases cited hereafter come from the general court, the Court of Chancery, or the Court of Appeals of the colonies. During this period the general court consisted of the governor and council, meeting quarterly in judicial session. The council was in existence in Virginia from the beginning of the colony and its members, as was the governor, were named by the Vir-

* See Appendix, pp. 392-95, A Note on the Indentured Servant System.

ginia Company of London.[10] The general court was the highest distinctively judicial body in the province, but for some years in the earliest period, the general assembly had jurisdiction concurrent with that of this quarterly general court and criminal cases involving life were tried in whichever convened first. In 1641, the civil jurisdiction of the assembly was limited mainly to appellate cases.[11]

Illustrative of the fragile evidence available to determine the status of blacks is the first judicial decision in the colony to make reference to blacks, *Re Davis*. The full official court report reads as follows:

> Hugh Davis to be soundly whipt before an assembly of negroes & others for abusing himself to the dishonor of God and shame of Christianity by defiling his body in lying with a negro which fault he is to actk Next sabbath day.[12]

The *Davis* case raises more issues than it answers. As reported, it fails to reveal Davis's race or legal status: freeman, indentured servant, or slave? The decision notes that Davis's "mate" was black, but the court does not disclose that person's sex or legal status. And, finally, it gives us no clues to the significance of Davis's public whipping before an "assembly of negroes and others."

Although the full picture can never be reconstructed, some of its elements can be reasonably assumed. First, because Davis's mate was described as a "negro," but no corresponding racial identification was made of Davis, it can be inferred that Davis was white. The references to shame in the context of Christian doctrine suggest a second factor that must be considered—the impact of religious doctrine on the colonial legal system. Davis's and his partner's crime was more than an infraction of colonial codes; their behavior was contrary to that allowed by the church.

From *Davis* alone, it would be difficult and unwise to proffer any theory to explain the impact and relevance of the court's use of the racial term "negro." However, the colonists' perception of blacks as inferior becomes more apparent when other cases such as *Re Sweat*,[13] decided in 1640, are scrutinized. As in the *Davis* case, *Sweat* raises more questions and leaves us with more ambiguities than it resolves.

In *Sweat* the defendant "Robert Sweat hath begotten with

child a negro woman servant," belonging to Lieutenant Sheppard. The court ruled that:

> [T]he said negro woman shall be whipt at the whipping post and the said *Sweat* shall tomorrow in the forenoon do public penance for his offense at *James city* church in the time of devine service according to the laws of *England* in that the case provided.

Although she was described as a "negro woman servant," it is unclear whether use of the term "servant" is conclusive evidence that the woman was not a slave. The mere word "servant" does not precisely indicate the nature of the servitude. Conceivably, the woman could have had a status equal to that of white servants, with the court's use of the word "negro" merely descriptive of the woman's color, not her station. It is just as conceivable that "servant" and "slave" were terms used interchangeably.

Robert Sweat's race is not mentioned, but the failure to designate it again probably indicates that he was white. If one assumes Sweat was white, it becomes necessary to consider whether the racial difference of the parties had any impact on the different punishment imposed. Was public whipping the usual punishment for an unwed mother, white or black, and "public penance" the usual punishment for an unwed father, revealing judicial prejudice against women in general rather than against blacks? Can we believe that if the races of the parties had been reversed, the white woman would have been whipped and the black impregnator let off with public penance? Or, was the whipping of a black woman merely another example of the racial disparity being created in the legal process? In all probability, *Sweat* symbolized the burgeoning judicial tendency toward racially inspired disparities in the punishment of blacks and whites who had committed the same offense.

A year after the *Sweat* decision, the colonial court decided one of the most fascinating cases of this era. *In re Graweere*[14] was a pivotal case in that it highlighted the ambiguities of the black man's position in Virginia during the early years. While under the law he was not the complete equal of the white man, nevertheless he had not been fully stripped of all basic human rights. John Graweere, a "negro servant unto William Evans," petitioned the court for permission to purchase the freedom of his young child from a Lieutenant Sheppard, the owner of the child's mother, in order that the child "should be made a christian and be brought up in the fear of God and in the knowledge of religion taught and exercised by the church of England." The court ruled in favor of Graweere's petition and ordered:

> that the child shall be free from the said *Evans* or his assigns and to be and remain at the disposing and education of the said *Graweere* and the child's godfather—who undertaketh to see it brought up in the christian religion as aforesaid.

As in *Sweat* and *Davis,* the significance the *Graweere* court attached to the word "servant" is unclear; there is no indication as to whether Graweere's precise legal status was that of slave or indentured servant. It is clear, however, that Graweere was allowed some special privileges. His master permitted him "to keep hogs and make the best benefit thereof to himself provided that the said Evans [Graweere's master] might have half the increase which was accordingly rendered unto him by the said negro and the other half reserved for his own benefit."

By the later part of the seventeenth century, slavery would be defined as a lifetime and hereditary form of servitude. However, as *Graweere* indicates, at least in 1641 some black servants such as John Graweere were able to exercise legal rights inconsistent with the subsequently defined system of chattel slavery. Graweere was able to petition a court on behalf of his child and break the grip of hereditary servitude by purchasing the child's freedom. Further, his right to purchase his child's freedom was not an unrealizable dream: he was able to do so because he had been allowed to earn and keep the funds necessary to purchase the child. *Graweere* is a clear indication that Justice Ruffin's 1829 declaration that slaves could not make anything their own was historically inaccurate.[15]

The religious factor is as evident in *Graweere* as it was in the earlier *Davis* opinion. The court allowed Graweere to purchase his child's freedom only when the justices were assured by the child's godfather that the child would be "made a christian. . . ." Religious concerns would exert less influence in the outcome of cases as the institution of slavery became more rigid. In cases after *Graweere,* the fact that a black person had been a baptized Christian would not be a factor at all in attempts to establish freedom.[16]

Graweere illustrates the judicial system's early flexibility and its approval of masters who designed a labor system that gave even black servants or slaves some rights and privileges and their masters some rights to manumit. Yet the same legal process that sanctioned the right of Graweere's master to allow his slave some degree of economic autonomy also simultaneously sanctioned the right of other masters to impose perpetual servitude on blacks by will or contract. To be sure, a will or a contract was only an expression of the maker's desire and intent, and not a judicial or legislative pronouncement. Yet the presence and presumed validity of these agreements is significant for they reveal that prior to any statutory authorization blacks were being "singled out for special treatment which suggests a general debasement of Negroes as a group."[17] For instance, in a 1646 contract, Francis Potts sold a black woman and child to Stephen Carlton, "to the use of him forever." Another deed records William Whittington's sale of a girl merely ten years old; looking to the future he noted that she was sold along with any issue (children) she might produce for her and her children's "lifetime and their successors forever."[18]

Not all blacks in Virginia by the 1650s were slaves, but the above quoted deeds suggest that the white colonists by that early date were already beginning to establish a process of debasement and cruelty reserved for blacks only.

The Fear of an Alliance Among
White Indentured Servants, Indians, and Blacks

It soon became apparent to white masters that with the increase in white indentured servants and the even faster simultaneous expansion of the black population, a threat existed in the development of an alliance of underlings—white indentured servants, particularly non-English whites, and blacks. Three cases from this period deal with the response of the courts to that threat, twice as it directly manifested itself in runaway cases and once as it indirectly played a part in the successful attempt of one individual to avoid punishment for a crime by playing on the society's greater interest in maintaining a distinction between the lowest white servants and blacks.

In 1640, the General Virginia Court decided the *Emmanuel*[19] case, which involved a black who participated in a conspiracy to escape and who, along with six white servants, stole "the skiff of Pierce and corn, powder, and shot guns, which said persons sailed down to Elizabeth river." The group was captured, convicted, and sentenced. The leader of the group, Christopher Miller, a Dutchman, was required to wear shackles for one year. John Williams was sentenced to serve the colony for an extra seven years; Peter Willcocke, who was to be branded and whipped, was required to serve the colony for three years, Richard Cookson for two. The black man, Emmanuel, was whipped, branded with an "R" in his cheek, and required to wear shackles for one year. All the punishments, with the exception of Emmanuel's, included additions to the time of the original service.

Was the failure of the court to require extra service from Emmanuel due to judicial leniency or was it simply that Emmanuel was already a servant for life, making a sentence of extra years of service an empty gesture? If it was leniency, then the *Emmanuel* decision is certainly outside the pattern common to the period; if, more likely, Emmanuel was already a servant for life, there was, then, little further the court could do to punish him, certainly no more than the society had already done by taking away his freedom. We can unfortunately draw from this decision nothing specific about the court's response to Emmanuel, but in its treatment of the white members of this group, we can see another pattern that is as much of interest.

Although the total horrors and pervasive deprivations of racial chattel slavery had not fully evolved during the early seventeenth century, the foundation for its more harsh deprivations was being laid partially through the legal process's doctrinal attitude toward indentured servants. It becomes easier to comprehend that a legal system, which in 1641 could authorize branding both white and black runaway servants in the same manner as one would brand cattle, would later prove capable of treating certain humans as no more than beasts of burden.

In another decision that same month, the Virginia Court demonstrated that it would not be reluctant to subject blacks who were not already enslaved to lifetime servitude. *In Re Negro John Punch* three runaway servants, two white and one black (John Punch), were captured in Maryland and each sentenced to be whipped; but the judicial parity stopped with the whipping. The court then went on to impose different sentences for the same "crime":

> one called *Victor, a dutchman,* the other a *Scotchman* called *James Gregory,* shall first serve out their times with their master according to their Indentures, and one whole year apiece after the time of their service is Expired . . . and after that service . . . to serve the colony for three whole years apiece, and that the third being a negro named *John Punch* shall serve his said master or his assigns for the time of his natural Life here or elsewhere.[20]

Thus, although he committed the same crime as the Dutchman and the Scotsman, John Punch, a black man, was sentenced to lifetime slavery. For the white servants, an additional four years of service was deemed sufficient punishment.

In many ways, the *Punch* case is an astonishingly harsh decision. It exemplifies the court's intent to deliberately exercise partiality in its dealings with blacks. The 1640 imposition of lifetime servitude on the black participant alone was not predicated on any previous legislative enactment or any other colonial judicial precedent. Such differentiation of treatment reflected the legal process's early adoption of social values that saw blacks as inferior. To make rigid the social stratifications these values called for, the court turned social biases, at will, into hard legal judgments. In the true sense of the word, the colonial judges constituted an activist court, in order to perpetuate disparate cruelty on blacks.

What rationale was there in the *Punch* case for such disparity in the sentencing of a black? Was it the belief that a runaway black servant posed more of a menace to society and therefore was in need of greater chastisement than his white counterpart? Or was it some theory that a special warning was required as a deterrent to blacks? Or, in addition to any thought of deterrence, was the most compelling rationale, as we believe, an economic one—to establish a precedent that the master might derive a benefit by having converted a black transgressor's limited term to one of perpetual servitude? Whatever the answer to these questions, it is significant that blacks were in such a degraded status, with so few friends who might plead their cause in high enough places to do so, that the court did not even feel required to proffer a rationalization for the significantly different adverse punishment imposed on Punch.

The *Punch* case must also be analyzed in relation to *Graweere*,[21] which came a year later. *Punch* is indicative of the rather erratic and uneven response a black defendant might receive from the courts, which still vacillated in defining the legal status of black men and women. When compared to the greater restrictions imposed on slaves a half-century later,[22] *Punch* stands as a somewhat ambiguous statement, judging by its lack of reference to possible ultimate consequences. By the court's decree there was no adjudication precluding the possibility that his master might later manumit him, or that Punch, as Graweere, might have certain rights to manumit his children.

Emmanuel and *Punch* most clearly reveal the English colonists' difficulties in fostering a sense of community in a colony populated by Portuguese, Spanish, French, Turks, Dutch, blacks, and Indians.[23] The presence of Dutchmen and Scotsmen is acknowledged in each case; in fact, Dutchmen were leaders in both escapades. These cases which show some antagonism to non-Englishmen (white Dutchmen) also explain why the colonists were predisposed to racism, since of all the Virginians, blacks looked the most different. The national consciousness favoring the Englishmen could loosely be translated to racial consciousness disfavoring blacks.

In a third case, perhaps the most intriguing of the three, *Re Warwick*,[24] a case decided by the court in 1669, the court's entire opinion was its one-sentence conclusion:

> Hannah Warwick's case extenuated because she was overseen by a negro overseer.

Besides suggesting that a black overseer was not the usual situation, *Warwick* makes clear the very important direction in which Virginia was moving. There is a strong implication that Hannah Warwick, though a servant, was a white woman; otherwise, the fact that the overseer was black would not be of such legal significance. Additionally, Hannah, apparently guilty of some infraction, was able to escape punishment because the individual she was bound to obey was a black person. Even though *Warwick* indicates that as late as 1669 racial roles had not been so defined as to preclude a black person from exercising some control over any white person, the case signals the end of that era. There was apparently little question that Hannah Warwick had acted improperly, since there is no reference to any mitigating circumstances other than that her overseer was black. The clear inference to be drawn from the decision is that the society was more interested in making sure that blacks did not exercise authority over whites, and that white servants knew this, than in prosecuting the infractions of Hannah Warwick. Thus, the court intimated, by extension, that whites, although wrong, could refuse to submit to the authority of blacks, even when blacks were performing as agents of the common master. If we err in the inference that Hannah Warwick was white, the case nevertheless exemplifies a debasement of blacks. For even if Hannah Warwick had been black, the court's view presumed that blacks were so inferior that the black overseer could not legally command the compliance even of another black.

Whether Warwick was black or white, the decision warned white masters that they should be reluctant to entrust to blacks any position of power, and further communicated to white servants that the court would exonerate whites (or possibly blacks) who had committed wrongs while under the supervision of blacks. Thus, *Warwick* subscribes judicially the view that the function of blacks in Virginia was to be ordered, and never to order others.

Through the decisions of the colonial courts in Virginia during the first fifty years, the message became increasingly clear: the court's intent to promulgate legal doctrines was predicated on its assumption of the social standard that blacks were particularly inferior. By keeping its decisions consistent with that assumption, it made the legal sanctioning of slavery possible if not probable.

THE SPECIAL TREATMENT OF INDIANS

The colonists' attitude in this early period toward the other non-Europeans—the indigenous population—must also be considered. The 1610 *Lawes Divine, Morall and Martiall,* which governed the colonists with a militaristic code of laws, did not encourage meaningful coexistence with the Indians.[25] Some servants probably sought refuge among the Indians, particularly after 1618 when the *Lawes Divine, Morall and Martiall,* authorizing execution of all recaptured servants who had fled to the Indian settlements, were repealed. But increasing fear and hostility between Indians and whites made that avenue of escape both less feasible and less attractive.[26] Attempts were also made to separate Indian children from their parents in an effort to bring up the children surrounded by the English and away from the "evil" influence of their parents. When Indians came into Jamestown to visit or trade, they were placed under guard, ostensibly to prevent Indian thievery. As a further precaution no inhabitant was to speak to them without the governor's permission; and settlers were forbidden:"on pain of death to runne away from the Colonie, to Powhatan, or any savage Werowance else whatever."[27]

Indians and whites conducted guerilla raids against each other's settlements with ever increasing ruthlessness, particularly on the part of the English, although the Spanish atrocities in Hispanola were not repeated.[28] Constant warfare did reduce the Indian population, however. It has been estimated that the nine to ten thousand Indians in Virginia when Jamestown was founded were reduced to three or four thousand subjugated survivors living at the mercy of the English by 1670.[29] Bacon's Rebellion in 1675 and 1676, although obviously more than an attempt to prevent Indian attacks, suggests the ease with which a colonist could arouse the Virginians' zeal to annihilate the total Indian population.[30]

While perhaps not identified as such, racism had already become a prevalent characteristic in Virginia, and was expressed in societal acceptance of disparate treatment of individuals whose color, more than their culture, marked them different from English men and women.

Codification of Prejudice:
The Early Legislative Experience

Though the Virginia colonial courts often attempted to translate the moods and desires of the white power structure, on whose behalf they operated, into a series of written decisions giving legal force to social bias, the court's decisions were erratic and disjointed so far as precisely defining the legal status of blacks. The inclination of a judge in the immediate disposition of a case was usually to decide only the specific problems before him; thus, although a decision and sentence might show blatant discrimination, it did not always become the precedent or precursor for future acts of discrimination either in other courts or in other similar cases.

The legislature was in a different position. Within twenty years after the 1619 arrival of the "Negers" in Jamestown, the colonial council already had begun to write legislation uniquely excluding blacks from the normal protections provided by governments to those under their aegis. The first legislative enactment making reference to blacks was the statute of 1639:

> 1639. Act X. All persons except Negroes are to be provided with arms and ammunition or be fined at the pleasure of the governor and council.[31]

Although this statute excluded blacks (and perhaps Indians) from the subsidy of arms and ammunition, it did not specifically prohibit blacks from having and using arms and ammunition. Compared with the cruelty legislated in subsequent statutes, this initial enactment, while an affront to black pride, did indeed represent a small first step of deprivation.

The earliest Virginia statute dealing with servant obligations was enacted sometime in 1642. It required those servants brought to the colony without indenture to serve four years if older than twenty, five years if between twelve and twenty, and seven years if under twelve.[32] This legislation may also have been applicable to those blacks brought involuntarily to North America from the African continent. Between 1642 and 1660 further laws were passed pertaining to the length of service of colonial servants, as were other laws, generally favorable to the interests of the master, attempting to deal with the most frequent areas of conflict in the master-servant relationship. For example, Act LX, passed in 1642, sentenced those who traded with a servant without the master's consent to one month in prison, in addition to a fine of four times the value of the article traded.[33]

Two later statutes, dated 1657 and 1658 respectively, indicate that runaway servants was another repeating problem in the master-servant relationship. The earlier of the two authorized the establishment of a colonial militia to track down runaways:

> Act CXIII. Whereas hue and cry after runaway servants has been much neglected to the great loss of the inhabitants, it is enacted that all such hue and cry shall be signed either by the governor or some of the council and the same shall be conveyed from house to house with all convenient speed. Runaways, if found, shall be sent from constable to constable until delivered to their master or mistress.[34]

The second required that all masters, upon apprehending their runaways, "cut the hair of all such runaways close above the ears, whereby they may be with more ease discovered and apprehended [in the future]."

By 1654, legislation on master-servant relationships was already making distinctions based on ethnic and/or racial grounds. The first statute, Act VI, passed in 1654, required Irish servants arriving in the colony without indentures to serve longer terms than their English counterparts:

> 1654. Act VI. Irish servants brought in without indentures, if above sixteen years old, are to serve six years; if under sixteen years, to serve until twenty-four years of age.[35]

Indians, as well, were singled out. In 1657, the colonial legislature precluded masters of Indian children, confined to these masters for education or instruction, from selling said children; the children were to be freed when they reached twenty-five. In the same year, the English were prohibited from buying Indians.

It was not until 1659, forty years after the arrival of the first blacks in Virginia, that a direct reference to blacks as slaves appeared in Virginia legislation. A 1659 statute imposed reduced import duties on merchants bringing slaves into the colony:

> 1659. Act XVI. Dutch and all strangers of Christian nations are allowed free trade if they give bond and pay import of ten shillings per hogshead laid upon all tobacco exported to any foreign dominions; always provided that if Dutch or other foreigners shall import any Negro slaves they, the said Dutch or other foreigners, shall for the tobacco really produced by the said Negroes, pay only the impost of two shillings per hogshead, the like being paid by our own nation.[36]

The purpose of this statute was to encourage the international slave trade by providing financial incentives to the "Dutch and all strangers of Christian nations" participating in the slave trade. But of greater significance historically is the fact that this statute clearly reflects legislative recognition of the increasing value slave labor had acquired in colonial Virginia.

By 1660, it appears, the composition of the labor force in colonial Virginia—previously made up of whites and blacks in various degrees of servitude—began to include in increasing numbers another category of laborers, blacks in lifetime bondage. The eventual crossover to an almost total slave labor force would not be complete, it seems, until a century later. The statutes of the next few years, therefore, while reflecting recognition, if not direct sanctioning of perpetual servitude for some black laborers, concern themselves not with the minority of black slaves but with what were the special problems during the period of the transition—when both white indentured servants, black servants, and totally enslaved blacks worked side by side. One of the problems was apparently white-black alliances for the purposes of escape.

In 1660 a statute dealt with one of the early attempts of the legislature to put a stop to such attempts.

> 1660. Act XXII. It is enacted that in case any English servant shall run away in company with any Negroes who are incapable of making satisfaction by addition of time that the English so running away shall serve for the time of the Negroes' absence as they are to do for their own by a former act.[37]

The reference to "Negroes who are incapable of making satisfaction by addition of time" is an implicit acknowledgment of Negro life-time servitude, which some scholars have interpreted further to be an actual expression of legal recognition of Negro slavery.[38]

Further, this statute also recognizes the problem that would increasingly preoccupy Virginia legislators: black slave labor had no incentives to remain on the plantation and would, presumably, not hesitate to join whites even in open rebellion. Later the council passed a more comprehensive act rendering such "Christian servants" (who would run away with blacks) liable for the loss of slaves:

> in case any English servant shall run away in company of any negroes who are incapable of making satisfaction by addition of a time: . . . the English soe running away in the company with them shall at the time of service to their owne masters expired, serve the masters of the said negroes for their absence soe long as they should have done by this Act if they had not beene slaves, every christian in company serving his proportion; and if the negroes be lost or dye in such time of their being run away, the christian servants in company with them shall by proportion among them, either pay fewer thousand five hundred pounds of tobacco and caske or fewer yeares service for every negro so lost or dead.[39]

The reference to "serve the masters of the said negroes . . . as they should have done . . . if they had not beene slaves," leaves no doubt as to the fact that by then Negro slavery was perpetual slavery. Catterall has also suggested that the word "Christians" in the 1661 statute was used to specifically "includ[e] the Irish and other white servants."[40]

The 1661 statute was clearly intended as more of a deterrent to servants than to slaves; there was still no statutory mechanism that could compel slaves in the way servants could be compelled by threats of fines and extensions of time. But at that time the problem was the larger white servant population. Eight years later, when the problem was more limited to slaves, Virginians forthrightly and ruthlessly went about bringing slaves into line by making it socially, morally, and eventually legally acceptable to threaten a slave's life. Morgan has stated that, "Slaves could not be made to work for fear of losing liberty, so they had to be made to fear for their lives . . . in order to get an equal or greater amount of work, it was necessary to beat slaves harder than servants, so hard in fact, that there was a much larger chance of killing them than had been the case with servants."[41] In 1669, the Virginia legislature, by passing the following statute, notified slave owners that they would not be criminally prosecuted for the "casuall killing of slaves."

> 1669. *An Act about the casuall killings of slaves*
>   Whereas the only law in force for the punishment of refractory servants resisting their master, mistress or overseer, cannot be inflicted on negroes [because the punishment was extension of time], Nor the obstinacy of many of them by other than violent meanes supprest. *Be it enacted and declared by this grand assembly,* if any slave resist his master . . . and by the extremity of the correction should chance to die, that his death shall not be accompted Felony, but the master (or that other person appointed by the master to punish him) be acquit from molestation, since it cannot be presumed that propensed malice (which alone makes murther Felony) should induce any man to destroy his own estate.[42]

This 1669 statute indicated that Virginia was prepared to exploit the slave labor force to the maximum degrees possible. Virginians revealed that they were prepared to beat, mutilate, and even kill slaves in order to extract profits from their plantations.

CHRISTIANITY: MEANINGFUL FOR WHITES BUT IRRELEVANT FOR BLACKS

Virginians had to clarify how seriously they accepted the concept of true human brotherhood for those blacks who had adopted the white man's Christian faith. Did conversion to Christianity entitle the slave to freedom? That was the crucial question, and it was answered in 1667 when the colonial assembly passed an act providing that baptism would not affect the bondage of blacks or Indians.

> 1667. Act III. Whereas some doubts have arisen whether children that are slaves by birth, and by the charity and pity of their owners made partakers of the blessed sacrament of baptism, should by virtue of their baptism be made free, it is enacted that *baptism does not alter the condition of the person*

as to his bondage of freedom; masters freed from this doubt
may more carefully propagate Christianity by permitting slaves
to be admitted to that sacrament.[43]

Once masters were reassured that it was the skin color and
not the heathenism of their black and Indian slaves that "justified"
their subjugation, they were not as hesitant to have their slaves
baptized. In fact, a slave's baptism was often seen as a sign of his
docility. Eventually some ministers began to use even Christianity
as a means of extorting obedience from their slaves. In his sermon
to a Maryland slave congregation, Reverend Thomas Bacon
stressed that slaves who desired to be good Christians could become so only by being "good slaves":

> And pray, do not think that I want to deceive you, when I tell
> you, that your *masters* and *mistresses* are God's *overseers,*—
> and that if you are faulty towards them, God himself will pun-
> ish you severely for it in the next world, unless you repend it
> and strive to make amends, by your *faithfulness and Dili-*
> *gence.*[44]

In 1670, three years after the assembly had made clear that
baptism would not alter a black man's bondage, it passed an act
further clarifying the black servants' status in the colony by divid-
ing non-Christian servants into two classes: those imported into this
colony by shipping, who "shall be slaves for their lives"; and those
who "shall come by land," who "shall serve, if boys or girles; untill
thirty yeares of age: if men or women twelve yeares and no longer."[45]
This act favored the Indian, who usually came by land, and fixed
the status of the non-Christian African as that of slave for life. It
also anticipated later judicial and legislative pronouncements that all
Africans were presumed to be slaves.[46] The distinctions established
by the 1670 statute were eliminated in 1682 when all imported non-
Christians were made slaves.[47]

If one juxtaposes the 1670 statute (and the 1682 modification), which fixed the status of blacks and Indians upon entry into
the colony, with the earlier 1667 statute, which declared that baptism did not alter slave status, one realizes that by 1682 slavery was
placed squarely on a racial foundation. Yet even these legislative
enactments did not prevent masters who wanted to from creating

their own arrangements. For instance, in 1678, a "Spanish Mullato, by name Antonio," sold by John Indicott[48] of Boston to Richard Madlicott, to serve "But for Tenn yeares from the day he shall Disembarke in Virginia, and at the expiration of the said Tenn yeares the s'd Mullato, Antony, to be a free man to goe wherever he pleaseth."[49]

THE FIRST MAJOR SLAVE CODES

The first major slave codes were dated 1680-1682. They not only synthesized all the piecemeal legislative deprivations of the previous twenty years but introduced others incorporating some of the harshest customs and traditions that had evolved to control the colony's indentured servants. At the same time the codes were emphatic in denying slaves any of the privileges or rights that had accrued to white indentured servants in this same period.

Despite some limitations on their rights, white servants were never the victims of any legislative plan to deprive them of such basic options as the right to sue one's masters for ill treatment or for one's freedom and white servants were never precluded from owning property. Nor does the argument that masters feared slave revolts, which of course could destroy the colony, fully explain why the legislature denied basic rights to blacks, mulattoes, and Indians, while granting some of those privileges to white indentured servants. An argument can just as easily be made that the white indentured servant or freedman precluded from the decision-making processes of the government and subjected to harsher treatment was probably as dangerous as the slave. Certainly the totality of deprivations cannot be explained by any assumption that blacks were more necessarily prone to violence. There is no evidence to substantiate this. And whatever the relative threats posed by each group, the fact is that nonwhites alone were legally deprived of all basic human rights. Only against nonwhites did colonial society feel it could use anything and everything—the legal structure, the militia, even armed private citizens—to keep human beings in a submissive state.

With each succeeding decade, the Virginia legislators, expressing a mixture of fear, greed, and prejudice, simply reduced the privileges and rights of blacks. They rationalized their actions on the ground of security, without religious or moral qualm whatsoever.

They no doubt convinced themselves that blacks were so inferior that their subhuman status deserved no recognition of human rights. And just as often, they probably made no effort at all to find a rationale; they simply dehumanized those who were black because of the color of their skins and because blacks were largely powerless to prevent it.

It may be no more than the accident of black skin that precluded the empathy of white Virginians. The black looked enough different from the white Virginian to spare the white any guilt over his legal cannibalism. The white Virginian, enriching himself by depriving blacks of rights, was further spared by the convenient differences in skin color and hair texture from having the thought cross his mind: "There but for the grace of God go I."

The 1680 statute would become the model of repression throughout the South for the next 180 years. The following provisions are illustrative of its codification of prejudice and the degree to which the statute attempted to make sure that blacks would be recognized as legally inferior:

> 1680. Act X. Whereas the frequent meetings of considerable numbers of Negro slaves under pretense of feasts and burials is judged of dangerous consequence [it] enacted that no Negro or slave may carry arms, such as any club, staff, gun, sword, or other weapon, nor go from his owner's plantation without a certificate and then only on necessary occasions; the punishment twenty lashes on the bare back, well laid on. And further, if any Negro lift up his hand against any Christian he shall receive thirty lashes, and if he absent himself or lie out from his master's service and resist lawful apprehension, he may be killed and this *law* shall be published every six months.[50]

If blacks could not leave the owner's plantation without a certificate, their mobility was destroyed; if blacks could not carry arms, the potential to resist was reduced. And, if blacks could be whipped for lifting up a hand against any Christian—regardless of the provocation—then the dehumanization process was complete because blacks were legally precluded from responding in a manner thought normal for whites or most other human beings.

Two years later the legislature, not content with the prohibi-

tions of 1680, sanctioned punishment for any slave who remained
on the plantation of a white man other than his own master for more
than four hours without permission:

> 1682. Act III. Whereas the act of 1680 on Negro insurrection
> has not had the intended effect, it is enacted that church war-
> dens read this and the other act, twice every year, in the time
> of divine service, or forfeit each of them six hundred pounds
> of tobacco, and further to prevent insurrections no master or
> overseer shall allow a Negro slave of another to remain on his
> plantation above four hours without leave of the slave's own
> master.[51]

For those who still believe that the whole black population
went docilely into bondage, the words quoted above ought to be
reread. The harsh proscriptions of 1680 against freedom of assembly, against bearing arms, against freedom of movement, the requirement that blacks carry "papers" (a certificate)—in short,
those very devices despotic governments have employed into this
century in subjugating much more sophisticated cultures—did not
easily work against the seventeenth-century black. "The Act of
1680 on Negro insurrection," in the words of the Act of 1682, had
"not had the intended effect." Rather, the blacks' desire for dignity
and freedom remained to be beaten back over many years through
the repeated use of many cruel devices borrowed from the historical inventory of suppression.

White Male Domination
and Interracial Sexual Relations

As colonial America established the legal traditions expanding the human rights of whites while simultaneously cutting back
those of blacks, there was one subgroup of each being pulled
several ways—colonial America's white and black women. At times
the stratification became: 1) white males; 2) white females; 3)
black females; 4) black males. Always there was the purported concern for white racial integrity, but curiously both in practice and
by legislation there was not equal concern about white *male* integrity. The legal process was tolerant of white male illicit "escapades"

involving either white females or black females, but it was relatively harsh on infractions by white females (even when involving white males) and brutally harsh on infractions between black males and white females.

The law's greater sensitivity to interracial sexual activity and white male domination remained for centuries. As recently as 1974, though in a somewhat different factual context, the United States Supreme Court stated that women in America have been the victims of either "overt discrimination or . . . a socialization process of a male dominated culture."[52] Even the famed egalitarian, Thomas Jefferson, purportedly believed "that women should be neither seen nor heard in society's decision making councils."[53] The statutes that we study in this chapter were written by white males approximately 300 years ago. They exemplify the values, preferences, and standards of a socialization process of a white male-dominated culture. One should ascertain whether, by their language or their enforcement, the statutes were more advantageous to white males than to any other segment of society. The consequence of a white male-dominated culture has been inherent in the legal system. To this malaise must be added the additional factor of the law's different responses when interracial matters are involved.

Interracial sexual relations seem to have been always an even more sensitive and, for some, threatening area than the normal concerns about sexual relations. There are many contradictions between the practices and the legal prohibitions on interracial sexual relations. As one views the varying complexions of blacks in America, it is quite obvious that there has been extensive interracial sexual relations—despite the many purported taboos and legal pronouncements against it.

Colonial anxiety about interracial sexual activity cannot be attributed solely to seventeenth-century values, for it was not until 1967 that the United States Supreme Court finally declared unconstitutional those statutes prohibiting interracial marriages. The Supreme Court waited thirteen years after its *Brown* decision dealing with desegregation of schools before, in *Loving* v. *Virginia*,[54] it agreed to consider the issue of interracial marriages. Many commentators have suggested that the issue of interracial marriage was far more explosive than even the maelstrom involved over integrated education and that it was by design that the Court delayed accepting such cases until 1967.[55] As recently as 1967 more than sixteen states prohibited and punished interracial marriages, and in the celebrated *Loving* case the Virginia trial judge in January, 1959 stated his legal rationale justifying the constitutionality of the prohibition against interracial marriages as follows:

> Almighty God created the races white, black, yellow, malay and red, and he placed them on separate continents. And but for the interference with his arrangement there would be no cause for such marriages. The fact that he separated the races shows that he did not intend for the races to mix.[56]

Thus the colonial legal system can be better evaluated by recognizing that it was a system controlled by a white male-dominated culture, a society generally antagonistic toward blacks, a society wherein white males wanted to maintain their domination over *both* white and black females, and finally a society in which white males fervently desired to preclude any sexual relationships between black males and white females.

The data indicates that almost from the time blacks arrived in Virginia there were interracial sexual relations between Indians, blacks, and whites. The fact that legislators thought it was necessary to pass statutes pertaining to interracial sexual practices demonstrates their perception that this was a special problem requiring specific statutory prohibitions.

It is unclear whether prior to 1662 judicial punishments of miscegenation were merely the same punishments employed in all instances of fornication. For example, in the previously discussed *Davis* case[57] the punishment may have been solely for disobeying moral doctrine, rather than for crossing the color line. Court records show that prior to 1662, all fornicators, regardless of race, were fined or whipped.[58]

In typical piecemeal fashion, the Virginia legislature attacked in 1662 one facet of a "problem" caused by illicit sexual behavior— the problem of women indentured servants (white or black) having children out of wedlock; they passed a statute that penalized the unmarried mother by requiring her to serve an additional two years.

In the preamble the legislature noted that "some dissolute masters" had "gotten their maids with child" in order to "claim the benefit of their service," and that some loose women, hoping to gain their freedom, had laid "all their bastards to their masters." And accordingly, the following provision was enacted:

> each woman servant got with child by her master shall after her indenture is expired be sold for two years by the church wardens, the tobacco to be employed by the vestry for the use of the parish.[59]

Note the bias in favor of males in this statute. While conception of a child required a male's involvement and while often the father may even have been the master of the mother, it was the mother *only* who had the additional burden of servitude. Furthermore, the psychological forces affecting the female indentured servant may raise the question as to how voluntary her act was, if it involved the master. Yet, the master or male's act was clearly voluntary and he was at least equally culpable. Nevertheless the male had no additional penal burden. The society economically profited by obtaining a servant for two years without cost for her labor. The child of the union suffered the social stigmatization of being a bastard.

But in a struggling colony where the population was largely composed of Europe's undesirables and where women were scarce, it is unclear whether illegitimacy, per se, was so great a stigma. During the same year, however, the colonial assembly thought sexual relations between whites and blacks to be special problems requiring a special penalty:

> 1662. Act XII. Children got by an Englishman upon a Negro woman shall be bond or free according to the condition of the mother, and if any Christian shall commit fornication with a Negro man or woman, he shall pay double the fines of a former act.[60]

This statute, upon first reading, does not clearly reveal the built-in bias and preferences of its drafters. "Englishmen" as used here is probably a synonym for whites generally or at least white Englishmen. The fact that interracial fornication caused a double fine corroborates the thesis that an interracial sexual act was considered to be far more immoral or deviant than fornication by persons of the same race.

The statute also expressed more than mere social taboos or religious precepts. Implicit in the statute were the economic preferences and advantages to whites who sought to extend servitude and slavery. Prior to passage of this statute it had been an open question as to whether the normal doctrine of English law would be applicable—that the status of a child would be dependent upon the status of the child's father. However, the statute rejected the English doctrine and provided that children "got by an Englishman upon a Negro woman shall be bond or free according to the condition of the mother."[61]

Because (at least in part) of the scarcity of white women, there was probably far more sexual contact between Englishmen and black women than between white women and black men. It was, therefore, significant from an economic standpoint whether a child derived its status from its mother or its father. Once it was established that the black woman's child took the mother's status, the master class gained a crucial economic advantage—its labor force reproduced itself. If the legislature had followed the English legal doctrine that the status of the child was determined by the status of the father, the thousands of blacks or mulattoes whose fathers were white would have been free. However, contrary to English precedent, the legislators adopted the doctrine which would maximize their privileges; thus, even the children whose fathers were their mother's white masters were not only bastards, but slaves. By his illicit relations, a white male could eliminate the cost of purchasing an infant slave; by agreeing to enslave his progeny he became a breeder of slaves.

The subsequent 1691 statute (Act XVI) was far more comprehensive. By the language of its preamble, it was designed to prevent "that abominable mixture and spurious issue . . . by Negroes, mulattoes and Indians intermarrying with English or other white women" and provided that:

> whatsoever English or other white man or woman, bond or free, shall intermarry with a Negro, mulatto, or Indian man or woman, bond or free, he shall within three months be banished from this dominion forever.

And it is further enacted, that if any English woman being free shall have a bastard child by a Negro she shall pay fifteen pounds to the church wardens, and in default of such payment, she shall be taken into possession by the church wardens and disposed of for five years and the amount she brings shall be paid one-third to their majesties for the support of the government, one-third to the of the parish where the offense is committed and the other third to the informer. The child shall be bound out by the church wardens until he is thirty years of age. In case the English woman that shall have a bastard is a servant she shall be sold by the church wardens (after her time is expired) for five years, and the child serve as aforesaid.[62]

Several racial disparities were written into this statute. After 1691, the white man or woman was to be penalized if he or she legitimized the relationship with a black person by marriage; in that event they would be banished from the colony forever. Yet, apparently the white man could remain in the colony if he merely carried on a meretricious relationship with a black woman. The possibility of pregnancy significantly lessened the white woman's chances of maintaining a clandestine relationship with a black man. Yet, the statute did not penalize a white man for having sexual relations with his slave and it was not a crime for a black woman to have a bastard child by a white man. Both acts became a crime only when a white Englishwoman had a black man's child out of wedlock.

By 1705, the Virginia General Assembly had clarified all ambiguities and insured that all mulatto children would be servants at least until they were thirty-one years old.[63] The statute also provided harsher punishment for an unwed mother. A woman servant who had an illegitimate child by a black or a mulatto was fined fifteen pounds; if she was unable to pay the fine she was sold for five years at the expiration of her time of service.[64] If the unwed mother was a free white woman she was also subject to a fifteen pound fine or five years of service.

In one major aspect of interracial relationships, the 1705 statute mirrored those legislative enactments that preceded it; the harshest punishment was levied against those interracial couples who sought to legalize their relationships. Banishment, the penalty imposed by the 1691 act, was so ineffective a deterrent that sterner measures were enacted by the general assembly.[65] The statute required any white master or mistress, "having a Christian white servant," who married a black, mulatto, Indian, or a non-Christian, to free the servant. In addition, the statute authorized a fine and imprisonment:

> Whatsoever white man or woman being free shall intermarry with a Negro shall be committed to prison for six months without bail, and pay 10 pounds to the use of the parish. Ministers marrying such persons shall pay 10,000 pounds of tobacco.[66]

The 1705 prohibition against interracial marriage was reenacted in 1792; both statutes imposed a penalty of six months' imprisonment on whites, but curiously at that time no imprisonment penalty was imposed on blacks in the statutes. In 1848 the imprisonment for whites marrying blacks was increased to twelve months.[67] It was not until 1932, when the statute was amended, that imprisonment was imposed on *both* blacks and whites for intermarrying, and in 1932 the penalty was increased to confinement in the "penitentiary for from one to five years."[68]

Occasionally the legislature annulled a marriage between whites or granted a divorce on the ground that the white female had had sexual relations with a slave or a free black man:

> Chapter 6. The marriage between Benjamin Butt, Jr., and a certain Lydia Bright, who is of respectable family, and was at the time of the marriage supposed to be unsullied in her reputation, is dissolved because Lydia has been delivered of a mulatto child and has publicly acknowledged that the father of the child is a slave.[69]

> Chapter XCVIII. A marriage solemnized between Richard Jones, of the County of Northampton, and his wife, Peggy, is dissolved and Richard forever divorced from Peggy provided that a jury find that the child of Peggy is not the child of Richard, but is the offspring of a man of color.[70]

When white males impregnated black women, during the time when the above statutes were passed, no statutory annulments or divorces were granted.

But, the 1705 and 1792 acts did more than proscribe inter-racial relationships. The statutes minimized the economic options available to blacks, mulattoes, Indians, and non-Christians. All nonwhites were prohibited from obtaining white servants. Such leg-islation clearly limited freed blacks, Indians, and mulattoes from gaining a foothold in the colony's economy because purchasing a slave required more initial capital investment than securing the serv-ices of an indentured servant.[71]

With these rigid statutory restrictions written by white males, one might think that interracial sexual relationships during the co-lonial period would have become nonexistent. Instead, the statutes merely eliminated legitimization of marriages and encouraged the extensive exploitation of black women by their masters and other white men, thus explaining the presence of thousands of mulattoes in Virginia. The result was that there was probably more intermix-ture in the 1700s than since then.[72] Despite moral taboos and crimi-nal sanctions, "white men of every social rank slept with Negro women. The Colonists, as well as European travelers in the colonies frequently pointed to this facet of American life."[73] Where inter-racial sex relations were involved, the legal system was operation-ally effective to the extent that white men maximized their options, dehumanized blacks, white women—and themselves.

Manumission and Emancipation

Even before the Act of 1705, however, the Virginia legislature had begun to attack the normal human emotions of blacks by at-tempting to deprive slaves of any hope of eventual emancipation.[74] It did this by temporarily and conveniently reversing its philosophy and legislating that one right, at least, of the property holder was not inviolable—the right to give up his interest in his property. Leg-islation of 1699, in fact, had made manumission impossible in some instances: previously the master's right to determine the nature and length of servitude imposed on his slaves had not been challenged.

As early as 1645, a white master, A. Vanga, emancipated some blacks (who may have been either servants or slaves) by a will that "freed his negroes at certain ages; some of them he taught to read and make their own clothes. He left them land."[75] However, by 1691, there was an absolute prohibition against freeing a black or mulatto without also providing for transportation of "the negro out of the country within six months after such setting free." Free blacks were viewed as undesirable elements in the population, a clear indication that racist attitudes had hardened. The implication of such a statute is obvious—blacks had only one function in Virginia society and that was to labor perpetually for the benefit of their owners. Masters who, in "ill directed" generosity, sought to release blacks from such a condition, were to be penalized by having to pay for the removal of such unsavory additions to the population. The act stated:

> A great inconvenience may happen to this country by the setting of Negroes and mulattoes free, by their entertaining Negroes from their masters' service, or receiving stolen goods, or being grown old bringing a charge upon the country, it is enacted that no Negroes, or mulattoes be set free by any person whatsoever, unless such person pay for the transportation of such Negro out of the country within six months after such setting free, upon penalty of ten pounds sterling to the church wardens, with which the church wardens are to cause the Negro to be transported out of the country and the remainder given to the use of the poor of the parish.[76]

The option to free one's slaves was therefore exercisable only by masters with sufficient capital to pay the transportation costs. The poorer planter was forced to continue as a slaver even if he desired to do otherwise.

Later provisions further limited the master's right to manumit his slaves. Manumission became possible only upon approval of the governor and council as a reward for public service, which included, by definition, revealing a slave conspiracy.[77] Slaves were punished when their masters ignored such statutory mandates. The legislature authorized the seizure and reenslavement of blacks, mulattoes, and Indians who had been improperly freed.[78]

Throughout the eighteenth century many statutes were passed by either the colonial or the state legislatures granting approval for the manumission of slaves. The following 1779 and 1780 statutes are typical of probably more than 100 passed in the 1700s and early 1800s.

1779. Chapter XLIV. A Negro slave named Kitt, owned by Hinchia Mabry, of Brunswick, has rendered meritorious service in making the first information against several counterfeiters, and is hereby emancipated and his owner ordered paid 1,000 pounds out of the public treasury.[79]

1779. Chapter XLVII. Application has been made to the General Assembly that John Hope (called Barber Caesar), Wm. Beck and a mulatto girl, Peg, be emancipated. They are hereby declared free and may enjoy all the rights which free Negroes by the laws of this country enjoy, with a saving to all persons (except the present owners), any claim they may have to the said Negroes.[80]

1780. Chapter XXV. Ned and Kate, slaves, are declared free and may enjoy the rights of free Negroes.[81]

In 1782 the legislature passed a statute authorizing the manumission of slaves and provided that it shall hereafter be

lawful for any person, by his or her last Will and testament, or by any other instrument in writing, under his or her hand and seal . . . to emmancipate and set free, his or her slaves, or any of them, who shall thereupon be entirely and fully discharged from the performance of any contract entered into during Servitude, and enjoy as full freedom as if they had been particularly named and freed by this act.[82]

Throughout the early nineteenth century, several statutes were passed indicating how tenuous even was the freedom of free blacks; as an example the legislature provided: "Archy Higginbotham, a free man of color, is permitted to remain, subject to the power of the court to revoke the leave. . . . Daniel Higginbotham is permitted to remain four years to acquire the means of removing himself and family."[83]

Virginia vacillated on the issue of freeing slaves until its constitution of 1850-1851, when it provided:

Slaves hereafter emancipated shall forfeit their freedom by remaining in the commonwealth more than twelve months after they become actually free, and shall be reduced to slavery under such regulations as may be prescribed by law. . . . The General Assembly shall not emancipate any slave, or the descendant of any slave, either before or after the birth of such descendent.[84]

Virginia indicated its hostility not merely against masters who wanted to emancipate or manumit their slaves but also against any individuals who acted as a friend of a black who filed a suit for freedom. The 1795 statute provided that "If any person aid or abet any person [slave] in such a claim for freedom and the claim is not established, he shall forfeit $100 to the owner of the slave."[85] The Act of 1798 further exemplified the hostility:

> It is further enacted that in cases where in the property of person held as a slave demanding freedom shall come for trial, no persons shall serve as a juror who shall belong to a society for the emancipation of negroes.[86]

Creditor and Estate Rights in Slaves: Were Slaves Like Horses and Dogs or Like Real Estate?

Though by 1700, the Virginia legal system—court and legislature alike—had boxed in the colony's black population, it was not until 1705 that the general assembly passed a comprehensive statute effectively removing blacks from the family of man and reassigning them to the classification of real property. Because the 1705 statute so clearly distinguished between the legal status of "slave" and that of "servant," the act became a model code for other colonies.

Prior to 1705, the courts often struggled to define the nature of the master's property interest in his slaves when creditors sought to collect on judgments for the master's debts. In a real estate context, that creditor who holds a mortgage on real estate usually has priority over other creditors in realizing what he can by foreclosure on that property; thus, he can sell the real estate to collect the amount owed, even if other creditors (without mortgages) have obtained court judgments against the owner of the real estate. The issue before the Virginia legislature in 1705 was where to place slaves: with the real estate portion of a man's estate or with his personal property. If slaves were to be considered real estate they could be sold to pay off the mortgage and other real estate debts when the owner defaulted. On the other hand, if slaves were to be treated like other types of personal property (such as horses and cattle), they were subject to sale to satisfy non–real estate debts. How painful it is to note that the problem was never phrased to reflect even slight recognition of the moral issue arising when the legislature assigns to human beings the status of either real estate or chattel.

In 1671, in dealing with the special problems of distributing an orphan's estate, the legislature had first attempted to define the status of slaves (i.e., whether they were more like real estate or personal property). The general assembly passed the following statute:

> 1671. Act IV. In a former act it is provided that sheep, horses, cattle should be delivered in kind to an orphan when he comes of age, to which some have desired that Negroes be added; this Assembly considering the difficulty of procuring Negroes in kind as also the value and hazard of their lives has doubted whether any sufficient men could be found who would engage themselves to deliver Negroes of equal ages if the special Negroes should die, or become by age or accident unserviceable; it is enacted, that at discretion of the courts Negroes may be appraised, sold at an outcry, or preserved in kind, as it is deemed most expedient for the preservation or advancement of the estates of orphans.[87]

The 1671 statute dealt with the issue in the administration of decedent's estate and the judgment as to how slaves would fit within that structure so they could be passed down from a decedent's master to his children. Normally a child, despite his father's death, could not hold title to property until he was twenty-one. When he became twenty-one, his inheritance would be turned over to him. The problem arose when, for example, a child at the age of seven who inherited property would have to wait fourteen years before he acquired title to it. If one were dealing with jewelry or undeveloped real estate, that property could be held during the interim normally without any significant diminution of its value and without any significant maintenance obligation. But when dealing with human beings who, like sheep, horses, and cattle, reproduce and die, to preserve the value of an estate for an orphan it may become necessary to sell the slaves or sheep or horses during the child's minority so that he will have their monetary equivalent when he comes of age. The problem of whether slaves should be treated like sheep, horses, or cattle, or like real estate had such complexity for the Virginia colonial legislators that the assembly wrote the above statute and left it to the judgment of the court to take whatever action was "most expedient for the preservation or advancement of the estates of orphans."

The ultimate irony in these legislative acts is that the courts recognized that slaves were human beings with all of the hazards of life that mark other human beings; yet ultimately the disposition of slaves was completed on a dehumanized level. The court's final judgment was to be predicated on what was best for the orphan, regardless of the human consequences to the slaves (separation of families, etc.).

In October, 1705, the governor, council, and House of Burgesses removed all ambiguities and passed the following act, relegating all black, mulatto, and Indian slaves to the status of real estate.

> Chapter XXIII. All Negro, mulatto, and Indian slaves within this dominion shall be held to be real estate and not chattels and shall descend unto heirs and widows according to the custom of land inheritance, and be held in *"fee simple."** Provided that any merchant bringing slaves into this dominion shall hold such slaves whilst they remain unsold as personal estate. All such slaves may be taken on execution as other chattels; slaves shall not be escheatable.
>
> No person selling any slave shall be obliged to have the sale recorded as upon the alienation of other real estate. Nothing in this act shall be construed to give the owner of a slave not seized of other real estate the right to vote as a freeholder.[88]

The statute makes it clear that ownership of slaves, without the ownership of any other real estate, would not render the master a "freeholder," entitled to vote.[89] Unfortunately, the statute did not

---

* *Fee Simple* is an ownership interest in land where the owner is entitled to the entire property with unconditional power of disposition during his life and descending to his heirs and legal representatives.

anticipate the problem caused when the number of slaves increased due to birth, or decreased because of death, after the master's death. That problem was addressed in *Tucker* v. *Sweney*[90] where the court allowed the executors to treat after-born children as "no otherwise than Horses or Cattle":

> Negroes notwithstanding the Act making them Real Estate remain in the Hands of the Ex'ors by that Act as Chatels and as such do vest in them for payment of Debts So that in this Case they are considered no otherwise than Horses or Cattle, And there is no doubt but the Increase of any living Creature after the death of the Testor, are looked upon as part of his Estate, and are liable to be taken for his Debts.[91]

The most comprehensive sections of the 1705 act distinguished the legal status of slaves from that of servants.

RIGHTS OF SERVANTS

All people brought into Virginia without indentures were presumed servants if they were Christian and of Christian parentage prior to entry. However, those servants who were non-Christians in their mother country (a label which included the vast majority of blacks and Indians) were presumed to be slaves by the 1705 statute:

> That all servants imported and brought into this country, by sea or land, who were not christians in their native country, (except Turks and Moors in amity with her majesty, and others that can make due proof of their being free in England, or any other christian country, before they were shipped, in order to transportation hither) shall be accounted and be slaves, and as such be here bought and sold notwithstanding a conversion to christianity afterwards.[92]

Direct provisions were passed to codify the duties masters owed to servants. In addition to the prohibition against publicly whipping a naked white Christian servant, masters were admonished to "find and provide for their servants wholesome and competent diet, clothing and lodging, by the discretion of the county court."[93] Church wardens were authorized to provide for servants who become so sick or lame that "he or she cannot be sold for such value . . . as shall satisfy the fees and other incident charges accrued."[94]

The masters were required to reimburse the church wardens. Masters were also precluded from discharging servants who became sick or lame before their indentured servitude was completed; a fine of ten pounds was assessed against offenders. Additionally, the law required the payment of "freedom dues," payable at the end of the indenture, for those servants who did not receive a yearly wage.

> That there shall be paid and allowed to every imported servant, not having yearly wages, at the time of service ended, by the master or owner of such servant, viz: To every male servant, ten bushels of indian corn, thirty shillings in money, or the value thereof, in goods, and one well fixed musket or fuzee, of the value of twenty shillings, at least: and to every woman servant, fifteen bushels of indian corn, and forty shillings in money, or the value thereof, in goods.

Servants were guaranteed the right to sue in county court masters who failed to make the proper payment.[95] In contrast to the detailed delineation of duties owed a servant by the master, the statute was silent as to any obligations owed to the slave by the master. Masters were apparently allowed to feed, clothe, and nurse their slaves in whatever manner they saw fit.

But, perhaps the most crucial demarcation made between slave and servant in the 1705 statute was the codification of a rather broad panoply of legal rights to be enjoyed exclusively by servants. And further, servants were given effective means to seek judicial protection of such rights. Expeditious procedures were created to insure quick settlement of servant problems. Complaints from servants were received by a justice of the peace who, upon finding cause, could order the master to answer the complaint in court. No formal process was needed to commence a legal action, particularly if the servant was suing for nonpayment of wages or freedom dues, for the master's failure to free the servant according to the indenture, or for maltreatment (which included public whipping without a permit from the justice of the peace).[96]

Finally, masters and servants were precluded by statute from extending the original indenture without court approval.

> that no master or owner of any servant shall during the time of such servant's servitude make any bargain with his or her

said servant for further service, or other matter or thing related to liberty, or personal profit, unless the same be made in
the presence, and with the approbation, of the court of that
county where the master or owner resides.[97]

The legal rights given servants greatly altered the attitudes of masters and white servants toward each other. The initial consequence
was to increase the cost of a white indentured servant, which in
turn rendered investment in slave labor the more economically rational choice. However, this increased cost was probably more than
offset by the racial affinity between masters and servants engen-
dered by the law. To be sure, white servants were "inferior" to their
masters in an economic and social sense, but such inferiority was
temporary by nature of the indenture agreement; providing servants
with legal rights prevented the creation of a lasting caste system.
Racial identification between white masters and servants further
precluded an alliance with black laborers. No one seeks an alliance
with "nonpersons."

NONRIGHTS OF SLAVES AND BLACKS

Not only did the Virginia council fail to enact parallel legislation to protect slaves, the council enacted no legislation at all extending to slaves any of the rights granted to servants. In fact, as
far as slaves were concerned, the 1705 statute increased their master's control over their lives. For example, Chapter 34 provided that
a master who killed his slave in an attempt to correct the slave
would not be held to have committed a felony:

XXXIV. And if any slave resist his master, or owner, or other
person, by his or her order, correcting such slave, and shall
happen to be killed in such correction, it shall not be accounted felony; but the master, owner, and every such other
person so giving correction, shall be free and acquit of all
punishment and accusation for the same, as if such accident
had never happened.[98]

In contrast, any Negro, mulatto, or Indian, bond or free, was
precluded from lifting his or her hand "at anytime, in opposition
against any christian, not being negro, mulatto or Indian." The
punishment—"30 lashes, well laid on."[99]

Slaves were prohibited from carrying any arms, including guns, swords, clubs, or staffs, or from leaving their plantation without written permission from their masters. Any slave caught violating these provisions could be apprehended by any person, and brought before the constable who, without any other warrant, was authorized to give the slave twenty lashes on his or her bare back. Slaves were also prohibited from owning any cattle; the statute authorized the seizure and sale of all slave cattle, with proceeds of the sales being used to aid the colony's poor. Thus, in addition to producing wealth for their masters, slaves who had been enterprising enough to have accumulated some valuable property were required to help sustain Virginia's poor whites.

Virginia's 1705 statute culminates the beginning of the legislature's partnership with masters to ensure the total subjugation of the slave and the colored population.* Two justices of the peace, upon receiving information that a runaway slave was in the area, were authorized to empower sheriffs to search for the runaway; such proclamation, which included a description of the runaway, was published on the Sabbath and nailed to the church doors. Once the proclamation was made public:

> it shall be lawful for any person or persons whatsoever, to kill and destroy such slaves by such ways and means as he, she, or they shall think fit, without accusation or impeachment of any crime for the same: And if any slave, that hath run away and lain out as aforesaid, shall be apprehended by the sheriff, or any other person, upon the application of the owner of the said slave, it shall and may be lawful for the county court, to order such punishment to the said slave, either *by dismembring,* or any other way, not touching his life, as they in their discretion shall think fit, for the reclaiming any such incorrigible slave, and terrifying others from the like practices.[100]

The above statute exemplifies the "maturation" of the Virginians' legislative process and their views of blacks as nonhuman beings. They seemed to view blacks as if they were fungible products— just like trees, tobacco, or other disposable commodities. They

---

* "Colored" refers to Indians, mulattoes, and mixtures of Indian and black.

seemed horrified over the fact that some slaves would become "incorrigible," without ever pausing to question why. Did the legislature in 1705 think that blacks might also have an innate desire for freedom—just as their white masters sought it? Was it the lust by blacks for freedom which made them incorrigible? The language of statutes so often masks the human suffering which is imposed by statutory fiat. The reference to "dismembring" indicates that just as branches could be cut from a tree, if the trunk remained upright, the limbs of the slaves could be dismembered with statutory justification providing it was "not touching his life." The statute permitted the court to sanction such punishment also for the purpose of "terrifying other blacks"—terrifying them so that they would not become incorrigible, so that they would not dare to seek freedom. Thus the judicial system, which historically is cited as a refuge of justice for the weak and dispossessed, was utilized by colonial Virginia to sanction brutalizing blacks rather than to protect them. One obligation did remain for the court. The legislature recognized at least one type of value inherent in each slave. It provided that:

> And to the end, the true value of every slave killed, or put to death, as aforesaid, may be the better known; and by that means, the assembly the better enabled to make a suitable allowance thereupon, *Be it enacted,* That upon application of the master or owner of any such slave, to the court appointed for proof of public claims, the said court shall value the slave in money, and the clerk of the court shall return a certificate thereof to the assembly, with the rest of the public claims.[101]

Thus, by their statute of 1705 the legislature most carefully protected the economic values of the master and disregarded the human value of a slave's life. So that there could be no doubt of their paramount concern for the masters' economic welfare, they declared:

> XXXVIII. Provided always, and it is further enacted, That for every slave killed, in pursuance of this act, or put to death by law, the master or owner of such slave shall be paid by the public.[102]

Virginia: An Evaluation

After the first blacks landed in 1619, they had an uncertain legal status for at least four decades. But as the years passed the freedom of blacks decreased and the deprivations they were forced to endure were transformed into legal dogma. By 1705 Virginia had rationalized, codified, and judicially affirmed its exclusion of blacks from any basic concept of human rights under the law. After the 1705 slave code, Virginia made several revisions, in acts passed in 1710, 1723, 1726, 1727, 1732, 1744, 1748, 1753, 1765, 1769, 1778, 1782, 1785, 1787, 1789, and 1792.[103] The 1792 act was the last and most comprehensive codification of the slave codes in eighteenth-century Virginia. Yet, from 1705 to 1792 there was no change of substantial significance to improve the status of slaves or free blacks.

In 1723, for instance, a free Negro or mulatto who was a house-keeper could keep one gun "[a]nd that all negroes, mullattoes or Indians bond or free, living at any frontier plantation [were] permitted to keep and use guns."[104] In this respect Virginia was not as restrictive as some other colonies and states.[105] A 1769 provision banned the dismemberment of blacks because it was often "disproportioned to the offense and contrary to the principles of humanity";[106] nevertheless, the statute authorized the castration of any slave who attempted to ravish a white woman, but it had no similar provision when white men either attempted or in fact ravished black women.[107]

In proceedings involving solely blacks, blacks were allowed to testify in court. But their testimony was admissible only against blacks.[108] No white man could ever be found guilty of a crime on the word of a black person.[109]

Thus, even upon reading all the late eighteenth-century legislative modifications in the light most favorable to Virginia, the pattern of debasement and degradation remains. The black slaves' plight was one of daily imposition of brutality by the laws which sanctioned his enslavement; no part of the legal process was his ally, the courts not his sanctuary. Virginia's later restrictions against the importation of slaves were probably attributable more to economic motivation than to humanitarian concern about the plight of blacks.[110]

As the legalized debasement of blacks continued, Virginia's primary statesmen were spouting the language of revolutionaries in their claims for freedom from King George. In their famous Virginia Bill of Rights of June 12, 1776, they declared as a first principle:

> 1. That all men are by nature equally free and independent, and have certain inherited rights, of which, when they enter into a state of society, they cannot by any compact deprive or divest their posterity; namely, the enjoyment of life and liberty, with the means of acquiring and possessing property, pursuing and obtaining happiness and safety.[111]

Of course, the happiness and safety of which they spoke was the happiness for whites *only*. The right to acquire and possess property included the right to acquire black human beings. They made clear that blacks were not "by nature equally free" because they reserve those rights only for those persons who "enter into a state of society." They did not intend for blacks to be considered as human beings within a state of society, and thus as free and independent persons with "inherent rights."

This first clause was considered by the Virginia Court of Appeals in 1806 in *Hudgins* v. *Wright*.[112] Judge St. George Tucker, one of Virginia's most famous justices, explored the issue of the presumption of freedom for all men (including blacks), and whether the Virginia Bill of Rights applied to blacks. He framed the issue as follows:

> Suppose three persons, a black or mulatto man or woman with a flat nose and woolly head; a coppor coloured person with long jetty black, straight hair; and one with a fair complexion, brown hair, not woolly or inclining thereto, with a prominent Roman nose, were brought together before a Judge upon a writ of Habeas Corpus, on the ground of false imprisonment and detention in slavery: How must a Judge act in such a case? . . . He must discharge the white person and the Indian out of custody . . . and he must redeliver [into slavery] the black or mulatto person, with a flat nose and woolly hair to the person who claiming to hold him or her as a slave, un-

less the black person or mulatto could . . . produce proof of his descent, in the maternal line, from a free female ancestor.[113]

Judge Tucker vigorously disagreed with the lower court chancellor, who had ruled that freedom was the birthright of every human being and that the Virginia Bill of Rights had established a presumption of freedom, thereby putting the burden of proof of ownership on the person who wanted to enslave any black. Judge Tucker said the Virginia Bill of Rights had been framed "with a cautious eye," that it was "meant to embrace the case of free citizens, or aliens only; and not be a side wind to overturn the rights of property, and give freedom to those very people whom we have been compelled from imperious circumstances to retain, generally, in the same state of bondage that they were in at the revolution, in which they had no concern, agency, or interest."[114] Thus, Judge Tucker's ruling was a definitive holding that Virginia law imposed a different burden on all black people because of the coincidence of their woolier hair, their flatter noses, or their darker skin—thus deprivations that even "aliens" would never be subjected to, if they were white.

Thus, in 1806 Virginia was continuing its ambivalence as to whether blacks were human beings or whether, as Virginians had declared in their creditors' laws, they were more like horses, dogs, and real estate.[115] Virginia's leadership in drafting these slave codes was followed by other colonies; such is part of Virginia's legacy to the nation. Later on, Virginia legislators did occasionally pause to recognize by statute that blacks had some humanitarian rights, for in Chapter 12 of the 1805 statute, they declared "it is not unlawful for a master to permit slaves to accompany them, or any party of a family to a religious worship if it is conducted by a *white* man."[116]

3

MASSACHUSETTS
SLAVES AND THE PILGRIMS

I N 1700, sixty-two years after the first black slaves had been brought to the Massachusetts Bay Colony,[1] Samuel Sewall, noted Boston churchman and jurist, published New England's first public antislavery tract, "The Selling of Joseph." Liberty, he wrote, being "the real value unto Life; [n]one ought to part with it themselves or deprive others of it but upon mature consideration."[2] This statement underscores the ambivalent attitude toward slavery even within the "God-fearing" Puritan Massachusetts Bay Colony, a point not always dealt with fully by historians and scholars. William Sumner's allegation that "Slavery was repugnant to the Puritans and was regarded by them with abhorrence"[3] may have accurately reflected the moral pretensions of the colonists, but Sewall's statement revealed the true picture: to deny an individual his liberty was indeed a serious act, but it was an act that was legal and justifiable under the auspices of the legal process, on condition only that the deprivation of liberty was the result of "mature consideration."

John Winthrop's Journal entry of 1638 is apparently "the earliest recorded account of Negro slavery in New England. . . . Negroes may have been enslaved before that time but earlier allusions to slavery are inferential and even contemporaries were apparently no more certain of the facts."[4] But from that early date on, slavery did not then develop in New England in any haphazard or piecemeal fashion. Unlike Virginia, for example, which developed a legal framework for slavery in response to societal custom, the Massachusetts Bay and Plymouth colonies statutorily sanctioned slavery as part of the 1641 Body of Liberties a mere three years after the first blacks arrived. Thus, Massachusetts was the first colony to authorize slavery by legislative enactment.

The 1641 Body of Liberties outlawed "bond slaverie, villenage, or captivitie" among the settlers, unless those to be held in bondage were:

> lawful captives taken in juste warres, and such strangers as willfully sell themselves or are sold to us. And these shall have all the liberties and Christian usages which the law of God established in Israell concerning such persons doth morally require. This exempts none from servitude who shall be judged thereto by Authoritie.[5]

Thus, although three types of servitude had been expressly prohibited, three forms of bondage had in turn been legislatively authorized.[6] Massachusetts colonists could rightly enslave those captured in just wars, strangers who were voluntarily or involuntarily sold into slavery, and those individuals who were required by "Authoritie" to be sold into servitude. But, when did a war become just? And which people were strangers? And under what conditions could the authorities sentence someone to servitude? Alone, the statute provides only an inkling of the colonists' acceptance of and participation in the institution of chattel slavery. As we follow and analyze the legal system's use and misuse of this early statutory framework, we will see in full detail the development of slavery in the New England colonies.

Participation in the International Slave Trade

When judicial and legislative decisions are analyzed, it becomes clear that from the earliest years of settlement, Massachusetts settlers were deeply involved in the kidnapping, transporting, and selling of black Africans. Further, even William Sumner's allegation that slavery was morally repugnant to the Puritans (if not legally prohibited) must be viewed skeptically. How repugnant could slavery have been to the Puritans if they allowed members of their closely controlled colony to participate in the lucrative slave trade? The profitability of this trade was such that New England merchants braved the tremendous dangers involved in transporting slaves through international waters. During most of the seventeenth century, a fierce international struggle was raging on the west coast of Africa between powerful European trading combinations, each trying to corner the markets that supplied slaves for the New World. While other small and independent traders were being virtually eliminated—their small size making them easy prey for all sides— the Bay Colony merchants survived and even prospered. By 1676, they were actively transporting slaves from Madagascar to the West Indies. Two years later, John Saffin, a Boston merchant and jurist, and John Endicott, also of Boston, were selling blacks in Virginia, sometimes as slaves, other times as indentured servants. In 1678, for instance, John Endicott sold a Spanish mulatto (Antonio) to Richard Medlicott to serve, "But for ten years from the day he shall Disembarke in Virginia, and to be a free man to goe wherever he pleaseth." Saffin sold another slave two months later under similar conditions.[7]

Changes in international politics further encouraged New England merchants to participate in the slave trade. In 1696 the English parliament revoked the monopoly granted to the Royal African Company for slave trading, thereby enabling all Englishmen to engage legally in the slave trade. Moreover, in 1713 England gained the *Assiento* (the privilege of supplying 4800 blacks a year for thirty years to Spain's American colonies) from Portugal. The New England settlers quickly seized the opportunity to utilize the region's "resources" in skilled shipbuilders, sailors, and profit-seeking merchants; by the 1700s New England was the most active slave-trading area in America.[8]

The Massachusetts colonists viewed the international slave trade as their English counterparts did—merely as another form of commercial activity. They required merchants and sailors to abide by no more than the usual rules. Thus, although some scholars[9] have argued that the 1646 case of *Smith* v. *Keyser*[10] was an indictment of slavery and the international slave trade, a careful examination of both the facts and the ultimate decision suggests that what was antagonistic to the court was the method by which the blacks were captured, and not the fact that the blacks were made slaves.

On a Sunday in 1645 two Massachusetts slave merchants, William S. Smith and Thomas Keyser, joined with London slave raiders in an attack upon an African village, killing about one hundred persons and wounding others. Two Negroes, one of whom was an interpreter, were brought to Massachusetts and sold.

The Massachusetts General Court first learned of the manstealing when Smith, the ship's captain, sued his first mate for damages that had occurred when the mate left the port too early and refused to deliver the remainder of the cargo—black human beings. Although the court felt compelled to register "indignation against ye haynos and crying sinn of manstealing," the court allowed the captain damages for the blacks who had been stolen from him.[11]

One magistrate before whom the case was tried presented a petition to the court to bring a separate indictment for the crimes of murder, manstealing, and Sabbath-breaking because he believed the acts to be directly contrary to the laws of God and the laws of the colony:

> The act (or acts) of murder (whether by force or fraude) are expressly contrary both to the law of God, and the law of this country.
>
> The act of stealing negers, or taking them by force (whether it be considered as theft or robbery) is (as I conceive) expressly contrary both to the law of God, and the law of this country.
>
> *The act of chaceing the negers (as aforesayde) upon the sabbath day (being a servile worke and such as cannot be considered under any other heade) is expressly capitall by the law of God.*[12]

The magistrate further requested that the court censure and imprison the offenders.

The indictment sought by the magistrate was well within the scope of actions the general court could take. The statute under which Smith and Keyser were charged, the 1641 Body of Liberties, did not authorize the taking of slaves without compensation; it did, however, provide a partial standard for distinguishing manstealing from slavery. The statute limited "lawful" slavery to those situations in which individuals were lawfully captured during "juste wars" or where strangers were willingly sold to New Englanders. Yet, the en-

actment proscribed that "he who stealeth a man and selleth him
. . . he shall surely be put to death."[13]

Manstealing and murder were crimes against the colony and
against God and therefore punishable by death; Sabbath-breaking
was also a capital crime. Yet, the general court ultimately considered only the charge of manstealing. It ordered the blacks returned
to Guinea in November, 1646, "by the first opportunity (at the
charge of the country for present)"[14] and neither Smith nor Keyser
was ever fined or prosecuted.

Despite its professed moral indignation, the court did not condemn slavery because slavery per se was not contrary to Massachusetts colonial law. The general court's emphasis on Smith and Keyser's acts of "manstealing" implies that no protests would have been
made on the blacks' behalf if they had been purchased or received
in exchange for rum, trinkets, or other commodities. "The Puritan
conscience, controlled as it was by the Biblical injunction could not
but revolt against the stealing of a man, even as it would have condemned the theft of an ox, a horse, or a keg of rum."[15]

Some colonists did protest against the selling of human beings
for profit. The most noted was missionary John Eliot, an English
pastor of a Puritan church from 1651 until his death in 1690. In a
letter dated June 13, 1675, to the Boston General Council, Eliot
argued that repression and slavery were in contradiction to the
teachings of the Bible.

> This usage of them is worse than death. It seemeth to me that
> to sell them away as slaves is to hinder the enlargement of His
> kingdom. To sell souls for money seemeth to me a dangerous
> merchandise. If they deserve to die it is far better to be put to
> death under godly persons who will take religious care that
> means may be used that they may die penitently. To sell them
> away from all means of grace when Christ hath provided
> means of grace for them is the way for us to be active in de-
> stroying their souls, when we are highly obliged to seek their
> conversion and salvation.[16]

But Eliot stood alone or nearly alone against the financial might of
a growing number of wealthy traders and New England slave
masters.

Enslavement as Punishment for Crime

Although slavery was not legally sanctioned until 1641, records dating as early as 1636 reveal that the Puritans had already evolved their own version of local slavery. Initially, the local slavery system was penal. Servitude could be imposed as punishment for a variety of crimes, ranging from robbery to nonpayment of fines; servitude imposed as punishment was usually labeled "slavery" by the Massachusetts colonial courts. Such punishment was applied to both sexes and all races, or at least Indians and whites, for one of three terms: a definite number of years; for the life of the individual; or until restitution was made. Most sentences were imposed against Indians captured in wars or against others as punishment for crimes. Colonial records indicate a disparity in that nonwhites (and particularly Indians) seemed to receive longer sentences.

One of the earliest references to slavery in the Massachusetts court records was the sentence of perpetual enslavement given to an Indian. Chousop, "the Indian of Black Island was adjudged to be sent to the island and there kept as a slave for life to worke, unless we see further cause." It is possible to read the last words, "unless we see further cause," as evidence that Chousop's enslavement was not necessarily irrevocable. Even the fact that there appears to be no further mention of Chousop in later records cannot be held to be conclusive.

In another case, the 1638 case of *Re Andro[w]s,* the flexibility of the colonial legal process in Massachusetts, even when the court clearly sought to impose a sentence of slavery, is conclusively demonstrated.

> William Androws, having made assault upon his mr, Henry Coggan, struck him diverse blowes, and wickedly conspired against the life of his said mr, and not only so, but did conspire also against the peace and welfare of this whole commonwelth, was censured to bee severely whiped, and delivered up as a slave to whom the Court shall appoint.[17]

One year later the court released Androws:

Willi: Androws, who was formerly committed to slavery for his ill and insolent carriage, is released (upon his good carriage) from his slavery, and put to Mr. Endecott, hee promising to pay Henry Coggan 8'; and so Androws is to serve Mr. Endecot the rest of his time.[18]

Other early cases suggest that when those who were not Indians were enslaved for criminal or antisocial activity, the court usually did not intend such slavery to be perpetual. The hallmark of the era, however, was judicial inconsistency. In some instances non-Indians were sentenced to slavery, and there are no concise records indicating the release of these persons from such terms of bondage.[19] For example, in 1640 Thomas Savory was made a slave "for breaking a house in the time of exercise [and] was censured to be severely whipped, and for his theft to be sould for a slave until he have made double restitution."[20] There is no further reference to Savory's release in later years, although he may very well have been voluntarily released by his owner once restitution had been made.

A comparison of the court's treatment of Androws with that of Chousop, however, highlights curious inconsistencies in the court's approach to servants. Chousop, an Indian, was sentenced to slavery for some unrevealed offense. The race of Androws, found to have attacked his master, was not disclosed, leading to the inference that he was white. An eventual reprieve ended Androws's slavery; no additional proceedings in Chousop's behalf were recorded.

These few cases of record are insufficient to clearly establish the argument that the New England colonists had developed any defined system of racial slavery prior to the 1660s. There is at least one instance in which the person enslaved was probably white. Marmaduke Barton was "condemned to slavery and to be branded, and to remain in slavery till the court take further order about him."[21] As in *Chousop,* there is no record that Barton was ever released.

The last time the general court attempted to impose enslavement on whites for their violations of the colony's laws was in the 1659 case of *Re Southwicke.*[22] The Southwickes had been fined by the county courts in Salem and Ipswich for not working and for siding with the dissident Quakers; their father, Lawrence Southwicke, had been banished by order of the general court on May 11, 1659 for his Quaker views. When the Southwicke children were brought before the general court, the court ruled:

> in answer to a question, what course shall be taken for the satisfaction of the fines, the Court, on perusall of the lawe, title Arrests, resolve, that the Treasurers of the several counties are and shall hereby be impowered to sell the said persons to any of the English nation at Virginia or Barbadoes.

However, the two were not taken out of the colony; Edward Butler, one of the treasurers, "sought out for passage, to send them to Barbadoes, for sale; but none were willing to take or carry them."[23]

Southwicke was probably the last time the general court ordered the enslavement of whites, whether free or indentured servants, for violating the criminal or religious laws of the colony, although in 1665 the general court in *Laborne*[24] authorized a debtor's enslavement to ensure that his creditors would be repaid. The court ruled that "the petitioner . . . be delivered to the creditors to be sold or serve, he having taken his oath that he is not worth five pounds." Laborne had petitioned the court for such a solution to his financial problems. The *Laborne* decision does not reveal whether the petitioner was made a slave, or a servant only until the debt was paid.

Since the Body of Liberties prohibited only bond slavery, villenage, or captivity, there was probably legislative authority to continue enslaving whites who fell within the permissible categories—particularly nonbond slavery.[25] The discontinuance of white enslavement and the perpetuation of nonwhite enslavement throughout this colonial period illustrates a societal decision to impose slavery only on nonwhites, particularly Indians. Records are admittedly scarce. Yet, despite the lack of conclusive evidence, it seems that the treatment accorded Indians by the Massachusetts colonists sharply contrasted the treatment accorded either white or black servants and slaves, even though the differential treatment was not mandated by the statute or judicial authority.

THE SPECIAL BRAND OF INDIAN ENSLAVEMENT

As the early cases suggest, the New Englanders' attitude toward Indians was at best ambivalent. The colonists depended on the Indians for trade and for instruction on how to survive in the wilderness during the early years of the settlement. Some religious zealots felt duty bound to convert to Christianity the very Indians whom the English considered less than human and against whom their prejudice was revealed in various ways, the most notable being the usurpation of lands.

Racial and cultural prejudices were never specifically cited as explanations for English action; instead, the colonists justified usurpation by the doctrine of *vacuum domiculium codit occupanti,* which held that those who enclosed, maintained, and domesticated the land obtained a civil right superior to the natural right of the possessor. Additional justification was grounded in the "revealed word of God," which told the chosen people to occupy the earth and to increase and multiply.[26] It was John Winthrop, governor of the Massachusetts colony, however, who revealed the more practical considerations prompting the usurpation of Indian territories:

> There is more than enough for them and us. 3dly, God hath consumed the natives with a miraculous plague, whereby the greater part of the country is left voide of inhabitants. 4thly, We shall come in the good leave of the natives.[27]

The general court of the colony enforced the English right to take the Indians' "unimproved" land in 1633. The court ruled that all land not cultivated by Indians lay open to any that could or would improve it.[28]

In the early (1640) case of *Re Hope, the Indian,* the court had ordered Hope to be severely whipped for running away and "other misdemeanor."[29] But within forty years the Massachusetts general court chose to treat Indians more harshly, as the 1674 decision in *Re Indian Hoken* demonstrates.[30] Indian Hoken, described by the court as a "notoriouse theife . . . being insolent in his carryage and an incorrigable theife . . ." was convicted of burglary, sentenced to prison and then escaped from prison. The court ruled that:

> whereby many persons are greatly in feare and danger of him; wherfore in Court doe order Mr. Hinckley and Leiftenant Freeman, or any other magistrate that can light off the said Hoken, that they cause him to be apprehended and sold or

sent to Barbadoes, for to satisfy his debts and to free the col-
lonie from so ill a member.

Hoken indicates the Massachusetts court's willingness not merely
to enslave but to banish Indians who violated the colony's laws.

In cases after *Hoken* the Massachusetts courts continued to
punish Indian criminals by enslavement, either for a term of years
or for life, or to banish them from the colony; occasionally, as in
Hoken, both forms of punishment were used. Yet this era was one
of considerable flexibility for the judiciary, as demonstrated by the
1674 *Re Indian Tom* decision.[31] Indian Tom was found guilty of
rape and sentenced to death. Pleading ignorance of the law, Tom
petitioned the court for leniency. The general court ruled that it
was:

> meet to grant his request as to saving of his life, but order,
> that he be sold for a slave for ten yeares, to be sent to the
> English living in some parts of the West Indies, remayning in
> prison till he be sent away.

In *Re Indian Popanooie,* decided in 1677,[32] neither Popanooie
nor his wife (the defendants) were as "fortunate" as Indian Tom.
Popanooie was convicted of "great crewlty" toward the colonists.
The court condemned Popanooie, his wife, and children to *per-*
petual servitude. Popanooie, alone, was banished. One year after
the *Popanooie* decision, the Massachusetts court imposed perpetual
slavery on yet another group of Indians. Three Indians were sold
into lifetime slavery because they were unable to reimburse the
colonists from whom they had stolen twenty-five pounds; in this
case, however, the court did not banish the Indians.[33]

The later cases are crucial if we are to trace the development
of slavery in Massachusetts. They mark the first time the court
imposed perpetual servitude on nonwhites as punishment, a retreat
from the previous position of treating all servants equally.[34] Of
course, even in the late seventeenth century all Indians (or blacks)
who were convicted were not sentenced to term or perpetual slavery. Yet, the record reveals that while during this era some nonwhites were made lifetime slaves, NO whites were perpetually enslaved.[35]

Black Slavery in New England

It is difficult to discern why, given the relatively small number of blacks in the New England colonies, slavery developed at all. Lorenzo Greene states that blacks numbered less than a thousand in 1700 and were never more than 3 percent of the total population in the eighteenth century.[36] Virginia and other colonies rationalized slavery on their need for a large labor force and one that could withstand the hot climate;[37] as that labor force grew, Virginians reasoned that the harshness of their slavery laws was due to a fear of slave revolts. In Massachusetts, where there was no staple crop, a large labor force was unnecessary; indentured servants were probably adequate. And, because the actual number of blacks in the colony was too small to prompt a fear of revolt, there seemed to be little reason for the development of a separate legal status repressive of them.[38]

Yet New England colonists showed a marked preference for black slaves as opposed to white indentured servants. As early as 1645, Edward Downing, Governor Winthrop's brother-in-law, was arguing that blacks were essential to the growth of the colony; he even went so far as to express his interest in a "juste warre" with the Indians whereby he could obtain Indian captives to exchange (presumably in the West Indies) for blacks. " 'The colony will never thrive,' [Downing] wrote Winthrop, 'untill we gett . . . a stock of slaves sufficient to doe all our business.' "[39] And as late as 1723 a visitor to Boston noted that the New England whites "will rather be burnt in their beds by them [the blacks] than suffer English servants to come hither to work, obliging all M[aste]rs of ships to carry them back again upon their own charge, or else they must not trade in this country."[40] Thus, although indentured servants did come in the original migrations during the 1630s and Governor Winthrop was noticeably upset that they stopped coming during the 1645 Civil War, they were always less welcome in New England than in the more southern colonies.

By the end of the 1600s some blacks in New England were perpetual slaves and that status was transmitted to their children. It is difficult to trace the development of this legal status, which came to be applied to blacks (even black Christians) and other nonwhites. We know that all blacks were not slaves for life. Yet, we do not know the proportion of the black population that was free or indentured.

If one finds merit in determining the comparative levels of deprivation, one will discover that the New England institution of slavery was probably the most "benign" system in the original English colonies.[41] There was often a fusion of the status of slave and servant; black servants and slaves were apparently accorded the same legal rights as white servants in terms of their ability to petition the court for protection against their masters, and in their ability to obtain the same panoply of legal protections available to whites when they were criminal defendants. Thus, in New England perpetual servitude did not involve complete removal of basic rights. The Body of Liberties, which authorized slavery as punishment for criminals and for war captives, did not authorize the denial of those basic rights enumerated in the Scriptures. "In Massachusetts, the magistrates demonstrated that they were not about to tolerate glaring breaches of 'the Law of God, established in Israel,' even if the victims were Negroes."[42]

An analysis of available court records is necessary to determine how blacks were treated in colonial Massachusetts, since blacks were involved in both voluntary servitude and involuntary penal slavery. Furthermore, the problem is compounded by the rather inconsistent references made to blacks in colonial records. For example, the earliest use of a term denoting blackness appears in a Massachusetts Bay Court of Assistants entry in 1642 noting that "Mincarry the blackmore was admonished, and dismissed."[43] The record failed to indicate Mincarry's legal status. After this initial entry, references to blacks tended to occur in the use of "negro" as the party's surname or after the party's full name; thus, when a colonist was not labeled a "negro" and/or when a colonist's full name alone was used, the colonist was probably white.

Two early cases underscore the flexibility with which the Massachusetts General Court treated blacks. In *Re Negro*[44] (1653) the court settled a controversy between a "neager maide servant of John Barnes," and John Smith of Plymouth (who was probably white). The court ruled that:

whatsoever could bee said on either side was heard; and with admonission, both parties were cleared.

This decision suggests that both parties, including the "neager maide servant," were given the opportunity to present evidence and to have their respective arguments considered. Whatever the nature of the controversy, the court did not assume that the "neager" woman was in the wrong.

The 1669 decision of *Re Franck Negro*[45] suggests that blacks were not deprived of more basic rights:

> Franck Negro is Indicted . . . for conspiracy: aiding or assisting John Pottell in his escape out of the prison in Boston of the 8th. of December last. the said Pottell being committed in order to his tryall for murdering of the Cooke of the ship *Golden Fox* . . . wee the Grand Jurie doe not find Franck Negro: guilty of the fact according unto this bill of Indictment.

Failure of the court in *Franck* to use the words "servant" or "slave" suggests that Franck could have been a freedman. But, whatever his status, Franck was tried for the crime in the same manner a white person would have been. He was formally accused and the grand jury evaluated the merits of the charge; there was nothing to indicate that special procedures were instituted or used because Franck was black.

Re Negro Sebastian[46] (1676) illustrates judicial leniency toward a black servant whose master petitioned the court to spare the servant's life; Sebastian had been found guilty of rape and was ordered hanged. The court granted the master's request for leniency and ordered that Sebastian receive thirty-nine stripes and to always "weare a roape about his neck, to hang downe two Foot, . . . and whenever he is found without his roape, on complaint thereof to be severely whipt with twenty stripes, and dischardging the prison charges, to be releast and dischardged the prison."

It is not clear whether the servant could have appealed the decision in his own right or whether the master's petition was required for the reduction of sentence. Whatever the circumstances, the black servant seems to have been accorded a just and fair hearing. And yet there is always the underlying question as to whether the court's motives were humanitarian and in consideration of Sebastian or whether the reduction in sentence was predominantly motivated by the court's concern that Sebastian's master not sustain a financial loss.[47]

A case that suggests parity in the legal treatment accorded blacks and that given whites by the Massachusetts colonial courts was *Re Hannah Bonny,* decided in 1685.[48] Hannah Bonny, a white woman, was convicted of fornication with two lovers, John Michell and Nimrod, a black man; Nimrod fathered Hannah's illegitimate child. Both Hannah and Nimrod were sentenced to be "severely whipt" and Nimrod was ordered to provide for the child's maintenance. John Michell was not racially identified and therefore was probably white. Michell was convicted of fornication with Hannah Bonny and for "lascivious carriages and speeches at sundry times." He was sentenced to be "severely whipt" and required to give a bond with surety "for his good behaviour." Both Nimrod and Michell were directed to be "severely whipt" and the sentences were tailored to fit the nature of their crimes. No racial animus is apparent in the court's decree.

Blacks and Indians were able to petition the courts for their freedom in much the same manner as white servants. In the 1737 case of *Re Negro James,*[49] the court announced that it was "pleased to Order that he might have a Writ of Protection for his security . . . so he might then further apply for his Freedom." James had initially petitioned the court to emancipate him as provided for in his master's will in 1735; at that time the court issued the Writ of Protection for James's "security until three months after the death of his mistress." When his mistress died in 1737 James re-petitioned the court. The court then declared him "to be absolutely free."

The significance of the *James* case is best understood when compared with the more restrictive decisions in other colonies.[50] Almost forty years before the *James* case, the Virginia legislature had rigidly restricted a master's right to manumit his slaves; the assembly prohibited manumission of slaves unless the masters paid for the transportation of the slaves out of the colony.[51] In 1723 the assembly forbade emancipation except by approval of the governor and council, which would approve the petition only as a reward for special public service.[52]

While Massachusetts legislation never approached the restrictiveness found in Virginia, the colony did impose some limits on a master's ability to manumit his slaves through legislation passed in 1703. This act, requiring masters to post security before freeing their slaves, was ostensibly caused by the "great charge and inconveniences . . . to divers towns and places" occasioned by the practice of freeing old or ill unskilled slaves who were unable to support themselves and thus had to be supported by the towns. Failure of a master to provide the required bond rendered the attempted manumission void and the slave became "liable at all times to be put forth to service by the selectmen of the town." That effective maintenance of indigent blacks was a main concern of the statute is shown by a petition to the House of Representatives in 1716, for an exception from the bond requirement. The petition was granted, "In as much as the Petitioner is a young able-bodied man & it cannot be supposed that he is Manumitted by his Master to avoid charge in supporting him."[53]

With the close of the seventeenth century, the Massachusetts colonists began to exhibit symptoms of paranoia and the fears of slave uprisings usually associated with southern colonists. Reports of slave unrest in other colonies may have caused the slave owners in Massachusetts to interpret disorders in their colony as insurrectionist plots. The 1681 case involving a black servant, Marja, reveals the developing Puritan attitude toward slave recalcitrance.[54] In *Re Marja,* a black woman servant was indicted for burning down a building in Roxbury; the court found that Marja did not have "the feare of God before her eyes."[55] Because her actions were "instigated by the divil," Marja was burned at the stake, the punishment traditionally used when the defendant was thought to be possessed by the devil. Three other black servants, Jack Negro, Cheffaleer, and another identified only as Jack Pemberton's Negro, were found to have joined Marja in the commission of the crime; Jack was ordered hanged and the other two men were ordered "kept in prison till his master send him out of the country."[56]

The Marja incident was not to be the only time when slave owners in Massachusetts were to attribute suspicious fires to discontented blacks. For example, there were a series of suspicious fires in Boston in April, 1723, shortly after an alleged "plot" had been discovered in Virginia and at a time when recollections of the 1712 insurrection in New York were still vivid.[57] These fires were viewed by the Massachusetts authorities as part of a black uprising. The governor of the colony offered a reward for the apprehension and arrest of the arsonists, proclaiming that the "fires have been designedly and industriously kindled by some villanous and desperate Negroes, or other dissolute people . . . it being vehemently suspected that they have entered into a combination to burn and destroy the town. . . ."[58]

A military force was added to the common watch. Whenever a fire was reported, a portion of the force was armed and sent out to keep the slaves. Even a year after the 1723 fires, a local newspaper, the *N. E. Courant* of November, 1724, reviewed the fires and concluded that blacks had been responsible:

> It is well known what loss the town of Boston sustained by fire not long since, *when almost every night* for a considerable time together, some building or other and sometimes several in the same night were either burned to the ground or some attempts made to do it. It is likewise well known that those villanies were carried on by Negro servants, the like whereof we never felt before from unruly servants, nor ever heard of the like happening in any place attended with the like circumstances.[59]

Immediately following these fires Boston selectmen revised their earlier regulations and passed a complex local act, applicable only to Boston, *Articles for the Better Regulating Indians, Negroes and Molattos Within this Town, that if approved they may be Endeavored to be Drawn into a Law or Lawes at the Next Session of the Great and Generall Court or Assembly.*[60]

The Boston articles required *all* Indians, blacks, and mulattoes to remain inside their masters' home between one hour after sunset and one hour before sunrise. It was illegal for them to wear or carry weapons or to idle or lurk together in groups of more than two, and to go to the common (training field) on training days after sunset even with their masters' permission.

The articles also required every free Indian, black, or mulatto to bind out his children to an English master when the children were between ages four and twenty-one. Finally, the articles precluded free nonwhites from entertaining any nonwhite slave in his "House, yard, garden or outhouse," unless the servant had been sent by his master; from selling liquor or provisions at the training field on all "Publick dayes"; and from receiving any goods from nonwhite servants or slaves. Apparently, the drafters assumed that either the social customs precluded free blacks from entertaining whites or that such relationships would not be as pernicious or potentially conspiratorial.

The penalties for violating these articles were a severe public whipping at the House of Corrections, plus a fine for the free nonwhites. Penalties stiffer than those in earlier ordinances were imposed for nonwhites who engaged in conduct previously prohibited, such as receiving stolen goods, stealing, breaking and entering, and assaulting "any of his Majesties Subjects."[61] Moreover, bond and free nonwhites alike could be "Sent beyond Sea"—a synonym for their banishment, sale, and transportation to the West Indies.[62]

There is no indication that the general assembly ever enacted such legislation on a colonywide scale. Although the earlier Province Laws dealing with nonwhites tended to treat specific problems as they arose,[63] by the beginning of the eighteenth century laws for the entire province sketched more broadly the parameters of the institution of black slavery. The Province Laws were couched in terms that stressed the inconveniences and disorders allegedly caused by nonwhites. However, the laws effectively defined and regulated nonwhite slavery in the colony and defined and limited the rights of the nonwhite population.

Another act passed in 1703 established a 9:00 P.M. curfew for Indians, black or mulatto servants, or slaves because "great disorders, insolences and burglaries are oft times raised and committed in the night time by Indians, negro and mulatto servants and slaves, to the disquiet and hurt of her majest's good subjects." The curfews reinforced the narrow path drawn for nonwhites in bondage; if found out of their masters' control without their masters' permission, nonwhite servants and slaves could be arrested and forced to spend the night in prison or be taken before a justice of the peace for immediate sentencing.[64]

Changing Legal Concepts of Blacks

Admittedly, these acts illustrate the distinctions made by the legal system between nonwhites and whites. But, it was not until 1705 that nonwhites were openly and obviously equated with *chattel*.* The 1705 act imposed a duty on imported blacks, which continued for several decades, despite opposition from the British home government. The act required ship captains to list all imported blacks and to pay "four pounds per head," or a fine of eight pounds if they refused or failed to make proper entry. A rebate was allowed if the slave died within six weeks or was sold out of the colony within one year; some slave owners petitioned for remittance of the duty because of hardship or because the slaves were not worth the money.

With each passing decade, black, Indian, and mulatto slaves were more and more closely identified as chattel, not people, in the colony's tax assessment statutes. A 1646 statute taxed black slaves as individuals (though their masters had to pay the charges); acts in 1692, 1696, and 1698 included nonwhite servants and slaves in assessments of personal property, and a 1707 law classified nonwhite slaves as personal estate and nonwhite servants as polls.[65] Despite protests by humanitarians such as Judge Sewall and the Reverend John Eliot, black and Indian "servants for life" continued to be rated with horses, oxen, cows, goats, and swine until the Revolutionary War.[66] On the local level, Boston selectmen were embellishing on this design by tabulating the number of "Houses Ware Houses Negroes Horses and Cows within the Town."[67]

Boston presents a special case. In that city, where as many as one-third of all the blacks in the colony lived, the selectmen were particularly concerned that public officials "take Especial care to keep the Indians, Negroes, and Melattoes in Good Order, and See that the Province Law Respecting them be Attended."[68] Free nonwhites were often included in the proscriptions of the black slave codes on the local level, and local regulations covered a wide range of situations, including burying, gambling, and curfew. Indeed,

---

* *Chattel* is used to mean goods or property.

many of the local ordinances seemed to assume some condition of servitude for all blacks; even the acts ostensibly regulating free blacks make references to the inconveniences to their masters or to permission required from their masters.[69] Several ordinances establishing watchmen's duties typically ordered the watchmen after 9:00 or 10:00 P.M. "to Walk the Streets, Lanes &c. in Order to take up all Negro and Molatto Servants, that shall be unseasonably Absent from their Masters Families, without giving a sufficient reason therefor."[70]

However, at one point the curfew was evidently not intended to apply to free nonwhites, for in 1740 the following matter was brought before the Boston selectmen:

> John Wood'by a free Negro man, appear'd and Complains, that on the 10 Instant, he was taken up in the Street by John Rice One of the Watchmen as he was going from his Day labour in the Evening to his Lodging, was Bound and Imprisoned, and Obliged to pay Thirteen Shillings before he could gain his Liberty, and all without any legal process— Which he humbly Apprehends is against Law and Justice, and Prays the Select men would advise him how to act in the affair.
>
> Voted, That mr. Savell be directed to Notify and Warn John Rice, to attend on the Select Men, next Wednesday, in the afternoon, to make answer to the Complaints exhibited against him as above.

On June 25, 1740, "John Rice . . . appeared . . . and gave the Select men an account of his proceeding in that Affair. But Woodby not appearing according to Order, the said Rice was dismiss'd, with a Caution to Act prudently in all such matters for the future."[71]

Blacks, Indians, and mulattoes in Boston were also forbidden to keep hogs because such an activity allegedly tempted them to steal from their masters, spend time away from their masters, and possibly plot together. On March 10, 1745, Captain John Steel made a motion "that some Method may be taken, to prevent Negroes keeping Hogs." Thomas Hubbard, Esq., petitioned for the same measure on March 25, 1745. On April 8, 1746, the town took the matter into consideration and voted for a committee to be chosen "to Consider what will be best for the Town to do hereon."

The committee, consisting of Thomas Hubbard, Esq., Mr. Edward Bromfield, and James Allen, Esq., reported on May 14, 1746, at "a meeting of the Freeholdors and other Inhabitants of the Town of Boston duly qualified and lawfully warned . . ." and made the following draft of a bylaw:

> Whereas great Damage arises to the Inhabitants of the Town of Boston by negro's and Indians keeping Hogs, not only by Occasioning very great Wast in the several Familys they respectively belong to, but as it Exposes them to great Temptations to Steal and purloin from their several Masters, provisions and other of their Substance and especially as it Occasions great Loss of time, and gives them an opportunity of Meeting and conferring together, whereby great Injuries have been done to the Inhabitants of said town.
>
> For the Prevention of so great an Evil
>
> Ordered that no Indian negro or molatto shall be permitted to Keep any Hog or Swine whatever within the Town of Boston either with or without the privity or Consent of his said Master or Mistress, under the Penalty of Twenty Shillings to be paid by the Master or Mistress of any Indian, negro or molatto so offending for the use of the poor of said Town, upon due conviction of any such Offence before any one of His Majesty's Justices of the Peace for the County of Suffolk.
>
> And if any person shall hire or let to hire to any Indian Negro or Molatto, any Sty or Penn, or peice of Ground whereon to Erect the same, or that shall suffer any Indian Negro or Molatto to keep any Swine on any of their Ground. Ordered that every person so Offending on due Conviction thereof as aforesaid shall also forfeit and pay the sum of twenty shillings for the use aforesaid.

This draft was accepted and the selectmen were requested "to present it to the next Court of General Sessions of the peace for their Approbation."[72]

BLACK CODES IN MASSACHUSETTS

Why did this extensive regulation of nonwhites suddenly spring full-blown at the beginning of the eighteenth century? Was this regulation merely to reinforce and protect the economic institution of slavery (as the southern slave codes of the period are interpreted)? Or were the regulations, as the law against interracial marriage might imply, the fruit of racial prejudice and perhaps fear, which ripened with the sudden and significant increase in the black population of the English colonies during the first quarter of the eighteenth century?[73]

During the first half of the eighteenth century the black population in Massachusetts more than doubled. This increase only raised the number of blacks to slightly over 2 percent of the total colony's population by 1755; the black population constituted approximately 8 percent of the total population of Boston during this era.[74] There were never as many blacks in Massachusetts as there were in the southern colonies, where blacks usually numbered over 30 percent of the total population.[75] At best, this numerical disparity may have produced regulations and black codes that were less harsh than those found in southern colonies such as Virginia.

The approaches in Massachusetts and Virginia tended to differ, but in both places there was always regulation. Virginia colonists sought to regulate whites and nonwhites primarily out of fear; slave masters were required by law to exercise strict discipline over their slaves, regardless of personal preferences, for the safety of the colony. In Massachusetts, certain transactions between whites and nonwhites were precluded by law (such as interracial sexual relationships), and fear of the nonwhite population was probably at least partially responsible for this. But there appears to have been no pervasive sense of civic duty to the codes. The codes seemed to have been drafted more as nuisance regulation.

Ordinances began with a litany of the inconvenience and disorder caused by the nonwhite behavior about to be limited. This nuisance image of nonwhite behavior necessarily assumed that wherever there were nuisances, nonwhites were involved. Thus the 1728 prohibitions of street gambling blamed "young People, Servants & Negroes," and a 1752 prohibition of commercial street pageants and shows assumed the "tumultous companies" contained "men, children, & negroes."[76]

The ultimate implication of this view—which the southern colonists seemed to reach early in their history—was that nonwhites were the cause of all disorder and inconvenience. In the eighteenth century, with the institution of slavery racially defined and the degradation of servitude stamped on all nonwhite skins, blacks and Indians free or unfree became the usual scapegoats for disturbances and inconsistencies between the white colonists' image of an English and Christian civilization and the day-to-day reality of their lives.

The question of which came first—formalization and protection of slavery, or racial prejudice and xenophobia—is of course unanswerable. And the answer may not even matter. What does matter is that in constructing the legal system to entrench nonwhite servitude and limit and dehumanize nonwhites, the white colonists were forced to confront the basic flaw in all systems of subjugation. There can be no successful, peaceful coexistence between master and slave: between those who are always considered human and those beings who are sometimes animal sometimes human, who are sometimes bought and sold like chattel and sometimes able to own chattel, and who are sometimes bound as perpetual slaves and sometimes free.

In the autumn of 1755, in Cambridge, Massachusetts, two slaves of John Codman of Charlestown were put to death. Mark was hanged and Phillis was burned alive. Having ascertained that their master had willed them freedom at his death, they poisoned him, to obtain liberty sooner.[77] This is the most the Puritans could have expected from their system of slavery.

Movement for Abolition

Almost before the formal institutionalization of slavery, Massachusetts colonists had attempted to stop the importation of black slaves. In 1701 Boston selectmen indicated their desire "to promote the Encouraging [of] the bringing of white servants and to put a Period to negros being Slaves."[78] In 1712 the colony passed a law prohibiting the importation of Indian servants or slaves because:

> divers conspiracies, outrages, barbarities, murders, burglaries, thefts, and other notorious crimes and enormies at sundry times, and especially of late, have been perpetrated and committed by Indians and other slaves within several of her majesty's plantations in America, being of a malicious, surly and

revengeful spirit . . . and discouragement to the importation
of white Christian servants . . .[79]

However, these measures were not aimed at equality for nonwhites.
Both showed concern over the presence of nonwhites and attempted
to use legal sanctions to minimize the numbers of nonwhites. The
1712 act was specifically intended as a check on the introduction of
the violent Tuscarora Indians from South Carolina. The practical
nonexistence of humanitarian reasons for ceasing the importation
of black slaves lends credence to Lorenzo Greene's description of
Judge Samuel Sewall as almost the only abolitionist in early eighteenth-century Massachusetts.[80] It was not until after mid-century—
the "revolutionary period"—that a humanitarian rationale for the
abolition of black slavery first appeared.

In March, 1767, a bill "to prevent the unwarrantable and unlawful Practice or Custom of inslaving Mankind in this Province,
and the importation of slaves into the same" was presented in the
Massachusetts House of Representatives. This March, 1767 bill
was countered with a "bill for laying an Impost on the Importation
of Negro and other Slaves" for one year. Both measures were defeated.[81] Meanwhile, the Boston selectmen voted to adhere to their
instructions to their representatives that "for the total abolishing
of Slavery among us that you move for a Law to prohibit the Importation and purchasing of Slaves for the future."[82]

In 1771 another "Bill to prevent the Importation and purchasing of Slaves into this Province" was passed by the legislature and
the council. Governor Hutchinson, however, refused to sign it. He
wrote, regarding this and two other bills, to Lord Hillsborough, Secretary of State for the colonies:

> The Bill which prohibited the importation of Negro Slaves ap-
> peared to me to come within his Majesty's Instruction to Sir
> Francis Bernard, which restrains the Governor from Assent-
> ing to any Laws of a new and unusual nature. I doubted be-
> sides whether the chief motive to this Bill which, it is said, was
> a scruple upon the minds of the People in many parts of the
> Province of the lawfulness, in a meerly moral respect of so
> great a restraint of Liberty, was well founded, slavery by the
> Provincial Laws giving no right to the life of the servant and a
> slave here considered as a Servant would be who had bound

himself for a term of years exceeding the ordinary term of human life, and I do not know that it has been determined he may not have a Property in Goods, notwithstanding he is called a Slave.

I have reason to think that these three Bills will be again offered to me in another session. I having intimated that I would transmit them to England that I might know his Majesty's pleasure concerning them.[83]

But the British government opposed any impediment to the slave trade.[84] Indeed, this opposition was one of the grievances listed in Jefferson's first draft of the Declaration of Independence.

Near the closing years of the French and Indian War, Massachusetts slaves began to appeal to the legal sensibilities of individual jurists by bringing "freedom cases"—civil lawsuits for their liberty. This was also a time of general awakening among white colonists to their political enslavement to the British.[85]

In 1765, "Jenny Slew of Ipswich in the County of Essex, spinster" sued "John Whipple, Jun., of said Ipswich Gentleman" for trespass. Slew charged Whipple with unlawfully taking her "with force and arms," keeping her as his slave from January 29, 1762 to March 5, 1765, and doing "other injuries against the peace" and to her, in the amount of twenty-five pounds damage. Defendant Whipple answered the charge with the novel plea that "there is no such person in nature as Jenny Slew of Ipswich aforesaid, Spinster." The Inferior Court of Common Pleas accepted Whipple's defense and charged Jenny Slew with the expense of the suit. But, one year later a jury for the Superior Court of Judicature reversed this ruling and granted Jenny Slew four pounds in damages plus expenses.[86] No general trend toward granting slaves freedom was yet in evidence, for in 1768 the highest court in the colony ruled against the slave Amon, finding "that said Amon [Newport] was not a freeman, as he alleged, but the proper slave of the said Joseph [Billing]."[87]

On May 2, 1769, a black slave named James sued Richard Lechmere of Cambridge "in trespass for assault and battery, and imprisoning and holding the plaintiff in servitude from April 11, 1758, to the date of the writ." Once again the Inferior Court of

Common Pleas ruled against the slave, but on October 31, 1769 the Superior Court of Suffolk had the case settled by compromise. Nineteenth-century abolitionists proudly cited this case as the legal destruction of slavery in Massachusetts; Charles Sumner later glorified the *Lechmere* case[88] in the United States Senate. However, later authorities examining the court records discovered that the case was not litigated to a definitive conclusion and that there was no real determination as to James's freedom.[89]

In later cases there were judicial determinations and the trend of the judiciary quickly shifted toward granting the slaves' freedom.[90] These cases illustrated the significant and generally unparalleled access Massachusetts blacks had to the colony's courts. Blacks were allowed to bring appeals and were permitted the general procedural safeguards available to all citizens. As one instance, in *Caesar* v. *Taylor* (Essex, 1772), a slave's wife was not allowed to testify against the slave and the defendant master was not permitted to answer a general charge of false imprisonment simply by demonstrating his ownership of the slave.[91] Later abolitionists found similarities between *Caesar* v. *Taylor* and other Massachusetts cases on the one hand, and Lord Mansfield's discharge in 1772 of the slave from Boston, Sommersett, on the other (see pp. 333-355). Yet, in fact, these decisions actually went beyond the *Sommersett* ruling. In 1785 Lord Mansfield himself referred to the *Sommersett* decision as going "no farther than that the master cannot by force compel the slave to go out of the kingdom."[92] In reference to the many British actions by black slaves for wages from their masters, Lord Mansfield said, "When slaves have been brought here, and have commenced actions for their wages, I have always . . ." denied the plaintiff's claim.[93]

In 1774, a jury, sitting in the Essex Inferior Court of Common, granted a verdict to the black slave Caleb Dodge of Beverly, Massachusetts, who had sued his master for restraining his liberty. The jury based its verdict on the ground that there was "no law of the Province to hold a man to serve for life."[94] It is not clear whether the jury reached this verdict from knowledge of the colony's charter, stating that "all subjects . . . shall have & enjoy all liberties & immunities . . . as if they . . . were born within . . . England,"[95] or because of specific instructions from the court. Nevertheless, the case stands as a significant recognition by white jurors that a black man had a right to his liberty.

This growing recognition and awareness among white juries was insufficient to bring about wholesale liberation. And so, blacks tried additional avenues. A "Petition of Slaves in Boston" was signed in January, 1773 and presented to Governor Hutchinson, his Council, and the House of Representatives. This "humble petition of many slaves living in the town of Boston, and other towns in the province" asked only "[t]hat Your Excellency and Honors, and the Honorable Representatives would be pleased to take their unhappy state and condition under your wise and just consideration." As this indicates, the petition was humble and subservient in its approach, with the blacks accepting their lot "so long as God, in his sovereign providence, shall *suffer* us to be holden in bondage," asking "for such relief as is consistent with your wisdom, justice, and goodness," and concluding with the note that "we pray for such relief only, which by no possibility can ever be productive of the least wrong or injury to our masters, but to us will be as life from the dead." Yet the petition also pointed out that "[a]lthough some of the negroes are vicious . . . there are many others of a quite different character." In a particularly poignant passage, the petition lamented: "We have no property! we have no wives! we have no children! we have no city! no country!"[96]

A later petition, submitted to the House in June, 1773, was more specific in its demands; this was the petition of "Felix Holbrook, and others, Negroes":

> praying that they may be liberated from a state of Bondage, and made Freemen of this Community; and that this Court would give and grant to them some part of the unimproved Lands belonging to the Province, for a settlement, or relieve them in such other Way as shall seem good & wise upon the Whole.

This petition, continued to the January, 1774 session, ultimately inspired "a Bill to prevent the Importation of Negroes and others as slaves into this Province." Governor Hutchinson did not sign the bill and in June, 1774 Governor Gage refused to sign it. At this point the concurrence of the governor became irrelevant—the general court dissolved itself the day after it concurred on the later bill.[97]

The problem then passed to the new state's legislature. In 1777 "Lancaster Hill, and a number of other negroes" asked that the legislature "take into consideration their state of bondage, and pass an act whereby they may be restored to the enjoyment of that freedom which is the natural right of all men. . . ."[98] Both the petition and the preamble to the suggested act reflected the current trends in revolutionary rhetoric. The preamble began:

> Whereas ye unnatural practice in this state of holding certain Persons in slavery, more particularly those transported from Africa and ye children born of such persons, is contrary to ye laws of Nature, a scandal to professors of ye Religion of Jesus, and a disgrace to all good Governments, more especially to such who are struggling against Oppression and in favor of ye natural and unalienable Rights of human nature—[99]

Nonetheless, the sincerity of this fervor was somewhat questionable: the legislature voted to table the act and make application on the subject to the predominantly slave-holding congress.[100]

As the conflict with England became more polarized, the British took advantage of this heterogeneous view of human liberty in the colonies. Tory propaganda played upon the inconsistency and some British soldiers conspired to turn it to a practical advantage.[101] In 1768 a British captain attempted to convince black slaves to rise against their masters on the assurance that foreign troops had come to procure their freedom and "with their assistance, they would be able to drive the Liberty Boys to the devil." Several of the slaves' owners complained to the Boston selectmen, who brought a complaint against the captain and caused his arrest. However, through the influence of the British, the indictment was quashed and the captain fled.[102] Meanwhile "the Several Constables of the Watch [were] directed by the Selectmen, to be watchful of the Negroes and take up those of them that may be in gangs at unseasonable hours."[103] In 1774 blacks in Boston approached the British on their own. They persuaded an Irishman to draw up a petition to Governor Gage, offering to fight for the British if he could arm them and liberate them when he conquered. Gage seriously considered the proposal, but the plot was discovered before it could be effected. This episode occasioned one of the most famous and telling comments on the ironic inconsistency among the revolutionaries. In describing the plot to her husband, Abigail Adams said:

> There is but little said, and what steps they will take in consequence of it I know not. I wish most sincerely there was not a slave in the province; it always appeared a most iniquitous scheme to me to fight ourselves for what we are daily robbing and plundering from those who have as good a right to freedom as we have. You know my mind upon this subject.[104]

When blacks were captured as prisoners of war, perhaps as a result of such conspiracies, the Americans were somewhat uncertain as to the appropriate treatment. In 1776 two such prisoners were about to be sold but the Massachusetts House of Representatives passed a resolve forbidding their sale and establishing a policy of treating all prisoners of war alike, regardless of color.[105]

The presence of slaves in the Revolutionary Army was recognized by the Massachusetts authorities as incongruous. In May, 1775, the Massachusetts Committee of Safety passed the following resolution:

> That it is the opinion of this Committee, as the contest now between Great Britain and the Colonies respects the liberties and privileges of the latter, which the Colonies are determined to maintain, that the admission of any persons, as soldiers, into the army now raising, but only such as are freemen, will be inconsistent with the principles that are to be supported, and reflect dishonor on this Colony, and that no slaves be admitted into this army upon any consideration whatever.[106]

The preclusion of blacks, Indians, and mulattoes from the colony's militia[107] lasted until the severe winter of 1776-1777 forced the authorities to admit nonwhites as draft substitutes and as actual soldiers. Nonwhites remained a vital part of the Massachusetts armed forces throughout the war, although after the war, the early policy was reinstated and "Negroes, Indians and Mulattoes" were "exempted" from the army in the First General Militia Act of 1785.[108]

Efforts to Enact a Constitution

The Massachusetts legislature established a Constitutional Convention in 1778 to write an American constitution for the new state. To an extent, the convention revolved around the conflict between those for and those against black equality. Those who opposed equality for blacks (even free blacks) won; the 1778 constitution the Massachusetts legislature sent to the towns for ratification included Article V, which provided:

> Every male inhabitant of any town in this state, being free, and twenty-one years of age, excepting Negroes, Indians and Mulattoes, shall be entitled to vote for a Representative or Representatives, as the case may be . . .[109]

The status of free blacks was particularly ambiguous during the period in which the state's constitution was pending passage. In February, 1780 blacks in Dartmouth, Massachusetts petitioned the general court for relief from taxation because the 1778 constitution denied them the privileges and duties of citizenship. The blacks complained that they had "no vote or influence in the election of those that tax us."[110]

The 1778 constitution was resoundingly defeated, with 9972 towns voting against the constitution and only 2083 of the towns voting for it; a margin of roughly five to one.[111] It can be easily argued that the proposed constitution was defeated primarily because of the restrictive suffrage requirements. There also seemed to have been a general dissatisfaction with a constitution lacking a Declaration of Rights, which would presumably have included a "free and equal clause," as had several of the declarations enacted prior to the Revolutionary War. Most important for the present analysis, however, are the declarations of those towns that viewed Article V as a condonation if not a legitimation of slavery. The town of Westminister rejected the constitution, for example, because the townspeople found:

> the following articles appears to us Exceptionable viz—Article 5th which deprives a part of the humane Race of their Natural

Rights, . . . Which in our opinion no power on Earth has a Just Right to Doe.[112]

The town of Sutton in Worcester County was even more explicit in its disapproval of the 1778 state constitution, particularly Article V, which was characterized as "wear[ing] a very gross complexion of slavery." It was further suggested by the townspeople that it:

> is diametrically repugnant to the grand and Fundamental Maxims of Human Rights, viz. *"That Law to boind all must be assented to by all."* which this Article by no means admits of, when it excludes free men, and men of Property from a voice in the Election of Representatives; Negroes &c. are excluded even tho they are free and are men of Property. This is manifestly adding to the already accumulated Load of guilt lying upon the Land in Supporting the Slave Trade. . . . We also can't but observe that by this Article the Convention had in contemplation of having many more Slaves beside the Poor Africans, when they say of others beside; being *Free* and twenty-one . . .[113]

The towns' selectmen voted to call a new constitutional convention, separate from the legislature, in Cambridge in 1779-1780. John Adams drafted the new constitution and without much discussion the convention agreed to include a Declaration of Rights,* unqualified male suffrage, and unqualified male eligibility for elective office.

Even with the addition of the Declaration of Rights and the extension of suffrage to *all* males, two decided improvements over the 1778 constitution, the status of nonwhites in Massachusetts was not secure. There was no explicit emancipation clause nor any language authorizing legislative action effecting emancipation. Clearly, slavery continued to exist within the state after the 1780 constitution was ratified. A 1781 statute assessing taxes recognized that some nonwhites were still enslaved, and required: "Negroes and

---

* "All men are born free & equal, & have certain natural, essential, & unalienable rights; among which may be reckoned the right of enjoying and defending their lives and liberties; that of acquiring, possessing, and protecting property; in fine, that of seeking and obtaining their safety and happiness." Massachusetts Constitution of 1780, Art. I, *Federal and State Constitutions* 3: 1889.

Molattoes . . . such of them as are under the government of a master or a mistress, to be taxed to said master and mistress." This statutory language was used until 1793.[114]

Quock Walker:
Did It Abolish Slavery in Massachusetts?

Massachusetts blacks turned to litigation in order to secure recognition of their humanity and equality. Historians have usually praised the Massachusetts judiciary, and particularly Chief Justice William Cushing, for abolishing slavery in 1783 by the decision in *Commonwealth* v. *Jennison*,[115] the final in a series of cases concerning the freedom of a black man, Quock Walker.

When Reverend Jeremy Belknap, a prominent Massachusetts abolitionist and founder of the Massachusetts Historical Society, was asked in 1795 by Virginia lawyer St. George Tucker how Massachusetts had abolished slavery, he concluded that both public opinion and the law were responsible: "The general answer is, that slavery had both been abolished here by publick opinion; which began to be established about 30 years ago."[116] Belknap concludes that it was the decision in the *Quock Walker* case that "was a mortal wound to slavery in Massachusetts."[117]

Quock Walker's legal difficulties began sometime in 1781 when he escaped from his master Nathaniel Jennison and fled to Seth and John Caldwell's nearby farm. The Caldwells had been brothers of Walker's former master, whose widow subsequently married Jennison. Jennison and some friends attempted to force Walker to return, and when he resisted, they severely beat him and brought him back to the Jennison farm. A few days after this incident, Walker sued Jennison for assault and battery; the justice of the peace referred the case to the next session of the Worcester County Court. The Caldwells consulted Levi Lincoln, who would later serve as lieutenant governor of Massachusetts and as attorney general for both Massachusetts and the United States. Lincoln was widely believed to be the most able attorney in Worcester; he assured the Caldwells that Quock Walker was legally able to work for them.[118]

The case of *Quock Walker* v. *Jennison* was heard in June,

1781. Walker charged Jennison with assault and battery, asking 300 pounds in damages. In defense Jennison produced a bill of sale to prove that he owned Walker, implying that as owner of a "proper slave," he was legally entitled to discipline the black man. The jury found that, "said Quo[c]k is a Freeman and not the proper Negro slave of the Deft." Walker was awarded fifty pounds in damages.[119] Though Jennison filed an appeal, he failed to appear when the case was called for argument and the lower court's decision was affirmed.

Jennison also filed suit against the Caldwell brothers, claiming that on April 2, 1781, the Caldwells "seduced Quock Walker from plaintiff's service," and "caused him . . . to absent himself and retained said negro for 6 weeks for their own benefit."[120] Levi Lincoln and Caleb Strong argued on behalf of the Caldwells, but the jury decided in favor of Jennison and awarded him twenty-five pounds. The case was appealed to the Supreme Judicial Court which found the Caldwells not guility and levied costs against Jennison.

The verdicts in the two trial cases were clearly contradictory. If Quock Walker was really a free man, as the jury in the first case had decided, how could the Caldwells have been found liable to Jennison for interfering with the use of his property? This inconsistency may be due to the proclivity of Massachusetts juries to rule in favor of slaves who challenged the legality of their enslavement.[121]

In the appeal of *Jennison* v. *Caldwell,* Lincoln and Strong, arguing on behalf of the Caldwells, asserted that Walker had not been enticed away from his master. But the fundamental issue before the appellate court was whether Walker was actually a slave or free to come and go as he pleased. Stearns, Jennison's attorney, argued that Walker had consented to be a slave; and even if there had been no consent, Walker became Jennison's property in 1754 when he and his parents were purchased by the Caldwells' older brother. When the original master died, Walker became his wife's property; and when she married Jennison, Walker became his property.[122]

In his brief and in his argument on behalf of the Caldwells, Lincoln did not rely on the new constitution. Instead, Lincoln argued that regardless of the constitution, slavery was a violation of natural rights guaranteed humanity by natural law and the law of God:

It will then be tried by the laws of reason and revelation. Is not a law of nature that all men are equal and free. Is not the laws of nature the laws of God? Is not the law of God then against slavery.[123]

According to Lincoln, if the constitution could be construed as authorizing slavery, the constitution conflicted with the law of God. The task before the jury, Lincoln summarized, was to choose between the law of the state and the law of God:

> We are all born in the same manner, have our bones clothed with the same kind of flesh—had the same breath of life breathed into us—are all under the same Gospel dispensation have one common Saviour—inhabit the same com[mon] Globe of earth, die in the same manner, the white may have their bodies wrapt in rather finer linnen—& his coffin a little more decorated—& then all distinctions of mens making ends —we all sleep in a level in the dust—Shall all be raised by the sound of one common trump—calling to all that are in their graves . . . to arise. Shall be arrained at one common bar shall have one common Judge, tried by one common jury— condemned or acquitted by one common law—by the Gospel the perfect law of liberty—
> This cause will then be tried over again, and your verdict will then be tried gentlemen of the jury. Therefore gent. of the jury let me conjure you to give such a verdict now as will stand the test, as will be approved of by your own minds in the last moments of your existence—by your Judge at the last day—.[124]

The last in the series of cases involving Quock Walker began in April, 1783: before the Supreme Judicial Court, meeting in Worcester, Jennison was indicted and charged with assault and battery committed on Quock Walker. The full state bench, consisting of Chief Justice Cushing, Justices Sargeant, Sewall, and Increase Sumner heard the case. Attorney General Robert Paine, arguing that Jennison had attacked a free citizen (Walker), not a chattel slave, produced testimony proving that Walker's former master had promised to manumit him once he reached the age of twenty-five, that his widow had renewed this promise, and that

Jennison was aware of the promise before his marriage to the widow.[125]

Jennison's defense counsel relied upon a showing of the existence of a master-servant relationship between Jennison and Quock Walker; the state's major arguments were not contested. Rather, Jennison's act was characterized as a proper disciplinary measure. Moreover, it was maintained that without a specific prohibition of slavery in the 1780 constitution, the traditional and widely recognized right of a person to hold property in slaves should not be contravened by implication or construction of the constitution.[126]

Despite defense counsel's admonitions, Chief Justice Cushing's charge to the jury relied extensively on the 1780 constitution. Directing the jury to find Jennison guilty on the basis of the facts presented at the trial, Cushing construed Article I of the constitution as *granting* rights incompatible with the institution of slavery:

> The defense set up in this case afforded much scope for discussion and has been fully considered. It is founded on the assumed proposition that slavery had been by law established in this province: that rights to slaves, as property, acquired by law, ought not to be divested by any construction of the Constitution by implication; and that slavery in that instrument is not expressly abolished. It is true, without investigating the rights of christians to hold Africans in perpetual servitude, that they had been considered by some of the Province laws as actually existing among us; but nowhere do we find it expressly established. It was a usage—a usage which took its origins from the practice of some of the European nations and the regulations for the benefit of trade of the British government respecting its then colonies. But whatever usages formerly prevailed or slid in upon us by the example of others on the subject, they can no longer exist. Sentiments more favorable to the natural rights of mankind, and to that innate desire for liberty which heaven, without regard to complexion or shape, has planted in the human breast—have prevailed since the glorious struggle for our rights began. And these sentiments led the framers of our constitution of government—by which the people of this commonwealth have solemnly bound themselves to each other—to declare—*that all men are born free and equal;* and that *every subject* is *entitled to liberty,*

and to have it guarded by the laws as well as his life and property. In short, without resorting to implication in constructing the constitution, slavery is in my judgment as effectively abolished as it can be by the granting of rights and privileges wholly incompatible and repugnant to its existence. The court are therefore fully of the opinion that perpetual servitude can no longer be tolerated in our government, and that liberty can only be forfeited by some criminal conduct or relinquished by personal consent or contract. And it is therefore unnecessary to consider whether the promises of freedom to Quaco, on the part of his master and mistress, amounted to a manumission or not. The Deft must be found guilty as the facts charged are not contraverted.[127]

The jury heeded the chief justice's charge and found Jennison guilty of assault and battery. This verdict was predicated on a finding that slavery was not legal in Massachusetts as of 1781.

Cushing read the language of the new constitution literally and concluded that the institution of slavery was inconsistent with the words "all men are born free and equal." There is no discussion of the intent of the framers of the document. It is not clear, however, whether this lack of discussion derived from Cushing's assumption that the framers intended to abolish slavery or whether he found their intention irrelevant, except insofar as to incorporate the doctrine of natural laws favoring liberty, in face of the actual words of the document.

Cushing's decision not to discuss the intentions of the framers may have been due to personal convictions against slavery. However, there is at least some evidence suggesting that Cushing was not as staunch an abolitionist as his words would lead one to believe. Cushing had owned at least one slave, Prince Warden, who complained to the attorney general of Massachusetts in 1779 that Cushing had failed to emancipate him as promised. The attorney general notified Cushing that Prince Warden was to be given "a proper manumission in the course of the week [or] an action will be carried to next court so that if he is your slave you may have an opportunity to prove it."[128] No record exists of any court proceedings on the matter, but Cushing's papers indicate that Prince Warden became a hired man in the late summer of 1779.

Still another episode involving slaves may appear to cast some doubts on the abolitionist sentiments of Chief Justice Cushing. In 1779 a ship carrying blacks was captured by the British in South Carolina, then recaptured by a Massachusetts ship and brought to Boston. The blacks were interned there until they could be claimed by their masters. Some of the slaves refused to return to slavery in South Carolina and these were held in the Suffolk County Jail until April, 1783, when they were freed by a writ of *habeas corpus* from the Supreme Judicial Court. South Carolina, considering the act an illegal emancipation of slaves belonging to its citizens, strongly protested the action to the governor of Massachusetts, Hancock, who in turn asked the Supreme Judicial Court for an advisory opinion on the matter.

Justices Cushing and Sargeant, both of whom had issued strong problack and antislavery charges to juries in the *Quock Walker* cases, considered the matter and Justice Cushing wrote the advisory opinion, which both signed. The best that can be said about the opinion is that it was masterful equivocation about the rights of blacks, and that it revealed more about the two justices by what it failed to say than by what it said. Although the justices agreed that the blacks had a right to a *habeas corpus* hearing at the time it was granted, the justices held that the slaves should have been turned over to their proper owners initially, whether the slaves went peaceably or not: "If a man has a right to the services of another, who deserts his service, undoubtably he has the right to take him up and carry him home to serve again. . . ." This right, Cushing continued, "has always been the case here [Massachusetts], without any sanction from the magistrate."[129] Perhaps the equivocation suggests not a lukewarm attitude toward the problems of slaves but rather a concern for peaceful relations with a sister state and for strengthening, not weakening, the loose confederation of states.

Traditionally, historians have concluded that the *Quock Walker* cases abolished slavery in the state of Massachusetts. But did Chief Justice Cushing's charge to the jury and the jury's verdict abolish slavery in Massachusetts? Even contemporary observers differed as to the effect of the decision. For example, in March, 1795 Judge James Winthrop complained that:

By a construction of our state Constitution, which declares all men by nature free and equal, a number of citizens have been deprived of property formerly acquired under the protection of law.[130]

Several prominent citizens, responding to a series of questions about slavery sent by Judge St. George Tucker of Virginia to Dr. Belknap,[131] indicated that in their view it was the Massachusetts Declaration of Rights of 1780, as interpreted by the courts in 1781 and 1783, which had abolished slavery. Some attributed the end of slavery to popular sentiment. For example, Dr. Eliot answered that: "The cause of abolition of slaves in the State may be traced entirely to the sentiment of the people."[132] Agreeing, Belknap found that although the *Quock Walker* cases severely undermined whatever legal foundation existed for slavery, public opinion had been opposed to slavery for more than thirty years.

John Adams, although not totally dismissing the moral arguments against slavery, found that it was economic considerations that propelled the antislavery missiles in Massachusetts. On March 21, 1795, Adams replied to the questions printed by Belknap in the following manner:

I was concerned in several causes in which negroes sued for their freedom, before the Revolution. The arguments in favour of their liberty were much the same as have been urged since . . . arising from the rights of mankind, . . . Argument might have some weight in the abolition of slavery in Massachusetts, but the real cause was the multiplication of labouring white people, who would no longer suffer the rich to employ these sable rivals so much to their injury. This principle has kept negro slavery out of France, England, and other parts of Europe. The common people would not suffer the labour, by which alone they could obtain a subsistence, to be done by slaves. If the gentlemen had been permitted by law to hold slaves the common people would have put the negroes to death, and their masters too, perhaps. . . . The common white people, or rather the labouring people, were the cause of rendering negroes unprofitable servants. Their scoffs and insults, their continual insinuations, filled the negroes with discontent, made them lazy, idle, proud, vicious, and at length wholly useless to their masters, to such a degree that the abolition of slavery became a measure of economy.[133]

Massachusetts: An Evaluation

Perhaps, as some historians have suggested, Massachusetts colonists spoke out in moral outrage against the institution of slavery in 1636. Yet, ownership of human property was endorsed by the power structure, for throughout the colonial period statutes sanctioned the ownership of human beings and the colonial courts protected the masters' ownership interests. Merchants from Massachusetts, the most vigorous slave traders in the New World, made enormous profits from the slave trade. Judicial records are scarce, but those available reveal the prevalence of slavery in the colony.

The institution of slavery remained ambivalently defined in colonial Massachusetts, however. The earliest cases and statutes suggest that at first slavery was viewed as punishment for criminal conduct. Slaves, who were sometimes white, were generally not thought to be perpetually bound to serve. But with succeeding decades, enslavement became perpetual for nonwhites. By 1700 slavery had evolved into a racially identifiable institution. Blacks were imported into the colony as perpetual chattel slaves; Indians were captured and made perpetual slaves. Color itself began to indicate a separate, and lower, social class; free nonwhites were statutorily limited in their movements and in the occupations they could pursue. Despite these deprivations, one factor was crucial and must not be omitted; the nonwhite population in Massachusetts never lost the right and ability to seek judicial determination of the legitimacy of their individual enslavement.

Domestic slavery never assumed the economic importance in Massachusetts that it had in the more southern colonies. In fact, a combination of this lack of economic dependence on the institution, an expanding white labor population, a nonwhite population able and eager to sue for its freedom in the courts, and a burgeoning moral and intellectual commitment to political and economic liberty contributed to the increase in the number of nonwhites who were granted their freedom.

The political milieu that produced much of the revolutionary ferment during the War of Independence aided the blacks and Indians enslaved in Massachusetts to obtain their freedom either through manumission or through the courts. Moreover, this milieu resulted in a 1780 constitution with a Declaration of Rights which, if read literally, prohibited slavery in the new state. This interpretation was adopted and sustained by the Chief Justice of the Massachusetts Supreme Court in his 1783 charge to the jury in the *Quock Walker* case. Admittedly, slavery continued after the *Quock Walker* decision; judicial decrees tend to affect immediately only the rights of the litigants involved in the case. However, by judicial activism, the state of Massachusetts signaled that it would no longer protect the legality of slavery, regardless of social custom.

4

NEW YORK

FROM HALF-FREEDOM TO SLAVERY

The New Netherland Experience

THE DUTCH SETTLERS: HUMANE MASTERS?

SLAVERY developed gradually in New York, a settlement founded by the Dutch as the colony of New Netherlands and under Dutch control until 1664, when the English conquered it and renamed it New York. Whether as New Netherlands or New York, however, the settlement never evolved as harsh a slave system as did colonies such as Virginia or the Carolinas.[1] Yet slavery and the treatment of free blacks should be viewed as significantly different institutions in New York dependent upon whether the Dutch or the English controlled the legal process. After they were subject to English governance blacks, whether free or slave, were worse off than their brethren in New England and somewhat better off than their southern counterparts.

Slavery was introduced into the Dutch settlement of New Netherlands in an early attempt by the Dutch West India Company to turn a losing colonial venture into a profitable one. The company, which had settled the area in 1623 with expectations of establishing a permanent colony, recognized within a couple of years that it was not attracting to the area homesteaders and the variety of craftsmen necessary to a developing community. For the most part, the early colony consisted of a relatively small number of transient fur traders. Moreover, the small size of the trader population made this New World venture an unprofitable enterprise for the company in its role as a shipping concern. In anticipation of a return cargo of only a few furs, the company was obliged to outfit practically empty vessels and sail them to the New World to supply these first few trader-settlers with goods and supplies. The "solution" for their underdevelopment was the same choice made by other English colonials —the importation of black labor to aid the whites regardless of its consequence to blacks.

Thus, in 1626, three years after the colony's establishment, the Dutch West India Company imported eleven black males into the area;[2] black women were imported in 1628. The early fur traders did not react enthusiastically to the prospect of owning slaves. Unable to provide for their own immediate needs, they were not eager to assume the responsibility for the care and feeding of other humans for whom there was only marginally profitable work. But in bringing in these first few slaves, the company was looking beyond the limited horizons of its early fur-trading population. Meanwhile, to offset its immediate financial losses, the company retained ownership of these blacks and put them to use building military posts, public buildings, and roads.

Despite the economic obstacles to immediate expansion of the slave labor force in New Netherlands, the ultimate value of this labor force was readily perceived by the company. In a company report, the Bureau of Accounts asserted:

> It would be wise to permit the patroons, colonists, and other farmers to import as many Negroes from the Brazils as they could purchase for cash, to assist them on their farms; as (it was maintained) these slaves could do more work for their masters, and were less expensive, than the hired laborers engaged in Holland, and conveyed to New Netherlands, *"by means of much money and large promises."*[3]

It took no sophisticated accounting to compute that the initial financial expenditure for a slave was very little more and sometimes even less than one year's salary of a free white worker. During the 1640s free workers earned 280 guilders a year excluding food and lodging; a slave from the West Indies could usually be purchased outright for 300 guilders, and those from Angola for even less.[4]

Although available evidence suggests that the Dutch West India Company may not have attempted to build up an extensive slave-trading center within its own colony, the company's increased participation elsewhere in the international slave trade undoubtedly encouraged the introduction of black slave labor on a wider basis within the colony. For instance, as an inducement to the use of blacks, the company at times sold slaves to buyers at a discount; "it also permitted slaveowners to exchange unsatisfactory slaves for company slaves free of charge."[5] Thus it was perhaps inevitable that upon long-term exposure to temptation the Dutch in New Netherlands would begin to perceive blacks as their English cousins did—as articles of commerce—and then rationalize the new perception. A poem by the Dutch colonist and poet, Jacob Steendam, written to his legitimate mulatto son in Guinea, reflected this perception:

> Since two bloods course within your veins,
> Both Jam's and Japhet's intermingling;
> *One race forever doomed to serve,*
> The other bearing freedom's likeness[6]

When some Dutch settlers began to express the idea that slavery was the *only* status appropriate to blacks, it was but a short step to treating the decision to exploit black labor simply as an amoral economic determination based solely on what constituted the most efficient allocation of financial resources. The purchase of slaves or black or white indentured servants simply became a way to ensure the continued prosperity of the master class and through them the colony.

Having made the decision to rely on slaves, most of the Dutch colonists preferred to purchase seasoned slaves who had been "broken in" in the West Indies (usually from the island of Curaçao) rather than slaves newly captured from Africa, even though those from Africa were less expensive. The colonists were mostly farmers. There would be few overseers skilled in breaking slaves into submission in the manner of the southern plantations. A slaveowner family in New York would own a single slave family, usually two working slaves (male and female) and their children. Most slaves were able to perform several tasks and were not required to work one staple crop, a clear contrast to their utilization in the tobacco plantations of Virginia and the rice plantations of South

Carolina.[7] Most male slaves worked in the fields and most female slaves were assigned domestic chores, a division of labor similar to that among indentured servants and free whites. As E. B. O'Callaghan notes in his history of early settlement in the area, the role played by black arrivals was a substantial one. He writes: "It is doubtful whether New Netherland would have survived without these slaves . . . they provided the labor which ultimately transformed the colony from a shaky commercial outpost into a permanent settlement."[8]

Yet, from the beginning, the treatment by the Dutch of their slaves was milder than that accorded blacks enslaved in other colonies. It is difficult to point to a single factor responsible for this phenomenon. Some historians have ascribed it to some characteristic in the Dutch settlers' culture and special perception of the world. Others have argued that the Dutch remained less cruel masters because even though Dutch participation in the international slave trade increased during the seventeenth century, the number of slaves held by the colonists (as opposed to those held by the company) remained small enough to obviate a general demand for harsh and disparate treatment of blacks. Still others have noted that the purpose of the settlement was more to create a "community" of Dutchmen in the New World than (as with the English) to provide a means for adventurers to get rich quickly and return to the mother country. Last and saddest, perhaps the milder treatment afforded blacks may not at all have been related to noble motives but simply to time. The Dutch occupation of New York ended while slavery was still in an infantile state and there is evidence to support the conjecture that had slavery been given the opportunity to develop and expand under Dutch authority, the colony might well have followed the harsher models of Massachusetts and Virginia.

Regardless of which explanation one accepts to account for the differences between the English colonies and the lone Dutch colony, the fact remains that during the forty years of Dutch rule in New York, black slaves were often accorded rights usually reserved for white indentured servants. Among the Dutch, in fact, the distinction between freedom and slavery was at times more social than legal. "The casual attitude of the master class together with the ill-defined legal status of the slave tempered the system to such an extent that it resembled in many ways an indenture system."[9] This "casual attitude" was evident in the reluctance of Dutch slave owners to separate slave families, especially women from the children. The slave owners were probably moved by more than compassion; since it was undoubtedly easier to have slave mothers care for their own children, economic expediency came into it as well. But at least the slave family was permitted some semblance of unity.

Negroes were able to own real property and to serve in the militia; slaves had certain tangible rights in the society. In fact, during the Indian Wars of 1641, 1642, and 1643, the Dutch frequently used slaves to track down fugitive Indians who had committed war crimes in the community. George W. Williams, the first great black American historian, wrote that during the entire period of Dutch control, blacks

> went and came among their class without let or hindrance. They were married, and given in marriage; they sowed, and, in many instances, gathered an equitable share of the fruits of their labors. If there were no schools for them, there were no laws against an honest attempt to acquire knowledge at seasonable times. . . . [The Dutch] could not habilitate slavery with all the hideous features it wore in Virginia and Massachusetts. The slaves could not escape the good influences of the mild government of the New Netherlands, nor could the Hollanders withhold the brightness and goodness of their hearts from their domestic slaves.[10]

In the courts, the status of a slave was nearly the same as that of a free man and woman. A slave could testify against other blacks and even in cases in which one or both of the litigating parties was white.

Black slaves were able to seek judicial relief when they were unlawfully held in bondage, as the 1654 case of Antony Jansen, a mulatto, demonstrates.

> *Antony Jansen, a Mulatto, pltf. v/s William Strengwits, deft.*
> For payment of 2 months' wages at 130 lbs. of tobacco per month, amounting to 260 lbs. Deft. says he does not know Antony Jansen, but that he had engaged Willem Schepmoes; requests, that he serve out his time to the last of August, he promising to pay him in full according to agreement. Willem Schepmoes being heard in Court, states, that he put Antony

Jansen in his place with Strengwits's consent, and he is not
bound to serve such a term. Parties being heard on either side,
it is decided that Will. Strengwits's shall pay Antony Jansen
for the 2 months he served in the place of W. Schepmoes, and
if Strengwits have any further claim, he may institute his action against Schepmoes.[11]

The *Jansen* case is unclear in regard to the nature of the relationship between the mulatto, Antony Jansen, and the man whom
he replaced, Willem Schepmoes. Jansen could have been either
Schepmoes's slave or his indentured servant; or, there could have
been no master-servant relationship between the two. But even if
Jansen had been Schepmoes's slave or servant, the court nevertheless required the defendant to reimburse the mulatto, *not* Schepmoes. The *Jansen* decision suggests that blacks and mulattoes could
sue in court for payment of wages and were, by inference, legally
able to hold property and to profit from their own labor. Race apparently posed no impediment to the prosecution of the suit since
each party was able to present its evidence.

A comparison of the *Jansen* decision, where the race of the
plaintiff was judicially recognized, with the *Pataddes* case of the
same year, where no mention was made of the race of either parties,
reveals that the New Netherland tribunals often used race simply
descriptively, in much the same manner in which the Massachusetts
courts employed such terms. There is nothing to suggest that the
court accorded different rights to whites and nonwhites. The plaintiff in *Pataddes* petitioned the court to release him from service because his master (the defendant) "ill-treats him abusing him and
threatening to sell him." The defendant produced the servant's indenture and swore that he had not mistreated him. The court ruled
that:

> Parties having been heard on either side, it is [ruled] Pataddes,
> must serve his time out, provided that Strengwits shall pay
> him and give him satisfaction for the wages he has already
> earned according to contract.[12]

THE HALF-FREEDOM STATUS

The "casual attitude" of the colony toward slavery and servitude made possible the emergence of several forms of less harsh

service for black laborers, perhaps the most unique of those forms
the "half-freedom" status. Under the half-freedom system, a black
slave was able to enjoy the total and full personal rights and liberties of a free person if he or she was able to pay an annual tax and
was willing to perform a specified amount of needed labor for the
Dutch West India Company. A typical half-freedom grant bound
the slave to pay the company annually "30 schepels of maize or
wheat and one fat hog, valued at twenty guilders."[13] Failure to pay
the yearly dues or to perform the tasks stipulated by the company
caused the half-free black to forfeit his quasi-free status. Despite
this drawback, several blacks were able to throw off some of the
shackles of slavery and to obtain the "freedom" certificates that ensured their status; the passes certified the half-free black to be free
and at liberty on the same footing as other free people.

In comparison with the status permitted black slaves in other
colonies, the Dutch half-free status was clearly a beneficial modification of chattel slavery. But though the half-freedom system appears to have been grounded on democratic and humanitarian principles, the system obviously served the more pragmatic economic
interests of the Dutch West Indian Company as well. The half-freedom agreements relieved the company of the burden of providing
for several adult slaves. At the same time, the agreements assured
the company of a percentage of the slaves' profits and a labor force
sufficient to perform the needed public works, since half-free blacks
remained obligated to perform certain tasks for the company.

The following 1644 act of the Director and Council of New
Netherlands emancipating certain Negroes reflects the ambiguous
and hybrid status of these "half-free" blacks in New Netherlands.

> WE, *William Kieft* and Council of *New Netherland* hav-
> ing considered the petition of the Negroes named *Paulo
> Angola, Big Manuel, Little Manuel, Manuel de Gerrit de
> Reus, Simon Congo, Anthony Portugis, Gracia, Peter San-
> tomee, Jan Francisco, Little Anthony, Jan Fort Orange,* who
> have served the Company 18 *a* 19 years, to be liberated from
> their servitude, and set at liberty, especially as they have been
> many years in the service of the Honorable West India Com-
> pany here, and have been long since promised their Freedom;

also, that they are burthened with many children so that it is impossible for them to support their wives and children, as they have been accustomed to do, if they must continue in the Company's service; Therefore, We the Director and Council do release, for the term of their natural lives, the above named and their Wives from Slavery, hereby setting them free and at liberty, on the same footing as other Free people here in *New Netherland,* where they shall be able to earn their livelihood by Agriculture, on the land shewn and granted to them, on condition that they, the abovenamed Negroes, shall be bound to pay for the freedom they receive, each man for himself annually, as long as he lives, to the West India Company, or its Deputy here, thirty skepels of Maize, or Wheat, Pease or Beans, and one Fat hog, valued at twenty guilders, with thirty skepels and the hog they, the Negroes, each for himself, promises to pay annually, beginning from the date hereof, on pain if any one of them shall fail to pay the yearly tribute he shall forfeit his freedom and return back into the said Company's slavery. With express condition, that their children at present born or yet to be born, shall be bound and obligated to serve the Honorable West India Company as Slaves; Likewise that the abovenamed men shall be obliged to serve the Honorable West India Company here, by water or on land, where their services are required, on receiving fair wages from the Company.

Done 25 February, 1644, in *Fort Amsterdam* in *New Netherland.*[14]

The above statute repudiates the claim of historians that half-free blacks were treated as equal to truly free whites. Certainly the half "freed" blacks were treated more harshly than were white indentured servants even under the English, for these blacks had already served eighteen or nineteen years. When freed their rights were supposed to have been "on the same footing as other Free people in New Netherlands," but in actuality the extent of their freedom was far less. If they failed to meet the annual quota of wheat and a fat hog they would be returned to slavery. An even more repressive limitation was that their children "born or yet to be born" were obligated to serve the West India Company as slaves.

The enslaving of the children of free Negroes was denounced by "some of the best citizens" as a "violation of the law of nature." It was asserted that "anyone born of a free Christian mother could never be a slave."[15]

Yet despite the limitations of the half-freedom system, half-freedom was better than total slavery. Thus, the existence of a half-freedom system prior to 1664 raises the inference that slavery, as it existed in every other colony, did not come into being while the Dutch governed New Netherlands. One can argue that slavery in the Dutch colony never granted the master rights of absolute possession over the slave; it constituted only a labor obligation. In this regard, perhaps, slavery during the period of Dutch rule closely approximated the villenage system of feudal England.[16] New Netherland remained one of the few colonies where "slavery" and "freedom" were not perceived as mutually exclusive conditions, but were instead inaccurate labels to describe blurred social distinctions and obligations of labor.

A certain number of blacks did manage to acquire total freedom, usually after a period of servitude. How far back we might have to go to find these first free blacks is difficult to determine. It was not until 1640 that any record was made of the status of blacks in the colony, and by then certain blacks had already obtained their freedom, which many were probably able to retain. Historians have not always recognized this fact. They have assumed instead, perhaps by reasoning backwards, that because practically all the blacks in the New York area in the 1700s, under English rule, were slaves, those blacks who arrived in 1628 and even years later had also all been slaves.

The predominant attitude of the Dutch settlers toward free blacks has been called nondiscriminatory. Free blacks were able to join the Dutch militia and to bear arms. They could own and inherit real estate and other property. No record exists of any legislation severely restricting the rights of free blacks. Free blacks could engage the services of indentured servants. Even interracial marital ties were recognized as valid.

Professor Edgar J. McManus, whose studies on slavery in New Netherlands and New York show a singular depth of penetrating and detailed scholarship, notes:

Neither the West India Company nor the settlers endorsed the specious theories of Negro inferiority used in other places to justify the system. No attempt was ever made to treat free Negroes differently from the white population.[17]

The prejudice and discrimination that existed in the colony was directed primarily against dissident religious groups, particularly Jews. New York City (then New Amsterdam) statutes dating from this era demonstrate that although free blacks might join the militia and buy real estate, Jews were barred from both. An ordinance of the Director and Council of New Netherlands passed August 28, 1655 exempted Jews from military service because "First, the disgust and dislike at the mass of citizens to be fellow soldiers" of Jews "to watch in the same guard house," but in lieu of service each male Jew between sixteen and sixty years of age was required to contribute sixty-five stivers each month.[18] While blacks could purchase real estate, a Jewish merchant named Salvador d'Andrada who had purchased a house and lot in New Amsterdam at a public auction was denied the deed and the sale was declared null and void.[19]

THE ORDINANCES AND JUDICIAL RULINGS
OF NEW NETHERLAND

Most commentators have emphasized that New Netherland, while under Dutch control, dealt far less harshly with blacks than did any of the English colonies. Unfortunately, these conclusions were not often based on a separate detailed analysis of the actual legislative acts. Thus it is particularly intriguing to trace the evolution of the legislative process under the Dutch as they categorized black-white relationships and defined the status of blacks. There still remains the question of whether, if blacks were indeed treated more fairly, it was basically because of custom, economics, and decency—or was it that greater humaneness was required by Dutch laws. Or in other words, how much did Dutch morality influence the evolution of New Netherlands law and how much did Dutch legal traditions preordain the special relationship between whites and blacks that developed in the Dutch colony?

A chronological analysis of the ordinances of New Netherland reveals that in their charter provision of June 7, 1629 defining the freedoms and exemptions for "all persons, masters, or private persons who will plant colonies in New Netherlands," it was provided that:

> The Company will use their endeavors to supply the colonists with as many Blacks as they conveniently can, on the conditions hereafter to be made, in such manner, however, that they shall not be bound to do it for a longer time than they shall think proper.[20]

Thus, ten years after the first blacks landed in Virginia, and as eager as the West India Company was to have blacks in New Netherlands, the colony's charter failed to establish definitively what the legal status of these blacks would be. By specifically providing "that they shall not be bound to do it for a longer time than they shall think proper," the council left the status of blacks to be decided on an *ad hoc* basis.

By their ordinance of April 15, 1638, the council stated:

> each and every one must refrain from Fighting, Adulterous intercourse with Heathens, Blacks, or other persons, Mutiny, Theft, False Swearing, Calumny and other Immoralities, as in all this the Contraveners shall, according to the circumstance of the case, be corrected and punished, as an example to others.[21]

By their inclusion of "other persons," the council revealed that it did not perceive intercourse with blacks as a more heinous type of adultery. We cannot tell conclusively, however, since the type and degree of punishment, as was customary in statutes of that time, was left to the discretion of the sentencing authorities. By 1642 the degraded status of some black slaves was alluded to in an ordinance that provided that "no one shall presume to draw a knife much less to wound any person, under the penalty of fl. 50, to be paid immediately, or in default, to work three months with the Negroes in chains. . . ."[22]

The legislative acts manumitting blacks also tell us little about the feelings of the society toward the rights of blacks. These manumission acts vary widely in their determinations of the future obligations of free Negroes. For example, a group of Negro men freed on February 25, 1644 had to pay annually at least thirty skepels of wheat and one fat hog,[23] while Jan Francisco, who was manumitted by Reverend Dom Johannes Megapolenisis, had to pay as a condition for his freedom merely ten skepels of wheat yearly.[24]

On January 20, 1648 the council passed a resolution opening trade to Brazil and Angola and authorizing the importation of slaves into New Netherlands. However, there are no surviving records documenting the departure of any vessel to Africa from New Netherlands in consequence of the resolution.[25]

Further, in one of the few statutes dealing directly with any aspect of slavery in the society, the general council passed a 1648 ordinance curbing runaways in response to what seems to have been pressure by slave owners against a segment of the population that was harboring fugitive slaves.

> Whereas the Director General and Council daily see and notice, that some inhabitants of New Netherland harbor and entertain in their houses and dwellings the servants of the Honorable Company and other servants, when they have run away from their masters, also those, who come from our neighbors, which causes, that many laborers, doing their duties unwillingly, are given the means and have the road opened to run away, which is done every day,—
>
> Therefore to prevent this as much as possible, the Director General and Council advise and warn everybody, not to entertain or lodge any servant of either the company or private parties, living here or elsewhere, for longer than 24 hours. If anybody is found to have acted contrary hereto, he shall pay a fine of 150 fl., to be given to him, who gives the notice.[26]

It should be noted that the statute deals with servants (undoubtedly both black and white); the word "slave" was not used. However, there is clear indication that by 1648 many of the Dutch opposed the institution of slavery, especially in its more repressive forms, and some began to harbor fugitives from other parts of New Netherlands and even from other colonies.

Slavery per se, however, was never legally sanctioned by the Dutch colony. This absence, coupled with the fact that few of the magistrates in the colony had any legal training, helped produce an improvisational or *ad hoc* slavery system. The informality of legal

slave regulations resulted in most cases concerning black slaves being decided upon their individual merits rather than according to
generally accepted and propagated beliefs and notions of the proper
place of the black race in white society or through the application
of inflexible slave codes. Black slave labor was effectively disci-
plined with a minimum of the usual coercive methods. There are, in
fact, few records of cases involving black defendants and few slave
conspiracies noted. Even those records available point toward a
tendency by the Dutch tribunals to deal leniently with slave defendants. Professor McManus details one such incident that occurred in
1647:

> a female slave convicted of arson was sentenced to death.
> After the public sentence had been pronounced, the magis-
> trates issued a secret pardon which the sheriff was ordered to
> withold until the last moment. Only when all preparations for
> the execution had been completed did the sheriff announce
> the pardon and return the terrified woman to her master.
> Magistrates loath to impose the death penalty in capital cases
> often arranged mock executions. And since offenders never
> knew whether a pardon would be forthcoming, the practice
> did not impair the deterrent effect of the sentence.[27]

When blacks were found guilty of serious crimes and were
punished by torture, such punishment was consistent with the type
of punishment used in Holland and throughout Europe. The testimony of slaves was acceptable in court and could outweigh the testimony of whites. In 1646, for example, a dispute over the ownership of some wood was decided on the testimony of a single slave,
even though his story had been contradicted by several white
witnesses.[28]

It would be an overstatement, nevertheless, to conclude that
the legal system was completely color blind. In some cases the race
of the individual was a determining factor in his or her legal status.
The 1642 incident involving the privateer *La Garce* is a case in
point. The ship brought to New York blacks captured from the
Spanish. The blacks asserted their freedom, but were summarily
sold into slavery without any inquiry into their status under Spanish
law. Thus, because of their race alone, the blacks were presumed to
be slaves. Unlike whites, blacks had the burden of proving them-

selves free rather than their claimants having the burden of proving them slave.

The presumption that black skin was synonymous with a condition of slavery was certainly not a notion peculiar to the Dutch colonies, and acknowledgment of that presumption does not destroy the argument that slavery among the Dutch never achieved the acceptance as a legal precept that it enjoyed among the English. Because of the "half-freedom system" even those blacks who were slaves were not uniformly treated as their master's chattel, and the colony never enacted repressive laws to govern free blacks. As one last example, by it's ordinance of May 12, 1653, requiring all "Burghers and Inhabitants, together with the Mechanics and Laborers" to generally assist in fortifying the city of New Amsterdam, the council (seemingly equitably) provided that for "free negroes, every fourth man in his term shall help to labor."[29] Similarly, the tax records confirm that blacks owned property openly: to pay the salary of the Reverend Polhemius, the court of Breuckelen assessed black Hans's 6 fl. on his land.[30]

These sporadic references to blacks, then, were the only surviving indications of how blacks fared under Dutch New World law. The council seemed far more concerned with its relationship with Indians and the prohibitions and regulations regarding trading with them.[31]

Apparently the first slaves imported into New Netherlands directly from Africa entered in 1654 or 1655, and after their arrival some were exported elsewhere. As a result, an ordinance of 1655 was passed requiring payment of 10 percent of either the slaves' worth or their purchase price.[32] By the 1660s nearly 10 percent of the colony's population of 8000 was black, although census reports failed to distinguish between free persons of color and slaves. Reports of slave ships docking at New Amsterdam to unload their "cargo" indicate that slavery became more firmly established as the settlement started to grow. This contention is further supported by the 1651 petition presented by the inhabitants of Gravesend requesting an increase in the supply of slaves brought into the colony.[33] But in New Netherlands, unlike most of the other colonies, including Massachusetts, an increase in the black population, slave or free, did not trigger the immediate enactment of new restrictions on blacks. During the entire period of Dutch control the enslavement of blacks was more a *de facto* institution based on custom and usage than it was a *de jure* status. It was not until the English assumed control of the colony that slavery gained undisputed legal recognition.

The Early New York Experience

On August 27, 1664 the Dutch governor, Peter Stuyvesant, surrendered the colony proper to the British.[34] By 1669, the Dutch had ceded the entire territory of New Netherlands to Great Britain, giving the English a link between their earlier settlements in Virginia and New England. With control of New York, as the colony was renamed, the English acquired a strategic advantage in the inland fur trade and in their increasing difficulties with the French in Canada. But the assumption of control by the English marked the first time an English colonial administration was confronted with the problem of ruling an alien population. And, perhaps most ominous, it marked the end of the period of nonhostile relations between blacks and whites in the colony.

Upon the surrender of the Dutch, the territory was entrusted to the Duke of York, whose personal finances were closely tied to those of the Royal African Company, the British trading outfit that held a monopoly on the slave trade in the latter part of the seventeenth century. Under the duke's guidance, the slave trade was strongly encouraged. All English governors, councilors, and customs officials were specifically instructed to promote the importation of slaves by every possible means.[35] For the first time in the colony's history, slaves were being imported for the sole purpose of providing their owners with profit opportunities on their sale.

STATUTORY RECOGNITION OF SLAVERY UNDER ENGLISH RULE

As sovereignty over the area passed from Dutch to English hands, slavery was altered from a *de facto* to a *de jure* institution. The Articles of Capitulation, which officially ceded New Netherlands to English control, confirmed the legality of all existing Dutch titles to property, including slaves. Specifically, masters were reassured that while no Christian would be enslaved or made a villein, nothing in the laws was intended to prejudice the masters or dames who had apprentices or servants for terms of years or life.

More explicit sanction of slavery came in 1665 when a group of New Englanders who had moved to Long Island, the overseer of Long Island, and the English governor wrote and enacted the Duke of York Laws,[36] the foundation of the legal system of colonial New York. These broad-ranging laws covered all major aspects of governance in the colony—its civil and criminal codes as well as its legislative organization. The laws dealt in minute detail with matters ranging from births and marriages to burial, from the rights of midwives to the obligations of churchwardens to the establishment of the court structure. From a slavery standpoint, these laws made significant changes in the number and role of slaves in the colony by variously promoting the use of slave labor, by limiting the desirability of white indentured servants, and last, by granting port privileges and warehouse priorities to ships participating in the international slave trade.

The Duke of York Laws served as a catalyst to those merchants, eager to reap the benefits readily available from the slave trade, but who had been given no impetus by the Dutch. As the colony became more prosperous, slave imports grew to such an extent that despite a rapid increase in the white population, blacks numbered about one-seventh of the total population by the eighteenth century and remained at that percentage throughout the first half of the century. In 1711 a market house came to be established in New York City as the central location for the hiring of all slaves in New York City.

This increase in the number of black slaves in colonial New York was also a direct consequence of several statutes whose effect was to decrease the economic feasibility of indentured servant labor. Under Dutch law indentured service was an informal, indefinite, and sometimes arbitrary form of service; individuals were able to modify custom to suit their individual needs. The English leaders of New York, however, by limiting indentured servitude to a specific length of time, increased the costs and decreased the utility of this particular labor source. In addition to stipulating the maximum duration of an indenture agreement, the Duke of York Laws limited indentured servitude to only those whites who would willingly sell themselves into bondage, thus further decreasing the availability of white indentured servants. Unlike their neighbors in New England, New Yorkers had initially expressed a desire for more indentured servants, but the nature of the legislation made compliance difficult for obtaining whites, so few were brought.[37] Indians were effectively eliminated from the available labor pool in 1679 when the colonial assembly prohibited the enslavement of Indians. There remained only one source of cheap dependable labor—Africans.

As the black slave population grew in New York State, and in New York City in particular, where the slave trade was centered, the colony's English rulers further defined the slave code and thereby more effectively regulated the slave population. In his masterful work, *The Negro in the Making of America,* Dr. Benjamin Quarles offers a perceptive explanation for the *ad hoc* development of slave codes: "As a rule, a slave code was an accurate reflection of the fears and apprehensions of the colony. Hence the more numerous the blacks, the more strict the slave codes."[38]

This argument is particularly persuasive when one reviews the development of black codes of the New York colony. In the late 1600s the legislature tended to deal with one problem at a time. But as New York's black and mulatto population grew larger, the colony's slave laws grew harsher. Most of the restrictive provisions were enacted by the early 1700s; several were codified in the basic slave code of November 27, 1702, entitled "An Act for Regulateing of Slaves."

Two objectives spurred the New York Common Council to pass its first restrictions on slaves. One clear objective was to eliminate the hazy distinctions between slavery and indentured servitude characteristic of the Dutch legal system. But, in addition to placing the slave in an inferior position in society, the restrictions were designed to prevent slave insurrections and to thwart runaway slaves.

The freedom of movement allowed slaves under the Dutch was drastically curtailed in October, 1682 when the General Court of Assizes passed an ordinance prohibiting "negro or Indian Slaves" from leaving their master's homes or plantations on Sundays or "any other unseasonable time or times . . ." without the handwritten consent of their masters. Slaves found to be out of their masters' custody without a valid pass were to be arrested, brought before

either a magistrate or a justice of the peace, and whipped. Moreover, anyone who traded with Negro or Indian slaves without the
master's permission was fined five pounds for each offsense. The
1682 ordinance, however, did not restrict the movement of blacks
and Indians who were *not* slaves.

A year later the Common Council further restricted the movement of Indian and black slaves:

> That noe Negro or Indian Slaves, Above the Number of four,
> doe Assemble or meet together On the Lords Day or att Any
> Other tyme att any Place, from their Masters Service within
> [the City] And the Libertyes thereof, And that noe such Slave
> doe goe Armed att Any tymes with gunns, Swords, Clubs,
> Staves Or Any Other kind of weapon wit Soever under the
> Penalty of being whipped att the Publique whipping poste
> Tenn Lashes, unless the master or Owners of Such Slave will
> Pay Six Shillings to Excuse the Same.[39]

The relatively small fee charged a master who permitted his slave to
gather with other slaves on property other than the master's was a
curious revenue-raising device that probably exacerbated existing
class distinctions. It gave wealthy masters the freedom to continue
to permit their slaves to accompany them, for example, to various
social and business functions. Yet, the tithe undoubtedly prevented
masters less well situated from bringing their slaves to such functions, a socially relevant fact in a society where the ownership of
slaves was deemed indicative of social, political, and economic
power.

As early as 1684, the general assembly enacted legislation that
curtailed the economic opportunities open to servants or slaves by
prohibiting both slaves and servants from trading "any Commodity
Whatsoever during ye Time of their service under ye penalty of
such Corporale punishment as shall be Ordered to be Inflicted by
Warrant under ye hands of two Justices of ye Peace of the County
where ye said servant or Slave doth Reside. . . ."[40] Those who
traded with servants and slaves were required to return the goods
received and were fined five pounds; moreover, anyone who gave a
servant or slave food, clothing, or any other goods was barred from
suing for payment.

In penalizing those who traded with servants and slaves, the general assembly's primary objective was to thwart thievery among servants and slaves, not implicitly to condone mistreatment of the servant population. The legislature expressly required all masters to provide for their servants.

Other statutes were passed that were decidedly racially discriminatory. In an apparent effort to lessen the resentment of white workers and to curtail the activities of blacks, free and slave, and Indians, the colonists passed several ordinances that made race a qualification for certain occupations; this type of ordinance was passed most frequently in New York City. The following ordinances are representative:

> Att a Comon Councell held in the Citty of Newyorke the 24th day of Jully, 1686: ORDERED that noe Negroe or Slave be Suffered to worke the bridge as a Porter about any goods either Exported or imported from or into this Citty.

> Att a Comon Councill held at the Citty hall of Said Citty on Saterday Aprill the 18th A. Dom 1691: No Boyes or Negroes to drive Cart upon the Penalty of three Shillings halfe to the Informer and the other halfe to ye Citty without Licence from ye Mayor.[41]

Such distinctions were not *class* distinctions, but racial ones, motivated by racist considerations. If slaves per se were deemed too unreliable to guard goods that were shipped into the city, free blacks would not have been precluded from this occupation. The second ordinance more directly illustrates this point. Had the legislation been solely motivated by a desire to protect white laborers from unfair competition from slave laborers, this ordinance should have read, "no Boyes not slaves," since there were also mulatto and Indian slaves.

Even more occupations became racially restricted in the period before the Revolutionary War. New York City's white coopers protested the "great number of Negroes entering their trade." In 1737 the coopers submitted a petition to the colonial assembly for protection against "the pernicious custom of breeding slaves to trades whereby the honest and industrious tradesmen are reduced to poverty for want of employ"; Lieutenant Governor Clarke supported the petition.[42]

Starting in 1702 the New York colonial assembly passed a series of comprehensive legislative statutes, which made clear that their intent was to relegate the colony's blacks and slaves to a status more similar to that of blacks and slaves in the southern colonies. Even the captions of the succeeding statutes convey the colony's increasing anxiety over the presence of blacks and the possibility of slave rebellions or revolts. The first comprehensive statute passed November 27, 1702, was merely encaptioned "An Act for Regulateing of Slaves."[43] A later, even more comprehensive statute, of December 10, 1712, was encaptioned "An Act for preventing Suppressing and punishing the Conspiracy and Insurrection of Negroes and other Slaves."[44] The act of November 2, 1717 was encaptioned "An Act for Explaining and Rendring more Effectual an Act of the Generall Assembly of this Colony, Entitled, An Act for preventing, Suppressing, and punishing the Conspiracy and Insurrection of Negroes, and other Slaves."[45] And finally there was passed the act of May 14, 1745, "An Act to Prevent the Runing away of Slaves out of the City and County of Albany to the French at Cannada," which was a reenactment of earlier laws pertaining to slaves fleeing to Canada.

The earlier economic restrictions seemed almost minor when compared to the repressive provisions in the 1702 slave code. The legislature explicitly provided that except for taking a slave's life or dismembering him, it was "lawful for any Master or Mistress of slaves to punish their slaves for their Crimes and offenses at [the master's] Discretion."[46] Slaves were forbidden to assemble in groups greater than three unless "for their Master's . . . proffitt, and by their Master's . . . consent." For assembling in groups more than three in violation of the statute, they were to be "whipt upon the naked back, at discretion of any Justice of the peace, not exceeding Forty Lashes." The statute created the office of a Common Whipper for slaves who was to be paid "three shillings P head" for all slaves he whipped. The statute made it a crime for any person to trade with any slave, "either in buying or selling," without the consent of the master and penalized a person so doing by trebling the value of the item traded plus the sum of five pounds, all of which was to be paid to the master of the slave. The statute prohibited any slave from testifying "in any matter" except in cases of conspiracy among slaves pertaining to running away, killing, or destroying their master's property, and then such testimony would only be permitted when one slave would be testifying "against another slave."

The statute exemplified the paradox of slaveholders who did not want the routine criminal laws applied to their slaves even when the slaves were guilty, because of the resulting economic loss to the master:

> And Whereas slaves are the property of Christians, and cannot without great loss or detriment to their Masters or Mistresses, be subjected in all Cases criminal, to the strict Rules of the Laws of England, Bee it Enacted by the Authority aforesaid, That hereafter if any slave by Theft or other Trespass shall damnifie any p'son or p'sons to the value of five pounds, or under, the Master or Mistress of such slave shall be lyable to make satisfaction for such damage to the party injured, to be recovered by action of Debt in any Court haveing Jurisdiction and Cognizance of Pleas to that value, and the slave shall receive Corporal Punishment, at Discretion of a Justice of the peace, and immediately thereafter be permitted to attend his or her Master or Mistress service, without further punishment.[47]

The right of a slave to protect himself or herself, or others, from the abuse of whites was denied by the following provision in the 1702 code:

> And in Case any slave presume to assault or strike any Freeman or Woman professing Christianity, it shall be in the power of any two Justices of the peace, who by this Act are thereunto authorized, to Comitt such slave to Prison, not exceeding fourteen days for one fact, and to inflict such other Corporeal punishment (not extending to life or limb) upon him, her, or them so offending, as to the said Justices shall seem meet and reasonable.[48]

As in other colonies, New York punished any slave who struck a Christian. It must be noticed, however, that while the statute authorized imprisonment and corporal punishment, such penalties were not mandated. Justices of the peace were required to determine the reasonableness of the punishment in each instance.

In substance, during the thirty-eight years from the English conquest of the New Netherlands in 1664 until 1702, the status of the black slave in New York diminished from a position in which he had some freedom to work for himself, to arm himself, and to attempt to secure his freedom to one in which he was stripped of all meaningful rights. The black slave in New York was relegated to so demeaning a position in the society that he was viewed as chattel. He could be treated by his master in any way the master desired; the master's prerogative of ownership was rarely the subject of judicial or legislative scrutiny.

In contrast to the 1702 statute, the 1705 enactment, "An Act to Prevent the running away of Negro Slaves out of the City and County of Albany to the French at Canada," did not leave punishment so completely to the discretion of the presiding justices. Upon the testimony of two or more witnesses, all slaves belonging to inhabitants of the city and county of Albany found more than forty miles north of the town of "Sarachtoge" (Saratoga) and not accompanied by their masters could be convicted of a felony and executed. Those slaves who were so accused were arrested and imprisoned without bail until the case came before the justice of the peace.[49]

The slaves' owners were not left without some recompense for the lost value of their property. The statute required the justice of the peace to notify the slaves' owners within two days. Upon receipt of this notice, the owners were authorized to appear before a justice of the peace in the county to "nominate one or more indifferent persons to Appraise and value the Negro slave or slaves so taken." The justice of the peace could also appoint other appraisers. After the appraisal was completed, the slave was tried. If the slave was convicted and executed, the costs were assessed as follows:

The . . . Court of Sessions is hereby directed and Impowered to Cause the Summ of the Appraisement of said Negro Slave or Slaves together with the Charges of prosecution Provided the said prosecution data not Exceed Tenn pounds to be Rated Assessed and levyed on all and every person and persons having Slave or Slaves within the Said Citty and County in Such ways and manners as other the publick charges of the Said City are levyed. . . .[50]

There is clear indication in the statute that its undeniable severity and cruelty were prompted not so much by racial animosity as by the fear that black slaves would flee to Canada and join forces with the French:

> this Act and every article and charge therein contained shall only be of force during this present warr with the French and no longer.[51]

The number of slaves executed under this statute cannot be determined. Nor is it clear exactly when the statute ceased to be effective. One fact is clear, though: the statute permanently established one key principle: that it was a *capital* offense, a crime against the colonial government, for a slave to try to obtain his or her freedom.

The 1702 statute had not provided for reimbursement of a master if a slave were to be executed pursuant to a judicial decree. However, on October 30, 1708, the assembly passed a compensation law in response to what was described in the statute as "the Execrable and Barberous Murder comitted on the Person and family of William Hallet Junr. late of New Town and Queens County." The statute provided that for those "Negro or Indian slave or slaves" who are executed pursuant to judicial decree the owner or owners should be paid in the same fashion as had been previously provided (in the Act of 1705) for slaves who ran away from the county of Albany to the French at Canada. The owner could receive a maximum of twenty-five pounds minus the cost and charge of prosecution.[52]

By the 1712 act the assembly significantly deterred blacks from becoming economically self-sufficient, under a statute captioned to imply that its purpose was to punish conspiracies and insurrection. This act precluded the rights of even innocent blacks by providing that "no Negro, Indian or mulatto, that shall hereafter be made free, shall enjoy, hold or possess any houses, lands, tenements, or Hereditaments within this colony" and any which they own would escheat (would be forfeited and transferred) to "her Majesty, her Heirs and successors." By the Act of May 19, 1715, it was made unlawful for any Negro, Indian or mulatto slave to sell any oysters in the city of New York upon the penalty of twenty shillings for each offense to be paid for by the master or mistress of the slave.[53]

PROCEDURAL RIGHTS OF SLAVES AND BLACKS

Even as the New York General Assembly expanded the list of crimes for which black slaves could be executed, interestingly it still provided a modicum of procedural rights to blacks and slaves. An October 30, 1708 act entitled "An Act for Preventing the Conspiracy of Slaves" is a curious example of this dichotomy involving the repression of the rights and dignity of nonwhites, and the maintenance of procedural decorum. This statute made it a capital crime for a Negro, Indian, or slave to murder, kill, or conspire or attempt to murder or kill any master, mistress, or "any other of her Majesties Leige People *not* being Negroes Mulattoes or Slaves within this Colony."[54] Thus, *by implication* it was not a capital offense for a slave to kill another slave, or a nonwhite freeman, or even a white indentured servant.

It was not until the 1712 statute that the assembly made it a statutory crime for a Negro, Indian, or other slave to "wilfully murder any Negro, Indian or mulatto slave within this colony."[55] By the 1708 statute, the slave was given an opportunity to have his case heard and determined by three or more justices of the peace, one to constitute a quorum.[56]

In 1709 Governor Hunter of New York was instructed by England to see to it that private slave discipline was not unduly severe and that the physical needs of slaves were not neglected by their masters. The colonial legislature implemented this policy by passing ordinances to deal with specific problems. For example, a master was fined for mistreating his slaves by providing such inadequate sustenance that they were forced to beg for food. Slaveholders were expressly forbidden to abandon slaves who had become too old or too sick to be of further service.

The willful killing, *deliberate* maiming, or mutilation of a slave were also prohibited. In theory, then, the slaves' lives and physical well being were to some extent protected from unscrupulous masters. In practice, however, even the rights given by the colonial assembly, as mandated by the English government, were limited. Slaveholders complained that these laws impaired their ability to control their slaves. In response to slaveholder pressure, the laws were modified to permit a slaveholder to use whatever degree of force he deemed necessary to enforce his commands; obviously, this modification undercut much of the protection afforded a slave. The masters' property interests remained protected, however, because prior to this, in 1706, the courts had been empowered to punish capital offenses committed by a slave "in such a manner and with such circumstances as the aggravation and enormity of the crime shall merit." Usually masters were fined for their slaves' minor crimes.

Even in cases extreme enough to be brought to court, the masters were acquitted. The *New York Weekly Journal* of January 5, 1735 reported a case in which a New York City resident had been accused of beating his slave to death. The coroner's jury held that the slave's death could be attributed to a "work of God"; judgment was rendered in favor of the defendant.[57] John Coaley was jailed until the coroner's jury exonerated him of wrongdoing in the death of his slave.[58]

BLACKS AS DEFENDANTS

The segregated judicial system was another important addition to the legal armament brought into play against blacks. Although the general assembly provided some of the common law procedural safeguards available to whites, other basic due process procedures were denied. Slaves could not testify either for or against a white or black freeman. Although in the trial of a slave the testimony of another slave was admissible, there was an exception to this rule in cases where the crime was conspiracy.[59]

As the 1708 statute suggested, a slave suspected of a criminal offense was arrested only upon a warrant issued by a justice of the peace. If evidence was sufficient to prosecute, the slave was jailed on suspicion. The justice would then assemble the panel—two other justices and five freeholders. A slave could not demand a regular jury. Yet, his master could do so by paying a nominal fee.

If the master did so, the slave was still denied the right to question the jurors or freeholders to establish bias or any other dis-

qualifying information. If the slave was convicted of a capital offense, the death penalty was mandatory although the chief justice
determined the method. In the case of an assault on a white person,
two justices of the peace, sitting without a jury, were authorized to
impose any punishment short of death or amputation. Slaves charged
with minor offenses received no court hearings; flogging was the
mandatory form of punishment.

The slaves' right to a judicial determination of guilt or inno-
cence was limited in New York, although these rights were protected to a greater extent in New York than in the more southern
colonies. Once the legislature had legally designated slaves to be
property, the legislature could have totally precluded slaves from
using the courts. Instead, the tendency was to invoke the chattel aspect of slavery to uphold commercial transactions involving slave
owners. Blacks were bought or hired as personal property, and regular bills of sale were executed to effect the transfer of title. They
were also mortgaged and assigned as collateral for the debts of their
masters. Any interference with these property rights constituted a
trespass for which damages could be recovered. For example, a free
man responsible for making a slave woman pregnant was liable for
any loss of services or diminution of the slave's value suffered by the
owner. And masters could recover pecuniary damages from individuals who were found to have enticed slaves to run away. On the
other hand, as property, slaves could be taken from their masters on
writs of attachment and sold to benefit creditors.

It is probable that slaves benefited from their position as chattel property in those instances in which they were charged with
criminal activity. English law, applicable in New York, required
death if the defendant was convicted for theft or any other felony by
which the injured party suffered a loss of five pounds sterling or
more. Slaves were often spared execution, though not, of course,
for humanitarian reasons. Legislators eager to avoid burdening
slave owners with financial losses protected the slave-owners' interests by allowing a slave defendant to live if his master reimbursed
the injured party and agreed to publicly whip his slave. But as the
1708 statute indicates, the sentence imposed on slaves for murdering whites was not tempered by economic concerns.

THE RELEVANCE OF RELIGION

New York colonists, like their Virginia counterparts, felt compelled to solve the problem created by slaves who had embraced Christianity. They were confronted with conflicting theological and jurisprudential theories on the consequence of slaves becoming Christians. Since one element of the earlier justification for enslavement had been that blacks were heathens, did their conversion to Christianity abrogate their enslavement?

The ambiguity starts with one of the major provisions in the 1665 Duke of York Laws pertaining to slavery. It provided:

> No Christian shall be kept in Bondslavery, villenage or Captivity, Except Such who shall be Judged thereunto by Autority, or such as willingly have sould, or shall sell themselves, In which Case a Record of such Servitude shall be entered in the Court of Sessions held for that Jurisdiction where Such Matters shall Inhabit, provided that nothing in the Law Contained shall be to the prejudice of Master or Dame who shall by any Indenture or Covenant take Apprentices for Terme of Years, or other Servants for Term of years or Life.[60]

The above provision in the Duke of York Laws was amazingly similar to the Body of Liberties laws passed in Massachusetts in 1641[61] and would be subject to the same conflicting construction. Thus, what was the meaning of the phrase "No Christian shall be kept in Bondslavery, villenage or Captivity . . ."? Did it imply that slaves who had become Christians had to be freed, or did the exceptions in the statute sanction their enslavement?

In New York, as in all English colonies, one's civil status was interrelated to, and often determined by, one's religious affiliation. The English common law tradition tended to imply that slaves and Christians were mutually exclusive groups. Several English cases had justified enslaving blacks because they were "heathen" and had served "an Infidel Prince." Religious affiliation was only one factor, however. No case had specifically held that a slave's conversion to Christianity entitled the slave to freedom, although the 1677 decision in *Butts* v. *Penny*[62] may have lent some judicial support for that proposition. In *Butts,* the court ruled that even though blacks were "usually bought and sold in America as Merchandise," the ten non-Christian black slaves, despite being "by usage *tanquam bona*"—goods worth as much as they can be sold for—were to "go to administrator until they become Christians; and thereby they are Infranchised."[63]

When the British authorities realized that some slaves had converted in order to obtain their freedom, the colonists appealed to the Bishop of London, leader of the Colonial Church, who reversed the decree and ruled that although a black might adopt Christianity his conversion would not result in manumission. The colonial government also responded to the problem in 1674 by providing that "no Negro slave who becomes a Christian after he had been bought shall be set at liberty."[64] In 1706 the colonial government further clarified its earlier position by declaring that the baptism of a slave did not entitle said slave to freedom.

> Whereas divers of her Maties good Subjects, Inhabitants of this Colony now are and have been willing that such Negro, Indian and Mulatto Slaves who belong to them and desire the same, should be Baptized, but are deterr'd and hindred therefrom by reason of a Groundless opinion that hath spread itself in this Colony, that by the Baptizing of such Negro, Indian or Mulatto slave they would become free and ought to be sett at Liberty. In order therefore to put an end to all such Doubts and Scruples as have or hereafter at any time may arise about the same. Be it Enacted by the Governr Council and Assembly and it is hereby Enacted by the authority of the same, That the Baptizing of any Negro, Indian or Mulatto Slave shall not be any Cause or reason for the setting them or any of them at Liberty.
>
> And be it declar'd and Enacted by the Governr. Council and Assembly and by the Authority of the same, That all and every Negro, Indian Mulatto and Mestee Bastard Child & Children who is, are, and shalbe born of any Negro, Indian, Mulatto or Mestee, shall follow ye State and Condition of the Mother and be esteemed reputed taken and adjudged a Slave and Slaves to all intents and purposes whatsoever.
>
> Provided, always and be it declared and Enacted by ye said Authority That no slave whatsoever in this Colony shall att any time be admitted as a Witness for, or against, any

Freeman, in any Case matter or Cause, Civill or Criminal whatsoever.[65]

Like their Virginia cousins, the New York colonists wanted their blacks to be saved by Christ but never free from their masters.[66] Once the 1706 statute was enacted, New Yorkers were legally committed to justify slavery solely on racial grounds, even though this commitment was not explicit. For example, the prevailing argument against manumission by baptism, made in the English case, *Chamberlaine* v. *Harvey,* decided in 1696, was cast in economic terms; yet, there is no doubt that all parties recognized that it was the *nonwhites* and non-Christians (with emphasis placed on "nonwhite") who were to be exploited to ensure the wealth of the English empire:

> If baptism should be accounted a manumission it would very much endanger the trade of the plantations, which can not be carried without the help and labor of these slaves; for the parsons are bound to baptize them as soon as they can give a reasonable account of the Christian faith; and if that would make them free, then few would be slaves.[67]

Interestingly, the 1706 act also provided that:

> all and every Negro, Indian Mulatto and Mestee Bastard Child and Children who is, are, and shalbe born of any Negro, Indian, Mulatto or Mestee, shall follow ye State and Condition of the Mother and be esteemed reputed taken and adjudged a Slave and Slaves to all intents and purposes whatsoever.

By declaring in the statute that the status of the child was determined by the status of the mother, the assembly protected those white males who caused black women to become pregnant from the normal application of English paternity doctrines. All these deprivations were imposed on blacks by a statute encaptioned "An Act to Incourage the Baptizing of Negro, Indian and Mulatto Slaves."

MANUMISSION IN NEW YORK

The colonial government began to regulate the master's right to manumit slaves in 1712 when the general assembly, in response to the 1712 slave uprising in New York City, passed a statute permitting manumission only after a master had posted both a bond of 200 pounds, guaranteeing the freeman's ability to be self-supporting, and thereafter annually paying twenty pounds to the freeman for the duration of the master's life.

> And Whereas it is found by Experience, that the free Negroes of this Colony are an Idle slothfull people and prove very often a charge on the place where they are, Be It therefore further Enacted by the Authority aforesaid, That any Master or Mistress, manumitting and setting at Liberty any Negro, Indian or Malatto Slave, shall enter into sufficient Security unto her Majesty her heires and Successors with two Sureties not less than the Sum of Two hundred pounds, to pay Yearly and every Year to such Negro Indian or Mallatto Slaves during their Lives the Sum of Twenty Pounds lawfull money of this Colony; And if such Negro Indian or Mallatto Slave shall be made free by the Will or Testament of any person deceased, that then the Executors of such person shall enter into Security as above immediately upon proving the said Will or Testament, which if refused to be given, the said manumission to be void and of none effect.[68]

Many slaveholders argued that this restriction on manumissions would cause rather than cure slave discontent. Even Governor Hunter argued that the ban on manumission was unjust and would provoke unrest; his solution was to substitute indentured servant labor for slave labor.

In 1717 the legislature acknowledged that the prior statute requiring the posting of the bond for manumission had been:

> found by Experience to be very Inconvenient, prejudicial, and in a manner, a prohibition to Liberty, and will very much Discourage and Dishearten such Negroe, Indian or Malatto Slaves from serveing their Masters or Mistresses truely and faithfully, as they ought to doe.[69]

Yet despite these findings the statute appeared to have reimposed the bond requirements, though some scholars have construed the statute as authorizing nominal bonds. Professor McManus claims that at least in one instance a surety was permitted to give his guarantee that the freedman "shall not be a charge to any town in this province."[70]

Although legislation intruded somewhat on the master's ability to dispose of his property by manumission, evidence suggests that to a large extent such masters and slaves were able to work out individual arrangements best suited to the particular circumstances. Some bondsmen were able to persuade their masters to give them freedom after a certain period of faithful service; still others purchased their freedom by hiring themselves out to others and paying for their freedom on an installment basis.[71]

The New York courts tended to strictly construe the manumission agreements, by applying the technical common law contract doctrines and their related burden of proof to manumission transactions. As an example, in *Kettletas* v. *Fleet*[72] the former owner sued for the purchase price of a slave he sold to the defendant. The issue was whether a promise to free the slave within eight years if "he conducted himself faithfully" was enforceable against the subsequent purchaser. Applying rigid contract doctrines, the court ruled:

> If, at the time of the sale, the defendant had known that a covenant to manumit had been solemnly executed [with a seal] in the manner the witnesses have stated, then the purchase would have been a purchase of right and title only. But all that does appear from the testimony, is his knowledge of *a verbal promise* to manumit; this being a mere voluntary promise, would not have been obligatory in the law on the plaintiff, and the defendant would have been entitled to the services of the slave for life.

As we will note in greater detail in our chapter on Pennsylvania, the Quakers were leaders in the abolition of slavery. They were so persistent in their efforts to have all Quakers manumit their slaves that by 1784 there was only one Quaker slave owner in the state of New York and he had been admonished to give up his slave by 1787.[73]

Yet because the emancipation process had proceeded so rapidly among the Quakers, the masters had often failed to record the emancipations as required by statute. Many slaves were, therefore, defectively manumitted, such manumissions acquiring the name

"Quaker freedoms"; these "Quaker freedoms" were not statutorily validated until 1798.[74]

SLAVE REVOLTS AND LEGISLATIVE REACTIONS

The New Yorkers' fears of slave revolts were not groundless. It was a popular belief that two incidents, in 1712 and 1741, were large-scale slave revolts, although conclusive proof of the scale of either event has been difficult to extricate from the rather hysterical accounts of eyewitnesses.

In 1712 about twenty-four slaves set fire to a building in New York; the slaves ambushed whites who came to put out the blaze. Most white New Yorkers agreed that the city barely escaped from total destruction and "had it not been for the Garrison there, that city would have been reduced to ashes, and the greatest part of the inhabitants murdered."[75]

The absence of evidence indicating that there was a broad-based conspiracy among slaves to burn New York City did not prevent the swift capture of several suspects; several blacks committed suicide rather than face capture. All were quickly brought to trial and those conspirators found guilty suffered horrible deaths even by eighteenth-century standards. Thirteen slaves were hanged, one was chained and starved to death, another was slowly burned for eight to ten hours, and another was broken on the wheel.[76] The hysteria that followed the 1712 incident precipitated additional restrictions on the city's black population aimed at "preventing and punishing of the conspiracy and insurrection of negroes and other slaves for the better regulating them."[77]

As an analysis of selected provisions has already suggested, the 1712 statute was the most inclusive and most restrictive enactment up to that date in the New York colony. All persons were prohibited from harboring any slaves. If any slaves happened to be killed or, in the language of the statute, "otherways destroyed, such persons or persons so harbouring, entertaining, concealing, assisting, or converying of them away, shall be also liable to pay the value of such slave to the Master or Mistress, to be recovered by Action of Debt." Negro, Indian, and mulatto slaves were also forbidden to carry or use a gun or pistol, except under the direction and in the presence of their masters; violators received up to twenty lashes on their bare backs for each offense.[78] This provision was extended in 1730 to prohibit slaves from carrying clubs and/or swords.

Prompted by the increased incidence of arson in New York City, the general assembly included a section in the 1712 statute that made burning a house, bar, stable, outhouse, corn, or hay crops a capital offense, punishable by death. Moreover, the 1712 statute made it a capital offense to physically harm "any of Her Majesty's people, not being Slaves"; if read literally, the following provisions protected the lives of slaves and protected free nonwhites from physical attack by slaves;

> all and every Negro Indian or other Slave, who after Publication of this Act Shall Murder or otherwise kill, unless by misadventure or in Execution of Justice, or conspire or attempt the Death of any of Her Majesty's liege people, not being Slaves, or shall commit or attempt The Death of any of Her Majesty's liege people, not being Slaves, . . . or shall willfully mutilate mayhem or dismember any of the said Subjects, *not being Slaves* as aforesaid, or shall willfully murder any Negro Indian or Mallatto Slave within this colony, and shall thereof be convicted before three or more of Her Majesty's Justices of the Peace, one whereof, to be of the Quorum . . . with five of the principal freeholders of the County wherein such fact shall be committed, without a Grand Jury, . . . he, she, or they so offending shall suffer the pains of Death. . . .[79]

The 1712 act contains one provision, however, that implies that perhaps some justices of the peace tended to be less than diligent in their enforcement of the slave codes:

> And Be It further Enacted, That every Justice of the Peace, Constable, or other Officer, neglecting, delaying or refusing to perform their several Dutys enjoyn'd by this Act shall for every such Offence forfeit the Sum of Two pounds to Her Majesty Her Heirs and Successors to be recovered by Action of Debt in any Court of Record within this Colony, and Every ffreeholder Summon'd as aforesaid and refusing to Serve shall forfeit the Sum of Twenty Shillings, to be levied by the Constable by Warrant of Distresse from the Justices of the Peace Assembled to try the said Slave, who are hereby

required imediately upon such Refusall to Issue their Warrant for levying the same accordingly.[80]

In 1730 the general assembly provided that persons who were found to entertain slaves, or who knew of someone else who entertained slaves but failed to report such acts to the Master, were fined forty shillings.[81] Free blacks, Indians, and mulattoes were also prohibited from entertaining slaves unless said slaves had first obtained permission from their owners; blacks, Indians, and mulattoes who violated this law were fined ten pounds recoverable by the slave's owners in an action of debt, for every day or night the slave was illegally entertained.[82]

Although the 1730 statute is replete with provisions tightening the government's control over nonwhites, whether free or enslaved, one section in the statute more clearly than all others undercuts the New York slave's ability to receive any semblance of fair treatment before the colony's courts: the slave was precluded from serving as a witness, except in cases where slaves were accused of capital offenses:

> hereafter no Slave or Slaves shall be allowed as Evidence or Evidences in any Matter Cause or thing whatsoever excepting in the Cases of Plotting or Confederacy among themselves, either to run away Kill or distroy their Master Mistress or any other Person, or burning of houses Barns, Barracks or Stocks of hay or of Corne or the killing of their Master or Mistresses Cattle or Horses and that only against one another, in which Case the evidence of one Slave shall be allowed good against another slave.[83]

Thus, a slave could never testify against a free person, even if that person had plotted to kill the slave or his master.

Changes continued to occur in New York in the years following the 1712 fires, including the institution of slave patrols to prevent curfew violations. Nevertheless, the scene of this disturbance— New York City—continued to pose special problems. It had always been extremely difficult to control the city's slaves. Most slaves in the city were artisans and were relatively free of supervision during their free time, despite restrictive statutes. Perhaps, as Professor McManus has asserted, "the masters found it convenient to close their eyes to violations so long as their slaves rendered satisfactory service."[84] Whatever the reason for their rather casual enforcement of the slave control laws, this lack of enforcement was flagrant. Taverns served black slaves in defiance of the law; stolen goods were frequently purchased from slaves in the homes of whites who operated illegal drinking places.

The hysteria over possible slave revolts increased in New York in the winter of 1740-1741 and culminated in panic in the summer of 1741 with a tragedy similar in scope and horror to the Salem, Massachusetts witch trials of 1690 and 1691. The cause of the panic was a series of unexplained fires in New York City in the summer of 1741 that damaged several buildings, including a fort, its chapel and barracks, and the governor's home. There was no concrete evidence to support the belief that the fires were part of a wide spread slave conspiracy. But the white population convinced itself that "so bloody and Destructive a Conspiracy was this, that had not the merciful hand of providence interposed and Confounded their Divices, in one and the Same night the Inhabitants would have been butcher'd in their houses, by their own Slaves, and the City laid in ashes."[85]

An informer, Mary Burton, a white indentured servant, was partially responsible for the hysteria. Burton was called as a witness in the trial of her white master, John Hughson, a tavern owner who was on trial for burglary; Hughson, deemed to be a suspect character because he served blacks, was charged with receiving stolen goods from blacks and selling them. In her testimony Burton indicated that there was a connection between Hughson's activities and the fires. Perhaps influenced by the 100 pound reward, Burton began to implicate almost every black who was brought to the court. Burton's word alone proved enough to convict several blacks. To further flush out the conspirators, the colony agreed to spare the lives of those convicted blacks who implicated others. Winthrop Jordan, in *White Over Black,* reports that this procedure was so effective and so conclusive of the named party's guilt that a black spectator at one hanging immediately turned himself over to a marshal when he heard the defendant name him as a conspirator.[86] It was only when Burton began to implicate upstanding white citizens and their slaves that the justices ended the hearings.

Despite Burton's fabrications and exaggerations most New Yorkers believed the essence of her story—that several whites and blacks had conspired to burn down New York City. In total 154 blacks, free and slave, and numerous whites were implicated, 18 blacks and 4 whites were hung, 13 blacks were burned to death, and 70 blacks were transported out of the colony. Later investigations revealed that at most, the "Great Conspiracy" was just a plan by John Hughson and his accomplices to set some fires to divert attention from their main objective—the burglary of the homes of several wealthy citizens.

The fact that blacks had participated in the violence prevented New Yorkers from treating the crimes as arson and burglary. Instead, the acts symbolized treasonous behavior. Leading citizens, including some of the justices at the hearing, attempted to justify the degree and intensity of judicial reaction. One justice, Daniel Horsmanden, published a lengthy justification of the court proceedings. Horsmanden argued that several factors supported a "conspiracy" charge. At times the court viewed the fires as a Roman Catholic plot, supported by the Spanish who were at war with England. Horsmanden at one point indicated that the fires demonstrated the "gross ingratitude" of blacks toward their benevolent masters. Unscrupulous whites were also blamed for "influencing" normally good slaves. But, the key factor was the nature of the black man. As Horsmanden addressed a condemned black in the courtroom: "[in] many, it may be said most, of your complexion" there was an "Untowardness, as it would seem, in the very Nature and Temper of ye . . . degenerated and debased below the Dignity of Human Species. . . ."[87]

REVOLUTIONARY WAR AND THE IMPETUS TOWARD ABOLITION

By the late 1760s New York colonists, like their counterparts in the other twelve American colonies, began to clamor for political and economic freedom from Britain. Many Revolutionary polemicists found that the natural rights doctrines that compelled them to seek their freedom from Britain also compelled them to assert the freedom of slaves from colonial masters. Whites who argued for political freedom for themselves could not logically justify maintaining black slavery. Newspapers carried editorials in which the condition of black slaves was lamented. For example, an editorial in the March 24, 1760 edition of the *New York Weekly Post-Boy* described black slaves as "poor pagans whom Christians have thought fit to consider cattle."[88]

As the Revolutionary conflict loomed larger, opposition to slavery and the English slave trade increased. In 1774 New York City distillers voted unanimously to refrain from distilling molasses and syrup intended for the slave trade. Admittedly, this position was as much a challenge to English economic domination as it was an indication of an abolitionist position. Many challenges to slavery were more direct, however. John Jay, the first Chief Justice of the U.S. Supreme Court and that person who may have been the staunchest advocate for abolition in New York, declared that unless the colonies were prepared to free the slaves, "her own prayers to Heaven for liberty were impious."[89]

Yet, however lenient the New York slave owners appeared to be in enforcing the laws against their slaves, slavery was a solidly entrenched economic institution. Although in New York City blacks constituted a much higher percentage of the total population, overall throughout New York blacks constituted approximately 10 percent of the total population.[90]

At the state's first constitutional convention, held in 1777, although most of the delegates were philosophically opposed to slavery, the convention was reluctant to include even a suggestion of future emancipation in the new constitution. Even Governor Morris, while proposing that the new constitution include a promise of abolition to be achieved as soon as it could be done "consistent with the public safety and the private property of individuals," concluded that "it would at present be productive of great dangers to liberate the slaves within this state."[91]

Although no emancipation provision was passed, the delegates, by a vote of 36 to 5, did adopt Morris's antislavery resolution, which declared that: "every human being who breathes the air of the state shall enjoy the priviledges of a freeman."

The British drove a wedge between the American masters and their slaves by treating the slaves as neutrals in the conflict. For example, in raids against Americans in several New York towns, slaves were not harmed unless they fought against the British. This was made a standard military policy by Sir Henry Clinton, the British commander-in-chief, in 1779 when he authorized the manumission of slaves who joined the British armed forces. Some Americans in loyalist militia units accepted blacks in their ranks.[92]

But the black who fought with the British, like the black who fought with the Americans, was, as Philip S. Foner so aptly described him, the man "behind the man behind the gun."[93] Black soldiers were often no more than equipment in the eyes of whites.

> They [blacks] occupied the last rung in the British military caste. . . . He was marked, like a piece of military equipment, with the number of the regiment or the initials of the department to which he was attached.[94]

Blacks were willing to endure these indignities because the British had agreed to free those blacks who joined and aided in the loyalist cause. The promise of freedom created severe problems among the American forces in New York, particularly in the northern section of the state. British sympathizers in the area encouraged unrest and dissension among the slaves.

As the war continued, it became clear that in New York the masters' control of their slaves was being undermined anyway by the British and by slaves who supported the British. Moreover, the state was in desperate need of troops. Still, it was not until March 20, 1781 that the general assembly overcame its reluctance, and responded to the desperate need for troops by authorizing the enlistment of slaves in the Revolutionary Army:

> And be it further enacted by the authority aforesaid That any person who shall deliver one or more of his or her able-bodied male slaves, to any warrant officer as aforesaid, to serve in either of the regiments or independent corps, and produce a certificate thereof, signed by any officer or person authorized to muster and recieve men, to be raised by virtue of this act, and produce such certificate to the surveyor-general, shall, for every male slave so entered or mustered as aforesaid be entitled to the location and grant of one right in manner as in and by this act is directed; and shall be, and hereby is discharged from any future maintenence of such slave; any law to the contrary notwithstanding; And such slave, so entered

as aforesaid, who shall serve for a term of three years, or
until regularly discharged, shall, immediately after such service
or discharge be, and is hereby declared to be a free man of
this state.[95]

The fourth paragraph of the statute defined the right the master was to receive as 500 acres of unappropriated public land for
each slave delivered and enlisted. Thus, the legislature had given
the master a real incentive while it had given the slave no greater
personal stake in the outcome of the war than that already offered him by the British. The statute probably appeased the pro-
Revolutionary whites to some extent in that the severe troop shortage was alleviated and nonslave-owning whites received a similar
opportunity to obtain a grant of 500 acres by their own enlistments.
The true winners, however, appear to have been the slaveholders,
who received 500 acres and were relieved of all duties to support
slaves over which they probably had little or no control, all without
risking their own lives in defending their country. The boon of 500
acres should not be overestimated, however. How securely could
one view a land grant made by a rebel government whose largest
city was under siege?

Blacks in New York After the War

The promises of manumission were honored both by New
York, by statute in 1781, and by the British commander, General
Sir Guy Carlton, who negotiated the British evacuation of New
York City. Blacks who joined the British prior to November 30,
1782, the date the provisional treaty was signed, were freed. Carlton resisted public pressure to surrender these blacks, stating that
to break the promises of freedom would be "a dishonorable violation of the public faith."[96] Those blacks who sought asylum with
the British after November 30, 1782, however, were returned.[97]

The New York legislature provided for the maintenance of
slaves whose masters' property had been confiscated or forfeited.
In 1784 the general assembly provided that:

the . . . commissioner or commissioners shall out of any
monies which may come in his or their hands for rents, make

suitable provision for the support and maintenance of any slave or slaves who may be found unable to support themselves, and have not been disposed of by any person or persons whose respective estates have become confiscated or forfeited to the people of the state.[98]

Although technically manumitted in 1781, slaves who served in the Revolutionary Army were forced to wait until 1785 for the legislative enactment to implement the convention's resolution on eventual emancipation. By 1785, there was a clear antislavery majority in both houses. This antislavery majority was united in a desire to end slavery, but there was no consensus as to the method necessary to achieve that end. A bill for gradual emancipation—which freed children born to slave women after 1785—was introduced into the assembly that session. But before the more moderate bill was brought to a vote, Aaron Burr, leader of a militant group of antislavery representatives, introduced a bill proposing the immediate and unconditional end of slavery. Burr's proposal was rejected 33 to 13, but they approved a gradual emancipation plan by a vote of 36 to 11.

The failure of the state legislature to endorse immediate emancipation is directly related to the State's first constitution, passed in 1777. By that document, the state gave the franchise to all free propertied men, without reference to color, prior conditions of servitude, or religion. Thus, in 1785 the situation in New York was such that emancipation would have given all blacks the same civil rights enjoyed by whites. Many representatives, while antagonistic toward slavery, were far from prepared to live in a society that treated blacks and whites equally.

The bill that ultimately passed in the assembly corrected this perhaps unforeseen coupling of freedom and civil rights. Although blacks were freed by the 1785 statute, their political rights were severely limited; blacks could not vote nor could they hold public office. Social restrictions were also placed on blacks—interracial marriage with whites was banned. And even the legal rights of blacks were curtailed; the 1785 statute precluded blacks from testifying against whites in any court in the state.[99]

The failure of the legislature to completely end slavery resulted in increased efforts to pass an emancipation statute, and to initiate legislation ending the slave trade.[100] Most of the pressure was created in 1785 by the New York Society for Promoting the Manumission of Slaves, an organization Professor McManus has called "The most effective single agency of antislavery in the state."[101] The society, founded in 1785 to push the emancipation statute, and sponsored by the Federalists, numbered as members some of the most prominent members of New York, including John Jay, who was the society's first president, and Alexander Hamilton, its second president.

In 1785, the legislature did succeed in passing a statute prohibiting the importation of slaves. Violators were fined 100 pounds and the slaves illegally imported were freed.[102] The statute was ineffective since masters who brought slaves in for their own use were exempted from the legislation. Technically, slaves could be brought in for the present owner's use and thereafter sold with impunity. Others evaded the law by hiring out imported slaves under leases that were usually disguised sales cancelable only with the consent of a hirer or his heirs. For example, one importer brought in a "free" man from New Jersey under a ninety-nine-year indenture.[103]

The legislature also sought to make manumission easier to achieve. Masters were able to free a slave without posting bonds if the overseers of the poor certified that the slave was under fifty and capable of self-support.

The publication and distribution of Jupiter Hammon's 1787 sermon, entitled "An Address to the Negroes in the State of New York," must have come as a blow to slaves and their abolitionist allies.[104] Jupiter Hammond, born a slave in the Lloyd's family in Oyster Bay, Long Island, in 1711, was the first black poet to be published; his first volume was published in 1760, thus thirteen years before Phyllis Wheatley's poems were published. Hammond's "Address," his last known work, exhorted slaves to become Christians and to rely on the Lord to secure their freedom. The sermon can be read as a plea that blacks reluctantly accept their own enslavement or at least that emancipation not be their goal of first priority. He stated:

That liberty is a great thing we may know from our own feelings, and we may likewise judge so from the conduct of the

white people in this war. . . . I must say that I have hoped
that God would open their eyes, when they were so much engaged for liberty, to think of the state of the poor blacks, and
to pity us. He has done it in some measure, and has raised us
up many friends. . . .

This my dear brethren, is by no means the greatest thing
we have to be concerned about. Getting our liberty in this
world is nothing to our having the liberty of the children of
God. . . . What is forty, fifty or sixty years, when compared
to eternity?[105]

In 1788 the general assembly, still unable to act on emancipation, passed a comprehensive slave code that sought to minimize
some of the most unpleasant aspects of slavery and to eliminate the
loopholes in the 1785 antislave trade bill. The statute made it illegal
to sell any slave imported into the state after 1785 and it declared
that all such slaves improperly imported "shall be free."[106]

It also precluded sales where both buyer and seller claimed to
be permanent residents but where one was actually an agent receiving the slave with the intention of transporting the slave out of
the state for sale. For each offense the violator would forfeit 100
pounds and the slave was to "be immediately after . . . pur-
chas[e]d . . . declared to be free."[107]

The 1788 statute is noteworthy, however, not only for these
antislavery prohibitions. It appears that the legislature's intent was
to minimize the burden of slavery but simultaneously to affirm slavery's continued legality in the state, perhaps to reassure owners con-
fused by the ambivalence in the 1785 attempts to enact an emancipation statute. The statute restated settled principles of slavery law:
it provided that all blacks, mulattoes, or Mestees who were slaves
for life on February 22, 1788 (date the statute was passed) were
to remain in that condition, unless properly manumitted; children of these slaves "shall follow the state and condition of the
mother. . . ."[108] This proviso was some assurance to slave mothers
that their manumission effectuated the manumission of their children. Baptism was, once again, held not to effectuate manumission.[109] Under the 1788 statute, it was still illegal for anyone to entertain or harbor a slave without the owner's consent; it was still

illegal for persons to trade with slaves; it was still illegal to sell rum or other alcoholic beverages to slaves.[110]

And the dual justice system was still very much in evidence. It was still a crime for a slave to strike a white person, regardless of the circumstances; the punishment was imprisonment. And the right of a slave to testify was limited to only capital cases.[111] The slave was given one benefit, however; he or she was given the right to a trial by jury when accused of a capital offense.[112]

Even though the state legislature on the record at least tacitly supported the slavery system, manumissions in New York increased after the 1780s. This increase was probably due to economic factors as well as philosophical beliefs. During the last half of the eighteenth century the supply of free labor, particularly white, rapidly increased.[113] Between 1771 and 1786 the free population increased by 57 percent while the slave population decreased by approximately 5 percent, so that the ratio of slaves to whites was about 1 to 12. By 1786, there were 219,996 whites in the state and only 18,889 slaves, 7 percent of the total population.

The New York Manumission Society played a critical role in enforcing the 1788 statutory prohibition on the slave trade. The society appointed watchers throughout the state to report unusual purchases of slaves by strangers and to keep under surveillance those ships known to be slavers when the ships were in port. The society also boycotted merchants and other businessmen who participated in the slave trade, including newspapers that accepted advertisements for slave auctions or private purchases or sales of slaves. The society provided direct assistance to freed blacks. Blacks who were illegally reenslaved were often provided legal counsel to regain their freedom at the society's expense, and the society won thirty-four of the thirty-six cases it litigated.[114]

Perhaps as important were the society's efforts in helping ease blacks into life as free people. Schools were established to teach black children academic as well as vocational subjects. Perhaps one of the best-known schools for blacks in the nation was the society's New York African Free School, established in New York City in 1787. Because of white opposition, enrolment was at first small. Until 1800 there were never more than sixty students. By 1810, however, enrolment expanded, probably due to a statute requiring masters to teach their slaves' children to read the Bible.[115]

THE EMANCIPATION STATUTE

Finally in 1799, fourteen years after the first emancipation statute had been introduced, the New York state legislature passed a bill that gradually eliminated the system of slavery. All male children born to slave mothers after July 4, 1799 were to be freed at age twenty-eight and all female children at age twenty-five. These children were to serve their mothers' masters as indentured servants until freed, provided the master properly registered their birth. Failure to do so resulted in a monetary fine against the master and freedom for the child.[116] Masters, however, were not required to accept the child as an indentured servant, and upon their refusal to do so, the child was to be "bound out by the overseers of the poor on the same terms and conditions that the children of paupers were subject to."[117] The master was obligated to support the child until one year old and thereafter the support was "at the expense of the state." The statute specifically encouraged manumission by allowing it upon delivery of a manumission certificate to the slave.[118]

It is noteworthy to recognize that in 1799 the legislature avoided the dilemma it created for itself in 1785. The statute was silent as to the black's civil and political rights once he or she was freed.

Once the statute became effective, the prices for slaves in the New York market plummeted so greatly that New York became a mecca for slave traders from other states. They flocked into New York, hoping to purchase slaves at bargain prices and, in violation of New York laws, sell the slaves out of state.[119] Masters assisted in this subterfuge and employed other devices to avoid the 1799 statute. For instance, masters often sent a pregnant slave woman out of the state until she had given birth; sometime after the child's birth the child was sold and the mother returned to New York.

Both slavery and the slave trade existed well after this 1799 statute, despite legislative and judicial efforts to limit its impact in the state. In 1801 the legislature passed a bill that, while recognizing and reassuring nonresidents of their rights to enter and leave

New York without losing ownership of their slaves, prevented New York residents from taking their slaves out of the state with them and not bringing them back upon their return. The statute also precluded residents from leaving the state with slaves that had been purchased for less than one year.[120]

The legislature continued to modify the harshness of slavery for those still in chains. In a three-paragraph statute the legislature, on February 17, 1809, initiated the process to ultimately legitimize the black family. Previously "marriages" between slaves had not been generally recognized by New York laws—even when the slaves had been manumitted subsequent to their marriage. Since such marriages had no legal status, the children were illegitimate. Thus, one of the tragic ironies of that entire era was that after having first denied slaves the right to have any valid marriage, that same legal process declared their children bastards—not because of any immorality or fault of the parents but solely because of the inherent cruelty of the applicable legal doctrines. Only black people had been denied the legal right to enter into an agreement for that ancient, holy, and honorable state—marriage. In 1809 the legislature provided:

> That all marriages contracted or which may hereafter be contracted, wherein one or more of the parties was, were, or may be slaves, shall be considered equally valid, as though the parties thereto were free, and the child or children of any such marriage shall be deemed legitimate, any law, usage or custom to the contrary notwithstanding: *Provided,* That nothing herein contained shall be deemed or construed to manumit any such slave or slaves.[121]

In 1807 the legislature repealed the one-year ownership requirement for exporting slaves and only permitted persons who had resided ten years within New York and who were planning to move permanently out of the state to take their slaves with them. They were required to prove to a judge or public official that they had owned the slave for at least ten years. Strict affidavits were required and the failure of the master of a vessel to obtain a license for each slave he took on board establishing compliance with the statute was made a crime.[122]

While the 1809 act recognized slave marriages regardless of

whether the marriage took place in or outside New York, the legislature was more restrictive in dealing with blacks' rights to inherit or own property. They provided that blacks who had been born slaves within the State of New York and who were thereafter manumitted were capable of inheriting property, real or personal, and could sue "in all courts, having the like remedy for the recovery of such estates, or for injuries done to the same, as if such person or persons had been free born citizens of this state." By implication the legislature was denying the right to inherit property to all blacks who were still slaves and also even to those slaves who had been manumitted but not born within the State of New York. Finally the legislature made it easier for an owner to manumit "any child born a slave" if the parent of the child was "able and willing" to provide the future maintenance.

The legislative balancing act of attempting simultaneously to expand options for emancipation while maintaining vestiges of slavery is reflected in the comprehensive Act of April 9, 1813.[123] Twenty-six years earlier at the Constitutional Convention in Philadelphia, the nation's forefathers had wrestled with the issue whether the law, for purposes of taxation and representation, should view slaves solely as property or as persons to be counted like all other human beings. In the political compromise, the framers agreed that for purposes of representation and taxes slaves would be counted as three-fifths of all other persons. In many respects the 1813 New York statute exemplifies New York's efforts to strike a balance between freedom and slavery. In the very first section, the framers made clear that the act was not a general emancipation statute, for they provided "that every negro mulatto or mestee within this state, who is now a slave for life, shall continue such unless such slave shall be manumitted according to law." They then assured masters that religion was legally irrelevant: "the baptizing of any slave shall not be deemed to be a manumission of such slave." In support of freedom for blacks, they reenacted previous provisions legitimizing marriages of manumitted slaves, and guaranteeing manumitted slaves the right to inherit property.

To tip the scales more favorably to freedom, they made it easier for owners to manumit slaves. If the slave was less than forty-five years of age any owner could manumit the slave either by will, testament, or certificate. For slaves over forty-five the owner would be obligated for the slave's maintenance if "such slave shall become a charge to any city or town within this state." Yet even this latter contingent liability was far less onerous than some of the earlier statutes that had required owners to post a 200 pound bond prior to manumitting their slave. The 1813 statute also provided a method to obtain exemption from financial responsibility if the owner had obtained a certificate from the overseers of the poor certifying that the slave "appears to be under the age of 45 and of sufficient ability to provide for himself or herself"; upon registering the certificate, the owner was relieved of any future obligation even if the slave became a pauper. The act legitimized those earlier manumissions "made by the people called Quakers and others" even though those manumissions had not been in strict conformity with the statute. Limitations were further imposed on the transportation of slaves into the state. One could be fined if by fraud or collusion one sold or pretended to sell any aged or infirmed slave to a person unable to maintain the slave.

On the issue of a slave's procedural and substantive rights in court, the legislature continued to make distinctions between slaves and free persons. They provided "that no slave shall be a witness in any case, except for or against another slave, in criminal cases." Thus slaves could not testify in a case when any person other than a slave abused them. Presumably a slave woman could not even testify to prove that she had been raped, mutilated, or dismembered if the assault had been committed by any white person or even a free black. The statute gave any and all white persons another special advantage by providing that the justices of the peace could commit any slave to jail who struck a white person without the slave having any right to a jury trial to contest the factual allegations. But as an expansion of the liberties of slaves, it noted that "in all other cases [except where a slave was charged with assaulting a white person] such slaves shall have the privilege to trial by jury." In 1813 the legislature also made it a crime to kidnap free Negroes and sell them into slavery.[124] The comprehensive April, 1813 statute was the last stage before the ultimate abolition of slavery.

Finally, in 1817 the legislature set a date for the absolute end of slavery:

> every negro, mulatto or mustee within this state, born before
> the fourth day of July, one thousand seven hundred and
> ninety-nine, shall, from and after the fourth day of July, one
> thousand eight hundred and twenty-seven, be free.[125]

Thus, every slave born before 1799 and after 1827 was freed. Slavery was not completely eradicated, for those born within the interim twenty-eight-year period (1799-1827) were to remain indentured servants until they reached the ages specified in the 1799 statute.

The only other exception in the statute allowed nonresidents to enter New York with their slaves and remain in the state for up to nine months without forfeiture of their slaves.[126] Such an exception was found necessary under the federal constitution, as the state's highest court ruled in *Jack* v. *Martin,* a case in which a black man brought suit against a woman claiming she was illegally detaining him as her slave:

> We may deplore the existence of slavery in any part of the
> Union, . . . yet as the right of the master to reclaim his fugitive is secured to him by the federal constitution, no good
> citizen, . . . will interfere to prevent this provision from
> being carried into full effect. . . . It stands . . . undenied
> that the defendant was entitled to the services of the plaintiff,
> under the guaranty of the federal constitution. . . .[127]

CIVIL RIGHTS ACCORDED FREED BLACKS

Emancipation was not the key that unlocked the door to full equality. As the 1785 debate demonstrated, if emancipation were tied to the granting of equal civil rights to blacks, the majority of New Yorkers were willing to allow slavery to continue in their midst. This attitude was most prevalent among New York's white working-class population, which felt particularly victimized by the slavery system; economically, whites did not profit under slavery, for several jobs were closed to them. As a group, working-class whites did not want to erect a system that gave blacks equal rights on the dismantled foundation of slavery. Many whites in New York, and their counterparts in other northern states, demonstrated nothing but antipathy for freed blacks. As deTocqueville observed, "Thus it is that in the United States the prejudice rejecting the Negroes seems to increase in proportion to their emancipation."[128]

The attack waged against free blacks was of great importance in New York where, since 1777, all free men, subject to property requirements applicable to all regardless of previous conditions of servitude, race, or creed, were able to vote.

Racial hatred soon began to chip away at blacks' political rights. By 1815, two years before the passage of the emancipation statute, the Republican-controlled state legislature had already passed a bill requiring blacks to obtain special permits in order to vote in state elections. And, in 1822, only five years after the emancipation statute was passed, the state constitution was amended abolishing for all whites the property qualification for voting. But the property requirement for blacks was increased from $100 to $250; this provision remained in effect until the ratification of the Fifteenth Amendment to the federal constitution in 1870.[129] Thus, although blacks were no longer property in New York, they were second-class citizens, unable to equally use the ballot to protect themselves from future economic, social and political deprivations.

New York: An Evaluation

What, therefore, is unique about the experiences of slaves and free nonwhites in the region now known as New York? Was this colony like the other northern colonies and states such as Pennsylvania, New Jersey, or Massachusetts? The answer is no. For it was New Netherland more than any other colony or state that successfully experimented with more humane alternatives to the chattel slavery system. It was New York that rejected those alternatives.

While under Dutch rule, the colony adopted a system of half-freedom for slaves that was productive for whites and productive for nonwhites as much as any system other than full freedom had been. And the colony was prosperous. Yet, when the British assumed control in the mid-1600s, the half-freedom system was eliminated. Slavery as it existed in other English colonies became the rule.

Yet slavery in New York did not reach the level of depravity and harshness found in Virginia, South Carolina, or Georgia. Slaves in New York had more basic rights protected by the legal process. When the masters desired to be more lenient, the New York slave codes were not as severely restrictive on the discretion of the master. But was this greater moderation because the colony was less economically dependent on slave labor than were the more southern colonies?

Despite its greater liberality, the master-slave relationship in New York still had persistent tensions and confrontations. In 1712 New York City was the scene of the first, and the most violent, slave revolt during the colonial era. Colonial legislators, and some commentators, argued that the violence was caused by the lenient slave system in New York and thus they enacted stricter provisions further curbing the slaves' freedom. But, it is equally as plausible that the violence was attributable to the increased restrictions the English imposed on the slaves.

Throughout the colonial era restrictions on both the slave and his master increased. Yet, the dichotomy continued to exist between the legislated restrictions and the more permissive and lenient attitudes of several masters. Masters tended to overlook curfew violations; and nonslave owners disregarded prohibitions against trading with slaves and serving them alcohol.

When in 1777 the general assembly enacted the state's first constitution, New York was presented with another opportunity to fashion a society composed of free people, where all residents were accorded basic rights. And, although there was some discussion of emancipation, such action was deferred because the delegates feared that emancipation would add to the disruption already caused by the impending War of Independence. The delegates did approve, perhaps unintentionally, a constitution giving all free male inhabitants, regardless of race, creed, or previous condition of servitude, the right to vote in state elections, subject to property qualifications that applied to *all*.

The state was unable to reconcile political and civil equality and emancipation even after the War of Independence. New York modified the system of slavery, encouraged manumission, and sought to end the slave trade in the state. But, it was only when the concept of civil rights was separated from the emancipation issue that the legislature could enact an emancipation statute; even then, in 1799, emancipation was to be gradual, probably because the legislators desired to minimize the economic loss to the masters.

Emancipation became absolute for slaves born before 1799 and after July 4, 1827, in 1817. But only five years later, blacks were precluded from voting in state elections.

Thus, New York is a case history where the traditional myths used to block black freedom and black civil equality were proven incorrect. Under the less harsh slave system, masters and slaves flourished economically. Under a constitution in which free blacks were able to vote, the state did not degenerate; chaos was not the norm. In fact, the social disruptions that did take place were most often caused by whites attacking blacks. The true reason for the deprivation of colonial blacks was exposed by the New York experience; and that reason was a perception that blacks were inferior human beings and thus not entitled to equality and fairness under the law.

5

SOUTH CAROLINA

WHITE MINORITY/BLACK MAJORITY

Introduction

IN 1787, one hundred sixty-one years after the first Africans were brought to the territory of South Carolina,[1] one of the colony's most prominent leaders and a delegate to the Constitutional Convention, General Charles Cotesworth Pinckney, declared:

> I am of the same opinion now as I was two years ago . . . that, while there remained one acre of swampland uncleared of South Carolina, I would raise my voice against restricting the importation of negroes [slaves]. I am as thoroughly convinced as that gentlemen is, that the nature of our climate, and the flat, swampy situation of our country, obliges us to cultivate our lands with negroes, and that without them South Carolina would soon be a desert waste.[2]

From its beginning, black labor was the primary factor in preventing South Carolina from becoming a "desert waste." The first black slaves to be recorded by name were brought into the colony in 1670 by Captain Nathaniel Sayle, brother of the first governor of Carolina.[3] According to the records, the three blacks imported, John Sr., Elizabeth, and John Jr., were members of a family brought over from Bermuda.[4]

Blacks were not imported in large numbers into South Carolina until the late 1690s with the development of rice as a profitable staple. In its initial years, the colony tried to some extent to enslave local Indians but gradually their representation in the labor force dropped to a minimum. To a larger extent, South Carolina, like every other developing American colony, first relied on whites— who were, generally, indentured servants.[5] Despite the colonists' efforts to encourage the importation of whites, white indentured servitude declined as a major labor source in South Carolina and, with the aid of the legislative process, the widespread enslavement of blacks developed. Soon after the decision to begin widespread use of black slave labor, the number of blacks in the colony exceeded the number of whites. By 1708, less than twenty years after the decision to move from white indentured labor to black slave labor, black slaves outnumbered white inhabitants, both free and bonded, 4100 to 4080. South Carolina was unique among the American colonies in becoming at this early date, and in remaining so throughout the colonial period, the only colony where blacks were a majority of the population.[6]

Many historians have asserted that racial slavery existed so early in South Carolina's history because the colony was originally populated by migrants largely from the West Indian colonies and particularly Barbados.[7] These scholars point out that the "natural" tendency for these transported Barbadians would have been to maintain slaves as a carryover from their experiences in Barbados.[8]

What the Barbadian heritage did determine, even prior to the first large importation of blacks as slaves, was the uncompromising attitude the colonists held toward the moral question of enslaving a black person against his will. Unlike those colonies where there was some hesitancy, experimentation, or delay in initiating a comprehensive slave system, South Carolina, even while still part of the original colony of Carolina, started with a relatively definitive legal structure on slavery based on a fierce determination to use slavery wherever it was profitable. The evolution of the colony of Carolina and, more specifically, the evolution of what will be analyzed in this chapter as the South Carolina slave law, can be understood only if one takes into account the fact that the West India human value system provided the basis for the institution of black slavery in South Carolina. In other aspects too—even in the production of goods—the early South Carolina economy was very much based upon the needs of Barbadians.[9] So great, in fact, was this economic dependence that Peter Wood, in his classic work, stated that the early South Carolina settlement "had been little more than the dependent servant of an island master—in short, the colony of a colony."[10]

Furthermore, South Carolina's special isolation from her American colonial neighbors acted to reinforce the Barbadian influence by excluding the colony from diverse and often more temperate influences. For instance, Virginia, Carolina's neighbor to the north, was not only distant given the transportation conditions at that time, but communications were impeded by the relatively rough territory between the settlements.[11] Even the Albermarle settlement, which later became North Carolina, was relatively isolated from the South Carolina settlement centering on Charlestown. Although the entire Carolina area was included under the same charter granted to the Proprietors, the settlements were established with two distinct governments.[12] The colonies were referred to as North and South Carolina before 1700 and the distinct reference to South Carolina appears in the *Statutes at Large of South Carolina* by 1696;[13] the colonies were not separated by law, however, until 1729. The two Carolina settlements also had differing concerns. North Carolina was geographically an extension of Virginia and there was, at one period, an attempt by Virginia to claim the area of North Carolina. North Carolina was not as preoccupied with the fear of European enemies—the Spanish and French—as South Carolina. The economies were also different; the North Carolina settlers were not generally involved in the Indian trade and their chief commodities were tobacco, corn, and livestock.[14] According to Charles M. Andrews:

> The province of Albermarle, known after 1691 as North Carolina, was far removed from its southern partner and in its history was pursuing an entirely different course. . . . It was an isolated settlement, singularly out of touch with the outside world.[15]

The separateness of the settlements was heightened after 1719 when South Carolina overthrew the proprietary government and attempted to become a royal colony, whereas North Carolina remained under the proprietary rule until 1729.[16]

What will be notable about the issue of race and the legal process in South Carolina will not be a gradual development toward slavery but rather the tracing of the growing restrictions placed upon blacks by the legal system. What began as a carryover of West Indian slave laws was reinforced in its severity by the perceived need to contain the growing black majority. Another notable aspect of South Carolina slave law is the absence of arguments—human and legal—over the existence of slavery within the colony. The primary legal evidence of the institution of slavery in the colony, the colonial statutes, are devoid of such debate. Likewise, there are no cases raising the issues so eloquently raised in the English case, *Sommersett* v. *Stuart*. The absence of one surviving judicial case challenging the validity of slavery tells almost as much about the treatment of blacks by the legal system as do the detailed descriptions of the key elements of the black slave codes. What makes this absence all the more depressing is that in South Carolina the evolution of legal rights was so markedly tied to race—an expansion of protections for white servants and a repression of liberties for blacks.

The Decline of Indentured Servitude for Whites and the Escalation of Slavery for Blacks

WHITE BONDAGE IN COLONIAL SOUTH CAROLINA*

White servants were introduced into the colony to settle the country, supply labor, and provide a population sufficient to defend the colony.[17] During the early colonial period efforts to obtain white servants resulted in the importation of indentured labor and convicts. Later, German redemptioners[18] constituted a substantial portion of the new arrivals.[19]

The number of convict laborers was small and those who

---

* In our analysis of the South Carolina law on servants, we use the term "servant" as a synonym for *white* servant. While there are scattered references to the existence of black servants in colonial South Carolina, their number was minuscule and they should be viewed as an aberrational phenomenon in a generally repressive system. In the first comprehensive census of the colony taken in 1708, there is reference to whites as free or servants and to Negroes as slaves. By 1717, the legislation regarding servants was entitled, "An Act for the Better Governing and Regulating White Servants"; no reference was made to black servants.

came had little effect on the general population.[20] In fact, the colony discouraged the importation of convicts and, at times, forbade their entry, resulting in fewer criminals being sent to South Carolina than to other colonies.[21]

While white servants were never as large a percentage of South Carolina's population as of Virginia's, Maryland's, or Pennsylvania's,[22] they were a major factor in the early settlement of the colony. For the period 1682 to 1708, white servants were one-third of the immigrant population.[23] Their large numbers are especially evident during the earlier part of this period.[24] For example, on board the *Carolina,* one of the first vessels to arrive in South Carolina, "sixteen were masters, one of whom had with him a wife, sixty-three servants, and thirteen persons who brought no servants."[25]

The fairness of any legal system can be measured by the availability of adequate remedies to protect one's rights. Thus, the essential question is, does one have free access to a court or legislative body to obtain vindication where a human right has been infringed? The legal system of South Carolina focused on concepts of fairness when adjudicating "the welfare of the white servant class."[26] Both procedural and substantive rights were legislated with specificity to protect them.

One of the protections afforded the servant in South Carolina was the assurance that he would serve only for a fixed period. By legislative action masters were prohibited from perpetrating fraud upon servants who arrived without indentures or contracts. In accordance with the statute, a master was required within six months from the servant's arrival to obtain a certificate from a judicial official to verify the age of the servant.[27] Once his period of service expired, a servant could demand a certificate of freedom.[28]

Upon the master's failure to obtain the certificate verifying the age of the servant, the servant was protected by a statute that made the maximum term of service five years.[29] As a further distinction from slave codes, the burden of proof was always on the master who sought the service of a white servant: this was in complete contrast with slavery law, where the burden was always on the black to prove that he was a free person.

Servants were provided a means to protect themselves from inhumane treatment by masters, and masters were directed by the legislature to treat their servants fairly. Under a 1690 act a servant could complain to the grand council and obtain liberty or other relief if he could demonstrate that the master had not provided adequate food, shelter and clothing, or if the servant had been unreasonably abused.[30] A later act of 1717 attempted to correct the "barbarous usage of servants by cruel masters,"[31] by declaring that servants could complain to a justice of the peace to ensure that their master provided a "competent diet, clothing and lodging, and that he [did] not exceed the bounds of moderation in correcting them beyond the merit of their offenses."[32] Servants could not be "unreasonably [burdened] beyond their strength with labour, or [deprived] of their necessary rest and sleep, or excessively beat or abuse[d]."[33] Masters would be admonished upon the first offense, fined after a second offense, and upon the third offense the servant would be sold. The legislature specified that the servant could be sold *only* to "any other white person."[34] The 1744 act increased the penalties by eliminating the mere admonishment of the master upon a first offense and replacing it with a fine.[35] That these protections were not merely illusory is established by the fact that it was not uncommon for a servant to bring a complaint against his master.[36]

Unlike slaves, servants could own property, the legislature having explicitly declared that servants could "have a property in their own goods, and dispose of the same for their own future advantage."[37] Also, servants could bring before any two justices of the peace complaints regarding wages, freedom, or any other labor problem.[38] At the end of their period of service, servants were given a clothing allowance.[39] Most important, as will be discussed later,[40] white servants were eligible for land grants under the "head right" system at the end of their term of service.*

Even when the indentured servant sought to illegally circumvent the terms of his indenture, either by absenting himself for short periods of time, or by participating in the theft and transfer of property belonging to the master, or ultimately by attempting to escape the jurisdiction—the South Carolina legislature acted with

---

* The "head right" system provided land grants to the early colonial settlers. Under this system, an individual was eligible for land, the amount of which was based upon status—age, sex, free, or servant—and persons importing slaves or servants were eligible for additional grants.

restraint, despite the fact that these crimes threatened the economic stability of the colony.*

Under a 1686 act entitled "An act inhibiting the trading with servants or slaves," the first act passed relating to servants and slaves, buying goods from or selling to a servant or slave was punishable by additional service, as to servants, and a fine, if committed by a free man or woman.[41] Slaves, perhaps in recognition of the fact that they were subjected to perpetual bondage and could not be punished by additional service, could:

> suffer and abide such punishment or censure, not extending to the taking away life or limb, as the Grand Counsell . . . or any two Justices of the Peace . . . shall think fit.[42]

The 1686 statute directed that any servant who "absented" himself from his work would serve for each day "absent" an additional twenty-eight days. By 1717, even that penalty was reduced—to one week of additional service for each day absent, not to exceed two years.[43] For striking or beating a master, mistress, or overseer, certainly serious offenses, under the 1686 act the punishment could be simply an additional period of service—often one additional year. Corporal punishment could be ordered under the 1717 statute for this offense; however, it could be inflicted only "by the hands of the constable or some other white person."[44]

It was not until 1744 that a white servant was required to carry a pass when he traveled more than two miles from his master's property.[45] Further, unlike the slave, the servant who was discovered without his pass could not be subjected to chastisement by his captor; only a justice could order that he be whipped and then no more than twenty stripes *after* his status as "fugitive servant" was determined.[46] Likewise, when a white servant stole a boat, a crime that implied the possible intent of escape, the white servant was nonetheless made liable to "the same penalties and punishments as any white free person," which were a fine, an assessment of damages, and possibly corporal punishment.[47] For the same crime a

---

* While one cannot maintain that the penalties placed upon the white criminal servant were mild, when one compares them to those exacted from the slave, *infra* pp. 162-199, the disparity is apparent.

black slave or an Indian would have been subject to thirty-nine lashes for the first offense and for the second, one ear cut off.[48]

Yet there was one crime that so concerned the power brokers in South Carolina, as it had those in Virginia,[49] that it was not treated with the comparative restraint common to other penalties for servant crimes: this was the attempt by the white poor or the white servant to join forces with the black slave against the common oppressor. For, perhaps if the white poor were to disregard the differences in the color of skin and unite with the enslaved black against those who exploited both poor whites and all blacks, the power of the master class would diminish. Thus, it is not surprising that to deter such alliances of white servants and slaves the servant who ran away in the company of slaves received harsher punishment; he was declared a felon and was to suffer death without the benefit of clergy.[50] The message was indisputably clear, a white runaway's alliance with slaves could cost him his life. An alliance with blacks was a crime of its own genre.

There is some evidence that during the early years of the colony it was somewhat tolerant of sexual relationships "between free white men and negro, Indian or mulatto women."[51] As the colony developed, the legislature sought to discourage sexual relations between white servants and blacks and to maintain a presumptive perception of the superiority of the white race. However, by a 1717 statute entitled "An Act for the Better Governing and Regulating White Servants,"[52] the colony dealt generally with illicit sexual relationships. Free white men who caused a servant woman to become pregnant could be fined and required to take care of her while pregnant and of the child during the woman's service.[53] The legislature differentiated the status of whites, placing upon the white male servant a greater burden than upon the white freeman; for the white male servant had to serve the woman servant's master after the expiration of his own indenture for a period equivalent to the remaining time the female servant had to serve when she became pregnant.[54]

Of course, the maximum penalty was imposed when the relationship was interracial. If the white woman was free she was obligated to serve seven years when she became pregnant by a black; if she was a servant her term was extended by an additional seven years plus her obligation to pay damages.[55] If the Negro man was free and the female white, the black male became a servant for seven years.[56] The child was to be a servant for twenty years if male or for eighteen years if female.[57] Surprisingly, when a free or servant white man impregnated a free or servant Negro woman, he was statutorily subject to the same penalties as a white woman impregnated by a black.[58] Most significantly, the child of an interracial relationship, even where the mother was not a slave, was condemned to servitude for the "indiscretions" of his parents; this process repudiated the current colonial doctrine of *partus sequitur ventrem,* where the status of the child was determined by the status of the mother. Thus, the child of a free mother should not have been enslaved.

Interestingly, the 1717 statute on illicit sexual relations did not refer to slaves. Did the legislature assume that there were no sexual relations between slaves and whites, or did it want to avoid categorizing as a crime the white sexual exploitation of black female slaves?

Although there were some technical differences between the South Carolina and Virginia statutes on interracial relationships in practice, the South Carolina statute probably resulted in the same types of disparities that favored white males and penalized, most harshly, interracial relationships between white females and black males.

As the number of black slaves began to increase substantially, efforts were made to encourage the importation of additional white servants. Initially, the head-right system provided the necessary incentive, but after it was altered legislative action was needed to further spur importation.[59] As early as 1698 an act was passed to pay masters of vessels or other nonresidents a bounty for each non-Irish, white male servant imported.[60] Planters owning six or more Negro slaves were to take on those servants imported until proportionate representation was achieved.[61] In 1716 another act similar to the 1698 act was passed. The bounty going to the importer of indentured servants was increased and persons owning ten slaves were required to purchase the servants imported under the act. In their choice of laborers the colonists revealed their belief that even all whites were not equally desirable and by the legal process they differentiated status levels, with the Irish and white Roman Catholics at the lowest level. They required all merchants or masters of vessels to certify:

> that to the best of their knowledge none of the servants by them imported be either what is commonly called native Irish or persons of known scandalous characters or Roman Catholics.[62]

The underlying concern in enacting the 1716 measure was one that would permeate much of the later legislation. The preamble declared:

> Whereas sad experience hath taught us that the small number of white inhabitants of this Province, is not sufficient to defend the same even against our Indian enemies, and whereas the number of slaves are daily increasing in this Province, which may likewise endanger the safety thereof, if speedy care be not taken to encourage the importation of white servants, . . .[63]

Despite the steady flow of white immigrants into the colony, there were never enough whites, servant and free combined, to offset the larger importation of black slaves.[64]

INDIAN SLAVERY

The enslavement of the Indian in the Americas preceded the arrival of the English. In his authoritative work, Edward McCrady notes that:

> the first Europeans who trod the soil of Carolina were Spaniards who had sailed in 1520 from Hispaniola for the purpose of securing in the island of Lucayos a supply of Indians to take back with them to work as slaves in the gold mines.[65]

Instead of reaching Lucayos, an island north of Cuba, the Europeans touched North America.[66]

With the arrival of the English settlers in the late 1600s, Indians were generally taken as captives in the many conflicts between early settlers and Indian tribes. Despite the fact that South Carolina enslaved a larger number of Indians than any other colony, most were not put to domestic labor tasks. After the Indians were captured, most frequently they were exported and sold, primarily in the West Indies.[67] South Carolina during the late seventeenth century became "more active than any other English colony in the export of Indian slaves."[68] The proceeds from selling Indians in the West Indies made possible purchase of another form of labor, one believed to be better suited to the colony—black slaves.[69]

Although the Proprietors enacted a temporary law as early as December, 1671, providing that no Indian, upon any occasion or pretense whatsoever, be made a slave or be carried out of the country[70] without his own consent, this provision was disregarded even by the Proprietors.[71] They continued, for example, to allow Indian captives to be sold to acquire the funds with which to compensate colonial soldiers,[72] a practice that appears to have been established early in the colony's history. Surviving records indicate that on September 23, 1671, the council "ordered open war, captives to be sold abroad as slaves, unless redeemed, and the proceeds to be distributed among the soldiers."[73] There is evidence that the "consent" required under the act was "readily obtainable" due to the Indians' fear of the captors and the ignorance of the white purchasers.[74]

The Act of 1708, entitled "An Act for Raising the Sum of Five Thousand Pounds," illustrates even later legislative sanction of the Indian export trade and a scheme of fostering divisiveness among the various Indian groups.[75] First, the act provided a reward in the form of a gun to "every [northern] Indian who shall take or kill an Indian man of the enemy."[76] Furthermore, the statute authorized the commanding officer:

> to buy all prisoners of the said Indian enemies, above the age of twelve years, that shall be taken captive either by white man or Indian in the said expedition . . . and the slaves so bought shall be taken care of and delivered by the said captain . . . to the public Receiver, who is hereby required and commanded to pay all such sum . . . for all such slave or slaves as he the said commissioner shall purchase not exceeding the sum of seven pounds for every Indian slave. And the public Receiver is hereby empowered to ship off to some islands of the West Indies the slaves so bought and delivered, to him by the commissioner . . . to be there sold, or dispose of them here for the use of the publick, . . .[77]

The statute specified that if the captured Indians were brought back into the province a penalty of 200 pounds would be imposed.

The frequent practice of exporting Indian slaves probably explains why enslaved Indians did not have a discernible influence on colonial slave law.[78] However, those Indians who did remain in South Carolina as slaves were generally regulated by statutes and codes made applicable to black slaves.

Just as there appeared to have been no moral qualms among the colonists regarding the propriety of black slavery in South Carolina, similarly there was no moral impediment to the widespread enslavement of Indians. Yet it did not flourish within the colony; other elements eventually made it impractical. Within miles of their own people, Indians, more easily than black Africans, could escape without being recaptured; thus, their value increased when they were sold away from their native regions.[79]

The colonists desired good trade relations with the Indian tribes and wanted to minimize armed conflict with them. Even though they did not enforce their enactment, still the Proprietors had condemned the enslavement of Indians.[80] Furthermore, the head-right system offered no incentive to the colonist to use Indians since he could not receive additional land for servants or slaves unless they had been imported.[81] Although there were always some Indian slaves within the colony, Peter Wood tells us, "any thought of utilizing such laborers as the core of the colonial work force had dissipated well before the end of the seventeenth century."[82]

BLACK SLAVERY: "WHEN I HAVE LAND,
WHAT SHALL I DOE WITH IT?"

The Early Colonial Period

While the institutions of white indentured servitude and Indian slavery were decreasingly relied upon, the South Carolina settler's favoritism of black slaves had grown such that by as early as 1682 Samuel Wilson, in "An Account of the Province of Carolina," told the Carolina Proprietors:

> But a rational man will certainly inquire, *when I have land, what shall I doe with it?* What comoditys shall I be able

to produce that will yeild me money in other countrys that I may be inabled to buy Negro slaves (without which a Planter can never do any great matter) and purchase other things for my pleasure and convenience, that Carolina doth not produce.[83]

The early assumption that black slaves were necessary for the developing South Carolina colony was made not only by incoming settlers. The first proposed legal system also revealed the colony's predisposition for black slavery. Prior to the arrival of the first black slaves into the colony of Carolina, a constitution was drafted for the governing of the colony making express provision for slavery and assuring slave owners that blacks could not be shielded under the umbrella of Christendom.

Every Freeman of Carolina shall have absolute power and authority over Negro slaves, of what opinion or Religion soever.[84]

The authors of that document, the so-called Fundamental Constitution of 1669, were John Locke and the first Earl of Shaftesbury. In matters of race, it seems, the understanding even of John Locke, to whom is attributed the whole concept of man's inalienable rights, was more a product of his times than of his conscience. It should be noted, of course, that Locke, as well as Shaftesbury, worked under the direction of the Carolina Proprietors, four of whom were members of the Royal African Company, which held a monopoly in the British African slave trade.[85]

Technically, the constitution never became legally operative in South Carolina because it never received the approval of the colonists, as required by the charter.[86] Nevertheless, the racial policies set forth in this Fundamental Constitution did become the accepted legal standard for South Carolina's treatment of blacks.

Although exact population statistics are not available, Peter Wood estimates that during the first twenty-five years of the colony's development "between one-fourth and one-third of the colony's new comers were Negroes. . . . Among these first several hundred black Carolinians at least three out of every four were men."[87] Then, importation from Africa was minimal, if at all, and most blacks were obtained through a variety of means, including piracy, "salvaging" from slaves abandoned in the Caribbean, and importation, primarily from the West Indies and occasionally from England.[88] By 1695 there were approximately two thousand blacks in the Carolina region, making the percentage of blacks in this colony higher than that in any other American colony.[89]

There are many hypotheses proffered as to why black slave labor overtook white indentured servitude and Indian enslavement so early in the colony's history. Some claim that South Carolinians brought their own established traditions on slavery over from Barbados. Others assert that the colony turned to slavery because of unsatisfactory results from free whites and indentured servants. While adverse publicity in England describing abuses under the indentured servant system may have deterred the emigration of white servants, certainly kidnappers of blacks in Africa were not adversely affected by public commentary on the cruelties of the international slave trade. Profitability was the sole determinant in the decision of whether or not to enslave black Africans. Also, unlike the retaliation that might ensue from enslaving Indians, the enslavement of blacks from distant societies created no risk to the security and stability of the colony. Finally, ownership of black slaves accorded the settler greater prestige.[90] Many political leaders were slave owners and the quantum of their slaves was a barometer of their authority and status.[91]

These factors notwithstanding, it is indisputable that blacks were not imported in large numbers until the development of the rice economy. Whether mistaken or not, the colonists believed that slaves were a better investment than other forms of unwaged labor. Purportedly, blacks survived better than whites or Indians in the torrid, mosquito-infested swamps where South Carolina's basic crop, rice, was cultivated.

Despite the long-term economic advantages, initially the purchase of African slaves did present difficulties. The immediate outlay required to purchase a slave was great compared to that for an indentured servant. Also, because money was relatively scarce, the risks that a slave would not endure for the length of time necessary to recoup the original investment became an important factor.[92]

To offset some of the economic disadvantages of Negro slave labor, the head-right system, giving land grants to new colonial arrivals, was modified by the Proprietors so that importers of black slaves became eligible for land grants. In response to the changes, the Barbadian planters more readily imported slaves to the colony, and thus automatically acquired more land.[93] Those arriving before March 25, 1670 received the most generous land grants. Each free person above sixteen years of age received 150 acres for each manservant or male slave imported and 100 acres for every woman servant or manservant under sixteen years of age imported. Also, each servant received 100 acres when he finished serving his term.[94] Through four statutory amendments in 1671, 1672, 1679, and 1682 the number of acres granted under the head-right system was gradually reduced so that by 1682 each free person received 50 acres and an additional 50 acres for each servant or slave imported. The servant received 40 acres upon expiration of his term.[95]

As the colony became more established, colonists could more easily purchase slaves on credit and thereby receive the benefits of the head-right system without any immediate cash outlay. David Wallace points to the colonial head-right system's tendency to depress economically the small white farmer and to escalate the larger planter's importation of slaves: "The planter could buy Negroes on credit; for the merchant knew that for every slave from pickaninny to patriarch his debtor would receive free fifty acres of land from the government, which increased his ability to pay."[96]

Once within the colony, most slaves during the early colonial period worked beside the Indian and white laborers, making the day-to-day distinctions between the black slave and white servant less significant than early legislative statutes might imply.[97] But with the widespread cultivation of rice, all this would rapidly change.

The Later Colonial Period:
Predominance of a Rice Economy

Much as in the 1800s cotton and the invention of the cotton gin economically shaped the entire institution of southern slavery, a century earlier the rice economy was the impetus to the entrenchment of slavery in South Carolina through the 1700s. The solidification of status distinctions between servants, free men, and slaves was concomitant with the extensive cultivation of rice. Blacks were increasingly relegated to field labor while white indentured servants worked as skilled laborers or as overseers on the plantations.[98] In the fields, because of the harshness of the conditions, blacks were "methodically slaughter[ed],"[99] and the high mortality rates on the South Carolina swamps were comparable to those in the West Indies.[100]

During the two decades after 1695, rice took permanent hold in South Carolina and the size of the African population grew until it exceeded the European.[101] By 1708, relatively early in the colony's history, black slaves outnumbered white inhabitants.

A complete rationale as to why black slaves were chosen as the mainstay of the labor force in rice production is, to a degree, unclear. Wood notes that many scholars of the early South state that the development of the rice economy closely paralleled the emergence of the colony's black majority; however, "none can be said to have explained it adequately."[102] He offers two factors that substantially explain why the use of black slaves predominated in rice production: the familiarity of many Africans to the production of rice acquired in their native lands,[103] and the ability of blacks to survive the health hazards of the rice-producing swamplands.[104]

McCrady suggests that it was the ultimate misfortune of South Carolina:

> not only that her climate suited the Negro race, but that rice—an article for foreign commerce as well as of home consumption—was found capable of production by negro labor at great profit, and that too in portions of her territory in which the white man could not continuously live. This made Charlestown an emporium of the trade which the English merchants were so vigorously prosecuting under the protection of the British government.[105]

As the economic viability of South Carolina became totally dependent on the coerced labor of blacks, the legal process escalated the codification of the deprivation of rights and encouraged an unbridled harshness on the very people who by their daily labor made the system profitable.

Legislative Enforcement of Racial Slavery

The wording of preambles is important, for drafters often seek the ambivalent goals of declaring the true purpose of the document while simultaneously masking its potentially harsh or inhumanitarian aspects. The drafters of the 1712 slave code pursued such goals when writing the preamble of the first comprehensive slave code enacted in South Carolina.[106]

The preamble to the 1712 slave code declared:

WHEREAS, the plantations and estates of this Province cannot be well and sufficiently managed and brought into use, without the labor and service of negroes and other slaves; and forasmuch as the said negroes and other slaves brought unto the people of this Province for that purpose, are of barbarous, wild, savage natures, and such as renders them wholly unqualified to be governed by the laws, customs, and practices of this Province; but that it is absolutely necessary, that such other constitutions, laws and orders, should in this Province be made and enacted, for the good regulating and ordering of them, as may restrain the disorders, rapines and inhumanity, to which they are naturally prone and inclined; and may also tend to the safety and security of the people of this Province and their estates; to which purpose, . . .[107]

Unless one reads this preamble critically, one may fail to perceive fully the state of mind and priorities of the whites then in power. This preamble, which was basically repeated in later acts of 1722[108] and 1735,[109] is primarily a statement of perceived economic necessity, in that the drafters seemed to be conceding that the province "cannot be well . . . [managed] without the labor and service of negroes and other slaves."[110] Thus, at the beginning, in their earliest preamble, they declare that exclusive utilization of white, indentured, and/or free labor will not be enough to sustain a sound economy. If necessity is the mother of invention, it is also the temptress of iniquity, for only after they have made their declaration of economic necessity (that they must have the service of Negroes and slaves), do they feel their reader is properly prepared to hear about the purported pernicious qualities of Negroes and slaves—that they "are of barbarous, wild, savage natures, and such as renders them wholly unqualified to be governed by the laws, customs and practices of this Province."[111] One must ask if these blacks who had been, or would be kidnapped from their homes in Africa were truly "wild and savage." It does seem a bit convenient that they were described as "wild and savage" directly after it had been pointed out that without black labor whites could not, on their own, make the province economically viable. It may be argued, on the other side, that little weight can be placed on the arguments of the preamble one way or the other since they were nothing more than a repetition of what had been said by Barbadians.[112] However, it is unlikely that the South Carolinians would have adopted so assertive a posture if it had been contrary to their own perceptions.

In 1740 the South Carolina legislature passed its most extensive, enduring slave code. That part of the earlier preamble in which reference was made to the economic necessity of slaves or the slaves' savage condition was deleted. Instead, the legislature rested its case by stating that its purpose was to have positive laws so that the slave "may be *kept in due subjection and obedience*."[113] While no record giving the reasons for the change has been found, we submit that the language change is significant. In the 1740 statute, the legislature asserted its goal of keeping blacks, Indians, mulattoes, and mestizos "in due subjection and obedience" regardless of whether they were savage, barbarous, or wild. With this change the legislature established justification for regulating the lives of nonwhites, not on the basis of the society's need to be protected from them, but to maintain slaves in a contained, restrictive, and profitable position.

This section will analyze the legislative process by which the colonists sought to keep slavery a profitable institution and maintain slaves in total subjection. As we analyze the provisions pertaining to the criminal laws, runaways, passes, or any other aspects of slave law, the legislature or the court always seemed to be making a judgment as to what was the most effective deterrent to preclude slave insurrections, while avoiding deterrents that would destroy the basic profitability of the system. The legal process tried to reap the harvest of fear by threatening a panoply of deterrents such as mutilation, castration, or even death, while at the same time trying to minimize the master's economic losses from too excessive enforcement of such deterrents. Of course, throughout this precarious balancing act, in pressing for the twin goals of profit maximization and total slave subjection, the legislature ignored the inherent desire of blacks for freedom and dignity.

EARLY LEGISLATION, 1690-1739

At a relatively early date, South Carolina resorted to statutory law as the primary vehicle for shaping its slave system. While the early legislation was not as restrictive as later acts, these early codes did regulate, generally, all the major areas of a slave's activities. To a large extent, the Barbadian tradition provided the basic framework for the South Carolina legislators. Yet, South Carolinians continually modified their slave law to respond to their unique position as an American colony with a black majority.

The first slave law was passed in 1690 by the South Carolina assembly;[114] however, it was subsequently disallowed by the Proprietors.[115] The 1712 act was the first comprehensive slave code of the colony.[116] It was followed by the codes of 1722 and 1735. Since there were no extensive revisions in the 1722 or 1735 codes, the 1712 code is exemplary of much of South Carolina's early slave legislation. At least five different aspects of the codes illustrate the evolutionary development of South Carolina's restrictive slave system and are, therefore, particularly appropriate for analysis: the legal status of slaves; the limitation of slaves' liberties; the capture and treatment of runaways; the criminal justice system; and finally, the protection of the slave.

Freehold vs. Chattel: Was There a Difference?

To regulate the legal status of slaves, the 1712 act provided: "All negroes, mulatoes, mustizoes or Indians" who were or will be bought or sold as slaves "are hereby declared slaves; and they, and their children, are hereby made and declared slaves, to all intents and purposes"; except for those who have been freed or who can prove their freedom.[117] The use of the phrase "they, and their children, are hereby made and declared slaves, to all intents and purposes" left the legal status and treatment of slaves determinable by custom.[118]

The disallowed 1690 act had provided that slaves were to

be "accounted as freehold" except "when other goods and chattels [were] not sufficient to satisfy" the debts of a master or in the settlement of certain estate matters.[119] The significance of freehold status was that, theoretically, the slave was accorded a higher position because the owner had a right to his services only and not an absolute right to the slave's person, as is the case with personal or chattel property.[120]

Thus, as "freehold" the slave was recognized under the law to have human qualities and personality and was thereby legally differentiated from chattels such as horses, dogs, and rice. The freehold concept was acquired from the Barbadian code.[121] Yet, despite the express language of the statute, South Carolinians disregarded the freehold definition of slavery and treated slaves as personal and chattel property.[122]

The 1712 act subtly repudiated the freehold concept in that it permitted the determination of slaves' status, whether freehold or chattel, to be made by custom. A little less than thirty years later, in 1740, the legislature would bluntly declare slaves chattel.[123]

The Limitation of Slaves' Liberties

Once slave status has been declared, most basic human rights are eradicated as a matter of law. The slave is denied the right to utilize the legal process in his behalf to stop injustices to himself, his body, or his family. Another aspect inherent in slavery law is its intent to protect above all else the institution of slavery so that no one master might individually do anything to weaken the system as it was practiced by others. Thus, even if a master wanted to give a slave more liberties or privileges than those minuscule protections the law required,[124] such additional privileges were subject to close scrutiny to assure that they would not cause unrest among other slaves or weaken the restraints of the slave system.

The basic limitations upon a slave's liberties, options, and mobility, regardless of whether or not the master was willing to grant such privileges, included the requirements that all slaves: carry passes or tickets any time they went beyond the limits of their owner's property; obtain their owner's explicit consent to carry on any form of trading; hold no property; and at no time hire themselves out to their own personal advantage. Simultaneously, rigid restrictions and prohibitions were placed on a master's right to free his slaves—even though a master might seek to do so on humanitarian grounds.

The pass system   The legislature limited slaves' mobility by the compulsory pass system. Under the 1712 act, traveling away from the plantation without a pass was prohibited unless slaves were in the company of "some white person."[125] Indicative of the legislature's attitude that vigilante powers be granted to whites to foster the implementation of slave laws, the 1712 statute obligated every white person to whip slaves apprehended without a ticket. If the white person did not apprehend the slave or failed to administer, whenever possible, such whipping, the white person "forfeit[ed] twenty shillings."[126] One half of the fine was "to be paid to the church wardens of the Parish" for the poor and the other half to the person who informed the authorities of the white person's failure to apprehend or beat the slave.[127] The white person apprehending the slave could "beat, maim or assault" his charge. If the slave refused to show his ticket and could not be apprehended alive, he could be killed with impunity.[128]

The 1712 act was far more restrictive and punitive than the 1690 act would have been had it been allowed. That earlier act would have excused slaves from traveling without a pass when there was "one more white men [sic] in their company."[129] Further, under that act the white person apprehending the slave (without a pass or not in the company of white men) was required to give him a "moderate" whipping and, if the slave violently resisted, he could be punished *only* by a judicial officer.[130] Under the 1690 act the judge could impose severe penalties. As an example, a slave could be severely whipped on the first offense of "offering violence" when questioned about his pass; for the second offense he was ordered to be severely whipped, nose slit, and "face burnt in some place," and, finally, on the third offense, the slave would suffer death.[131] Also unlike the 1712 act, the 1690 statute had provided that the white person could kill the slave *only* when the slave was a runaway and not when he resisted in the act of refusing to show a pass.[132] Though the penalties of the 1690 act were severe, they could be imposed only pursuant to judicial, and hopefully more impartial, decrees. In contrast the 1712 act, by eliminating the necessity of a judicial decree, adopted the arbitrariness, bias, and malevolency inherent in vigilante justice.

The provisions of the 1712 act were basically repeated in the later acts with a few changes. For example, in the 1722 act the slave could be whipped "not exceeding twenty lashes" when he traveled without a ticket, thus providing a standard for a moderate "whipping" as stated in the earlier acts.[133] However, by 1735 the legislature thought that the problem of resistance was so great that the supreme penalty, death, was ordered when the slave resisted with a stick or other instrument.[134] Thus, the practice of authorizing death only where it was the only means of apprehending the slave was changed to ensure the complete submissiveness of the black when challenged by his white examiner.

There were some instances where merely having a ticket would not suffice. The 1712 act provided that a slave could not go into Charlestown or travel to other plantations on Sunday unless he had a ticket that specified the urgent nature of his travels. This purpose had to be "for and about such particular business as cannot reasonably be delayed to another time."[135] If the owner failed to meet the statutory requirement, the slave, and not the owner, would bear the burden of the error. The slave, who had to obey his master and travel with the insufficient ticket, could be "dealt with as if he had no ticket."[136] Similar provisions were maintained throughout the early colonial period.[137]

Trading Slaves were forbidden to trade without the explicit consent of their owner.[138] The underlying concern reflected in these statutes was with numerous instances of purported theft by slaves. The 1712 act specifically made trading with a slave punishable when the party suspected that the goods were "unlawfully come by."[139] The act required the trader to prove that the goods were not stolen or lose the sum placed with the justice of the peace as "recognizance" or bond.[140] By 1714 the problems of having such a minor penalty were apparent, and when a party, against the "true intent and meaning of the laws," traded with a slave who did not have a license from his master, he could be punished by *fine or prosecuted* as an accessory for receiving stolen goods.[141]

Slave owners recognized that even the most cruel surveillance system relying on whites only might not be completely effective and thus they went to great efforts to encourage blacks to be informants. The 1714 act provided that when a slave informed the authorities of stolen goods being sold to any white person, he would receive from the white individual "the sum of two pounds."[142] Of course, the slave who stole was subject to criminal prosecution.[143]

Property held by slaves Property held by the slave with the owner's consent was liable to forfeiture. One of the main reasons for this liability was to ensure that slaves would not have weapons that could be later used during an attempted insurrection. For example, the 1712 act provided that slave quarters were to be searched by the master every fourteen days for items including "guns, swords, clubs and any other mischievous weapons."[144] These items were taken away and secured; thus, the owner was practically prohibited from allowing his slaves to have any item that could be used as a weapon regardless of whether the item was stolen. In 1722 the legislature expressed concern with slave possession of horses and "neat" (domesticated) cattle, which could serve to further insurrectionary plots by enabling the slave to travel and convey "intelligences." Instead of leaving the matter in the hands of the slave owner, the act gave justices of the peace the authority to take and sell these animals when informed of their being held by a slave.[145] The owner could retrieve the animals if he or another white person swore that the animal belonged to him. Private parties were given the authority to seize hogs, boats, and canoes that belonged to a slave, although they were required to give notice to a justice who would take and sell the items. This provision was repeated in the 1735 act.[146]

The best illustration of the extent to which a slave could be deprived of property held with his owner's consent is in the act of 1735.[147] When a slave managed to obtain clothing that might accord him some dignity or prestige, the act declared that when such clothing was "above" that which a slave should wear, it could be taken from the slave by "all and every constable and other persons" to be used for his or their own benefit.

The type of clothing that the slave could wear was:

negro cloth, duffelds, coarse kearsies, osnabrigs, blue linnen, checked linen or coarse garlix or calicoes, checked cottons, or scotch plaids, not exceeding ten shillings per yard for the said checked cottons, scotch plaids, garlix or calico, . . .[148]

A slave was to be forever aware of his degraded status; the requirement that he always wear the most inferior clothing—"negro cloth"—ensured that he never have an appearance giving him even minuscule status.[149] The slave was forced to "know his place" and never to reflect or symbolize any higher aspiration than that which the white society had irrevocably imposed upon him.

Hiring out   Masters were prohibited from granting a slave permission to hire himself out. The act of 1722 declared that no owner could permit a slave to work where he pleased under an agreement that the slave would pay the owner a sum from his earnings.[150] These agreements, according to the legislature, gave the slaves time to look for "opportunities to steal, in order to raise money to pay their masters, as well as to maintain themselves, and other slaves, their companions, in drunkeness and other evil courses."[151] The act also eliminated the ability of the owner to hire the slave out and give the slave a share of his earnings by stating that "the master is to receive the whole of what the slave shall earn."[152] Here, the legislature went beyond its stated purpose of eliminating the instances in which slaves could abuse the hiring-out system by prohibiting the slave from working for himself in any capacity. The master was required to reap all the benefits from his slaves' labor even when he was willing to share.

In eliminating hiring-out agreements under which the slave could profit, the slave code, once again, placed restrictions on the master class in an effort to maintain systemwide control over slaves. It is not surprising that the benefits to the slave of being hired out under this system were eliminated. Yet, here, the individual interests of a master in allowing his slave to work for himself had to yield to the broader benefits of the colony, which profited most when all slaves were kept under the master's dominion. They did not want any slave to have discretion or control over his economic welfare—regardless of his master's concurrence.

The problems in enforcing the statutory provisions on hiring out became apparent and in 1722 the legislature provided for a reward to informants, which was paid by the individual who hired the slave under the illegal conditions.[153] Finally, in the 1735 act, the penalty and reward were increased from five shillings per day to a ten pound reward to the informer paid by the owner as well as a five pound penalty for each day the slave was employed by the hirer.[154]

Manumission   During the early colonial period slave manumissions were generally left to the private sphere; the legislature made no provision restricting the right of the master to manumit his slaves and in certain situations made express provision for legislative manumissions. For example, a 1708 act entitled "an act for enlisting trusting slaves as shall be thought serviceable to this province in time of alarms" had provided that slaves who, "in actual invasion," killed or captured an enemy would be set free as a reward.[155] A curious feature was added, however, that *required* proof of the slave's action "by any white person." Thus, while freedom was theoretically obtainable, it was possible that deserving slaves would not be able to provide satisfactory proof.

It was not until 1722 that the colony regulated private slave manumissions in its slave code. Under the act it was provided:

> XXXIX.   And be it further enacted by the authority aforesaid, That all owners of slaves, who, at any time hereafter, shall manumit or set free any slave, for any particular service, shall make provision for his departure out of this Province; and such slave who shall not depart this Province by the space of twelve months next after such manumission, (being at liberty so to do,) shall lose the benefit of such manumission, and continue to be a slave, to all intents and purposes whatsoever, unless such manumission shall be approved of and confirmed by an order of both Houses of Assembly.[156]

In order for a slave to be manumitted and to stay in South Carolina, legislative approval was required. Under the 1735 act a black had to depart within six months after being manumitted by his owner, and freed blacks who returned within seven years from departure were to be reenslaved.[157] By statutory direction, upon violation of the act the manumitted black would be sold "by the public treasurer for the use of the public."[158]

The 1722 provision was not as restrictive as those that would follow; yet, it did represent the legislature's belief that private actions, when in the form of slave manumissions, needed official approval for lasting effect in South Carolina.

The Runaway Slave

Concomitant with the placement of greater restrictions on the ability of the owner to free the slave came heightened penalties on those slaves who sought to procure their own freedom—runaways.

In the 1712 act several provisions regulated the capture, maintenance, and punishment of runaways. As slaves traveling without passes, runaways would receive a moderate whipping or more severe punishment if resistance occurred.[159] However, there was an elaborate procedure for ensuring the capture and delivery of the slave to a marshal.[160] The marshal kept the runaway until the owner claimed him, reimbursed the marshal for the sums paid to the captor, and paid him an additional bonus.[161] The marshal was held liable for the value of the slave if he escaped or died through some fault of the marshal. While maintaining the slave, the marshal could not employ the slave. This, no doubt, was a form of protection against misappropriation of the slave's labor.

The statute made it clear that all members of the community were to be involved in the capture of runaway slaves. Incentives were offered. Special patrols received a reward of forty shillings for capturing a slave who had been away for more than six months. If the slave had escaped over twelve months previous and was taken alive, the members received four pounds from the master; but if he was killed, they received forty shillings from the public treasury.[162] If an Indian or a slave captured a runaway slave and delivered the slave to the owner or marshal, he received twenty shillings,[163] significantly less than the maximum amount of forty shillings provided to white captors.[164] This provision of the 1712 code was a radical change from the 1690 act, which gave any slave "the whole benefit" that any other captor received.[165]

The runaway slave was subject to criminal penalties. Slaves found guilty of attempting to escape from the province "in order to deprive [their] master or mistress of [their] service" were sentenced to death.[166] Those who persuaded or enticed another slave to do so were whipped and branded. Those slaves who participated further in an actual or attempted escape from the province received death sentences. A later act repealed the section mandating death to those slaves who merely urged another runaway to escape out of the province without taking any steps to aid in the escape.[167] In the later codes, death would not result in either case, not from humanitarian motives, but to minimize economic loss.

Those slaves above sixteen years of age who did not intend to run away from the province were punishable under another provision when they were away for at least twenty days.[168] Upon the first offense, the slave was to be "publicly and severely whipped, not exceeding forty lashes" by the owner or someone under his authority within ten days after the offense. Second offenses mandated being branded "with the letter R, on the right cheek." After a third offense, the slave was to be severely whipped, not exceeding forty lashes, and one ear was to be cut off. As for males, a third offense warranted being castrated and, if the slave died without any fault of the owner or person under his authority, the owner could be compensated for the value of the slave out of the public treasury. A female who ran away four times would be severely whipped, branded on the left cheek with the letter R, and mutilated, by having her left ear cut off. Finally, for a fifth offense, the "cord of the slave's legs" would be cut above the heel or the slave would suffer death.[169]

One must be mindful that these statutes directing the branding, mutilation, amputation, and killing of blacks were imposed by whites under English law, a legal process supposedly notable for its sensitivity to the rights of mankind.[170] But to the extent that this sensitivity existed it was for whites alone; the most brutal displays of inhumanity to blacks were sanctioned under the colony's rule of law.

The 1712 statute is notable not only for the type of punishment the runaway received, but also for the penalties to the owner who failed to whip, brand, cut the ear off, castrate, or make his slave lame. When an informant complained of the master's failure to punish his slave, the owner could be fined. After the slave's fourth offense, the owner might forfeit his slave.[171]

One can only wonder whether a master would actually inflict

the punishments knowing that the result might affect the slave's usefulness and value upon subsequent resale.[172] Yet, owners who wanted to commit these barbaric acts could do so under the sanction and encouragement of the law.

The provisions directing cruel punishment to runaways were not repeated in the 1722 act (which repealed the act of 1712) or in the 1735 act. Perhaps this was in recognition of most owners' reluctance to impair the value of their property.

The 1722 act made running away "with intent to go off from this Province" punishable by death.[173] But, in recognition of the extent of property loss, where slaves ran away in groups, only one or two of the most "notorious offenders" would die. The others suffered "such corporal punishment as to the said justices and freeholders shall deem reasonable."[174] The owners of the slaves who were spared were required to contribute to compensate the owners of the "notorious offenders" who were killed. But if all the slaves belonged to the same owner, he had to bear the losses.

On the other hand, the 1722 act apparently eliminated the reward to a slave who captured a runaway. There were no specific provisions granting him any benefits.

Both the 1722 and 1735 acts contained provisions allowing relief for persons who were injured while capturing a runaway.[175] The 1735 act specifically provided for recovery whether the person injured was slave or free.

Whether the severe penalties of the acts directing the maiming or death of a slave were enforced, the legal system provided a mechanism for minimizing escapes.

No one has captured the plight of South Carolina blacks more perceptively than Peter Wood, who states:

> As agricultural production intensified during the first half of the eighteenth century, the pressure on Negroes to run away increased, but at the same time the machinery for their containment multiplied: tickets were required, patrols were strengthened, punishments were enforced. Perhaps hardest of all, rewards were offered to buy the loyalty of slaves. Individually and collectively, therefore, Negroes felt their situation becoming more desperate. As the incentives grew higher on the one hand to rebel or escape, the inducements mounted on

the other hand to submit and even to inform. For slaves caught in such a vicious circle, running away represented a personal and partial kind of resistance which at one moment seemed too bold and at another moment did not seem bold enough. If the majority of slaves never actually broke out of the circle and ran away, even for a short time, it was due not to any ignorance of the variables involved but to an acute awareness of them.[176]

Tensions in Dealing with Criminal Slaves

The criminal provisions of the early slave codes established several basic concerns that would characterize the criminal justice system for the remaining years in the colonial period. These include: the broad discretion of the magistrate's court; the apparent desire of the colony to protect the economic interests of the master in his slave and the minimal protections afforded the slave in mandating punishment for "criminal conduct." In several instances these elements were in conflict; however, resolutions generally favored the interests of the master or the power of the magistrate's court and were against the seldom recognized individual interests of the slave.

The magistrate's court   The 1712 act provided for a magistrate's court wherein slaves were tried for criminal offenses.[177] First, a complaint against the slave, as a criminal defendant, would be made before a justice of the peace. The justice would then issue a warrant against the slave and all others having evidence. If it appeared that the slave was "probably" guilty, the slave could be committed to prison, immediately tried, or released with security given. The justice would then organize the court by calling another justice and summoning three freeholders to hear the case. Apparently, there were different standards of review: for nonmurder cases the justice and freeholders were supposed to "diligently weigh . . . and examine . . . all evidences, proofs and testimonies"; however, "in case of murder only," they were permitted to make their judgment "on violent presumption and circumstances."[178] Thus, less evidence was required in murder cases for a conviction, where the penalty was death, than in nonmurder cases. Where death could be ordered it was to occur immediately, "in such manner as they shall think fit, the kind of death to be inflicted to be left to their judgment and discretion."[179] Where death was not mandated, the court could inflict "any other punishment, but not extending to limb or disabling him, without a particular law directing such punishment."[180] It was not until 1833 that appeals were allowed to the circuit court by slave or free Negroes convicted of capital offenses.[181]

The abuses of the magistrate's court have been noted by several individuals, including Judge John Belton O'Neall. In his famous critique, he notes:

> The tribunal for the trial of slaves and free negroes . . . is the worst system which could be devised. The consequence is, that the passions and prejudices of the neighborhood arising from a recent offense, enter into trial, and often lead to the condemnation of the innocent.[182]

Concern for "swift justice" and the inherent flaws in the magistrate court system are shown in the following example:

> in Charleston in 1733, on a Saturday afternoon, "a negro fellow" stole a horse from a boy who was riding him. The negro was caught on Sunday, tried by the tribunal for negroes on Monday and about noon on Tuesday paid the penalty on the gallows.[183]

H. M. Henry continues, none "of the safeguards cherished by Englishmen, such as trial by jury, were thrown around the negro. It was a court given large discretion and unhampered by technicalities."[184]

The statutes reflected the decreasing concern for the prevention of the slave being unjustly convicted in the magistrate's court. One area in which this trend is most apparent is in the changes in evidentiary requirements. Under the 1712 act the court was always permitted to use the "confession of any slave accused";[185] but, when the trial concerned a crime for which the slave could suffer loss of life or limb or which involved a petty larceny exceeding forty shillings, there were limitations on the use of other slaves' testimony.[186] In those instances, except in the case of murder, the statute required "the plain and positive evidence of two negroes or slaves, so circumstantiated as that there shall not be sufficient reason to doubt the truth thereof. . . ." Also, the court had to inquire as to whether the slaves bore "any malice to the other slave accused."[187] For murder cases the court required less stringent proof than the testimony of two slaves. In murder, the testimony of *one* slave, regardless of bias, with strong attending circumstances, was sufficient.

In the 1722 act slave testimony was permitted in all noncapital cases.[188] As for capital cases, the limitations were similar to those previously specified in the 1712 act. By 1735 the legislature removed the limitations to slave testimony by permitting slave testimony "attended with circumstances of truth and credit," in all criminal trials of slaves. The testimony was permitted and the court was left to determine the weight it would be given.[189]

Criminal offenses and penalties   The 1712 act articulated a broad spectrum of criminal offenses and corresponding penalties. There were a large number of offenses that had not been proscribed in the act for which a slave could be punished. Those crimes declared "heinous or grievous" when committed by a slave included murder, burglary, robbery, and the burning of houses.[190] Lesser crimes included "killing or stealing any neat or other cattle, maiming one another, stealing of fowls, provisions, or such like trespasses or injuries."[191] For these crimes it would appear that the punishments were to be determined by common law, since the act states that the sentence will be imposed as the crime by law deserveth.[192] Where the slave committed an act that would indicate rebellion or an attempt to overthrow the government's authority, a sentence of death or "any other punishment . . . in such manner as they shall think fitting," was mandated.[193] However, if more than one black slave was involved in the "rebellion," the statute tempered the loss to the owners by declaring that the governor and council could select one or more of the slaves who would "suffer death as exemplary."[194]

An indication of the regard given to a slave's person is the fact that the maiming of one slave by another was called a "lesser crime" than burglary, robbery, or the burning of houses. It was placed on the level of a "trespass," comparable to the "stealing of fowls [or] provisions."[195] Thus, the legislature viewed the "maim-

ing" of one slave by another as a trespass or injury to the slave owner's property, not as a personal injury to the slave.

The 1722 act set up separate provisions and more specific
penalties for capital and noncapital crimes. Those crimes that were
felonies punishable by death included:

> murder, burglary, robbery, wilfull burning of dwelling houses,
> barnes, stables, kitchens, or stacks or rice, or tar kilns, barrels
> of pitch or tarr, or any other capital offenses, where clergy is
> taken away by the laws of England or this Province.[196]

As for felonies not named in the act, for the first offense "where a
white man is allowed the benefit of clergy, and ought to be punished by burning in the hand, a slave shall be burned with the letter
R in the forehead. . . ."[197] For a second offense, the slave would
suffer death.

In branding the slave on his forehead so that all persons
would know of his prior "criminal conduct," the state, in effect,
made a public announcement that the rights of this slave might be
compromised. If branding was not an effective deterrent, and there
was a second offense, the slave could be put to death.

If one wanted to single out one crime whose penalties one
would then trace throughout the colonial period, it ought to be
theft, for the obsession of the state with slave thefts permeated much
of its legislation. The 1712 act had provided for a series of punishments for multiple offenses. For the first offense of stealing or destroying another's goods valued under twelve pence (except for
those of the master), an adult slave would be "publicly and severely
whipped, not exceeding forty lashes."[198] Upon a second offense the
slave could be either "branded in the forehead with a hot iron, *that
the mark thereof may remain,*"[199] or have one of his ears cut off.
After a third offense, the slave would have his nose slit. The fourth
time the slave was tried as if he was accused of murder, burglary, or
other like offenses and the court could order death, "or other punishment, as the said justices shall think fitting."[200]

The legislature soon recognized that many thefts were in response to hunger, and in the 1722 act it openly admitted that
"negroes and slaves, under pretence of hunger, do frequently break
open corn houses and rice-houses, and steal from them corn and

rice. . . ."[201] If these slaves sought food when inadequate amounts were provided, was it in the master's interest to kill them for burglaries committed to alleviate hunger pangs?

A slave owner's brand of "humanitarianism" was incorporated into the 1722 statute by making the penalty for the first burglary a "whipping only, not exceeding forty lashes."[202] Another reduction in punishment was provided in the 1735 act. When a slave stole "any fowls, lambs, pigs, hogs, calves or poultry, or any other edible matter or other thing, under the value of twenty shillings,"[203] these offenses warranted a "whipping only, not exceeding thirty lashes."[204] The slave owner could be required to "answer" for the damages done by his slave. This punishment is less than that ordered under the 1712 act, where, for the stealing of goods valued under twelve pence, a slave could receive forty lashes for a first offense and death upon a fourth.[205] Under the 1722 act, for stealing a hog, sheep, pig, etc., the slave could be branded and upon multiple offenses he would suffer death.[206] Thus, by 1735 the legislature determined that the slave should suffer less and the master should be held partially responsible for those crimes due to inadequate provisions. Yet, in the final analysis one must ask: was this partial decriminalization process attributable to slave owners' humanitarian motives or to a concern for preserving the base of the economy—healthy, nonmutilated slaves?

Detection of criminal offenses   The 1712 act provided for a means of detecting offenses by slaves that demonstrated the slave's lack of privacy. The act required the master to search "all his negro houses" every fourteen days in order to find, among other items,* anything one could "suspect or know to be stolen goods."[207] These items would be seized, delivered to an officer who would post a list of the items in a public place, whereupon an individual could claim the items as his lost goods. Although the problem of theft among slaves has been well documented,[208] the act displays a presumption that goods not accounted for by the owner were stolen. Also, the responsibility for detecting the stolen goods is placed upon the

* The 1712 act also provided for the detection of items that could be used as weapons, regardless as to whether they were stolen, *supra* at p. 173. However, this provision regarding stolen goods was intended to serve a different purpose.

master, who after seizing the goods had to return them to the true owner or suffer a penalty of twenty shillings.[209] The problems of enforcement are obvious and will be discussed later.

In 1722 the legislature moved to improve the means by which crimes by slaves would be detected and brought before the tribunals. When the owner was required to search his Negro houses every fourteen days for mischievous weapons and stolen goods under the 1712 act,[210] the 1722 act transferred the responsibility for searching Negro homes for weapons to the justices of the peace.[211] Restrictions were made as to the circumstances under which a slave could possess or use arms. As always, the predominant theme was that use of a firearm was contingent upon the specific approval of whites. If a slave had a weapon it was conditioned upon a "ticket or license in writing, under the hand of the master, mistress or manager, to hunt and kill game, a month at farthest. . . ."[212] One of the exceptions to the ticket requirement was when the slave used the weapon for hunting or shooting when there was "some *white* person in the company of such slave."[213] Also, one slave could use a gun for "keeping off rice-birds and other birds, in the daytime,"[214] as long as the gun was kept in the master's chief dwelling house at night. Whenever a slave was found illegally possessing a "gun, pistole, sword, cutlace, or other offensive weapon," the finder was "empowered to seize and keep the same to their own use, without further law or process."[215] Certainly, rewarding the finder with the weapons illegally held by slaves was an important incentive in encouraging a continuing surveillance system.

Compensation and incentives to enforce criminal penalties As to specific crimes by slaves and the penalties accorded, there was a constant conflict between protecting the property interest of the master and assuring that crimes by slaves were punished and deterred. To ensure that the owner did not totally remove his slave from the penalties of the criminal process, the 1712 act declared that if a slave was sent out of the province after killing a white person, the owner forfeited five hundred pounds to the executor of the deceased white individual if the owner knew "the negro [was] guilty of such crime."[216] A curious paradox existed in the situation where one slave killed another slave and the supposed perpetrator had been sent out of the province by his master; the owner of the "fugitive slave" was obligated to pay "the full value of such negro so killed," regardless of whether or not the "fugitive's" master thought his slave was guilty of the crime.[217]

Even if the owner did not attempt to remove his slave from the province, the legislature recognized that owners would not always willingly report crimes or subject their slaves to criminal prosecution. To eliminate economic reasons for not reporting crimes the legislature provided that the owner should receive from the public treasury the full value of the slave, as determined by the justices and those freeholders who had condemned the slave to death.[218] Later this system of reimbursement was thought to be too costly. In 1714 the legislature found that "the public treasury hath been very much exhausted by the extraordinary sums that have been allowed for criminal slaves of all sorts, without distinction . . ." and compensation was limited to a maximum of fifty pounds.[219] The legislature stated that it had:

> found by experience, that the executing of several negroes for felonies of a smaller nature, by which they have been condemned to die, have been of great charge and expense to the public, and will continue (if some remedy be not found) to be very chargeable and burthensome to this Province . . .[220]

To offset this economic cost to their treasury, but apparently without any moral concern over the killing of blacks for lesser offenses, the legislature provided that:

> all negroes or other slaves who shall be convicted and found guilty of any capital crime (murder excepted,) for which they used to receive sentence of death, as the law directs, shall be transported from this Province, by the public receiver for the time being, to any other of his Majesty's plantations, or other foreign part, where he shall think fitting to send them for the use of the public . . .[221]

This program was short-lived, for by 1717 the 1714 provision regarding the transportation of slaves out of the colony was repealed and the 1712 act revived.[222] The cause for its repeal is stated:

> it has proved by experience, that this encouraged negroes and other slaves to commit great numbers of robberies, burglaries

and other felonies, well knowing they were to suffer no other punishment for their crimes, but transportation, which to them was rather an encouragement to pursue their villainies.[223]

Whether slaves committed these serious offenses in order to be transferred to another colony is questionable. Yet, the legislature did recognize that slaves, as rational beings, might take advantage of a legislative loophole. Thus, the perception of slaves as unintelligent creatures was implicitly negated.

To aid in the reporting of crimes the 1722 act increased to 100 pounds the amount for which an owner could be compensated when his slave was killed in accordance to law.[224]

Other problems of enforcement arose. Apparently, probably because of the harshness of the sentences, the legislature found that "the marshals and constables have refused to execute the sentence [of slaves] awarded against them by the justices and freeholders."[225] In response, the legislature provided for a penalty of fifty shillings where marshals or constables failed to execute the sentence. The legislature simultaneously provided incentives for compliance with court orders. For whipping, branding, or cutting off the ear of a slave, the marshal received two shillings and six pence payable by the owner, attorney, or manager of the slave's plantation.[226] From 1722 to 1735 the marshal's compensation was significantly increased to twenty shillings for whipping, branding, or cutting off a slave's ear.[227] Where the marshal executed a death sentence he received the maximum bonus—five pounds.

Slave assaults   The extent to which a slave had to submit to whites was best exemplified by the treatment of slave assaults on whites. Regardless of the brutality that the slave might have been subjected to, under the 1712 act he could be whipped for the first time he struck or "offered any violence" to a white or Christian, branded or whipped and mutilated (his nose could be slit) for the second offense, and killed upon a third offense.[228] The act specifically stated that when the slave was branded it would be "in some part of his face with a hot iron, *that the mark thereof may remain.*"[229]

The 1714 act conspicuously limited the offense to assaults on whites, thereby eliminating possible instances where a slave struck a nonwhite Christian—most likely a slave, freed black, or Indian.[230] Although the forms of mutilation possible in the 1712 act were eliminated, the 1714 act declared that the form of punishment would be left to the judges. The 1714 act thus eradicated the limitations of punishment that earlier could not extend "to life or limb," and the penalty of death was made discretionary even for the first offense of assault on a white person.[231] The act also declared that the testimony of the white person "so struck or maimed" would be sufficient to prove the slave's guilt "if the said white person's oath be deemed credible and valid by the judges."[232]

The 1722 act reinstituted varied penalties for multiple offenses, but added that if the white victim was in any way injured or bruised, death would result. Otherwise, the offense was not punishable by death.[233]

Throughout the era, hitting in self-defense or in protection of a member of the slave's family was not an acceptable defense if the victim was white. Yet, the slave could initiate action at his owner's command or in defense of his owner and his family or their goods.[234] In sum, blacks were deemed agents to protect whites, but were villains if they dared protect themselves.

Protection of the Slave

Since a slave could neither protect himself from physical abuse nor obtain adequate food, shelter, or clothing if his owner failed to provide these minimum necessities, the ultimate measure of justice or cruelty of the legal process becomes: what protections were assured the slave from starvation, serious bodily harm, or the denial of those minimum items that make living possible? Of course, those limited provisions dealing with protection of the slave approached the issue primarily from the master's perspective. While the statutes prohibited and penalized third parties from stealing or damaging the master's property, those provisions that recognized the independent rights of the slave in opposition to the preference of his master were rare and generally ineffective.

The 1712 act recognized that:

> divers evil and ill-disposed persons have hitherto attempted to steal away negroes or other slaves, by specious pretence of

promising them freedom in another country, against which
pernicious practice no punishment suitable hath been yet provided . . .[235]

A penalty of twenty-five pounds payable to the slave owner was
placed upon "any white person, either freeman or servant" who
persuaded any slave to escape.[236] Where more than two slaves were
involved, a penalty of ten pounds for each slave was imposed. If
the payment was not forthcoming the white person—free or servant—could become a servant of the person aggrieved for up to five
years. Where the slave was either carried away or in the process of
being taken, death was ordered upon conviction.

In the 1722 and 1735 acts, persons convicted of stealing a
slave or attempting to do so were put to death. In the instances
where the defendant persuaded slaves to escape, the penalties varied. In the 1722 act, if the slave stealer was merely fined, he could
not be jailed upon failure to pay the penalty; instead, he would be
publicly whipped.[237] However, under the 1735 act, more stringent
measures were enacted.[238] The penalty against whites for enticing
slaves rose to 500 pounds and, in default of payment, the individual could be branded and whipped. Apparently, this is one of the
few instances where free whites were subjected to branding.[239]

In ignoring any independent interest of the slave in the protection of his body, the legislature assumed that the slave would not
be unduly abused by the master because of his economic investment. McCrady expressed this view:

Indeed, the negro slave had the great security that if he died
his owner lost his pecuniary value; whereas by the death of a
white indentured servant the loss was only that of two or
three year's wages. The master was accordingly rendered
more careful of his slaves than of hired servants.[240]

The 1690 act "practically placed the life or death of the slave
in the hands of the master."[241] This act provided that the willful,
wanton killing of a slave would be a crime where death was not a
result of "punishment from the owner for running away or other
offence."[242] Thus, the master was virtually free to inflict mortal
wounds and, whether justifiable or not, these acts would practically
be beyond the purview of the law. Third parties received light

punishment where they killed a slave "out of wilfulness, wantoness, or bloody mindedness." For this they would be imprisoned for three months and had to pay fifty pounds to the deceased slave's owner. If the murderer was a servant, he received thirty-nine lashes and served the deceased slave's owner for a period of four years. But, where a slave was found stealing at a house or plantation at night and refused to submit, it was no crime to kill the slave and no damages were recoverable by the owner.

Gradually, the legislature began to recognize that slaves were subjected to brutal acts by their masters, whether in the form of physical injury or failure to provide adequate provisions, and the legislature then made some efforts to protect the slaves. The tension between the master's absolute right to control his slave and a societal concern for the minimum well-being of slaves and for maintaining a viable slave system becomes apparent. However, the statutes were devoid of any enforcement power to protect the slave from his master's abuses.

For the first time, in 1712 the legislature declared that an owner could be fined a maximum of fifty pounds when the slave was violently killed from "wantoness, or only of bloody-mindedness."[243] No imprisonment penalty was imposed. Where the victim was a slave of another, the full value of the slave was due to the master and a sum of twenty-five pounds was payable to the public treasury. Like the 1690 statute, the 1712 statute exemplified a class stratification in penalties. For if the killing was by a white servant, he would be imprisoned for three months and then required to serve for four years the master of the slave he killed. Where the slave's death was the result of an "accident" or when the slave was caught stealing and refused to submit, no criminal or civil damage actions were possible.

In an attempt to soothe their consciences, the legislature declared that slave deaths were unfortunate and "seldom happen[ed]."[244] The evidence is sparse for corroboration or repudiation of this legislative statement. However, the problems of detecting these crimes and proving the circumstances as required by the statute probably presented insurmountable obstacles in many instances.

Under the 1722 act, for killing a slave the servant could be liable to five years' service instead of four as provided in the 1712 act.[245] By 1735, greater sanctions were needed to protect slaves from their masters and the penalty rose to 500 pounds for an owner who "cruelly" killed his own slave. Interestingly, in 1735 the legislature deleted their findings in the early acts of 1712 and 1722 that the murdering of slaves "seldom happen[ed]." This deletion is significant, not in proving that slave murders in 1712 seldom happened, but in establishing that the problem was perceived as a frequent one, even by a legislature predominantly composed of slave masters. To provide some means of detection, the legislature resorted to the use of informants. One-half of the penalty went to the informant and the other half to the government.[246]

One of the most ineffective aspects of the statutes related to adequate provisions for slaves. Unlike the 1722 and 1735 acts, the 1712 act made no reference to the treatment of slaves.[247] The 1722 act acknowledged that "there [was] sometimes reason to suspect that slaves do run away for want of a sufficient allowance of provisions."[248] Justices of the peace were given the authority to "inquire, by the best means they [could], whether slaves, throughout the several plantations, [were] sufficiently provided with corn and other provisions."[249] Once a master was found to be inadequately providing for his slaves he could be fined a maximum of fifty shillings. The 1735 act increased the amount of the fine to a maximum of twenty pounds.[250]

Both acts recognized that inadequate provisions were often a basis for slaves' running away, as the statutes regarding theft had recognized. Also, the owner was made subject to criminal penalty. However, even if a justice of the peace were willing to enforce the statute and penalize his fellow slave owner, there was no organized means of detecting the crime. And, as in other areas of mistreatment, there was no method by which the slave could himself seek redress for insufficient provisions.

LEGISLATIVE EFFORTS TO RAISE REVENUE AND RESTRICT THE BLACK POPULATION

As the number of slaves within the colony increased, the ineffectiveness of the codes became manifest. The fear of slave rebellion became more intense and, in response, several laws were enacted, including statutes imposing duties on imported black slaves

and others encouraging the importation of additional white servants. Legislation dealing with the imposition of duties on slave
importations began as early as 1703. In that year the assembly
adopted a provision imposing a duty of twenty shillings on each
slave above eight years of age imported for sale from any place
other than Africa, and ten shillings on each slave imported from
Africa.[251] In 1706 the legislature exempted from taxation those
slaves brought into South Carolina by settlers who took an oath
that such slaves would not be sold within a year.[252] This exemption
was designed to encourage more affluent settlers.

Reflecting the colonists' perception of slaves as solely property, duties on slaves were generally part of broad-based revenue
acts such as the 1716 statute, "for laying imposition on liquors,
goods and merchandizes, imported into and exported out of this
province, for the raising of a fund of money towards the defraying
the publick charges and expences of the government."[253] This statute imposed a duty of thirty pounds on anyone who brought into
the colony from another American colony a slave above the age of
ten who had resided five months therein.[254] In the preamble to the
1716 act the legislature did not bother to distinguish blacks from
"liquors, goods and merchandizes," for they were perceived as mere
merchandise.

Blacks served a twofold purpose for the plantation economy.
First, the colony received thousands of pounds in revenue[255] from
the mere fact of importation and, second, it obtained the right to
work blacks for a lifetime without paying them for their labors.
Several other statutes were passed throughout the colonial era imposing duties on imported slaves, one of which tied the amount of
duty to the slave's height.[256]

Stressing that the "providence of God" deterred a percentage
increase of white persons because "negroes do extremely increas[e],"
the legislature declared in 1714:

> safety of the said Province is greatly endangered . . . [and
> that] all negro slaves from twelve years old and upwards, im-
> ported [six months after the ratification of the act] into this
> part of this Province from any part of Africa . . . [shall pay
> two additional pounds within thirty days.][257]

This legislation displayed one of the major concerns of the colonists when they enacted statutes exacting additional duties from importers of black slaves. Their desire to check the growth of the slave population had not been premised on moral grounds, but had developed from a fear of being outnumbered by blacks and the possibility that blacks would join in rebellion with the colonists' other enemies—the Indians, Spanish, or French.[258]

Another concern was that of providing funds for poor white settlers within the colony. Part of the duties on the importation of slaves went by statute "for the poor" and were, in fact, distributed to white Protestants by the colonial government.[259] Much of the money collected from fines and penalties imposed through the slave codes also went to aid the poor.[260]

Despite the sporadic efforts of the legislature to check the imbalanced racial composition, the importation and percentage of blacks steadily increased.[261] From 1715 to 1724 the number of whites doubled, from 6,250 to about 14,000, whereas the black population trebled, from 10,500 to 32,000.[262] In 1737 Samuel Dyssli, a Swiss immigrant, said, "Carolina looks more like a negro country than like a country settled by white people."[263] As the slave population grew so did the fears of white colonists that slaves would rebel against, resist, or even kill their oppressors.

SLAVE RESISTANCE: THE STONO REBELLION OF 1739

The Stono Rebellion* was the "most serious outbreak of the colonial period."[264] Slave resistance in the South Carolina colony

---

* The following account of the Stono Rebellion is primarily based on Wood, *Black Majority*, pp. 314-23; McCrady, "Slavery in the Province of South Carolina, 1670-1770," 657.
The Stono Rebellion began Sunday, September 9, 1739, approximately twenty miles from Charlestown. A group of twenty slaves broke into a store, stole guns and powder, and killed the storekeepers, leaving their heads on the front steps. The group moved southward toward St. Augustine burning and killing whites as other slaves joined the band. The group was seen by Lt. Gov. Bull while riding on horseback to Charlestown, whereupon he alerted whites (whether Bull was the first to do so is unclear). The Negroes had proceeded on, dancing, singing, and beating drums so as to attract more slaves. By Sunday afternoon the group stopped after having traveled more than ten miles and decided to wait until morning before crossing the Edisto River. The Negro group, numbering sixty to one hundred, was met by a group of white planters, numbering twenty to one hundred, whereupon a battle ensued. The uprising was suppressed by nightfall according to some secondary ac-

did not begin with the publicized Stono Rebellion of 1739, however; previously there were a series of incidents that could have reached the proportion of the Stono Rebellion.[265] Nevertheless, according to Wood, "[t]he Stono Uprising [could] be seen as a turning point in the history of South Carolina's black population."[266] However, "the odds against successful assertion were overwhelming; it was slightly too late, or far too soon, for realistic thoughts of freedom among black Americans."[267]

The impact of the Stono Rebellion was reflected in the 1740 statute. After noting that "several negroes did lately rise in rebellion and did commit many barbarous murders at Stono and other parts adjacent thereto,"[268] the legislature granted total immunity to all persons aiding in the suppression of the rebellion.[269] So that there would be no doubt, they declared that the killing of "rebellious" Negroes was:

> hereby declared lawful, to all intents and purposes whatsoever, as fully and amply as if such rebellious negroes had undergone a formal trial and condemnation . . .[270]

The 1740 act was not a copy or slight modification of Barbadian law; it was the first time that South Carolina developed its own slave code, directed to its particular needs.[271]

THE 1740 CODE AND SUBSEQUENT SLAVE LEGISLATION

The 1740 Slave Code: To Be Kept in Due Subjection and Obedience

In their request for approval of the 1740 slave code the general assembly asserted that:

> the extent of . . . power over . . . slaves ought to be settled and limited by positive laws, so that the slave may be *kept in due subjection and obedience,* and the owners and

---

counts. Others show that a small band of slaves had continued to the southern border and was met by whites the following Saturday. The colonists were on guard for some time after the rebellion, several moved for better security, and a special patrol was placed in the area in January. One ringleader of the slaves was not captured until three years later by two runaway slaves. He was tried and immediately hanged. McCrady estimates that twenty-one whites and forty-four Negroes died in the Stono Rebellion.

> other persons having the care and government of slaves may
> be restrained from exercising too great rigour and cruelty
> over them, and that the public peace and order of this Prov-
> ince may be preserved: We pray your most sacred Majesty
> that it may be enacted. . . .[272]

The preamble to the 1740 slave code assumed that in the American colonies racial slavery was the rule and that slaves were mere "subjects of property in the hands of particular persons."[273] The assembly correlated public peace in the colony with total "subjection and obedience" of blacks. The wish that slaves not be subjected to "too great rigour and cruelty"[274] was predicated more on the possibility that such cruelty might precipitate slave rebellions than as an expression of legislative compassion for the suffering of slaves. After the Stono Rebellion, the colonists legislatively recognized that while regulation of slaves is required, there must also be some restraints on those whose acts provoked slave resistance. Yet, on the whole, the most pervasive restraints of the 1740 slave code were on blacks, thereby creating an extensive system depriving blacks of their few personal liberties.[275] This statute continued in effect throughout the colonial period.

The first paragraph of the act defined those persons "deemed" slaves by stating that all Negroes, Indians, mulattoes, and mestizos who were then slaves "are hereby declared to be, and remain forever hereafter, absolute slaves."[276] The status of a black or Indian child would be determined by the mother's status; thus, the civil law doctrine of *partus sequitur ventrem*[277] was applicable. Once slave status was determined, a slave would be treated as personal property. Finally, the legislature explicitly sanctioned the actual treatment of slaves as chattel property, converting the 1712 code's allowance for "custom"[278] into a definitive statutory classification.

Formidable barriers were placed before those who chose to challenge their alleged slave status. A Negro, Indian, mulatto, or mestizo could claim freedom in a suit before the common pleas court *only* if represented by a guardian. This incapacity of non-whites to bring their own suit was not mentioned in earlier acts in regard to suits for freedom, thereby making the 1740 act the first South Carolina legislative declaration that slaves lacked legal capacity. Where slavery was in question there was a legal presumption that every Negro, Indian (except those in amity with the government), mulatto, and mestizo was a slave. If in the struggle to surmount this legal obstacle the slave lost, he not only returned to slavery but also was subject to "corporal punishment, not extending to life or limb, . . . as they [the court], in their discretion, shall think fit."[279] The litigation process was used as a means of penalizing blacks whose sole wrong was seeking freedom.

As for the protection of the slave's life, while some theoretical protections were provided, the legislature expanded the situations in which private parties could kill a slave without penalty or reprisal. Unlike the earlier codes, the 1740 act prohibited slave injuries by persons "not having sufficient cause or lawful authority for so doing,"[280] but even this prohibition was grounded more in concern for protection of the master's investment than for the slave's well-being. Although no award was given to the slave for pain and suffering caused by an unwarranted attack of a third party, the owner was compensated "for every day of his [slave's] loss time" and inability to perform his work along with the "charge of the cure of such slave."[281] No criminal penalty was imposed for unlawfully injuring the slave except for commitment upon nonpayment of fine. The slave had no legal rights in the security of his own body, though the master, who was neither mutilated nor bleeding, could collect "full compensation" for the economic injury.

The statute extended the rights of any white to require any slave "to submit . . . or undergo the examination of any white person," if the slave was away from the house or plantation. Blacks who were not meek and submissive could be subjected to the pursuit, apprehension, and moderate correction of "any white person."[282] If in the process any slave dared assault or strike any white person the legislature in 1740 directed "such slave may be lawfully killed." Previously, in the 1735 statute a slave could be killed by his captor *only* when he resisted with a stick or weapon,[283] or, if without a stick or weapon, he struck a white person *and* was subsequently found guilty of the offense by the magistrate's court.[284] Thus, in 1740, for certain offenses, the necessity of a judicial decree was eliminated in favor of the apprehender's right to execute the black "on the scene" even if the resistance was slight, nonphysical, and without a stick or weapon.

Purportedly stating its concern for the welfare of the slave, in the 1740 code the legislature declared:

by reason of the extent and distance of plantations in this Province [and that the] inhabitants are far removed from each other and many cruelties may be committed on slaves, because no white person may be present to give evidence . . . unless some method be provided for the better discovery of such offences . . .[285]

The statute provided that "if any slave shall suffer in life, limb or member, or shall be maimed, beaten or abused" contrary to the meaning of the statute when no white person was present or willing to give evidence, the owner was assumed to be guilty of the injury or death of the slave.[286] This assumption of guilt could be rebutted in two ways. The owner could prove that he did not commit the offense or he could exculpate himself by swearing that he did not commit the offense. If at least two white witnesses were not available to rebut his statement, the owner was acquitted. It would seem that the original burden of proof imposed on the owner could be easily nullified; one who would inflict cruelties upon his slaves would probably not be unwilling to swear falsely.

Steps were taken to encourage owners to provide their slaves with adequate food and care. The justice could order such relief as he "in his discretion [thought] fit," and impose a fine not exceeding twenty pounds upon persons in charge of slaves who did not provide them sufficient food and clothing.[287] Funds collected went to benefit the poor whites within the parish.

While the provisions penalizing owners for the inadequate treatment of slaves were a step toward ameliorating the conditions of slaves, there were several problems in enforcing the statute. Significantly, only whites could file the complaint initiating the investigation procedure by alleging that an owner had failed to provide the minimum necessities of food and clothing. Since an owner would not initiate a prosecution against himself, the slave's actual protection was contingent on the rare possibility that some white person would know about the cruelty *and* be willing to file a complaint. Like the statute pertaining to physical injuries to the slave, the owner or person in charge who allegedly failed to provide adequate food or clothing was allowed to exculpate himself upon his own oath where "positive proof [was] not given of the offence."[288] Once again, the slave was given theoretical rights that were not part of the reality of his existence. The impediments to his receiving the statutory protections included the difficulty of initiating a complaint, the ease of an owner to exculpate himself, and the absence of any imprisonment for violation of the act.

Indicative of his plight, the slave could not testify in court to protect his health against the master's abuses, but he was statutorily privileged to testify against other slaves being prosecuted. In explicit language the legislature declared:

> And for the preventing the concealment of crimes and offences committed by slaves, and for the more effectual discovery and bringing slaves to . . . punishment, *Be it further enacted* . . . That not only the evidence of all free Indians, without oath, but the evidence of any slave, without oath, shall be allowed and admitted in all causes whatsoever, for or against another slave accused of any crime or offence whatsoever; the weight of which evidence being seriously considered, and compared with all other circumstances attending the case, shall be left to the conscience of the justices and freeholders.[289]

One of the greatest ironies was the legislature's authorization for marshals to compel slaves to implement the judicial penalties. A slave could be required, at the direction of the marshal, to kill, cut off the ears, or brutally whip a fellow slave.[290] Slaves were obligated to be "obedient to and observe the orders and directions of the constable," and if they refused to execute the punishments against a fellow slave, such disobedience would subject them to twenty lashes on their bare back. Of course, the marshal collected his fee of twenty shillings for whipping a slave, five pounds for an execution, and other compensation for maintaining the slave; but, he could be obligated to pay five shillings to the black who aided in the execution.

Catching slaves who escaped beyond the south side of the Savannah River on their way to Florida was a profitable enterprise, whether the slave was returned dead or alive. The rewards were as follows:

for each grown man slave brought alive, the sum of fifty pounds; for every grown woman or boy slave above the age of twelve years brought alive, the sum of twenty five pounds; for every negro child under the age of twelve years, brought alive, the sum of five pounds; for every scalp of a grown negro slave, with the two ears, twenty pounds; and for every negro grown slave, found on the south side of St. John's river, and brought alive as aforesaid, the sum of one hundred pounds; and for every scalp of a grown negro slave with the two ears, taken on the South side of St. John's river, the sum of fifty pounds.[291]

While white persons or free Indians were eligible for the reward, blacks, whether slave or free, could not receive bonuses for aiding in the capture of slaves.

It was a crime to teach a slave to write or employ a slave as a scribe in any manner.[292] The fine for teaching slaves or using them as scribes was 100 pounds, one of the most severe fines under the colonial legislation.

The reward for killing a runaway slave was far less than the fine for teaching him to write. Thus, the legislature deemed educating slaves an act far more malevolent than even slaves fleeing their masters. They preferred to keep slaves as ignorant as possible and they feared that educating them could ultimately become a risk greater than the violence that ensued at Stono.

The 1751 Slave Legislation

Additional restrictions were placed upon the activities of slaves in the Act of 1751. Slaves could not be employed in an apothecary for fear that they would learn poisons; nor could they be taught anything about poisons. The statute directed death for any slave who taught another slave any knowledge about poisoning.[293] There was no provision proscribing others from teaching slaves about poison, probably on the assumption that no other individual with "common sense" would so teach a slave. The slave who received instruction on poisons could receive any punishment, not extending to life or limb, as the justice determined. All persons who employed a slave in a shop where they kept medicines or drugs would be fined twenty pounds.[294] Slaves could not be doctors, for fear that they could convey insurrectionary plots or other "danger-ous information."[295] Violation of this act would result in a whipping not exceeding fifty stripes. An exception was provided when any "negroes or other slaves (commonly called doctors)" treated a slave "at the instance or by the direction of some white person."[296] Slaves were prohibited from dealing in rice or coin as a measure to protect the colony from inducing slaves to steal.[297]

While it has been debated whether the 1740 act was vigorously enforced,[298] it is still indisputable that the 1740 code and the 1751 legislation clearly relegated the slave to a position of nonrights and assured whites greater control over the life and "protection" of the slave. These statutes contained provisions that were geared to elimi-nate the possibility of slave insurrections; any activity that could reach the height of the Stono Rebellion was to be eliminated at its incipient stage.

The 1740 code must be understood not only for what it did to blacks and slaves—assuring their submissiveness, guaranteeing their ignorance, and sanctioning great brutality; but it also im-posed an obligation on white inhabitants to set aside any natural human compassion and granted extraordinary inducements to those who would revel in brutality against blacks.

Christianity and Slavery

Slavery was encouraged by many of the religious organizations in colonial South Carolina; the major group, the Society for the Propagation of the Gospel in Foreign Parts (SPG), actually owned slaves. The SPG entered South Carolina in 1702.[299] As Frank Klingberg states: "In the beginning, the Society based its programs on an acceptance of slavery and racial inequality of status."[300] The legislature raised no questions about this behavior; in fact, in a 1704 act the legislature provided encouragement to ministers com-ing into the province by granting these ministers certain rights, in-cluding the right to hold:

all such negroes as shall be given and allotted to the severall
parishes by the Society founded by royal charter in the king-

dom of England, by the name of the Society for the Propagation of the Gospell in Foreign Parts, or by any other chari-
tably disposed persons; . . .[301]

While several colonial legal systems were confronted with the
issue of whether a black Christian could be kept enslaved, the South
Carolina view on the matter was stated rather early in its history.
Prior to the settlement of the colony the Fundamental Constitution
of 1669 had provided that the owner had total control over his slave
regardless of the slave's religion; however, this document was never
law in the colony. The 1690 act likewise had declared "no slave
shall be free by becoming a christian."[302] Although the 1690 act was
disallowed by the Proprietors, this concept became indisputably the
law by the 1712 act. The 1712 statute declared: "[s]ince . . . religion may not be made a pretence to alter any man's property and
right," and since whites might "neglect to baptize their negroes or
slaves, or suffer them to be baptized, for fear that thereby they
should be manumitted and set free,"

> it shall be, and is hereby declared, lawful for any negro or
> Indian slave, . . . to receive and profess the Christian faith,
> and be thereinto baptized; but that notwithstanding . . . he
> or they shall not thereby be manumitted or set free . . .[303]

Despite the fact that converting slaves had no impact on their
status, missionary groups sought blacks particularly in an effort to
educate them. The SPG was most active in the education of Negroes
and in 1743 it opened the Charleston Negro School, employing two
slaves who were purchased to serve as instructors.

> The school was established and the experiment tried in the
> hope that the negroes would receive instruction from teachers
> of their own race with more facility and willingness than from
> white teachers.[304]

The school continued for twenty-two years and was closed only
when the last Negro teacher died and no one was found to fill the
vacancy.[305]

The significance of the Charleston Negro School is highlighted by the fact that it existed after the 1740 act prohibited
teaching a slave how to write. Some missionaries had agreed earlier

that care should be taken in instructing Negroes because of "the ingratitude of some bloody villains who have returned them the greatest of evils for the greatest good" by participating in insurrectionary
plots.[306] The Reverend Le Jau had been convinced that it was "most
convenient not to urge too far that Indians and Negroes should be
indifferently admitted to learn to read."[307] Yet, despite opposition
both statutory and internal, the Negro school commenced. Klingberg indicates that:

> in spite of a prohibitory law, the Negro, both slave and free,
> continued to receive, from SPG missionaries, the opportu-
> nity for instruction.[308]

Henry speculates that the law was probably directed against slaves
only.[309] McCrady contends that the Negroes at the Charleston Negro School were only taught reading, not writing.[310] Birnie states
that probably only free persons received instruction.[311] Despite the
activities of the SPG, only a small number of Negroes were converted.[312]

The Protestant religious groups aided the master in his efforts
to control his Christian slaves. Unlike the Catholic practice of chris-
tening any black who requested it,[313] many Protestant groups limited the number of slave baptisms. This difference probably contributed to the colonists' reluctance to view blacks as members of a
universal human family. Because baptism would not free the slave,
the church could have been more active in baptizing the slaves and
urging the master to accord full "humanity" to the slave.[314] This may
have resulted in a less severe slave system. An exception was the
Quakers, who came into colonial South Carolina as early as 1675.[315]
In response to their antislavery stance, during 1790 to 1820 they
emancipated their slaves, thereby, in part, accounting for the large
increase in freed blacks during the period: from 1,801 in 1790 to
3,185 in 1800 to 6,826 in 1820.[316]

Free Blacks in Colonial South Carolina

NUMBER AND ORIGIN OF FREE BLACKS

Little is known of the white population profile during the early
colonial period and far less is known about the free black popula-

tion. Wood estimates that during the proprietary period, 1670-1719, the free black population may have slightly exceeded 1 percent of the total black population.[317] There are only a few references to free blacks in the early colonial materials. For example, Reverend Thomas Hasell, a Society for the Propagation of the Gospel missionary, recorded in 1712 that between twenty and thirty Negro men and women attended his "chapel of ease,"[318] and one of them was free.[319]

During the era South Carolina was under the royal government, 1719-1776, the estimated free black population never exceeded 1 percent of the black population.[320] In 1726, Reverend Francis Varnod sent a list of the inhabitants in his parish to a David Humphreys, and on that list he included the following:[321]

[Household]	Free Negroes and Indians			[Slaves Owned][322]		
	[Men]	[Women]	[Children]	[Men]	[Women]	[Children]
Robin Johnson, Negro	1	1	4	3	3	3
Guy, a negro	1	–	–	–	–	–
Nero, an Indian	1	–	–	–	–	–
Sam Pickins, Indian	1	1	4	–	–	–
Sarah	1	–	–	–	–	–

This parish had as members 537 whites, 1300 slaves, 16 Indians, and 8 free blacks.[323] The minuscule number of free blacks within St. Georges parish was reflective of their representation in the general population.[324]

According to tax receipts for the period 1761-1769, there were less than 200 free blacks registered in the entire colony.[325] By 1790, the year of the first census, better statistics are available. In 1790 there were 1,801 recorded free blacks in South Carolina in comparison to 107,094 slaves and 140,178 whites.[326] A majority of the free blacks lived in the city of Charlestown or in close proximity to it.

Slave manumissions were, by far, the largest source of growth for the free black population.[327] There is some indication that a limited number of blacks who came into South Carolina as indentured servants might have slightly added to the free black population.[328] Also, some blacks may have claimed freedom as children of a white, free Indian, or free black mother.

LEGAL STATUS OF FREE BLACKS

One of the most significant legal incapacities placed upon the free black was the legislative declaration that he could not vote. Although there is no information as to whether blacks voted in the elections held in the infant colony before 1700, there are references that free blacks voted in the elections of 1701 and 1703. In the colonial records of 1702, individuals were required to bring to the assembly "all Such Papers or Powers which they have for Quallifieing them to have Right to vote for members of Assembly."[329] Among those summoned to come before the assembly was "Black Natt."[330] Other references to black voters were made by dissenters who protested against "alien" suffrage. According to McCrady:

> A new Assembly was called and every exertion was made to control its composition. The election took place in November, 1701, and the dissenters of Colleton County charged that unqualified aliens, *i.e.* French Protestants, strangers, paupers, servants, and even free negroes, were allowed to vote.[331]

A similar protest was made after the 1703 election, where "all sorts of people, even aliens, Jews, servants, common sailors and negroes were admitted to vote. . . ."[332] Despite these protests, the governor failed to explicitly limit voting rights, basically because his instructions from the Lord Proprietors did not allow for such limitations.[333] After the royal government was established, a statute was passed in 1721 specifically limiting the right of suffrage to "every free white man . . . professing the Christian religion," who met the age and property qualifications.[334]

While there is no evidence to suggest that the 1721 statute excluding blacks from voting was not enforced, a curious reference appeared in the colonial records during the formulation of the 1740 slave code. One of the general headings proposed for one section of the act stated:

> First, All Negroes, Mulattos, Indians and Mustees shall be deemed Slaves and Chattels Personal and that their offspring shall follow the Condition of the Mother, except such Persons can prove they were born free *or have been manumitted or enfranchised.*[335]

Despite the proposed heading, the 1740 act did not state that non-whites who could prove enfranchisement were free; however, the fact that a committee proposed such a heading as a ground for establishing freedom implicitly contradicts the text of the 1721 statute that limited enfranchisement to free white men. By its proposed heading for the 1740 slave code, the committee perhaps intended to mandate freedom for those blacks who voted *prior* to 1721, or else it did not view enfranchisement as limited only to white men.

Free blacks could own property; in fact, several free blacks owned slaves.* The fact that free blacks owned slaves is often erroneously construed as a blanket approval of slavery by free blacks. Often free blacks owned slaves solely because of the innumerable legal barriers and consequences to manumitting slaves; thus, this was "a truly benevolent slavery."[336] It was far easier for a free black to purchase a slave than to comply with the intricate processes of manumission. Thus, it is not improbable that the ownership of slaves by free blacks was, as in Virginia, merely a process whereby "free blacks became instrumental in procuring freedom for many of their less fortunate kinsmen."[337] For example, a freed slave who inherited a life interest in twenty acres of land in 1783, acquired two slaves (a woman and child) and manumitted them in 1791.[338] In contrast, Abraham Jackson, a freed slave, executed his will in 1785 with the provision that his plantation would be worked by his slaves and that sufficient income would remain to pay his debts and provide money to several of his relatives.[339]

---

* As noted in the chart above, Robin Johnson, a free Negro, owned nine slaves, *supra* at p. 202.

Despite the fact that free blacks were legislatively denied the right of representation, these "denizens" were subjected to the same tax assessments regularly imposed upon white citizens.[340] Moreover, a capitation tax of two dollars was imposed in 1792 upon all free blacks regardless of their ability to pay.[341]

The growing trend toward using free blacks as an economic resource was accompanied by a movement to regulate their lives and treat them more like slaves. In 1740, the legislature noted its concern that "free negroes may escape the punishment" set out by the legislature for harboring slaves or encouraging them to commit offenses "for want of sufficient and legal evidence. . . ." It then declared that the testimony of free Indians *and* slaves without oath would be admissible in trials against free Negroes. Moreover, the legislature eliminated other safeguards in the trials of free blacks by stating, "all crimes and offences committed by free negroes, . . . shall be proceeded in, heard . . . and determined by the justices and freeholders . . . for the trial of slaves. . . ."[342] Revealing the same concerns about free blacks aiding the slave population, the same act declared that free blacks could be subjected to a fine for harboring a runaway slave, and for failure to pay the fine, he would be sold at "public outcry."[343] The penalty for failure to pay the fine was particularly harsh, since the free black was not given the option of being hired out for a period of time for a sum sufficient to pay his fine; instead, he was *sold* with the surplus funds going to the public treasury. The public treasury, which had always benefited from the various duties collected on slaves,[344] could now be further augmented by the sale of free blacks.

In a 1751 act, the legislature provided that the penalty for the crime of poisoning was death for all Negroes involved, "whether free or bond."[345] In this act, the legislature was continuing a trend of reducing distinctions between free blacks and slaves.

While the legislature continued to pass more restrictive acts regulating free blacks, the courts were not as adamant in the denial of rights to free blacks. In 1764, *John Mayrant* v. *John Williams*[346] held that a free Negro could bring a civil suit in chancery court and that he was capable of swearing to the truth of his pleading. The record is skimpy and appears, in full, as follows:

JOHN MAYRANT V. JOHN WILLIAMS [16 Feb. 1764]

Objection that Defendant was a free Mulattoe and could not swear to his Answer was disallowed and Injunction issued and Defendant required to Answer.

Mr. Pinckney Sollicitor for the Complainant moved (for Reasons in Bill set forth) that a Writt of Injunction might Issue, the Complainant having complied with the Directions of the Act of Assembly by making a Deposit with the Master. Mr. Leigh Sollicitor for the Defendant objected against the Injunction's issuing alledging that the Defendant being a free Mulattoe, his Answer could not be taken upon Oath The Court did Order that the Injunction do issue and that the Defendant do Answer by Tuesday next.

John Troup, Register in Chancery[347]

While no transcript is available, the perfunctory treatment of the case indicates that free blacks could maintain legal actions in the colonial era.

In cases arising after the American Revolution, the courts often held that free blacks could not generally testify in civil suits in the courts of South Carolina. As an example, in 1831, the court in *Groning* v. *Devann*[348] held that "a free person of color is not a competent witness in any case in the courts of record of the state, although both the parties to the suit are of the same class with himself; nor can book entries, made by a free negro, be received in evidence, on the oath of a white person to his handwriting."[349] As a result of the preclusion of black testimony, the plaintiff's case was dismissed.[350]

Two other cases prior to 1800 reflect the South Carolina court's comparatively liberal view, in these instances favoring claims to freedom. *The Guardian of Sally (a negro)* v. *Beaty*,[351] upheld a jury verdict for a Negro girl who had been purchased and granted her freedom by a black slave woman. The slave woman saved money above the sum she was required by agreement to give her master after being hired out. The court affirmed the verdict below, basing its decision to a degree on the injustice of denying the slave girl, Sally, her freedom. The master who hired the slave woman out received the portion of her wages he had demanded. The trial judge's instructions were summarized as follows:

> if the wench chose to appropriate the savings of her extra labour to the purchase of this girl, in order afterwards to set her free, would a jury of the country say no? He [the trial judge] trusted not. They were too humane and upright, he hoped, to do such manifest violence to so singular and extraordinary an act of benevolence.[352]

After the court's instructions, "the jury, without retiring from their box, returned a verdict for the plaintiff's ward, and she was set at liberty."[353] In this unique factual situation, a slave could buy another slave and free her despite the master's attempt to nullify the girl's manumission.

A second case, *Snow* v. *Callum*,[354] was in the same tradition. There the court decided that a slave woman's children would be free despite the technical problem that the bequest of freedom could not take effect as stated in the will.[355] In construing the will, the court could have declared that the children could not be freed; however, the court took a more liberal stance by saying that the master's "intention is so plain that there can be no doubt but the children were emancipated."[356] The court's minimum requirement of manifest intent by the testator was eventually changed in later cases and, more directly, by the legislature's declaration in the Act of 1800, which placed greater restrictions on manumissions.[357]

The legislature displayed its fear of the rising black population, whether slave or free, in another 1800 act that prohibited the entry into South Carolina of any free Negro or any "slave or servant of color, [brought in] for sale within this State. . . ."[358] Free blacks entering or brought into South Carolina in violation of this act were ordered to be sold after the violation was established by jury verdict.[359] After compensation was provided for the capture, commitment, and maintenance, the proceeds were distributed to the informers and the party of officers and privates who captured the black. Finally, free blacks, like slaves, could be banned from the state and sold upon the failure to strictly abide by the act's provisions.

The Judicial System and Slavery

While the legislature was actively declaring and modifying colonial slave policy,[360] the early judicial system was less vigorous in denying slaves basic human rights. The courts made no affirmative declarations sanctioning slavery; however, the decisions reflect an implicit acceptance and reinforcement of racial slavery. In part, the courts' inactivity in the area of slave law stemmed from a general ineffectiveness in declaring and implementing any judicial policies.

Some of the problems of the colonial courts may have stemmed from the fact that the decisions were made by persons not trained in the law; in fact, there was a relative scarcity of lawyers in the colony. This scarcity is perhaps attributable, in part, to the hostility against lawyers as exemplified in the Fundamental Constitution of 1669, which, while never validly enacted, declared:

> It shall be a base and vile thing to plead for money or reward;
> nor shall any one be permitted to plead another man's cause,
> till before the Judge, in open Court, he hath taken an oath
> that he doth not plead for money or reward, nor hath, nor will
> receive, nor directly, nor indirectly, bargained with the party
> whose cause he is going to plead, for money, or any other re-
> ward for pleading his cause.[361]

Although the impact of the 1669 declaration is not clear, apparently the first professional lawyer, Nicholas Trott, did not arrive in the colony until almost thirty years later.[362] Trott was the only trained lawyer who held the office of Chief Justice under the proprietary government; the position of assistant judge was held only by laymen.[363]

The provisional (1719-1729) and royal governments also had problems in obtaining quality appointments. One of the diatribes on the purported inabilities of Chief Justice Charles Skinner was published in the *South Carolina Gazette,* May 6, 1766, four years after his appointment:

> Skinner was an Irishman of the lowest class, with no better
> education than is usually given to qualify one for the meanest
> mechanical trade. And to such a trade Skinner had indeed

been brought up, but had quitted it as too confined for his enterprising genius, and had risen through a series of those various shifts and changes which checker the lives of needy adventurers to the respectable office of messenger to carry backward and forward for hire between the courts of England and Ireland Bills and Answers in Equity which had to be authenticated. Having had the good fortune to render some service to a lady who was engaged in a lawsuit in Ireland, she recommended him to her brother, then in a high office. The complacent brother, after considering for some time what could be done for the vulgar, illiterate ignoramus, unfit for any place of Credit at home, thought proper to send him as Chief Justice to one of the principal colonies of America to sit in judgment on the fortunes, liberties, and lives of his Majesty's subjects there.[364]

Another factor contributing to the relative inactivity of the judicial system was that the courts were, in many instances, composed of individuals who were also in the legislative branch of the colonial system. Since there was no truly independent court system, there was little reason for a significantly distinctive judicial policy, granted the activity of the legislative branch.[365]

The effect of having several colonial legislators also sitting on the courts is best revealed in this statement by Judge Desaussure, who was appointed to the chancery court in 1808:

A Court of Chancery appears to have existed in this State, very early after the settlement of the colony. . . . The court was composed of the governor and council, who dispensed this brand of justice. It could not be expected that a court so constituted could have been celebrated for its learning or legal judgment. Governors appointed for their military skill, or their parliamentary connections, and a council composed generally of private and unlearned men, could not be expected to be eminent judges. The effect was natural. Little confidence was reposed in their judgment, and no valuable decrees are recorded which illustrate the science, or furnish lights to guide succeeding times.[366]

The available cases show: 1) the general conditions of slaves during the colonial period; 2) the practice of dealing with slaves as chattel property; and 3) the court's protection of white servants.[367]

GENERAL CONDITIONS OF SLAVES DURING THE COLONIAL PERIOD

The cases reveal that during the earlier colonial period the slave system was less restrictive and that black slaves originally worked with Indian slaves. By the 1750s the cases also reflect the existing preference for black slaves over Indians.[368]

Two chancery court cases depict plantations where there were relatively small land holdings with both black and Indian slaves. *John Brown* v. *Eleana Wright* (1717)[369] involved a dispute over a lease. The plantation was being worked with the labor of "fifteen Negroe and Indian slaves."[370] In the same year *Thomas Murray and Wife* v. *Elizabeth Nairne, Administratrix of Henry Quentin,*[371] which concerned the division of an intestate estate, was litigated. The decedent's estate consisted of "negros, Mustee, Mulatta and Indian Slaves to a very great Value."[372]

John Kineard v. *Matthew Beard* (1715)[373] reflects a less restrictive slave system. There eleven blacks and one Indian slave worked a plantation of approximately one thousand acres. The case involved a dispute over the existence of an oral or parole lease allegedly made by the defendant's deceased brother. According to the plantation owner, when he attempted to come upon the land the alleged lessee's slaves acted impudently. He responded by threatening "to break their heads," and instead of humbly submitting to him, the slaves replied:

> If he . . . attempted any such thing they would break [his] head again and gave [him] other bold and threatening language . . .[374]

In the opinion it was stated that the black slaves would not have acted so impudently unless instructed to do so by their masters. This type of conduct and hostility to the plantation owner would have been intolerable under the later restrictive system.

Court records offer declarations that the minimum subsistence level of food deemed adequate for blacks was thought to be grossly inadequate for whites. One example is *John Brown* v. *Eleana Wright* (1717),[375] a case involving a dispute over the leasing of a plantation. To establish the inadequate treatment of the deceased white lessor's children, it was pleaded that when the children asked for milk Mrs. Brown: "Lett them have some Skim'd Milk such as was Commonly given to the Negroes. . . ."[376] Feeling that this was inadequate, the children complained and the use of two cows was requested.

There is reason to believe that the above rationale sanctioning disparity in food would be similarly argued as to housing or clothing in that blacks, as a matter of law, were not entitled to as high a subsistence standard in those areas as well.[377]

The growing preference for black slaves[378] was demonstrated in the later cases where executors requested permission to use funds to purchase black slaves for employment upon the estate. The court in *Raper Administrator of Beswicke Complainant* v. *The Executors of Hill Defendants* (1753)[379] granted the administrator permission to purchase black slaves. The administrators "apprehended the best Method of Improving the said Infants Estate would be by purchasing Negroes from time to time to be employed on their Lands in the Planting way. . . ."[380] *Petition of James Skirving only acting Exor, and Guardian of Infant Children, of Lawrence Sanders* (1755)[381] provides another example. Skirving, acting as executor, revealed his concern for providing profit to lands belonging to the children by pleading to the court that "the best method of Improving the said Children's Estate would be by purchasing some more Negroes. . . ."[382] The request was approved. Thus, the courts felt that the estate of children would be more profitable when black adults were denied their freedom and, as slaves, thereby conserve the children's estate. Thus, the cases reflect the already established trend of equating profitable labor with black slaves.

THE PRACTICE OF DEALING WITH SLAVES
AS CHATTEL PROPERTY

Although generally the judicial system exerted a role secondary to that of the legislature, in one area the courts were "ahead"— in decreeing that slaves had the status of chattel rather than freehold property. As noted previously, if a slave was considered to have freehold status, the owner had a right to the slave's services only. If a slave was deemed chattel property, his owner had a right to his services *and* total control over the slave's person; as such, the slave's position was similar to that of a horse, dog, or cow in the owner's possession. It was not until 1740 that the South Carolina legislature affirmatively declared that slaves were merely chattel property. Long before 1740, in a series of cases the chancery court[383] issued decrees and distributed estates in accordance with a rationale that presupposed slaves to be chattel property.

In *Benjamin Schenkingh, et al.* v. *Job Howes and Hugh Grange* (1704),[384] a case involving an estate issue, the complaint declared:

> That the said Bernard in his life time was possessed of a very considerable personal Estate, consisting of Negroes, Horses, Sheep, Cattle, Household stuff, Plate, ready money and of Divers other things of Vallue . . .[385]

No objection by the opposing party or court was made to this treatment of slaves as chattel property.[386]

In *Order on the Petition of William Ramsay's Executors* (1736),[387] the court included slaves as chattel, or in other words, part of the decedent's personal estate. The distribution of Ramsay's estate, which consisted of "[a]ll his Negro slaves and . . . other . . . personal estate,"[388] was made to the parties by the court. Again, as in the *Schenkingh* case, no objections were raised as to the court's treatment of the slave property.[389]

While the 1712 act had left the status of slaves determinable by "custom,"[390] the courts interpreted this provision to give them the authority to relegate slaves to the status of chattel property long before the slave code made its explicit declaration in 1740 that slaves: "shall be deemed, held, taken, reputed and adjudged in law to be chattels personal."[391]

THE COURT'S PROTECTION OF WHITE SERVANTS

The major aspect in which slaves were treated differently from white servants becomes apparent in the few cases in which white servants brought actions in the colonial courts. While several early colonial cases involved the protection of the servant's rights, there were no similar reported and available cases involving black slaves.

From the grand council records for the period of August 28, 1671 to July 9, 1672, there were two cases brought by servants; in one instance the grand council rewarded the servants, in the other liberty was granted after a finding that the servant's labor contract had expired. The first case was decided September 9, 1671. Two servants, Richard Rowser and Philip Jones, were awarded ten acres of land each after the grand council noted "how industrious and useful the said persons have been in this Collony, [and] for their better encouragement."[392] The second case, decided June 8, 1672, held that a servant, Christopher Edwards, was to be "reputed a Freeman, and ha[ve] liberty granted him to take warrants for the land due him in the Province aforesaid."[393] The servant, Christopher Edwards, established his right to freedom by having three individuals testify that the employment contract was for two years and had expired.

In 1692, in the chancery court, an unnamed case arose in which a master alleged that his servant had run away; in addition, there was a second dispute to be litigated regarding the existence and amount of an account between the master and his servant.[394] The court resolved the dispute by finding that an account had existed between the parties and that in order to determine the exact liabilities the master and servant had to file another suit at law. The chancery court ordered that the money deposited with the court at this point was to be equally divided between the master and his servant. While the record is admittedly succinct, it does illustrate the use of the courts by servants to resolve disputes with their masters. Unlike the slave, who was dependent upon others to vindicate his personal grievances, the servant could sue and be provided with personal relief.

The colonial courts did not hear servant cases only when they were suing for their legal rights. In November, 1671, Dennis Mahoon, a servant, was found guilty of encouraging some of his fellow servants to run away from the colony. Previous to this charge, Mahoon, along with others unnamed, had been found guilty of an earlier attempt to run away, that time to the nearby Spanish settlement; however, punishment for that offense had been suspended "in consideration of his penitency and amendment of life."[395] After being found guilty a second time of enticing "some of his fellow servants, namely, John Rivers and John Cooke, to run away and depart this

Collony," Mahoon was now punished. For this second attempt he was to "be stript naked to his waiste, and receive thirty-nine lashes upon his naked back."[396]

Cumulatively, the servant cases illustrate the collective attitude of the early colonial court that they had a responsibility to uphold the legislative provisions designed to protect white indentured servants in the colony. Also, the cases reflect a judicial attitude toward the lenient treatment of white servants. In contrast the cases, particularly those in the chancery courts, are devoid of doctrinal developments designed to protect the rights of black slaves involuntarily brought to the colony. Instead, the issue was how best to maintain the master's, or the estate's, property right in the slave.

In the Grand Council Journals for the period August 28, 1671 to July 9, 1672, the only reference to black slaves is made in an order regarding preparations upon attack of the area.

> And that all other the inhabitants of the Collony of Charles Towne (except the negroes in the Governour's plantation, who are left to defend the same, being an outward place,) repaire to Charles Towne with their armes and ammunition well fitted, as aforesaid, there to receive such orders as by the Grand Councill shall be thought most convenient.[397]

This provision reflects the steady ambiguity wherein colonists sought aid from the very blacks who were being denied freedom by the colonists. That white masters were also willing to leave their slaves at "an outward place" probably reflects nothing more than the recognition by the masters that the successful defense of outlying places was difficult and slaves' lives were expendable. The South Carolina colonists were willing to forsake their valuable interest in slave property—not in the interest of the slaves, but only when their own lives were at stake.

South Carolina: An Evaluation

South Carolina's slave law was unique because it was, in many ways, a direct response to the Barbadian heritage and the distinctive economic and safety needs of the colony.

The Barbadian tradition eliminated any questioning of the validity of the institution of racial slavery. The colonists who had slaves in Barbados simply carried them to the American mainland colony. The status of these first blacks and those who would arrive later was clear—they were subjected to perpetual bondage. The legal system simply sanctioned this treatment.

While the Barbadian tradition gave the colony its initial reasons for having black slaves, the developing South Carolina economy added impetus to maintaining slavery and increasing the number of black slaves. No one can underestimate the importance of the interaction between two essential factors of the South Carolina economy—rice and black slaves.

The South Carolina slave laws reflect the tension between the economic needs of the colony and its safety needs. While the colonists urged the increased importation of slaves, the legal system tried to develop methods of containing the growing black population. Whether by providing incentives for the immigration of white servants or by enacting restrictive pass laws, the legislature revealed its major focus of providing a "check" on the black population.

This chapter on South Carolina slave law does not capture all of the physical brutality that black slaves were subjected to during the colonial era. This is not a work on the condition of the slave in the mosquito-infested swamplands of South Carolina or any other brutal aspect of slavery. Yet, the materials do reveal the inhumane treatment of blacks as imposed by one of the highest, most lasting authorities of the colonial era—the legislature.

GEORGIA

FROM ANTISLAVERY TO SLAVERY

The Importance of Georgia

WAS GEORGIA FOUNDED WITH HUMANITARIAN MOTIVES
TOWARD BLACKS?

IN 1735, three years after Georgia's charter was issued, there was reason to believe that the harsh racial practices of the other colonies might not be repeated in this, the last of the thirteen original colonies.[1] In January of that year the English trustees, as the principal political and governing authority for the colony of Georgia, passed a law expressly banning the importation of blacks into Georgia after June 24, 1735 and, more significantly, prohibiting the use of blacks within the colony as slaves.[2] Clearly, Georgia had the potential to formulate a more humane policy toward blacks than was the case elsewhere. In 1735, when every other American colony was upholding the practice of racial slavery within its borders, the trustees of Georgia "refused . . . to make a law permitting such a horrid crime."[3] James Oglethorpe, Georgia's best-known trustee and *de facto* governor during the colony's early development, later asserted that the trustees had passed the slavery prohibition because "slavery . . . is against the Gospel, as well as the fundamental law of England. . . ."[4]

When treating Georgia's early prohibition of slavery, historians are confronted with the questions: did the authors of the prohibition truly believe, as some Quakers in Pennsylvania were then asserting, that, regardless of race, it was immoral and un-Christian to enslave any human being?[5] If so, did this moral repugnance to slavery extend itself into the Georgia courts, where the rights of black Georgians would be tested?

Sadly, as we will demonstrate in this chapter, the 1735 law was not passed for humanitarian reasons; nor did it move Georgia courts to a more sympathetic view of their responsibilities toward black Georgians. That unique antislavery law contained racist provisions, and subsequent judicial decisions based on these provisions were unnecessarily harsh and attest to the absence of any widely held Georgian regard for black welfare. Indeed, even the specific antislavery provisions in the 1735 law were themselves often disregarded or ineffectively enforced by judicial and administrative officials. In 1750, in response to mounting opposition to the law, Georgia repealed it by passing a statute sanctioning and encouraging slavery within its borders. The ban on slavery had lasted only fifteen years.

Despite the introduction of slavery, an opportunity still existed for Georgia to formulate a more humane slave policy than that of its southern slave neighbors. Immediately before the new slavery law was drafted, the chief colonial administrative officers proposed the establishment of regulations on the care of the slaves soon to be imported. They wrote to the trustees that it was their "inclination to make the condition of slavery as easy as may be consistent with the safety of his majesty's subjects, by putting the [slaves] under the protection of the Laws. . . ." The "restrictions" they would enforce for the protection of slaves would "set so fair an example of Humanity" that other colonists would "be induced to imitate" Georgia.[6]

Nevertheless, with the writing and passage of slave codes of 1755, 1765, and 1770, Georgia quickly became as strict as any other American colony in the prohibitions on freedom enforced against enslaved blacks.

On the surface, Georgia had traveled full circle from antislavery to an entrenched slave colony. In this chapter we will examine this legal development of slavery, which was made unique by the influence of social and institutional forces pressing for abolition of and restrictions on slavery. Only a careful examination of this process can reveal the inherent moral limitations of the opposition to slavery and help explain the quickness with which Georgia adopted a brutal slave code. While superficially the development of slavery in Georgia was subtly different from what we have observed elsewhere, in substance it reflected the same basic disregard for the humanity of blacks.

The need to understand Georgia's reversal is also important because it ultimately contributed to the continued enslavement of millions of blacks throughout the United States, as well as assured the immediate enslavement of thousands of blacks in Georgia. By the time of the 1787 constitutional convention, the pervasive presence of slavery in Georgia was a controlling factor in determining the votes of the Georgia representatives in support of the constitutional provisions guaranteeing any state the right to permit the importation of slaves until 1808, mandating the return of fugitive slaves, and counting slaves as three-fifths of the whites to bolster southern white federal influence[7]—all necessary supports to the entrenchment of southern slavery. For decades to come, federal attempts to limit slavery were blocked constitutionally by the efforts of Georgia and other southern states. Despite charter trustee Oglethorpe's pronouncements that slavery was against the "gospel" as well as the "fundamental law of England," for blacks throughout the United States, Georgia never was nor did it ever become in the colonial or even pre–Civil War years, an "example of humanity."

ORIGINS OF THE ANTISLAVERY LAW: THE GEORGIA CHARTER

The powers by which the trustees made provision to prohibit slavery in Georgia were given to them under the peculiar structure of the original charter government. Under that charter, which was approved by the Privy Council of England on June 9, 1732, the twenty-one English charter petitioners became a Board of Trustees for Georgia with special powers to guide the development of this colony.[8] The extensiveness of the powers granted to the trustees by the charter coupled with various conditions it placed on the exercise of those powers paved the way for the decision to ban slavery and allowed the continuation of that ban in the face of rising protest by colonial Georgians.

The charter gave the trustees absolute ownership over all land in the colony and extensive political authority for twenty-one years to establish and direct the government of Georgia.[9] They had the power to "Nominate, make constitute, commission, ordain and appoint . . . all . . . governors, judges, magistrates, ministers, and

officers, civil and military, . . . [as they] thought fit and needful
. . ." for the government of the colony.[10] They could pass all
Georgia laws with the approval of only the king in council[11] and
decide appeals from the Georgia courts.[12] To a great extent, the
trustees were the governor, legislature, and supreme court of
Georgia.[13]

While the trustees had the authority to make most of the major
decisions for Georgia,[14] the structure of the charter government insulated them from many local Georgia pressures, which were generally supportive of the admission of slaves. Unlike the charters in
other colonies, the Georgia charter did not require the establishment of a local colonial legislature. The result was that the trustees
were able to formulate their slavery policy without the approval
of a Georgia assembly, and without facing institutionalized criticism
of their policy from a local legislature.[15] This political independence
was given further meaning by the trustees' geographical distance,
for the charter, like the charters in other colonies, did not require
the trustees to become citizens of Georgia or even to reside in
Georgia. With the notable exception of Oglethorpe, none of the
trustees lived in the colony. Had they, they would have been forced
into frequent contact with the proslavery views of the Georgia
population.

Finally, unique charter restrictions on the personal financial
affairs of the trustees insulated them from the economic pressures
for slavery. No member or officer of the Board of Trustees could
reap financial gain from his position, either directly through slavery
or indirectly through Georgia investments. No grant of Georgia
land could be made to any trustee as an individual and no person
having an interest in such land could be a trustee.[16] Unable to participate individually in a Georgia slave trade or own Georgia land
whose value would rise with the introduction of slaves, the trustees
reached decisions on slavery without having to weigh the potential
for personal economic gain arising from the enslavement of blacks.
Other goals and interests could thus guide their policy. As Professor
Albert Saye has written, "this removal of the possibility of gain
from the Trustees was sufficient to make a 'radical difference between Georgia and all the other proprietary provinces.' Whatever
service any Trustee rendered the colony had to be without a view of

profit, 'a condition precisely the opposite of that which lay at the base of all other proprietorships.' "[17]

The detachment of the trustees also contributed, indirectly, to the disorganization of local Georgia government. The trustees' policy, under charter sanction, was to retain authority in the board, in order to pursue best the goals of the philanthropic adventure. Rather than delegate responsibility to a local governor or legislature, the board ruled through numerous *ad hoc* ordinances sent to particular Georgia appointees. Unfortunately, this system could not be administered well by a Board of Trustees geographically and politically distant from Georgia. Most authorities describe the Georgia government and judiciary as highly disorganized and generally ineffective, creating numerous difficulties even in the enforcement of the slave prohibition.[18] The trustees' willingness to accept this general inefficiency can only be explained by their pursuit of what they judged to be more important goals. Concludes historian Kenneth Coleman:

> given the intelligence of the Trustees, this insistence upon retaining all authority in their own hands is strange, because it went against English and colonial experience. The only explanation for this is that the Trustees put other priorities higher than government, that they did not understand the importance of government and participation in it to the colonists, and that they believed they could ensure the success of their experiment only by retaining authority in their own hands.[19]

THE GOALS OF GEORGIA

The distinct goals for the new colony of Georgia, set forth in the original charter, tell us much about the elements that brought about the formation of the colony under a trusteeship, and, as we shall examine, their decision to abolish slavery. While the structure of the colonial charter government permitted the trustees to abolish slavery, the goals for the colony—aiding the English poor, protecting the mercantile system, and providing military defense—were catalysts for the prohibition of slavery.

The first of these objectives was the improvement of the financial welfare of the English poor by their immigration to Georgia. While many of the poor, so the charter noted, were "not able to provide a maintenance for themselves and families" in England, "if they had means to defray their charges of passage, and other expenses incident to new settlements, they would be glad to settle in any of our provinces in America. . . . [B]y cultivating the lands at present waste and desolate, they might . . . gain a comfortable subsistence for themselves and families."[20]

The legislative proposal for the foundation of Georgia had, in fact, originated in a parliamentary committee charged with investigating the conditions of debtors in English prisons. This "committee on jails," which was organized and chaired by Oglethorpe, had concluded that the emigration of English debtors to a new American colony would provide these poor with a second chance at economic self-sufficiency. The actual proposal for the Georgia charter was later made by twenty-one petitioners, ten of whom were from the committee on jails.[21]

As it turned out, the aiding of debtors was more an ideal than a reality since no more than a dozen debtors were actually sent to Georgia.[22] Most of those whom the trustees ultimately financed were the "poor people from the English Towns." These "worthy poor," chiefly small tradesmen and artisans, were probably considered by the trustees to be sufficiently productive to flourish in Georgia, but not so valuable as to drain productive labor from the British economy.[23] The philanthropic goal of the originators was carried out, though perhaps not as substantially as the authors of the charter believed it would be.

The Georgia charter also noted that a prosperous settlement of former English poor would "strengthen our colonies and increase the trade, navigation, and wealth of these our realms."[24] According to eighteenth-century mercantile theory, Georgia colonization was supposed to provide a fruitful market for English products, as well as a rich supply of various commodities like silk and grapes. England hoped to end her dependence on outside suppliers of these items, and Georgia was considered, incorrectly, a likely source. Removing the financial burden of the English poor also contributed to the financial stability of the country.

The final purpose of Georgia's establishment was military defense. The charter framed this objective, narrowly, as providing protection for the (white) population of South Carolina from Indian attacks. The South Carolina frontier had been ravaged by several serious conflicts with the Indians, and their inhabitants "by reason of the smallness of their numbers, [would] in case of a new war, be exposed to the like calamities; inasmuch as their whole southern frontier continueth unsettled, and lieth open to the said savages. . . ." Since it was "highly becoming our crown and royal dignity to protect all our loving subjects, be they never so distant from us [and] to extend our fatherly compassion even to the meanest and most infatuate of our people, . . . a regular colony of the said poor people [was to] be settled and established in the southern territories of Carolina."[25]

Although the charter did not mention it, South Carolina was also vulnerable militarily because it had more blacks than whites and thus could muster few "dependable" (i.e., white) fighting men to ward off an Indian attack—or a slave uprising. Georgia's position was equally precarious because of the proximity to her border of Spanish (and French) military forces. The Spanish held Florida and claimed the lands far to the north, including much of the land that was settled as Georgia. Their encouragement of slave uprisings made their presence especially troublesome. South Carolina slaves who managed to make it into Spanish-held areas were free men in these Spanish settlements. This conflict later culminated in open warfare during the 1740s, when Oglethorpe successfully led Georgia and South Carolina troops (and slaves) against the Spanish forts to the south.[26]

For blacks, these military, philanthropic, and mercantilistic goals were of more fundamental importance *after* the founding of the colony, since the trustees' decision to ban slavery was based on the original objectives. Both the positive and negative characteristics of the 1735 law as well as the roots of Georgia's later slave history can be traced to these priorities.

The 1735 Antislavery Law

THE DECISION TO BAN SLAVERY:
A PROCESS OF AMORAL DECISION-MAKING

Inclusion of these goals in the charter did not itself serve to outlaw slavery from Georgia, nor did it lead to the immediate pass-

age by the trustees of a law banning slavery. When the first contingent of English settlers arrived in Georgia in 1733, one year after
the passage of the charter, the trustees' opposition to slavery was
somewhat ambiguous. For example, the trustees authorized the use
of black slaves in the construction of the first settlement of Savannah.[27] Later, about twelve slaves were used to help build the settlement at Ebenezer and a road between Ebenezer and another settlement at Abercorn.

That the trustees had taken no special action to protect these
slaves from abuse is suggested by two incidents. When some of the
slaves attempted to run away, they received what Salzburgians
Johann Bolzius and Israel Gronau characterized as "their regular
punishment," whereby they were "tied to a tree half naked and
beaten with a number of long sticks and whips." The lack of protection is also revealed by an instance in which Gronau reportedly
had no idea how to deal with a slave who had threatened his overseer with an axe. After Gronau asked the overseer "what to do in
order to be just," the overseer "beat the [slave] who had threatened
him."[28]

Another example of the trustees' ambiguous policy toward
blacks can be found in the terms of numerous trustee land grants,
which implied that settlers might be permitted slaves at some point
in the future. One 1733 lease of land by the trustees, for example,
forbade its recipients to "keep . . . or Employ within . . . Georgia any . . . Black . . . without the special . . . Licence of the
said Common Council. . . ."[29]

Despite these scattered cases, the trustees certainly did not
intend to permit the widespread use of slaves and probably did not
intend to permit slavery at all after the initial settlement had been
completed. Contemporary Georgians widely expected the trustees
to abolish slavery, and indeed several South Carolinians unsuccessfully proffered a bribe to Oglethorpe in an attempt to obtain special
permission to bring in slave labor to work certain pieces of Georgia
land they had requested. Oglethorpe's disgust over this incident and
his conviction that "our men were encouraged in Idleness by [slaves]
working for them" led him to return to South Carolina the slaves
used in Savannah.[30]

Oglethorpe, who was then the colony's *de facto* governor and the only trustee residing in Georgia, made the proposal to ban blacks. He had been instrumental in the political movement to create Georgia and had been the leader of the first immigrants. Now his evaluations of the progress of the colony prompted him to write to the other trustees proposing that blacks be prohibited.[31] As chairman of the trustees' committee on laws and regulations for the colony of Georgia, he later helped draft the 1735 slave law.[32]

According to later documents published by the trustees, their decision to prohibit both free and enslaved blacks from Georgia was based on their belief that the purpose of Georgia's settlement, as outlined in the charter, was inconsistent with the existence of slavery in Georgia. Since Georgia was supposed to provide a haven for the English poor, they concluded that its inhabitants would be financially unable to purchase slaves, or reduced to abject poverty if they tried. The vision of poor whites performing the same menial tasks black slaves engaged in would also be socially divisive. Economically, the production of silk and grapes did not require the physical stamina uniquely attributed to blacks.

When evaluating the military needs of the colony, the trustees raised the further argument that the rebelliousness of slaves would threaten the stability of Georgia as well as nearby South Carolina, which already had more slaves than whites. The cost of slaves, who could not serve as soldiers, reduced the fund for financing the immigration of militarily dependable and socially desirable whites.[33] Finally, the mere presence of blacks in the Georgia countryside would complicate the apprehension of runaway South Carolina slaves.

None of these explanations of the trustees' slave policy reveals any concern for the welfare of blacks. Rather, it appears that the trustees saw the antislavery prohibition as a protection of white interests in the colony. Even Trustee Oglethorpe, a major opponent of slavery in Georgia, had many slaves on his plantation in South Carolina and had profited from the international slave trade as a Deputy Governor of the Royal African Company.[34]

The reasons for the trustees' prohibition against free blacks in Georgia are less clear, and probably even less commendable. As noted previously, the 1735 antislavery provisions prohibited the importation of *all* blacks—thus, both slaves and free blacks. Yet, even given the trustees' rationale that slaves were a possible social or military threat, those fears would not justify the exclusion of free blacks. The immigration of free blacks would not have drained funds from the trustees' budget or reduced poor white colonists to greater poverty. Instead, it would have provided a much needed source of cheap labor as a substitute for the slaves banned from the colony. Presumably free blacks presented also less of a military threat than enslaved blacks.

Indeed, in 1740, several of the trustees discussed whether they ought to permit free blacks into Georgia, but they pragmatically concluded that the 1735 law was too explicit to now sanction the immigration of free blacks. The fact that they debated this issue indicates that they ultimately recognized that the importation of free blacks would not have been incompatible with the original goals for the colony.[35]

PROVISIONS OF THE ANTISLAVERY LAW

The preamble and provisions of the 1735 law repeated the amoral objectives of the law, titled "An Act for rendering the Colony of Georgia more Defencible by Prohibiting the Importation and use of Black Slaves or Negroes into the same."[36] According to the preamble, the settling of "Black Slaves and Negroes" in other colonies had "Obstructed the Increase of English and Christian Inhabitants . . . who alone can in case of a War be relyed on for . . . Defense and Security. . . ." It exposed settlers "to the Insurrections Tumults and Rebellions of . . . Slaves & Negroes . . ." and with the encouragement by foreign powers of slave rebellions "might Occasion the utter Ruin and loss" of English colonies.[37] Just as Georgia had been originally founded partially because of the military precariousness of southern white settlements, now all blacks were prohibited from Georgia to further protect those same white settlements. The law made no mention of a provision in the original charter declaring free "all people who shall at any time hereafter inhabit or reside within" Georgia,[38] though, on first examination, one would expect these charter "liberties" to have been cited by the authors of the antislavery law. One can only conclude that *these* precepts were not to be the basis of the law.

The law's substantive provisions on blacks furthered what the trustees viewed as the true interests of white Georgians—the banishment of all blacks from the colony. The first of these provisions imposed a maximum fine of fifty pounds on any person who imported, bought, sold, bartered, or used any black in Georgia.[39] While the provision did protect enslaved blacks by penalizing persons who imported or used slaves, it also injured free blacks by penalizing persons who imported or used them. Moreover, the penalty itself, which was principally a penalty against the enslavement of blacks, was merely a fine, not imprisonment or physical punishment. Blacks were thus being treated as property since the violation of their human rights elicited only a financial penalty. In practice, if enforcement was lax, as it later proved to be, slave owners could afford to violate the law, because the punishment was merely a fine and could be absorbed as an "operating cost."

A second provision regulated all blacks more directly by providing that any black (thus free or slave) "found in the . . . province of Georgia" could be seized by the government.[40] Of course, if the 1735 law had granted freedom to all blacks seized by the government, its prohibition might be viewed less harshly. But no such policy was enunciated. To the contrary, under one provision in the law, runaway slaves from other colonies who were found in Georgia *had* to be returned to their former owners, so long as the owner paid all court fees, costs of apprehension, and any damages, and entered a claim in Savannah court within three months of the capture. A judge could not free such slaves or order them sold to another owner, for either financial or humanitarian reasons. So long as the former owner could prove his title, the court could not even question the inhumanity of the treatment of his former owner, or the inhumanity of slavery in general.[41]

To "dispose" of the free or enslaved *Georgia* blacks who had been seized by the government, the law declared that they were "the Sole property of . . . the said Trustees . . . and shall and may be Exported Sold and disposed of in such manner as the said Common Council of the said Trustees . . . shall think most for the benefit and good of the said Colony. . . ."[42] Thus, rather than freeing captured blacks, the law permitted the government to sell formerly free or enslaved Georgia blacks into slavery outside the state. At least over the short run, Georgia's government could profit from its slave prohibition. Admittedly, the law left the *option* open for the government to free blacks, but, as we shall see, the courts did not follow that course in the case of captured slaves.

Lackadaisical Enforcement of the 1735 Antislavery Law

JUDICIAL ANTAGONISM TO THE PROHIBITION OF SLAVERY: A STUDY IN JUDICIAL ACTIVISM AGAINST BLACKS

The destruction of most pre-1776 Georgia court opinions severely hampers investigation of any of the original cases pertaining to the enforcement of the 1735 statute.[43] Several slave cases during this period are discussed in the official Journal of Trustee William Stephens, who served as the Secretary of the Colony for the Trustees from 1737 to 1750;[44] unfortunately, existing records of Stephens's Journal cover only eight of the fifteen years during which slavery was prohibited,[45] contain merely a limited selection of the cases, and make terse and sometimes ambiguous references to the specifics of the cases reported. The loss of records of Stephens's Journal from after 1745 is especially troublesome, since historical accounts suggest that the violation of the antislavery law was greatest toward the end of the 1740s. Nevertheless, when integrated with other historical descriptions of judicial enforcement, Stephens's cases furnish a modest foundation for evaluating the policies of the Georgia courts.

The court decisions disposing of free or enslaved Georgia blacks portray a judicial process that exercised the options under the 1735 law with the worst possible consequences for blacks. In two cases reported in Stephens's Journal, the Georgia courts sold captured Georgia blacks into slavery outside the state, thereby failing to free them, as permitted under the 1735 law.[46] In the case of "a Negro slave that belonged to the later Mr. Dyson," Trustee Oglethorpe ordered Mr. Jones (a magistrate) to sell Dyson's captured slave. The slave had been "kept in a clandestine Manner to and fro betwixt the two Provinces [of Georgia and South Carolina], being laid hold on by the Magistrates, after his Master's Decease here, and kept in Custody." Jones made a public advertisement of the impending auction and subsequently sold the slave to a Captain Thompson.[47]

Similarly, Stephens reports the case of "A Negro who had been seized a long while past and kept in Prison ever since." He adds that the imprisonment "in my own Opinion was a great Hardship upon him, and that he ought sooner to have been exposed to Sale, and discharged." After a public advertisement, the Negro "was now set up at publick Auction, and sold for 8/ & 10s."[48] Since Stephens describes the prisoner as a "Negro," not a slave, and makes no reference to a previous owner, as he did in the earlier case, it is possible that the court imprisoned a free black captured in Georgia and sold him into slavery.

One 1741 case, reported elsewhere, reveals that it was a practice to assign a portion of the profits from the sale of a captured slave to the private parties who reported the owner to the authorities. After a captured slave was sold at auction for thirteen pounds, Henry Manley and William German received one pound six shillings and five pounds four shillings respectively from the sale for notifying authorities of the prior illegal use of the slave by Thomas Upton. The two constables involved in the case were given one pound ten shillings and one pound as "compensation" for "certain charges and loss of time in Holding and Trying the said Negro." The balance of the profit from the sale was "to be applyed to such charitable uses as shall from time to time Appear necessary."[49]

The large number of cases resulting in the return, or attempted return, of foreign runaway slaves reveals vigorous enforcement of the 1735 clause on runaways.[50] In the cases Stephens describes, Georgia officials and citizens actively pursued suspected runaway slaves[51] and received financial reward under the law for their efforts.[52] The Savannah courts imprisoned suspected runaway slaves in order to give the owner opportunity to claim title,[53] published "proper advertisements . . . for the Benefit of any claiming a Property in him &c.,"[54] and quickly returned them to South Carolina slave owners who paid for their costs.[55]

This policy of vigorously returning runaway slaves, as Stephens repeatedly points out, was in sharp contrast to the failure of South Carolina officials to return runaway Georgia *white* servants. Following one case in which Stephens publicized the capture of three runaway slaves, he writes in his Journal: "we thought it would not be amiss to let the President and Council of Carolina know, how different a Course we took with Regard" to the Carolina slaves captured in Georgia, than were the hostile practices of Carolina magistrates, "who in many Instances of late had been so far from giving any assistance . . . in stopping Deserters [runaway white Georgia indentured servants]." Stephens claims that South Carolina officials were "inclined to protect and conceal such [white] Fugitives, to the great Detriment of this Colony; and such as if not soon remitted, would be of pernicious Consequence."[56]

After suspected runaway slaves were captured and imprisoned, the courts placed the burden of proof on *them* to show that they were free and not runaways. This probably imposed an immense, if not impossible, evidentiary task. For example, in a 1745 case a Negro "had been taken up a little while since, as a deserter from Carolina"; he claimed he was "a free man, and a subject to the State of Holland, living in Curassoe. . . ."[57] When at the first hearing no one appeared to claim him as his slave, the case was continued for a further hearing. The court required the prisoner to remain in prison until the second hearing unless he could post a bond assuring his appearance at the second hearing and indemnifying the alleged master "for all costs and damages" if the master's claim was good. In this case two entrepreneurs, apparently desiring the prisoner's labor, posted the bond.[58]

At the second hearing, Mr. Mulraynes, the alleged master, proved only that he had purchased the title for twenty-five pounds, but failed to establish that the title he purchased was actually valid. Stephens adds that "there were Strong Circumstances, to perswade the belief of foul play being used, and that the Seller had not a legal property in him seemed plain, for . . . the person and Stature of this Negroe was so comely and well put together, that instead of the price he was sold at, he would unquestionably have yielded more than double that Sum at any Markett, and if it appears at last that Mr. Mulrayne has been imposed on twas presumed he must seek his remedy against the Seller."[59]

Nevertheless, "since the *Onus probandi** [lay] upon the Negroe to make it appear that he is a Free Man, the Court thought fit to allow him Six Months or more, . . . to produce an Authentick

* burden of proof

publick Testimoney from Curassoe of his being a free Subject to the States of Holland. And the same Sureties remained as before, to answer for his appearance at the Court then to be holden, and also all Costs and damage &c."[60] By putting the burden on the slave to prove he was free, the decree may have been tantamount to a judgment of enslavement because of the difficulty for a black to acquire the prerequisite documentation.

Georgia's policy regarding runaway slaves may have permitted even the execution of runaway South Carolina slaves captured in Georgia. According to an October 3, 1739 entry in Stephens's Journal, Trustee Oglethorpe directed that a paper be written "cautioning all persons in this province to have a watchful eye upon any Negroes, who might attempt to get a foot in it." Oglethorpe promised "as a Reward for taking them, what the [1735 antislavery] Act here directs [i.e., reimbursement for costs], and withal, what the Government at Carolina promises to pay, for every such runaway Negro, delivered at Charles-Town, *alive* or *dead.*"[61]

JUDICIAL DISREGARD OF EXPLICIT PROVISIONS
OF THE 1735 LAW

In addition to construing provisions of the 1735 law in a manner contrary to the interests of blacks, the Georgia courts sometimes disregarded its explicit provisions outlawing slavery in Georgia. Evidence of this practice can only be gleaned inferentially from cases in which the use of slaves in Georgia appeared to have been brought to the attention of the courts, yet the courts failed to deal with the violations.

One such instance was a 1739 case involving a controversy between Captain Davis, a slave master, and his white boat captain, Pope. In describing the dispute between Captain Davis and Pope, Stephens unwittingly reveals an extraordinary, intimate relationship between the white master Davis and his black female slave, whose enslavement in Georgia appears never to have been challenged. Stephens's description of the highly visible involvement of the slave in Savannah trade and in the events leading to the suit suggests that her residence in Georgia must have been readily apparent to the Savannah community and to the Savannah court. Stephens's summary is also revealing of his own sexual attitude toward blacks. According to Stephens's entry, Davis's

> most visible Foible, was keeping a Mulatto Servant (or Slave) who in Reality was his Mistress: For he had in former Years by trading much in the hottest Parts of America, contracted such Distempers, as well nigh bereft him of the Use of both his Legs and Arms: And this Girl (who was of an exceeding fine Shape, and setting aside her swarthy Countenance, might compare with an European) was of much Use to him; not only as an Helper to put on his Cloaths, dress him, and look after his Linen, &c. which she did to great Perfection; but having very good natural Parts also, and by Length of Time having obtained good Knowledge of his Business, and learnt to look into Accounts; he suffered almost every Thing to pass through her Hands, having such Confidence in her, that she had the Custody of all his Cash, as well as Books; and whenever he ordered any Parcel of Silver to be weighed out for any Use, whether it were two or three hundred Ounces, more or less, in Dollars, she had the doing of it: And as this had been the Course for several Years past, wherein he had found her very faithful, and of great Service to him; it may easily be supposed the Life of such Slavery was not a heavy Burden upon her, and that she had Art enough to shew, all Persons who had any Business with Captain Davis, were expected not to treat her with Contempt . . .[62]

Davis's dispute with Pope began when

> Pope, who is a rough Tar, and naturally surly, upon some Difference with this Damsel, made Use of some Words she did not like; and she wanted not to return in softer Terms what was not a Jot less provoking; whereupon he gave her a Stripe across the Face with her own Fan; and having raised such a Flame in the House, left it.[63]

Later Davis heard "some words falling from [Pope] which Davis could not well relish. . . ." With "the abuse of Madam [the female slave] being also fresh in memory, . . . he discharged [Pope] from being master of the Snow. . . ."[64] The subsequent litigation between Captain Davis and Pope dealt with, among other issues, the legality of Pope's firing. Yet despite the obvious importance of Davis's slave to this point, the court never questioned or even discussed the illegality of the presence of Davis's mistress, and thereby left the impression that her presence was not considered illegal by the courts.

Another case arising in 1741 exemplifies the fact that the courts and governmental officials were neither surprised nor critical of the presence of slaves in Georgia despite the antislavery prohibition. Stephens reports on October 24 that he had just learned of two "negroes . . . who were taken into custody [in Savannah] and in a while since had broken prison and made their escape. Their crimes had been committed after their master, Captain Kent of the fort at Augusta, had been "allowed the Use of a Boy and Girl, Dutch Servants, to help him and his Wife in the Family. . . ." The servants "were cruelly treated by him, not allowed competent Food and Cloathing, and sent far off to a Plantation of his, where they were tasked at the Discretion of these Negroes, who likewise were authorized to punish them, if they did not fulfil their Task." One of the blacks "attempted to commit a Rape upon the Girl, [but was] prevented by some Person, who hearing her Shrieks, came to her Relief. . . . [W]hen she made Complaint to her Master, he first beat her with his Cane, and then ordered her to be stript stark naked, haul'd up to a Beam by her Arms tied, in Presence of these two Negroes, and afterwards to be terribly whipped."[65]

When the Savannah court dealt with the accused slaves, they do not appear to have considered the illegality of Kent's ownership of slaves in Georgia or to have fined him for his transgression of the antislavery law. "The cause of [the slaves'] commitment," according to Stephens, "was, for that [sic] they had been guilty of many foul crimes," and thus presumably not because they were illegally imported.[66] The Savannah magistrate implicitly recognized Kent's ownership of the "Negroes," for he apprehended them by sending notice to Kent "recommending to him to send [the white servants] hither, together with the two Negroes."[67]

At the end of the report, Stephens, the official secretary of the colony for the trustees, recognized the use of slaves by the people of Augusta, Georgia.

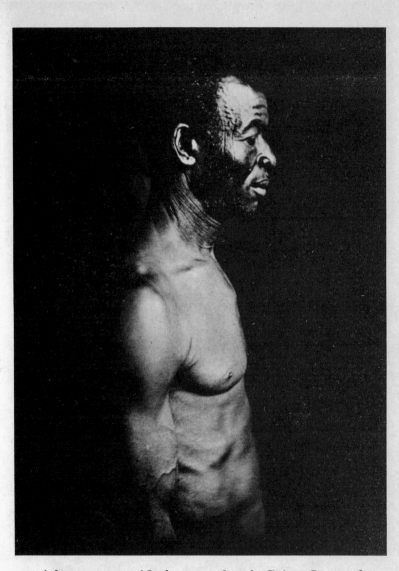

A daguerreotype of Jack, captured on the Guinea Coast and later a slave on a South Carolina plantation.

Bringing in Slaves to the Shaka Market
(Library of Congress)

Throwing Slaves Overboard
(Library of Congress)

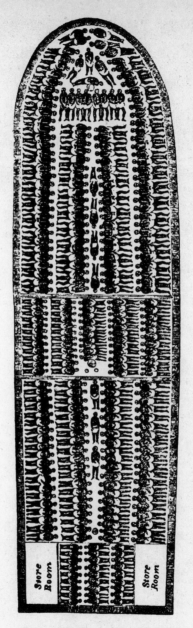

Lower Deck of Slave Ship
(London Museum)

Slave Branding
(Culver Pictures)

Inspection and Sale of a Negro
(Library of Congress)

A Slave Auction
(Culver Pictures)

Selling Female Slaves by the Pound
(Library of Congress)

TO BE SOLD,

A VERY likely young Mulatto Man Slave, an excellent taylor by trade, as well as a very good servant for a gentleman : He has had the small-pox and measles, is very healthy, and understands waiting at table well, taking care of horses, riding, and driving a carriage. Enquire of the Printer.

N. B. As the money will not be wanted till September 1780, it may lay at interest in the purchaser's hands on giving security, or the emissions out of circulation will be taken.

TO BE SOLD,

A LIKELY, healthy NEGRO MAN, about thirty years of age; has had the small-pox, and is fit for town or country; is sold for no fault but want of employ. Enquire at William Hodge's, in Front-street, between Race and Vine-streets.

Moore's-Town, Burlington County, Feb. 18.
One Hundred and Fifty Dollars Reward.

R AN AWAY last evening, from the subscriber, a Dutch servant man named JUSTUS CRAMMAR, about twenty-one years of age, five feet six or seven inches high, a well built, likely fellow, with black curled hair, dark eyes, has a scar cross-ways betwixt his under lip and chin, speaks tolerable good English, and 'tis thought speaks Dutch but imperfectly : Had on and took with him, a lead coloured homespun broadcloth coattee with a small falling collar, almost new, an old patched upper broadcloth jacket nearly of the same colour, a striped worsted and wool under jacket, patched on the fore part with cloth of the same; had two pairs of breeches, one of the same cloth of his coattee, almost new, the other of leather, old and patched; he had wooden buttons to all his cloaths except his leather breeches, part of which were brass : He had on an old shirt made of tow and linen, a pair of double soaled neats leather shoes with plated buckles in them; he had also a pair of plated knee-buckles, a pair of old yarn stockings mixed red and black, and a castor hat about half worn. Whoever takes up said servant and secures him in any gaol, and gives notice to his master so that he may be had again, shall have the above reward, and if brought home all reasonable charges defrayed, by
EPHRAIM HAINES.

Advertisements from the Pennsylvania Packet, February 27, 1779.
(Reprinted, by permission, from the George Beach Library.)

First Meeting of the Assembly in Virginia
(Library of Congress)

The Appeal
(Culver Pictures)

Slavers' Devices for Restraint
(Library of Congress)

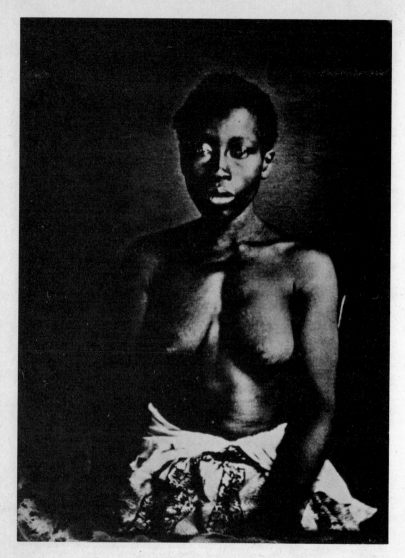

A daguerreotype of Delia, daughter of slaves
who had been captured in Africa.

Some of the People of Augusta having Plantations on the
Carolina Side of the River, as well as in Georgia, where they
find it more advantageous to settle, and carry on the Trade
with the Indians, together with making great Improvements
on their Lands; by such Means they have an Opportunity of
sliding two or three Negroes now and then at a Pinch into
their Plantations, where during their skulking a while (which
is not hard to conceive, considering the great Extent of the
Township of Augusta, by reason of large Tracts of Land)
they are not presently to be discovered.[68]

In another case, the Georgia magistrates apparently did not
question the use of slaves by a sloop's master who had stopped in
Georgia "with diverse goods of value," including slaves. The master,
identified only as "one Brace in a small sloop," had fallen ill and
therefore was obliged to remain in Georgia. Later, the magistrates
did seize at least some of his slaves, but only because they were
claimed by South Carolina creditors. Thus, not only did the magistrates permit the temporary use of slaves in Georgia, but they also
honored South Carolina's requests for those slaves—requests that
need not have been honored since the blacks were, arguably, not
runaway slaves.[69]

The Georgia courts also facilitated the illegal ownership and
use of slaves in Georgia by accepting the fraudulent claims of South
Carolina citizens to captured Georgia black slaves. Toward the second half of the slave prohibition period, Georgians found they
could hire South Carolina slaves as servants for short terms without
fear of presecution. Their ruse was that if the slave was discovered,
the real South Carolina owner would then come forward and claim
the slave as a runaway. The success of these fraudulent tactics led
Georgians to "lease" slaves from South Carolina owners for 100
years, with the advance lease payment being the equivalent of the
purchase price of a slave. The South Carolina owner claimed title
only if the slave was apprehended. Then, the court sanctioned this
ruse by returning the "leased" slaves to the South Carolina owners,
who could reimburse the Georgian for the loss. By a process of
deception and fraud sanctioned by the courts, violators incurred
no economic loss.[70]

While exceedingly ambiguous at several points, Stephens's 1743-1744 report of the trial of a black for a "foul murder" hints at the willingness of the court to use flimsy evidence against the defendant and its failure to enforce the 1735 law. According to a November 10, 1743 entry in Stephens's Journal, Captain Mackay, the head of the fort at Augusta, reported that "a Negro belonging to a trading Boat" had committed a "foul murder" by "Stabbing his Comrade with a Knife." Mackay requested that the Savannah magistrates be informed "so that they might take proper care to send for the criminal."[71] However, he asked that they not issue a warrant to him for the transportation of the slave to Savannah for trial, because criticisms of his authority in Augusta had "occasioned some Disturbance among the people there, insomuch that he feared" that the sending of such a warrant "would be attended with ill-Consequences; and as for his part he would act no farther in any shape till farther Directions from England."[72] Consequently, the magistrates sent a "Messenger" to bring the prisoner to Savannah, "being apprehensive otherwise that the Murderer might escape. . . ."[73]

At the trial, the court and jury not only disregarded what was probably the illegal importation of the black defendant, but also convicted the defendant on seemingly flimsy evidence. It appeared "by the Evidence that the deceased was the Aggressor, and had fallen upon him and beat him cruelly and soon after returned and followed him into his Hutt renewed his Blows, when he received the wound of which he died within few minutes after. But it being dark no proof was made of the Prisoner Stabbing him, nor was any White man with them in the Hutt. So the Jury brought it in Man Slaughter."[74] Ironically, what may have saved the Negro from a murder conviction was the fact that no "White man" witnessed the killing and that probably the victim was black.

Judicial support of slavery in Georgia was also illustrated by the political activities of some Georgia magistrates and other Georgia officials. So vigorous were they in their opposition to the prohibition on slavery that they took a public stand by sending proslavery petitions to their superiors, the trustees. The first major leader of the malcontents, a Savannah based proslavery group, was Peter Gordon, First Bailiff of Savannah. In 1738 he and ten other Georgia officials, including several magistrates, signed a 1738 Savannah petition to the trustees urging repeal of the slavery prohibition. Benjamin Martyn, Secretary of the Board of Trustees, replied that "the Trustees cannot but express their Astonishment that you the Magistrates, appointed by them to be Guardians of the People, by putting those Laws in Execution should so far forget your Duty, as to put yourselves at the Head of this Attempt."[75] Later, in 1740, five officials signed another petition to the trustees supporting slavery in Georgia.[76]

The absence of records of Stephens's Journal from the end of the trustee period prevents us from analyzing the most flagrant violations of the antislavery law. According to historical accounts, however, toward the end of the trustee period the magistrates were so favorably disposed to the introduction of slaves that the statute was almost a nullity and those few who supported the trustees to prohibit slavery were "denounced . . . threatened and persecuted."[77]

SLAVERY DURING THE ANTISLAVERY PERIOD

These few surviving decisions of the Georgia courts reflected not only judicial tolerance of slaves but the widespread and increasing hostility of the Georgia public and officials toward the antislavery law. In the Augusta region, slaves were widely used as early as the late 1730s without reported legal prosecutions.[78] Augusta was geographically, economically, and demographically distinct from the rest of Georgia, since it bordered on South Carolina and counted as residents many former and current citizens of South Carolina.[79] Slaves were frequently transported back and forth from South Carolina plantations to Georgia plantations in the process of being rented and even sold to Georgia slave owners.[80] A 1740 complaint to the Savannah authorities charged that the widespread use of slaves in the area had made it difficult for workingmen to find employment.[81]

In 1746, the trustees officially chastised Georgia's President William Stephens and his assistants for failing to enforce the antislave prohibition in this area.[82] In their reply, Stephens and his assistants not only admitted the widespread and long-term violation of the law around Augusta, but pleaded that continued enforcement would compel more Augustans to flee to South Carolina. They prefaced their remarks by asserting that they had "always acted an uniform Part in discouraging the Use of Negroes in this Colony, well knowing it to be disagreeable to the Trust as well as contrary to an Act existing for Prohibition of them. . . ." Yet they admitted that "the whole Inhabitants of Augusta . . . have had Negroes among them for many Years past, and now declare that if they cannot obtain that Liberty, they will remove to the Carolina Side, where they can carry on their Trade and Plantations with the same Advantage as where they now are. . . ."[83]

Outside Augusta, at least initially, Georgia officials appear to have enforced the prohibition. In 1736, the first reported attempt to smuggle slaves permanently into Georgia occurred when a group of South Carolinians established a plantation, with "Negroes," near an Indian town close to Ebenezer. Oglethorpe "ordered back the Cattle & sent away the Negroes."[84] Later, the trustees denied the land applications of several South Carolinians who claimed that the blacks they brought across the border to farm were indentured servants.[85] In several of the judicial cases already discussed courts did enforce the prohibition, albeit in a manner contrary to the interests of captured blacks.[86]

However, after the early 1740s, violations became commonplace throughout the colony, and, as we have seen, they were sometimes sanctioned by the courts. Oglethorpe's regiment used slaves at the Frederica fort, apparently without Oglethorpe's opposition.[87] Toward the end of the 1740s, slaves were sold openly in Savannah.[88] One citizen wrote in 1748, "Its well known to every one in the Colony that Negroes have been in and about Savannah for these several Years that the Magistrates knew and wink'd at it and that their constant Toast is (the one thing needful) by which is meant Negroes. . . ."[89]

The Failure of the Indentured Servant System

In order to evaluate how effective the Georgia government was in pursuing the antislavery goals of the 1735 law, we must also analyze how effective it was in establishing policies that induced nonslave labor to come to the colony. A colony without slaves had to have a sufficient number of white residents to defend it against attack, and a labor supply of indentured servants.

Several different methods were tried by the trustees to increase the number of white residents and to assure an adequate and cheap labor supply. They financed the transportation to Georgia of many free unindentured persons (called charity colonists) and granted them up to fifty acres of land.[90] Another group of emigrants (called adventurers) paid their own passage and received up to 500 acres of land.[91]

To increase the number of indentured servants, the trustees,[92] under the "Rules of the Year 1735," gave "Leave to every Freeholder to take over with him one Male Servant, or Apprentice, of the Age of Eighteen Years, and upwards, to be bound for not less than Four Years."[93] Loans were advanced to help freeholders pay for their servant's passage, clothing, and certain other provisions.[94] The trustees also *required* adventurers to import six[95] and later ten[96] indentured servants in order to receive the maximum trustee adventurer grant of 500 acres.

As an inducement for persons to enlist as indentured servants, the trustees first granted twenty-five acres of land to any servant who successfully completed his indenture. Later this figure was reduced to twenty acres and then it was increased in 1737 to fifty.[97] Under the 1737 ordinance servants also received a cow and a sow. A 1743 ordinance bestowed upon servants completing an indenture of more than four years, eight pence a day for men, six pence a day for women, various farming utensils, fifty acres of land, a cow, and a sow.[98]

Further, the trustees hired agents in Europe to recruit indentured servants armed with the promises of both enlistment bonuses and free transportation to Georgia.[99] After 1738, as the requests for servants increased, the trustees generally stopped financing the immigration of charity colonists and paid only for the transportation of indentured servants.[100] These indentured servants were usually owned by the trust and either employed directly on trustee projects,[101] rented out to colonists,[102] or sold to colonists.[103]

Despite these inducements, the trustees' efforts to attract indentured servants to the colony proved inadequate. While slaves made up well over half of the South Carolina population, Georgia normally counted no more than 20 percent of its population as indentured servants.[104] Some of the servants who were among the original settlers died or became ill. Throughout the period a significant number of indentured servants successfully fled to South Carolina, which obstructed their return.[105] Although there were numerous requests for more indentured servants, the trustees and private citizens were unable or unwilling to finance the transportation of sufficient replacements.[106] Even the Salzburgians, a German group who opposed the admission of slaves, made repeated requests for more indentured servants.[107] The scarcity of supply only increased the cost of white servants and the demands for slave labor.

Many factors contributed to the scarcity of efficient white labor. The limited supply of servants from Europe[108] and competition from cheap South Carolina slave labor were certainly factors.[109] With reductions in appropriations from parliament, the trustees discontinued in 1745 the financing of indentured servants.[110] William Stephens and other colonists also complained of the physical and moral deficiencies of European servants.[111] One group of forty Irish convicts purchased by Oglethorpe proved to be a particular source of problems, committing various crimes, running away, and creating popular unrest.[112]

However, the legal system must share a major part of the responsibility for the scarcity of white labor. The return of all indentured servants who escaped to South Carolina was critical to Georgia's maintenance of a viable indentured servant system and therefore to the antislavery experiment. Yet the South Carolina courts often ignored direct requests for indentured servants who had escaped from Georgia. Stephens discusses one 1738 case in which three runaway servants were "overtaken about twelve miles beyond Purysburgh on their travel thence toward Charlestown and brought back." The pursuers reported that in South Carolina "they were Apprehensive of being mobbed, and having those prisoners rescued." They had requested assistance from Mr. Leffette, a Carolina justice of the peace, showing him a letter from Mr. Causton[113] "directed to all Magistrates there, and praying their Aid in apprehending those People, who were described in a hue and cry requiring all Persons in the Province of Georgia to assist in it. . . ."

Leffette "threw the letter aside with Contempt, saying Mr. Causton had nothing to do in Carolina." Stevens concludes sarcastically that this was "Another notable Instance of the Good-will too many of that Province bear towards the Colony of Georgia."[114]

In a 1750 letter to Benjamyn Martyn, secretary to the trustees, Reverend Balzius refers to several cases where the South Carolina governor simply ignored presumably valid requests for indentured servants. In one case Balzius and several other prominent Georgians all informed the governor of Carolina that Ischarioth Richardson and several members of his family had left Georgia before their indentures were completed and had moved to the Carolina settlement of Congrees. Balzius reports that at the time of his letter "the whole Family is settled at the Congrees, and enjoy with other Settlers their equal Encouragements from the Governor of Carolina. . . ." In a 1749 case Balzius unsuccessfully "begged of the Governour in Charles Town to deliver up by lawful means" two escaping indentured servants, certifying to the governor "the two well attested Indentures of both Embarkations of servants."[115]

This South Carolina practice was in striking contrast to Georgia's policy toward escaped South Carolina slaves. As we have seen, whenever South Carolina slaves were captured in Georgia, government officials, acting under the provisions of the 1735 anti-slavery law, quickly returned them to their masters. In one of his frequent discussions of this difference, Stephens reported that the Carolina Magistrates "in many instances of late had been so far from giving any assistance (if desired) in stopping [white servants] from hence, that they discountenanced their Pursuers, and rather inclined to protect and conceal such fugitives, to The Great Detriment of this colony; and such as if not soon remitted, would be of pernicious Consequence."[116]

South Carolina's protection of runaway servants not only decreased the supply of indentured servants in Georgia, but also, according to Balzius, reduced the efficiency of those servants who remained. Fearing that servants would run to South Carolina, masters were "obliged to deal very tenderly with ill natured Servants to our great Disappointment and Losses. . . ."[117] As a consequence, the cost of white indentured servants had to rise, further stimulating the movement for the repeal of the slave law.

The apprehension of Georgia indentured servants was also obstructed by the policies of the Georgia courts. Balzius noted in his letter that when a servant deserted, his master had to "copy the whole Indenture, and get it attested and sealed by the Magistrates at Savannah" before he could pursue the servant and have him arrested. By the time he made such a trip to Savannah, the runaway servant had often already escaped to South Carolina, where the chances of capture, as we have seen, were much lower.[118]

The historical significance of this restrained policy toward the capture of white servants can be viewed best by comparison with the subsequent Georgia legislative policy toward the capture of escaped Georgia slaves. These later Georgia legislatures gave pursuers of slaves virtually unlimited authority to capture escaped slaves. Under their laws any white person had the right to pursue, detain, and, if need be, kill any black who did not have sufficient authority to be outside his plantation.[119] They also passed laws establishing an extensive patrol system to apprehend runaway slaves and prevent slave uprisings;[120] in contrast, no patrol system was ever established to prevent the escape of white indentured servants.

Finally, the viability of the white indentured servant system was also undermined by the trustees' decision to include provisions in the 1735 antislavery law prohibiting free blacks, who could have provided substitutes for white indentured labor.[121] Indeed, as the need for servants increased, the trustees once again considered but refused to permit the immigration of free blacks. The Earl of Egmont, one of the trustees and a major opponent of slavery in Georgia, noted in his journal in 1740 that the trustees debated whether to loosen further the restriction on Georgians' land tenure and to permit Georgians "the use of Negroes in some shape or other." Trustee Lopotre "was against humouring them in either." Trustee James Vernon suggested that the 1735 antislavery law "does not forbid Free Negroes from settling in the colony, but only the use of them as slaves. That the preamble of the Act shows the prohibition is only of slaves, and by the Law of England a free Negro is as much a subject as a white man and may set up any Trade." According to Egmont, Trustee John LaRoche agreed with Vernon, but warned that the presence of free blacks would complicate the apprehension of "slaves flying from Carolina and passing through our province in their way to Augustine."[122]

Lord Egmont himself argued against admitting free Negroes, fearing that they would "discourage and drive away white servants," unless their wages were restricted by statute: "I said I was against allowing free Negroes for the reason Mr. LaRoche had given, and because as they work cheaper, they would discourage & drive away white servants. That I saw no other inconvenience than this by admitting them; and possibly this might be remedied by passing an Act to regulate wages, for then a free Negro would demand as high wages as a hired white servant could demand, and it would be indifferent to a Master whether he hired a Negro or white servant, for tho the Negro can work some hours in the day whilst for the heat the white servant cannot; yet this is made up by the white man's doing his work after a better manner than a Negro does, as appears from Cap. Dunbars deposition. As to the Colonies being endanger'd by admitting Free Negroes, I thought there was not the least likelyhood of their running to the Spaniards, since they could not better themselves."[123] In the end nothing came of the proposal because the provisions in the 1735 law were too explicit on the subject of free blacks.[124]

The Growing Political Support for Slavery

The failure of judicial and administrative officials to enforce the 1735 antislavery law and to provide sufficient white indentured servants paralleled the increasing and ultimately widespread opposition in Georgia to the law. Initially, the main criticisms were voiced by South Carolinans who hoped to move their plantations to Georgia.[125] Soon many Georgians joined the movement as the Lowland Scots and *ad hoc* groups called malcontents and memorialists led the drive for repeal of the slavery prohibition.

In the late 1730s and throughout the 1740s opponents presented a series of proslavery petitions to the trustees. The first major petition was written in 1738, only three years after slaves were first prohibited, and was signed by 121 freeholders of Savannah, who were later known as the memorialists. The authors painted a

discouraging picture of the economic predicament of Georgia settlers. Planters were only "able to raise sufficient Produce to maintain their Families in Bread-kind," despite exerting as much effort
"as could be done by the Men engaged in an Affair, on which they
believe the Welfare of themselves and Posterity so much depended,
and which they imagine must require more than ordinary Pains to
make succeed. . . ."[126] The petitioners blamed the slavery prohibition for their economic plight, "since the Cultivation of Land with
White Servants only, cannot raise Provisions for our Families. . . ."

> It is very well known that Carolina can raise everything that
> this Colony can; and they having their Labour so much
> cheaper, will always ruin our Market, unless we are in some
> measure on a Footing with them . . .[127]

Another subject of their complaint was the trustees' land restrictions, which Daniel Boorstin has called "the most basic, most
ill-conceived, and most disastrous of the Trustees policies. . . ."[128]
The trustees had originally prohibited Georgians from alienating
title to their land (in effect denying them the right to sell it or to
purchase additional lands from others who were likewise so restricted) or from bequeathing it to anyone other than their male
children. These restrictions were intended to advance the social
and military goals of the colony by preventing the formation of
large plantations and by spreading the male population. Unfortunately, they had the effect of financially strapping many colonists,
who had received only 50 or 100 acres from the trust. The petition
pointed out that these restrictions prevented Georgians from obtaining credit and "goods upon commission, because no person
here can make any security of their lands or improvements. . . ."[129]
The only recourse for the trustees, concluded the malcontents,
was to permit free title or fee simple ownership of land and the importation of blacks "with proper Limitations." This would "induce
great Numbers of White People to come here, and also render
us capable to subsist ourselves by raising Provisions upon our
Lands. . . ." Like many others who would protest the slavery prohibition during the next decade, the petitioners quickly added how
"sensible" they were to the "Inconveniences and Mischiefs that have
already, and do daily arise, from the unlimited Use of Negroes."

But they were just "as sensible, that these may be prevented by a due Limitation, such as so many to each White Man, or so many to such a Quantity of Land; or any other manner which [the trustees] shall think most proper."[130]

After the trustees denied the petition,[131] the leaders of a Savannah-based club called the malcontents, Dr. Patrick Tailfer, Hugh Anderson, and David Douglass, along with others, published a comprehensive critique of the trustees' policies in their pamphlet, "A True and Historical Narrative of the Colony of Georgia in America" (1741).[132] The authors broadened the attack on the trustees by challenging not only the trustees' regulation of slavery and land title, but also the high land rents they charged, their right to control the location of an individual's settlement in the colony, and their power over the selection of magistrates and justices of the peace.[133] The radical nature of their demands was recognized by Trustee Lord Egmont, who observed that what Tailfer "clamours for is the use of negroes, the liberty to sell and take up land at will when and where he pleases, the choice of Magistrates independent of the Trustees etc."[134]

Since the "chief" error of the trustees' policy was "the denying the use of negroes," the narrative outlined many alleged inadequacies of the white labor force in Georgia. "[T]he strength and Constitution of white servants" was "very unequal" to the physical demands of timber production. "Hoeing the ground" by whites was "insupportable," since "whites were exposed to the sultry heat of the sun."

> it is well known, that this labour is one of the hardest upon the Negroes; even though their constitutions are much stronger than white people, and the heat no way disagreeable nor hurtful to them . . .

The loss in labor resulting from the sickness of white servants cost masters as much as it would have taken to maintain a "Negro" for four years.[135]

The narrative reproduced and praised the texts of several earlier petitions to the trustees that had bemoaned the absence of slaves.[136] One 1740 letter sent to the trustees by malcontents David Douglass, William Stirling, and Theodore Bailee had once again emphasized the protections that should be provided against the abuse of slaves if the trustees would permit their use.

> Because our neighbouring province (of which you are pleased to take notice) has, by an introduction of *too* great numbers, abused the use of Negroes . . . it does not at all follow that we should be debarred the use of Negroes for the field, or for the more laborous parts of culture, under prudent limitations . . .[137]

The authors of the 1741 narrative based their legal claim to slaves and to other rights on the provision of the original charter guaranteeing Georgians the rights of British citizens. According to the preface of their petition, "not even the flourishing of wine and silk can make a colony of British subjects happy, if they are deprived of the liberties and properties of their birthright."[138] They later quoted the original charter in full, implying that slavery could not be prohibited under it. Had the trustees pursued the "gracious purposes and ample privelages" contained in the charter, they lamented, "then would the colony, at this time, have been a flourishing condition, answerable to all those glorious ends that were proposed and expected from it. . . ."[139] The trustees' "laws and restrictions . . . were never heard in any British Settlement." Put bluntly, they claimed it was the right of free *British* citizens, and therefore of *Georgia* citizens, to deny blacks freedom by holding them as slaves.[140]

While proponents of slavery presented major petitions to the trustees several times during the 1740s, one incident may have marked a turning point. In 1741, the malcontents sent to England as their emissary Thomas Stephens, son of William Stephens, secretary of the province of Georgia and president from 1741 to 1751.[141] The young Stephens personally presented a 1741 petition to the crown and parliament, alleging various trustee abuses. Though his efforts were unsuccessful and the subject of official rebuke by parliament, he did meet some sympathy in parliament, which subsequently cut off appropriations to the trustees partially because of the slave prohibition.[142]

On July 14, 1742, probably in response to this pressure, the trustees appointed a committee to "consider how far it may be convenient or proper to admit the use or introduction of Negroes" and concomitantly instructed William Stephens to survey Georgia opinions on the subject.[143] In his reply Stephens, while proclaiming his "natural Aversion" to slavery, admitted that there was a labor shortage in Georgia and "little or no likelyhood of supplying the colony with a competent number of indentured servants." If the trustees were to permit slavery, however, he recommended that they wait until after the war with Spain. Slaves used in Georgia during the war would flee to Spanish Augusta and "become a part of their Army to fight against us." He concluded with a specific list of suggested regulations on the use of slaves for after the war.[144]

Although the actions of the trustees left the impression that they were considering repeal of the antislavery law, they made no attempt to permit slavery at this point. On several occasions they even reaffirmed their commitment to the prohibition of slavery.[145] However, the whole controversy on the antislavery law was weakening the trustees' position and further inciting domestic violations of the law.

With the removal of the immediate military threat from Spain in the early 1740s, yet another—the military—justification for the prohibition against slavery fell. The termination of major hostilities also led to the departure from Georgia of Oglethorpe, who had been the guiding force in the passage and enforcement of the antislavery law. By the mid-1740s violations of the antislavery law were becoming much more widespread.[146]

For the most part, the Georgia clergy, with the notable exceptions of Reverends John Martin Balzius and John Charles Wesley, did not oppose the enslavement of blacks.[147] The Scottish minister of Darien, John McLeod, actively supported the admission of slaves by signing an affidavit in 1739 claiming that the 1739 antislavery petition presented by Darien residents did not represent their true views.[148] The Reverend George Whitefield was perhaps as adamant and was as important a proponent of the admission of slaves as anyone else in the colony.[149] Whitefield's position, summarized by Balzius in a 1745 letter to Whitefield, proclaimed that "the Providence of God has Appointed this Colony rather for the work of black Slaves than for Europians, because of the hot climate, to which the Negroes are better used than white people."[150]

The trustees did enjoy some, though diminishing, native support for the slavery prohibition during the 1730s and early 1740s. The Highlander Scots of Darien, the Salzburgers of Ebenezer, and the residents of Frederica all sent antislavery petitions in response to the 1738 malcontent petition, though they probably acted at the request of Oglethorpe.

These groups stressed the social and economic arguments against slavery more than its immorality and never argued for the admission of free blacks. The Salzburgian petition reported that they were able to "lead a quiet and peaceable life" without slaves, causing them to "laugh at such talking" by proponents of slavery that it was "impossible and dangerous for White People to plant and manufacture any Rice. . . ."[151] Although they admitted that the community was experiencing a labor shortage, they argued that their labor needs could be met by the emigration of Salzburgian indentured servants, who were specifically requested in another part of the petition. The importation of "Negroes" would break up the close independent Salzburgian community and threaten its safety:

> We humbly beseech the honourable Trustees not to allow it, that any Negro might be brought to our Place, or in our Neighborhood, knowing by Experience, that Houses and Gardens will be robbed always by them, and White People are in Danger of Life because of them, besides other great Inconveniences . . .[152]

The petition from the residents of Darien did mention the immorality of slavery, but cited it as the last of five reasons for retaining the law.

> V. It's shocking to human Nature, that any Race of Mankind, and their Posterity, should be sentenced to perpetual Slavery; nor in Justice can we think otherwise of it, than they are thrown amongst us to be our Scourge one Day or another for our Sins; and as Freedom to them must be as dear as to us, what a Scene of Horror must it bring about! And the longer it is unexecuted, the bloody Scene must be the greater. We therefore, for our own sakes, our Wives and Children, and our Posterity, beg your Consideration, and intreat, that instead of introducing Slaves, you'll put us in the way to get us

some of our Countrymen, who with their Labour in time of
Peace, and our Vigilance, if we are invaded, with the Help of
those, will render it a difficult thing to hurt us, or that Part of
the Province we possess. We will for ever pray for your Excellency, and are, with all Submission,

New Inverness, 3d   Your Excellency's most obliged
January 1738-9.   Humble Servants,

John Mackintosh Moore   Daniel Clark, First
John Mackintosh Lynvilge Alexander Clarke, Son to the above
Ranald M'Donald   Donald Clark, Third, his Mark.[153]

The petition reflects the ambiguities in most statements of that
time against slavery: was the primary concern of those who spoke
out against the importation of black slaves into the colony no more
than their own physical safety—a response to the possibility of
slave uprisings—or was it in response to the inherent injustice of
slavery by its affront to man's highest moral ideals?

With time however, even these groups relented and eventually
they even came to support the admission of slaves. In 1748 Reverend John Balzius, the spiritual and political leader of the Salzburgians and formerly the major opponent of slavery in the colony,
wrote:

> Things being now here in such a melancholy situation I must
> humbly beseech their Honors not to regard any more our or
> Friend's Petition against Negroes but if they are bountifully
> disposed to forgive the present bold step of several Inhabitants
> in bringing our black Slaves from Carolina to our province
> and to allow the introduction of them We beg humbly to lay
> the use of them under such wise restrictions that it be not a
> discouragement but rather an encouragement to poor white
> Industrious people to settle and live happily on this Climate.[154]

THE BURDEN OF COMPETITION

Georgia's judicial and administrative officials and general population must all share the responsibility for the failure of the Georgia antislavery experiment. However, Georgia's unique position as
the last colony to be settled and thus the last to reach a decision on

slavery did place special pressures on those groups to permit slavery.

When Georgia was first settled as a colony in 1733, the harsh slave codes of Virginia (1705) and South Carolina (1712) were already in force.[155] The New York legislature had already enacted the 1706, 1708, and 1712 slave laws, shutting the door on the limited freedoms provided under the earlier Dutch half-free system.[156] South Carolina, which was nearest to Georgia in distance and in geography, already held more than 25,000 slaves, well over 50 percent of her population.[157]

This pervasive presence of slavery, especially in nearby South Carolina, gave rise to numerous violations in Georgia of the antislavery law and energized the local Georgia movement for the admission of slaves.

Economic competition from cheaper South Carolina labor depressed the sale of Georgia goods, thereby indirectly adding impetus to the repeal movement. No other colony faced such adverse economic competition when making decisions on slavery. In the 1740s the Georgia economy stagnated because of their competitive labor disadvantage and because of fears arising from war with Spain. Planters closed their farms and indentured servants moved to South Carolina after their terms were completed. This emigration compounded the colony's economic difficulties by decreasing the availability of already scarce white labor.[158]

The existence of so close and visible a slave system may also have caused Georgians to feel that they had less status than their neighbors because of their inability to own a special class of property that South Carolinians had in abundance.

The Introduction of Slavery: The 1750 Slavery Law

In 1750, the trustees finally relented. A new slavery law was enacted, ending the fifteen-year theoretical prohibition of slavery in Georgia.[159]

from and after the first day of January in the Year of Lord One Thousand seven hundred and fifty it shall and may be lawful to import or bring Black Slaves or Negroes into the

Province of Georgia in America to keep and use the same therein under the Restrictions and Regulations hereinafter mentioned and directed to be observed . . .[160]

These words stand as conclusive and public testimony of the lack of humanitarian motives in the slavery prohibitions of the 1735 law. Though racism was apparent in several of the provisions of the statute and certainly in the courts' biased enforcement of it, nevertheless, up to 1750 Georgia had been the only colony to declare illegal the enslavement of blacks within her borders. Now even this distinction was abandoned as Georgia enthusiastically joined the other colonies.

But still there was hope that perhaps Georgia's brand of slavery would not be as harsh as that practiced and legislatively sanctioned in the other colonies. Strict regulations on the number of slaves allowed into the colony and on their proper care had been called for in the petitions demanding their introduction into the colony. On the eve of the repeal, the Georgia president and others reemphasized to the trustees the need for making slavery "as easy as may be consistent with the Safety of His Majesty's subjects."[161] Precedent for the humanitarian protection of slaves could have been extracted from the ancient villenage system in England and from the Dutch half-free system.[162] If those more liberal precedents were adopted, "the fledgling province"[163] might nevertheless have become a symbol for other colonies to emulate.

RESTRAINTS OF THE 1750 LAW

By its language, the 1750 law may have been marginally less harsh than the slave codes of other colonies. It held that a "proprietor" who endangered the "limb" of a slave while chastising him forfeited a financial penalty, while one who murdered a slave was tried according to the same English laws that applied to whites.[164] The statute restricted the importation of slaves indirectly by requiring that the number of black males on each plantation be limited to four times the number of white male servants.[165] A master who did not "permit or even oblige" his slaves to attend religious service on Sunday could be fined ten pounds.[166] To regulate the slave trade, the law held that the captain of a ship carrying slaves to Georgia ports had to obtain a certificate of health before disembarkation, on penalty of 500 pounds.[167] The president and magistrates were also ordered to build a lazaretto on Tybee Island "where the whole crews of such infected ships and the Negroes brought therein may be conveniently lodged and assisted with medicines and accommodated with Refreshments for their more speedy recovery"—all at the expense of the ship's captain.[168] While the motive behind such regulations may have been primarily to protect the master class, nevertheless, if the provisions were enforced their consequence would be a marginal improvement of the welfare of blacks.

The 1750 law was not as comprehensive as those slave laws passed in some other southern colonies. It created no special justifications for a white man's restraint of, or attack on, a slave; it set up no special patrol system overseeing the movement of slaves beyond their master's property; it made no distinctions in the penalties imposed on slaves and whites for the commission of the same crimes; and finally, it did not categorize as a crime slave activities, such as learning to read or traveling on the road unsupervised, that would be considered normal and acceptable when engaged in by whites. In effect, the introduction of slaves into Georgia did not immediately bring with it the full panoply of harsh slave regulations that Virginia and South Carolina had already adopted. Whatever the reasons for these initial omissions (whether or not Georgia's antislavery past did have an effect), it remained to be seen how long these distinctions would be maintained.[169]

Despite the *comparative* differences, Georgia's first slave law was still a harsh one. In most situations violent, unprovoked, and unjustified attacks on slaves were absolutely legal. A "proprieter" possessed unrestrained authority over his slave, as long as he did not "endanger the limb" or take the life of his property. Indeed, all whites may have been immune to even the modest restraints of the law, since the statute did not prohibit the courts from independently formulating doctrines sanctioning or excusing assaults on slaves. In any event, such crimes were difficult to detect and prove when committed on slave plantations, and the penalty for "endangering the limb" was only five pounds.

Moreover, the 1750 law prohibited all slaves from being apprenticed to an "Artificer" (where they might have competed with white labor) and all plantation slaves from being lent out to another planter for any employment other than "manuring and cultivating their plantations in the country."[170] Marriages between whites and blacks were illegal.[171] A white "convicted of lying" with a black or a black "convicted of lying with a white" could receive such corporal punishment "as the court before whom such conviction shall . . . judge proper to inflict." The court had the option of imposing on whites convicted of interracial sex a fine rather than corporal punishment, but no substitution was permitted for blacks. This potential disparity in punishment gave recognition to the fact that blacks were generally destitute, and that fines would be uncollectable unless their masters paid them. Furthermore, after diligent search, we have not been able to find one case in which a white master was convicted for lying with his black slave, and we doubt whether any master was ever so prosecuted.

The provisions of the 1750 slavery statute technically never became law, since the privy council never officially approved it.[172] However, Georgia and English officials recognized its legality, and the number of blacks in Georgia increased significantly after its passage.[173] South Carolina and West Indian planters imported most of the first blacks, while later many more were brought directly from Africa.[174] Though colonial Georgia never had as many blacks as her neighbor South Carolina, by 1773 it counted among its inhabitants 15,000 blacks and 18,000 whites.[175]

Shortly after the passage of the 1750 slave law, on June 25, 1752, the trustees voluntarily relinquished control over the colony to the crown of England,[176] giving final recognition to the failure of their experiment. After this transferral of power, Georgia became a "model royal colony," technically ruled by the king sitting with his privy council, but in practice governed by the Board of Trade.[177] In Georgia a royal governor, his council, and a local representative assembly passed laws, subject to veto by the privy council.[178] Laws enacted during this period, unlike those few passed during the trustee period, were generally drafted and approved by Georgians themselves.

The Slave Codes of Georgia

THE 1755 SLAVE CODE

In 1755 royal Georgia passed its first law comprehensively regulating the status of slaves, entitled "An Act for the Better Ordering and Governing Negroes and Other Slaves in This Province."[179] This law, along with several others passed at the same time, immediately adopted many of the restrictions on slaves that had taken decades to develop in South Carolina and Virginia.

The contrast between the 1755 law[180] and the 1750 law is dramatic. The new law increased the number of slaves that could be legally held on each plantation. It ended the protection of a slave's life by adding a host of special justifications and reduced penalties for the murder of a slave. It created numerous new crimes for which slaves could be executed and placed strict limitations on slaves' everyday activities and movements. It introduced procedural requirements in a slave's suit for freedom, which made it difficult for a slave ever to gain his freedom. Georgia was quickly and tragically catching up with the slave colonies immediately to her north.

The very first provision of the new law exemplified the greater hostility that would characterize the remainder of the code toward blacks. While the 1750 law had *permitted* the enslavement of blacks, the 1755 act established at the outset a firm presumption in favor of the enslavement of *all* blacks and certain Indians.

> all Negroes Indians (free Indians in Amity with this Government and Negroes Mulatos or Mestizos who are now free Excepted) Mulatos or Mestizos who now are or shall hereafter be in this Province and all their Issue and offspring Born or to be Born shall be and they are hereby declared to be and remain for ever hereafter absolute Slaves and shall follow the Condition of the Mother and shall be deemed in Law to be Chattels personal in the Hands of their Owners and possessors and their Executors Administrators and Assigns to all intents and purposes whatsoever . . .[181]

A later provision indicated that Georgia slaves could theoretically gain their freedom, since it gave white "guardians" of slaves the right to prosecute a slave's suit for freedom. Unfortunately, the provision implied that slaves could not institute such suits without a guardian.[182] Moreover, the burden of the proof lay upon the plaintiff. It was "always presumed that every Negro Indian Mulato and Mestizo is a Slave unless the Contrary can be made appear (the Indians in Amity with this Government Excepted) in which Case the burthen of the proof shall lie on the Defendant."[183] If the slave lost the suit, the court could "Inflict such Corporal punishment not Extending to Life or Limb of the [slave] as they in their Discretion shall think fit."[184] Thus, the law proclaimed that all blacks were to be considered slaves; required slaves to secure a guardian to prosecute a suit for their freedom; placed the legal burden of proof on slaves to demonstrate that they were not slaves; and subjected slaves to corporal punishment if they unsuccessfully prosecuted a suit under this extra burden.

This new policy toward slavery also included a drastic loosening of the earlier limitations on the number of slaves that could be used—limitations which, according to all existing evidence, had not even been enforced.[185] Under the 1750 slavery law a plantation owner supposedly had to have kept "one white man servant on his own land capable of bearing arms and aged between 16 and 65 years . . . for every four male negroes or blacks on his plantation."[186] Now in 1755, every owner had to have one "white servant . . . capable of bearing arms" for the first twenty slaves, only two white servants for fifty slaves, and one white servant for each twenty-five slaves after that.[187]

Protection of the Slave's Life Under the Code

The life of the slave was no longer protected by the laws of England, as it had been under the 1750 trustee law. In the case where a person "willfully" murdered his own or another person's slave he was merely "adjudged guilty of Felony for the first Offense and [had] the Benefit of the Clergy making Satisfaction to the Owner of such Slave. . . ."[188] Only on the second offense of *willful* murder did the "offender Suffer for the said Crime according to the Laws of England except that he shall forfeit no more of his Lands and Tenemants Goods and Chattels than what may be Sufficient to Satisfy the owner of such Slave so killed as aforesaid. . . ."[189] Conviction for willful murder of a slave also required after 1755 the "oath of two witnesses," an extremely difficult burden of evidence for most criminal prosecutions.[190]

In other circumstances, the new law reduced or even eliminated the penalty for killing a slave because the murderer was supposedly justified or excused. A defendant merely forfeited fifty pounds sterling if he killed his own or another person's slave "on a Sudden heat or Passion or by undue Correction."[191] He received no penalty if he killed a slave who refused to "undergo examination" outside his master's property and assaulted and struck the white person.[192]

There was no prohibition for killing runaway slaves, since under the law they could be returned dead or alive.[193] The only inducement the pursuer had *not* to kill the slave was the *lower reward* he normally received from the government if he brought back the dead runaway's "scalp with Two ears," rather than the live slave. Free persons who captured a runaway "grown Man Slave . . . on the Southside of the Altamaha River" and more than twenty miles from his plantation won a five pound sterling reward for the live slave, or a one pound sterling reward for the dead slave's "scalp with Two Ears." There was no reward for the scalp of female or minor slave runaways.[194] The statute also permitted the *courts* to execute slaves "deserting out of this province." Reimbursements were made to the master out of the public treasury.[195]

The comprehensiveness of the runaway slave provision illustrates how irrelevant were the human rights of the slave. The assembly's primary concern was to preserve the slave system by deterring any slaves "who will be tempted to desert from their masters." Perhaps the Georgia legislature thought it was demonstrating "human compassion" by not offering rewards for the scalp and ears of women and children. In Georgia one could not profit from killing a "woman, boy or girl above the age of twelve years." For in that category they had to be "brought [back] a Live"; the reward for bringing a woman, boy, or girl above the age of twelve years found on the south side of the Altamaha River was two pounds sterling; however, if one killed a "grown man slave" and brought back his scalp and two ears, the reward was one pound—half that provided for returning a woman, boy, or girl alive. Thus, the Georgia legislative equation was: 1 *dead* grown man runaway slave $= \frac{1}{2}$ *live* woman or child slave.[196]

While almost all the records of judicial decisions during this period have been destroyed, the minutes of the Governor's Council, the Georgia Court of Appeals, did include discussion of a few cases. In one 1763 case of a slave who had murdered his overseer Alexander Crawford, the council offered bounty hunters a ten pound sterling reward for returning the fugitive slave alive, and a five pound sterling reward "in case the said Negro shall be killed in the Attempt to apprehend him."[197] Since the account does not mention the conviction of the slave, it is probable that no trial had occurred.

Assaults on Slaves

The assembly expressed their "humanitarian" concerns for blacks by providing that if any person

> wilfully cut the Tongue put out the Eye Castrate or Cruelly Scald burn or deprive any Slave of any Limb or Member or shall inflict any other Cruel punishment other than by whipping or beating with a Horse Whip Cow Skin Switch or Small Stick or by putting Irons on or Confining or Imprisoning such Slave every such person shall for every such Offence forfeit the Sum of Ten pounds Sterling.[198]

However, in those rare instances when such cruelty could be proven, the maximum penalty was merely a fine. Furthermore, the acts of whipping or beating, even if done cruelly, were not crimes under this provision.[199] The statute added another fine of six shillings if a slave was "beaten Bruised Maimed or Disabled," at the hands of "any person or persons not having sufficient Cause or Lawfull Authority for so doing." In such cases the master was entitled to reimbursement for his economic loss. However, these cruel acts of bruising, maiming, or disabling became a crime only when perpetrated without the master's authorization. Thus, the determining factor was not the slave's well-being, but solely whether an outsider was damaging the master's economic interest in the slave.[200]

Theoretically, the law benignly shifted the burden of proof to the murderer or assaulter of slaves "when no white person was present, or if present he refused to give evidence under oath." However, if a person simply gave a "clear" oath that exculpated himself, then the state had the burden of proof.[201]

Slaves as Defendants

The law also named as capital crimes when committed by slaves various new deeds, many of which would have elicited less severe punishment, or none at all, under the former law. Every homicide of a white person by a slave resulted in that slave's execution, except when he had acted by a "misadventure [i.e., by accident] or in defense of his master or other person under whose care and government such slave shall be."[202] Technically, any slave who killed a white person in order to defend himself, his family, a fellow slave, or a white third party had to be executed. The courts or government could grant no mercy in such cases.

In addition, a slave could be executed if he "raise[d] or attempt[ed] to raise an Insurrection in this Province or endeavor[ed] to delude or entice any slave to run away and leave thie Province," or if he acted as an accomplice, aider, or abettor to anyone else who had run away.[203] Death could likewise be imposed if a slave "greviously wound[ed] maim[ed] or bruise[d] any white person";[204] was convicted for the third time of striking a white person;[205] or, as we have seen, if he attempted to run away from his master out of the province.[206]

Finally, it was a capital offense for a slave, a free black, a mulatto, a mestizo, and certain of the Indians[207] to "willfully and Maliciously burn or destroy any Stack of Rice corn or other grain of the product growth or Manufacture of this province";[208] "feloniously Steal any Slave being the property of Another";[209] "willfully and Maliciously poison or administer any poison to any person";[210] or "willfully or Maliciously set fire to burn or destroy any tar kiln Barrels of pitch Tar Turpentine or Rozin, or any other goods or commodities of the growth produce of manufactures of this Province."[211]

Our analysis indicates that in those instances when a slave was convicted of a capital crime, in not one case did an appeal to the governor's council (the appeals court of Georgia) reverse the conviction or grant mercy to the slave.[212] Fortunately, despite the number of offenses that theoretically warranted the death penalty, the evidence available suggests that the Georgia courts seldom imposed that extreme sentence. One method by which one can determine the number of court-ordered executions is through a survey of Georgia tax laws, which recorded reimbursements to masters for the value of slaves executed pursuant to judicial decrees. A review of these statutes shows few reimbursements.[213]

However, the fact that there were few instances of master reimbursement tells us very little about the value the legal system placed on the life of the slave. Tax laws, for example, would not record instances, which were many, where slaves were "legally killed" by their masters, bounty hunters, or third parties, since no reimbursements were made to masters in such cases. Moreover, the paucity of judicially approved executions is probably explained by the court's desire to protect the master's property, rather than its recognition of the value of the life of the slave.

One 1765 case illustrates that when there were executions they were highly publicized to put fear into the minds of any other slave who dared violate the law. "[T]hree runaway Negro fellows, and to [sic] Negro Wenches" were charged with murdering "Durham Hancock A White Man and an Indian Fellow" and reportedly confessed to the murders. The governor

> proposed that Directions be sent to Mr. Baillie to cause the said Negroes to be tried for the said Murder comformable to the Directions of the Negro Law and on Conviction that Execution of them be in various Ports of the Province as an Example; And to invite the Indians to see the Executions; and acquaint them that the Invitation is in Consequence of the late Treaty made at Augusta Which was approved of by the Board.[214]

The directive of having the execution "in various Parts of the Province as an Example" no doubt reflects the desire of the colony to publicize for deterrent purposes such executions.

Trial Procedures for Slaves

The 1755 law also established special criminal procedures for the trial of slaves. In capital cases, two justices of the peace and from three to five freeholders "examined tried adjudged and finally determined" the cases.[215] The number was lowered to one justice and two freeholders in noncapital cases.[216] So that the master would not lose the labor of his slave, the slave had to be brought to trial within three days of his apprehension.[217] The testimony of a freed Indian or a slave "without oath" was admissible at the trial but, of course, only because they were testifying against a slave.[218] Upon the conviction of a slave, the constable might enlist other slaves to do the actual inflicting of the punishment. Slaves so enlisted who refused to inflict the punishment against the defendant could themselves be punished for their refusal.[219] This latter provision was also part of the deterrent process, the logic being that a slave who was forced to whip or even execute a fellow slave was vividly reminded that total submission was a slave's only safe option.

The list of legal restrictions on the everyday activities of slaves was extensive. Slaves could not travel outside Savannah or their own plantation without a ticket or letter from their master.[220] Nor could they travel in groups of more than seven slaves without a "White person."[221] They could not "buy, sell, or exchange any goods, wares, provision, grains, victuals, or commodities of any sort or kind whatsoever," unless they lived or worked in Savannah and had a special license.[222] They could not carry firearms during the week without a ticket and the supervision of a white person, and from sundown Saturday to sunrise Monday they could not carry firearms under any circumstances.[223] Slaves also could not keep any "boat, perryauger or canoe";[224] breed any "Horse Mares and Neat Cattle";[225] or "Rent or Hire any house Room Store or plantation on his or her own Account."[226]

Particularly revealing was the prohibition against teaching a slave to read or write—an act that elicited a penalty of fifteen pounds sterling. Previously, the trustees had not only permitted the education of Georgia slaves, but had affirmatively financed a catechist for their instruction.[227] Now, the financial penalty for teaching a slave was 50 percent greater than that for willfully castrating or cutting off the limb of a slave.[228]

The law did detail several obligations of the master for the care of slaves. A master could not work his slaves on Sunday (unless there were "works of absolute necessity [or] occasions of the family . . .")[229] or during the rest of the week for more than sixteen hours a day.[230] Violations could bring a penalty of up to six-teen shillings and three pounds, respectively. A master also had to provide his slave with "sufficient" food and clothing, on penalty of three pounds.[231] However, Georgia officials almost never enforced these restrictions.[232] And even when they did, the penalties could not have been burdensome in contrast to the ten pound fine for those whose only crime was teaching a slave to read and write.

Finally, the manumission of a slave was not prohibited or reg-ulated under the 1755 law or even under the later and more strin-gent 1765 and 1770 codes. In contrast to several other states, colo-nial Georgia never required the posting of security for the welfare of a slave whom the master desired to manumit; nor was there any requirement that the legislature approve the manumission or that the freed slave be transported out of the state. Copies of Geor-gia colonial wills reveal that a few slaves were freed throughout the post-1750 colonial period, though the overall number was minuscule.[233]

PATROL SYSTEMS

While the legal restraints on slaves tightened with the passage of royal Georgia's first slave code, the colony lacked the organiza-tion for physically monitoring the increasing number of black slaves. The first law passed to provide for direct oversight of blacks was a 1755 act regulating the militia.[234] One provision in that act noted the vulnerability of "many inland places [which] . . . are frequently infested with fugitive Slaves, whose sudden attempts may prove fatal to many of his majesty's subjects before Notice can be given to his Majesty's Governor. . . ."[235] To deal with this prob-lem, commissioned officers in the militia received special powers to enlist militia members "to disperse, suppress, kill, destroy, appre-hend take or subdue . . . any Company of Slaves, who shall be met together, or who Shall be lurking in any suspected places, where they may do Mischief or who shall have absented themselves from the Service of their Owners."[236] By prohibiting "mischief" without first defining it, the statute granted commissioned officers dictatorial powers over slaves discovered outside their plantation.

Ironically, the law also sought to use slaves to help defend the colony. While the trustees had originally prohibited slavery par-

tially because of Georgia's uncertain military position, now royal
Georgia chose to use slaves in the militia for similar reasons. Annually, every slave owner had to provide the captain or commanding officer of the local company of militia with a list of all his male
slaves from the ages sixteen to sixty. The governor could order the
enlistment of those slaves "which Shall be Recommended . . . by
the respective Owners or Managers of such Slaves to be most faithful and fit for Service,"[237] which ensured the military dependability
of enlisted slaves. By an additional limit, the total number of slaves
in a particular company could not exceed one-third the number of
white men.[238] Owners could not arm their slaves for service until a
"Time of General Alarm and Actual Invasion."[239]

The government was obligated to pay masters one shilling per
day for each day of service by an inducted slave and full compensation for the injury or death of a slave, compensation due the
master for the loss of his property.[240] In contrast, masters of *white
servants* received no compensation for their servants' induction or injuries, thereby further decreasing the profitability of white servants
as against black slaves, since masters of white servants would not
be compensated for their loss.[241] Normally, the servants, slaves, and
freemen who actually served in the militia were also not paid for
their service. In all probability the favorable treatment given masters of slaves exemplifies the legislature's bias toward the wealthier
class.[242] They were to suffer the least economic loss from the common defense of all.

The law did reward slaves, poor freemen, and servants "who
shall behave themselves manfully in fight against the enemy." "Poor
freeman or White Servant who shall boldly and chearfully oppose
the common Enemy, and Shall in fight happen to be maimed or disabled from Labour" received nine pounds annually, or thirteen if
married. In the event of their death their wife (or where there is no
widow, their children below the age of twelve) received nine pounds
annually.[243] Any slaves (or white servant) who should "manfully
Behave themselves in fight with the enemy . . . so as to deserve
public Notice . . . shall be entitled to and receive from the public
Treasury Yearly, and every Yr. a Livery Coat, and pair of Breeches,
made of good red Negro Cloth turn'd up with Blue, and a Black
Hat and pair of Black Shoes, and shall that Day in every Year (dur-

ing their Lives) on which such Action Shall be perform'd be free'd
and exempted from all personal Labour & Service to their owner or
Manager."[244] In the special case when slaves (or white servants)
"shall actually engage the Enemy, in times of Invasion of this Province, and Shall Couragiously behave themselves in Battle so as to
kill any one of the Enemy, or take a prisoner alive or Shall take any
of their Colours" the heroes would be freed, and their masters reimbursed for their loss out of the public treasury.[245] Theoretically,
Georgia government not only permitted manumissions, but mandated them in special circumstances.

Two years after the militia law was passed, the legislature enacted two new laws that were intended to increase even further the
supervision of slaves. One of these laws created a "watch" in Savannah, and the other, more extensive law established a slave patrol
system throughout the province.

The statute for Savannah made all Savannah male inhabitants
between sixteen and sixty liable to do watch duty. Each night from
five to ten men were to keep watch from nine o'clock to sunrise.

> And Whereas it may prove of dangerous Consequence to the
> Peace and Security of the said Town to suffer Negroes and
> other Slaves to be lurking and caballing about the Streets of
> the said Town after night, for preventing whereof & that all
> negroes & other Slaves who go abroad may be known Be it
> Enacted by the authority aforesaid that if any Negroes or
> other Slaves shall after the hour of ten O'clock be found in
> any of the Streets, Lanes, Alleys or other places in Savannah
> without a Ticket from his or their Master Owner or Overseer
> it shall & may be lawfull for the said Watch aforesaid to whip
> such Negroe or other Slave as is directed in and by the Negroe
> Law of this province made & provided . . .[246]

The second patrol law was more comprehensive and specifically intended "for the better keeping of Negroes and other Slaves
in Order and prevention of any Cabals Insurrections or other Irregularities amongst them. . . ."[247] It subdivided each militia "company district" (created under 1755 militia law) into "patrol dis-
tricts," which could be no wider than twelve miles. The commanding
officer of each company made up a patrol list of all male white

residents and female plantation owners in the district.[248] On every "muster day" the commanding officer of each patrol district chose from the list no more than seven male persons between the ages of sixteen and sixty to do service.

The patrols in each district were to "go to and examine" *every* plantation at least once a month. They could "take up" and whip up to twenty lashes any slave

> which they shall see without the Fences or cleared Ground of their Owners Plantations, who have not a Ticket or Letter or other Token to shew the reasonableness of their Absence or who have not some white Person in Company to give an Account, of his her or their business . . .[249]

The penalty for beating or abusing a slave not fitting this description was ten shillings to be paid to the master. Patrols could "search and examine all Negro Houses for offensive Weapons and Ammunition,"[250] enter any "disorderly tipling-house, or other house suspected of harboring, trafficing or dealing with negroes, either of white persons, free negroes or others," and "apprehend and correct all disorderly Slaves there found by whiping as hereinbefore directed. . . ."[251]

THE 1765 AND 1770 SLAVE CODES

While most of the provisions in the main 1755 slave law were continued in the 1765 and 1770 slave laws, both of those later laws introduced several harsher provisions that progressively tightened the restraints on blacks.[252] The greatest number of changes appeared in the new list of capital crimes that could be committed by "slaves, free negroes, Indians, mulattoes, or mestizoes." Both the 1765 and 1770 laws held that it was a capital offense for a slave, free black, mulatto, or mestizo to fail to reveal "the furnishing, procuring, or conveying of any poison to be administered to any person"; to "teach or instruct another Slave in the Knowledge of any Poisonous Root, Plant, Herb, or other sort of a poison whatever"; or to be convicted for the *second* time of striking a white person.[253] A slave who was "convicted of having given false information, whereby any other slave may have suffered wrongfully" would "suffer the same punishment as was inflicted upon the party accused," including death.[254]

Under the 1770 statute any slave, free black, mulatto, mestizo, or Indian (not in amity with the government) could be executed if he should attempt to rape or rape any white person; "break open, burn or destroy any dwelling house or other building whatsoever"; or be "accomplices, aiders, and abettors" of anyone who did.[255] The 1770 law also made several capital crimes, which had formerly pertained only to slaves, applicable to free blacks, mulattoes, mestizos, and some Indians.[256]

Many of the modest protections of slaves written into the 1755 code were dropped from the 1765 and 1770 laws. After 1765, there was no requirement that a slave's work day be limited to sixteen hours or that he be provided with "sufficient" food and clothing. After 1770 the provision shifting the burden of proof in certain cases to the person accused of assaulting a slave disappeared. The 1755 limitation on the permissible number of slaves for each white servant on a plantation was modified by both laws to permit more slaves.[257]

A few new provisions in the 1765 and 1770 laws were a marginal improvement for blacks. One provided that a person convicted for the first time of willfully killing a slave should, in addition to paying the fine imposed in the 1755 law, be "forever uncapable of holding any place of Trust, or exercising, enjoying or receiving the profits of any Office, place or employment, civil or Military within this Province."[258] Another unique provision contained in the 1765 law but dropped in 1770 provided that mulattoes and mestizos born outside Georgia should under certain circumstances be admitted into Georgia with many of the rights of British citizens.[259] This relatively benign statutory policy toward mulattoes was a sign of the new colony's uncertain military position. The threat of slave or Indian uprisings as well as external attack made the immigration of free mulattoes seem militarily advantageous to the Georgia legislators. Unfortunately, the provision never aided mulattoes since no one was ever naturalized during the life of the act. When the legislators wrote the 1770 slave law they dropped the protection from the code.[260]

TAXATION OF DOMESTIC AND IMPORTED SLAVES

Throughout the colonial period, Georgia never adopted a tax policy designed to discourage the enslavement of blacks through taxation. Though masters paid taxes on their slaves, the rates were moderate and the main objective of the levies was undoubtedly to raise revenue, rather than discourage slavery.

The 1750 law taxed masters one shilling for each black slave twelve years or older.[261] Later, head taxes on "all Negroes and other slaves" were enacted in 1755,[262] 1757,[263] 1758 (with some variation),[264] 1759,[265] and 1760.[266] The rate of taxation rose during the period until it was two shillings six pence in 1760 for all blacks within the province. Since the taxes applied to "all Negroes and other slaves within the limits of this Province," it appears that both free blacks and the masters of slaves were subject to the same level of taxation.[267]

There was an ambiguity in Georgia's dealings with free blacks after this point. By the 1765 slave code it granted several citizenship privileges to immigrating free mulattoes.[268] Yet three years later it established a special fifteen shilling tax on all "free Negroes, Mulattoes, and Mustizoes" over the age of sixteen within the province. At the same time, the tax on masters remained at the relatively low level of two shillings six pence per slave. Thus, a free mulatto was taxed six times more than a master was taxed per slave.[269] In order to prevent mulattoes from escaping the levy, the 1768 law also placed the burden on persons alleged to be mulattoes or mestizos to prove that they were not subject to the tax.[270]

Those laws we have located on the taxation of imported slaves demonstrate no desire by the legislature to restrict the importation of slaves in colonial Georgia, when there was a limited supply of slaves. For example, the 1750 trustee slavery law placed a tax of fifteen shillings on every slave over twelve who was imported for sale, a sharp contrast to the South Carolina levy of one pound, eight shillings, six pence, three farthings sterling.[271]

LAWS ON THE HIRING OF BLACKS

Georgia also strictly limited the type of occupations in which slaves or blacks could be employed. The first such law was passed in 1758, and had as its purpose "to encourage White Tradesman to Settle in the Several Towns within this Province of Georgia by preventing the employing of negroes and other Slaves being handicraft Tradesman in the said Towns."[272] No person could hire "any Negroe or other Slave in any handicraft trade in any of the towns of Georgia," though there were some exceptions.[273] Fearing the extent to which this discrimination would raise the fees of white tradesmen, which was, of course, one of the objects of the law, the drafters of the law established a Board of Commissioners to limit and set rates for "all Carpenters Joiners Bricklayers and Plaisterers . . . or other Tradesmens worn where the prices of the same can be Ascertained. . . ."[274]

In 1774 the legislature passed a law regulating and licensing the hire of slaves as laborers or porters in Savannah. Slaves "sent out for hire" could be required to constantly wear a public badge. They were to go to the Savannah Market House for employment by the "break of day" and remain until employed. A fee schedule was to be established by the commissioners appointed under the statute. Any slave sent for hire who did not go to the marketplace or refused to work at the proper time or at the rates set by the commissioners could receive up to thirty lashes on his bare back.[275]

The list of other colonial laws discriminating against blacks and slaves is extensive. No black, mulatto, or mestizo could legally serve as constables after 1759[276] or vote after 1761.[277] Under a 1759 statute no slave could "brand or Mark any horses or Neat Cattle but in the presence of some white person under the penalty of being severely whiped . . ."[278] A 1773 law prohibited any slave from driving "any Horses or Neat Cattle from their usual place of Feeding" on penalty of not more than thirty-nine lashes, unless he possessed a ticket from his master.[279]

In 1763 the Georgia legislature established a special "work house for the custody and Punishment of Negroes" where convicted slaves, runaway slaves, or simply "incorrigible" slaves (as adjudged by their masters) could be sent for incarceration and/or punishment.[280] One 1773 statute detailing the fees of various public officers provided a lower reimbursement for the meals served by the provost marshal to black prisoners than those served to white prisoners.

Diet of White Persons each day allowing One pound of Flesh and two pounds of Bread all Wholesome provisions Ten pence. Dieting Negroes each day; Six pence Three Farthings.[281]

Georgia: An Evaluation

The staunch defense of slavery by the Georgia delegates at the Constitutional Convention[282] reveals no hint that the delegates or the colony of Georgia had ever questioned the desirability or legality of slavery. At the convention there were no references to the fact that once slavery was prohibited during Georgia's early years. Yet the colony's history reveals dramatic changes from when slavery was banned in 1735 to the time of its legalization and the imposition of many statutory restrictions against blacks. In retrospect, the reversal was not totally unpredictable. The original slave prohibition never enjoyed the support of the Georgia population. When experience showed that the prohibition imposed economic hardships on whites, administrative and judicial officials increasingly failed to enforce the law, and the general population argued vehemently for its repeal. The trustees' vision of a nonslave, self-sufficient debtor colony proved to be unrealistic and the trustees were never able to formulate a more workable but humane policy for the colony.

After slavery was permitted, the diverse nature of Georgia's antislavery past presented, at best, an ambiguous precedent for the protection of blacks. The purpose of the antislavery law had not been to aid the welfare of blacks, but merely to further what the trustees believed were the social, economic, and military interests of whites. Moreover, experience had shown the trustees' interpretation of white Georgians' interests to be misguided, or so most Georgians felt. The subsequent termination of the trustees' authority over the colony weakened Georgia's link with even this modestly humanitarian past. Released from the restraints imposed by the trustees' authority, Georgia could follow what it believed were the true social and economic interests of the colony. The result was the imposition of a slave code ultimately as harsh as any found elsewhere in America.

7

PENNSYLVANIA
THE QUAKER AND GERMAN LIBERAL INFLUENCE

Introduction

IN 1688, prior to any enactment by the Pennsylvania legislature or any decision of any court of the area sanctioning slavery in Pennsylvania, a small group of German Mennonites and Quakers gathered near Philadelphia to consider the morality of this institution. The resolution passed by this congregation condemned the "traffic of Men-body" and stood as the first recorded official protest against slavery in any of the American colonies:

> we hear that the most part of such negers are brought hither against their will and consent, and that many of them are stolen. Now, though they are black, we cannot conceive there is more liberty to have them slaves, as it is to have other white ones. There is a saying that we should do to all men like as we will be done ourselves; making no difference of what generation, descent, or colour they are. And those who steal or rob men, and those who buy or purchase them, are they not all alike?[1]

Protests such as this would become increasingly frequent in Pennsylvania as the legal and social foundations of slavery solidified, making the development of slavery in Pennsylvania somewhat different from that in the southern slave states and the other northern colonies. Pennsylvania enjoyed the distinction of sponsoring the first organized protest against slavery in the colonies. A century later the Pennsylvania Society for Promoting Abolition of Slavery was organized with Benjamin Franklin as its president, and again Pennsylvania was the forerunner in establishing organized abolition societies. The number of manumissions undertaken by masters in Pennsylvania was probably greater than that in any other colony and the taxes on the importation of slaves, for various reasons, were in comparison with others also higher. As a consequence of these political factors, as well as other economic factors, Pennsylvania, though the most southern of the major northern colonies, generally counted within its population a smaller percentage of blacks and black slaves than New York, New Jersey, Maryland, or Delaware. This relatively small number made Pennsylvania a definite exception to the "rule" that the farther south one traveled, the larger the percentage of black slaves.[2]

In 1780 the abolitionists in Pennsylvania achieved perhaps their most significant triumph with the passage of the gradual emancipation statute, the first statute enacted in the eighteenth century to abolish slavery in any American colony.[3] John Hope Franklin describes the character of race relations in the Quaker colony as one of "some respect for blacks as human beings" with an absence of "the wholesale and indiscriminate enslavement of black people." Pennsylvania was "relatively free from violence and interracial strife. . . ." He emphasizes that in Pennsylvania "the Negro family achieved a stability unlike that reached by blacks in most English colonies."[4]

Despite Pennsylvania's more liberal attitude, the gap between the political rhetoric of the colonial period and the legal realities for blacks was often monumental. In this chapter we will examine the extent to which the social, economic, and political forces antagonistic to slavery actually had a substantive effect on Pennsylvania's legal treatment of blacks. Before 1700, when there was no statutory recognition of slavery, this assessment is confined to tentative interpretations of somewhat ambiguous judicial and statutory materials on white indentured servants and on black "servants," who were probably slaves. In the 1700s, after the Pennsylvania legislature had given direct statutory sanction to slavery and explicit direction to the regulation of blacks, we can determine more directly the legal regard for both free and enslaved blacks in the Quaker colony.

Throughout the period, two persistent themes stand out. First, although the well-publicized opposition to slavery in Pennsylvania was effective in partially limiting the pervasiveness and repressiveness of slavery, it was inadequate in preventing the actual development and solidification of a racial slave system in the Quaker colony. Prophetically, the very first antislavery petition of the German Mennonites was *not* adopted by the monthly, quarterly, or yearly Quaker meetings because, in the words of the monthly meeting, "we think it not expedient for us to meddle with it here."[5]

Quaker Pennsylvania followed Virginia, South Carolina, New York, and Massachusetts in legislatively and judicially sanctioning racial slavery within its borders. As Edward Turner has written in his definitive work, *The Negro in Pennsylvania,*

> the upholders of the idea that Negroes should be held only as servants, for a term of years, waged a losing fight. It is true that they did not desist, and in the course of one hundred years their view won a complete triumph; but their success came in abolition, and in overthrowing a system established, long after they had utterly failed to prevent the swift growth and the statutory recognition of legal slavery for life and in perpetuity.[6]

Second, the legal treatment of *free* blacks in colonial Pennsylvania appears to have been as restrictive and discriminatory as in any other colony—a sign perhaps that the antislavery forces were concerned more with the symbol of slavery than with the well-being of all blacks. For "crimes" as relatively benign as marrying a white person, engaging in interracial sexual intercourse, loitering on the street, or simply being under the age of twenty-one, free blacks were sold into indentured servitude or slavery. Thus, despite the existence of a determined movement to end the enslavement of blacks in the colony, not only did Pennsylvania's legal system steadfastly defend the enslavement of blacks, but it severely restricted and punished those blacks who escaped that system.

SLAVERY IN PRE-1700 PENNSYLVANIA

Before William Penn and the Quakers ever arrived in what was to become Pennsylvania, racial slavery—or at least lifetime servitude for blacks—already existed in the area around the Delaware River. There were reports of blacks (of unidentified status) in the region as early as 1639[7] and later references made to the holding of black slaves along the Delaware by the Dutch of New Netherlands and the Swedes.[8] One of the earliest records we have of a black in Pennsylvania refers in 1664 to a Negro named Anthony in the service of Governor Prince, caring for his cattle and accompanying him on his yacht.[9] Interestingly, according to the Virginia records, one of the first blacks to arrive in Virginia, in 1619, was also named Anthony.[10]

Slavery received statutory recognition for a brief period after the Pennsylvania region passed under English authority in 1664. For the regulation of this area as well as New York, the British passed the Duke of York's Laws, which gave indirect legislative sanction to the holding of slaves.[11] While these laws "were not passed by the people of the country and [were] not typical of the state of thought and feeling either in Pa. or in Deleware,"[12] there is evidence that they were enforced in the Delaware River region of Pennsylvania after 1676.[13] Thus, it is significant that the Duke of York's Laws prohibited any Christian—but not *non*-Christians—from being

> kept in Bond Slavery, Villenage or Captivity except Such as shall be judged thereunto by Authority or Such as willingly have sould or shall sell themselves. . . . Provided that nothing in This Law conteyned shall be to the prejudice of Master or Dame who have or shall by Any Indenture or Covenant take Apprentices for terme of yeares or Other Servants for terme of yeares or life; *And also provided that This Law shall not extend to sett at liberty Any Negroe or Indian Servant who shall turne Christian after he shall have been bought by Any Person.*[14]

This language gave direct statutory recognition to "Bond Slavery" and "Servants for . . . life," while, at the same time, it specifically excluded heathens—which, practically speaking, meant all blacks—from the freedom accorded to Christians. This policy toward blacks was somewhat similar to that outlined in the 1641 Massachusetts Body of Liberties,[15] which made exceptions to its general prohibition against slavery that also could have—paradoxically—justified racial slavery. The Duke of York's Laws, however, made it even more certain that "Negroes or Indian servants" were not to be the beneficiaries of its freedoms, since it *specifically* excluded blacks or Indians who should "turne Christian" after their enslavement from the freedoms accorded to every other Christian. Thus, the Duke of York's Laws avoided much of the ambiguity concerning black slavery that existed under the 1641 Massachusetts statute; the clear implication was that the enslavement of blacks was legal, while the enslavement of whites was not.

Although this limited statutory recognition of slavery ended soon after William Penn and the Quakers arrived in Pennsylvania in 1682 and the Duke of York's Laws were superseded by Pennsylvania laws, *de facto* slavery continued in the Quaker colony. In 1684, for example, a Cornelius Bonn had a black whom he "bought," and a William Pomfret had among his goods "one man" who was evidently a black slave.[16] In the legal records, the Court of Upland mentions in a 1677 list of "Tradable Persons" one "James Sanderling and slave."[17] Similarly, a black valued at thirty pounds in a 1686 lawsuit was probably a slave.[18]

Indeed, Penn tacitly recognized the institution of slavery when he failed to oppose a provision of the bylaws of the Free Society of Traders in 1682, implicitly sanctioning certain forms of slavery. While the provision allowed the society to free any of its black "servants," it required as a condition that they give the society's warehouse two-thirds of the crops they produced on the land allotted to them by the society with their freedom. If they were unwilling to accept the terms, the blacks were obliged to remain "servants" until they changed their minds, which could have led to slavery for life.[19] Later, in 1685, William Penn wrote his steward that it was preferable to have blacks to work on his farms because "a man has them while they live."[20] Three years later, in 1688, the famous German Mennonite protest against slavery took place.

Despite the public evidence of the use of black slaves in the colony, the precise legal status of blacks during this pre-1700 period can be determined only indirectly. Before 1700 no court or legislature took an explicit position on the legality of slavery; nor did they define precisely the status or rights of either enslaved or free blacks in comparison with the rights of whites in the legal hierarchy.

There is no evidence that black indentured servants or slaves were held for anything except lifelong terms,[21] in contrast to conditions in Virginia where records indicate that many of its early blacks were probably indentured servants for a limited term.[22] Despite the perpetuity of their servitude, however, Pennsylvania black slaves enjoyed some of the rights accorded to freemen and white indentured servants in other colonies. They were tried in the same courts and by the same judges as were whites, were subject to some of the same laws, and for similar acts often received the same punishments.

Several cases demonstrate the fact that prior to 1700 the Pennsylvania courts used the same judicial procedure for blacks and whites. In a 1687 case regarding Prudence, "The negro of An fforeft," the Bucks County court "oblidged" Prudence to "appeare at this Court." The fact that Prudence had "departed the same without examination" led the court to order "that warrant to Issue to apprehend the Said Negro for the apprehending & for the Safe Keeping of the Said negro, that She may [answer] all such Complaints as Shall be layd against her. . . ." Thus, Prudence was charged and was to be tried in the regular Bucks court, where "she may [answer] all such Complaints as Shall be layd against her. . . ."[23] In another 1687 case tried in the Sussex County court, a "negro" named Francis Jnoson successfully sued William Orion, who was evidently white, and received a judgment of twenty shillings. The subject of the dispute is not identified. Jnoson appeared in court against Orion for, according to the account, he "verbally complained agst Wm. Orion . . . [and there was] pleading to on both sides [before] the court passed judgment. . . ."[24]

The Jnoson case is important not only in its revelation concerning the procedural rights of blacks, but also because it suggests that blacks may have been treated similarly to whites in the substantive and sentencing determinations of the courts. A 1687 court decision punishing two runaways, "a negro man and a white woman servant," may be another example. The two runaways were "taken" and brought before the same judge, John Simcocke, "Justice in

Commission for runaways." Simcocke found that "they had no law-full passes [and] committed them to prison. . . ." They were both "delivered by order of Court into ye custody of Thomas Smith and John Henson with a black nagg."[25] This brief record reveals not only that the same passes were required of white or black servants, but that black and white violators of the same requirements were tried in the same courts, if not in the same proceedings; and that, at least in this case, they probably received the same punishment.

A 1677 case implied that the courts did not punish premarital interracial sexual activity more severely than it did intraracial pre-marital sex. Richard Duckett, the servant of Lace Cock, was in-dicted in 1677 because he "hath Kept Company & got with Child a certaine molato wooman called Swart anna. . . . Contrary to the Lawes of the Government and Contrary to his Masters Con-sent. . . ." Richard confessed, but he claimed that he had acted with the intention of marrying Anna and "Ingages to the Court to maintain the said child as soon he is free etc. . . ." The court par-doned Richard because of his "humiliation" and his master's plea that he not be punished.[26]

This account suggests that the court's decision was not condi-tioned by the interracial component of the violation. The court never mentioned the race of the female as grounds for special or more harsh punishment and indeed imposed no punishment upon the defendant. Richard's assertion that his intention to marry Anna should be a mitigating factor would imply that it was the illicit na-ture of the sex that was legally significant, not the race of the par-ticipants. That the lack of consent from the master was also cited as a factor would likewise suggest that the status of the servant, not his race, was the determining factor. Moreover, Richard must have ex-pected no judicial penalty against the offspring of this union, who would have been a mulatto, since he "Ingages to the Court to main-tain the . . . child" until he is free—presumably because he wanted to raise the child himself. This treatment by the court pro-vides a strong contrast to the excessive punishments already im-posed by the Virginia courts by this time against blacks convicted of interracial fornication.[27]

While the case of Richard Duckett may support the hypothesis that blacks were not identified for special judicial penalties in seventeenth-century Pennsylvania, several other cases suggest a developing discrimination against blacks. In a 1702 case, for example, a Bucks County court found a Negro slave called Hugo and a white woman named Sarah Cooper guilty of commiting fornication. Sarah had had a bastard child, evidently from this union. The court ordered that Hugo be "whipped with twenty one lashes upon his bare back well laid on" and that Sarah receive the same punishment. However, had Sarah been able to "pay a fine as the law in this case directs," the court noted, she could have escaped the corporal punishment. Thus, in this case the court gave the white defendant the option to pay a fine and avoid the corporal punishment that was mandatory for the black. Moreover, in this case the court imposed some punishment on both Hugo and Sarah, although the court in the Duckett and Anna case imposed no penalty on either defendant for committing (interracial) fornication. This decision not to pardon the defendants may have been attributable to a growing hostility toward interracial premarital sex and to the fact that Hugo was a black male and Sarah a white female, while Duckett was a white male and Anna a black female.[28]

In 1698 a Chester court took an even harsher view toward the "commingling" of the races. A black man and white woman were charged with having a bastard child. Both parties testified that the white woman had "intised" the black and promised to marry him. While the court held that the white woman should receive "twenty one lashes on her beare Backe" it also "ordered the negro never more to meddle with any white women *upon pane of his life.*"[29] Thus, a second conviction of the black for having premarital sex with any white female could have led to his execution, even if both parties had acted voluntarily. The decree illustrates the fact that interracial premarital sex was cause for brutal punishments, and that those punishments were imposed only on the black male violators; the court certainly did not threaten the white woman with loss of *her* life for future sexual violations. The ruling also suggests that interracial sex between black males and white females was the object of harsher punishments than interracial sex involving white males and black females, for it is unlikely that these punishments would have been imposed in the latter type of relationship. It is inconceivable, moreover, that a court would ever have executed or threatened to execute a white man for engaging in sex with a black woman.

A 1688 case demonstrates the courts' early efforts to grapple with the competing priorities and policy alternatives presented by the punishment of slaves:[30] should a slave who had committed a criminal offense be subject to the same, a lesser, or a harsher penalty than that for which an indentured servant would be liable? The issue was further complicated by the fact that the slave was also a fugitive from another state and his master was neither known nor locatable for the proceeding. The defendant, George, a runaway slave from Virginia,[31] was tried in the Pennsylvania courts where he pled guilty to three counts of theft. The Pennsylvania court issued a multifaceted judgment. Just as it would have ordered physical punishment of an indentured servant for a theft, it ordered that George be whipped—but much more severely than the standard punishment for white indentured servants. Just as it would have protected the victim of a theft by requiring additional servitude by a white indentured servant to reimburse the victim, it also imposed servitude on George—but here again, the penalty (of fifteen years) was much more severe than that for a white servant.[32] Presumably because the defendant's master was not known, the court let out the defendant to a new master, who was obligated to pay the court for the ultimate reimbursement to the victim of the theft.

At the end of its decision, the court ordered that after completion of his fifteen-year indenture, George should be returned to the Virginia master if the master should claim him. Thus, in 1688, the Pennsylvania courts were already honoring requests for runaway slaves. Indeed in this case, they did not even wait for the actual request before issuing the conditional order permitting the slave's return if the request should be made.

Another and much later case in which the Pennsylvania judicial system supported the return of runaway slaves occurred in 1738.[33] In this case, Daniel Cheston had arrived from Bonavista, one of the Cape de Verde Islands, with two of the Bonavista governor's black slaves whom Cheston had stolen. Cheston claimed his theft and other actions were justified because he had suffered "sundry Impositions and Abuses . . . from the Governour and Inhabitants of that Island. . . ." The Pennsylvania governor sought the advice of the provincial council, which was of the unanimous opinion

> that the said Cheston's behaviour was highly criminal, and a Breach of the Amity Subsisting between the King of Great Britain and the King of Portugal; And that the said Cheston ought to be obliged to enter into Security in the Penal Sum of Two Hundred pounds Sterling, conditioned for the returning of the said Negroes. . . . [I]f the said Cheston *shall refuse so to, . . . the Governour [should] issue his Warrant for committing him to Custody till he shall give such Security, and the Negroes be seized for the use of the Owner, and be returned by the first convenient Opportunity.*[34]

Cheston was subsequently jailed pending trial, but he returned the two Negroes to the Bonavista governor. The provincial council agreed to let him out on his own recognizance "in Consideration of the two Negroes being already returned. . . ."[35]

The first *explicit* legal restriction on blacks was recorded in 1693 and served as a harbinger for the racial restrictions on blacks that were to follow in the early 1700s. The Court of Quarter Sessions for the County of Philadelphia, acting on a "presentment" of the grand jury, directed

> the Constables of Philadelphia, or anie other person whatsoever, to have power to take up negroes, male or female, whom they should find gadding abroad on the first dayes of the week, without a tickett from their Mr. or Mris. or not in their Company, or to carry them to goale, there to remain that night, and that without meat or drink, and to cause them to be publickly whipt next morning, with 39 lashes well laid on, on their bare backs, for which their said Mr. or Mris, should pay 15d to the whipper att his deliverie of ym to their Mr. or Mris. and that the said order should be confirmed by the Lieut. Governor and Councill.[36]

Since the presentment required that all Negroes carry passes from their master, it is probable that its authors did not consider the distinction between free and enslaved blacks important. Technically, any person in Philadelphia could "take up" any Negro who was simply "gadding abroad" without a ticket from his master. The black was to be imprisoned overnight without food and given thirty-nine lashes, more physical punishment than white servants generally received for a major theft.[37]

It is appropriate to note, however, that the Pennsylvania 1693 presentment occurred more than thirty years after Virginia had enacted its far more harsh slave code, and comparatively, the Pennsylvania presentment was not as restrictive as the slave codes that had been already enacted in other colonies.[38] With continued complaints in Pennsylvania concerning the congregating and traveling of blacks without their masters, subsequent restrictions would be imposed in 1725, though they also would not be equal in their severity to the southern codes.

COMPARATIVE LEGAL STATUS OF 17TH-CENTURY WHITE SERVANTS AND BLACKS

The existence of greater restrictions on black servants than on white servants in seventeenth-century Pennsylvania, which is strongly suggested by these later cases, has not been adequately recognized. Historians have generally given Pennsylvania a "good press" in regard to its benign treatment of slaves, especially during this seventeenth-century period. Edward Turner, for example, writes authoritatively that before 1700 the Negro in Pennsylvania held for life was "subject to the same restrictions, tried in the same courts, and punished with the same punishments as white servants," leading him to conclude that the treatment of white servants and blacks was "nearly the same."[39] The only difference was the length of their servitude.

Of course, when compared with several other colonies, Pennsylvania may have been more liberal by statute and in practice. It may have had more residents opposed to slavery. It does not follow, however, that the Pennsylvania experience was one in which the legal process assured blacks the same protections accorded whites.

Turner's comparison of the treatment of white servants and black slaves ignores the fact that virtually all blacks during the pre-1700 period were slaves, while only a small proportion of whites were indentured servants. A comparison of blacks to white "servants" totally obscures many of the legal differences between blacks and whites as groups.

Moreover, Turner's extraordinary scholarship and detailed research ignores the overwhelming significance of the one difference between blacks and white "servants" he does admit to—namely, the length of their servitude. For Turner, this distinction between a *lifetime* of slavery for blacks in contrast to the limited terms of a *few* years that white servants had to endure meant that their legal status was "nearly the same." Yet this one exception was the critical factor in differentiating a system that was repressive *perpetually* versus one probably tolerable if it did not have to be endured more than a few years. Who would view a lifetime sentence as only slightly different than a three-year term? Who would consider a decree that all one's children be bound to slavery as nearly the same as one making no claim whatsoever on one's children? Think of the difference in hope, aspiration, and potential between the legal preclusion of any future freedom versus the ultimate assurance of full liberty. Perhaps blacks would have been far better off in Pennsylvania if slavery had been illegal, even if they were treated more harshly than whites but in exchange had only to serve a limited term of indenture. We submit that even benign slavery for life is a thousand times more harsh than a five-year indenture.

Even exclusive of the disparity in length of their servitudes, it is still very doubtful whether slaves and white servants were actually subjected to the same restrictions and punishments, as Turner asserts so vigorously. Several of the judicial decisions we have already discussed bring this argument into serious question. We submit further that there is abundant evidence to infer that the statutes on white servants, contrary to Turner's hypothesis, did not require that blacks be treated the same as white servants. Even in the seventeenth century there was no "separate but equal" concept applicable to black slaves and white servants; rather it was separate and *un*equal, separate and far more harsh. From our view, Turner's charitable construction of the indentured servitude statutes is suspect, and in all probability the indentured servitude statutes protected whites only.

For example, the first major law relating to servants, which was passed in 1682, provided

that Servants Shall not be kept Longer than their time and
Such as are Carefull shall Be boath Justly and Kindly Used in
their Service and put in fitting Equipage at the Expiration
thereof according to Custom . . . and if any Master abuse
his Servant on Complaint to the next Justices of the Peace he
shall take Care to redress the Said Grievance.

A registry of all servants was to be made "where theire Names time
Wages and days of freedom or Payment Shall be Registred."[40] Since
the law was intended to limit the "time" of servants, it is probable
that white indentured servants—rather than black "servants" or
slaves who were kept for life—were to be the beneficiaries of its
protection.

More comprehensive but equally ambiguous regulations of the
activities of "servants" and their masters were enacted in laws
passed in 1683 and 1692. No servants "bound to serve their time
in the Province of Pennsylvania" could be sold into another province, under penalty to the transgressing master of ten pounds and
return of the servant.[41] No "servant" imported into Pennsylvania
"without Indentures of Covenant" could be made to serve for more
than five years, or until the age of twenty-one if he or she was under sixteen upon entrance. Masters were also to provide "Every
Servant at the Expiration of their term," according to the custom
of the country, with "One new Sute of aparrell, tenn bushells of
wheat or 14 bushells of Indian-Corn, one Ax, two howes, one broad
& another narrow, and a discharge from their Service."[42] However,
once again, the inclusion of a provision regulating the time of servitude would suggest that slaves were not the object of the regulation.

A further suggestion that blacks were not the intended beneficiaries of these statutes can be gleaned from the judicial cases applying them during the period. We have not been able to uncover
one case where the sale, care, indenture, or discharge benefits of a
black slave or servant were litigated, though there are cases in
which white servants obtained judicial decrees against their masters to meet their obligations toward servants in all those categories.[43] Indeed, in one notable case a white individual charged
with harboring a runaway white servant was acquitted after evidence was admitted that the runaway he had sheltered had departed
from an abusive master.[44]

These laws also introduced various punishments whose purpose was to restrict the activity of "servants," though, once again, the exact definition of the term "servant" was left unclear. Servants could not "give, trust, sell or dispose" of their masters' goods without their consent[45] or "presume to travel or go without the Limits of the County wherein they reside, without a pass Or certificat Under the seal of that County. . . ."[46] Inhabitants who concealed a runaway servant were fined five shillings for every day of their protection, but won a twenty shilling reward from the owner if they captured or delivered a runaway to the sheriff and the justice of the peace.[47]

In only one provision did either of those laws, or for that matter any seventeenth-century Pennsylvania law, make reference to black servants (or slaves). Chapter 136 of the 1683 law provided

> That no Servant White or Black within this Province & territories therunto belonging, shall at anie time after publication hereof be Attached or taken in Execution for his M[aste]r or M[istres]s's debt or debts, To the end that the means of Lively-hood may not be taken away from the said M[aste]r or M[istres]s.[48]

This explicit reference to black servants in the 1683 provision and the failure to refer to blacks in the other servant provisions of this and other laws lends support to our position that blacks were covered only in the above 1683 provision. Yet the inclusion here of blacks was certainly not for their benefit, but merely to help a master in debt so that he could have his livelihood protected. Obviously the welfare of the black servant was irrelevant as far as this provision was concerned.

STATUTORY RESTRICTIONS ON BLACKS: THE POST-1700 ERA

While before 1700 judicial and legislative judgments on slavery can only be inferred from ambiguous texts, in 1700 the Pennsylvania legislature passed "An Act for the better regulation of servants in this province and territories," which appeared to give the first—though admittedly indirect—legal sanction to the holding of blacks for life. To punish "servants imbezzling their masters or owners goods," the law provided that *white* servants "shall make satisfaction to his or her master or owner by servitude, after the expiration of his or her time, to double the value of the said goods. . . ." Black servants, instead of having their "servitude" extended, were to be "severely whipped, in the most public place of the township where the offence was committed."[49] Presumably, this special sanction against blacks was a result of the fact that blacks were enslaved for life and thus could not be penalized by having their servitude extended.[50]

The Pennsylvania legislature's solution to the problem of punishing the criminal acts of black slaves (who already had been sentenced to lifetime servitude for the crime of simply being black) was developed more explicitly in a 1700 act on the trial of Negroes.[51] Previous attempts to punish slaves had led to frequent petitions by masters for the commutations of their slaves' sentences in recognition of the masters' economic investment in these slaves.[52] As the preamble to the act put it, "difficulties" had arisen in the punishment of "negroes" and a special effort needed to be taken to assure the "speedy trial and condign punishment of such . . . negroes. . . ." Thus, to better reconcile the master's and the victim's interests, as well as to expedite the adjudicatory proceeding during which the master was deprived of his property, the act established a special court for the trial of "negroes," composed of two justices of the peace and "six of the most substantial freeholders of the neighborhood." The judges were to "hold a court for the hearing, trying, judging, determining and conviction of such negro or negroes as shall be before them charged or accused of committing any murder, manslaughter, buggery, burglary, rapes, attempts of rapes, or any other high or heinous offenses. . . ." There was to be no jury; nor were distinctions to be made between free blacks and black slaves. All blacks, free and slave, were subject to trials before the Negro courts. Special sanctions were also introduced against justices or freeholders who should "neglect or delay to do their duty herein . . ."—another indication that pressure from masters had led to the circumvention of the criminal laws against slaves.[53] William Penn supported the establishment of the special courts for blacks because he thought that a separate judicial system would more fairly protect blacks.[54] From 1700 until 1780, when the special courts were abolished by "An Act for the gradual abolition of slavery," all trials of blacks in the colony were removed to these special courts.[55]

Whether the special courts or the regular courts had jurisdiction over civil suits involving blacks is unclear. In civil suits where both parties were black the regular courts theoretically might have retained jurisdiction, though we have found no record of such a proceeding. One can surmise that after 1700 blacks could not be witnesses against whites in the regular courts, since this right was not affirmatively given to free blacks until 1780[56] and to slaves until 1847.[57]

The law on the trial of Negroes also established various special crimes and punishments for blacks. These additional deprivations precariously balanced the increasing fears of whites against the requirement that the society not deprive masters of their slaves' labor. Imprisonment or extended "indenture" was rejected as a punishment for blacks. All blacks—both "free" and enslaved—found guilty of *attempts* to rape a white woman or maid were to be castrated.[58] Those convicted of "robbing, stealing or fraudulent taking or carrying away any goods, living or dead"; or carrying "any guns, swords, pistols, fowling pieces or other arms or other weapons whatsoever, without his master's special license"; or meeting in groups over four were *all* to be publicly whipped.

For crimes such as raping a white woman or maid, committing murder, buggery, or burglary, all blacks could be executed. Here, the legislature obviously deemed the state's interest in "controlling" blacks of paramount importance. With the exception of murder, these crimes were not capital for whites until 1718.[59]

Once again, the 1700 statute reveals the degraded legal status of the black woman, even when she was a victim of rape or attempted rape. First, it provided no punishment if the victim was black. Apparently, the degradation of the black women was not enough to subject a master to acute economic loss. If a black woman was raped by a *white* male again the law was silent, though arguably he might have been subject to the penalties involved in the rape of a white woman. But we doubt it.

In 1725-1726, Pennsylvania passed its most comprehensive statute on blacks, "An Act for the better regulation of Negroes."[60] This far-reaching law made more explicit and expanded the re-

straints on blacks in three areas: the trial procedures for enslaved
blacks, the substantive restrictions on free blacks, and the substantive restrictions on enslaved blacks.

First, in order to remove continuing pressure from masters to
acquit their accused slaves, it provided for reimbursement of a master for his financial loss resulting from the execution of his slave
pursuant to judicial decree. The preamble noted that:

> it too often happens that negroes commit felony and other
> heinous crimes which by the law of this province are punish-
> able by death, but the loss in such case falling wholly on the
> owner is so great a hardship that sometimes may induce him
> to conceal such crimes or to convey his negro to some other
> place and so suffer him to escape justice to the ill examples of
> others to commit the like offenses . . .[61]

Thus, *immediately* after a "negro owned by any of the inhabitants
of this province shall hereafter be convicted of any capital crime,"
the justice and freeholders who sat as judges were to appraise his
value and pay that sum to the owner from "the duties fees and penalties arising from this and one other act laying a duty on negroes
imported into this province. . . ."[62]

As in Virginia, South Carolina, and Georgia, the decision to
reimburse such masters revealed a legislative judgment to resolve
the conflict between punishment of the slave and loss of the master's
property in the slave by reimbursing the master for his loss, rather
than by reducing the punishment of the slave. This reimbursement,
moreover, was to be paid out of the taxes on imported slaves, which
some legislators then claimed and some historians later claimed
had been instituted to penalize the holding of slaves in the Quaker
colony.[63] The description of those taxes as a deterrent to slavery is
brought into question by the use of these tax funds to assure the
legal system's rigid control over slaves and to protect masters' economic interests in their slaves.

The most distinctive change wrought by the enactment of the
1725-1726 law was those restrictions placed on free blacks in Pennsylvania. According to the preamble, which is as revealing of the
Pennsylvania legislators' view of blacks as are the restrictions themselves, "experience" had demonstrated that "free negroes are an

idle, slothful people, and often burdensome to the neighborhood and afford ill examples to other negroes."[64] Thus for the first time free blacks were categorized separately from slaves and subjected to special restrictions by the law.

One method the legislators chose for reducing the "burden" of free blacks was to limit the size of the free black population in the Quaker colony. There had been instances of manumission occurring in Pennsylvania as early as 1701.[65] There were successful suits for freedom as early as 1703.[66] Though the overall number of manumissions was probably not great, by 1725 it evidently had become a source of some concern to the legislature. It required, therefore, that "sufficient surities in the sum of thirty pounds" be provided by every master *before* he manumit his slave to indemnify the government for "any charge or incumbrance [his slave] may bring upon the same in case such negro by sickness or otherwise be rendered incapable to support him or herself. . . ."[67]

This restriction on the private actions of slave masters was significant, since the destruction of slavery in Pennsylvania was achieved to a great extent through the private actions of Quakers and Germans freeing their own slaves and cajoling their neighbors to act likewise.[68] As a result of the 1725-1726 law, however, masters contemplating the manumission of their slaves now had to consider not only the loss of their slaves' value but the possible forfeiture of the thirty pound surety. The specter of this added financial loss led to a marked reduction in the number of manumissions in Pennsylvania.[69]

This was the first time in Pennsylvania that an individual master's benign treatment of his slaves was restricted and thus may reflect a growing realization by the legislature of the interests of the master class as a whole.[70] Pennsylvania did not go as far as several southern states, which restricted individual masters even further by banning manumission altogether, or requiring a legislative enactment validating the emancipation, or demanding the exportation of the freed blacks out of the state. Neither did it follow the example set in Georgia, however, which never limited the manumission of slaves during the entire colonial period.

In fact the Pennsylvania legislature did not even stop here— at restricting the manumission of slaves. Those blacks who were lucky enough to be freed from slavery or servitude found that the legislature instituted numerous devices for returning blacks to slavery or servitude. "[A]ny one negro fit and able to work" who should "neglect so to do and loiter and misspend his or her time of traveling from place [to place] . . ." was to be bound out to service "from year to year" as the magistrates shall "seem meet."[71] Thus, virtually every free black in the colony could be returned to servitude or, practically speaking, lifetime slavery, merely at the whim of a magistrate.

In one significant respect Pennsylvania treated free blacks even more harshly than did any of the southern colonies. The standard legal doctrine had always been that the children of free Negroes were free, but in its 1725-1726 statute Pennsylvania provided that all children of free Negroes or mulattoes or any black children freed when under twenty-one were to be bound out until they were twenty-one, in the case of women, and twenty-four, in the case of men.[72]

Shockingly, the penalty was *not* discretionary and required no finding that the parents were unable to take care of the children or that the children had done anything wrong. Rather, the statute *ordered* that all children of free blacks be bound out for service. This one statute deflates the more extravagant praise of Pennsylvania for its purported benign treatment of blacks.

Pennsylvania's fear of free blacks probably found its most visible expression in the emotion-tinged area of interracial sex. A free black convicted of committing fornication or adultery with a white was to be sold into servitude for seven years; the guilty white was merely punished "as the law directs in cases of adultory or fornication," which meant in cases of adultery his imprisonment for one year and payment of a fifty pound fine.[73] *Technically* whites guilty of interracial fornication might also have been subject to a period of seven years' servitude, for under another provision, whites who "shall cohabit or dwell with any negro under pretense of being married" could also receive such a punishment.[74] However they could avoid that sentence simply by paying a thirty pound penalty and we doubt whether either of these stern penalties was imposed on whites ever.

While there is much speculation as to the extent of interracial sexual activities occurring in Pennsylvania, Turner notes "There had doubtless been some [interracial] intercourse from the first."[75] One tract of land in Pennsylvania was known as "Mulatto Hall."[76] Despite the prohibitions of the 1725-1726 statute it "did not succeed in checking cohabitation, though of marriages of slaves with white people there is almost no record."[77] Advertisements for runaway slaves indicated that there were "very many" mulattoes.[78]

Throughout the colonial literature there is a continuous debate as to whether interracial sexual relations occurred primarily between blacks and "servants, outcasts, and the lowlier class of whites" or whether it included the master class as well.[79] Turner believes that the stigma of such illicit intercourse in Pennsylvania would "not generally seem to rest upon the masters."[80] But it is perhaps not without significance that one of Pennsylvania's leading statesmen, Benjamin Franklin, "was openly accused of keeping negro paramours."[81]

In cases of interracial marriage, the statute ordered that the free black be sold into slavery, but provided no punishment of the guilty white for the marriage itself. Perhaps the white could have received some penalty, since he might have been punished under the above prohibition against "cohabit[ing] or dwell[ing] with any negro under pretense of being married," though again we doubt this penalty was ever imposed. The children from such a marriage were to be "put out to service" until they reached the age of thirty-one, and the minister who performed the ceremony was to be fined 100 pounds.[82] The whole policy toward interracial sex contrasts with the holding and dicta of the court in the 1677 case of Anna, reported earlier, which implied that the *marriage* of a white and mulatto could have been legal at that time.

Free Negroes or mulattoes were also subject to punishments for merely harboring or trading with slaves, and the penalties were greater than those imposed on whites guilty of the same offenses. If convicted of trading, harboring, or in any way dealing with any "negro or other slave without license," blacks could receive up to twenty-one lashes and be forced to pay restitution.[83] Whites were exempt from corporal punishment but could be forced to make restitution for three times the value of the goods.[84] The punishment for free blacks or mulattoes "harbouring or entertaining any negro,

Indian, or mulatto slave or servant in his or her house without the leave or consent of their respective master or mistress" was "five shillings for the first hour and one shilling for every hour afterwards they shall be harboured or entertained."[85] Whites paid thirty shillings for every twenty-four hours.[86] While these restrictions may seem minor when compared to the excessive brutality of the southern colonies, they do reveal a fear among Pennsylvania legislators that whites—and especially free blacks—would provide assistance to slaves seeking freedom.

Finally, the 1725-1726 law expanded the restrictions on the geographical movement of slaves and their ability to seek work. As in previous provisions, these restrictions technically applied to "negroes" but references to masters would imply that they were intended mainly for slaves. Any "negro" discovered more than ten miles from his master's house and without leave in writing could receive up to ten lashes with the apprehending party winning five shillings. Any "negro" found "tippling or drinking" in any house or shop where strong liquors were sold or found away from his master after 9:00 P.M. without license received up to ten lashes on his bare back. Reciprocal restrictions on masters fined them twenty shillings for letting their "negroes" "ramble under pretence of getting work, [or] giv[ing] liberty to their negroes to seek their own employ . . ." Finally, as we have seen, persons entertaining or harboring other people's slaves without their masters' consent paid thirty shillings for every twenty-four hours, unless the violation occurred "in distress of weather or other extraordinary occasion."[87]

With the passage of the 1725-1726 law, the basic underpinnings of the Pennsylvania slave code were cemented. Until the passage of the 1780 gradual emancipation statute, subsequent laws did not designate special crimes for slaves; both slaves and free citizens (white and black) were subject to the same criminal statutes though special (physical) *punishments* were added solely for slaves. Like the 1700 law on servants, which had imposed a special physical penalty against black "servants," these provisions merely gave public evidence to the financial destitution and perpetual servitude of slaves. Instead of being punished by the imposition of an uncollectable fine or by imprisonment amidst a lifetime of enslavement, slaves were to be publicly whipped for such crimes as using fireworks without the governor's permission, setting fire to the wood-lands, or participating in a horse race.[88] Often, the laws did *not* give the master the right to pay the state in lieu of the corporal punish-ment, though this option was provided for on occasion.[89]

Curiously, some of these laws that imposed special physical punishment on slaves did not impose such additional punishment on whites convicted for the commission of the same crimes.[90] In the past no statute except the 1725-1726 law had made an explicit distinction between free and enslaved blacks, and that law had done so only in order to subject free blacks to special crimes, not to exempt them from crimes or penalties applicable to slaves. By the time of these later laws, however, the legislature may have recognized that there was no utility in always lumping free and enslaved blacks in the same category, especially for the purpose of punishment, since the imprisonment of free blacks would not deprive any white master of his property. Of course, this change did not provide any great benefit to free blacks, who were still subject to the punishment im-posed on whites—usually imprisonment. Moreover, free blacks were still treated like slaves under all the other laws on blacks and they were subject to the special penalties for free blacks under the 1725-1726 law.

JUDICIAL POLICY TOWARD BLACKS

Though William Penn suggested that the special court for the trial of Negroes created by the 1700 statute was for the better pro-tection of Negroes, in all probability the court was created because "in such courts it was doubtless easier to regard the slaves as prop-erty, and do full justice to the rights of the *masters.*"[91]

Tragically, all the official trial court records of the special court for Negroes seem to have been lost or destroyed, but in the archives of the Historical Society of Chester County we have found what appear to be accurate copies of seven original reports by the special court of Chester County on cases litigated between 1762 and 1772.[92] These cases include one prosecution for murder,[93] four for burglary or stealing,[94] and two for "attempt at rape."[95] In each of the seven cases the defendant was a slave.[96] Thus, no cases were found where a free black was prosecuted in the special court for Ne-groes.[97] The records reveal that the 1700 statute was complied with in that blacks were denied a jury trial; the triers of facts were commissioners appointed because they were "six of the most substantial freeholders of the Neighborhood."[98]

Our review of the seven Chester County cases indicates that the commissioners' major priority was protecting the interest of the property class. The most harsh penalty was imposed on slave Phobe, apparently a woman who was charged with "burglariously entering house of Thomas Barnard and stealing divers goods." She was sentenced to be hung, and apparently was, in fact, hung. She was valued at fifty-five pounds and per a court order her owner, Joseph Richardson, received that amount from the provincial treasurer.[99] The least harsh penalty of the special court was one imposed on December 4, 1772 when Negro Prime, slave of Sam Kennedy, was charged with stealing a pair of gold sleeve buttons; he was sentenced to receive "7 lashes on bare back & master to pay costs."[100]

It appears that greater procedural due process was granted the black defendant when his victim was also black. In 1762 Abraham Johnson, a slave of Humphrey Marshall, was charged with murdering a slave named Glascow; counsel was assigned the defendant, and he was "adjudged not guilty of murder but of homicide" and was to be discharged upon payment of costs.[101]

Curiously, for the three cases (*King v. Phobe, King v. Martin, King v. Dick*) on which the most serious penalties were imposed (attempt at rape and burglary), there was no notation on the court record that the commissioners had actually found the slave guilty of the offense charged. Thus, despite the fact that the slave, Phobe, was apparently hanged, and the record noted that she was "sentenced to be hung," there is no notation that she had been adjudged guilty. This omission of a finding of guilt is significant in view of the fact that in two earlier cases the commission had noted on the record their findings of guilty or not guilty. As to the two cases involving an "attempt at rape," the court's disposition was:

> sentenced to 39 lashes and to be branded with R on his forehead and be exported out of this province within 6 months and imprisoned till exportation at master's charge and cost of prosecution.[102]

> 39 lashes, branded R and to be exported never to return upon pain of death.[103]

But despite the above sentences, they did not note on the record a finding of guilt. One of the slaves charged with "an attempted rape" apparently was owned by a black, since the record notes "Negro Dick the slave of a mulatto Dinah otherwise Dinah Jones."[104]

In 1763 slaves Negro Sam and Negro Cambridge were found not guilty of burglary and were "to be discharged on payment of costs." They were, nevertheless, found guilty of stealing "some rum & molasses the property of Gervase Burgess" and were "sentenced to 39 lashes each at whipping post."[105]

Our analysis of the relatively few Chester County cases found indicates that in all probability the special court provided blacks no significantly greater protection than they would have otherwise received if the cases had been tried in the regular criminal courts of Pennsylvania where jurors were triers of facts. For minor offenses the masters did not have their property interest—the slave—adversely damaged, since even thirty-nine lashes would not constitute a permanent injury or a diminution of economic value. For the more serious offense, attempted rape, the masters' interest was protected in that the slaves were exported, which means that the masters could recover the economic value by selling the blacks to a slave trader.

While only secondary records were available as to the special Negro courts for the trial court proceedings, we found several official recorded decisions on blacks at the Governor's Provincial Council, which was a court of appeals to review the adjudications of the special Negro court. In virtually all the cases we have located, it was the master who brought the appeal to the council, suggesting that the main justification for review of the lower court decision was its impact on the master. These appellate cases corroborate our conclusion that both at the trial court and the appellate court levels there was an absence of any primary concern for the liberties or well-being of the blacks, but there was a steady concern for protecting the economic interest of the individual master or the master class generally.

To Make "Slaves Examples of Terror to Others of Their Complexion"

In a 1707 case, for example, two black slaves named Toney and Quashy were condemned to death in the special courts for the crime of burglary. The two masters of the slaves petitioned the council to spare the lives of their slaves in order that the masters may be "suffered to transport them." This presumably was a request to deport the slaves out of the province, where they would represent no further actual or symbolic threat to Pennsylvania, but could be sold by the masters for compensation. The masters proposed as punishment that they "may have liberty to inflict on [their slaves] such corporal punishment as may be requisite for a terror to others of their color, wch the said Owners will take care to have duly executed upon ym." The Council readily agreed, since "[t]he Death of these Slaves would be a greater Loss to The Owners than they could well bear, and. . . . There is no Provision made for restitution for The Loss by the Publick. . . ." It was "as convenient to make the Slaves examples of Terror to others of their Complexion, by a most Severe Corporal Punishment, and that the Petitioners may have Liberty to transport them as requested." It was resolved, therefore, to have the slaves

> led from the Market place, up ye Second Street and down thro' the front street to ye Bridge, with their arms extended and tied to a pole across their Necks, a Cart going before them, and that they shall be severely Whipt all the way as they pass, upon the bare back and shoulders; this punishment shall be repeated for 3 market days successively; in the meantime they shall lie in Irons, in the prison, at the Owners Charge, until they have such an Opportunity as shall best please them for transportation; All which being duly perform'd, the Sentence of Death shall be intirely remitted.[106]

The desire to make a vivid example in the punishment of a black also precipitated the council members' decision in a 1737 case. The facts of the case and the vacillating position of the council reveal a startling lack of legal protections for the trials of blacks. The special Negro court, the lower trial court, had convicted the black slave and had sentenced him to death. The flimsiness of the evidence against the slave, however, led several of the assistant freeholders who had sat as judges at the trial to petition the council for a reversal of the conviction.

The review by the council was clouded by the fact that its president was the victim in the case. The president, who presented the evidence for the meeting, openly admitted that the conviction was based solely on the defendant's confession and that the prosecutor had been "deficient in the prosecution." The prosecutor had only been "furnished with sufficient Proofs to show the wicked Disposition of the Criminal, his Malice, and Threatened Resentments against the Owner of the House, and the person who then lived in it, together with the Criminals former bad character. . . ." Yet the president, having virtually conceded that the evidence against the defendant was insufficient and that as the victim, he should not take part in the decision, he nevertheless warned that "a Compliance with [the freeholders'] Request in suffering so henious a Crime to pass unpunished cannot be attended with many ill consequences. . . ." His fear was based not on the possible guilt of the defendant, but on "the insolent Behaviour of the Negroes in and about the city, which has of late been so much taken notice of, requires a strict hand to be kept over them, & shows the Necessity of some further Regulations than our laws have yet provided."[107]

The board itself agreed with the position of the president that the conviction must stand. Like the president, their reasoning, as reported in the minutes, was *not* that the *defendant* was guilty, but merely that "so daring a *crime* ought not to pass unpunished. . . ."[108] Presumably, any black, whether guilty or innocent, would have served their purposes of making an example. They were unsure, however, whether the slave should be executed, since they were "willing to pay some Regard to the Application" of the freeholders. They decided, therefore, to have the execution "respited" for three months. It was only after this three months had elapsed that they resolved at a later meeting not to execute the slave. Instead they ordered that the slave be transported out of the province by his master.[109]

Manumission of Slaves

During the same period in which legislative restrictions on free and enslaved blacks were being institutionalized, the social and political movement for the abolition of slavery was gaining momentum. These antislavery forces, as we have seen, were ineffective in preventing the legal development of slavery and, for a long time after its establishment, procuring its legal abolition. But this movement did have a significant impact on *private* decisions to hold slaves, inducing Germans, then Quakers, and finally much of the public at large to remove themselves from the holding of and trafficking in slaves. Acts of manumission, which can be found from as early as 1701, multiplied throughout the eighteenth century. The Deed Book of Pennsylvania counties records numerous manumissions that upon registration became freedom certificates.

The repeated passage of laws levying heavy taxes on the importation of slaves was also a result partly of abolitionist efforts. In 1780, when the Pennsylvania legislature finally voted on the issue of the legality of slavery, it was not imbedded in the social and economic fabric of Pennsylvania, in part due to the efforts of the abolitionists, and thus could be evaluated with more objectivity by the legislators.

Germans made up the first, and probably the most vehement, group opposing slavery. While there is some dispute as to whether or not they were members of the Society of Friends,[110] their opposition appears to have been based on both religious and moral grounds, as well as a predisposition toward self-reliance and independence.[111] Few Germans ever held slaves and their protests against this institution, which almost none had observed before their arrival in Pennsylvania, began soon after their arrival in Pennsylvania. It is certainly not surprising that they were the source of the first organized protest against slavery in America when, as we have seen, they gathered at the Germantown meeting in 1688 to discuss the propriety of slavery.

Opposition to slavery among the Quakers was more ambiguous at the end of the 1600s and beginning of the 1700s, though the roots of their later opposition were visible. In 1671, before Pennsylvania was ever created, the prominent Quaker leader George Fox, while traveling in the West Indies, had advocated the mild treatment of slaves and their manumission after a "reasonable period of time."[112] Some Pennsylvania Quakers, such as George Keith, also opposed slavery on religious and moral grounds. In 1693 George Keith wrote a paper condemning slavery entitled, "An Exhortation and Caution to Friends Concerning Buying or Keeping

Negroes," which he delivered to a Philadelphia Quaker meeting.[113] He argued that slaves were men and that true Christians would not buy slaves, and that those who owned slaves free them.[114]

While Keith and other individuals spoke out against slavery over the years, their opinions did not hold much weight with many early Pennsylvania Quakers, who as a group held from one-third to one-half of all slaves in the colony.[115] The early *official* pronouncements against slavery by the Quakers only related to the participation of Quakers in the importation of slaves and, in any event, those early declarations never rose above mere suggestions for the proper conduct of their followers.[116] Indeed when William Southeby, a Pennsylvania Quaker, wrote to his friends in Barbados to implore them to cease the shipping of blacks into the United States, he was expelled from the Quaker community. Most Quakers at that time were in favor of placing some controls on slavery, but Mr. Southeby's suggestions were apparently too drastic for some.[117] It was only in the 1730s that Quaker sentiment against slavery led to a reduction in their importation of slaves. By 1745, Quakers had virtually ceased to be involved in the importation of slaves.[118]

A review of various quarterly meetings of Friends indicates that steady pressure was often applied on members either to free their slaves or to sell them to fellow Quakers who in turn would set these slaves free. Those members who refused to free their slaves were often "disowned for encouraging warlike measures."

Quakers also seem to have been instrumental in reducing the overall number of slaves imported into Pennsylvania by supporting the passage of numerous laws levying increasingly high taxes on the importation of slaves. In 1700 the Pennsylvania legislature imposed an import tax of twenty shillings for every black,[119] which sum was doubled in 1702.[120] The 1712 statute raising the Pennsylvania levy to twenty pounds[121] was not approved in England.[122]

From 1712 until 1729, a legislative battle was waged between the Pennsylvania legislature and the crown. Of the Pennsylvania legislature import tax laws on slaves during this period (1715, 1717-1718, 1720-1721, 1722, 1725-1726), most had been disallowed by an English Board of Trade, which was sensitive to the economic interests of the British slave trading companies. The Pennsylvania legislature, however, was able to circumvent the

Board of Trade's vetoes by enforcing the laws before their rescission and then reinstituting a new tax before the old law was repealed. With a decline in the demand for and importation of slaves, a much lower 1729 duty of two pounds was not vetoed by the crown and remained in effect for over thirty years.[123] A 1761 law raised the rate to ten pounds[124] and after being renewed in 1768,[125] the tax was made "perpetual" in 1773 at a rate of twenty pounds per slave.[126] By this time the actual importation of slaves had dwindled to a trickle anyway, and seven years later the importation of slaves was completely outlawed with the passage of the gradual emancipation statute.

The reasons for the passage of these taxes on the importation of slaves by the legislature are ambiguous and probably vary according to the particular law. Fear of slave insurrections, complaints concerning competition from black labor, and the need for revenue undoubtedly animated different legislators at different times. But the moral influence of the Quakers cannot be denied. Turner writes that when the texts of the laws are analyzed:

> in connection with matters which they themselves do not mention, namely, the predominance of the Quakers in the colonial Assembly together with the abhorrence which they felt for the slave-trade and later for slavery itself, it becomes probable that the predominant motive was restriction.[127]

For many Quakers, as well as the public at large, ending their participation in the importation or purchase of slaves was a different moral and economic question from the manumission of the slaves they already owned. The first resolutions of the Quaker meeting concerning the propriety of Quaker participation in slavery were limited to admonitions against importing and buying slaves, and it was not until the 1750s that the coercive step was taken to "disown" members of Quaker meetings who continued to buy slaves.[128] Finally, in 1758, the yearly meeting dealt with the problem of Quaker ownership of slaves. The meeting commanded Quakers to manumit the slaves they already owned and penalized violators by excluding them from participating in the affairs of the society.[129] After the 1750s the ownership of slaves by Quakers dwindled steadily because of private emancipations of slaves.

FREEDOM CERTIFICATES

John Alexander to Hector and Sallo His Negroes

THESE ARE TO WHOM IT MAY CONCERN: That the Bearer Hereof, Black Hector and his wife Black Sallo, is now free from me mye heirs, executors and administrators and at full liberty to act and do for themselves, to pass and repass about their Lawful concerns, without trouble, let, or molestation of me the Subscriber, as WITNESS my Hand and Seal, This Twenty-first Day of April, One-Thousand, Seven-Hundred and Fifty-eight (1758)

JOHN ALEXANDER (Seal)

Witness present: John Scott, Esq., Chester County, Penna.

BE IT REMEMBERD: This, Twenty-first Day of April, One-thousand-Seven-hundred and Fifty-eight, Came John Alexander of London Britain, Before me, John Scott, Esquire, And acknowledged the above Certificate of Freedom for the above named, Black Hector, and his wife Black Sallo (two of his negroes) to be his Act and Deed as Witness to my Hand and Seal and desire that they might be recorded this Twenty-first Day of April, 1758,

John Scott (Justice of Peace) (Seal)

[Recorded May 9th., 1758 #(14) Sˢ
IN MISCELLANEOUS DEED BOOK]

Whereas I Anne Tomkins of the Township of Charles Town in the County of Chester and Province of Pennsylvania, feeling a disposition of mind to do upright and impartial justice unto all Men, and having a Negroe Man in my Possession named Solomon, about Twenty three years of Age; and being mindful that he should have his freedom believing it to be his Just Right and it is my will and Pleasure, and I hereby declare that from the day of the date hereof, that he the said Solomon shall be free from me my heirs and assigns, and at his liberty to dispose of himself like other men, and that from this time forward he shall not be taken into slavery by me my Heirs or assigns or by any of our procurement.

In Witness whereof I have hereunto set my hand and seal this 7th day of the 7th month 1775.

Anne Tomkins (Seal)

Witness present: Willᵐ Lightfoot Jonatⁿ Coates Isaac Jacobs

SLAVES

From Records of Mochlan Mo. Mtg.

At Muchlan 8-8-1776—The Committee formerly appointed to join the Committee of the Quarterly Meeting in visiting those who hold slaves, reported in Writing as follows, viz: "We visited John Jacobs, who has a Negro Woman near 50 years of Age, who has a lameness: She has two Children, one a Boy of about 8 years old, the other a Girl about 6. He has also a Boy of about 18, and a Mulatto Girl that he purchased of about 14 years of Age, bound to the Age of 31 years:—the four first belonged to his Father-in-law.—We imparted to him and his Wife our best Advice, who appeared to us to be very unsensible of the Concern among Friends on Account of the Bondage of the Negroes, and he in a particular Manner contended against the Rule of Friends in that Case"—Therefore Robert Milhous and William Trimble are appointed to visit John respecting his Mullatto slave and report of their service and his Disposition, to next Meeting. (answer to 7th query)—"One Friends has bought a Mullatto Girl: None sold, and the few who are detained in Bondage well supplied with Food and Clothing; but little can be said respecting their religious Education, tho' some Endeavours are used to give them Learning."

9-5-1776—"The Friends appointed to visit John Jacobs respecting purchasing his Mullatto Slave, reported that they were with him, that he seemed friendly; that he informed them he made the Purchase 7 or 8 years ago, not with any view to keep her longer than till she arrived to the Age of 21 years, or than till she paid him for bringing her up. This matter is now left under the Consideration of the Meeting; and if any Friend feel an Openness in the Truth to labour further with him on the subject they are desired to do it & report thereof to next meeting." (He was soon after *disowned* for encouraging warlike measures)

8-7-77 "A few [slaves] yet remain unfreed, their mistresses only belonging to Frd."

9-4-1777—"Cadwallader Jones, William Lightfoot and Simon Meredith are appointed to join Women Friends in visiting those who are Mistresses of Slaves."

"This Meeting is Informed by men Friends that it was the mind of our last Quarterly Meeting that such Women Friends whose Husbands hold Slaves in Bondage should be visited. Mercy Baldwin & Dinah Meredith are appointed to join with Men Friends to visit them and report of their service to next Meeting."

1-7-1779—A Committee apptd to visit such negroes as have been set free to promote their welfare and that of their children.

3-8-1781—"The preparative Meeting brings a Complaint against Elizabeth Jacobs, for refusing to take Friends Advice respecting a Molatto Woman and several Negroes (Minors) under her Care: Samuel Bond and Dougall Cameron are appointed to join Women friends in a visit to her and report of her Disposition to our Next."

4-5-1781—They report "that there does not appear in her a Disposition to comply with the Advice of Friends, and signified that they need not take any more Trouble on her Account: Yet a Tenderness appearing in this Meeting towards her it is left under the Care of James Kenny and Robert Milhous, who are desired with Women friends, to visit her again and make Report thereof to next Meeting."

5-10-1781—Report—"She heard them patiently but signified she could not comply with Friends Advice respecting her slaves." disowned 6-7-1781.

4-10-1783—"Several Slaves having been manumitted by Friends within the Compass of this Meeting some years ago, and no Book having been yet provided for recording their Manumissions, agreeable to the Advice of the Yearly Meeting. Thomas Lightfoot is now appointed to procure one and record all said Manumissions, and report to a future Meeting."

8-7-1783—In answer to 7th Query "We are clear of Slaves for anything that appears."

LEGISLATIVE ABOLITION OF SLAVERY

Mounting agitation against slavery finally led Pennsylvania to become the first state to abolish slavery in the eighteenth century by *legislative* enactment when, in 1780, it passed "An Act for the Gradual Abolition of Slavery."[130] "Gradual" was the key word in the act, if one were asked to describe its effect on the majority of black people in the state. Those who were already slaves when the statute was passed were not freed by its enactment; only the black and mulatto children born *after* the passage of the law were to be freed and those only after serving their mothers' masters for twenty-eight years.[131] Freedom was thus conferred upon a generation yet unborn, and "the living [slaves] were given merely the consolation of a free posterity."[132]

Section 5 of the act required all slaveowners to register their slaves with the county clerk before November 1, 1780. The registration process required the full name and address of the owner, his occupation, and the name, age, and sex of each of his slaves. This provision was enacted "in order to ascertain and distinguish the slaves and servants for life . . . within this state, who shall be such on the said first day of November next from all other persons."[133] The penalty for nonregistration was the loss of the slave because "no negro or mulatto now within this state shall . . . be deemed a slave or servant for life . . . unless his or her name shall be entered as aforesaid on such record."[134]

The statute also provided in section 7 that the offenses and crimes of Negroes and mulattoes would be "enquired of, adjudged, corrected and punished, in like manner as the offenses and crimes of the other inhabitants of this state";[135] one restriction was that a slave could not testify against a freeman.

Exempted from the obligation of registration and the related freeing of slaves for noncompliance with section 5 were the "domestic slaves attending on members of Congress . . . and persons passing through or sojourning in this state, and not becoming residents therein."[136] Residency was defined as more than a six-month sojourn in Pennsylvania.[137] Thus, a person could not visit in Pennsylvania for more than six months without the slave or slaves who accompanied him becoming free. Visitors who came to Pennsylvania after November 1, 1780 (the last day of registration under the 1780 act) could not register their slaves. If the legislature had allowed visitors to register slaves after the residents' deadline of November 1, there would have been easy options for the evasion of the statute. More important, it would have made more difficult the gradual abolition of slavery in Pennsylvania.

Two aspects of the law were particularly significant in the gradual abolition process. First, the statute's registration provisions provided substantial penalties for noncompliance. Unregistered slaves were automatically emancipated. Inaction on the part of the slave owners out of laziness, ignorance, or contempt for the law would result in freedom for the slave, thus creating a significant financial loss for the owner. The registration requirement resulted in substantial litigation between master and slave, most of which was initiated by the Pennsylvania abolition societies after a thorough search of the records.[138] In response to this abolitionist litigation, the slave owners in 1781 initiated a strenuous political effort to amend the 1780 statute, by extending the deadline for the registration of slaves. The antislavery forces had sufficient political strength, however, to defeat them.[139] The specificity of the registration requirement resulted in some slaves being freed as a consequence of such technical errors as the failure of the master to write down the slave's precise name. At least one judge, Gibson, held the masters to strict compliance with the law in registration cases.[140] Such interpretations resulted, according to Turner, in "constructions which favored freedom wherever possible."[141] It is not apparent whether most judges adopted this presumption of freedom for the slaves.[142] The presumption of freedom was of profound legal significance since it required proof by the *master* that the black was in fact his slave, rather than proof by the black that he was free. Thus, if the master's evidence was not convincing the slave could go free without his having to prove anything.[143]

A second significant factor in the 1780 act is that in its preamble it incorporated the religious rhetoric common to the Declaration of Independence and the revolutionary era and extended those precepts to blacks. The preamble provided:

> we conceive that it is our duty, and we rejoice that it is in our power, to extend a portion of that freedom to other, which hath been extended to us, and release from that state of thraldom, to which we ourselves were tyrannically doomed, and from which we have now every prospect of being delivered. It is not for us to enquire why, in the creation of mankind, the inhabitants of the several parts of the earth were distinguished by a difference in feature or complexion. It is sufficient to know, that all are the work of an Almighty hand. We find, in the distribution of the human species, that the most fertile as well as the most barren parts of the earth are inhabited by men of complexions different from ours, and from each other; from whence we may reasonably, as well as religiously, infer, that He, who placed them in their various situations, hath extended equally his care and protection to all, and that it becometh not us to counteract his mercies. We esteem it a peculiar blessing granted to us, that we are enabled this day to add one more step to universal civilization, by removing, as much as possible, the sorrows of those, who have lived in undeserved bondage, and from which, by the assumed authority of the Kings of Great Britain, no effectual, legal relief could be obtained. Weaned, by a long course of experience, from those narrow prejudices and partialities we had imbibed, we find our hearts enlarged with kindness and benevolence towards men of all conditions and nations; and we conceive ourselves at this particular period extraordinarily called upon, by the blessings which we have received to manifest the sincerity of our profession, and to give a substantial proof of our gratitude.[144]

Though revolutionary, religious, and humanitarian concepts are incorporated into the 1780 act—and particularly in the above preamble—the drafters nevertheless were deliberately vague on the issue of the rights blacks would be entitled to once freed. Were blacks to be given *all* the white men's privileges or did the preamble advocate merely the abolition of slavery without any assurance of total citizenship rights for blacks. Though the Pennsylvania legislature noted that God "has extended equally his care and protection to *all*," the legislature itself made no such comparative commitment, at least not in this preamble. The drift of the Preamble was such that although it seemed committed to a humanitarian stance—in fact it had some of the inherent vagueness blacks most often had known: fully equal under God's laws, but less than equal under man's.

By 1780, then, Pennsylvanians would condemn the basic inconsistency in protesting the tyranny and the "assumed authority of the Kings of Great Britain," while simultaneously tolerating the legally enforced tyranny upon blacks by sanctioning slavery. But they were not prepared to ignore the economic and property consideration that would be jeopardized by the freeing of all slaves and they had not even begun to face the next issue of how far they would go to demand total equality for freed blacks. Even at the first stage of their moral obligation to at least *free* all blacks, they compromised. They denied slaves born before March 1, 1780 any freedom, and they delayed freedom for twenty-eight years to any children born thereafter of slave mothers.

The twenty-eight-year time period was probably adopted on the theory that it would compensate the master for the expenses of raising the children.[145] With hindsight, one sees clearly the competing tensions of values in the political compromise—the delicate effort to balance the economic losses of a master against the moral imperative that slaves should be free.

Pennsylvania's population was only 2½ percent black when the act was passed.[146] The smallness of the black population was another important factor favoring the passage of the 1780 statute. Other states with larger black populations had been more reluctant to start loosening the shackles of slavery and had emphasized the threat of being overrun by free black people if slavery were to be abolished.[147] Even in Pennsylvania, with its small black population, the freedom granted by the 1780 act was never intended to include a grant of full citizenship to the freedmen. It was to be decades before blacks had access to some of the most fundamental concomitants of citizenship, such as the ballot box, and more than a century and a half before the nondiscrimination legislation in housing, employment, and public accommodations was enacted.[148]

There were positive aspects to the statute that ought not be ignored. The language of the preamble was at least a legislative starting point for people honestly interested in eradicating slavery and one day securing total equality for free blacks in Pennsylvania and throughout the nation. The preamble to the Pennsylvania statute, like the Declaration of Independence, created a dynamism of its own to permit the principle to expand to the limit of its rhetoric. Thus, once written down legislatively, even in a vague preamble, that "God hath extended equally his care and protection to all, and that it becometh not us to counteract his mercies," it became easier to make more specific assurances of equal rights to all men under the law by the legislative and judicial processes. At that time there was a persistent interrelationship between religious concern and legislative enactment. Thus, William Jay, antislavery lawyer of New York and son of Chief Justice John Jay, wrote: "I do not depend on anyone as an abolitionist who does not act from a sense of religious obligation."[149] By the limited substantive provisions in the statute, the Pennsylvania legislators had already indicated how far they were willing to let revolutionary rhetoric carry them. The language of the preamble to the 1780 act remained, however, for anyone to read and at a later date, in arguing for full freedom and equality for blacks, to expand.

It must also be remembered that there were alternatives available to the 1780 legislators, if so inclined, that could have emasculated the act. No restrictions were imposed on the immigration of free blacks to Pennsylvania nor were those slaves freed by the act required to leave the state. Most important, the 1780 act represented the first time the legislature of a state had included blacks within the revolutionary rhetoric that possessed the country at that time.

LEGISLATIVE REFINEMENTS OF THE 1780 ACT

The 1782 Act

The residents of two Pennsylvania counties, Westmoreland and Washington, considered themselves to be under the jurisdiction of the state of Virginia because of an uncertain boundary. Pursuant to an agreement between the states, both counties were designated as part of Pennsylvania. In response, the residents of these counties petitioned Pennsylvania to declare them free inhabitants of the state and thus grant them the privileges assured under the Pennsylvania constitution to free inhabitants. They also requested an extension of time to register their slaves since previously they had believed they were subject solely to Virginia law. Thus, the legislature passed an act in April, 1782, extending the registration date for slaves in Westmoreland and Washington counties to January 1, 1783.[150]

The 1788 Act

In 1788 the legislature passed an act "explaining" the 1780 act for the gradual abolition of slavery. This later act was an attempt to "prevent many ills and abuses arising from ill-disposed persons availing themselves of certain defects" in the 1780 act.[151]

The first section clarified the tenth section of the 1780 act, which dealt with the status of visitors' slaves. It said that "all and every slave and slaves who shall be brought into this state by persons inhabiting or residing therein or intending to inhabit or reside therein shall be immediately considered, deemed and taken to be free to all intents and purposes."[152] The intention to reside in Pennsylvania was now proof enough to free slaves. No mention is made of the six-month period that was the key to residency in section ten of the 1780 act; at least one case construing the 1788 act held that a six-month stay in Pennsylvania would still operate to free the visitor's slaves.[153]

Section 2 dealt with the efforts of slave owners to avoid the impact of the 1780 act. As previously noted, all children born of slaves after March 1, 1780 would be free on their twenty-eighth birthday. Apparently, in an effort to avoid the mandated freeing at age twenty-eight, some slave owners were removing pregnant slaves from Pennsylvania for the birth of the child to an area where slavery for life was sanctioned. The 1788 act provided:

> That no negro or mulatto slave or servant for terms of years
> . . . shall be removed out of this state with the design and intention that the place of abode or residence of such slave or servant shall be thereby altered or changed or with the design and intention that such slave or servant if a female and preg-

nant shall be detained and kept out of this state till her delivery of the child of which she is or shall be pregnant.[154]

Another method of softening the impact of the 1780 act was for visitors who planned to stay in Pennsylvania more than six months to take their slaves out of the state within the six-month period and sell them. The 1788 act further provided:

> That no negro or mulatto slave or servant for term of years . . . shall be removed out of this state . . . *with the design and intention that such slave or servant shall be brought again into this state* . . .

The statute prohibited the selling of a slave or a servant outside Pennsylvania when "such a slave or servant would lose those benefits and privileges" of the gradual emancipation statute. The penalty was a fine of seventy-five pounds.[155]

Section 3 provided that all children born of slaves after March 1, 1780 and liable under the 1780 act to serve for twenty-eight years must be registered before April 1, 1789 or "within six months next after the birth of any such child." The registration of these children would secure their right to freedom at age twenty-eight and eliminate any hopes of the masters of retaining them in slavery for life. The penalty for nonregistration of these children within the time limits was their immediate freedom.

Section 5 provided a fifty pound fine for the master who "separated or removed a wife from her husband or a child from his or her parent to a distance of greater than ten miles with the design and intention of changing the habitation or place of abode of such husband, wife, parent or child, . . . unless the consent of such slave or servant for life or years shall have been obtained. . . ."[156]

Pennsylvania's Tolerance and Opposition to Slavery: An Evaluation

The Pennsylvania colonial legislature constructed a more benign slave code than its southern neighbors, yet provided for the subjugation of blacks within this more moderate framework. While slaves and free blacks were not to be brutalized to the extent sanctioned and encouraged by the southern colonies, every effort was made to assure that they would never be equal to whites.

After the revolution of 1776, Pennsylvania continued its relative enlightenment by passage of the gradual emancipation acts of 1780 and 1788. If one were to measure history solely by the absolute of *total* freedom or *complete* equality, obviously any state or nation would have some significant deficiencies against such absolute calibrations. However, Pennsylvania must be evaluated as part of the era when racial slavery was almost universally sanctioned by the legal process. It is indisputable that in Pennsylvania slaves and free blacks were not brutalized to the extent sanctioned and encouraged by the southern colonies, even though there was every effort made to assure that they would never be fully equal to whites under the law. As Massachusetts was abolishing slavery by the judicial process,[157] Pennsylvania significantly distinguished itself from most of its northern neighbors by being the first to initiate legislation for the gradual demise of slavery.

Perhaps the most notable instance in which Pennsylvania distinguished itself from its southern neighbors was in its refusal to sanction physical attacks on slaves by masters or third parties. While Georgia and South Carolina permitted masters and bounty hunters to execute those slaves who merely challenged their authority, Pennsylvania never created a special list of justifications or excuses for the murder or beating of slaves.[158] The laws governing the physical abuse of slaves and blacks were the same as those that applied to whites. Pennsylvania blacks and slaves were also not subjected to as many special judicial sanctions—capital or otherwise—for the commission of various acts. In Georgia and South Carolina, for example, blacks could be executed for merely striking a white person for the third time, for running away out of the province, or for destroying any crop such as corn or rice.[159]

Of course, this does not mean that physical assaults on blacks did not occur in Pennsylvania under the sanction of the courts. Pennsylvania never enacted a *positive* bill of rights for blacks that would have protected them against the discretion judges enjoyed in exonerating masters for the abuse of their slaves. Peter Kalm, writing in 1770, noted that there was no record of any punishment of a master for killing his slave, though it is a near certainty that such criminal acts took place. Kalm cited one case in which a white accused of killing a slave was covertly advised by the Pennsylvania magistrates to leave the country before the trial "as otherwise they could not avoid taking him prisoner, and that he would be condemned to die according to the laws of the county, without any hope of saving him."[160]

Another type of restriction never employed by the Pennsylvania legislature was the restrictive patrols frequently found in the South. Virginia, South Carolina, and Georgia all required tight overseeing of slaves through daily patrols of the countryside and mandated inspection of slaves' quarters on all plantations. One explanation for the absence of such laws in Pennsylvania was the influence of the Quakers on the legislature preventing the establishment of a militia altogether in the Quaker colony until the revolutionary period. Perhaps the lower percentage of blacks and their more scattered distribution on small farms and in individual houses also made this military surveillance less necessary.[161]

But while Pennsylvania never created an extensive patrol system, it used many related techniques to supervise the public activities of blacks. Beginning in 1693, as we have seen, any black could be stopped on the street and imprisoned by any magistrate or citizen if the black did not hold a ticket from his master.[162] The 1700 slave law prohibited blacks from meeting in groups of more than four or carrying any guns or other weapons without a special license from their master.[163] The 1725-1726 law granted a reward of five shillings to any person who should "take up" a Negro found more than ten miles from his master's house and without "leave in writing" from his master; the guilty slave, while not subject to the capital punishment that could have been imposed had his transgression occurred in Georgia or South Carolina, was to be given up to ten lashes.[164] Other provisions imposed similar penalties upon blacks discovered away from their master's house after 9:00 P.M. without special leave, or at any tippling house. Reciprocal restrictions on whites prohibited them from employing or harboring such blacks.[165]

Finally, the more restrained policy of the Pennsylvania legislature toward the human debasement of enslaved blacks was symbolized by its refusal to import some of the southern restrictions denying the personality or basic humanity of blacks. Neither the Pennsylvania legislature nor the Pennsylvania courts ever classified slaves as property, as was the case in Virginia, Georgia, and South Carolina. Slaves were never prohibited from receiving an education, nor from engaging in many common activities and occupations, as was the case, for example, in Georgia, which prohibited any black from slaughtering a cow, even under a master's supervision.[166] There was no gruesome bounty system, as there was in Georgia and South Carolina, reimbursing bounty hunters for the return of a runaway slave's "scalp with two ears." Innocent slaves could not be forced to impose judicially ordered punishments on other slaves—a device employed by the Georgia and South Carolina legislatures to force absolute submission to and participation in the harsh southern system. The Quaker colony constructed an extensive slave code, but failed to retain many of the sharpest edges of slavery in the southern colonies.

But if the repression of blacks in the Quaker colony did not extend to the full brutalization of slaves, it did include the subtle legal and social debasement of free blacks. Numerous special provisions limited their freedom or relegated them back into servitude or slavery for the slightest infraction. As Turner has demonstrated so persuasively, for blacks as a group, the rise from slavery did not lead to freedom, but rather to servitude, and later to a semifree legal status. This halfway process is perhaps best exemplified by the 1780 Pennsylvania gradual emancipation statute, which did not give immediate freedom to children born to slaves after that date, but enforced decades of servitude before freedom.

Pennsylvania's hostility toward the free black population is best shown by its restrictions on manumissions. Technically, the state never closed the door to freedom for enslaved blacks, for it never prohibited manumission, never required the deportation of emancipated blacks, and never placed the burden of proof on slaves suing for their freedom, as was the case in various parts of the South. It did, however, demand that masters wishing to free a slave produce a thirty pound surety for the state's expenses for the emancipated slave. The proviso had the effect of reducing the number of manumissions and the size of the overall free black population.

Other restrictions had the effect of returning free blacks into servitude for a period of time—a status that was certainly an improvement over slavery, but one that clearly was intended to distinguish blacks from the rest of the population. Free blacks convicted of marrying whites were sold into slavery, and their children into servitude until the age of thirty-one. Blacks who were adjudged to be "loiterers"—a vague term for which there was no generally agreed specific definition—could be sold into servitude "from year to year"—a sentence that could have been tantamount to enslavement. All children of a free black could be sold into servitude until their twenty-first (for females) or twenty-fourth (for males) birthdays, thereby potentially removing every free black child from his family during his childhood.

These stringent colonial restrictions on free blacks are not surprising, for they were part of a determination to differentiate the status of free blacks from the status of free whites so that blacks were cast by the law in an inferior position. Yet these disparities were not necessary even in the colonial period. The presence of free blacks would not have presented the same economic and military threat to the Pennsylvania slave system as it might have in the South, where every free black represented a symbolic as well as potentially a military challenge to the profitable enslavement of other blacks. On a more subtle level, however, free blacks in the North may have constituted a psychological challenge to the status of free whites; the greater the number of free blacks and the higher their status, the more their presence undermined the status of the general white population. Restrictions on the loitering of free blacks and the indenturing of free black children assured whites that the new "freedoms" of free blacks were not equivalent to the inherent liberties assured all whites. Pennsylvania may have punished interracial sex and interracial marriage harshly because the perceived inferiority of blacks in this emotionally explosive area needed to be vigorously demonstrated.

Colonial Pennsylvania's failure to assure blacks, as it had whites, full equality and liberty under the law tells us much about its true perception of blacks. Even the Quaker colony could not, or at least did not, accept blacks in anything but an inferior status. Pennsylvania did not brutalize blacks as severely as the southern colonies did, but it took every effort—indeed, in contrast to the moderation of its slave code, perhaps greater effort than any other colony—to assure that blacks who aspired to legal equality would not achieve that status in colonial Pennsylvania.

A review of these restrictions may place in perspective many of the later restrictions in the North on free blacks. The black in the "benevolent" North during the twentieth century, particularly 1900 to 1950, suffered acute deprivations, for the legal process was often geared to make sure that blacks did not enjoy the full equal options proffered to white citizens.[167] This disparity was not a phenomenon unique to the post–Civil War period; its origins were written into the legal process even in Pennsylvania during the colonial period.

Pennsylvania's accomplishment in passing the gradual emancipation acts cannot be underestimated. It was a significant changing of the tide toward ultimate freedom for blacks. Its impact went beyond Pennsylvania and helped trigger similar legislation in other northern states. In succeeding years northern states such as New Jersey, New York, and Connecticut would follow Pennsylvania, often adopting almost verbatim portions of the Pennsylvania statute.[168] On the basis of the Pennsylvania experience, other northern abolitionists could argue that the proposed moderate and gradual emancipation statutes would not bring about the havoc proslavery advocates had predicted would be the consequence if slaves were ever systematically freed.

The distinguished black abolitionist Frederick Douglass once said:

> No one can tell the day of the month, or the month of the year, upon which slavery was abolished in the United States. We cannot even tell when it began to be abolished. Like the movement of the sea, no man can tell where one wave begins and another ends. The chains of slavery with us were loosened by degrees.[169]

Pennsylvania was an important force in the abolition movement whereby, as Douglass phrased it, the chains of slavery were loosened by degrees.

III

The English Experience with Slavery

8

THE SETTING

O N the eve of their break with England, the American colonies, with the exception of Rhode Island,[1] had each individually, acting by legislative act or judicial ruling, sanctioned racial slavery. Admittedly, enthusiasm for slave labor was at no time universal among the colonists, and each region had tailored its legal model to protect its own special needs in regard to slave labor. Despite variations in application, however, on the issue itself —whether or not it was legal for one individual to hold another in perpetual bondage—the colonial courts had consistently upheld racial slavery. Indeed, until the violent upheaval of the Civil War a century later, and the subsequent passage of the 13th, 14th, and 15th Amendments to the Constitution, no federal court in America had ruled that slavery was inconsistent with the national legal tradition. Only on the state level, and even then only in rare instances, did courts support any opposition—whether on idealistic, humane, or pragmatic grounds—to legal slavery.[2]

In contrast, by 1772 a relatively humanitarian attitude toward slavery had been established under English common law, resting on the landmark decision *Sommersett* v. *Stuart*,[3] written by Lord Mansfield of the King's Bench of England. In that remarkable decision, which profoundly influenced American and English legal opinions for decades, Lord Mansfield proclaimed that neither moral nor political grounds existed to support slavery; the institution could be justified only by positive law.

Scholars have disagreed on the significance of Lord Mansfield's holding. Some suggest that the *Sommersett* case represented one of the English court's "finest hours" by its abolition of slavery within the shores of England. Further, the argument can be made that in the long run this decision provided the intellectual and legal foundation used subsequently by others to secure passage of the parliamentary statutes outlawing British participation in the international slave trade in 1807 and slavery in the British colonies in 1833. Professor Reginald Coupland has asserted that behind the legal judgment in *Sommersett* lay the moral breakthrough, and as a result, Lord Mansfield's opinion marked the beginning of the end of slavery throughout the British empire.[4] In contrast, others assert that the case was of only slight significance since it did not reach the core problems of slavery—that is, the international slave trade and slavery in the English colonies of North America and the West Indies—involving millions of slaves physically outside of England. Benjamin Franklin, when commenting on the case, condemned "the hypocrisy of [England], which encourages such a detestable commerce, while it piqued itself on its virtue, love of liberty, and the equity of its courts, in setting free a single negro. . . ."[5] With time, in England and the English Caribbean the *Sommersett* view gradually prevailed, and "it was no longer possible to take for granted the universal legality of slave property."[6]

Yet, as Franklin had correctly observed, *Sommersett* was not the *coup de grâce* to the institution of slavery in the eighteenth-century British empire—as, for instance, the 13th, 14th, and 15th Amendments to the U.S. Constitution were for the nineteenth-century United States. Even by the most liberal and broad reading the decision dealt narrowly with the right to treat blacks as slaves within England, where Englishmen gained least from the maintenance of slaves, and where, in fact, there were never more than twenty thousand slaves in total. Critics of the day, like Franklin, were derisive of the failure of the English courts to address themselves to the Englishmen's more invidious role in the perpetuation of slavery within the empire. The international slave trade was a business dominated by English merchants, and slavery within the English colonies of North America and the West Indies involved millions of black human beings.

The *Sommersett* decision, despite its limited applicability, accomplished more than the freeing of a single Negro. Prior decisions by the English courts had vacillated on the legality of racial enslavement on English soil, and their precedents gave only limited guidance for Mansfield's task. At best, the pattern was one in which the English had established very special conditions in applying individual liberty concepts to slave-master disputes. Thus, Mansfield had the vision to rise above the rationalizations of his time, reconcile ambiguous and seemingly contradictory holdings of English common law, and forge a more humane path for English society.

This first chapter on the English experience will present an overview of the events, issues, and cases setting the stage for the *Sommersett* case in order to clarify the dynamics of the British response to slavery prior to this important decision. It will further delimit many of the special conditions separating the English and American experiences. These differences culminated in and are symbolized by the *Sommersett* case, which stands as the historical watershed in the evolution of British attitudes toward racial slavery.

The following chapter will offer a detailed recounting of the case itself, presenting extensive argument from both counsel for the slave Sommersett and for the defendant Stuart. The third chapter in this section will follow the events that proceeded from *Sommersett* all the way to the end of English participation in the international slave trade, the final legacy of the *Sommersett* controversy.

That the *Sommersett* decision expressed and established a new standard of justice under English common law is a position most scholars will not question.* But what is less often understood is that in so doing, it advanced one step further the cumulative understanding and expression of social justice by which English society civilized itself.

Why then we may ask, did the American courts, which relied on

---

* The common law "consists of a few broad and comprehensive principles, founded on *reason, natural justice, and enlightened public policy*. It has its foundation in the principles of equality, natural justice, and that general convenience which is public policy." *Edgerly* v. *Barker,* 31 A. 900, 905, 66 N.H. 434, 28, L.R.A. 328, quoting *Norway Plains Co.* v. *Boston & M.R. Co.,* 67 Mass. (1 Gray) 263, 267, 268, 61 Am. Dec. 423). Others have said: "The common law is but the crystallized conclusion of judges arrived at from applying the principles of natural right and justice to the facts actually experienced in cases before them." *Scott* v. *Kirtley,* 152 So. 721, 722, 113 Fla. 637, 93 A.L.R. 661.

English common law for guidance and precedent in so many other matters both during the American colonial period and, to a lesser extent, even after the revolution, reject this guidance when it came to the issue of racial slavery? A full assessment of the contrasting responses requires, of course, an analysis of the historical context as well as the legal arguments made in each response. Thus, this chapter will also focus on the political and economic factors that directed the English and the Americans onto different courses.

The Economics of English Slavery

In contrast to her European neighbors, Britain was a late entrant into the slave trade. Although the first English slave-trading expedition set sail in 1562, under the leadership of Sir John Hawkins,[7] it was not until 100 years later, in the 1660s, that England began to participate vigorously in that trade. This late entry was related to practical impediments, including civil war in England, and not to any special objection on the part of English merchants to the kidnapping and enslaving of human beings.

The English slave trade was established in 1663 as a monopoly granted to the Company of Royal Adventurers for 1000 years; a new company, the Royal African Company, was incorporated in 1672 when the Royal Adventurers had proved insolvent and been dissolved. In 1698 the Royal African Company lost its monopoly right, thereby ensuring, as Eric Williams has put it, that the "right of a free trade in slaves was recognized as a fundamental and natural right of Englishmen."[8]

After 1698, English participation in the slave trade increased extensively; it has been estimated that by 1756 over two million blacks had been sent to the British colonies. By 1772, the year of the *Sommersett* decision, Britain had developed into the foremost slave trader in the world, having kidnapped or transported millions of blacks from Africa to the Americas in the course of her profitable triangular trade[9] with groups on these two continents. About two-thirds of the British commercial export of slaves from Africa were eventually sold in non-English colonies. This trade, a key factor in the mercantile wealth of eighteenth-century England, was consistently supported by both the British monarchy and parliament until about 1783, the year the Revolutionary War in America ended.[10]

As Thomas Clarkson wrote in 1788: "As long as America was our own . . . there was no chance that a minister would have attended to the groans of the sons and daughters of Africa, however he might feel their distress."[11] Whenever colonial legislatures imposed high import duties on newly imported slaves in an attempt to impede the rapid growth of the colonial black population and to raise revenue, parliament invariably disallowed such duties. Indeed, the Board of Trade, heeding British merchants, had ruled as far back as 1708 that it was "absolutely necessary that a trade so beneficial to the Kingdom should be carried on to the greatest advantage. The well supplying of the plantations and colonies with sufficient numbers of negroes at reasonable prices is in our opinion the chief point to be considered."[12] It was only when the American colonies became independent of the old mercantile system, which required the entire empire to pay tribute to the sugar plantation by paying a grossly inflated price for British brown sugar, that the system was no longer viable.[13]

But the importance of slave trading was not felt only in increases in the mercantile wealth of England; the domestic economy of Great Britain also was altered. Its impact on the latter may be appreciated by examining the striking influence of slave trading on the city of Liverpool, which attributed much of its wealth to the English involvement in the slave trade. By 1752 the city's fleet of eighty-seven slave-trader ships could hold twenty-five thousand slaves, although the number actually shipped "if not actually delivered in good order and condition was probably much higher as it was customary to overload with the most frightful results."[14] Liverpool's eighty-seven ships were used solely for the transporting of slaves, and by 1795 the city had five-eighths of the British slave trade and three-sevenths of the whole European trade.[15]

This traffic in human beings clearly became the most lucrative form of commercial activity in Liverpool. Even with a large portion of the Liverpool trade monopolized by ten large firms, many small vessels were outfitted by the local merchants. It was stated at the time that "almost every man in Liverpool is a merchant . . . almost every order of people is interested in a Guinea cargo; it is [due] to this influenza that [there are] so many small ships."[16]

Yet other businesses directly and indirectly connected with the slave trade also prospered greatly. The building and outfitting of slave ships gave employment to many tradesmen and laborers. In addition, numerous articles necessary for the transportation of slaves to Guinea needed to be produced, as was illustrated by one representative advertisement in the Liverpool paper for such items as "83 pairs of shackles, 11 neck collars, 22 handcuffs for the traveling chain, [and] 4 long chains for the slaves."[17] Other sectors of the domestic English economy were also spurred to development because of the triangular trade and the processing of colonial raw produce.

The dependence of nonmerchant Englishmen as well as slave traders on this peculiar institution created a broad-based and powerful opposition to all attempts to attack or limit slavery. Many of the men who participated in the slave trade continued to come from all levels of English society, illustrating the fact that slave trading was apparently viewed merely as one more form of commerce— albeit a particularly lucrative one. A large number of slave traders were of English nobility; others who had no previous access to social acceptance or political power were recognized on the strength of their successful slave trading. The Royal Adventurers, the first trading company, for example, was composed of two aldermen, three dukes, eight earls, seven lords, a countess, and twenty-seven knights. Many slave traders were members of Parliament. Ellis Cunliffe, whose family owned four slave ships capable of holding 1120 slaves, represented the city of Liverpool in Parliament from 1767 to 1775. The conservative House of Lords also contained several "noble slavetraders," many of whom would probably not argue with the Earl of Westmoreland's remark that they owed their seats in the upper house to the slave trade.[18]

Yet, as the effects of her participation in this form of commerce reached its peak, one consequence of slave trading troubling the English was the rise of a slave population in England. Masters who returned to England from the colonies invariably arrived with retinues of personal slaves and many of these were sold or transferred into the permanent population of the British isles. In 1764, the *Gentlemen's Magazine* estimated that there were over twenty thousand black slaves in London alone and that slaves were openly bought and sold in the center of London. The new visibility of slaves to the eighteenth-century English citizen was noted by Eric Williams:

> Negro servants were common. Little black boys were the appendage of slave captains, fashionable ladies or women of easy virtue. . . . Freed Negroes were conspicuous among London beggars and were known as St. Giles black birds.[19]

Further, slave auctions were held in several large cities, especially Liverpool, where advertisements for the sale of slaves and for the capture and return of runaways appeared with some regularity. Williamson's *Advertiser* of June 24, 1757 carried the following advertisement:

> For sale immediately, One stout Negro young fellow about 20 years of age, that has been employed for 12 months on board a ship, and is a very serviceable hand. And a Negro boy, about 12 years old, that has been used since Sept. last to wait at a table, and is of a very good disposition, both warranted sound. Apply to Robert Williamson, Broker.[20]

About six months later, on February 17, 1758, the same newspaper carried the following advertisement for the return of an escaped slave:

> Run away from Dent, in Yorkshire, on Monday the 28th August last, Thomas Anson, a negro man, about 5 ft. 6 ins. high, aged 20 years and upwards and broad set. Whoever will bring the said man back to Dent, or give any information that he may be had again, shall receive a handsome reward from Mr. Edmund Sill of Dent; or Mr. David Kenyon, Merchant, in Liverpool.[21]

English abolitionists, then, confronted an institution that, though perhaps not as deep-rooted in England as in the colonies, had many influential defenders at home. Restrictions on English slaveholding invited strong reactions from slave traders, who foretold the economic chaos that would result from the application of egalitarian ideals to England's own foreign slave trade and to the colonial slaveholders. Any attempts to limit slavery on the British isles so that proper English gentlemen and women would not be offended by the sight of slave auctions would, and did, stir vehement criticism. On the other hand, the legal system was charged with hypocrisy for its failure to extend to its logical conclusion the English ideal of personal equality before the law.

The Developing English Case Law of Slavery

As a matter of theoretical choices, the English legal system— through its courts or parliament—could have exercised various options foreclosing different levels of participation in slavery. For example, they could have merely outlawed British domestic slavery, either through total or gradual manumission. They could have reduced the harshness of slavery by granting a minimal bill of rights for slaves. They might have attacked the incidence of foreign slavery in England by prohibiting the temporary use of slaves in England by foreigners or the forced deportation of blacks from England into slavery in another country. Or, finally, they could have outlawed the sale or holding of slaves by foreigners or British citizens throughout the British empire. A decision abolishing slavery in England and in the English colonies could have precluded Englishmen and colonists from engaging in the international slave trade.

The decisions in the cases leading up to *Sommersett* attempted to reconcile these pressures in their vacillating interpretations of English common law. The courts seldom confronted directly the legality of slavery as an institution, but instead relied on technical matters of pleadings, such as whether the particular writ was in the proper form to establish ownership of a slave or a right to his service.[22] The choice of the proper common law pleadings (the various forms of which had developed over centuries of adjudication) often became the determinant factor in the judges' finding for or against the plaintiff. The courts' evolving attitude toward these writs and slavery in general illustrates the halting steps made by the English judiciary to endorse the motto *in favorem liberatis*—in other words, to presume all parties free until proven otherwise. But it was not until *Sommersett,* as we shall see, that Lord Mansfield finally set a common law standard that was to be the starting point for parliament's ultimate abolition of all incidents of slavery in the British empire.

The 1569 *Cartwright*[23] case was the first proceeding in which slavery was found to be inconsistent with English traditions. The short report of the holding states that a slave imported from Russia must be manumitted because, in words that would be the subject of much later debate and interpretation, "England was too pure an aire for slaves to breath in."[24] Unfortunately, the decision did not specify the race of the slave, though it is probable that a slave imported from Russia at that time would have been white. It was not until the eighteenth-century case of *Smith* v. *Brown and Cooper*[25] that we can be sure that the *Cartwright* principle had been applied to a case involving a black slave.

Indeed, the first time an English court was faced with a legal controversy involving black slaves, in *Butts* v. *Penny* (1677),[26] the court explicitly sanctioned black slavery under English law and failed even to mention the earlier *Cartwright* case, which had clearly stated that slavery was antithetical to English law and society. The plaintiff in *Butts* had brought a suit in *trover*[27] for the value of a slave. This was a type of common law action used generally to recover the value of personal property wrongfully converted (sold or used) by another. The issue before the courts then was not one based on philosophical or legal arguments for or against slavery, but simply on whether or not and under what conditions Negroes constituted personal property to the extent that an action in *trover* could be maintained.

In a special verdict for the plaintiff, the court found that since Negroes were "usually bought and sold among merchants, as merchandise, and also being infidels, there might be a Property in them sufficient to maintain trover, and gave judgment for the Plaintiff *nisi Causa,* this *Term."*[*28]

The opinion in *Butts* does not specify the particular factor, or combination of factors, that justified the decision. Perhaps the

---

* The judgment *nisi causa* indicates that the decision was valid *unless* the party affected came to show cause within the specified time why it should not stand. In other words, the ruling was not necessarily final. There is no record, however, of future adjudication of the matter.

judges thought that the sale was enforceable because they had been informed that it had occurred outside England. The record presently available unfortunately does not reveal where the sale of the particular blacks took place; the court does state that blacks were "usually bought and sold in India."[29] The court's failure to refer to the earlier *Cartwright* case may support the view that either the sale took place outside England or the slaves were never in England. Thus, a decision holding that the air of England was incompatible with slavery would not be controlling if the individuals were not actually held in bondage in England.

Since the court in *Cartwright* discussed neither the religion nor the race of the slave, in *Butts,* the "heathenism" of the blacks might have justified their enslavement. The court emphasized that they were "infidels" and the "Subjects of an Infidel Prince."[30] However, the court failed to differentiate the heathenism from the blackness of skin; it remains unclear after *Butts* whether either characteristic alone would have been enough to justify enslavement and thereby override the English law's preference for liberty.

The court in *Butts* also considered for the first time whether the ancient English system of bondage, called villenage, was relevant precedent for the enslavement of blacks. Counsel for the slave had argued as a defense that an action of *trover* would not lie for any person since the laws on villenage only permitted the acquisition of a property right in a person by reason of compact or conquest, and there was no evidence that Butts had acquired the slave, Penny, in either of these ways.

The court ruled against the slave's defense but gave no explanation of its views as to whether villenage was a precedent for slavery. Nevertheless the system of villenage repeatedly came up as a defense in later cases. Thus, an understanding of villenage is essential to evaluate the cases subsequent to *Butts.*

The ancient feudal system of villenage, referred to by the defense in *Butts* v. *Penny,* provided an arguable legal and social precedent for slavery in England. Such legal treatises as Littleton's work on *Tenures* (1268), Cowell's legal dictionary, *The Interpreter* (1607), and Lord Coke's first volume of *Institutes of the Laws of England* continued through the time of *Sommersett* to include writings on villenage within their texts, suggesting that however loosely

slavery and villenage were related, slavery had some form of prece-
dential support.[31] As chattel slavery became more completely developed, English lawyers tended to characterize the institution as a
New World version of villenage.[32] Lawyers hoping to confirm a
common law preference for liberty would need to reconcile their
positions with the prior existence of villenage in England and the
laws technically still in force that had supported or at least permitted it at an earlier time.

The feudal villenage labor system bound the worker to the
master's estate in a status comparable to that of a serf. A villein
was a person attached to a manor, substantially in the condition of
a slave, who performed the base and servile work upon the manor
for the lord and was the lord's property. A villein was incapable of
owning property. The master possessed a limited physical dominion
over the villein and his direct descendants through the male. There
were basically two types of villeins, *villeins in gross* and *villeins regardant*. A *villein in gross* was annexed to the person of the lord
and could be transferred by deed from one owner to another. A
villein regardant, on the other hand, was annexed to the manor
of the lord and was a serf.[33]

The fact that a villein was "attached" to a lord's person or land
did not, however, imply that the villein lacked social status. As
Winthrop Jordan has noted, "In the middle ages being a villein had
meant dependence on the will of a feudal lord but by no means
deprivation of all social and legal rights. . . ."[34] The physical and
legal protections a villein enjoyed were, not surprisingly, more extensive than the nonrights of black slaves.[35]

The system of villenage, which had arisen, according to one of
the counsels for the slave Sommersett, during "the wars between
our British, Saxon, Danish, and Norman ancestors," had already
begun to decline sometime after the Norman conquest of England
in 1066. By the "latter end of Elizabeth's reign or soon after the
accession of [her successor], James," the system became virtually
extinct.[36] All the counsel arguing in *Sommersett* agreed that no
English court had had to deal with a case of villenage since the early
seventeenth century. In the 13th and 14th centuries, as Winthrop
Jordan observed, "villenage had decayed markedly, and it may be
said not to have existed as a viable social institution in the second

half of the sixteenth century. Personal freedom had become the normal status of Englishmen."[37]

Following *Butts* v. *Penny,* two later cases, *Noel* v. *Robinson* (1687)[38] and *Gelly* v. *Cleve* (1694)[39] recognized the legality of property interests in blacks who were not Christian. In *Noel* v. *Robinson,* the court implicitly sanctioned a slaveholder's property interest in black slaves by holding that Sir Martin Noel's devise of a moiety (one of two equal portions) of his West Indian plantation, including slaves, was a valid disposition of property. The court in *Gelly* v. *Cleve* upheld an Englishman's claim to a property interest in black slaves because they were heathens:

> adjudged that *trover* will be for a *Negro* boy; for they are heathens, and therefore a man may have property in them, and that the court . . . will take notice that they are heathens.[40]

In all these early cases, the student of the history of racial slavery must be wary of references to "slaves" and "slavery" during this time. The word "slave" did not always signify the same level of repression and lack of humanity during the 1600s and early 1700s that the term would imply during the later 1700s and 1800s. Obviously, even in the 1600s a slave was not a free person, but it was not until the 1700s that social customs, legislative enactments, and judicial decisions determined the exact place in the social and legal hierarchy that the slave would be allowed to occupy. One cannot be certain, therefore, of the true social and legal ramifications attending the use of the term "slave" when used in these early cases.[41]

Judicial acceptance of the right of an Englishman to own black "heathen" slaves was qualified in the 1696 case of *Chamberlaine* v. *Harvey.*[42] In *Chamberlaine,* suit was brought in trespass* against the defendant (Harvey) for detaining a black, allegedly owned by Chamberlaine. The black had originally been owned by Chamberlaine's father, a planter in Barbados, who died leaving the black to Chamberlaine's mother. The widow remarried and moved to England, taking the slave with her. While in England, the slave was baptized without the plaintiff's permission. When Chamber-

---

* Trespass was an action for financial redress for unlawful injury done to the plaintiff's person or property by the improper act of the defendant.

laine's mother died, her second husband "put the negro slave out of his service."[43] The slave hired himself out to several masters, and when suit was instituted, he was working for the defendant at a wage of six pounds a year.

The court's decision for the defendant did not address the two contentions of the defendant that the black's migration to England and his baptism justified a grant of freedom, although the legal uncertainty surrounding the effect of a slave's baptism on his or her slave status had caused considerable anxiety among slaveholders. Rather, the narrow ruling merely found that a slave could not be assigned the legal status of moveable personal (chattel) property, and therefore an ordinary action in trespass for damages was not appropriate in this case.

> An action of trespass will not lie, because a Negro cannot be demanded as a chattel; neither can his price be recovered in damages in an action of trespass, as in case of a chattel for he is no other than a slavish servant, and the master can maintain no other action of trespass for taking his servant, but only such which concludes *per quod servitium amisit,* in which the master shall recover for the loss of his service, and not for the value, or for any damages done to the servant.[44]

Throughout the eighteenth century, the English courts were often antagonistic toward the institution of slavery and sought to discourage its growth in England. At the same time, the concept of capturing and selling blacks into slavery or using black slave labor in West Indian colonies, sanctioned in *Butts* v. *Penny,* was not challenged. Whatever challenge there was to the legality of slavery in England, slavery in the colonies was not seriously questioned in the courts.

Two cases after *Chamberlaine* highlight this dualistic position. In *Smith* v. *Brown and Cooper** the court found that a plaintiff could not sue in *assumpsit* (an action for the recovery of damages for the nonperformance of a contract) for the purchase price of a slave because, according to Chief Justice Holt, who repeated the dicta of

---

* The exact date of *Smith* v. *Brown and Cooper* is not known. However this case and *Smith* v. *Gould,* discussed *infra,* appear one below the other at 2 Salkeld 666. The possibility exists that the plaintiff may have been the same in both cases and the date probably the same. See Note 25.

Chamberlaine and *Cartwright,* no man can be a slave in England—only a villein. More important, Holt announced that "as soon as a negro comes into *England,* he becomes free."[45]

However, Chief Justice Holt's remarks were gratuitous and afforded little comfort to either the black or the defendant. The Chief Justice volunteered that the plaintiff could have prevailed had he "averred in the declaration that the sale was in *Virginia,* and, by the law of that country, negroes are saleable; for the laws of *England* do not extend to Virginia, being a conquered country their law is what the king pleases. . . ."[46] He recommended that the plaintiff amend his complaint to show that the black at the time of the sale was in Virginia and subject to Virginia laws. (The fact that the sale was in exchange for a Negro previously transferred in England did not undermine this reasoning, evidently.) Thus, the Chief Justice managed to reach a decision that sustained the "purity of the English air" and simultaneously supported the impurity of racial slavery by utilizing the technical nuances of common law pleading.[47]

Mechanistic pleading was a crucial element in the *Smith* v. *Gould* (1706) case as well.[48] The *Smith* plaintiff instituted an action in *trover* against the defendant for, among other things, a *de uno Aethiope vocat* (a singing African). The defendant's argument against Smith's request for relief was essentially that made in *Chamberlaine;* namely, that *trover* was not an appropriate pleading to recover a slave because "the owner had not an absolute property in him; he could not kill him as he could an ox. . . . Men may be the owners and therefore cannot be the subject of property." However, the court did seem to think that by using another form of common law pleading the plaintiff might have been able to place into evidence the fact that the party in question was "his negro" and he had purchased him. The court further noted:

> this action does not lie for a negro, no more than for any other man; for the common law takes no notice of negroes being different from other men. By the common law no man can have a property in another, but in special cases, as in a villain, but even in him not to kill him: so in captives took in war, but the taker cannot kill them, but may sell them to ransom them: there is no such thing as a slave by the law of England. And if

a man's servant is took from him, the master cannot maintain an action for taking him, unless it is laid *per quod servitium amisit*. . . . And the court denied the opinion in the case of *Butts and Penny,* and therefore judgment was given for the plaintiff, for all but the negro as to the damages for him. . . .[49]

Because of these contradictory precedents, there was increasing uncertainty as to whether or not blacks brought to England by slave masters became free. To respond to these concerns, the then Attorney General, Sir Phillip Yorke, and the Solicitor General, Mr. Talbot, were invited in 1729 to a special dinner meeting arranged in Lincoln's Inn Hall to informally express their comments after dinner to a delegation of merchants and planters.

The colonial planters wanted to know whether the mere arrival in London of slaves, or their baptism, would invalidate the planters' authority over their slaves, in view of a growing disapproval of slavery in England. The brief off-the-record opinion of the attorney general and the solicitor general assured the traders and plantation owners that:

[A] slave, by coming from the West Indies, either with or without his master, to Great Britain or Ireland, doth not become free; and that his master's property or right in him is not thereby determined or varied; and baptism doth not bestow freedom on him, nor make any alteration in his temporal condition in these kingdoms. We are also of opinion, the master may legally compel him to return to the plantations.[50]

This advisory opinion lacked the force of a judicial decree. However, the prestige and influence of its authors gave their opinion a legal imprimatur that was gratifying to proslavery interests.[51]

In *Pearne* v. *Lisle*[52] (1749), some twenty years later, their interpretation gained official recognition in the opinion by Sir Phillip Yorke, who had become chancellor and was then known as Lord Hardwicke. In *Pearne,* the plaintiff had hired out to the defendant in Antigua fourteen black slaves at a yearly rate of 100 pounds. Pearne (the plaintiff) claimed that the defendant had refused to pay for the slaves and had refused to return them.

Lord Hardwicke first ruled that the plaintiff would be required to pursue his claim in the colonial court in Antigua. Although it was unnecessary for the court to discuss any other issue, Lord Hard-wicke was eager to imprint in a judicial decree that which he had expressed unofficially. Thus, in gratuitous comments, he attempted to legitimize slavery, adding to a judicial legacy that confronted *Sommersett* twenty years later. First, Hardwicke contended that a *trover* would lie for a Negro slave, just as it had for a villein in ancient English history, because "it [the slave] is as much property as any other thing."[53] He stated that no legal differences existed between enforcing service contracts of English servants or villeins and black slaves. Lord Holt's holding in *Smith* v. *Gould*[54] (1706) was distinguished by Hardwicke as turning on a mere procedural mistake by the plaintiff. He also criticized Lord Holt's notion that setting foot in England established a slave's freedom because it could not explain why a slave would not be freed upon landing in British-controlled Jamaica, whose slavery practices were presumably unchallengeable. Finally, Hardwicke reaffirmed his earlier opinion that baptism of a slave did not lead to emancipation.

In addition to the legal arguments, Hardwicke's opinion evinces a stark commercialistic attitude toward slaves—one that was probably necessary before a person could accept the enslave-ment of a fellow human being. The opinion concludes, for ex-ample, that a delivery of the specific Negroes at issue in the case "is not necessary, others are as good; indeed in the case of a cherry stone, very finely engraved, and likewise of a extraordinary piece of plate for the specific delivery of which bills were brought in this Court, they could not be satisfied in any other way. . . . The Negroes cannot be delivered in the plight in which they were at the time of the demand, for they wear out with labour, as cattle or other things; nor could they be delivered on demand, for they are like stock on a farm, the occupier could not do without them, but would be obliged, in case of a sudden delivery to quit the plantation."[55]

The harsh but definite rule of *Pearne* (1749) was not followed even before *Sommersett*. Ten years before Lord Mansfield's deci-sion in *Sommersett,* Lord Chancellor Henley ruled in favor of a former slave's claim to freedom in *Shanley* v. *Harvey*[56] (1762). Edward Shanley, owner of the defendant, Joseph Harvey, had brought the defendant, then a child, to England in 1750. The plain-tiff gave the slave to his niece (Margaret Hamilton) who baptized him and changed his name. When she was near death, Margaret Hamilton gave the defendant 700 or 800 pounds in bank notes. Plaintiff Shanley tried to resume control over Harvey, but the black man resisted. Lord Chancellor Henley ruled that Harvey could exercise the rights any freeman was able to enjoy.

> As soon as a man sets foot on English ground he is free:
> a negro may maintain an action against his master for ill usage,
> and may have a *Habeas Corpus* if restrained of his liberty.[57]

The Influence of the Abolitionists

Though the judicial decisions of the British courts did not reflect any constant hostility toward the institution of slavery, the slave trade was admittedly an established form of English commerce at the time of the *Sommersett* case. Nevertheless, abolitionist sentiment, led and perhaps epitomized by Granville Sharp, was rising during the latter half of the 1700s.[58] Sharp was the most influential abolitionist during this period, and his ideas undoubtedly helped shape the position of Sommersett's lawyers, with whom he discussed the case. He came from a noted family, even though he was apprenticed to a draper; his grandfather had been the Archbishop of York and his father the Archdeacon of Northumberland. His wealthy older brothers were leading philanthropists.[59] Sharp's interest in the slavery issue began in 1765 when he helped a young black slave, Jonathan Strong. Strong's master had attempted to kidnap Strong and ship him to Jamaica for sale, even though two years earlier Strong had been abandoned by this master, a lawyer from Barbados, after being savagely beaten. Sharp successfully intervened and prevented Strong's reenslavement, but was sued by the slave's master. In his defense, Sharp planned to rebut the prevailing legal view, most likely still shared by the current Chief-Justice, Lord Mansfield, that no slave could claim freedom merely because he had come to England.[60]

This prevailing view had been accepted even by Blackstone, one of the leading legal minds of the century, whom Sharp had consulted about the legal foundations of slavery. In the first edition of his famous treatise, the *Commentaries,* Blackstone had seemed to reiterate the doctrine of such cases as *Cartwright.* "A slave or negro,

the moment he lands in England," he wrote, "falls under the protection of the laws and without regard to all natural rights becomes
eo instanti a freedman." In the third edition, however, this sentence
was qualified to read a slave or Negro, the moment he lands in
England, "falls under the protection of the laws, and so far becomes
a freeman; *though the master's right to his service may probably still
continue.*"[61] Although wishing Sharp success "in his human under-
taking," Blackstone emphasized the qualifications of a slave's purported rights to claim protection of the English laws:

> with regard to any right which the master may have acquired,
> by contract or the like, to the perpetual service of John or
> Thomas, this will remain exactly in the same state as before.
> . . . [T]he slave is entitled to the same liberty [the word be-
> came "protection" in later editions] in England before, as
> after, baptism; and whatever service the heathen negro owed
> to his English master, the same he is bound to render when a
> christian.[62]

The position Granville Sharp ultimately fashioned on behalf
of slaves in England therefore did not rest solely upon judicial
authority. Sharp developed a two-pronged attack on slavery that
challenged both the right of a master to claim a property interest
in a black and the accuracy of previous jurists' reading of English
common law. The 1769 essay, *A Representation of the Injustice
and Dangerous Tendency of Tolerating Slavery; or of Admitting
the Least Claim of Private Property in the Persons of Men in England,*[63] revealed one facet of Sharp's position. Sharp maintained that
no one could claim a black person as a species of private property,
as one would claim a horse or cattle, unless it could first be shown
that blacks were not human beings and therefore not subjects of the
king. "All men, women, and children, including aliens and strangers,
were in a relative sense the 'property' of the King; as subjects, they
were bound by the King's laws and were entitled to the King's protection." . . .[64] This protection, claimed Sharp, included the protection of the Habeaus Corpus Act of 1679, which protected subjects from arbitrary imprisonment or involuntary shipment out of
England.

By the time of the *Thomas Lewis* decision in 1771,[65] Granville

Sharp had a chance to argue his second line of attack. As a result of his intensive study of English law over the preceding few years, Sharp was now ready to challenge those previous jurists' readings of English common law that had sustained slave interests.

Lewis, the former slave of Robert Staplyton, had been forcibly seized by his ex-master and two watermen, dragged to the Thames, and placed on a ship bound for Jamaica, where he was to be sold into slavery. Sharp procured a writ of *habeaus corpus*, temporarily halting the deportation. An action was then commenced against Staplyton, with the able barrister John Dunning hired to serve as counsel for Lewis.

Dunning argued at the trial that villenage had been found to be contrary to English common law and natural law; since villenage itself was illegal it could not be viewed as a precedent for chattel slavery. The jury apparently accepted Dunning's argument and found that Staplyton had no property in the former slave Lewis. But the judge, in this case Lord Mansfield, Chief Justice of the King's Bench, was unwilling to issue a judgment against the defendants, expressing his doubts as to the quality of the evidence. He advised that the proceedings be dropped. Mansfield reportedly told Dunning, Lewis's attorney:

> You will see more in this question than you see at present.
> . . . There are a great many opinions given upon it; I am
> aware of many of them; but perhaps it is much better it
> should never be finally discussed or settled. I don't know what
> the consequences may be, if the masters were to lose their
> property by accidentally bringing their slaevs to England. I
> hope it will never be finally discussed; for I would have all
> masters think them free, and all Negroes think they were not,
> because then they would both behave better.[66]

In this statement, his initial recorded encounter with the problem of a slave's being forcibly transported out of England, Lord Mansfield's advice to Dunning (which noticeably deals with factors other than the quality of the evidence) avoided the pivotal question of whether a master in England had so strong a coercive power over a black person (his former slave) that the forcible exportation of that person might be justified. Mansfield wanted to avoid firmly deciding the controversial issue of the legality of slavery in England.

But the problem remained: the societal pressure to have the matter legally resolved could not much longer be deferred. Less than one year later, Lord Mansfield would again find himself presiding over a trial brought on by the attempt of a master to forcibly transport his slave out of England. Again Mansfield would struggle in an eleventh-hour move to bring about an out-of-court disposition of the case. Again attempts to settle the matter out of the court would be unsuccessful.

Who knows what pressures weighed on this man who had twice attempted to relieve himself of the obligation of imposing a judicial solution on a moral matter? During one of the early oral arguments, with carefully chosen words, Lord Mansfield brushed aside any consideration of the grave social inconveniences and dislocations that might befall his beloved English society, and commented *"Fiat Justitia, ruat coelumtet"*—let justice be done whatever the consequences. With this case, the stage would now be set for an explicit debate in England on the survival of slavery.

9

THE CASE OF
JAMES SOMMERSETT,
A NEGRO

The facts of *Sommersett* fell within the hazy area of ambiguous precedents. The plaintiff, Sommersett, was challenging his master's efforts to deport him from England for sale in Jamaica. Since, arguably, either English law or (indirectly) foreign law could be applied in determining the legality of his enslavement in England, counsel on both sides found ample justification for what were contradictory positions. The constant tension between the existence and legality by default of the British foreign trade and the British common law principles *in favoram liberatis* resurfaced in *Sommersett,* allowing Lord Mansfield to strike a new balance.

The conflict arose when Charles Stuart attempted to forcibly transport his escaped slave, James Sommersett, back to Jamaica. Stuart had originally purchased the slave in Virginia and had in 1769 brought him to England. In October, 1771 Sommersett escaped. Stuart's agents seized Sommersett in November of 1771 and had him chained in a Jamaica-bound ship, commanded by Captain Knowles. In order to end this abduction three English citizens—Thomas Watkins, Elizabeth Cade, and John Marlow—submitted affidavits in support of a motion to Lord Mansfield for a writ of *habeaus corpus* against Captain Knowles. Mansfield granted the writ, ordering the captain to bring Sommersett to court and justify the detention.

On December 9, 1771, upon producing Sommersett before

Lord Mansfield, Captain Knowles replied that Sommersett was owned by Charles Stuart and had been left in Mr. Knowles's custody, "in order to carry him to Jamaica, and there sell him as a slave."[1] Knowles filed a lengthy answer averring that Sommersett had been a slave in Africa even before he was purchased by Stuart. Knowles also stated that Sommersett, who "hath not at any time since [the purchase by Stuart] been manumitted, enfranchised, set free or discharged," had "without the consent, and against the will of the said Charles Stuart, and without any lawful authority whatsoever, departed and absented himself from the service of the said Charles Stuart."[2]

Due to the importance of the case, a hearing on the plaintiff's objection to the return was postponed until February 7, when Mr. Serj. Davy and Mr. Serj. Glynn argued against the return.[3] The most penetrating and consequential debate between counsel, however, would not occur until the Easter term, when Mr. Hargrave, Mr. Alleyne, and Mr. Serj. Davy spoke for freeing the slave and Mr. Wallace and Mr. Dunning for his continued bondage.

The legal issue presented in *Sommersett* did not require a general determination on the legality of slavery on English soil, though certainly the decision could and did bear on that question. Rather, the precise issue was whether it was legal for a slave master from another country to forceably *remove* his slave from England. Thus, counsel on both sides needed to discuss which laws were to be applied to the enforcement of restrictions on foreign slaves being transported through or held in Britain: Was it English common law or the laws of the country from which they had been imported or purchased? And second, assuming that British common law was chosen as the relevant standard, then the court had to determine how it should be interpreted to apply to the facts of *Sommersett*. The decision as to which law would be honored involved that elusive field known as conflicts of law—thus, should Lord Mansfield honor the laws of Virginia, under which Sommersett had been purchased and which sanctioned slavery, or should he look only at the laws of England, where the case was being prosecuted, to determine whether slavery was legal in England.

Of course, the two issues often merged, for the choice of what law pertained to the enslavement of foreign blacks depended in part on one's interpretation of English common law. Throughout his presentation Hargrave on behalf of Sommersett argued that slavery was antagonistic to the tradition of English common law, thereby assuming that Virginia law was irrelevant. On the other side, Dunning maintained consistently that the decision had to be based on foreign law, particularly that of colonial Virginia where Sommersett was purchased. While never conceding that the common law required freedom, he urged that certain relationships involving foreign citizens (master-slave, husband-wife, master-apprentice) should generally be protected by British courts deferring to foreign interests by applying foreign law. The type of slavery involved in this case, he added, was distinguishable from other more pernicious types of foreign slavery that should not be enforced by British courts.

The oral argument in *Sommersett* could have easily become sidetracked into a general discussion of the economic, moral, and political necessities of either sanctioning or prohibiting all slavery throughout the world. Such an exercise might have endeared each counsel to the purists supporting his view, but given the legal and political tenor of the period, it would not have advanced either side's legal position, and all counsel knew it. The brilliance of counsel, especially Hargrave and Dunning, lay in their skill in structuring their positions in the most limited but forceful fashion, marshaling arguments from moral philosophy, public policy, but most of all from judicial precedent, so as to maximize the probabilities of a favorable outcome.

Thus, John Dunning in behalf of the owner repeatedly stressed the limited and restrained form of slavery that would be sanctioned by Sommersett's enslavement and rejected support for more destructive forms or a more pervasive presence of slavery. Hargrave, to the contrary, accepted the legality of various types of slavery, such as villenage or slavery in the colonies, which were supposedly distinguished from the form of bondage holding Sommersett.

Sommersett v. *Stuart* is a classic example of public policy changing because of the intellectual strength of an advocate's argument. Most notably, the resourcefulness of Francis Hargrave's presentation for Sommersett's freedom may have been crucial in the slave's ultimate victory, and it is especially noteworthy in light of the fact that Hargrave was opposed by one of the ablest barristers in England, John Dunning. It is for this reason that we will now present and analyze Sommersett's legal issues in the chronological order and in the format in which they were introduced by the primary counsel for each side, Hargrave and Dunning. The subtleties of the debate would not survive in general summaries of the legal positions; the order, structure, phraseology, and emphases of the actual arguments are themselves keys to the various elements of the decision.

HARGRAVE'S ARGUMENTS IN BEHALF OF SOMMERSETT

Francis Hargrave was the first to present the case for Sommersett's freedom. This was the first time Hargrave had publicly argued a case, but he was thoroughly familiar with the views of the famous abolitionist Granville Sharp, with whom he had corresponded as early as May, 1769. Hargrave assured Sharp that his zeal for abolition would outweigh his lack of experience.

Hargrave presented a forceful and skilled argument limited to the contention that the common law forbade chattel slavery on English soil.[4] Though observing that slavery was a "pernicious institution," he adroitly chose not to attack the legality of slavery in the colonies or the extinct villenage system in England—issues that he claimed were tangential to Sommersett's case. It was only slavery on English soil that he wanted established as clearly unenforceable by British courts.

Admittedly, this position did not make use of several of the broader moral and legal arguments against slavery that abolitionists such as Granville Sharp believed made slavery illegal and immoral wherever it existed. Yet Hargrave's seemingly logical consistency with ancient common law precedent and his modest but pragmatic objectives undoubtedly weighed heavily upon Mansfield and helped stimulate a receptive response.

Hargrave and the other counsel repeatedly stressed that English political interests, moral responsibilities, and legal doctrines were undermined by the importation of foreign slaves. Thus, by emphasizing the extent to which the institution of slavery was antagonistic to the traditions of English common law, Hargrave, in fact, avoided the traps of the opposition.

In his opening remarks, Hargrave moved immediately to emphasize the importance of Sommersett's freedom to the interests and liberties of all British citizens. A finding for the defendant, he predicted, would permit the lawful importation of foreign slaves "with its horrid train of evils, . . . at the discretion of every individual foreign and native."[5] With this statement Hargrave not only commenced his own argument but simultaneously undercut the contention he may have anticipated would be that of the opposition, namely that the importation of foreign slaves did not challenge English liberty[6] and affected the interests only of those foreigners who happened to bring slaves to England. Hargrave stressed that if slavery gained such a sanction from English law, it "will be transmitted to use in all of its various forms in all gradations of inventive cruelty: and by an universal reception of slavery, this country, so famous for public liberty, will become the chief seat of private tyranny."[7] Foreign slavery, he reasoned, could not be imported into England without fundamentally undermining the common law doctrine in favor of personal rights and freedom of all Englishmen.

Hargrave's substantive critique of slavery emphasized its pernicious impact on white masters, English society in general, and slaves. Slavery, he noted,

> corrupts the morals of the master, by freeing him from those restraints with respect to his slave, so necessary for control of the human passions, so beneficial in promoting the practice and confirming the habit of virtue—it is dangerous to the master; because his oppression excites implacable resentment and hatred in the slave, and the extreme misery of his condition continually prompts him to risk the gratification of them, and his situation daily furnishes the opportunity—To the slave it communicates all the afflictions of life, without leaving for him scarce any of its pleasures; and it depresses the excellence of his nature, by denying the ordinary means and motives of improvement. It is dangerous to the state, by its corruption of those citizens on whom its prosperity depends; and by admitting within it a multitude of persons, who being excluded from the common benefits of the constitution, are interested in scheming its destruction.—Hence it is, that slavery, in whatever light we view it, may be deemed a most pernicous institution; immediately so, to the unhappy person who suffers under

it; finally so, to the master who triumphs in it, and to the state which allows it.[8]

By emphasizing that slavery corrupted the morals of the master, Hargrave raised the issue to a new level of consciousness for a court's adjudication. It was more than mere sympathy for the despicable plight that the slave endured. He was begging the court to recognize that slavery caused the master to have a malevolence irrespective of the harm caused the slave.[9] Hargrave in effect introduced the social and moral costs of slavery to whites as a factor the court would have to consider in its final adjudication of the case.

The particular form of slavery under review, Hargrave continued, lacked any philosophical justification, since it was distinguishable from those types of slavery that retained, according to some authors, limited moral legitimacy. Slavery established through warfare had some, though doubtful, moral justification, and in any event, it was permissible only until reparations were paid for the aggression against the triumphant country. In contrast, Stuart sought to enslave Sommersett permanently, and there was no evidence that Sommersett's bondage had originated in war. Similarly, slavery by contract was rejected by Hargrave as a possible basis because "freedom from arbitrary power is essential to the exercise of the right [of preserving title]; and therefore . . . no man can by compact enslave himself."[10] He also argued that the justification of slavery—punishment for crimes against the state—was inapplicable to Sommersett because it never extended to the offender's issue and seldom required family service to satisfy the debt of service owed to the state by the original defendant. Hargrave concluded that except when imposed as punishment for a crime, the legality of slavery was "at least doubtful." Thus, "the oppressive manner in which [slavery] has generally commenced, the cruel means necessary to enforce its continuance, and the mischiefs ensuing from the permission of it, furnish very strong presumption against its justice."[11]

THE LEGAL PRECEDENTS FOR AND AGAINST SLAVERY

The greatness of Hargrave's argument lay in his adroit analysis of the legal precedents against slavery. The position he fashioned took full advantage of the legal existence of villenage in distant

English history to demonstrate the illegality of slavery. He admitted that human bondage, present from the earliest years of recorded history, had continued in many areas through advanced civilization, but observed that its subsequent decline in most of Europe evidenced a developing legal as well as pragmatic disapproval of the institution. The recent resurgence of this subjugation in the new and more debilitating form of New World racial slavery was therefore inconsistent with the legal doctrines that had evolved to limit villenage. Thus, Hargrave's acceptance of the limited legality of villenage, which was anathema to Sharp in any form, permitted him to apply those same common law doctrines *in favorem liberatis* to the eradication of modern slavery in England, rather than restricting himself to the more nebulous concepts of natural law.[12]

Hargrave willingly acknowledged that villenage and slavery shared many similar characteristics. "The condition of a villein," he said, "had most of the incidents which [give] the idea of slavery in general."[13] In both systems the service was uncertain and indeterminate; the master could beat, imprison, or chastise his slave without reproach; and the slave was incapable of acquiring property. Hargrave used the similarity of conditions between villeins and slaves as a basis to apply those decisions and rules that limited and ultimately caused the eradication of villenage in England. And, of course, those *differences* that did exist between the two systems, such as the greater legal protection and local character of villenage, established the illegality of the more destructive chattel slavery.

Hargrave detailed the common law doctrines that had restricted villenage and hopefully would not permit the commencement of any new form of slavery. Developed after the Norman conquest of England, these rules evidenced a bias generally assumed in all common law decisions in favor of liberty—or what was called *in favorem liberatis*. The *onus probandi* (burden of proof) for demonstrating the servitude of a villein was always placed upon the lord whether he was the defendant, in a suit called *Liberate Probanda*, or the plaintiff, in a suit called *Nativo Habendo*. A ruling for a landlord in one of those suits, moreover, did not bar future actions by the villein, though a decision for a villein's freedom precluded the landlord from asserting the villein's bondage in any future action. The landlord's legal costs were increased by the requirement that he prosecute no more than two villeins in one *Nativo Habendo,* though several villeins could join together, so as to reduce costs, and sue for their freedom in a *Liberate Probanda.*

Constructive manumissions were also imposed by the courts on "the slightest circumstances of mistake or negligence in the law, from every act or omission which legal refinement could strain into an acknowledgment of the villein's liberty."[14] A variety of unintentional acts by the landlord automatically triggered manumission; a lord would forfeit his ownership of a villein if he permitted him to own land, vote, serve on a jury, join a religion, or simply bring an action against the lord without a protestation of villenage by the master. The financial and legal burden of owning a villein increased significantly with these proscriptions.

While these rules certainly hastened the decline of villenage and, as Hargrave emphasized, demonstrated for later generations the preference of the common law for freedom, other parallel legal restrictions on the title to villenage specifically prevented the commencement of any *new* villenage or slavery. Hargrave declared that the enslavement of every villein required either his confession in a court of record or a prescriptive showing that the ancestors of the slave had entered bondage at a time "ancient and immemorial." Villenage originating in contract, war, or sale was not legal; only "slavery" (i.e., villenage) that had commenced before the "time of memory" and had continued by birth without interruption up to the present time was sanctioned.[15]

These requirements had continued after the demise of villenage and "now furnishes one of the chief obstacles to the introduction of slavery attempted to be revived."[16] "The law of England," Hargrave stressed, "only knows slavery by birth; it requires prescription in making title to a slave; it receives on the lord's part no testimony except such as proves the slavery to have been always in the blood and family, on the villein's part every testimony which proves the slave to have been once out of his blood and family; it allows nothing to sustain the slavery except what shews its commencement beyond the time of memory, everything to defeat the slavery which evinces its commencement within the time of memory."[17] Black chattel slavery clearly did not fall within the protection of these laws, as no form of slavery could, since the only slavery the English common law recognized was now irreversibly extinct.[18]

The antislavery arguments that were based on the precedent of villenage were summarized by Hargrave:

> The law of England then excludes every slavery not commencing in England, every slavery though commencing there not being ancient and immemorial. Villenage is the only slavery which can possibly answer to such a description, and that has long expired by the deaths and emancipations of all those who were once the objects of it. Consequently there is now no slavery which can be lawful in England, until the legislature shall interpose its authority to make it so.[19]

The fact that no slavery had arisen in England after the extinction of villenage, Hargrave stressed, gave further evidence of an English common law-prohibition against all forms of slavery within England.

Hargrave found supporting evidence in the legal presumption against slavery by the law of contracts. He explained that the English courts had refused to enforce contracts of self-enslavement, probably one of the less pernicious of the various forms of slavery.[20] If English law would not permit this type of bondage, then, Hargrave urged, certainly the more devastating forms, such as slavery based on captivity in war and introduced from another country, could not be sanctioned. Hargrave asked:

> Will the law of England condemn a new slavery commencing by consent of the party and at the same time approve of one founded on force, and most probably on oppression also? Will the law of England invalidate a new slavery commencing in this country; when the title to the slavery may be fairly examined; and at the same time give effect to a new slavery introduced from another country, when disproof of the slavery must generally be impossible? This would be . . . rejecting slavery the least odious, receiving slavery the most odious; and by such an inconsistency, the wisdom and justice of the English law would be completely dishonored.[21]

Hargrave wisely did not contest the legality of colonial slavery. He refused to assert that the libertarian protections of the English common law applied to slaves who were physically in American colonies. Slavery in America, he conceded, "may be by captivity or contract as well as birth; no prescription is requisite; nor is it necessary that slavery should be in the blood and family and immemorial."[22] Politically, the admission undoubtedly assuaged fears that a ruling for Sommersett would undermine the legal foundations of the international slave trade; thus, he maximized the popular pressures for a favorable decision.

The admission may have improved Hargrave's logical position, since it allowed him to argue that if the American colonies were exempt from foreign British law then the English legal system was exempt from the enforcement of foreign slave laws.[23] His concession also undermined Lord Hardwicke's earlier contention[24] in *Pearne* v. *Lisle* that the acceptance of slavery in the colonies proved the legality of slavery generally under English law, including domestic slavery in England. Hargrave had argued that the legality of slavery was limited to the boundaries of the colonies. America could no longer be pointed to as proof of the legality of slavery under English common law. Thus, by extricating the colonies from English domestic precedent, Hargrave pragmatically thinned out the ranks of his opposition; he buttressed his argument that English law should be applied to *domestic* slavery and that such English common law mandated liberty for Sommersett.

Having concluded his principal arguments, Hargrave then moved to rebut in advance several possible objections to his position. He asserted the mere fact that villenage had *arisen* in England at one point also did not undermine his position, since the institution "had a commencement here prior to the establishment of those rules which the common law furnishes against slavery by contract."[25]

Of course, Hargrave's argument on the common law would have been irrelevant if his opponent were able to find a legislative sanction of slavery in England. Hargrave responded to this hypothetical challenge by pointing out that the only act of parliament giving official sanction to slavery implied that slavery was in the colonies. To extend that sanction judicially would undermine the sovereignty of parliament.[26]

[T]he utmost which can be said of these statutes is that they impliedly authorize the slavery of negroes in America; and it would be a strange thing to say that permitting slavery there, includes a permission of slavery here. By an unhappy concurrence of circumstances, the slavery of negroes is thought to have become necessary in America; and therefore in America our legislature has permitted the slavery of Negroes. But the slavery of Negroes is unnecessary in England, and therefore the legislation has not extended the permission of it to England; and not having done so, how can this court be warranted to make such an extension?[27]

Hargrave argued that slavery could not be sanctioned by the common law in England out of deference to the slave laws of *other* countries and English colonies, because, as several European countries had also concluded: "To prevent the revival of domestic slavery effectively, its introduction must be resisted universally, without regard to the place of its commencement; and therefore in the instance of slavery, the *lex loci* [the law of the country in which the relation originated] must yield to the municipal law [the law of the country where the case is being tried]."[28]

Hargrave's opponents would also make a related argument that the court was not being asked to enforce slavery in England, but merely to enforce various types of service obligations that were also routinely enforced by the British courts, except in this case they happened to be exacted from slaves. The legal fiction supporting this position was that foreign slaves in England had entered into a service contract to perform services in England. In a sense this argument attempted to justify the enforcement of foreign contracts involving slaves in those areas where they might not be inconsistent with British law. Hargrave, however, urged the court not to accept such an obfuscation of the realities. Black slaves had not been parties to any contract because their status denied them the power to enter any contract. Thus, such fictional contracts were unenforceable by the courts. But even assuming there were such an agreement in the instant case, the contract ultimately would need to include, if the defendant was to prevail, a provision for Negro Sommersett to return to America and slavery. Thus, a service contract became finally a slave contract—what Hargrave called "a contract to go into slavery whenever the master's occasions shall require"[29]—and this clearly was illegal. Hargrave wondered, "Will the law of England disallow the introduction of slavery, and therefore emancipate the Negro from it; and yet give effect to a contract founded solely upon slavery. . . ."[30]

In general, all attempts to soften the effect of slavery in England, either through implied contracts or outright modification, would invariably insist that the slave regain all the severe burdens of slavery on his departure; and this, Hargrave insisted, the common law would not permit.[31]

MR. DUNNING, COUNSEL FOR STUART AND KNOWLES

Mr. Dunning was by far the most eloquent and forceful defender of Stuart's right to keep Sommersett a slave. Just one year earlier he had been retained to argue for the freedom of the slave in the *Lewis* case[32] for, according to William Holdsworth, he was "universally acknowledged to be at the head of the common law and equity bars."[33] He was "doubtless retained [in *Sommersett* so] that his formidable powers might not be called into action for Sommersett," one historian concluded.[34]

Dunning's acceptance of his position in *Sommersett* raised several ethical issues, since he argued in the *Lewis* case that no man could be legally detained as a slave in Great Britain. Sharp was indignant because Dunning was advocating a position in which he did not believe and because Dunning had already taken a stand against slavery in *Lewis*. However, the practice of the English legal profession supported Dunning's action; in England a barrister was traditionally obligated to accept a client unless the barrister was otherwise retained.[35]

In his opening remarks in *Sommersett,* Dunning attempted to soften the emotional intensity of the slavery issue and limit the natural sympathy the court and the public probably felt toward the slave. He pictured himself as the underdog, faced by an overly emotional opposition that failed to appreciate the legal aspects of the issues. He remarked:

> It is my misfortune to address an audience, the great part of which, I fear, are prejudiced the other way. But wishes, I am

well convinced, will never enter into your lordships' mind, to influence the determination of the point: this cause must be what in fact and law it is; its fate, I trust, therefore, depends upon fixt invariable rules, resulting by law from the nature of the case.[36]

Dunning's speech was sprinkled with references to the benign and restrained nature of slavery in England. He was not pleading for the right to physically abuse or sell slaves or to enslave their descendants. The case was solely concerned with the judicially enforced performance of certain services, which might have been required of a servant, but happened to be exacted from a slave. Hargrave's morbid description of slavery was inapplicable to the case at hand. Dunning argued that the more moderate form of servitude did possess legal and philosophical justification.[37]

Dunning began, as Hargrave did, by emphasizing the pragmatic considerations supporting his position. Freedom for all English slaves would loosen the legal and psychological restraints on over fourteen thousand slaves and appropriate their value from their English owners, he said. In time more slaves would come from Jamaica and further burden the country. Perhaps wisely, Dunning never clearly articulated *what* would occur if all the slaves were manumitted, except to say, "There are very strong and particular grounds of apprehension, if the relation in which [the slaves] stand to their master is utterly to be dissolved on the instant of their coming into England."[38]

Dunning's legal defense of slavery was based initially on the *possibility* that Sommersett had become enslaved through legitimate criminal or civil litigation—a process Hargrave had admitted earlier might provide legal and moral grounds for certain types of enslavement.[39] African law provided for explicit punishment through involuntary servitude for the commission of various crimes against property. Dunning detailed the legal procedures that were often used to enslave lawbreakers, implying that such institutionalized legal proceedings were the basis of Stuart's legitimate expectations that his authority over Sommersett would be enforced in England. There was no way of proving that this was the process by which Sommersett had been forced into slavery; but Dunning argued that it was the *plaintiff's* burden to prove that he did *not* fall under this supposedly legal category of slavery: "I do not aim at proving these points; not because they want of evidence, but because they have not been contoverted, to my recollection, and are, I think, incapable of denial."[40]

But even if this were not the method by which the present slavery commenced, Dunning asserted that other types of slavery found legal precedent in English history. The laws protecting villenage, though that feudal system was now extinct, continued to permit forms of involuntary servitude.

Dunning conceded that some especially destructive forms of slavery (evidently distinguishable from Sommersett's bondage) were illegal. In particular, the supposedly unique characteristics of Russian slavery did not find precedent in the more moderate system of villenage. Dunning noted that under the *Cartwright* case, "Russian slavery and even the subordination among themselves, in the degree they use it, is not here to be tolerated."[41] But, Dunning repeated, the case at bar was different: the court was not being asked to support the sale or physical abuse of a slave, but merely to require reasonable service.

Dunning's reliance on the precedent of villenage meant that he still had to explain why the common law rules preventing the formation of any new villenage or slavery did not free Sommersett. He suggested that since the *institution* of slavery found precedent in England, the *process* by which any slavery came into being was irrelevant to the judiciary. "Mr. Alleyne [counsel for Sommersett] justly observes, the municipal regulations of one court are not binding on another . . . but does the relation cease where the modes of creating it, the degrees in which it subsists, vary? I have not heard, nor, I fancy, is there any intention to affirm, the relation of master and servant ceases here?"[42] The fact that it was often impossible to specify how a foreigner became enslaved reinforced Dunning's argument. While Hargrave argued that it would be wrong to enforce a more pernicious type of servitude merely because it arose in another country, Dunning replied that it would be unjust *not* to enforce servitude merely because it commenced in another country in a different (albeit more pernicious) manner.

Dunning went on to describe the restrictions on slaves as fundamentally no different from those found in most service contracts.

The refusal to enforce such "obligations" would be equivalent to a refusal to enforce standard English contracts that take effect abroad.

> It would be a great surprise, and some inconvenience, if a foreigner bringing over a servant, as soon as he got hither, must take care of his carriage, his horse, and himself in whatever method he might have the luck to invent. He must find his way to London on foot. He tells his servant, Do this; the servant replies; Before I do it, I think fit to inform you, Sir, the first step on this happy land sets all men on a perfect level; you are just as much obliged to obey my commands. Thus, neither superior, or inferior, both go without their dinner. We should find singular comfort, on entering the limits of a foreign country, to be thus at once devested of all attendance and all accommodation.[43]

Finally, Dunning noted several other examples of English servitude that reinforced his proposition that the institution of slavery was recognized by the courts. Apprentices bound out by a parish could not choose their trade or employer. And contracts for life were recognized as valid, although several procedural prerequisites were required. He also distinguished several of the cases freeing slaves as having been based on property principles of *trover*. Had those slave owners sued *per quod servitium amisit,* for loss of service, they would have prevailed.

MR. DAVY, COUNSEL FOR SOMMERSETT

Davy presented a point-by-point rebuttal of Dunning. First, he argued that political pragmatism called for the emancipation, not the continued bondage, of the fourteen thousand British slaves, since the proliferation of such "superfluous inhabitants" with no interest "in the prosperity of the country is very pernicious." They formed "a nation of enemies in the heart of a state."[44]

The relation of master and slave—which Dunning had believed universally enforceable—was illegal in Great Britain because it was "utterly foreign to the laws and customs of this country, the law cannot recognize such relation."[45] Certain moral obligations such as marriage or business contracts normally were enforced across national boundaries. However, the relation between a master and servant was not based on such a moral obligation and should not be protected.[46]

But even if one were to accept the relation between master and servant that Dunning had outlined, Davy stressed that the court "certainly would not allow the most exceptionable part of slavery; that of being obliged to remove, at the will of the master, from the protection of this land of liberty, to a country where there are no laws; or hard laws to insult him. It will not permit slavery suspended for a while, suspended during the pleasure of the master."[47] These words undercut Dunning's contention that the court was merely being asked to enforce a service contract. Those forms of slavery that even Dunning had found legally and philosophically inconsistent with English heritage would be sanctioned indirectly by the forced deportation of Sommersett and other slaves.

Later, Davy chided Dunning for his obvious deemphasis of the dehumanizing aspects of British slavery:

> For the air of England; I think, however, it has been gradually purifying ever since the reign of Elizabeth. Mr. Dunning seems to have discovered so much, as he finds it changes a slave into a servant; though unhappily he does not think it of efficacy enough to prevent that pestilent disease reviving the instant the poor man is obliged to quit . . . this happy country.[48]

Lord Mansfield: An Able and Independent Jurist

The Justice to whom these speeches were directed, Lord Mansfield, was not only an influential politician, but also a noted legal scholar whose decision in the *Sommersett* case was probative and well considered, unlike the 1729 extrajudicial opinion of Talbot and Yorke.[49]

As a further distinction, whereas Talbot and Yorke's *ex parte* advisory opinion in 1729 was judicially gratuitous, Lord Mansfield's decision was within what is still considered good judicial practice: it was written only after sincere attempts to settle the case and thereby avoid establishing a precedent of wide applicability.

The life of William Murray, later Lord Mansfield, spanned the bulk of the eighteenth century, during which Britain was becoming the most powerful Western commercial nation. Perhaps no other eighteenth-century jurist was regarded as being more able to cope with these changing conditions than Lord Mansfield; he can be credited with the formation of much of the commercial law of England.[50]

Despite his linkage to the development of English commercial law, there were a series of incidents prior and subsequent to the *Sommersett* case that indicated that Mansfield had greater sensitivity and concern than his peers for the rights of all persons—even those of minorities and the unpopular. In 1767, in *Rex* v. *Webb*,[51] a defendant was prosecuted for celebrating mass, an act that had been made a criminal offense under a statute of William III. Mansfield directed an acquittal ruling that the jury must not infer that defendant is a "priest because he said mass, and that he said mass because he is a priest." His ruling led to such public condemnation that some called him a Jesuit in disguise. In *Chamberlin* v. *Evans*,[52] Mansfield reversed a practice that had been previously upheld by Lord Holt, whereby under the Test Act all persons elected to municipal office who refused to take office because they were unable to take the sacrament of the English church were subject to fines. Mansfield ruled that the Toleration Act of 1689[53] had established the right of dissenters to worship as they chose and that the failure to assume office from which they were disqualified was no ground on which to support a fine. In Mansfield's words:

> bare nonconformity is no sin by the common law; and all positive laws, inflicting any pains or penalties for nonconformity to the established rites or modes, are repealed by the act of toleration, and dissenters are thereby exempted from all ecclesiastical censures.[54]

Just as he had protected the Catholics' freedom of religion, in *Atcheson* v. *Everitt* (1775)[55] he defended a Quaker, whose adversary sought to disqualify the Quaker from testifying because he did not take the traditional oath of a witness. Speaking for tolerance, Mansfield said:

> Upon general principles, I think the affirmation of a Quaker ought to be admitted in all cases, as well as the oath of a Jew, or a Gentile, or of any other person who thinks himself really

bound by the mode and form in which he attests. * * *

A scruple of conscience entitles a party to indulgence and protection so far as not to suffer for it . . .[56]

Perhaps the strongest example of Lord Mansfield's independence was his ruling involving John Wilkes, who had been prosecuted for publishing a libel against King George III and for publishing an obscene poem entitled "Essay on Women." He had been expelled from the House of Commons for his libelous publication and outlawed from Britain because of his failure to appear to receive judgment at the Bar of the Commons. In 1768 Wilkes reappeared in an attempt to reverse his outlawry. Mansfield denied him bail, thereby becoming most unpopular with the public, which ultimately rioted outside the King's Bench prison.

On June 8, 1768, Mansfield delivered his judgment on Wilkes. The following extract is quoted in such detail because it reveals Mansfield's independence and obliviousness to the pressures of an intense public that may want a contrary result. Mansfield said:

But here let me pause!—It is fit to take some notice of the various terrors being held out; the numerous crowds which have attended and now attend in and about the hall, out of all reach of hearing what passes in court; and the tumults which, in other places, have shamefully insulted all order and government. Audacious addresses in print dictate to us, from those they call the people, the judgment to be given now, and afterwards upon the conviction. Reasons of policy are urged, from danger to the kingdom by commotions and general confusion.

Give me leave to take the opportunity of this great and respectable audience to let the world know that all such attempts are vain. Unless we have been able to find an error which will bear us out to reverse the outlawry, it must be affirmed. The constitution does not allow reasons of state to influence our judgments. God forbid it should! We must not regard political consequences, how formidable soever they might be; if rebellion, was the certain consequence, we are bound to say "Fiat justitia, ruat coelum." * * * We are to say what we take the law to be: if we do not speak our real opinions, we prevaricate with God and our own consciences.

I pass over many anonymous letters I have received. Those in print are public, and some of them have been brought judicially before the court. Whoever the writers are, they take the wrong way. I will do my duty unawed. What am I to fear? That *menax infamia* from the press, which daily coins false facts and false motives? The lies of calumny carry no terror to me. I trust that my temper of mind, and the color and conduct of my life, have given me a suit of armour against these arrows. * * * Once and for all, let it be understood, that no endeavours of this kind will influence any man who at present sits here. * * * The only effect I feel from such outrages is an anxiety to be able to explain the grounds upon which we proceed; so as to satisfy all mankind that a flaw of form given way to in this case could not have been got over in any other.[57]

Ultimately, Mansfield reversed the outlawry of Wilkes but affirmed a verdict of guilty for the libelous publication. Wilkes was sentenced to two years' imprisonment, fined one thousand pounds and was to find two securities of five hundred pounds each for his good behavior for seven years. While we do not suggest that the physical abuse of a public official is an appropriate vindication of his integrity, perhaps it is not without significance that in 1780 Mansfield's house in Bloomsbury Square was burned down, his library completely destroyed, together with his notes and correspondence, and Mansfield is said to have "narrowly escaped in safety." This destruction occurred as a result of the "Gordon riots" in opposition to the Roman Catholic Relief Act of 1778. While Mansfield was not an instigator in the formation of the act, his well-known sympathy to that act made him subject to the type of violence that occurred at the site of his home.

These cases and experiences demonstrate that Sommersett's case was presided over by a jurist of profound intellectual ability and extraordinary independence. He was not inclined to make a judgment solely for the sake of winning popular plaudits.

The Decision-making Process

Lord Mansfield's preliminary opinion in *Sommersett,* perhaps as well as his final opinion, reflected his reluctance to interject judicial coercion into this one area. His first move was to prod the parties toward an out-of-court settlement, reporting that "in five or six cases of this nature, I have known [the controversy] to be accommodated by agreement between the parties."[58]

Yet both sides were unwilling or unable to settle the issue, and Mansfield was thereby required to give judgment in accordance with English law. It was here that the chief justice spoke the famous words *"fiat Justitia, ruat coelumtet"*—let justice be done whatever the consequences. Just as four years before, when confronted by a howling mob outside King's Bench prison during the Wilkes case, the court was now committed to decide the nature of Stuart's dominion, deriving from a valid contract over Sommersett.[59]

Mansfield first noted the conflicting arguments for both sides. There were legal and pragmatic liabilities to the enforcement of any aspect of slavery as well as disagreeable effects threatened by the emancipation of fourteen thousand slaves. He ended with another attempt to avoid the decision by suggesting that the merchants should apply to parliament as "perhaps the only method of settling the point for the future."[60]

Yet, ultimately, Mansfield resolved the issue in a decision that would remain a landmark in English legal history. The core of the *Sommersett* opinion is excerpted below:

> We pay all due attention to the opinion of Sir Philip Yorke, and lord chancellor Talbot, whereby they pledged themselves to the British planters, for all the legal consequences of slaves coming over to this kingdom or being baptized, recognized by lord Hardwicke, sitting as chancellor on the 19th of October, 1749, [when he found] that trover would lie [for slaves]; that a notion had prevailed, if a negro came over, or became a Christian, he was emancipated, but [it had] no ground in law; that he and lord Talbot, when attorney and solicitor-general, were of opinion that no such claim for freedom was valid; that though the statute of tenures had abolished villeins regardant to a manor, yet he did not conceive but that a man might still become a villein in gross, by confessing himself such in open court. We are so well agreed, that we think there is no occasion of having it argued (as I intimated an intention at first,) before all the judges, as is usual, for obvious reasons, on a return to a Habeas Corpus.
>
> The only question before us is, whether the cause on the

return is sufficient? If it is, the negro must be remanded; if it is not, he must be discharged. Accordingly, the return states, that the slave departed and refused to serve; whereupon he was kept, to be sold abroad. So high an act of dominion must be recognized by the law of the country where it is used. The power of a master over his slave has been extremely different, in different countries. The state of slavery is of such a nature, that it is incapable of being introduced on any reasons, moral or political, but only by positive law, which preserves its force long after the reasons, occasion, and time itself from whence it was created, is erased from memory. It is so odious, that nothing can be suffered to support it, but positive law. Whatever inconveniences, therefore, may follow from the decision, I cannot say this case is allowed or approved by the law of England; and therefore the black must be discharged.[61]

The Significance and Impact of Sommersett

By its very nature, the Anglo-American legal process has traditionally operated as a system of selection. Advocates present what they believe to be the best options before the judiciary; the "best" options usually being those most favorable to their client. The judge or jury carefully considers the choices and selects one side's alternative as the "better," the "fairer," the "most just," solution to the problem. That is, of course, an abstract of the system in its purest form. Any student of legal history can recite a host of occasions when the system has gone awry. And, when one narrows the field to a consideration of only those cases involving blacks and slaveholders, the response of the legal system has regularly displayed a potential for the distortion of justice, probably because racial prejudice itself is twisted and irrational.

Yet, Lord Mansfield's decision in *Sommersett* is one of the few cases approaching the model of the judicial system. Prior to *Sommersett,* Mansfield's positions on race and slavery were unclear. The chancellor had successfully avoided the issue in the 1771 *Lewis* case, apparently believing that parliament, rather than the courts, was the appropriate institution to decide the slavery issue. Few judges on few cases can be totally neutral, however, and it is probable that Mansfield's dedication to the modernization of commercial law and his commitment to the concept of a British empire might have led one to expect that commercial interests supportive of slavery would be favored.

But, as an eminent jurist, Lord Mansfield was undoubtedly also familiar with the common law tradition of liberty and of the courts' growing reluctance to sanction villenage as obviously inconsistent with notions of British freedom. But, as the *Sommersett* case demonstrates, the commercial interests profiting from slavery were antagonistic to the broader English concepts of freedom. The ultimate question in *Sommersett* called for a balancing of the interests of each side of the issue.

Lord Mansfield would rather not have had this momentous selection forced on him. His initial response was an open suggestion to the parties to "accommodate by agreement" between them. Thus, it is not surprising that once settlement was impossible, the Chief Justice would seek to deal with the case as presented to him and not use the case as a vehicle to deliver an opinion broader than the merits of the case required. Mansfield, still the cautious eighteenth-century jurist, framed the issue as: "Whether any dominion, authority or coercion can be exercised in this country, on a slave according to American laws?"[62]

Even though Mansfield's decision was not as broad in scope as some scholars would like to suggest, some crucial questions affecting the total slavery question were answered in the case. Mansfield categorized slavery as a municipal (governmental) system—that is, a system that can be justified only if a local governmental unit had specifically approved of slavery. These following lines from his opinion were repeated and followed in hundreds of American decisions and pamphlets for the next several decades:

> So high an act of dominion [slavery] must be recognized by the law of the country where it is used. * * *
> The state of slavery is of such a nature, that it is incapable of being introduced on any reasons, moral or political, but only by positive law which preserves its force long after the reason, occasion, and time itself when it was created, is erased from memory. It is so odious that nothing can be suffered to support it, but positive law.[63]

Once slavery was so labeled to require the positive law of one's jurisdiction, it became possible, at least in Mansfield's view, for England not to enforce the municipal law of another jurisdiction—even if it involved a colony of England. Despite the antislavery posture, one could infer that Mansfield was not condemning the institution of domestic slavery per se, but merely prohibiting a master's attempt to kidnap or imprison his slave when seeking to remove the slave from England.

10

THE LEGACY OF SOMMERSETT

ansfield did not intend for *Sommersett* to upset the international slave trade. Three years later, Mansfield had an opportunity to expand the humanitarianism implied in *Sommersett* to a condemnation of the international slave trade. The case, *Jones* v. *Schmoll,*[1] involved an insurance policy taken out on slaves shipped from Africa to the West Indies; but Mansfield did not question the morality or legality of the slavery issue in the *Jones* case involving Englishmen profiting from the international slave trade. He treated it as a standard commercial matter construing one's rights under an insurance policy. He rendered a verdict:

> That all the slaves who were killed in the mutiny, or died of their wounds, were to be paid for [by the insurance company]. That all those who died of their bruises, which they received in the mutiny, though accompanied with other causes, were to be paid for. That all who had swallowed salt water, or leaped into the sea, and hung upon the sides of the ship without being otherwise bruised, or died of chagrin, were not to be paid for.

In nearby Scotland, a jurist extended the rationale of the *Sommersett* case and found slavery per se inconsistent with local law in *Joseph Knight* v. *Wedderburn* (1778).[2] Knight had been one of a cargo of Negroes imported into Jamaica by the commander of a vessel involved in the African slave trade. At the age of twelve or thirteen he was sold to Wedderburn and later accompanied Wedderburn to Scotland as the latter's personal servant. Several years later, Knight left and Wedderburn apprehended him on a warrant from the justice of the peace. The issue was substantially similar to *Sommersett,* that is, whether a protesting or fleeing "slave" could be forced into slavery or continuous service in Scotland. Without equivocation the court held:

> the dominion assumed over this Negro, under the law of Jamaica, being unjust, could not be supported in this country to any extent: That, therefore, the defender had no right to the Negro's service for any space of time, nor to send him out of the country against his consent.[3]

While the *Knight* case was unequivocal in declaring that both slavery and/or perpetual unremunerated service was illegal, seven years later Mansfield had the opportunity, in *King* v. *Inhabitants of Thames Ditton* (1785),[4] to assess the scope of his prior ruling in *Sommersett* and to decide whether the broad rationale of the *Knight* case would be adopted in England. The *King* case concerned Charlotte House, a pauper slave. She had been purchased in America by a Captain Howe, who brought her to England in 1781. She continued in this service until Howe's death in June, 1783. Shortly thereafter she was baptized and lived with her master's widow for approximately six months. She then left and "served" as a pauper for forty days in the parish of St. Chelsea. Apparently, she filed suit for wages due, and in denying her claim, Lord Mansfield noted and ruled:

> The case of *Sommersett* is the only one on this subject. Where slaves have been brought here, and have commenced actions for their wages, I have always [denied the plaintiff's claim]. The condition of slavery is not totally rescinded by the coming to *England.* With regard to the right to wages it still subsists. 1 *Blacst. Com.* 425. But wages are no necessary part of the contract for the purposes of a settlement. It cannot be contended that this was a voluntary hiring, and therefore not a service; and if the service with the captain be admitted, it continues with his widow. The odious part of slavery, which is contrary to the laws of *England,* determines on the slave coming to *England;* and if the relationship of master and servant subsists on the coming to *England,* the master has the common legal remedy for his servant being taken from him

per quod servitium amisit; Chamberlain v. Harvey. The reason why a negro is not entitled to wages is because there never
was a contract for wages. . . .[5]

Mansfield's decision in the *King* case rejected the rationale of
Knight and undermined the most crucial tenet of the *Sommersett*
opinion, that slavery existed only where authorized by positive law.
While he had been reluctant to sanction the magnitude of dominion
the master sought to exert over his slave when the master endeavored to remove a reluctant slave from England, Mansfield apparently found that other badges and incidents of slavery were *less* offensive. Perhaps on a purely theoretical basis predicated on legal
factors that reject actual reality, Mansfield's argument can be justified, since under English law a servant must have been "hired" in
order to receive a settlement.

While he argued that her race and purported station were not
precluding her from the statute's protection, he failed to acknowledge that a service or hiring by contract and chattel slavery were
mutually exclusive legal and economic categories. Mansfield's ruling
implied that while in England a slave was required to serve his or
her master even when the slave had not been provided for. Thus,
while under *Sommersett* the master could not have the protesting
slave deported from England and sold in another jurisdiction, nevertheless under *King* v. *Inhabitants of Thames Ditton* the master was
apparently as free as he would have been in Jamaica or Virginia to
exercise dominion over the slave by requiring his service.

In two later cases, *Williams* v. *Brown*[6] and *Slave Grace,*[7] English courts considered the applicability of *Sommersett* to persons enslaved in the colonies. In *Williams* the plaintiff, a black sailor, entered London on a ship bound for Grenada; the defendant was the
master of the ship. When the ship arrived in Grenada the plaintiff
was claimed as a runaway by his former master, Mr. Hardman. At a
meeting between the plaintiff, defendant, and Mr. Hardman, the
former master agreed to manumit the plaintiff if the defendant paid
a certain sum to Mr. Hardman. In return, the plaintiff, describing
himself as a "free black man of the island of Grenada," entered into
an indenture to serve the defendant for a set salary for three years.
When Mr. Williams arrived in London at the end of the three-year

period, he sued for wages (apparently for more than he had been promised) commensurate with the value of the services he performed.

The court ruled that the plaintiff was estopped from claiming more than he agreed to in the indenture instrument; the only contract that would not have been enforced was an agreement in which the plaintiff contracted to be the defendant's slave, as slavery was not recognized in England. Williams, of course, with some very justifiable fears that he might forfeit his new freedom, had prejudged such an interpretation by referring to himself as a "free black man."

All three justices deciding the *Williams* case agreed that the plaintiff was capable of making a binding contract; only one, Justice Chambre, delved into the most pertinent issue—whether Williams, a runaway slave, could obtain a fair bargain when bargaining for his freedom. Wasn't it likely that Williams was taken advantage of? Ironically, Justice Chambre managed to find the contract conscionable (legally valid) not because it was fair to Williams but because any finding that this contract was unenforceable would tend to make masters less likely to agree to manumit their slaves.

It is supposed that [the black plaintiff] has been driven to an unreasonable and unconscientious bargain: but I cannot say that it so appears to me. What was his condition at Grenada? Being claimed as a runaway slave he was considered as a criminal, he was liable to very severe punishment, he was incapable of recovering for his own benefit the money which he had earned upon the outward bound voyage, and he was unable to fulfill his contract with the Defendant. . . . It is true that by the articles he had contracted with the Defendant for a greater rate of wages; but from that contract he could derive no benefit, for his master was entitled to all the wages he might earn. . . . By rescinding such a contract as this I think we should be guilty of great inhumanity; for unless such a contract can be enforced, no master of a slave would agree to his manumission, nor any person be willing to pay the price of his freedom; the consequence of which would be that the present Plaintiff and all others in similar situations must remain in perpetual slavery.[8]

The opinion of the Chief Justice, Lord Alvanely, reveals the English court's dichotomous view toward slavery. Since there was no law authorizing slavery on English soil, the plaintiff, according to the *Sommersett* case, was "as free as any one of us while in England." By the quirk of international law, however, the plaintiff's freedom was curiously limited *only* to England. "When the plaintiff was claimed in Grenada as a runaway slave, he was not only liable to be remanded to slavery, but by the laws of the island he was amenable to severe punishment for his desertion."

It was not until 1827 in the *Slave Grace* case that the English courts determined the type of freedom a black person gained when he or she had come into England as a slave and then later left England. In 1822 a Mrs. Allan from Antigua brought her female slave, Grace, to England; when Mrs. Allan returned to her home in 1823 Grace went "voluntarily" back to Antigua. She continued as Mrs. Allan's slave until 1825 when she was seized by a customs official, who contended that Grace "being a free subject of His Majesty was unlawfully imported as a slave from Great Britain into Antigua and there illegally held and detained in slavery." The trial judge ruled that Grace should be returned to her mistress.

On appeal by the government, the issue was framed as, "whether under the circumstances, slavery was so divested by landing in England that it would not revive on a return to the place of birth and servitude." The appellate court affirmed the lower court's ruling. Lord Stowell found that Grace "'was not a free person" and found the *Sommersett* case inapplicable. Stowell ruled that the right to liberty claimed by Grace was conveyed by "a mere residence in England." Once the slave woman left England, this right "had totally expired when the residence ceased and she was imported in Antigua." Stowell noted that despite the fact that the air of England had been found to be too pure for slavery:

> The personal traffic in slaves resident in *England* had been as public and as authorised in *London* as in any of our *West India* islands. They were sold on the Exchange and other places of public resort by parties themselves resident in *London*, and with as little reserve as they would have been in any of our *West India* possessions . . .[9]

The language of the *Sommersett* decision was further qualified by Justice Stowell, who ruled that all *Sommersett* allowed and sanctioned was a "limited liberation":

> The fact certainly is, that it never has happened that the slavery of an African, returned from England, has been interrupted in the colonies in consequence of this sort of limited liberation conferred upon him in England . . . he goes back to a place where slavery awaits him, and where experience has taught him that slavery is not to be avoided. . . . It has been said that in the decline of the ancient villenage, it became a maxim of very popular and legal use, "Once free for an hour, free for ever!" And this has been applied as a maxim that ought to govern in the case of negro slavery . . . it has never been once applied, since the case of Sommersett, to overrule the authority of the transmarine law. . . . This cry has not, as far as we know, attended the state of slavery in any other country, though that has been a state so prevalent in every other part of the world, . . .
>
> [S]lavery was a very favoured introduction into the colonies: it was deemed a great source of the mercantile interest of the country; and was, on that account, largely considered by the mother country as a great source of its wealth and strength. Treaties were made on that account and the colonies compelled to submit to those treaties by the authority of this country. . . . Instead of being condemned as malus usus, it was regarded as a most eminent source of its riches and power . . . in affirming the sentence of the Judge of the Court below, I am conscious only of following that result which the facts not only authorize but compel me to adopt.[10]

Lord Stowell's opinion, praised by U.S. Supreme Court Justice Story, the American authority on conflict of laws, as an "impregnable decision," granted slaves only a limited liberation.[11] Stowell found that the common law maxim, "once free for an hour, free for ever," applied only to English villeins and, per *Sommersett,* to black slaves *only while in England.* The maxim had never been recognized in international (transmarine) law. Admittedly, Stowell placed the slave woman in an anomalous position. If the slave in the instant case, Grace Jones, had decided to remain in England, she would have been entitled to the same legal rights as free people in England. Once the woman voluntarily left England, however, she lost all legal rights; the limited liberation she enjoyed while in England did not prevent her "re-enslavement" once she reached a jurisdiction that recognized slavery. But what is a "voluntary" leaving? Does it assume that, as in current constitutional law, one knows of one's actual rights and then voluntarily waives them? Did Grace know of her right to remain in England, of her right to resist deportation, and did she have counsel available to advise her of her rights and to defend her freedom? The legal assumption that she left voluntarily was just another legal fiction sanctioning a harsh result.

Neither Stowell nor Story found *Sommersett* and *Slave Grace* to be inconsistent. In a letter to Story dated May 17, 1828, Lord Stowell, describing himself as an abolitionist, did not consider *Slave Grace* to be supportive of slavery.

> I desire to be understood as not at all deciding the question upon the lawfulness of the slave trade, upon which I am rather a stern Abolitionist, but merely this narrow question, whether the Court of King's Bench, in the case of Sommersett, meant to declare that our non-execution of the slave code in England was a new [mere] suspension of it as respected England, but left it in full operation with respect to the colonies—which some of our Abolitionists here and some of our Judges there resolutely contend for. My clear opinion is for its limited effect. The execution of the Code laws is suspended in England, as being thought inconsistent with the nature as well as the institutions of this country. So far as it goes, but no farther, it does not at all derogate from the law of the colonies upon the return of the person so far liberated in England, but left exposed to the severity of the law in the colonies, upon the return of the party so partially liberated here; this is the whole of the question which I had occasion to consider, and is a question which has nothing to do with the general legality of the slave trade in the colonies. How the laws in respect of that trade made in England and enforced by our courts of law, the King's Privy Council, and the Court of Chancery, to their utmost extent, can consist with any notion of its entire abolition here, is, in my view of it, an utter impossibility.
>
> I am a friend to abolition generally, but I wish it to be

effected with justice to individuals. Our Parliaments have long recognized it and have not only invited, but actually compelled our colonists to adopt it, and how, under such circumstances, it is to be broken up at the sole expense of the colonist, I cannot see consistent with either common reason or common justice; it must be done at the common expense of both countries; and upon that part of the case very great difficulties exist. Our zealots are for leaping over them all, but in that disposition I cannot hold them to be within the wise or the just part of this nation.[12]

By juxtaposing *Slave Grace* and *Sommersett,* the English judiciary was able to achieve a pragmatic balance between the domestically held myth about England's concern for freedom and the still forceful commercial and imperial interests. The British were assured by *Sommersett* of their nation's moral integrity. About fifty years later, the commercial interests were assured by *Slave Grace* of the validity of their investments in human property. As David Brion Davis states in *The Problem of Slavery in the Age of Revolution:*

> English law was flexible enough to recognize the validity of slave property, to uphold contracts for the sale of slaves, and to provide room for a qualified servitude, even a servitude without wages. It simply told masters that they should not repeat Stuart's mistake of locking a slave in irons for forcible shipment out of the country. . . . [R]egardless of legal forms, English courts endorsed no principles that undermined colonial slave law.[13]

The English Abolition of the International Slave Trade and of Slavery

As the *Slave Grace* decision demonstrates, English jurists were reluctant to confront the total problem presented by slavery. Both Mansfield and Stowell were unwilling (and perhaps unable) either to end British involvement in the international slave trade or to abolish slavery in the West Indies. Such tasks were matters for parliament. Unlike the federal legislative branches in the United States, the British parliament did eradicate both evils.

It is probable that, as most events in political history, various threads of self-interest and humanitarianism were woven to create the political, economic, and moral fabric that was necessary to support British action against slavery and the slave trade. Some historians have found that the moral and religious concerns of the English precipitated abolition. For example, in an imaginary interview with the foremost leader of the English abolitionists, Wilberforce, Professor Coupland asked, "What do you think, . . . is the primary significance of your work, the lesson of the abolition of the slave system?" Wilberforce answered, "It was God's work. It signifies the triumph of His will over human selfishness. It teaches that no obstacle of interest or prejudice is irremovable by faith and prayer."[14]

Wilberforce's sincerity cannot be doubted. Yet, as one studies the efforts of the British humanitarians to end English involvement in the international slave trade, two analytic problems arise: one, how can one reconcile the abolitionists' selective attack on the evils of slavery; and two, how can one determine the reason for parliament's decision to end Britain's involvement in the slave trade.

Wilberforce, and others such as Ramsay, Wesley, Thorton, and Macaillay, were not radicals; their attitudes toward domestic problems were reactionary. Therefore, as expected, in their attempts to end the evils of slavery they did not seek to undermine or overthrow the existing governmental structure, but to work within its confines. Sir Stephen characterized Wilberforce in the following manner:

> He deprecated extreme measures and feared popular agitation. He relied for success upon aristocratic patronage, parliamentary displomacy and private influence with men in office. He was a lobbyist. . . .[15]

None of the abolitionists openly contended that his ultimate goal was emancipation. The Abolition Committee repeatedly denied any intentions of advocating legislative emancipation, and in 1807 Wilberforce also publicly denied this. Even as late as 1815 the African Institution stated clearly that it looked for emancipation from the slave owners and not from abolitionists in England.[16] But, however limited their vision or their ability to suppress it the abolitionists succeeded in gaining passage (by a margin of 100 to 34 in the House of Lords and by 283 to 16 in the House of Commons) of the 1807 Foreign Slave Trade Bill, which stated that the slave trade was "contrary to the principles of justice humanity and sound policy."[17]

Even though the Foreign Slave Trade Bill attacked only one aspect of the slavery problem, its importance and impact should not be underestimated. By 1807 the British had obtained a virtual monopoly over the international slave trade. Given this extraordinary degree of control, it is perhaps more comprehensible that those laboring for an end to the British slave trade viewed the 1807 bill as an act so destructive of slavery that without additional legislation the system would decline.

But the increasing moral opposition to the slave trade was hardly the sole factor in this decline; both economics and the fear of slave rebellions were crucial factors. As a sudden shift, it became in the best economic interests of those who profited from the West Indian cash crop, sugar, to end the slave trade. By the early 1800s, the price of West Indian sugar had dropped drastically, primarily because Napoleon Bonaparte's continental blockade against English goods had backed up the supply of sugar so that it far outweighed the demand in the remaining available market. In 1806 the surplus of sugar in England was about six thousand tons.[18] A parliamentary committee set up in 1807 discovered that British West Indian planters were producing at a loss. In 1800 the planter's average profit was reported to be 2½ percent; in 1807 he had no profit.[19]

One solution found for the planters' rather deplorable financial position was to reduce production. And, to restrict production it became advantageous to have the slave trade abolished. Since the older, more established British colonies such as Jamaica and Barbados were "saturated" and needed no new importations of slaves, it was hoped that the competitive capabilities of the newer non-British colonies, particularly Brazil and Cuba, would suffer most by the end of the British slave trade.

Besides fearing for the economic stability of the islands, Parliament also had before it the specter of Haiti, which was established as an independent nation in 1804 after a violent slave revolt against the French. Undoubtedly, the West Indian planters were eager to limit the black population in the islands in order to limit the successful prospects of any future slave revolts.

Another crucial economic factor supporting abolition of the slave trade was the desire of British merchants and industrialists to normalize trade conditions with Africa. It was generally agreed that the slave trade "severely hampered ordinary trade, . . . kept the [African countries] in turmoil, and even directly competed with honest merchants by dumping cargo on the African market at low prices."[20] British anti–slave trade patrols of the African coast, therefore, served the purpose of "aiding humanity, helping hard-pressed planters in Jamaica and Mauritius, and increasing the profits of British merchants and manufacturers."

The abolitionists remained convinced that emancipation would be gradual. Slavery would never be abolished, they believed, but it will "subside; it will decline; it will expire; it will, as it were burn itself down into its socket and go out. . . . We shall leave it gently to decay—slowly, silently, almost imperceptibly, to die away and to be forgotten."[21]

Apparently the abolitionists underestimated the planters' ability to thwart the strategy of the abolitionists and their resolve to resist even minimum modification of the chattel slavery system. In 1823 the British government tried unsuccessfully to introduce some reform measures aimed at lessening the harshness of West Indian slavery. The policy called for an end to whipping and the black Sunday market (by giving the slaves another day off) to permit religious instruction. It instituted a nine-hour day, established savings banks for slaves, allowed slaves' testimony in courts of law, and prohibited the flogging of female slaves. It also manumitted all domestic and field slaves and all female children born after 1823.[22] The planters in the crown colonies of Trinidad and British Guiana and the self-governing colonies emphatically refused to pass any act that served to ameliorate slavery's harshness, fearing that these "concesssions" would invariably lead to total emancipation.

Understandably, the slaves tended to view the planters' actions as a refusal to carry out the crown's manumission policy. From 1807 until emancipation, slave revolts increased. Revolts came to Barbados in 1816, and British Guiana had two slave uprisings, the second involving fifty plantations and approximately twelve thousand slaves.[23] An insurrectionary movement among slaves was formed in 1831 in Antigua and instigated a revolt that year in Jamaica, the largest and most important British West Indian colony, with more than half the slaves in the entire British West Indies.

Within two years slaves throughout the colonies were emancipated by the 1833 act, which provided:

> An Act for the Abolition of slavery throughout the British Colonies; for promoting the Industry of manumitted slaves; and for compensating the persons hitherto entitled to the Services of such Slave.
>
> Sect. LXIV: Provided, "That nothing in this Act contained doth or shall extend to any of the Territories in the Possession of the East India Company, or to the Island of Ceylon or to the Island of Saint Helena.[24]

Parliament voted a sum of twenty million pounds to compensate slave owners.[25] The compensation formula, which paid the slave owners less than the market value of the slaves, was approved by the English courts on the 1835 case, *Case of Compensation Commissioners Under the Act for the Abolition of Slavery.*[26]

In earlier chapters we have seen the ambiguity of the American colonial experience, where in some northern colonies there was a "slackening" of the harshness of slavery even before the Declaration of Independence. Yet, in the southern colonies we have observed slavery becoming more and more repressive for blacks while simultaneously the legal process became more supportive of privileges for whites and particularly in aid of white indentured servants. The *Sommersett* case and the general legal experience of the motherland in England as to its treatment of domestic slaves were well known to all leading colonists. Prior to any colony's abolition of slavery, we see in England a series of cases climaxing in *Sommersett* that exemplify a judicial attitude far more hostile to domestic slavery than the American colonial legal system of 1772.

The *Sommersett* case was a significant starting point, and probably a turning point, in the British empire's ultimate abolition of slavery and the international slave trade. Though it could be debated forever whether this famed 1772 decision and the later events abolishing slavery were attributable to basic English humanitarian motives or to mere economic necessity, it is appropriate to compare these English legal events with those taking place in America as the colonists were moving toward their birth of freedom in 1776. One should evaluate the English legal process and the moral tone inherent in the *Sommersett* case along with the ambiguity and hypocrisy of most in the colonies, who in 1776 were demanding equal rights for themselves—the whites—while simultaneously denying to blacks any semblance of justice in that new nation the "revolutionaries" were about to create.

While current historians reflect on those momentous events of more than two centuries ago, some become critical of Mansfield for not taking a broader judicial position for the total eradication of slavery. They complain that after the *Sommersett* case he tolerated slavery outside of England and sanctioned the lesser form of servitude and unremunerated forced services exemplified in *King* v. *Inhabitants of Thames Ditton*. True, with a stroke of his pen he did not declare total freedom for black slaves (wherever they might be on British soil), but he synthesized most of the essential ingredients or rationale for future generations to eradicate slavery. Many of his current critics are tainted with insights gained by current jurisprudential doctrines and seem oblivious to the times in which Mansfield lived. For his generation he was a giant in the cause of human freedom and a significant contributor to the ultimate abolition process. His condemnation of slavery as an odious institution "incapable of being introduced on any reasons, moral or political, but only by positive [statutory] law" gave abolitionists a broader platform of respectability from which to assert that the enslavement of blacks was incompatible with the basic rights of all men. Mansfield's holding moved the rhetoric from a theological base to a jurisprudential condemnation. Shortly after his opinion, the forefathers of the new nation would have to decide whether their standards of morality and law were as high as Mansfield's.

IV

The Revolution

11

THE DECLARATION OF INDEPENDENCE

A SELF-EVIDENT TRUTH
OR A SELF-EVIDENT LIE?

When we were the political slaves of King George, and wanted to be free, we called the maxim that "all men are created equal" a self-evident truth; but now when we have grown fat, and have lost all dread of being slaves ourselves, we have become so greedy to be masters that we call the same maxim "a self-evident lie." The Fourth of July has not quite dwindled away; it is still a great day for burning fire-crackers![1]

—Abraham Lincoln, 1855

Roots of the Revolution

DID the Declaration of Independence announce a self-evident truth or a self-evident lie? The answer depends on whose equality one considers. As Abraham Lincoln later noted, the success of the first Revolution in no way altered the degraded status of most[2] black Americans. Nor did it free the more than one-half million slaves in the colonies. As we have noted in the introduction of this book, Frederick Douglass spoke out three years before Lincoln, much to the same point when he noted: "This Fourth [of] July is yours, not mine . . . the sunlight that brought light and healing to you, has brought stripes and death to me."[3] From the perspective of the black masses, the Revolution merely assured the plantation owners of their right to continue the legal tyranny of slavery.

It is sad to note that the first emancipation proclamation applying to American slaves was issued during the Revolutionary era by the representatives of George III. On November 7, 1775, John Murray, Earl of Dunmore and Governor-General of the Colony and Dominion of Virginia, issued a proclamation that freed "all indented Servants, Negroes or others . . . able and willing to bear Arms . . ." with His Majesty's troops.[4] In contrast, some of the colonists equivocated as to whether they would free blacks who fought for the colonists' cause. Tragically the colonists wanted both their freedom from the King and simultaneously the right to deny that freedom to blacks.

Some blacks were active on the battlefronts and behind the lines. In his illuminative work, Professor Benjamin Quarles noted:

> The Negro's role in the Revolution can best be understood by realizing that his major loyalty was not to a place nor to a people, but to a principle. Insofar as he had freedom of choice, he was likely to join the side that made him the quickest and best offer in terms of those "unalienable rights" of which Mr. Jefferson had spoken.[5]

As to those blacks who fought for the independence of the new nation, Harriet Beecher Stowe observed:

> We are to reflect upon them as far more magnanimous [because they served] a nation which did not acknowledge them as citizens and equals, and in whose interests and prosperity they had less at stake. It was not for their own land they fought, not even for a land which had adopted them, but for a land which had enslaved them, and whose laws, even in freedom, oftener oppressed than protected. Bravery, under such circumstances, has a peculiar beauty and merit.[6]

Relatively few blacks were freed by the colonists, by either Lord Dunmore's proclamation or the fact that several thousand blacks had fought on behalf of the American forces.[7] The war had no immediate impact on the struggle to deny slavery its legitimacy as an institution. Yet half a century later, the documents and rhetoric of this successful "white" revolution did indeed become catalysts, if not rallying points, for blacks and their white allies in the abolitionist struggles. In the decades preceding the Civil War, abolitionists would point to the forefathers' Revolutionary assertion of inalienable rights and the obligation of those who govern to obtain the consent of the governed. Affirming the essential dignity of all mankind, they stressed the inherent hypocrisy in this nation's exclusion of blacks from those rights of mankind that at its very birth this nation proclaimed inalienable.[8]

Paradoxically, then, the first Declaration, impotent though it was to change black servitude, did ultimately play a part in the evolutionary process that was to free blacks from slavery. Accordingly, the history of the first Declaration of Independence is relevant to an understanding of the process through which blacks came to be freed from slavery and through which post-emancipation gains were made.

Though the temptation exists to equate the opening of hostilities with the start of revolutions, revolutions do not begin in the hour when the first shots are fired. Revolutions, like most historic moments, are born and acted out in men's minds well before they become history. As Chateaubriand noted with regard to the revolution in France, it was "accomplished before it occurred."[9] Similarly, among its more radical leaders, the American Revolution started long before 1776. As John Adams wrote:

> What do we mean by the revolution? The war with Britain? That was no part of the revolution; it was only the effect and consequence of it. The revolution was in the minds and hearts of the people, and this was effected from 1760 to 1775, in the course of fifteen years, before a drop of blood was shed at Lexington.[10]

Though Adams and a few revolutionary thinkers were manifestly discontent even before 1760, until 1764 the colonists "were in the main well satisfied" despite some occasional tensions with Great Britain.[11] The vast majority seemed "proud to be counted British subjects and citizens within the empire, the burdens of which, such as they were, had never rested heavily upon them."[12] They had been displeased with those Imperial regulations that hindered the manufacture of iron products, hats, or woolen cloth, but the vast majority "had inspired no thoughts of outright resistance."[13] However, upon the passage of the 1764 Sugar Act, this "gentle current of tranquility"[14] was shaken.

The 1764 Sugar Act put the American colonists in a significantly disadvantageous position in their competition in the triangular trade. This trade involved the shipping of products, basically molasses, from the West Indies to the New England colonies for distillation into rum, generally at Boston or Newport. The rum and other New England products were shipped to Africa in exchange for slaves; the slaves were then transported to the American colonies. The 1764 Act precluded American colonies from obtaining molasses at the French Islands, such as Santo Domingo, where the products were superior and cheaper.[15] This one act of Parliament had, as James Otis declared, "set people a-thinking in six months, more than they had done in their whole lives before."[16] Starting with the protest to the 1764 Act, more colonists began to agree with Patrick Henry's later prediction that England would:

> drive us to extremities; no accommodation *will* take place; hostilities *will soon* commence; and a desperate and bloody touch it will be.[17]

In their new thinking the soon to be revolutionary leaders were greatly influenced by the concepts of natural rights that John Locke and others had articulated. Locke's categorization of the natural rights of "property, liberty and estate" were broadened to "life, liberty and the pursuit of happiness" by Jefferson. Armed with the natural rights arguments asserted by Locke and the earlier declared "liberties of Englishmen" it was but an "easy step" for these men to move "to the universalist assertion that all men had a right to be free."[18]

Though influenced by these Lockean concepts, when the representatives to the First Continental Congress met in Philadelphia in 1774 they still did not plan "to set in train a movement for independence from Great Britain."[19] The delegates had been charged by their constituencies "to reestablish the harmony that before 1763 had characterized colonial relations with the mother country."[20] Their primary task was "to persuade the British government to abandon its efforts to tax the colonies without their consent" and to free the colonies from the Coercive Acts.[21] Yet while they were meeting, King George III declared: "The dye is now cast, the Colonies must either submit or triumph."[22] As the colonists became more and more reluctant to submit, the argument that the

British denial to them of the natural rights of man constituted an enslavement gained wider appeal.

The White Colonists' Perception of Their Enslavement

Although the enslavement of whites was never legally permissible at any time in any of the colonies, nevertheless revolutionary leaders persistently described the political plight of the colonists as one of enslavement. In noting his opposition to the Sugar Act of 1764, Governor Stephen Hopkins of Rhode Island started his diatribe by asserting that "Liberty is the greatest blessing that men enjoy, and slavery the heaviest curse that human nature is capable of."[23] Of course, Governor Hopkins was not speaking of the enslavement of blacks. Ironically, he argued that white colonists were being enslaved by England because the Sugar Act of 1764 decreased the profits from Rhode Island's involvement in the international slave trade.

Pennsylvania's John Dickinson in 1768 likewise argued:

> *Those* who are *taxed* without their own consent expressed by themselves or their representatives . . . are *slaves. We are taxed* without our consent expressed by ourselves or our representatives. *We* are therefore—SLAVES.[24]

Five years later Boston's Josiah Quincy proclaimed:

> I speak it with grief—I speak it with anguish—Britons are our oppressors: I speak it with shame—I speak it with indignation —*we are slaves.*[25]

John Adams concurred that we are "the most abject sort of slaves, to the worst sort of masters!"[26] Almost every statement of political principles linked the status of white colonists to a concept of slavery.

As a political term then, slavery had two meanings. For whites it described any enactment that limited their economic freedom of action or reduced the value of their property when they had not previously elected representatives to vote on that impediment. Concurrently, however, those arbitrary acts of physically enslaving blacks, despite the absence of black consent, were not embraced within the slavery definition whites used in condemning the king's abuses.

Nowhere is this racially bifurcated construction of slavery more manifest than in the July 6, 1775 Declaration of the Causes and Necessities of Taking Up Arms.[27] Franklin, John Rutledge, Johnson, Livingston, John Jay, Jefferson, and Dickinson constituted the committee that drew up this declaration, though the final draft appeared to be primarily the work of Dickinson and Jefferson. They started the Declaration by asking whether it was possible for men "who exercise their reason to believe that the Divine author of our existence intended a part of the human race to hold an absolute power in, and an unbounded power over others . . . as the objects of a legal domination never rightfully resistable, however severe and oppressive." Then they responded that:

> the great Creator['s] principles of humanity, and the dictates of common sense, must convince all those who reflect upon the subject, that government was instituted to promote the welfare of mankind, and ought to be administered for the attainment of that end.

They condemned the legislature of Great Britain for "enslaving these colonies by violence," which acts "have thereby rendered it necessary for us to close with [our] last appeal from reasons to arms." They emphasized that when "reduced to the alternative of chosing an unconditional submission to the tyranny of irritated ministers, or resistance by force" that they must respond by force:

> We have counted the cost of this contest, . . . *and find nothing so dreadful as voluntary slavery.*—Honour, justice, and humanity, forbid us tamely to surrender that freedom which we received from our gallant ancestors, and which our innocent posterity have a right to receive from us. We cannot endure the infamy and guilt of resigning succeeding generations to that wretchedness which inevitably awaits them, if we basely entail hereditary bondage upon them.

Several times in their Declaration they referred to their slavery or enslavement. "With hearts fortified" they pledged "before God and the world" that they would use arms "in defiance of every hazard with unabating firmness and perseverance," and they resolved that "we are of one mind" *determined "to die freemen rather than to live slaves."*

Yet while the revolutionary leaders had resolved to die freemen rather than to live slaves, they did not perceive blacks as having the same human right to be free. By their statutes the colonists had made it an act of treason, often punishable by death, for blacks to dare to flee from slavery and seek to live as free men.

The colonists were ridiculed often in England because the protest against their alleged enslavement was inconsistent with their insistence that blacks should be slaves. In 1775 in response to the resolution and address of the American Congress, Dr. Samuel Johnson said:

> If slavery be thus fatally contagious, how is it that we hear the loudest yelps for liberty among the drivers of negroes.[28]

Finally, Johnson summed up the colonists' arguments as "too foolish for buffoonery [and] too wild for madness."[29]

The Moral Antecedents for Challenging, in 1776, the Continuance of Slavery

Although the 1776 statesmen were insistent on their right to revolt for their freedom, they did not mean to even inferentially condemn their enslavement of a half-million blacks. Long before July 4, 1776, many forceful arguments had been asserted as to the immorality of slavery, had our forefathers sought precedent for a commitment to universal freedom. The first organizational resolution as a protest against slavery had occurred, as we have noted in our chapter on the Pennsylvania colony, eighty-eight years previously in the same city where the Declaration of Independence was ultimately written. On February 18, 1688, the Germantown Mennonites at Philadelphia had asserted that maintenance of slavery was inconsistent with Christian principles. They concluded by recognizing the moral right of slaves to revolt and the contradictions of principle if Christians opposed the slaves' fight for freedom:

> If once these slaves (which they say are so wicked and stubborn men,) should join themselves—fight for their freedom, and handel their masters and mistresses, as they did handel

them before; will these masters and mistresses take the swoard at hand and war against these poor slaves, like, as we were able to believe, some will not refuse to do? Or, have these poor negers not as much right to fight for their freedom, as you have to keep them slaves?

After this 1688 resolution there were many further protestations against slavery. Some challenged slavery on moral grounds. Others opposed slavery because of fears of revolt. Some argued that the existence of slavery precluded white settlers from coming to the new country and still others asserted that slavery deterred the general economic growth of the country.

During this pre-Revolutionary era, none wrote more eloquently in condemnation of slavery than James Otis and Anthony Benezet. In 1764, James Otis wrote "The Rights of the British Colonies Asserted and Proved."[30] First he asserted that all men, black and white, were born equal. Then he asked:

Does it follow that 'tis right to enslave a man because he is black? Will short curled hair like wool instead of Christian hair . . . help the argument? Can any logical inference in favor of slavery be drawn from a flat nose, a long or short face?[31]

He condemned the slave trade as a "most shocking violation of the law of nature" for it "makes every dealer in it [slavery] a tyrant." Otis also argued that "those who every day barter away other men's liberty will soon care little for their own."[32] Benezet, as the leading Quaker spokesman, argued unrelentingly against slavery.[33]

After reading Benezet's 1772 book, which attacked the slave trade, Patrick Henry noted the incompatibility of Christian precepts and enlightenment values, on the one hand, and the practice of slavery on the other.[34] Then, moving from the serene level of abstract analysis to the more difficult task of facing these same contradictions within himself, he noted:

Would any one believe that I am Master of Slaves of my own purchase! I am drawn along by ye general Inconvenience of living without them; I will not, I cannot justify it.[35]

Yet Patrick Henry was able, as were most "enlightened" slave holders, to soothe his conscience by proclaiming that "a time will come when an opportunity will be offered to abolish this lamentable evil." He urged that if he and his fellow man failed to abolish this evil within "our day" then "let us transmit to our descendants together with our Slaves a pity for their unhappy Lot, and an abhorrence for Slavery."

Even the Harvard University Commencement of July 21, 1773 included "A Forensic Dispute On The Legality of Enslaving Africans."[36] The opponent to slavery argued:

> To me, I confess, it is matter of painful astonishment, that in this enlightened age and land, where the principles of natural and civil Liberty, and consequently the natural rights of mankind are so generally understood, the case of these unhappy *Africans* should gain no more attention;—that those, who are so readily disposed to urge the principles of natural equality in defense of their own Liberties, should, with so little reluctance, continue to exert a power, by the operation of which they are so flagrantly contradicted. For what less can be said of that exercise of power, whereby such multitudes of our fellow-men, descendants, my friend from the same common parent with you and me, and between whom and us nature has made no distinction, save what arises from the stronger influence of the sun in the climate whence they originated, are held to groan under the insupportable burden of the most abject slavery, without one chearing beam to refresh their desponding souls; and upon whose dreary path not even the feeblest ray of hope is permitted to dawn, and whose only prospect of deliverance is—in death. If indeed the law protects their lives, (which is all that can be said even here, and more—shame to mankind!—more than can be said in some of our sister colonies) the only favor these unhappy people receive, from such protection, is a continuation of their misery; the preservation of a life, every moment of which is worse than non-existence.[37]

From Benezet to Patrick Henry, from the Germantown Mennonnites to the Harvard commencement, the moral issue had been pleaded with escalating vigor. Shortly before the Declaration of Independence was drafted, theologian Samuel Hopkins petitioned the Continental Congress for the abolishment of slavery.[38] Like others, he linked slavery with immorality and on his cover page he quoted, "Open thy mouth, judge righteously, and plead the cause of the poor and needy" [Pr. XXXI: 9] and "as ye would that men should do to you, do ye also to them likewise" [Luke VI: 31]. Through these biblical precepts, he argued that slavery was a "shocking, intolerable . . . bare faced inconsistence."

During this era the revolutionaries at Carpenter's Hall were all men—thus, in a political participatory context we had no foremothers. But Abigail Adams also had made clear her concerns on the slavery issue. Writing to her husband, John, who was then in Philadelphia, she commented on some petitions slaves in Massachusetts had filed with the governor seeking their freedom, "telling him they would fight for him provided he would arm them, and engage to liberate them if he conquered."

> I wish most sincerely there was not a slave in the province; it always appeared a most iniquitous scheme to me to fight ourselves for what we are daily robbing and plundering from those who have as good a right to freedom as we have.[39]

Obviously, Thomas Jefferson, the man to whom would fall the ominous task of drafting the Declaration of Independence, was aware of these compelling indictments on the immorality of slavery. It is intriguing to observe how he ignored them and instead attempted to single out the international slave trade for condemnation, perhaps thereby partially soothing his conscience as to the injustices which he, a purported spokesman for liberty, perpetuated by his ownership of slaves.

The Discarded July 2 Draft:[40]
A Futile Diatribe on the International Slave Trade

THE DELETED CLAUSE

As finally adopted, the Declaration of Independence contained no references at all to the plight of blacks or slaves, or to the international slave trade. It is particularly ironic that the revolutionary forefathers struck out the one and only provision in an earlier draft that even condemned by inference the international slave trade. Between June 11, 1776[41] and June 28, 1776,[42] Jefferson had written a passage condemning the international slave trade. Basically, this provision was not altered in the final draft presented by the Committee of Five to the Continental Congress for their debate and deliberations on July 2. The full significance of the deletion at this July 2 debate stage is apparent only to those familiar with the different stages in the writing of the Declaration of Independence.

There were at least three stages in the writing of the Declaration of Independence. On June 11, 1776 the Committee of Five— Jefferson, Franklin, Sherman, Adams, and Robert R. Livingston— was appointed to prepare the Declaration of Independence.[43] The committee gave Jefferson the responsibility to prepare the first draft.[44]

In Jefferson's original rough draft and in the draft approved by the Committee of Five as submitted on June 28 to the Congress, the climax of charges against the king was a significant diatribe against the international slave trade:

> He has waged cruel war against human nature itself, violating it's most sacred rights of life and liberty in the persons of a distant people who never offended him, captivating and carry them into slavery in another hemisphere or to incur miserable death in their transportation thither. This piratical warfare, the opprobrium of *infidel* powers, is the warfare of the Christian king of Great Britain. Determined to keep open a market where MEN should be bought and sold, he has prostituted his negative for suppressing every legislative attempt to prohibit or to restrain this execrable commerce. And that this assemblage of horrors might want no fact of distinguished die, he is now exciting these very people to rise in arms among us, and to purchase that liberty of which *he* has deprived them, by murdering the people on whom *he* also obtruded them; thus paying off former crimes committed against the *Liberties* of one people, with crimes which he urges them to commit against the *lives* of another.[45]

As a matter of logic, in many respects the diatribe was substantively deficient. For George III did not initiate the slave trade; it had been started centuries before. Further, there is an inherent hypocrisy wherein Jefferson is so vehement against the international slave trade and yet is totally silent about the continuance of slavery in the colonies. If, in Jefferson's phrase, the international slave trade was initiated by "cruel war against human nature itself," why was it not just as depraved for him to keep in lifetime servitude in the colonies those who had been so cruelly captured abroad or their children?

Furthermore, even in 1776 many of the colonies had never taken steps to prevent the further importation of slaves, and most had profited from it. Even Virginia's sporadic opposition to the international slave trade may have been based more on a fear of slave revolts or on economic considerations than on any concern about the immorality of either the international slave trade or slavery itself.[46]

Unfortunately, there is just as much reason to believe that Jefferson was not truly troubled about the international slave trade. Perhaps his insertion of this provision had more pragmatic ends, one being to mitigate the impact of Lord Dunmore's emancipation proclamation.[47] Jefferson had responded to Dunmore's proclamation by arguing that the king was:

> now exciting those very people to rise in arms among us, and to purchase that liberty of which *he* has deprived them, by murdering the people upon whom *he* also obtruded them: thus paying off former crimes committed against the *liberties* of one people, with crimes which he urges them to commit against the *lives* of another.[48]

Was Jefferson's greatest fear that the slaves might believe that they too were entitled to the natural rights of man Jefferson had proclaimed for the white colonists? Was Jefferson most fearful that the slaves believing in the natural rights of man might take arms against their slave master oppressors, just as the colonists felt they had the obligation to take arms against the king? Was he merely fearful of the economic loss that Dunmore's proclamation might cause because Jefferson's "livelihood depended" on the continuance of slavery?[49]

Nevertheless, when Jefferson's draft was debated by the Congress on July 2 to 4, the members eliminated even this one reference to slavery. Jefferson's notes of July 2 state:

> The clause too, reprobating the enslaving the inhabitants of Africa, was struck out in complaisance to South Carolina and Georgia, . . . Our Northern brethren felt a little tender for they had been pretty considerable carriers of [slaves].[50]

Rather than risk any negative votes from South Carolina and Georgia, the Congress opted for unanimity because of an attitude that Franklin reportedly expressed: "We must, indeed all hang together, or most assuredly we shall all hang separately."[51] Despite Thomas Jefferson's purported chagrin over the deletion, as John Hope Franklin pointedly observed, "The record does not indicate that Jefferson made any effort to save the section" against the international slave trade. For a mulatto slave Sandy, the following excerpted advertisement of Thomas Jefferson's was far more significant than his flourish of words condemning the international slave trade:

> Run away a Mulatto slave Sandy, 35 years, complexion light, shoemaker by trade, can do coarse carpenters work, a horse jockey, when drunk insolent and disorderly, swears much, and his behaviour is artful and knavish. Took a horse. Whoever conveys the said slave to me shall have reward, if taken up within the county, 4 l. if elsewhere within the colony, and 10 l. if in any other colony, from
>
> THOMAS JEFFERSON[52]

The July 2nd draft probably reflected the tensions within Jefferson—his simultaneous desire to protect his estate and his moral inability to justify slavery. Five years later, Jefferson, once again commenting on slavery, further noted:

> Indeed I tremble for my country when I reflect that God is just; that his justice cannot sleep forever.[53]

The Impact of the Declaration of Independence: "The Tendency of a Principle to Expand Itself to the Limit of its Logic"[54]

After reading the sordid history of a nation that spoke nobly that all men are created equal and then, nevertheless, excluded blacks from the equality promised all, the unsophisticated might argue that the Declaration of Independence had no ultimate impact or significance in eradicating slavery or diminishing racial discrimination. Yet in the corridors of history, there is a direct nexus between the egalitarian words uttered, even if not yet meant, and many of the changes that later took place.

No one has written more precisely than has Dean Louis Pollak of the University of Pennsylvania law school on the ultimate impact of the embryonic idea of equality expressed in the Declaration of Independence.

> The ever-widening impact of the nation's early commitment to the equality of "all men" compellingly illustrates what Benjamin N. Cardozo, one of the handful of great American judges, termed "the tendency of a principle to expand itself to the limit of its logic." In this sense, the Declaration of Independence is the apt progenitor of the Emancipation Proclamation, the Gettysburg Address, the Fourteenth Amendment's guarantee of "the equal protection of the laws," and the Supreme Court's recent decisions invalidating governmentally ordained racial segregation in public schools and elsewhere.[55]

If the authors of the Declaration of Independence had said— "all *white* men are created equal" or even "all white men who own property . . ." they would have more honestly conveyed the general consensus. But when they declared, as they did, that "all men are created equal" without introducing any qualifications, they created a document that put moral demands on all Americans who would ever quote it. Thus, on the authority of the Declaration of Independence blacks and their white sympathizers urged that they were obligated to abolish the present government that denied blacks "Life, liberty and the pursuit of happiness."

The irony of the unfulfilled American dream of equality is that of all those in the long line of dreamers who have sought the ultimately just society, none had to seek out alien sources for moral authority. They had only to say to the American people: fulfill the largest promise in your first statement as a nation.

By its very language, the Declaration of Independence introduced to the nation, from its inception, the problem of a "moral overstrain," a burden from which it has ever since suffered in varying degrees—that ". . . tension caused between high ideals and low achievement, between the American creed including equalitarian individualism and the historical American reality of unjust, unequal and class treatment for blacks."[56]

From 1776 to 1863 abolitionists repeatedly used the language and logic of the Declaration of Independence to stoke the American conscience. Abolitionist William Lloyd Garrison, in commencing his newspaper, "The Liberator," stressed that because he:

> Assent[ed] to the "self-evident truths" maintained in the American Declaration of Independence, "that all men are created equal, and endowed by their Creator with certain inalienable rights—. . ." I shall strenuously contend for the immediate enfranchisement of our slave population . . .[57]

After quoting from the Declaration, the Quaker David Cooper asserted:

> If these solemn *truths,* uttered at such an awful crisis, are *self-evident:* unless we can shew that the African race are not *men,* words can hardly express the amazement which naturally arises on reflecting, that the very people who make these pompous declarations are slave-holders, and by their legislative conduct, tell us, that these blessings were only meant to be the *rights* of *white-men* not of all *men.*[58]

At the end of the Revolutionary War, Cooper wrote:

> We need not now turn over the libraries of Europe for authorities to prove that blacks are born equally free with whites: it is declared and recorded as the sense of America.[59]

Further, reflect on the following cry of outrage by Frederick Douglass regarding Independence Day celebrations and consider how much less moral force his arguments would have had if the framers of the Declaration of Independence had not declared all men created equal.

> . . . your denunciation of tyrants, [are] brass fronted impudence; your shouts of liberty and equality, hollow mockery; your prayers and hymns, your sermons and thanksgivings, with all your religious parade and solemnity, are, to Him, mere bombast, fraud, deception, impiety, and *hypocrisy*—a thin veil to cover up crimes which would disgrace a nation of savages. There is not a nation on the earth guilty of practices more shocking and bloody than are the people of the United States, at this very hour.[60]

But the impact of the Declaration of Independence goes beyond its implied criticism of the hypocrisy of slavery; for the document not only asserts that all men were endowed with these inalienable rights but "That whenever any Form of Government becomes destructive of those ends, it is the Right of the People to alter or to abolish it, and to institute new Government. . . ."

In 1831 black abolitionist David Walker wrote:

> that if any people were ever justified in throwing off the yoke of their tyrants, the slaves are that people. It is not we, but our guilty countrymen, who put arguments into the mouths, and swords into the hands of the slaves. Every sentence that they write—every word that they speak—every resistance that they make, against foreign oppression, is a call upon their slaves to destroy them. Every Fourth of July celebration must embitter and inflame the minds of the slaves.[61]

Born to a free black woman, David Walker wrote a series of tracts that placed fear in the hearts of every slaveholder, partially because he cited their Declaration of Independence as his justification for inciting blacks to rise with force and militancy to destroy their white oppressors. In "Walker's Appeal in Four Articles Together with a Preamble to the Colored Citizens of the World, But in Particular and very Expressly to those of the United States of America," he asserted:

> Are we men!!—I ask you . . . are we MEN? Did our creator make us to be slaves to dust and ashes like ourselves? Are they not dying worms as well as we? . . . How we could be so *submissive* to a gang of men, whom we cannot tell whether they are as *good* as ourselves or not, I never could conceive. . . . America is more our country than it is the whites—we have enriched it with our *blood and tears*. The greatest riches in all America have arisen from our blood and tears:—and will they drive us from our property and homes, which we have earned with our *blood?*[62]

In one letter to "The Liberator," a free Negro wrote:

> Nothing was ever more true, sir, than the sentiment put forth by Mr. Jefferson in the Declaration of Independence, that all men are born free and equal;—and there is no stronger proof of this truth, than to see, wherever an opportunity presents itself, the oppressed grasping the banner of liberty and breath-

ing forth this sentiment in peals of thunder. That the spirit of liberty is born in the breast of every man is an undeniable truth: it is also true that the sensation accompanies him from his cradle to the grave; and though sometimes suppression by the sword and bayonet, it often bursts forth, like the smoking volcano, striking terror into the heart of the oppressor. May its mighty power shake the pillars of oppression until they crumble like "the baseless fabric of a vision."[63]

The Declaration of Independence's relevance to blacks was not debated solely in the political and religious forums. Finally the courts were asked to adjudicate its applicability to blacks. In the *Amistad* case, when arguing before the United States Supreme Court for the freedom of Africans who had mutinied against a slave trader, former President of the United States, John Quincy Adams, arguing in behalf of the slaves said:

> The moment you come, to the Declaration of Independence, that every man has a right to life and liberty, an inalienable right, this case is decided. I ask nothing more in behalf of these unfortunate men, than this Declaration.[64]

Shortly before the Civil War Abraham Lincoln construed the Declaration of Independence as having a broader scope and impact than that suggested by Taney. President Lincoln said the framers:

> meant to set up a standard maxim for free society, which should be . . . constantly looked to, constantly labored for, and even though never perfectly attained, constantly approximated, and thereby constantly spreading and deepening its influence, and augmenting the happiness and value of life to all people of all colors everywhere.[65]

Even after slavery was abolished, Charles Sumner, the major author of the 14th and 15th Amendments, emphasized the continuing relevance of the Declaration. In his moving letter to the American Antislavery Society for their final meeting on April 8, 1870, he said:

> The Antislavery Society may now die in peace. Slavery is ended. But I do not doubt that the same courage and fidelity which through long years warred against this prodigious Bar-

barism will continue determined to the end in protecting and advancing the work begun.

I do not think the work finished, so long as the word "white" is allowed to play any part in legislation,—so long as it constrains the courts in naturalization,—so long as it rules public conveyances, steamboats, and railroads,—so long as it bars the doors of houses bound by law to receive people for food and lodging, or licensed as places of amusement,—so long as it is inscribed on our common schools;—nor do I think the work finished until the power of the Nation is recognized, supreme and beyond question, to fix the definition of a "republican government," and to enforce the same by the perfect maintenance of rights everywhere throughout the land, *according to the promises of the Declaration of Independence,* without any check or hindrance from the old proslavery pretension of State Rights.[66]

Even after legal emancipation, the Declaration of Independence continued to be part of the moral authority for the dream of true equality. Martin Luther King in his dramatic speech on August *28,* 1963 in the celebrated March on Washington referred to it:

I still have a dream. It is a dream deeply rooted in the American dream that one day this nation will rise up and live out the true meaning of its creed—we hold these truths to be self-evident, that all men are created equal.[67]

U.S. Supreme Court Chief Justice Earl Warren emphasized its relevance when stating:

There are many causes of the crises [in American justice], but none I believe as basic as our neglect in reaching the ideal we fashioned for ourselves in the Declaration of Independence that "All men are created equal . . ."[68]

The impact of the Declaration of Independence can be seen in the Civil Rights acts of the 1960s; fortunately the scope has been expanded beyond the Declaration's chauvinistic categorization of "men" to the Civil Rights acts' guarantees for all persons. Title II provides:

All persons shall be entitled to the full and equal enjoyment of the goods, services, facilities, privileges, advantages, and ac-

commodations of any place of public accommodation, . . .
without discrimination or segregation on the ground of race,
color, religion, or national origin.[69]

In Title VII, these rights are expanded to preclude discrimination
against any *individual* "with respect to his compensation, terms,
conditions, or privileges of employment, because of such individual's race, color, religion, sex, or national origin."[70]

Thus the recent Civil Rights act exemplifies the formation of
an idea expanded far beyond what the forefathers intended when
they said "all men are created equal." Perhaps if the framers of
1776 had not declared the concept of equality in such universal
terms it may have been more difficult to challenge and partially
eradicate the pervasive barriers of discrimination on race and sex.
But once the drafters and signers of our Declaration made the decision not to weaken their moral argument for nationhood by attempting to rationalize the lie many of them were living, they made
inevitable the irony that the truth they espoused, and not their example, would eventually guide their progeny to a society more just
than their own.

EPILOGUE
IN THE MATTER OF COLOR

W E conclude this volume at approximately 1776, as the whites of this new nation prepare to start their revolution against oppression. Yet this new nation, "conceived in liberty and dedicated to the proposition that all men are created equal," began its experiment in self-government with a legacy of more than one-half million enslaved blacks—persons denied citizenship and enslaved, not for criminal infractions, but solely as a matter of color.

Unless their color was their crime, these blacks were innocent. Under the colonial rule of law, however, blacks who sought the same freedom that was now demanded as the inalienable right of whites could be scalped, mutilated, or even killed. In every major respect, the colonial law itself was an instrument of injustice. Even on the birth of the new nation, the founding fathers still subjected blacks to a persistent cruelty that was far more oppressive than the deprivations over which white Americans waged the Revolution.

But it need not have been that way. The branding of any group as inferior or less than human on the basis of color was not inevitable. There were sufficient legal, theological, and philosophical foundations upon which a more uniformly just and humane social structure could have been built.

In future volumes I hope to trace the painful process through which the law shifted from the role of brutal oppressor, to tolerant oppressor, to silent accomplice of injustice, and finally to the supposed ally of blacks as it had long been in America for those of lighter hue.

Shortly before Chief Justice Earl Warren died, I spoke with him in great detail about my ten year research effort on the issue of colonial slavery. He responded:

> I would be especially interested in seeing you at this particular time because of a reappraisal of my own thinking concerning slavery—not only what it meant in the past but the danger of what it will still mean to the future.

I concur with the concern expressed by Chief Justice Warren that the impact of our heritage of slave laws will continue to make itself felt into the future. For there is a nexus between the brutal centuries of colonial slavery and the racial polarization and anxieties of today. The poisonous legacy of legalized oppression based upon the matter of color can never be adequately purged from our society if we act as if slave laws had never existed.

APPENDIX

A NOTE ON THE INDENTURED
SERVANT SYSTEM

BEFORE focusing on the harsh legal process whereby blacks were gradually enslaved in the American colonies, one must first understand another labor system which was purportedly in competition with slavery—indentured servitude. The question remains whether there could have been a viable labor system as an alternative to human beings being deprived of all their freedoms solely because of their race. The persistent deprivation of rights imposed on blacks by the early colonial legal system cannot be studied in isolation. The entire seventeenth and eighteenth centuries must be put into perspective, for throughout that era the colonial system was generally harsh on *all* who were powerless—poor whites, Indians, or blacks. Among the propertyless whites in the weakest positions were those collectively referred to as indentured servants.

There were different types of indentured servitude, each allowing varying degrees of harshness and terms of service. In its simplest form, an indentured servant was a person obligated to serve a master for a period of years, generally four to seven years. In return for this service, the master often paid the indentured person's fare to America, and, throughout the entire period of the indenture, was required to provide a minimum level of subsistence—food, shelter, clothing—for the servant. Often the master also agreed to give the servant a specified award at the end of service, which became known as "freedom dues" (most commonly in money, tools and clothing). Because few planters could go to England and select their own servants, the servant was usually indentured to a merchant, a ship captain, or sometimes even to seamen, and then exported like other cargo. When the servants landed in the colonial port, they were sold to the highest bidder; the new owner, often a planter, was bound to abide by the terms of the original indenture.

The early indentured servant system remained primarily a contractual arrangement between two parties; it took into account the interests of only the two signatory parties and generally its terms could be modified any time both parties agreed. By 1636, printed indenture forms appeared, complete with blank spaces for specifics such as length of service. Skilled workmen were often able to obtain annual wages in addition to shelter, food and clothing. A child's indenture might specify that the master was also bound to see that the child obtained a rudimentary education. A typical contract of servitude as developed in the latter half of the seventeenth century is the following:

This Indenture made the *21st February 1682/3* Between *Rich. Browne aged 33 years* of the one party, and *Francis Richardson* of the other party, witnesseth, that the said *Rich. Browne* doth thereby covenant, promise, and grant to & with the said *Francis Richardson* his Executors & Assigns, from the day of the date hereof, until h*is* first & next arrival *att New York or New Jersey* and after, for and during the term of *foure* years, to serve in such service & imployment, as he the said *Francis Richardson* or his Assigns shall there imploy h*im* according to the custom of the Country in the like kind—In consideration whereof, the said *Francis Richardson* doth hereby covenant and grant to and with the said *Richard Browne* to pay for h*is* passing, and to find and allow h*im* meat, drink, apparrel, and lodging, with other necessaries, during the said term, & at the end of the said term to pay unto *him according to the Custom of the Country*

    In Witness thereof the parties above mentioned to these Indentures have interchangeably set their Hands and Seals the day and year above written.[1]

A tour of duty in America was not the first preference for many of the indentured servants. Many came because they had been convicted of crimes, and chose indentured servitude in America as an alternative to the death penalty or lengthy imprisonment. Some had been kidnapped; often innocent persons were convicted of crimes as part of a conspiracy of shipowners and judicial authorities. Eric Williams described the process:

> In the transportation of felons, a whole hierarchy from courtly secretaries and grave judges down to the jailers and turnkeys, insisted on having a share in the spoils . . . The leading merchants and public officials were all involved in the practice.[2]

When the mayor of Bristol in the 1660s was preparing to sentence a pickpocket to Jamaica, Judge Jeffrey sent the mayor himself to the prisoner's dock and said of him:

> Sir, Mr. Mayor, you meane, Kidnapper, and an old Justice of the Peace on the bench. . . . I doe not knowe him, and old knave: he goes to the taverne, and for a pint of sack he will bind people servants to the Indies at the taverne. A kidnapping knave! I will have his ears off, before I goe forth of towne. . . . Kidnapper, you, I mean, Sir. . . . If it were not in respect of the sword, which is over your head, I would send you to Newgate, you kidnapping knave. You are worse than the pick-pockett who stands there. . . . I hear the trade of kidnapping is of great request. They can discharge a felon or a traitor, provided they will go to Mr. Alderman's plantation at the West Indies.[3]

In 1661 a colonial board was finally created in England to regulate the trade of indentured servants. A year earlier, an act had been proposed prohibiting the transportation of English prisoners overseas and imposing a penalty on those who stole children for the purposes of placing them in involuntary indenture. Despite the villainy exposed, the bill was not then enacted. After further exposés in the press on the horrors of the voyages of indentured servants, a commission was appointed headed by the king's brother to report on the conditions of exportation of indentured servants.

In the later part of the seventeenth century a modification of the earlier indentured system, known as redemption, was also developed, although the indenture system remained the primary means by which planters obtained white laborers. A redemptioner, unlike an indentured servant, was often able to pay a part of the cost of passage. Merchants took whatever money the redemptioner had and provided him and his family with passage aboard ship and a contract to deliver them to America. The redemptioner was usually allowed fourteen days to try to secure the balance due; if he could not, he was sold into indentured servitude for a length of time roughly equivalent to the amount of money due the captain. Also, unlike most indentured servants, redemptioners (usually Germans or Swiss) would often come as a family, with the entire family contracting with the ship's captain.[4]

The primary purpose of the indentured servitude or redemptioner systems was that of obtaining a cheap and abundant labor supply, for the aristocrats could not or would not do their own planting and farm their own land. They preferred that their labor force be composed of whites from England, but despite the kidnapping, the conspiracies, and the eventual acceptance of even non-English whites, there was still an inadequate supply of white indentured servants.

As it became increasingly evident that the supply of indentured servants and redemptioners was inadequate for the colonists' maximization of their profits, a far more cruel system of human bondage was chosen—slavery, where one's darker skin became a justification for whites to subject blacks to a depravity that had never been used against indentured servants.

BIBLIOGRAPHY

Allen, James Egert. *The Negro in New York.* (New York: Exposition Press, 1964).

Andrews, C. M. *The Colonial Period of American History.* (New Haven: Yale University Press, 1934-1938).

Aptheker, Herbert. *American Negro Slave Revolts,* 2nd ed. (New York: International Publishing Co., 1969).

Bailyn, Bernard. *The Ideological Origins of the American Revolution.* (Cambridge, Mass.: The Belknap Press of Harvard University Press, 1971).

————. *Pamphlets of the American Revolution 1750-1776* (Cambridge, Mass.: The Belknap Press of Harvard University Press, 1965).

Ballagh, J. C. *A History of Slavery in Virginia.* (reprint of 1902 edition, New York: Johnson, 1969).

Bardolph, Richard, ed. *The Civil Rights Record: Black Americans and the Law, 1849-1970.* (New York: Crowell, 1970).

Becker, Carl. *The Declaration of Independence, A Study in the History of Political Ideas.* (New York: Alfred A. Knopf, 1956).

Bell, Derrick A. *Race, Racism and American Law.* (Boston: Little, Brown, 1973, 1975 Supp.).

Benezet, Anthony. *Serious Considerations on Several Important Subjects* . . . (Philadelphia: Joseph Crukshank, 1778).

Bennett, Lerone. *Before the Mayflower: A History of Black America,* rev. ed. (Chicago: Johnson, 1969).

Bergman, Peter M. *The Chronological History of the Negro in America.* (New York: Harper and Row, 1969).

Berlin, Ira. *Slaves Without Masters: The Free Negro in the Antebellum South.* (New York: Pantheon, 1975).

Berry, Mary Francis. *Black Resistance/White Law.* (Englewood Cliffs, N.J.: Prentice-Hall, 1971).

————. *Military Necessity and Civil-Rights Policy*. (Port Washington, N.Y.: Kennikat Press, 1977).

Birkenhead, F. *Fourteen English Judges*. (London: Cassell and Co., 1926).

Blassingame, John W. *The Slave Community*. (New York: Oxford University Press, 1972).

Boorstin, Daniel. *The Americans: The Colonial Experience*. (New York: Random House, 1958).

Boyd, Julian P. *The Declaration of Independence: the Evolution of the Text as Shown in Facsimiles of Various Drafts by its Author, Thomas Jefferson*. (Princeton: Princeton University Press, 1945).

————. *The Papers of Thomas Jefferson*. (Princeton: Princeton University Press, 1950).

Brookes, George S. *Friend Anthony Benezet*. (Philadelphia: University of Pennsylvania Press, 1937).

Burnett, Edmund Cody. *The Continental Congress*. (New York: The Macmillan Company, 1941).

Campbell, Lord. *The Lives of the Chief Justices of England*. (Boston: Estes and Lauriat, 1873).

Cardozo, Benjamin N. *The Nature of the Judicial Process*. (New Haven: Yale University Press, 1932).

Catterall, Helen. *Judicial Cases Concerning American Slavery and the Negro*, 5 vols. (reprint ed. New York: Negro University Press, 1968).

Clarkson, Thomas. *History of the Rise, Progress and Accomplishment of the Abolition of the African Slave Trade By the British Parliament*. (Philadelphia: James P. Parke, 1808).

Coleman, Kenneth. *Colonial Georgia: A History*. (New York: Scribner's, 1976).

Coupland, Reginald. *The British Anti-Slavery Movement*. (London: Home University Library, 1933).

————. *The Empire in These Days*. (London: Macmillan, 1935).

Cover, Richard M. *Justice Accused: Anti-Slavery and the Judicial Process*. (New Haven, Conn.: Yale University Press, 1975).

Craven, Wesley Frank. *The Colonies in Transition 1660-1713*. (New York: Harper and Row, 1968).

Davie, Maurice R. *Negroes in American Society*. (New York: McGraw-Hill, 1949).

Davis, David Brion. *The Problem of Slavery in the Age of Revolution 1770-1823*. (Ithaca, N.Y.: Cornell University Press, 1975).

————. *The Problem of Slavery in Western Culture*. (New York: Pelican Books, 1970).

————. *Was Thomas Jefferson an Authentic Enemy of Slavery?* (Oxford: The Clarendon Press, 1970).

Degler, Carl. *Neither Black Nor White: Slavery and Race Relations in Brazil and the United States.* (New York: Macmillan, 1971).

Donnan, Elizabeth (ed.). *Documents Illustrative of the History of the Slave Trade to America.* (Washington, D.C.: Carnegie Institution of Washington, 1930-1935). (reprint ed., New York: Octagon Books, 1965).

DuBois, W. E. B. *The Suppression of the African Slave-Trade to the United States of America, 1638-1870.* (New York, 1896).

Dunmore's Proclamation of Emancipation. (The Tracy W. McGregor Library, University of Virginia, 1941).

Elkins, Stanley. *Slavery: A Problem in American Institutional and Intellectual Life.* (Chicago: University of Chicago Press, 1959).

Farrand, Max (ed.). *The Laws and Liberties of Massachusetts.* (Cambridge, Mass: 1929).

————. *The Records of the Federal Convention of 1787,* rev. ed. (New Haven: Yale University Press, 1966).

Fernow, Berthold. *Records of New Amsterdam.* (reprint edition, Baltimore: Genealogical Publishing Co., 1976).

Fifoot, C. H. S. *Lord Mansfield.* (Oxford: Clarendon Press, 1936).

Flanders, Ralph Betts. *Plantation Slavery in Georgia.* (Cos Cob, Conn.: John E. Edward, 1967).

Fleming, Donald and Bernard Bailyn (eds.). *Perspectives in American History.* (Cambridge, Mass.: Charles Warren Center for Studies in American History, 1971).

Foner, Philip S. *History of Black Americans: From Africa to The Emergence of the Cotton Kingdom.* (Westport, Conn.: Greenwood Press, 1975).

————. *The Life and Writings of Frederick Douglass.* (New York: International Publishers, 1950).

————. *Organized Labor and the Black Worker, 1619-1673.* (New York: Praeger Publishers, 1974).

————. *The Voice of Black America.* (New York: Simon and Schuster, 1975).

Franklin, John Hope. *From Slavery to Freedom,* 4th ed. (New York: Alfred A. Knopf, 1974).

————. *Racial Equality in America.* (Chicago: The University of Chicago Press, 1976).

————. *The Free Negro in North Carolina 1790-1860.* (New York: W. W. Norton, 1971).

————. *The Militant South, 1800-1860.* (Boston: Harvard University Press, 1970).

———— in United States Commission on Civil Rights, Freedom to the Free. (Washington, D.C.: U.S.G.P.O., 1963).

Frederickson, G. *The Black Image in the White Mind.* (New York: Harper & Row, 1971).

Garrison, William Lloyd. *Selections from the Writings and Speeches of William Lloyd Garrison.* (New York: The New American Library, 1969).

Genovese, Eugene D. *The Political Economy of Slavery.* (New York: Random House, 1965).

Goodell, William. *The American Slave Code in Theory and Practice.* (1853; reprint ed., New York: New American Library, 1969).

Greene, Lorenzo J. *The Negro in Colonial New England.* (New York: Columbia University Press, 1942).

Greenberg, Jack. *Race Relations and American Law.* (New York: Columbia University Press, 1959).

————. *Judicial Process and Social Change.* (St. Paul, Minn.: West Publishing Co., 1977).

Guild, June Purcell. *Black Laws of Virginia.* (reprint ed., New York: Negro University Press, 1969).

Handlin, Oscar. *Race and Nationality in American Life.* (Boston: Little, Brown, 1957).

Haskins, George Lee. *Law and Authority in Early Massachusetts.* (New York: Macmillan, 1960).

Holdsworth, William. *A History of English Law XII.* (London: Methuen & Co., Ltd., 1938).

————. *Some Makers of English Law.* (Cambridge: The University Press, 1938).

Holliday, J. *The Life of William, late Earl of Mansfield.* (London: printed for P. Elmsley, 1797).

Hornsbury, Jr., Alton. *The Black Almanac,* 2nd. rev. ed. (New York: Barren, 1975).

Horowitz, Harold W., and Karst, Kenneth L. (eds.). *Law, Lawyers and Social Change.* (New York: Bobbs Merrill, 1969).

Hurd, John C. *The Law of Freedom and Bondage in the United States,* 2 vols. (1858; reprint ed., New York: Negro University Press).

Jefferson, Thomas. *Notes on the State of Virginia.* (New York: Harpers, 1964).

Jones, Charles C. *History of Georgia.* (Boston: Houghton, Mifflin and Co., 1883).

Jordan, Winthrop. *White Over Black*. (Chapel Hill: University of North Carolina Press, 1968).

Kaplan, Sidney. *The Black Presence in the Era of the American Revolution 1770-1800*. (Washington, D.C.: New York Graphic Society Ltd. in association with the Smithsonian Institution Press, 1973).

Katz, William L. *Eyewitness: The Negro in American History*. (New York: Pitman Publishing Corp., 1967).

Klein, Herbert S. *Slavery in the Americas: A Contemporary Study of Virginia and Cuba*. (Chicago: University of Chicago Press, 1967).

Kobrin, David. *The Black Minority in Early New York*. (Albany, N.Y., 1971).

Litwack, Leon. *North of Slavery*. (Chicago: University of Chicago Press, 1961).

Logan, Rayford W. (ed.). *Memoirs of a Monticello Slave*. (Charlottesville: University of Virginia Press, 1951).

———. *The Negro in the United States, Vol. 1: A History to 1945: from Slavery to Second-Class Citizenship*. (reprint ed., New York: Van Nostrand, 1970).

Logan, Rayford W., and Winston, Michael R. *The Negro in the United States, Vol. 2: The Ordeal of Democracy*. (New York: Van Nostrand, 1971).

McColley, Robert. *Slavery and Jeffersonian Virginia*. (Urbana: University of Illinois Press, 1964).

McIlwaine, H. R. (ed.). *Minutes of the Council and General Court of Colonial Virginia, 1622-1632, 1670-1676*. (Richmond, Va.: Richmond Colonial Press, 1924).

McManus, Edgar. *Black Bondage in the North*. (Syracuse, N.Y.: Syracuse University Press, 1973).

———. *A History of Negro Slavery in New York*. (Syracuse, N.Y.: Syracuse University Press, 1970).

Malone, Dumas. *The Story of the Declaration of Independence*. (New York: Oxford University Press, 1954).

Mangum, Charles S. *The Legal Status of the Negro*. (Chapel Hill: University of North Carolina Press, 1940).

Meier, August, and Rudwick, Elliott. *From Plantation to Ghetto: An Interpretive History of American Negroes*. (New York: Hill and Wang, 1970).

Moore, George H. *Notes on Slavery in Massachusetts*. (reprint ed., New York: Negro University Press, 1968).

Morgan, Edmond S. *American Slavery, American Freedom: The Ordeal of Colonial Virginia*. (New York: W. W. Norton, 1975).

Morgan, Edwin V. *Slavery in New York.* (Washington, 1891).

Mullin, Gerald W. *Flight and Rebellion.* (New York: Oxford University Press, 1972).

Myrdal, Gunnar. *An American Dilemma: The Negro Problem and Modern Democracy.* (New York: Pantheon, 1944, 1964).

O'Callaghan, E. B. *Voyage of the Slaver St. John and Arms of Amsterdam.* (Albany: J. Munsell, 1867).

O'Neall, John Belton. *The Negro Law of South Carolina.* (Columbia, S.C.: John G. Bowman, 1848).

Otley, Roy, and Weatherby, Wm. J. (eds.). *The Negro in New York.* (New York: The New York Public Library, 1967).

Painter, Nell. *Exodusters.* (New York: Knopf, 1977).

Pease and Pease. *The Antislavery Argument.* (Indianapolis: Bobbs Merrill, 1965).

Phillips, Ulrich. *American Negro Slavery.* (Baton Rouge, La.: Louisiana University Press, 1966).

————. *Life and Labor in the Old South.* (Boston: Little, Brown, 1929).

————. *Plantation and Frontier: 1649-1863.* 2 vols. (Cleveland: B. Franklin, 1910).

Pollak, Louis H. (ed.). *The Constitution and the Supreme Court.* (Cleveland: World Publishing Co., 1966).

Quarles, Benjamin. *The Negro in the American Revolution.* (New York: The Norton Library, W. W. Norton, 1973).

————. *The Negro in the Making of America.* (New York: Collier Macmillan, 1969).

Robinson, Donald L. *Slavery in the Structure of American Politics, 1765-1820.* (New York: Harcourt Brace Jovanovich, 1971).

Saye, Albert. *New Viewpoints in Georgia History.* (Athens, Ga.: University of Georgia Press, 1943).

Sharp, Granville. *A Representation of the Injustice and Dangerous Tendency of Tolerating Slavery; or of Admitting the Least Claim of Private Property in the Persons of Men in England.* (London: Benjamin White and Robert Horsefield, 1764).

Smith, Abbott E. *Colonists in Bondage.* (Chapel Hill: University of North Carolina Press, 1947).

Smith, Warren B. *White Servitude in Colonial South Carolina.* (Columbia, S.C.: University of South Carolina Press, 1961).

Stampp, Kenneth M. *The Peculiar Institution.* (New York, Random House, 1956).

Stroud, George M. *Sketch of the Laws Relating to Slavery in the Several States of the United States of America.* (Philadelphia: Henry Longstreth, 1856).

Styles, Fitzhugh Lee. *Negroes and the Law.* (Boston, 1937).

Tannenbaum, Frank. *Slave and Citizen.* (New York: Random House, 1947).

Turner, Edward R. *The Negro in Pennsylvania.* (Washington, D.C.: The American Historical Assoc., 1911).

Ward, W. E. P. *The Royal Navy and the Slavers: The Suppression of the Atlantic Slave Trade.* (New York: Schocken, 1969).

Ware, Gilbert (ed.). *From the Black Bar: Voices for Equal Justice.* (New York: G. P. Putnam's Sons, 1976).

Weinstein, A., and Gatell, F. (eds.). *American Negro Slavery, A Modern Reader.* (New York: Oxford University Press, 1968).

Williams, Eric. *Capitalism and Slavery,* 4th ed. (New York: Penguin Books, 1966).

Williams, George Washington. *History of the Negro Race in America from 1619 to 1880.* 2 vols. (New York: Arno Press and the New York Times, 1968).

Winthrop, John. *The History of New England, 1630-1649,* edited by James K. Hosmer. 2 vols. (1908; repr. New York: Barnes and Noble, 1959).

Wood, Peter H. *Black Majority: Negroes in Colonial South Carolina from 1670 through the Stono Rebellion.* (New York: W. W. Norton, 1974).

Woodson, Carter G., and Wesley, Charles H. *The Negro In Our History,* 11th ed. (Washington, D.C.: Associated Publishers, 1966).

Woodward, C. Vann. *The Strange Career of Jim Crow,* 3rd. rev. ed. (New York: Oxford University Press, 1974).

———. *Origins of the New South 1877-1913.* (Baton Rouge: Louisiana State University Press, 1951).

NOTES

INTRODUCTION

1. Leon Friedman, ed., *Argument: The Oral Argument Before the Supreme Court in Brown v. Board of Education of Topeka, 1952-55* (New York: Chelsea House Publishers, 1969), p. 239.
2. Coretta Scott King, *My Life With Martin Luther King, Jr.* (New York: Holt, Rinehart and Winston, 1969), p. 317.
3. Ben W. Gilbert and the staff of the *Washington Post, Ten Blocks from the White House* (New York: Frederick A. Praeger, 1968).
4. *New York Times* articles: Earl Caldwell, "Guard called out curfew is ordered in Memphis but Fires and Looting Erupt" (April 5, 1968); Thomas A. Johnson, "Scattered Violence occurs in Harlem and Brooklyn" (April 5, 1968); "Army Troops in Capital as Negroes Riot; Guard Sent Into Chicago, Detroit, Boston; Johnson Asks a Joint Session of Congress" (April 6, 1968).
5. Others present were: Richard Hatcher, Mayor of Gary, Indiana; Walter Washington, Mayor of Washington, D.C.; Joseph Califano, Special Assistant to President Johnson; Harry McPherson, Counsel to the President.
6. This theme has been further developed by A. Leon Higginbotham, Jr., in the articles: "Racism and the Early American Legal Process, 1619-1896," *The Annals of the American Academy of Political and Social Science,* vol. 407, May, 1973; and "To the Scale and Standing of Men," *The Journal of Negro History,* vol. 60, no. 3, July, 1975; and in chapters in several books including: "Double Standards for Black Judges" and "Labor Union: Racial Violence" in Gilbert Ware, ed., *From the Black Bar: Voices for Equal Justice* (New York: G. P. Putnam's Sons, 1976), pp. 61-72 and 255-61; "The Black Prisoner: America's Caged Canary," in Hugh Davis Graham, ed., *Violence, The Crisis of American Confidence* (Baltimore, Md.: Johns Hopkins Press, 1971), Chapter 7.
7. See generally, *Report of the National Advisory Commission on Civil Disorders,* "Why Did It Happen?," part 2 (Washington, D.C.: U.S.G.P.O., 1968), pp. 91-145.
8. See articles by A. Leon Higginbotham, Jr.: "Racism and the American Legal Process: Many Deeds Cry Out to be Done," *Progress in Africa and America,* Scholars-Statesmen Lecture Series, Number Three, Dillard University, New

Orleans, La., 1971-1972; "Race, Racism and American Law," 122 *University of Pennsylvania Law Review,* April, 1974; "Civil Rights Litigation in the Federal Courts: The Constitutional and Statutory Prerequisites," paper presented at the Regional Meeting of The Judicial Council of the National Bar Association, Philadelphia, Pa., April 5, 1975; "The Impact of the Declaration of Independence?," *The Crisis* (November, 1975), p. 360, reprinted in Marr and Ward, eds., *Minorities and the American Dream: A Bicentennial Perspective* (New York: Arno Press, 1976), p. 35; "The Priority of Human Rights in Court Reform," paper presented at the National Conference on The Causes of Popular Dissatisfaction with the Administration of Justice, sponsored by the Judicial Conference of the United States, the Conference of Chief Justices and the American Bar Association, St. Paul, Minn., April 8, 1976, 70 F.R.D. 134, republished in *The Judges' Journal,* vol. 15, p. 34; "Race in American Law," paper presented at the Bicentennial Conference on American Law: The Third Century, sponsored by New York University School of Law, New York, April 27, 1976, reprinted in Schwartz, ed., *American Law: The Third Century* (South Hackensack, N.J.: Fred B. Rothman and Co., 1976), p. 45.

9. Recorded message of President R. M. Nixon on July 4, 1970 at the Honor America Day Celebration in Washington, D.C. from *Weekly Compilation of Presidential Documents* 6 (July 13, 1970): 892.

10. "The Meaning of July Fourth to the Negro," 1852, in Philip S. Foner, ed., *The Life and Writings of Frederick Douglass* (New York: International Publishers, 1950), vol. 2, p. 189.

11. 60 U.S. 393, 407 (1857).

12. Mark Twain, *The Adventures of Huckleberry Finn* (New York: Harper & Brothers, 1884), pp. 306-7.

13. James Otis, "The Rights of the British Colonies asserted and Proved," in Bailyn, *Pamphlets,* vol. 1, p. 437.

14. William Goodell, *The American Slave Code in Theory and Practice* (1853; reprint ed., New York: New American Library, 1969), p. 17. William Goodell attributes this statement to Dr. Priestly.

15. My views differ from those apologists who have implied that as an institution slavery was not severely harsh. See Ulrich Phillips, *American Negro Slavery* (1918; reprint ed., Baton Rouge: Louisiana State University Press, 1966). Illustrative of the views which are far too complimentary of the southern justice system are the series of articles by A. E. Kier Nash: "Fairness and Formalism In the Trials of Blacks in the State Supreme Courts of the Old South," *Virginia Law Review* 56 (1970), p. 63; "A More Equitable Past? Southern Supreme Courts and the Protection of the Antebellum Negro," *North Carolina Law Review* 48 (1970), p. 197; "Negro Rights, Unionism and Greatness on the South Carolina Court of Appeals: The Extraordinary Chief Justice John Belton O'Neil," *South Carolina Law Review* 21 (1969), p. 141.

16. Winthrop Jordan, *White Over Black* (Chapel Hill: University of North Carolina Press, 1968), p. 588.

17. C. Vann Woodward, *The Strange Career of Jim Crow,* 3rd. rev. ed. (New York: Oxford University Press, 1974), p. xiii.

18. For general background, see bibliography at pp. 397-403.

19. 13 N.C. 263 (1829).

20. 13 N.C. at 266.

21. Id. at 266-67.

22. Frederick Douglass, *Life and Times of Frederick Douglass* (New York: Collier Books, 1962), p. 150.

23. See Cotton Mather, *The Negro Christianized: An Essay to Encite and Assist that Good Work the Instruction of Negro Servants in Christianity* (Boston, 1706), pp. 18-27; Thomas Bacon, *Sermons Addressed to Masters and Servants and Published in the Year 1743* . . . (Winchester, Va., 1813?), pp. 104-11; Theodore D. Weld, *The Bible Against Slavery: An Inquiry into the Patriarchal and Mosaic Systems on the Subject of Human Rights,* 4th ed. (New York, 1838).

24. Angelina Grimke Weld, daughter of Judge Grimke of South Carolina, stated: "Slaveholders regard their slaves as *property,* the mere instruments of their convenience and pleasure. One who is a slave holder at heart, *never recognizes a human being in a slave.*" Mr. L. Turner, "a regular and respectable member of the Second Presbyterian Church in Springfield, Innilois," said: "Slaves are neither considered or treated as human beings." Mr. Gnolson, of the Virginia legislature, when opposing persons who had proposed abolition, said: "Why, I really have been under the impression that I *owned* my slaves. I lately purchased *four women* and ten children, in whom I thought I obtained a great bargain, for I really supposed they were *my property,* as were my *brood mares.*" Goodell, *The American Slave Code,* pp. 36, 38, 39.

25. G. Frederickson, *The Black Image in the White Mind* (New York: Harper & Row, 1971), pp. 71-96; William R. Stanton, *The Leopards' Spots. Scientific Attitudes Toward Race in America 1815-1859* (Chicago, 1960), pp. 3-14.

26. State v. Mann, 13 N.C. 263 (1829); also, when speaking to the State Agricultural Society of North Carolina in 1855, Judge Ruffin said: Slavery "has a beneficial influence on the prosperity of the country and the physical and moral state of both races, rendering both better and happier than either would be here, without the other." *Publications of the North Carolina Historical Commission,* vol. 8, part 4, "The Papers of Thomas Ruffin," IV, p. 329.

27. Thomas Jefferson, *Notes on the State of Virginia* (New York: Harpers, 1964), p. 138, see also John Hope Franklin, *Racial Equality in America* (Chicago: University of Chicago Press, 1976), pp. 12-20.

28. Ibid., pp. 136, 138.

29. *Report of the National Advisory Commission on Civil Disorders* (Washington, D.C.: U.S.G.P.O., 1968), p. 1.

30. Goodell, *The American Slave Code,* pp. 54-55.

31. Ibid.

32. Vilhelm Aubert, ed., *Sociology of Law* (Baltimore, Md.: Penguin Books, 1969), p. 11.

33. Charles Warren, *The Supreme Court in United States History* (Boston: Little, Brown, 1926), vol. 1, p. 2.

34. Oliver Wendell Holmes, *The Common Law* (Boston: Little, Brown, 1881), p. 1.

VIRGINIA

1. John Smith, *Travels of John Smith*, ed. Edward Arber and A. G. Bradley (Edinburgh: Grant, 1910), vol. 2, p. 41; Winthrop Jordan, *White Over Black* (Chapel Hill: University of North Carolina Press, 1968), p. 3.
2. Carl Degler, "Slavery and the Genesis of American Race Prejudice," *Comparative Studies in Sociology and History* 2 (October 6, 1959): 52.
3. Helen Catterall, *Judicial Cases Concerning American Slavery and the Negro,* reprint ed. (New York: Negro University Press, 1968), vol. 1, p. 55. During the early years of settlement in Virginia, others as well as blacks provided the labor needed by the colony. Orphan boys, convicts, workingmen, and some who might truthfully be described as gentlemen worked as indentured servants alongside their black counterparts. See also June Purcell Guild, *Black Laws of Virginia,* reprint ed. (New York: Negro University Press, 1969), Introduction. For a description of a similar cruise in 1625 made by the *Black Bess,* a Dutch man-of-war commanded by the same captain, see McIlwaine 66, 68; 24 *Va. Mag. Hist.* 46, n. 1. Both captain and crew were English, as was the name of the Dutch ship. Catterall, *Judicial Cases,* vol. 1, p. 55, n. 12.
4. 3 Keble 585 (1677). For full discussion of this case, see pp. 320-324 *infra.*
5. McIlwaine 33 (1624). Primary source used has been the *Minutes of the Council and General Court of Colonial Virginia, 1622-1632, 1670-1676,* ed. H. R. McIlwaine (Richmond, Va.: Richmond Colonial Press, 1924). The original records of the General Court at Virginia were destroyed in the burning of the state capitol building on April 2 and 3, 1865, when Richmond was evacuated by Confederate troops, McIlwaine Preface; Guild, *Black Laws,* p. 21.

   Catterall, *Judicial Cases,* vol. 1, p. 55, n. 14. The names of eleven of the original twenty have been recorded. One, a Negro woman owned by John Rolfe's (the Secretary of the colonies) father-in-law, was called Angelo, a name uncommon in England and unknown in Africa. Others were Anthony, and Isabella, who had a child apparently born after the census at 1623, whose name is recorded as William, in Captain Tucker's muster in 1625. There were two other Anthonys, two Johns, and William, Frances, Edward, and Margaret. Catterall suggests that these names were Anglicizations of Antonio, Juan, Guillen, Francisca, Eduardo, and Margarita. One of the Anthonys in this first group was freed within a few years and as Anthony Johnson became an owner of slaves and considerable property.

   See also *Freedom to the Free,* p. 7; and Woodson and Wesley, *The Negro in our History,* 10th ed. (Washington, D.C.: 1962), p. 82, n. 3; Susie M. Ames, *Studies of the Virginia Eastern Shore in the Seventeenth Century* (Richmond, 1940), p. 99; John H. Russell, *The Free Negro in Virginia,* 1619-1685 (Baltimore: Johns Hopkins University Press, 1913), pp. 23-39; and his "Colored Freemen as Slave Owners in Virginia," *Journal of Negro History* 1 (1916): 234-37, from Jordan, *White Over Black,* p. 74, n. 67.

   Other Negroes came in 1619 with names suggesting antecedent Spanish baptism. See Catterall, *Judicial Cases,* vol. 1, p. 56. And, finally, in the 1640s one notices a difference in names between the second generation of Negroes and their elders. The child of Anthony and Isabella is named William.

By 1649, there were 300 blacks among Virginia's population of 15,000, thus about 2 percent. Jordan, *White Over Black*, p. 72; Peter Force, ed., "A Perfect Description of Virginia," *Tracts* (Washington, D.C.: P. Force, 1836-1846), vol. II, #8. But as Negroes were increasing in substantial number to the colonists, there was similarly a dramatic growth of white indentured servants.

6. Philip A. Bruce, *Economic History of Virginia in the Seventeenth Century,* vol. 2 (New York: Macmillan, 1896), p. 73; J. C. Ballagh, *A History of Slavery in Virginia* (New York: Johnson Reprint Corporation, 1968).

7. John Hope Franklin in United States Commission on Civil Rights, *Freedom to the Free* (Washington, D.C.: U.S.G.P.O., 1963), p. 71; Philip S. Foner, *Organized Labor and the Black Worker* 1619-1673 (New York: Praeger, 1974), p. 73.

8. Oscar and Mary Handlin, "Origins of the Southern Labor System," *William and Mary Quarterly* 8 (1950).

9. Catterall, *Judicial Cases,* pp. 53, 54.

10. McIlwaine, pp. x, xi.

11. Catterall, *Judicial Cases,* p. 75.

12. McIlwaine 479 (September, 1630).

13. McIlwaine 477 (October, 1640).

14. McIlwaine 477 (March, 1641).

15. State v. Mann, 13 N.C. 263 (1829).

16. See generally, "The English Experience," *infra.*

17. Jordan, *White Over Black,* p. 77.

18. Northampton City, Va. *Deeds, Wills, etc.* (Virginia St. Library Edition, Richmond, Va.), Deeds #4, #28.

19. McIlwaine 467 (July, 1640).

20. McIlwaine 466 (July, 1640).

21. Re Graweere, McIlwaine 477 (March, 1641).

22. See pp. 38-57, *infra.*

23. Edmund S. Morgan, *American Slavery, American Freedom: The Ordeal of Colonial Virginia* (New York: W. W. Norton, 1975), p. 153.

24. Re Warwick, McIlwaine 513 (April, 1669).

25. Morgan, *American Slavery,* p. 130.

26. Ibid.

27. William Strachey, *For the Colony in Virginia: Laws Divine Morall and Maritale,* ed. D. H. Flaherty (Charlottesville, Va.: published for the Association for the Preservation of Virginia Antiquities by the University Press of Virginia, 1969), p. 20.

28. In the creation of a ruthless form of slavery in Hispanola, the Arawak Indian population of the island, estimated at approximately eight million when Columbus landed, was reduced to about two hundred during fifty years of Spanish rule. Sherburne F. Cook and Woodrow Borah, *Essays on Population History: Mexico and the Caribbean I* (Berkeley, Calif., 1971), pp. 376-410, cited by Morgan, *American Slavery,* p. 7.

29. Wesley Frank Craven, *The Colonies in Transition 1660-1713* (New York: Harper and Row, 1968), p. 109.

30. See generally, Morgan, *American Slavery,* pp. 250-59; T. J. Wertenbaker, *Torchbearer at the Revolution* (Princeton, N.J.: Princeton University Press, 1940); and Wilcomb Washburn, *The Governor and Rebel* (Chapel Hill: University of North Carolina Press, 1957).

31. William W. Hening, *Statutes at Large of Virginia,* vol. 1 (Richmond, Va.: Franklin Press, 1819-1820), p. 226.

32. Ibid. It is unclear whether all blacks who came to the American continent came as slaves. Some may have been servants without indentures.

33. Guild, *Black Laws,* p. 38. See also Hening, *Statutes,* vol. 1, pp. 274-75. While I am aware that Hening *Statutes* are the official or preferred source for citation of Virginia statutes for the period covered by this chapter, nevertheless I have quoted the statute as republished in Guild, *Black Laws of Virginia,* because Guild has revised the official statutes into modern English usage and is therefore more readable. I have checked each Guild "revision" to make certain that it substantially complies with the Hening version.

34. Act CXIII, Guild, *Black Laws,* p. 39. See also Hening, *Statutes,* vol. 1, p. 483.

35. Act VI (1654), Hening, *Statutes,* vol. 1, p. 226.

36. Hening, *Statutes,* vol. 1, p. 540 (page misnumbered 450). See also Guild, *Black Laws,* p. 40.

37. Hening, *Statutes,* vol. 2, p. 26.

38. Guild, *Black Laws,* p. 40, n. 5.

39. Hening, *Statutes,* vol. 2, p. 116. Emphasis added.

40. Catterall, *Judicial Cases,* vol. 1, p. 60.

41. Morgan, *American Slavery,* p. 312.

42. Hening, *Statutes,* vol. 2, p. 270.

43. Hening, *Statutes,* vol. 2, p. 260. A Maryland law passed in 1639 provided that "all persons being Christians (slaves excepted) over eighteen who were imported without indentures would serve four years." Archives Md. I, 41, 80, also 409, 453-54.

44. Thomas Bacon, *Sermons Addressed to Masters and Servants, Published in the Year 1743* (Winchester, Va., 1813), p. 104.

45. Hening, *Statutes,* vol. 2, p. 283.

46. Hudgins v. Wright, I Hen. and M. 134 (November, 1806).

47. Hening, *Statutes,* vol. 2, pp. 490, 492.

48. The alternate spelling, Endicott, is also used.

49. Catterall, *Judicial Cases,* vol. 1, p. 60.

50. Act X, 1680; Guild, *Black Laws,* p. 45. See also Hening, *Statutes,* vol. 1.

51. Guild, *Black Laws,* p. 46. See also Hening, *Statutes,* vol. 2, p. 18.

52. Kahn v. Shevin, 416 U.S. at 353 (1974).

53. As quoted in Frontiero v. Richardson, 93 S. Ct. 1769, n. 13 (1973). Thomas Jefferson also stated "Were our state a pure democracy, there would still be excluded from our deliberations . . . women, who, to prevent deprivation of morals and ambiguity of issues, should not mix promiscuously in gatherings of men." M. Grueberg, *Women in American Politics* (1968).

54. Loving v. Virginia, 388 U.S. I, 87 S. Ct. 1817 (1967).

55. For an insightful analysis of the sociological and legal ramifications of the miscegenation issue, see Derrick A. Bell, Jr., *Race, Racism and American Law* (Boston: Little, Brown, 1973), pp. 258-94. See also Applebaum, "Mis-

cegenation Statutes: A Constitutional and Social Problem," 53 Geo. L. J. 49, 50, 56, 57, 62-64 (1964); Awins, "Anti-Miscegenation Laws and the Fourteenth Amendment," 52 Va. L. Rev. 1224, 1231 (1969); Note, 58 Yale L. J. 472 (1949); Note, 41 Va. L. Rev. 860 (1955); Weinberger, "A Reappraisal of the Constitution of Miscegenation Statutes," 42 Cornell L. Q. 208, 210-11 (1957). Oliver Cox offers an economic explanation of the antagonism whites have felt toward miscegenation in *Caste, Class and Race* (New York: Doubleday, 1948), pp. 386-87, 526-27. For a psychological inquiry into this issue, see William Grier and Price Cobbs, *Black Rage* (New York: Basic Books, 1968), pp. 91-100; and Goel Kovel, *White Racism: A Psychohistory* (New York: Vintage Books, 1970), pp. 67-71.

56. As quoted in Loving v. Virginia, 388 U.S. 3 (1967).
57. See pp. 23-25, *supra*.
58. Morgan, *American Slavery,* p. 333, citing to Norfolk, *Wills and Deeds,* 1646, 113a: 1666-1675, 55.
59. Hening, *Statutes,* vol. 2, p. 167.
60. Ibid., p. 170.
61. Id.
62. Act XVI, Hening, *Statutes,* vol. 3, pp. 86-88; see also Guild, *Black Laws,* p. 24.
63. Act XLLX, 1705 in Hening, *Statutes,* vol. 3, pp. 447-62. The period of servitude, thirty-one years, was a substantial portion of a servant's life in a colony with so high a mortality rate. Morgan, *American Slavery,* pp. 175-76. In 1769, the statute was amended reducing mullatoes' terms of service to eighteen years of age for females and twenty-one years of age for males. Hening, *Statutes,* vol. 8, p. 376.
64. Morgan, *American Slavery,* p. 335.
65. Id.
66. 1705 Act. Guild, *Black Laws,* p. 24. See also Hening, *Statutes,* vol. 3, pp. 453-54.
67. 1848 Criminal Code, Chapter 120; Guild, *Black Laws,* p. 32.
68. Va. Code Ann. §20-59 (1960) Repl. Vol. See also Guild, *Black Laws,* p. 36.
69. Guild, *Black Laws,* p. 31.
70. Id.
71. Guild, *Black Laws,* p. 49.

"1705. Act XLIX. This act, on servants and slaves, states that for a further Christian care of all Christian slaves it is enacted that no Negro, mulatto, or Indian, although Christian, or Jew, Moor, Mohamedan, or other infidel, shall purchase any Christian servant nor any other except of their own complexion, or such as are declared slaves, but if any Negro or other infidel or such as are declared slaves (i.e., those not Christians in their native country, except Turks and Moors in amity) shall notwithstanding purchase any Christian white servant, the said servant shall become free."

This statute was reincorporated in the 1792 Act, Chapter 67. Shepherd Samuel, ed., *The Statutes at Large of Va.,* vol. 1, p. 181.

72. Jordan, *White Over Black,* p. 137.
73. Id.
74. For a detailed analysis of manumission in Virginia, see unpublished manuscript of Linda Lee Walker: "A Comparative Analysis of Manumission in

Virginia and Louisiana: 1803-1863." University of Pennsylvania, Dept. of Sociology.

75. Catterall, *Judicial Cases*, vol. 1, p. 58, n. 37; Northampton County Records, 5 *Va. Mag. Hist.* 40.

76. Guild, *Black Laws*, p. 47. See also Hening, *Statutes*, vol. 3, p. 87.

77. Hening, *Statutes*, vol. 3, p. 537 reports one such incident in 1710: "Whereas a Negro slave belonging to Robt. Ruffin, of the County of Surry, was signally serviceable in discovering a conspiracy of Negroes for levying war in this colony, for a reward of his fidelity, it is enacted that the said Will is and forever hereafter shall be free and shall continue to be within this colony, if he think fit to continue. The sum of forty pounds sterling shall be paid the said Robt. Ruffin for the price of Will."

78. Hening, *Statutes* (1723), vol. 4, p. 132.

79. Guild, *Black Laws*, p. 60. See also Hening, *Statutes* (May, 1779), vol. 10, p. 115.

80. Guild, *Black Laws*, p. 60. See also Hening, *Statutes* (1779), vol. 10, p. 211.

81. Guild, *Black Laws*, p. 94. See also Hening, *Statutes*, vol. 10, p. 372.

82. Hening, *Statutes*, vol. 11, p. 39.

83. Guild, *Black Laws*, pp. 110-11.

84. Ibid., p. 209. See also general discussion on emancipation and manumission in Virginia in Jordan, *White Over Black*, pp. 551-60.

85. Ibid., p. 68.

86. Ibid., p. 69.

87. Hening, *Statutes* (1671).

88. Hening, *Statutes*, vol. 3, pp. 333-35. Chapter XXIII was repealed in 1748 (Chapter II). The 1748 provision relegated slaves to the status of personal property. Hening, *Statutes*, vol. 5, pp. 432-54.

89. Chapter XXIII (1705) in Hening, *Statutes*, vol. 3, p. 334.

90. Rand, Sir. G. 39 (April, 1730).

91. Chapter XLIX, sec. I (1705), in Hening, *Statutes*, vol. 3, p. 447.

92. Hening, *Statutes* (1705), vol. 3, sec. 4, pp. 447, 448.

93. Hening, *Statutes* (1705), vol. 3, p. 448.

94. Ibid., sec. 9, p. 449.

95. Ibid., p. 451.

96. Ibid., pp. 448, 449.

97. Ibid., sec. 12, p. 450.

98. Ibid., sec. 34, p. 459.

99. Id.

100. Hening, *Statutes*, vol. 3, sec. 37, pp. 460, 461. Emphasis added.

101. Ibid., sec. 39, p. 461.

102. Ibid., sec. 37, p. 461.

103. Hening, *Statutes*, Chapters 16, 17 (1710), vol. 3, pp. 537-40; Chapter 4 (1723), vol. 4, pp. 126-34; Chapter 4 (1726), vol. 4, pp. 169-75; Chapter 15 (1727), vol. 4, pp. 222-28; Chapter 3 (1732), vol. 4, pp. 317-21; Chapter 6 (1732), vol. 4, pp. 324-25; Chapter 7 (1732), vol. 4, pp. 325-26; Chapter 12 (1744), vol. 5, p. 244; Chapter 13 (1744), vol. 5, pp. 244-45; Chapter 32 (1748), vol. 6, p. 31; Chapter 2 (1748), vol. 5, pp. 432-39; Chapter 14 (1748), vol. 5, pp. 547-58; Chapter 21 (1748), vol. 5, p. 38; Chapter

41 (1748), vol. 6, pp. 121-23; Chapter 38 (1748), vol. 6, pp. 104-12; Chapter 7 (1753), vol. 6, pp. 356-57; Chapter 24 (1765), vol. 8, pp. 133-37; Chapter 26 (1765), vol. 8, pp. 137-39; Chapter 27 (1769), vol. 8, pp. 374-77; Chapter 37 (1769), vol. 8, p. 393; Chapter 19 (1769), vol. 8, pp. 358-61; Chapter 1 (1778), vol. 9, pp. 471-72; Chapter 21 (1782), vol. 11, pp. 39-40; Chapter 32 (1782), vol. 11, p. 59; Chapter 78 (1785), vol. 12, p. 184; Chapter 78 (1786), vol. 12, p. 345; Chapter 22 (1787), vol. 12, p. 505; Chap-37 (1787), vol. 12, p. 531; Chapter 45 (1789), vol. 13, p. 62. Shepherd, *The Statutes at Large of Virginia*, Chapter 41 (1792), vol. 1, pp. 122-30; Chapter 42 (1792), vol. 1, pp. 130-36.

104. Hening, *Statutes,* vol. 4, p. 131.
105. See pp. 258, 262, *infra.*
106. Hening, *Statutes* (1769), vol. 9, p. 358.
107. Id.
108. Shepherd, *Statutes at Large,* Chapter 41, vol. 1, p. 123.
109. Id. The statute limits the admissibility of testimony by blacks to those situations where either a criminal charge is brought against another black or in the case of civil suits to those in which blacks *alone* are parties.
110. See generally, A. Leon Higginbotham, Jr. unpub. ms., "Slavery and the Constitution," pp. 33-46; see also Max Farrand, ed., *The Records of the Federal Convention of 1787* (New Haven: Yale University Press, 1911), vol. 2, p. 371.
111. Henry Steele Commager, ed., *Documents of American History,* 8th ed. (New York: Appleton-Century-Crofts, Meredith Corp., 1968), p. 103.
112. Hudgins v. Wright, Hen. and M. 1 Va., 134 (1806).
113. Id. at 140.
114. Id. at 136; for an excellent discussion of this case, see Robert M. Cover, *Justice Accused* (New Haven: Yale University Press, 1975), pp. 50-55.
115. See pp. 50-53, *supra.*
116. Guild, *Black Laws,* p. 72.

MASSACHUSETTS

1. On December 10, 1638, Captain W. Pierce returned to Salem on the ship *Desire* from the Tortugas, where he had exchanged a group of Pequod Indian warriors for "salt, cotton, tobacco, and Negroes." John Winthrop, *The History of New England,* 1630-1649, ed. James K. Hosmer (New York: C. Scribner's, 1908), vol. 1, p. 260.
2. Samuel Sewall, "The Selling of Joseph" (a sermon first published in 1700), in L. H. Fishel and B. Quarles, *The Negro American: A Documentary History* (Glenview, Ill.: Scott, Foresman, 1967), pp. 34-35; reprinted from George H. Moore, *Notes on the History of Slavery in Massachusetts* (New York: 1968), pp. 83-87.
3. William Sumner, *History of East Boston* (Boston, 1858), pp. 90, 91.
4. Lorenzo G. Greene, *The Negro in Colonial New England,* 1620-1776 (New York: Columbia University Press, 1942), p. 17.
5. Colonial Laws of Massachusetts Rep. From 1660 Supp. to 1672 (Boston:

Rockwell & Churchill, 1889), p. 91; also found in Greene, *The Negro in Colonial New England*, p. 63, *Codification of Laws of 1649-1672, General Laws and Liberties for the Massachusetts Colony.*

6. Professor Haskins in his classic treatise describes five social classes identifiable in Massachusetts Bay Colony: 1) the upper class, men of wealth and education; 2) the middle class, artists and tradesmen; independent farmers; 3) the lower class, common and unskilled labor; 4) the servant class; and 5) slaves. George Lee Haskins, *Law and Authority in Early Massachusetts* (New York: Macmillan, 1960), pp. 99-103.

7. Helen Catterall, *Judicial Cases Concerning American Slavery and the Negro* (reprint ed., New York: Negro University Press, 1968), vol. 1, p. 60, citing to a deed dated March 6, 1677 from Middlesex City, Virginia Recs., 8 *Va. Mag. Hist.* 187.

8. Greene, *The Negro in Colonial New England,* pp. 20, 22-23.

9. Moore, *Notes,* pp. 20-22; G. W. Williams, *History of the Negro Race in America from 1619 to 1880* (New York: Arno Press & The New York Times, 1968), vol. 1, p. 179.

10. N. Shurtleff, ed., *Records of the Governor and Company of the Massachusetts Bay in New England* (Boston, 1853), vol. 2, 1642-1649, p. 129 (hereinafter referred to as "Mass. Recs."); case also appears as "Kaezar."

11. 2 Mass. Recs. 168 (1646).

12. Elizabeth Donnan, ed., *Documents Illustrative of the History of the Slave Trade to America* (reprint ed., New York: Octagon Books, 1965), vol. 3, p. 7.

13. Whitemore, ed., *Colonial Laws of Mass.* (reprint 1660), p. 55; Greene, *The Negro in Colonial New England,* p. 68.

14. 2 Mass. Recs. 168 (1646).

15. Greene, *The Negro in Colonial New England,* p. 68.

16. John Eliot, "A Protest," originally printed in John Winsor, *The Memorial History of Boston* (Boston, 1880), vol. 1, p. 322. See also Louis Ruchamies, *Racial Thought in America: From the Puritans to Abraham Lincoln* (New York, 1970), vol. 1, pp. 33-35. For detailed accounts of American Indian and white relations, dating from colonial times, see William T. Hagan, *American Indians* (Chicago: University of Chicago Press, 1961) and Roy Harvey Pearce, *The Savages of America* (Baltimore: Johns Hopkins Press, 1953).

17. 1 Mass. Recs. 246 (1638); For Chousop see 1 Mass. Recs. 181. (1636).

18. 1 Mass. Recs. 269 (1639).

19. Re Gyles Player, 1 Mass. Recs. 246 (1638). Two years later Player was again ordered committed to slavery as punishment for stealing from the master he was given to in the first case; Records of Court of Assistants of the Colony of the Massachusetts (Boston, 1904), vol. 2, 1630-1692, p. 99 (1640) (hereinafter referred to as "Mass. Bay Ct. of Assts."); Re John Kempe, 1 Mass. Recs. 269 (1639), Kempe was made a slave as punishment for "filthy uncleave attempts with 3 young girles"); Re Johnathan Hatch, 2 Mass. Bay Ct. of Assts. 97 (1640).

20. 2 Mass. Bay Ct. of Assts. 94 (1640); see also Re Dickerson, 1 Mass. Recs. 284 (1639), 1 Mass. Recs. 300 (1640), Dickerson released from slavery, and Re Elizabeth Sedgwicke, 2 Mass. Bay Ct. of Assts. 118 (1641-1642), who,

"for hir many theftes and lyes was censured to be severely whipt, and condemned to slavery, till shee have recompenced double for all hir thefts."

21. 2 Mass. Recs. 21 (1642).
22. 4 Mass Recs. (part 1) 366 (1659).
23. Sewall, *History of the Quakers*, vol. 1, p. 278; Catterall, *Judicial Cases*, vol. 4, p. 471, n. 5.
24. 4 Mass. Recs. (part 2) 153 (1665).
25. See generally, Winthrop Jordan, *White Over Black* (Chapel Hill: University of North Carolina Press, 1968), p. 67; Donnan, *Documents*, vol. 3, p. 4.
26. C. E. Eisinger, "The Puritans' Justification for Taking the Land," in M. E. Price, ed., *Law and the American Indian* (New York, 1973), p. 367.
27. John Winthrop, "General Considerations for the Plantation in New England, with an Answer to Several Objections," quoted in Jennings C. Wise, *The Red Man in the New World Drama*, ed. and rev. by V. Deloria, Jr. (New York: Macmillan, 1971), p. 79.
28. Wise, *The Red Man*, p. 8.
29. 1 Mass. Recs. 298 (1640).
30. N. Shurtleff, ed., Records of the Colony of New Plymouth in New England (Boston, 1856), vol. 5, 1678-1691, pp. 151-52 (1674) (hereinafter referred to as "Plym. Col. Recs.").
31. 5 Mass. Recs. 25 (1674).
32. 5 Plym. Col. Recs. 243-44 (1677).
33. See Re Indian Slaves, 5 Plym. Col. Recs. 270 (1678).
34. In *Chousop*, the court noted that he would be a slave for life "unless we see further cause"; thus, there was a reservation that his enslavement need not be for life and could be reduced to a term of years.

   The earlier cases apparently did not provide for the enslavement of the defendant's chillren, but enslaved only the defendant, while in *Popanooie* the court also subjected the children to perpetual slavery, solely because of the acts of their parents.
35. For other instances where nonwhites were sentenced to serve for an established period of years, see Re Indian Joseph Peter, 6 Plym. Col. Recs. 32 (1680); three years later Joseph Peter was found to be incorrigible and was ordered sold out of the country, 6 Plym. Col. Recs. 108 (1683); Re Indian Isacke Tetatan, 7 Plym. Col. Recs. 237-38 (1681); Re Indian Imdah, 6 Plym. Col. Recs. 116 (1683), Imdah was branded and banished; Re Indian Timothy, 6 Plym. Col. Recs. 152 (1685). For instances where Indians were sold as perpetual servants see Re Indian Thomas Wappatucke, 6 Plym. Col. Recs. 153 (1685).
36. Greene, *The Negro in Colonial New England*, p. 23; Jordan, *White Over Black*, p. 66.
37. In his work *American Negro Slavery*, Ulrich Philips had argued that the availability of land, "virtually to be had for the taking" in the southern colonies, and the lack of affordable free labor required the importation of workers who, unlike indentured servants, would not eventually gain their freedom and produce crops in competition with their former masters. *American Negro Slavery* (Baton Rouge: Louisiana University Press, 1966), pp.

73, 74. See also Chief Justice Taney's opinion in Dred Scott v. Sandford, 60 U.S. 393, 412 (1856):

It is very true, that in that portion of the Union where the labor of the negro race was found to be unsuited to the climate, and unprofitable to the master, but few slaves were held at the time of the Declaration of Independence; and when the Constitution was adopted, it had entirely worn out in one of them, and measures had been taken for its gradual abolition in several others. But this change had not been produced by any change of opinion in relation to this race; but because it was discovered, from experience, that slave labor was unsuited to the climate and productions of these States: for some of the States, where it had ceased or nearly ceased to exist, were actively engaged in the slave trade, procuring cargoes on the coast of Africa, and transporting them for sale to those parts of the Union where their labor was found to be profitable, and suited to the climate and productions. And this traffic was openly carried on, and fortunes accumulated by it, without reproach from the people of the States where they resided. And it can hardly be supposed that, in the States where it was then countenanced in its worst form—that is, in the seizure and transportation—the people could have regarded those who were emancipated as entitled to equal rights with themselves.

Cf. Eugene D. Genovese, *The Political Economy of Slavery* (New York: Random House, 1965); Kenneth M. Stampp, *The Peculiar Institution* (New York: Random House, 1956).

38. Jordan, *White Over Black*, p. 66.
39. Greene, *The Negro in Colonial New England*, p. 60.
40. Abbott E. Smith, *Colonists in Bondage* (Chapel Hill: University of North Carolina Press, 1947), p. 29.
41. New York did not become an English colony until 1664. See section on New York, *infra*, for a detailed analysis of the New York colonial history.
42. Jordan, *White Over Black*, p. 69.
43. 2 Mass. Bay Ct. of Assts. 118 (1642).
44. 3 Plym. Col. Recs. 39 (1653).
45. 3 Mass. Bay Ct. of Assts. 194 (1669).
46. 5 Mass. Recs. 117 (1676).
47. The 1684 case of Robert Trayes, Negro, 6 Plym. Col. Recs. 141 (1684) is a further example of the degree to which Massachusetts courts sought to treat blacks as equal to whites, at least in the legal arena. Robert Trayes was indicted for firing a gun at Richard Standlake, and wounding and shattering the leg of Daniel Standlake who subsequently died from the wound. The court found that Trayes had caused the death by misadventure and cleared him of murder; Trayes was transported.
48. Re Hannah Bonny, 6 Plym. Col. Recs. 177 (1685).
49. The Acts and Resolves, Public and Private, of the Province of Massachusetts Bay, 1734-1741 (Boston, 1904), vol. 12, p. 413 (1737).
50. For more detailed analysis of manumission see generally David B. Davis, *The Problem of Slavery in Western Culture* (Ithaca, N.Y.: Cornell University Press, 1966); June P. Guild, *Black Laws of Virginia* (New York: Negro University Press, 1969); John C. Hurd, *The Law of Freedom and Bondage in the United States* (Boston: Little, Brown, 1858), vol. 1 & 2; John D.

Russell, *The Free Negro in Virginia: 1619-1685* (Baltimore, Md.: Johns Hopkins Press, 1913).

51. W. Hening, *Statutes at Large; being a Collection of all the Laws of Virginia* (Philadelphia, 1823), vol. 3, p. 87 (hereinafter referred to as Hening, *Statutes*).

52. Hening, *Statutes,* vol. 4, p. 132.

53. Moore, *Notes,* pp. 246, 247.

54. Re Marja, A Servant, 1 Mass. Bay Ct. of Assts. 198, 199 (1681).

55. Id.

56. Id.

57. See *infra,* pp. 131-134 on New York.

58. Joshua Coffin, *Slave Insurrections,* New York American Anti Slavery Society (1860), [reprinted (Detroit) Negro Hist. Press.], pp. 11-13.

59. Ibid., pp. 12, 13. Article in the *Boston Weekly Journal* of April 8, 1724, also excerpted by Coffin, linked the Boston fires with those in New York in 1712. Ibid., p. 11.

60. A Report of the Record Commissioners of the City of Boston (Boston, 1883), vol. 8, 1700-1728, pp. 173-75 (hereinafter referred to as "Boston Recs.").

61. 8 Boston Recs. 174.

62. Id.

63. For example, John Hope Franklin cites a 1680 law in which blacks were forbidden to board ships in Massachusetts ports without permits, probably because of runaway or kidnapping problems. Franklin, *From Slavery to Freedom: A History of Negro Americans,* 3rd ed. (New York: Vintage Books, 1969), p. 105. In 1698 the first of many laws regulating the availability to nonwhites of businesses licensed by the government prohibited innholders from selling liquor to "any apprentice, servant, or negro" or allowing them to sit drinking liquor in his or her house without permission from their masters. Later extensions of this law were enacted on a local level—the Boston selectmen, for example, enacted this ordinance in 1759 and 1761. See generally Moore, *Notes.*

64. Moore, *Notes,* p. 54; Charters and General Laws of the Colony and Province of Massachusetts Bay (Boston, 1814), pp. 745, 746 (hereinafter referred to as "Charters"). Boston selectmen's version (1757) included proscription of strolling "unnecessarily abroad or . . . loitering and idling in any of the Streets or Lanes, or in the Common during the time of divine Service on the Lord's Day." 14 Boston Recs. 315 (1742-1757).

65. Greene, *The Negro in Colonial New England,* pp. 169, 170.

66. Ibid., pp. 169-71; Williams, *History,* vol. 1, p. 188.

67. 15 Boston Recs. 368-70.

68. Greene, *The Negro in Colonial New England,* p. 84; 8 Boston Recs. 170 (1722).

69. A Boston ordinance of 1723 limited burial of all Indians, blacks, and mulattoes under penalty of a fine, to "halfe an hour before Sun Set at the least," at "the nearest burying place (where Negroes are usually buried)." A petition from the Grave Diggers in 1744 complained of overcrowding in the "South Burying Place" and requested the town to "provide some place to Bury Strangers and Negroes." 14 Boston Recs. 53.

Free Boston blacks were not permitted to choose an undertaker until 1792. 27 Boston Recs. 103, 159, 189, 327.

Another ordinance passed in 1728, forbade Indians, blacks, or mulattoes to carry a stick or cane "that may be fit for Quarelling or Fighting with," prohibited servants or slaves from buying provisions "of any of the Country People," that drove up prices.

70. Proposed regulations, April 28, 1736, 12 Boston Recs. 139. See also 19 Boston Recs. 188 (1761); at least one regulation simply ordered "Watchmen to take care of Negroes after 9 o'clock." 19 Boston Recs. 109 (1759).

71. 15 Boston Recs. 245.

72. 14 Boston Recs. 62, 77, 91, 96-97.

73. Jordan, *White Over Black*, p. 101.

74. Greene, *The Negro in Colonial New England*, p. 81; Jordan, *White Over Black*, p. 103.

75. Jordan, *White Over Black*, p. 102.

76. Charters, pp. 595-97.

77. Coffin, *Slave Insurrections*, p. 15.

78. 11 Boston Recs. 5.

79. Charters, p. 749.

80. Greene, *The Negro in Colonial New England*, p. 51.

81. Moore, *Notes*, pp. 126-28.

82. 16 Boston Recs. 200.

83. Moore, *Notes*, pp. 131-32.

84. Greene, *The Negro in Colonial New England*, p. 56.

85. Franklin, *From Slavery to Freedom*, 4th ed., pp. 85-86.

86. This case was noted in John Adams' Diary as follows: Wed., 11/5/1766, "Attended Court; heard the trial of an action of trespass brought by a mulatto woman . . ."; Williams, *History*, p. 228.

87. Ibid., pp. 229-30.

88. Ibid., p. 230; Williams cites *Records*, 1769, fol. p. 196.

89. Moore reports that the case had "been brought up from the Inferior Court by sham demurrer, and after one or two continuances, settled by the parties." Moore, *Notes*, p. 116. A demurrer under the rules of common law pleadings was a pleading mechanism by which the party could dispute the sufficiency in law of the other side's case.

90. See generally, Hendrick v. Greenleaf (Essex, 1773); Caesar v. Taylor (Essex, 1772); Caleb Dodge v. Z. (Essex, 1774); Moore, *Notes*, pp. 118-19; Williams, *History*, pp. 230-33.

91. Moore, *Notes*, p. 118; Quincy's Reports, 30, (1772).

92. Williams, *History*, p. 230.

93. R. V. Inhabitants of Thames Ditton, 4 Douglass K. B. 300 (1785).

94. Williams, *History*, p. 231.

95. Charters, p. 31 (1691 Charter of the Province).

96. Williams, *History*, p. 462.

97. Ibid., pp. 233-37.

98. Moore, *Notes*, p. 180.

99. Ibid., p. 184.

100. Ibid., p. 181.

101. Ibid., pp. 145-46, quotes the following Tory propaganda: "Negro slaves in Boston! It cannot be! It is nevertheless very true. For though the Bostonians have grounded their rebellions on the 'immutable laws of nature,' and have resolved in their Town Meetings, that 'It is the first principle in civil society, founded in nature and reason, that no law of society can be binding on any individual, without his consent given by himself in person, or by his representative of his own free election; yet, notwithstanding . . . they actually have in town two thousand Negro slaves, who neither by themselves in person, nor by representatives of their own free election, ever gave consent to their present state of bondage.'"

102. Coffin, *Slave Insurrections,* p. 16.

103. 20 Boston Recs. 314.

104. Williams, *History,* p. 227; Herbert Aptheker, *American Negro Slave Revolts* (New York: International Publishers, 1943), pp. 87, 201.

105. Williams, *History,* p. 371, see also pp. 379-80; Moore, *Notes,* p. 171.

106. Moore, *Notes,* pp. 144-45.

107. Although a 1630 order of the Massachusetts Bay Court of Assistants directed "every person within their Towne . . . as well servants as others, be finished with good and sufficient armes . . . ," 2 Mass. Bay Ct. of Assts. 12, and a 1652 order of the General Court directed "all Scotsmen, Negeres and Indians inhabiting with or servant to English . . ." to be listed and train with the English, generally blacks were specifically excepted from military drafts. Moore, *Notes,* pp. 243-45.

108. A 1793 act authorized the enrollment of "each and every free, able-bodied white male citizen of this . . . Commonweath," between 18 and 45, with exceptions. It was not until 1863 that the state legislature, matching its laws to federal military law during the Civil War, enacted legislation that accepted blacks as soldiers. Moore, *Notes,* p. 246.

109. Ibid., p. 191.

110. Williams, *History,* vol. 2, pp. 125-27. Perhaps in response to the new state constitution passed in 1780, two of the Dartmouth blacks petitioned the Dartmouth selectmen in 1781 to ascertain whether the townspeople agreed that free nonwhites had the same privileges as whites; the answer, if any, is not known.

111. Francis H. Fox, *Discrimination and Anti Discrimination in Massachusetts Law,* 30 Bur 30, 47 (1964).

112. Robert Taylor, ed., *Massachusetts Colony to Commonwealth* (Chapel Hill: University of North Carolina Press, 1961), p. 69; See also Richard M. Cover, *Justice Accused: Anti-Slavery and the Judicial Process* (New Haven, Conn.: Yale University Press, 1975), p. 43.

113. Taylor, *Massachusetts Colony,* p. 64; Cover, *Justice Accused,* p. 44.

114. See Moore, *Notes,* p. 222 as to petitions in 1790's of "pauper negroes."

115. Commonwealth v. Jennison, Proc. Mass. Hist. Soc., 1873-1875, 293 (April, 1783).

116. Queries Respecting the Slavery and Emancipation of Negroes in Massachusetts, Proposed by the Hon. Judge Tucker of Virginia & Answered by the Rev. Dr. Belknap, Mass. Hist. Soc., *Collections* 1st Ser.

117. Ibid.

118. John D. Cushing, "The Cushing Court and the Abolition of Slavery in Massachusetts: More Notes on the Quock Walker Case," 5 Am. J. Legal Hist. (1961): 118-19.

119. Quock Walker v. Jennison, Proc. Mass. Hist. Soc., 1873-1875, 296 (September, 1781).

120. Jennison v. Caldwell, Proc. Mass. Hist. Soc., 1873-1875, 296 (September, 1781).

121. Jennison's appeal in the Quock Walker case was the first of the two to be "called" for trial. Because of a procedural mistake, however, Jennison's case was postponed. The case was later called on two separate occasions, but as Jennison had never corrected the procedural error, the court found him in default. Jennison petitioned the legislature for a reinstatement of the case but he was unsuccessful. According to J. D. Cushing, Jennison's attorneys could have corrected the error by retrieving the necessary papers from the court chambers a few yards away, but this was never done. Jennison waited nine months before he petitioned the legislature for a rehearing of the case. Cushing, "The Cushing Court," pp. 123, 124.

122. More detailed insights into these cases are available in the brief or notes of Levi Lincoln in the Jennison v. Caldwell case in the *Collections of the Massachusetts Historical Society,* 1st. Series 4 (1795), p. 438. And, for analysis of the criminal case, Commonwealth v. Jennison, two sources exist for Cushing's charge to the jury: that found in J. D. Cushing's article, "The Cushing Court," and used in this text as the more definitive version, and the copy of the charge which appears in the Proceedings of the Massachusetts Historical Society. See note 126 *infra.*

123. Letters and Documents Relating to Slavery, *Collect. of the Mass. Hist. Soc.* 5th Ser. 3 (1877), 442.

124. The account of the trial can be found in Levi Lincoln's brief in the William Lincoln Papers, *American Antiquarian Society;* See also Cushing, "The Cushing Court," pp. 122, 123.

125. Cushing, *supra* at 131, citing to "S.J.C. Record, Worcester Session, 1783, fol. 85"; Paine, Minutes & Trial of the Case, Worcester, 1783; *Paine Papers,* vol. 1.

126. For a most illuminating discussion on the Massachusetts 1780 constitutional provision, see Cover, *Justice Accused,* Chapter 3.

127. This version appears in a manuscript notebook in the Harvard University Law Library entitled "Notes of Cases decided in the Superior and Supreme Judicial Courts of Massachusetts from 1772-1789 taken by the Honorable Wm. Cushing, one of the Judges during that period and most of the time Chief Justice"; this version first appeared in Cushing, *supra* at 132, 133.

 Another version, probably Cushing's rough draft, appears as follows in Proc. Mass. Hist. Soc. 1873-1875, 293, 294 (April, 1783):

CUSHING, C. J. As to the doctrine of slavery and the right of Christians to hold Africans in perpetual servitude, and sell and treat them as we do our horses and cattle, that (it is true) has been heretofore countenanced by the Province Laws formerly, but nowhere is it expressly enacted or established. It has been a usage—a usage which took its origin from the practice of some of the European nations, and the regulations of British government respecting the then Colonies, for the benefit of trade and wealth. But whatever sentiments have formerly prevailed in this particular or slid in upon us by the example of others, a different idea has taken place with the people of America, more favorable to the natural rights of mankind, and to that natural, innate desire of Liberty, which with Heaven (without regard to color, complexion, or shape of noses-features) has inspired all the human race. And upon this ground our Constitution of Government, by which the people of this Commonwealth have solemnly bound themselves, sets out with declaring that all men are born free and equal—and that every subject is entitled to liberty, and to have it guarded by the laws, as well as life and property—and in short is totally repugnant to the idea of being born slaves. This being the case, I think the idea of slavery is inconsistent with our own conduct and Constitution; and there can be no such thing as perpetual servitude of a rational creature, unless his liberty is forfeited by some criminal conduct or given up by personal consent or contract . . . *Verdict Guilty.*

128. Robert Treat Paine to William Cushing, August 21, 1779, *Paine Papers,* vol. 4.
129. Cushing & Sargeant to Hancock, December 20, 1783, *Cushing Papers,* vol. 2.
130. Belknap Papers, 2 vols., *Mass. Hist. Soc. Collections,* 5th Ser. 3 (1877), pp. 389–90.
131. Tucker wrote to Belknap in January 24, 1795 that: "That introduction of slavery into this country is at this day considered among its greatest misfortunes by a very great majority of those who are reproached for an evil which the present generation could no more have avoided than an hereditary gout or leprosy . . . having observed, with much pleasure, that slavery has been wholly exterminated from the Massachusetts, . . . I have cherished a hope that we may, from the example of our sister State, learn what methods are most likely to succeed in removing the same evil from among ourselves." 3 Mass. Hist. Soc. *Collections,* 5th Ser., 378, 380.
132. 3 Mass. Hist. Coll. (5th Ser.) 379.
133. 3 Mass. Hist. Coll. (5th Ser.) 401.

NEW YORK

1. Winthrop Jordan, *White Over Black* (Chapel Hill: University of North Carolina Press, 1968), p. 84. Cf. Frank Tannenbaum, *Slave and Citizen* (New York: Random House, 1947), p. 65, n. 153.
2. Edgar McManus, *A History of Negro Slavery in New York* (Syracuse, N.Y.: Syracuse University Press, 1970), p. 11.
3. George W. Williams, *History of the Negro Race in America, 1619-1880* (1883; repr. New York: Arno Press, 1968), vol. 1, p. 136.
4. Edgar McManus, *Black Bondage in the North* (Syracuse, N.Y.: Syracuse University Press, 1973), p. 3.
5. McManus, *A History,* p. 9.
6. Emphasis added. Ellis Lawrence Raesly, *Portraits of New Netherland* (New York: Columbia University Press, 1945), pp. 160, 162, 269-84 (quoting the poem with permission of Columbia University); Jordan, *White Over Black,* p. 84.

7. For detailed analysis of the development of the South Carolina colony, see Peter H. Wood, *Black Majority: Negroes in Colonial South Carolina from 1670 through the Stovo Rebellion* (New York: Alfred A. Knopf, 1974), particularly pp. 35-62.

8. E. B. O'Callaghan, *Voyage of the Slaver St. John and Arms of Amsterdam* (Albany, N.Y., 1861), p. 12.

9. McManus, *A History*, p. 12.

10. Williams, *History of the Negro Race*, p. 137.

11. Berthold Fernow, *Records of New Amsterdam* (New York: Knickerbocker, 1897), vol. 1, p. 204.

12. Id.

13. E. B. O'Callaghan, *Laws and Ordinances of New Netherlands 1638-1674* (Albany, N.Y.: Weed Parsons and Co., 1868), pp. 36, 37.

14. Ibid.

15. Williams, *History of the Negro Race*, p. 136.

16. See Chapter 8, section on villenage.

17. McManus, *A History*, p. 12.

18. O'Callaghan, *Laws and Ordinances of New Netherlands*, pp. 191-92.

19. Ibid., p. 193.

20. O'Callaghan, *Laws and Ordinances of New Netherlands*, p. 10.

21. Ibid., p. 12.

22. Ibid., p. 33.

23. Ibid., p. 36.

24. Ibid., p. 60.

25. Ibid., pp. 81-82. See also note, p. 127, as to a similar resolution of April 4, 1652.

26. Fernow, *Records*, pp. 11-12.

27. McManus, *A History*, pp. 17, 18.

28. Ibid., p. 18.

29. O'Callaghan, *Laws and Ordinances of New Netherlands*, pp. 144-45.

30. Ibid., p. 305.

31. Ibid., pp. 21, 22, 28, 100, 103, 182-83, 228, 234-35, 259-60, 366, 384, 451, 463, 446.

32. Ibid., p. 191.

33. Ulrich Phillips, *American Negro Slavery* (repr. Baton Rouge, La.: Louisiana State University Press, 1966), p. 108.

34. For a more detailed analysis of the English conquest of New Netherlands, see Wesley Frank Craver, *The Colonies in Transition 1660-1713* (New York, 1968), pp. 70-88. See also John R. Brodhead, *History of the State of New York*, vol. 2, pp. 22-41.

35. McManus, *A History*, p. 23.

36. Act of 1665 (Duke of York Laws); *Colonial Laws of New York* (Albany, N.Y.: James B. Lyon, 1894), p. 18.

37. A. E. Smith, *Colonists in Bondage* (Chapel Hill: University of North Carolina Press, 1947), p. 35.

38. Benjamin Quarles, *The Negro in the Making of America* (New York: Collier McMillan, 1969), p. 40.

39. *Minutes of the Common Council of the City of New York, 1675–1776*, (New

York: Dodd, Mead and Company, 1905), vol. 1, p. 134.

40. McManus, *Black Bondage*, pp. 18, 41, 42.

41. *Minutes of the Common Council of the City of New York, 1675-1776*, vol. 1, pp. 179, 219.

42. McManus, *Black Bondage*, p. 45.

43. *Colonial Laws of New York*, ch. 123, pp. 519-21 (November 27, 1702).

44. Ibid., ch. 250, pp. 761-67 (December 10, 1712).

45. Ibid., ch. 790, pp. 448-49 (May 14, 1745).

46. Ibid., ch. 123, pp. 519-21 (November 27, 1702).

47. Id.

48. Ibid., ch. 123, p. 520 (November 27, 1702).

49. Ibid., ch. 149, pp. 582-84 (August 4, 1705).

50. Ibid., p. 583.

51. Ibid., p. 584.

52. Ibid., ch. 181, p. 631 (October 30, 1708).

53. The 1706 statute modified the 1682 law which allowed up to four slaves to assemble. Governor Cornbury's proclamation of 1706 stated: "Requiring and commanding (all officers) to take all proper methods for the storin and apprehending of all such Negroes as shall be found to be assembled—. & if any of them refuse to submit, then fire upon them, kill or destroy them, if they cannot otherwise be taken—I am informed that several Ns in Kings County (Brooklyn) have assembled themselves in a riotous manner, which if not prevented may prove of ill consequence." Otley and Weatherby, *The Negro in New York*, p. 22.

54. *Colonial Laws of New York*, ch. 181, p. 631 (October 30, 1708). Emphasis added.

55. Ibid., ch. 250, p. 765 (December 10, 1712).

56. Ibid., ch. 181, p. 631 (October 30, 1708).

57. *New York Weekly Journal*, January 5, 1735, p. 36; as cited by McManus, *Black Bondage*, p. 19.

58. McManus, *Black Bondage*, p. 91.

59. *Colonial Laws of New York*, ch. 123, p. 521 (November 27, 1702).

60. Act of 1665 (Duke of York Laws); *Colonial Laws of New York* (Albany, N.Y.: James B. Lyon, 1894), p. 18; the several existing copies of the Duke's Laws vary partly from errors in transcribing and partly from amendments. Id., p. 6. See Beckman, *The Statutes at Large of Pennsylvania in the Time of William Penn* (New York: Vantage Press, 1976), vol. 1, pp. 27-29.

61. See p. 62, *supra*.

62. 3 Keble 785 (Jones, 1677). There are two reported versions of this decision. The version cited in the text implies that slavery may have been justified because of the blacks' present status, i.e. "heathen." The other version, reported in 2 Levinz 20 (Irinn 1677), strongly suggests that slavery was a permanent condition, not to be modified by any altered religious status.

63. Accord, Gelly v. Cleve, 1 Ld. Raym. 147; Chamberlaine v. Harvey, 3 Ld. Raym. 129 (1696, 1697). See generally "The English Experience," *infra*.

64. Roi Otley & William J. Weatherby, eds., *The Negro in New York* (New York: The New York Public Library, 1967), pp. 15-16. Cf. Williams, *History of the Negro Race*, p. 139.

65. *Colonial Laws of New York,* ch. 160, pp. 597-98 (October 21, 1706). For the English precedent see pp. 324, 327-329, *infra.*

66. By 1700 the colonies of Maryland, Virginia, North and South Carolina, and New Jersey had passed laws stating that conversion did not require manumission. The fact that such laws were necessary suggest that prior to their enactment heathenism was a crucial factor in determining who was and who was not a slave. For further detail on the above mentioned colonies, see *Archives of Maryland* (Baltimore, Md., 1883-) vol. 1, pp. 526, 533 (1664), vol. 2, p. 272; Hening, ed., *Statutes of Virginia* (Richmond, 1809-1823) vol. 2, p. 260 (1667); William L. Saunders, ed., *The Colonial Records at North Carolina* (Raleigh, 1886-1890) vol. 1, p. 204 (1670), vol. 2, p. 857. Thomas Cooper and David v. McCard, eds., *Statutes at Large of South Carolina* (Columbia, S.C., 1830-1841, vol. 7, p. 343 (1691). See also Jordan, *White Over Black,* pp. 91-98.

67. *Chamberlaine,* 3 Ld. Raym. at 129. See also *Modern Repts.—Select Cases adjudged in the Courts of Kings Bench, Chancery, Common Pleas & Exchequer,* vol. 5, pp. 186, 188.

68. *Colonial Laws of New York,* ch. 250, pp. 764-65 (December 10, 1712).

69. Ibid., ch. 341, pp. 922-23 (November 2, 1717).

70. *Court of General Sessions of the Peace, Ulster County, Kingston,* November 4, 1740, May 1, 1750, Hist. Doc. Coll., Klapper Library, Queens College. As cited by McManus, *A History,* p. 143.

71. See generally Register of Manumissions, Jamaica Town Records, vol. 3, pp. 346-47, 349-50; *Abstracts of Wills,* vol. 15, pp. 114-16. As cited by McManus, *A History,* p. 145.

72. Kettletas v. Fleet, 1 Antou's Nisi Pruis Repts. 36 (New York, 1808).

73. Leo Hirsch, "The Negro and New York 1783-1865," *Journal of Negro History* 16 (1931): 385.

74. *Laws of New York,* ch. 188, pp. 612-19 (April 8, 1801).

75. Kenneth Scott, "The Slave Insurrection in New York in 1712," N.Y. Hist. Soc. Quarterly (1961); Jordan, *White Over Black,* p. 116.

76. Jordan, *White Over Black,* p. 116.

77. *Colonial Laws of New York,* ch. 250, p. 761 (December 10, 1712).

78. Ibid., pp. 763, 766-67.

79. Ibid., p. 765. Emphasis added. Contrast this statute with the 1708 act, discussed *infra.*

80. Ibid., p. 767.

81. Ibid., p. 682.

82. Ibid., pp. 682-83.

83. Ibid., p. 684.

84. McManus, *A History,* p. 86.

85. Daniel Horsmanden to Cadwallader Colden, From on Board the *Admiral Winne* near the mouth of the Highlands, Aug. 7, 1741. *The Letters and Papers of Cadwallader Colden,* 9 vols. (N.Y. Hist. Soc., *Collections,* 50-56, 1917-1923), vol. 2, p. 225. As cited by Jordan, *White Over Black,* p. 117, n. 36.

86. Jordan, *White Over Black,* p. 118.

87. Ibid., p. 119.

88. *New York Weekly Post-Boy,* March 24, 1760. As cited by McManus, *A History,* p. 151.

89. Henry P. Johnson, ed., *The Correspondence and Public Papers of John Jay* (New York: G.P. Putnam's Sons, 1890-1893), vol. 1, p. 407.

90. Philip S. Foner, *History of Black Americans: From Africa to The Emergence of the Cotton Kingdom* (Westport, Conn.: Greenwood Press, 1975), p. 366.

91. Ibid. See also McManus, "Antislavery Legislation in New York" *Journal of Negro History* 46 (1961).

92. McManus, *A History,* pp. 154-55.

93. Foner, *History,* p. 338.

94. Ibid., quoting from Sylvia Freys's study, "The British Soldier in the American Revolution."

95. *Laws of New York,* ch. 32, p. 42 (March 20, 1781).

96. Quarles, *Negro in Making America,* p. 171.

97. Ibid.

98. *Laws of New York,* ch. 44, p. 143 (May 12, 1784).

99. *Journal of the Assembly of the State of New York,* March 9, 1785. As cited by McManus, *A History,* p. 162.

100. This tactic, an attack on the international slave trade, was used by the English abolitionists with hopes that domestic slavery would gradually disappear.

101. McManus, *A History,* p. 168.

102. *Laws of New York,* ch. 15, p. 85 (February 22, 1788).

103. For a discussion of this common practice, see Soble v. Hitchcock, 2 Johnson's Cases 68 (N.Y. Sup. Ct. 1800); *Minutes of the New York Manumission Society,* June 23, 1795. As cited by McManus, *A History,* p. 169.

104. See Carter G. Woodson, ed., *The Mind of the Negro As Reflected in Letters Written During The Crisis,* 1800-1860 (Washington, D.C., 1926) p. IV. Sidney Kaplan, *The Black Presence in The Era of the American Revolution 1770-1800* (Smithsonian Institution Press & N.Y. Graphic Society, 1973), pp. 171-77.

105. Kaplan, *Black Presence,* p. 177.

106. *Laws of New York,* ch. 40, p. 85 (February 22, 1788).

107. Id.

108. Id.

109. Id.

110. Ibid., p. 86.

111. Ibid., pp. 86-87.

112. Ibid., p. 87. For discussion of the 1788 provisions regarding manumissions, see pp. 141-142, *infra.*

113. E. Wilder Spaulding, *New York in the Critical Period* (New York: Columbia University Press, 1932), pp. 30-31. As cited by McManus, *A History,* p. 172.

114. Hirsch, "The Negro and New York," pp. 387-88.

115. *Minutes,* August 8 and November 15, 20, 1787; January 17, 1797. As cited by McManus, *A History,* p. 173. Carter G. Woodson, *Education of the Negro Prior to 1861* (New York, 1915); see also John Hope Franklin, *From Slavery to Freedom,* 3rd ed., p. 160.

116. *Laws of New York,* ch. 62, pp. 388-89 (March 29, 1799).

117. Ibid., p. 389.
118. Ibid.
119. For a discussion of similar efforts to avoid compliance with the gradual emancipation statute, see pp. 299-305 on the Pennsylvania experience.
120. *Laws of New York*, ch. 188, p. 615 (April 8, 1801).
121. *Laws of New York*, ch. 44, p. 450 (February 17, 1809).
122. *Laws of New York*, ch. 77, pp. 92-93 (March 31, 1807).
123. William P. Van Ness and John Woodworth, eds., *Laws of the State of New York Revised & Passed at the 36th Session of the Legislature* (Albany, N.Y.: H. C. Southwick and Co., 1813), vol. 2, p. 207.
124. Ibid., ch. 15, p. 209 (February 25, 1813).
125. *Laws of New York*, ch. 137, p. 144 (March 31, 1817).
126. Ibid., p. 140.
127. Jack v. Martin, 14 Wendell 507, 528, 530 (Court of Corrections, December, 1835).
128. Alexis De Tocqueville, *Democracy in America* (New York: Doubleday, 1969), p. 344.
129. Fox, *The Negro Vote*, pp. 256, 257, 262. As cited by McManus, *A History*, p. 187.

SOUTH CAROLINA

1. Peter H. Wood, *Black Majority* (New York: W. W. Norton, 1974), p. 3.
2. Max Farrand, ed., *The Records of the Federal Convention of 1787*, rev. ed. (New Haven: Yale University Press, 1966), vol. 3, p. 254.
3. Wood, *Black Majority*, p. 21.
4. Ibid.; Alexander S. Salley, *Warrants for Lands in South Carolina, 1672-1679* (Columbia, S.C., 1910), p. 52.
5. Warren B. Smith, *White Servitude in Colonial South Carolina* (Columbia: University of South Carolina Press, 1961), p. 5.
6. Wood, *Black Majority*, p. 144.
7. Edward McCrady, *The History of South Carolina under the Proprietary Government, 1670-1719* (New York: Macmillan, 1897), p. 8.
8. McCrady, "Slavery in the Province of South Carolina, 1670-1770," pp. 643-44; David Duncan Wallace, *South Carolina, A Short History 1520-1948* (Chapel Hill: University of North Carolina Press, 1951), p. 31; Wood, *Black Majority*, p. 43.
9. Wood, *Black Majority*, p. 32.
10. Ibid., p. 34.
11. McCrady, *The History of South Carolina under the Proprietary Government, 1670-1719*, pp. 2-3.
12. William J. Rivers, *A Sketch of the History of South Carolina to the Close of the Proprietary Government, 1719* (Charleston, 1856), p. 71; Edward McCrady, *The History of South Carolina under the Royal Government, 1719-1776* (New York: Macmillan, 1899), p. 3; Wesley F. Craven, *The Southern Colonies in the Seventeenth Century, 1607-1689*, in Wendell Stephenson and E. Merton Coulter, eds., *A History of the South, I* (Baton Rouge: Louisiana State University Press, 1949), p. 326. The colony of Carolina was settled by

several individuals called Proprietors, who received a charter dated March 24, 1663, from Charles II. A second charter, dated June 30, 1665, granted to the same noblemen, extended the bounds of the province to include lands from the Atlantic to the South Seas and with a latitude of 29° south to 36°30' north. This second charter gave the Proprietors the authority to subdivide the territory and constituted the basis of the colonial government until the demise of the proprietary government. Rivers, *A Sketch of the History of South Carolina,* pp. 61, 73.

13. Thomas Cooper and David J. McCord, eds., *The Statutes at Large of South Carolina* (Columbia, S.C., 1836-41), vol. 2, p. 124.
14. Charles M. Andrews, *The Colonial Period of American History* (New Haven: Yale University Press, 1937), vol. 3, pp. 247-50.
15. Ibid., p. 247.
16. There was a provisional government in South Carolina from 1719-1729; the royal government was established in 1729. See McCrady, *The History of South Carolina under the Royal Government, 1719-1776,* pp. 4-5.
17. Smith, *White Servitude,* p. 7.
18. For a discussion of redemptioners, see *supra* at pp. 394-395.
19. Smith, *White Servitude,* pp. 48-49.
20. McCrady, "Slavery in the Province of South Carolina, 1670-1770," American Historical Association *Report* (1895): 631.
21. Wallace, *South Carolina,* pp. 187-88; McCrady, *The History of South Carolina under the Proprietary Government, 1670-1719,* p. 357; Smith, *White Servitude,* p. 39.
22. Wallace, *South Carolina,* pp. 186-87.
23. Karl F. Geiser, "Redemptioners and Indentured Servants in the Colony and Commonwealth of Pennsylvania," *Yale Review Supplement* 10 (1901): 41.
24. Wallace, *South Carolina,* p. 35.
25. McCrady, *The History of South Carolina under the Proprietary Government, 1670-1719,* p. 212.
26. Smith, *White Servitude,* p. 82.
27. Act of 1717, *Statutes at Large of South Carolina,* vol. 3, p. 15.
28. Ibid.; Act of 1744, *Statutes at Large of South Carolina,* vol. 3, p. 623.
29. Act of 1717, *Statutes at Large of South Carolina,* vol. 3, p. 15; Act of 1744, *Statutes at Large of South Carolina,* vol. 3, p. 622.
30. *Statutes at Large of South Carolina,* vol. 2, p. 52.
31. Ibid., vol. 3, p. 17.
32. Ibid.
33. Ibid.
34. Ibid., p. 18.
35. Ibid., p. 624.
36. Smith, *White Servitude,* p. 78. For an example of the type of summons delivered to the master on complaint of a servant and an order granting that a servant be freed from his master after a finding of ill treatment, see William Simpson, *The Practical Justice of the Peace and Parish-Officer of His Majesty's Province of South Carolina* (1761; reprint ed., New York: Arno Press, 1972), pp. 237-38.
37. Act of 1717, *Statutes at Large of South Carolina,* vol. 3, p. 19; Act of 1744, *Statutes at Large of South Carolina,* vol. 3, p. 628.

38. Act of 1717, *Statutes at Large of South Carolina*, vol. 3, p. 20; Act of 1744, *Statutes at Large of South Carolina*, vol. 3, p. 628.
39. Ibid.
40. See *infra*, p. 165.
41. *Statutes at Large of South Carolina*, vol. 2, p. 22; McCrady, "Slavery in the Province of South Carolina," 633-34.
42. *Statutes at Large of South Carolina*, vol. 2, p. 22.
43. Ibid., vol. 3, p. 16.
44. Ibid.
45. Ibid., p. 625.
46. Ibid.
47. Act of 1695, *Statutes at Large of South Carolina*, vol. 2, p. 105.
48. Ibid.
49. See Virginia chapter *supra* at pp. 40-47.
50. *Statutes at Large of South Carolina*, vol. 3, p. 17.
51. Wood, *Black Majority*, p. 98.
52. *Statutes at Large of South Carolina*, vol. 3, p. 14.
53. Ibid., p. 19.
54. Ibid., pp. 19-20.
55. Ibid., p. 20.
56. Ibid. This was one of the few, if not the only, instances where black servants were referred to in the earlier colonial statutes.
57. Ibid.
58. Ibid.
59. Smith, *White Servitude*, pp. 19-20.
60. *Statutes at Large of South Carolina*, vol. 2, p. 154.
61. Ibid.
62. Ibid., p. 647.
63. Ibid., p. 646.
64. As to how adverse publicity in Europe and England about the harsh treatment of servants contributed to the difficulties of importing white servants, see Wood, *Black Majority*, pp. 40-43, 55.
65. McCrady, "Slavery in the Province of South Carolina," 641.
66. Rivers, *A Sketch of the History of South Carolina to the Close of the Proprietary Government, 1719*, p. 15.
67. McCrady, *The History of South Carolina under the Royal Government, 1719-1776*, p. 399; M. Eugene Sirmans, "The Legal Status of the Slave in South Carolina, 1670-1740," *Journal of Southern History* 28 (1962): 464.
68. Wood, *Black Majority*, p. 39.
69. McCrady, *The History of South Carolina under the Proprietary Government, 1670-1719*, p. 399.
70. Ibid., p. 189; Rivers, *A Sketch of the History of South Carolina to the Close of the Proprietary Government, 1719*, p. 353.
71. McCrady, *The History of South Carolina under the Proprietary Government, 1670-1719*, p. 189.
72. Ibid.; Rivers, *A Sketch of the History of South Carolina to the Close of the Proprietary Government, 1719*, p. 132. An example of the use of Indian slaves as a direct reward to colonial soldiers can be found in A. S. Salley, ed., *Journals of the Commons House of Assembly of South Carolina for*

1702 (Columbia, S.C., 1932), p. 84. A committee reporting on the best means to conduct an expedition to St. Augustine stipulated: "The Encouragement [to the soldiers] to be free Plunder and share of all slaves, . . ."

73. Wallace, *South Carolina*, p. 35.

74. Wood, *Black Majority*, p. 39.

75. *Statutes at Large of South Carolina*, vol. 2, p. 324.

76. Ibid.

77. Ibid., p. 325. Not all Indian slaves were acquired as prisoners of war. An account of a complaint against John Musgrove for, among other allegations, enslaving and selling free Indians can be found in A. S. Salley, ed., *Journal of the Commons House of Assembly of South Carolina, November 20, 1706-February 8, 1706/7*, pp. 21-23.

78. Sirmans, "The Legal Status of the Slave in South Carolina, 1670-1740," p. 464, n. 9.

79. Wood, *Black Majority*, p. 39.

80. Ibid.

81. For a discussion of the head-right system, see *infra*, p. 165.

82. Wood, *Black Majority*, p. 40.

83. Alexander S. Salley, ed., *Narratives of Early Carolina, 1650-1708* (New York: Charles Scribner's Sons, 1911), p. 174. Emphasis added.

84. *Statutes at Large of South Carolina*, vol. 1, p. 55. Another provision of the Fundamental Constitution stated: "Since charity obliges us to wish well to the souls of all men, and religion ought to alter nothing in any man's civil estate or right, it shall be lawful for slaves as well as others, to enter themselves and be of what church or profession any of them shall think best, and thereof be as fully members as any freeman. But yet no slave shall hereby be exempted from that civil dominion his master hath over him, but be in all things in the same state and condition he was in before." *Id*.

85. McCrady, "Slavery in the Province of South Carolina," 643.

86. While the Fundamental Constitution of 1669 was accepted by the Proprietors, this document, drawn up by John Locke and the first Earl of Shaftesbury, never became legally operative in South Carolina because it was not accepted by the freemen as required by the charter. McCrady, *The History of South Carolina under the Proprietary Government, 1670-1719*, p. 110.

87. Wood, *Black Majority*, pp. 25, 131.

88. Ibid., p. 45.

89. Ibid., p. 26, n. 36.

90. Wood, *Black Majority*, p. 46.

91. Ibid. Those early governors owning slaves included William Sayle, Sir John Yeamans, Joseph Morton, James Colleton, Seth Sothell, and Sir Nathaniel Johnson. Ibid., pp. 46-47.

92. Ibid., p. 48.

93. Ibid., pp. 19-20; Craven, *The Southern Colonies in the Seventeenth Century, 1607-1689*, p. 338.

94. Rivers, *A Sketch of the History of South Carolina to the Close of the Proprietary Government*, p. 347.

95. Smith, *White Servitude*, p. 11.

96. Wallace, *South Carolina*, p. 147. See also McCrady, *The History of South Carolina under the Royal Government, 1719-1776*, pp. 183-84, in regard to

the colonists' tendency to purchase more slaves on credit than they could pay for and the fear of the rising Negro population.

97. See Wood, *Black Majority*, pp. 54-55.

98. Smith, *White Servitude*, pp. 21-22.

99. Jordan, *White Over Black*, p. 233.

100. Ibid.

101. McCrady, *The History of South Carolina under the Proprietary Government, 1670-1719*, p. 688.

102. Wood, *Black Majority*, p. 36.

103. Ibid., pp. 56-62.

104. Ibid., pp. 79-91.

105. McCrady, *The History of South Carolina under the Proprietary Government, 1670-1719*, p. 350. As to the profound Barbadian influence upon the colony, Winthrop D. Jordan states: "By the end of the seventeenth century the development of rice plantations and the Barbadian example had combined to yield in South Carolina the most rigorous deprivation of freedom to exist in institutionalized form anywhere in the English continental colonies." Jordan, *White Over Black*, p. 85.

106. As to the 1690 slave code whih was not ultimately adopted see *infra*, p. 169.

107. *Statutes at Large of South Carolina*, vol. 7, p. 352.

108. Ibid., p. 371.

109. Ibid., p. 385.

110. Ibid., p. 352.

111. Ibid.

112. See McCrady, "Slavery in the Province of South Carolina," 646.

113. *Statutes at Large of South Carolina*, vol. 7, p. 397. Emphasis added.

114. *Statutes at Large of South Carolina*, vol. 7, pp. 343-47.

115. Sirmans, "The Legal Status of the Slave in South Carolina, 1670-1740," 465.

116. Ibid.; H. M. Henry, *The Police Control of the Slave in South Carolina* (diss., Vanderbilt University) (Emory, 1914), p. 6; see also McCrady, "Slavery in the Province of South Carolina, 1670-1770," 645. In 1696, the abortive 1690 statute was validly reenacted with some additional provisions extracted from other Barbadian legislation. Sirmans, "The Legal Status of the Slave in South Carolina," 466. The official reporters did not include this statute as emanating in 1696, but instead make reference to the 1712 statute, which actually was a reenactment of the 1696 statute. Ibid, n. 13. For convenience and clarity, the codes will be referred to as reported in *Statutes at Large of South Carolina*, which omits the original 1696 act and lists its provisions as the 1712 act.

117. *Statutes at Large of South Carolina*, vol. 7, p. 352.

118. This provision was retained in the 1722 and 1735 acts. *Statutes at Large of South Carolina*, vol. 7, pp. 371, 385.

119. Ibid., pp. 343-44.

120. Sirmans, "The Legal Status of the Slave in South Carolina," 465.

121. Ibid., p. 464.

122. Ibid., p. 468; McCrady, "Slavery in the Province of South Carolina," 645.

123. See *infra*, p. 194.

124. See *infra*, pp. 187-190.

125. *Statutes at Large of South Carolina*, vol. 7, p. 352. White servants were not subjected to a pass system until 1744, see *infra*, p. 157.

126. Ibid.
127. Ibid.
128. Ibid., p. 353.
129. Ibid., p. 343.
130. Ibid.
131. Ibid.
132. Ibid., p. 346.
133. Ibid., p. 371.
134. Ibid., p. 386.
135. Ibid., p. 354.
136. Ibid.
137. Act of 1722, *Statutes at Large of South Carolina*, vol. 7, p. 373; Act of 1735, *Statutes at Large of South Carolina*, vol. 7, p. 387.
138. For earlier acts relating to servants and slaves trading, see *infra*, p. 157; *Statutes at Large of South Carolina*, vol. 2, pp. 22, 598.
139. *Statutes at Large of South Carolina*, vol. 7, p. 353.
140. Ibid.
141. Ibid., p. 367. Emphasis added.
142. Ibid.
143. See *infra*, pp. 182-183.
144. *Statutes at Large of South Carolina*, vol. 7, p. 353.
145. Ibid., pp. 382-83.
146. Ibid., p. 394.
147. Ibid., p. 396.
148. Ibid.
149. Wood notes how these laws furthered the process of economic and social subjugation by eliminating the incentives for earning or otherwise obtaining money to purchase good clothes. Wood, *Black Majority*, p. 232.
150. *Statutes at Large of South Carolina*, vol. 7, p. 363.
151. Ibid.
152. Ibid.
153. Ibid., p. 380.
154. Ibid., p. 393.
155. Ibid., p. 350.
156. Ibid., p. 384.
157. Ibid., p. 396.
158. Ibid.
159. Ibid., pp. 352-53.
160. Persons capturing runaways were to return them to the owner, if known, or to a marshal, receiving ten shillings and one ryal per mile for the first eight miles and sixpence per additional mile not exceeding forty shillings. The captor was given a reasonable time for the distance traveled and ten additional days to return the slave or he would forfeit twenty shillings per slave for each day exceeding the allowed period. The individual delivering the runaway had to, under oath, give an account of his name, residence, and facts concerning the apprehension of the slave including that he did not know the slave's owner or know of any ticket possessed by the slave.
161. *Statutes at Large of South Carolina*, vol. 7, p. 361.
162. Ibid., p. 362.

163. Ibid.
164. Ibid., p. 361.
165. Ibid., p. 345.
166. Ibid., p. 357.
167. Ibid., p. 648.
168. Ibid., pp. 359-60.
169. Ibid., p. 360.
170. See *infra*, "The English Experience," pp. 336-338 and the arguments of Hargrave, counsel for the slave, in Sommersett v. Stuart, 20 How. St. Tr. 23, 47-49, 65.
171. *Statutes at Large of South Carolina*, vol. 7, p. 360.
172. Henry notes that this provision of the 1712 act was "the most striking stupidity perhaps to be found in slave legislation," because of the unlikelihood that an owner would actually inflict the directed punishment and make his slave less useful to him or less valuable on resale. Henry, *The Police Control of the Slave in South Carolina*, p. 119.
173. *Statutes at Large of South Carolina*, vol. 7, p. 376.
174. Ibid.
175. Act of 1722, *Statutes at Large of South Carolina*, vol. 7, p. 380; Act of 1735, *Statutes at Large of South Carolina*, vol. 7, p. 392.
176. Wood, *Black Majority*, p. 268.
177. *Statutes at Large of South Carolina*, vol. 7, pp. 354-55; see also Act of 1690, *Statutes at Large of South Carolina*, vol. 7, pp. 345-46.
178. *Statutes at Large of South Carolina*, vol. 7, p. 355.
179. Ibid.
180. Ibid.
181. Ibid., vol. 6, pp. 457, 489; Henry, *The Police Control of the Slave in South Carolina*, p. 64.
182. John Belton O'Neall, *The Negro Law of South Carolina* (Columbia, S.C.: John G. Bowman, 1848), p. 35. John Belton O'Neall was born on Bush River, Newberry District, South Carolina on April 10, 1793. After serving in the militia, he began an active political career until he was elected by the legislature to serve as a circuit judge in 1828. O'Neall served in the South Carolina circuit court, the court of law appeals, and the court of errors. In 1859 he became the chief justice of South Carolina. Not limited to judicial matters, O'Neall was also active in several organizations and was an author of many essays and longer works, including *The Negro Law of South Carolina*. Dumas Malone, ed., *Dictionary of American Biography* (New York: Charles Scribner's Sons, 1934), vol. 14, pp. 42-43.
183. *South Carolina Gazette*, January 27, 1733, cited in Henry, *The Police Control of the Slave in South Carolina*, p. 58.
184. Henry, *The Police Control of the Slave in South Carolina*, p. 58.
185. *Statutes at Large of South Carolina*, vol. 7, p. 356.
186. Ibid., pp. 356-57.
187. Ibid., p. 357.
188. Ibid., pp. 375-76.
189. Ibid., p. 389. The trend in broadening the use of slave testimony and the discretion of the court in cases where slaves were defendants should be compared to the incapacities of slaves in other areas, *infra*, pp. 170-175.

190. Ibid., p. 354.
191. Ibid.
192. Ibid., p. 355.
193. Ibid., p. 356.
194. Ibid.
195. Ibid., p. 354.
196. Ibid., pp. 373-74.
197. Ibid., p. 374.
198. Ibid., p. 355.
199. Ibid. Emphasis added.
200. Ibid.
201. Ibid., p. 374.
202. Ibid., p. 375.
203. Ibid., p. 388.
204. Ibid.
205. Ibid., p. 355; *infra*, p. 182.
206. *Statutes at Large of South Carolina*, vol. 7, p. 374.
207. Ibid., p. 353.
208. Wood, *Black Majority*, pp. 211-17.
209. *Statutes at Large of South Carolina*, vol. 7, p. 353.
210. Ibid., *infra*, p. 173.
211. *Statutes at Large of South Carolina*, vol. 7, p. 372.
212. Ibid.
213. Ibid. Emphasis added.
214. Ibid.
215. Ibid.
216. Ibid., p. 356.
217. Ibid.
218. Ibid., p. 358.
219. Ibid., p. 366.
220. Ibid.
221. Ibid.
222. Ibid., p. 370.
223. Ibid.
224. Ibid., p. 383.
225. Ibid.
226. Ibid., p. 384.
227. Ibid., p. 395.
228. Ibid., pp. 358-59.
229. Ibid., p. 359. Emphasis added.
230. Ibid., p. 366.
231. Ibid., p. 367.
232. Ibid., p. 366.
233. Ibid., p. 377.
234. Act of 1735, *Statutes at Large of South Carolina*, vol. 7, p. 390.
235. Ibid., p. 357.
236. Ibid.
237. Ibid., p. 376.
238. Ibid., pp. 389-90.

239. Ibid., p. 390.

240. McCrady, *The History of South Carolina under the Proprietary Government, 1670-1719*, p. 357.

241. Ibid., p. 359.

242. *Statutes at Large of South Carolina*, vol. 7, p. 346.

243. Ibid., p. 363.

244. Ibid.

245. Ibid., p. 381.

246. Ibid., pp. 393-94.

247. The 1690 act attempted to make some provisions for the slave by stating, "all slaves shall have convenient clothes, once every year"; but, there was no fine or other penalty placed upon the owner who did not provide the minimum clothing stipulated. *Statutes at Large of South Carolina*, vol. 7, p. 343.

248. Ibid., p. 378.

249. Ibid.

250. Ibid., p. 391.

251. Ibid., vol. 2, p. 201.

252. Ibid., p. 280.

253. Ibid., p. 649.

254. Ibid., p. 651.

255. One of the more detailed records of the sums obtained from the tax on black slaves can be found in the colonial records for the period November 10, 1736 to June 7, 1739. Sums received from the tax on imported slaves constituted a substantial portion of those duties collected by the colony for the years 1733, 1734, 1736, and 1737. J. H. Easterby, ed., *The Colonial Records of South Carolina: The Journal of the Commons House of Assembly, November 10, 1736-June 7, 1739* (Columbia: Historical Commission of South Carolina, 1951), pp. 405, 524.

256. See, e.g., Act of 1719, *Statutes at Large of South Carolina*, vol. 3, pp. 57, 59; Act of 1722, *Statutes at Large of South Carolina*, vol. 3, p. 195; Act of 1740, *Statutes at Large of South Carolina*, vol. 3, p. 556 (duty placed on imported slaves based upon height); Act of 1751, *Statutes at Large of South Carolina*, vol. 3, p. 739; Act of 1764, *Statutes at Large of South Carolina*, vol. 4, p. 187; see also *infra*, p. 159.

257. Act of 1714, *Statutes at Large of South Carolina*, vol. 7, p. 367.

258. McCrady, *The History of South Carolina under the Proprietary Government, 1670-1719*, p. 9. Also, there were antislavery sentiments from the nonslaveholders of South Carolina who felt that the legislation and policies of South Carolina favored the slaveholding class. One example of a complaint by small farmers in the "back country" reads: "It is the number of *free men*, not *black* slaves, that constitute the strength and riches of a state." Wallace, *South Carolina*, p. 224. While this view was held by some South Carolinians, it did not dominate the legislation and general policy.

259. *Statutes at Large of South Carolina*, vol. 3, pp. 409, 556.

260. See, e.g., Act of 1712, *Statutes at Large of South Carolina*, vol. 7, p. 364; Act of 1735, *Statutes at Large of South Carolina*, vol. 7, p. 395.

261. Wood, *Black Majority*, p. 227; McCrady, *The History of South Carolina under the Royal Government, 1719-1776*, p. 378.

262. McCrady, "Slavery in the Province of South Carolina, 1670-1770," 654; Wallace, *South Carolina,* p. 709.

263. *South Carolina Historical and Genealogical Magazine,* December 3, 1737, p. 90, as cited in Wood, *Black Majority,* p. 132.

264. Jordan, *White Over Black,* p. 120.

265. Wood, *Black Majority,* pp. 308-9.

266. Ibid., p. 308.

267. Wood, *Black Majority,* p. 309.

268. *Statutes at Large of South Carolina,* vol. 7, p. 416.

269. Ibid.

270. Ibid., pp. 416-17.

271. Sirmans, "The Legal Status of the Slave in South Carolina, 1670-1740," 471; *infra,* pp. 167-169.

272. *Statutes at Large of South Carolina,* vol. 7, p. 397. Emphasis added.

273. Ibid.

274. Ibid.

275. A contrary interpretation has been offered by David D. Wallace and Edward McCrady, who refer to the 1740 code as on the whole benefiting the slave. Wallace, *South Carolina,* p. 186; McCrady, "Slavery in the Province of South Carolina, 1670-1770," 657. In his usual perceptiveness, Wood puts the matter into focus by asserting that the 1740 code "did more than any other single piece of legislation in the colony's history to curtail certain *de facto* personal liberties, which slaves had been able to cling to against formidable odds during the first three generations of settlement." Wood, *Black Majority,* p. 324.

276. *Statutes at Large of South Carolina,* vol. 7, p. 397.

277. For a discussion of this doctrine, see *infra,* p. 44.

278. *Infra,* p. 169.

279. *Statutes at Large of South Carolina,* vol. 7, p. 398.

280. Ibid., p. 399.

281. Ibid.

282. Ibid.

283. Ibid., p. 386.

284. Ibid., p. 390.

285. Ibid., p. 411.

286. Ibid., pp. 411-12.

287. Ibid., p. 411.

288. Ibid.

289. Ibid., p. 401.

290. Ibid., p. 404.

291. Ibid., p. 415. A comparable Georgia statute granted the largest reward to scalps of grown *male* slaves with two ears; no reward was given for scalps of female slaves. See *infra,* p. 254 (Georgia chapter).

292. Ibid., p. 413.

293. Ibid., p. 423.

294. Ibid.

295. Ibid.

296. Ibid.

297. Ibid.

298. Henry, *The Police Control of the Slave in South Carolina*, p. 7; Sirmans, "The Legal Status of the Slave in South Carolina, 1670-1740," 470.

299. Frank J. Klingberg, *An Appraisal of the Negro in Colonial South Carolina* (Washington, D.C.: Associated Publishers, 1941), p. 4.

300. Ibid., p. 123.

301. *Statutes at Large of South Carolina*, vol. 2, p. 239.

302. Ibid., vol. 7, p. 343.

303. Ibid., p. 365.

304. McCrady, "Slavery in the Province of South Carolina, 1670-1770," 664.

305. Ibid.; Klingberg, *An Appraisal of the Negro in Colonial South Carolina*, p. 121.

306. Richard Ludlam to David Humphreys, St. James, Goose Creek, South Carolina, March 22, 1725, in SPG MSS. (L.C. Trans.) A19, pp. 62-63, from Klingberg, *An Appraisal of the Negro in Colonial South Carolina*, p. 47.

307. Wood, *Black Majority*, p. 187.

308. Klingberg, *An Appraisal of the Negro in Colonial South Carolina*, p. 70.

309. Henry, *The Police Control of the Slave in South Carolina*, p. 167.

310. McCrady, "Slavery in the Province of South Carolina, 1670-1770," 664.

311. C. W. Birnie, "Education of the Negro in Charleston," *Journal of Negro History* 22 (1927): 13-14.

312. McCrady, *The History of South Carolina under the Royal Government, 1719-1776*, p. 243; Wood, *Black Majority*, p. 141.

313. Wood, *Black Majority*, p. 142.

314. Ibid.

315. Wallace, *South Carolina*, p. 60.

316. W. A. Schaper, "Sectionalism in South Carolina," American Historical Association *Report* 1 (1900): 393.

317. Wood, *Black Majority*, p. 103.

318. Technically, a "chapel of ease" is a chapel erected for the accommodation of an expanding parish; however, it is possible that this structural addition was built to "accommodate" the black members of the parish.

319. Klingberg, *An Appraisal of the Negro in Colonial South Carolina*, p. 31.

320. Wood, *Black Majority*, p. 103.

321. Klingberg, *An Appraisal of the Negro in Colonial South Carolina*, p. 60.

322. As to the ownership of slaves by free blacks, see *infra*, p. 204.

323. Wood, *Black Majority*, pp. 157, 159.

324. For further discussion of these statistics, see Wood, *Black Majority*, pp. 156-66.

325. Ibid., p. 103.

326. Marina Wikramanayake, *A World in Shadow: The Free Black in Antebellum South Carolina* (Columbia: University of South Carolina Press, 1973), p. 21; William L. Katz, ed., *Negro Population in the United States, 1790-1915* (New York: Arno Press, 1968), p. 45.

327. Wikramanayake, *World in Shadow*, pp. 73, 109.

328. Ibid., p. 9; see also Wood, *Black Majority*, p. 24.

329. A. S. Salley, ed., *Journal of the Commons House of Assembly of South Carolina for 1702* (Columbia: Historical Commission of South Carolina, 1932), p. 56.

330. Ibid., p. 57.

331. McCrady, *The History of South Carolina under the Proprietary Government, 1670-1719*, p. 374.

332. Ibid., p. 431.

333. Ibid., p. 462.

334. *Statutes at Large of South Carolina*, vol. 3, p. 136.

335. Easterby, *The Colonial Records of South Carolina*, p. 362. Emphasis added.

336. John H. Russell, "Colored Freemen as Slave Owners in Virginia," *Journal of Negro History* vol. 1 (1916): 239.

337. Ibid.

338. Wikramanayake, *A World in Shadow*, p. 33 (quoting Anne King Gregorie, *History of Sumter County*, p. 131).

339. Ibid., p. 109.

340. Ibid., p. 66.

341. *Statutes at Large of South Carolina*, vol. 5, p. 209.

342. Ibid., vol. 7, p. 402.

343. Ibid.

344. See *infra*, pp. 190-192.

345. *Statutes at Large of South Carolina*, vol. 7, p. 422.

346. Anne King Gregorie, *Records of the Court of Chancery of South Carolina, 1671-1779* (Washington, D.C.: American Historical Association, 1950), p. 526. (Hereinafter, *Records of the Court of Chancery.*)

347. Ibid.

348. 2 Bailey 192 (S.C. Ct. of App., 1831).

349. Id.

350. *Compare* Chartram v. Schmidt, Rice 229 (S.C. Ct. of App., 1839) where a free black woman was permitted to use the *affidavit* of a third person since she could not testify in support of her suit for her slaves. The court stated: "It would be gross injustice to allow a free person of color to bring an action and withhold the means of making it effectual." Id. at 231.

351. 1 Bay 260 (S.C. Super. Ct., 1792).

352. Id. at 262-63.

353. Id.

354. 1 Des. 542 (S.C. Ch. Ct., 1797).

355. The will declared that freedom was to be granted to the slave woman and her children ten years after the testator's death; however, the slave woman died before the ten-year period expired.

356. Snow v. Callum, 1 Des. 541, 543 (1797).

357. *Statutes at Large of South Carolina*, vol. 7, pp. 442-43.

358. Ibid., p. 436.

359. Ibid., p. 438. Black informants were specifically made competent to testify.

360. See *infra*, pp. 167-169, on legislative action.

361. *Statutes at Large of South Carolina*, vol. 1, p. 51.

362. McCrady, *The History of South Carolina under the Royal Government, 1719-1776*, p. 459 (there is some dispute on whether Trott was first; McCrady notes this point).

363. Ibid., p. 460.

364. Cited by McCrady, *The History of South Carolina under the Royal Government, 1719-1776*, p. 466.

365. For example, during the early years, the court system was administered by

the grand council. Basically, the grand council consisted of the governor, deputies of the Proprietors, members of the colony's nobility, and others selected by the Parliament. McCrady, *The History of South Carolina under the Proprietary Government, 1670-1719*, p. 141. From 1698 to 1719 the appellate court in civil and criminal cases and the chancery courts were composed of the governor and council. Ibid., pp. 692-93. This basic framework continued throughout the colonial era. McCrady, *The History of South Carolina under the Royal Government, 1719-1776*, p. 43; *Records of the Court of Chancery*, p. 3.

366. Desaussure, I., *Reports of Cases Argued and Determined in the Court of Chancery of the State of South Carolina, from the Revolution to December, 1813: Inclusive* 53 (as cited in *Records of the Court of Chancery*, p. 30).

367. No records are available from the Court of Common Pleas before 1733 and records after that period until 1791 are primarily judgment books, providing only the disposition of the case. Sirmans, "The Legal Status of the Slave in South Carolina, 1670-1740," 464-66. Those court records which are available and indicative of the treatment of slaves are the chancery records and the grand council journals.

368. While there are limitations in abstracting, from a few cases, general propositions as to the conditions of slaves during the colonial period, the cases reinforce the statutes and the findings in other secondary material.

369. *Records of the Court of Chancery*, p. 178.

370. Ibid.

371. Ibid., p. 237.

372. Ibid.

373. Ibid., p. 120.

374. Ibid., p. 123.

375. Ibid., p. 178.

376. Ibid., pp. 180-81.

377. For example, in the colonial records there are differences in the amounts allowed to compensate for or provide food, clothing, or other provisions to blacks and whites. In an account of a surveyor who used a white assistant, four slaves, and a pack horse in surveying the boundaries of several parishes, he allowed four pounds per day for his provisions, twenty shillings per day for his white assistant, and ten shillings per day for the slaves and pack horse. Easterby, *The Colonial Records of South Carolina: The Journal of the Commons House of Assembly, September 12, 1739-March 26, 1741*, p. 282. This form of discrimination was also practiced by the legislature. After examining the account of a marshal who kept several criminals, a committee concluded that five shillings was sufficient to maintain a white man for one day and that three shillings and nine pence was "rather more than a full compensation" for maintaining a slave for a day. Ibid., p. 284. For further discussion, see Wood, *Black Majority*, pp. 232-33.

378. See *infra*, pp. 165-166.

379. *Records of the Court of Chancery*, p. 465.

380. Ibid., p. 468.

381. Ibid., p. 480.

382. Ibid.

383. Although the chancery court cases are reviewed here, the colonial probate

records and records of slave sales also support the conclusion that slaves were treated as chattel property before 1740. Sirmans, after reviewing the various records, concluded: "The available evidence, then, indicates that under the vague definition of slavery in the code of 1696 South Carolinians began treating their slaves as personal chattels nearly half a century before the code of 1740 formally inaugurated chattel slavery." Sirmans, "The Legal Status of the Slave in South Carolina, 1670-1740," 468; see McCrady, *The History of South Carolina under the Proprietary Government, 1670-1719*, p. 390.

384. *Records of the Court of Chancery,* p. 82.
385. Ibid.
386. See also Christopher Arthur, by Christian Arthur, his Prockien Amie and Guardian v. John Gough (1714), *Records of the Court of Chancery*, p. 106.
387. *Records of the Court of Chancery,* p. 384.
388. Ibid., p. 385.
389. See also George Bassett v. Christopher Wilkinson (1721/2), *Records of the Court of Chancery,* p. 278; Order on the Petition of John Baker's Executors (1736), *Records of the Court of Chancery,* p. 383.
390. *Statutes at Large of South Carolina,* vol. 7, p. 352; *infra,* pp. 169-170.
391. Ibid., p. 397.
392. Rivers, *A Sketch of the History of South Carolina to the Close of the Proprietary Government, 1719,* p. 372.
393. Ibid., p. 379.
394. *Records of the Court of Chancery,* p. 64.
395. Rivers, *A Sketch of the History of South Carolina to the Close of the Proprietary Government, 1719,* p. 376.
396. Ibid.
397. Ibid., p. 381.

GEORGIA

1. Albert Saye, *New Viewpoints in Georgia History* (*NVIGH*) (Athens, Ga.: University of Georgia Press, 1943), p. 51.
2. Allen D. Candler, ed., *Colonial Records of Georgia* (*CROG*), (Atlanta, Ga.: Franklin Printing and Publishing Co., 1904), vol. 1, pp. 49-52.
3. Letter from James Oglethorpe to Granville Sharp, October 13, 1776 in *The African Repository* (Washington, D.C., 1826), vol. II, pp. 104-5, as cited by Ruth Scarborough, *Opposition to Slavery in Georgia* (Nashville, Tenn.: George Peabody College for Teachers, 1933), p. 62.
4. Ibid.
5. The development of support for and opposition to slavery in colonial Pennsylvania is discussed *supra,* pp. 267, 284, 292-299.
6. "Letter from the President, Assistants, and Councilmen to Benjamin Martin, Esquire," Secretary to the Board of Trustees, January 10, 1748/9, *CROG,* vol. 25, p. 349.

They went on to say: "We have reason to believe that Negroes under such protection will not quit their Master's Service to fly into abject Slavery. We also think that no Man of an inhuman Disposition will think of making

Georgia the place of his Abode where such exemplary Laws are made."
Ibid., p. 350.

This letter was in response to an earlier trustee letter of August 26, 1748, evidently soliciting the opinions of Georgia officials on the proper restrictions to be placed on the admission of slaves. See ibid., p. 347.

The trustees responded to the January 10, 1749 proposals in a July 7, 1749 letter, reproduced in part by Charles C. Jones, *History of Georgia.* (Boston: Houghton, Mifflin and Company, 1883), vol. 1, pp. 422-25. The president and his assistants gave further proposals on the admission of slaves in an October 26, 1749 letter, which includes most of the provisions of the later 1750 slavery law. *CROG,* vol. 25, pp. 430-37.

7. See Higginbotham, *Slavery and the Constitution,* unpublished monograph, see also D. D. Wax, "Georgia and the Negro before the American Revolution," 51 *Georgia Historical Quarterly (GHQ)* 63, 55 (1967).

8. *Acts of Privy Council,* vol. III, p. 305.

9. Many of the charter powers of the Trustees were to be exercised by a Common Council, which was a fifteen- (later increased to twenty-four-) member subsidiary body of the full Board of Trustees. The Common Council was supposed to oversee the day-to-day operation of the colonial government. It had the power "to dispose of, expend, and apply all the moneys and effects" of the Trustees as it thought best to promote "the good purposes herein mentioned and determined," and to enter into covenants or contracts for effectuating those same goals. It could appoint "all . . . governors, judges, magistrates, ministers, and officers, as well as appoint and fix the salaries of "treasurers, . . . secretaries, and all such other officers, ministers, and servants as often as they think fit to do so." It also could make grants of land to Georgia settlers. Later the 1735 antislavery law gave the Common Council authority over the disposition of captured slaves. *CROG,* vol. 1, pp. 14-15, 19-22, 24. See *infra,* note 46.

Despite the importance of the authority granted to the Common Council of Trustees, it is probable that the full Board of Trustees assumed many of their powers, especially toward the latter part of the trustee period. Since the charter required a quorum of eight trustees for official council meetings, dwindling attendance by its members reduced the importance of the body. Ibid., pp. 23-24. See generally, Saye, *NVIGH,* pp. 56-57, 82. Many meetings supposedly called for the Common Council became meetings of the full Board of Trustees simply because the council quorum of eight was not met. See Kenneth Coleman, *Colonial Georgia: A History* (New York: Charles Scribner's Sons, 1976), p. 89.

10. *CROG,* vol. 1, p. 24. Technically, this power was possessed by the Common Council of the Trustees.

11. Ibid., p. 19. The Board of Trustees could "form and prepare laws, statutes and ordinances, fit and necessary for and concerning the government of the said colony, and not repugnant to the laws and statutes of England, and the same shall and may present, under their common seal, to us, our heirs and successors, in our or their privy council, for our or their approbation or disallowance. . . ."

12. The Board of Trustees could "erect and constitute judicatories and courts of record, or other courts, to be held in the name of us, our heirs and suc-

cessors, for the hearing and determining of all manner of crimes, offences, pleas, processes, plaints, actions, matters, causes, and things whatsoever, arising or happening within the said province of Georgia or between persons of Georgia. . . ." Ibid., p. 22.

13. In addition, the charter gave the trustees authority to "constitute, ordain and make such and so many by-laws, constitutions, orders and ordinances, as to them . . . shall seem necessary and convenient for the well ordering and governing of the said corporation" (ibid., p. 17); "to set impose and inflict reasonable pains and penalties upon any offender or offenders who shall transgress, break or violate the said by-laws, constitutions, orders and ordinances" (id.); "to train, instruct, exercise and govern a militia for the special defence and safety of our said colony, to assemble in martial array the inhabitants of the said colony, and to lead and conduct them, and with them to encounter, expulse, repel, resist and pursue, by force of arms, as well by sea as by land, within or without the limits of our said colony . . ." (ibid., p. 24); and "to import and export their goods at and from any port or ports that shall be appointed by us, our heirs and successors, within the said province of Georgia for that purpose, without being obliged to touch at any other port in South Carolina" (ibid., p. 25). They also could increase the number of persons on the Board of Trustees, and select the new members of the Board and the Common Council. Ibid., pp. 13-14.

To aid the financing of the Georgia settlement, the Trustees were granted authority

to purchase have, take, receive and enjoy, to them and their successors, any manors, messuages, lands, tenements, rents, advowsons, liberties, privileges, jurisdictions, franchises, and other hereditaments whatsoever, lying and being in Great Britain, or any part thereof, of whatsoever nature, kind or quality, or value they be, life and in perpetuity: not exceeding the yearly value of one thousand pounds, beyond reprises; also estates for lives and for years; and all other manner of goods, chattels and things whatsoever they be; for the better settling and supporting and maintaining the said colony, and other uses aforesaid; and to give, grant, let and demise the said manors, messuages, lands, tenements, hereditaments, goods, chattels and things whatsoever aforesaid, by lease or leases, for term of years, in possession at the time of granting thereof, and not in reversion, not exceeding the term of thirty-one years from the time of granting thereof: on which in case no fine be taken, shall be reserved the full; and in case a fine be taken, shall be reserved at least a moiety of the value that the same shall reasonably and bona fide be worth at the time of such demise; and that they and their successors, by the name aforesaid, shall and may forever hereafter be persons able, capable in the law, to purchase, have, take, receive and enjoy, to them and their successors, any lands, territories, possessions, tenements, jurisdictions, franchises and hereditaments whatsoever, lying and being in America, of what quantity, quality or value whatsoever they be, for the better settling and supporting, and maintaining the said colony; and that by the name aforesaid they shall and may be able to sue and be sued, plead and be impleaded, answer and be answered unto, defend and be defended in all courts and places whatsoever, and before whatsoever judges, justices and other officers, of us, our heirs, and successors, in all and singular actions, plaints, pleas, matters, suits and demands, of what kind, nature or quality soever they be; and to act and do all other matters and things in as ample manner and form as any other our liege subjects of this realm of Great Britain; and that they and their successors forever hereafter, shall and may have a common seal to serve, for the causes and businesses of them and their successors; and that it shall and may be lawful for them and their successors, to change, break, alter and make new the said seal, from time to time, and at their pleasure, as they shall think best. Ibid., pp. 12-13.

14. There were several charter provisions theoretically ensuring royal oversight of the trustees' decisions. The most important was the limitation of the trustees' authority to twenty-one years. Ibid., pp. 18-19. In addition, all laws passed by the trustees needed to be consistent with the laws of England and approved by the King in Council. Ibid., p. 19. Any governor nominated by the Common Council of the Trustees had to be approved by the king and had to give "good and sufficient security for observing the several acts of Parliament relating to trade and navigation, and to observe and obey all instructions that shall be sent to him [by the King] pursuant to the said acts. . . ." Ibid., p. 24.

Although these restrictions were intended to hold the trustees accountable to the crown, in practice the trustees enjoyed wider discretion than the wording of the charter would suggest. Officially, they passed only three laws (one of which was the antislavery law) during the entire period of their rule, through a system of "ordinances," which did not require royal approval. Each year, hundreds of these directives were sent to particular Georgia officials regarding their activities in the colony. The trustees also avoided undergoing royal scrutiny of their gubernatorial appointments for Georgia by naming instead presidents for the colony, who served in a similar, though less powerful, capacity.

One mechanism of indirect oversight the trustees could not circumvent was the review incident to the annual parliamentary appropriations to the trustees. Since the establishment of Georgia was supposed to provide various military and economic benefits to England and the other colonies, parliament made appropriations each year to the trustees during much of the period of their authority. The threat that these appropriations would be terminated because of the antislavery law was probably a factor in the trustees' final decision to repeal the prohibition.

To facilitate oversight of the trustees' activities by the crown and parliament, the charter stipulated that the trustees should annually record all receipts and expenditures with certain royal officers (ibid., p. 17) and file "from time to time" with "one of the principal secretaries of state and to the commissioners of trade and plantations, accounts of the progress of the said colony," Ibid., p. 23. To provide oversight of the collections of taxes owed to the crown, the trustees were obliged to register all "leases, grants, plantings, conveyances, settlements, and improvements . . . made by and in the name of the said corporations, of any lands, tenements or hereditaments within the said province" and forward a copy to the royal auditor and the South Carolina royal surveyor. Ibid., pp. 22-23.

15. Saye, *NVIGH*, pp. 56-57.
16. *CROG*, vol. 1, pp. 16, 22. The Secretary and Treasurer of the Board of Trustees, who did receive salaries, could not be trustees while serving in that capacity. Ibid., p. 20. The presidency of the board and the chairmanship of the common council were rotated, so no one trustee was forced to sacrifice too much of his unpaid time for the colony. Ibid., p. 15.
17. Saye, *NVIGH*, p. 55, quoting in part, Herbert L. Osgood, *The American Colonies in the Eighteenth Century* (New York: Columbia University Press, 1924), vol. III, pp. 36-37.
18. The disorganization of the trustee administration is discussed by Randall M. Miller, "The Failure of the Colony of Georgia Under the Trustees", 53 *GHQ* 1-17 (1969); Coleman, *Colonial Georgia*, pp. 89-110; Saye, *NVIGH*, pp. 83-84; Daniel Boorstin, *The Americans: The Colonial Experience* (New York: Random House, 1958), p. 77.
19. Coleman, *Colonial Georgia*, p. 109.
20. *CROG*, vol. 1, p. 11.
21. Saye, *NVIGH*, pp. 10-26.
22. Ibid., preface and pp. 31-42.
23. Coleman, *Colonial Georgia*, p. 22.
24. *CROG*, vol. 1, p. 11.
25. Id.
26. For a more detailed discussion of the motives behind the establishment of Georgia, see Saye, *NVIGH*, pp. 3-50; Saye, "The Genesis of Georgia Reviewed," 50 *GHQ* 153-161 (1966); Ralph Betts Flanders, *Plantation Slavery in Georgia* (Cob Cob, Conn.: John E. Edward, 1967), pp. 3-5; Boorstin, *The Americans*, pp. 76-84; Scarborough, *Opposition to Slavery*, pp. 2-7.
27. Letter from Benjamin Martyn to Governor Johnson, London, 18 October 1732. *CROG*, vol. 29, pp. 1-2. Martyn, Secretary for the Board of Trustees, requested that "twenty Negro labourers and Four Pair of Sawyers be hired to assist in clearing the grounds for this new settlement." Colonel William Bull and Mr. Bryan of South Carolina supplied "20 slaves whose Labour they gave as a free gift to the Colony." Oglethorpe to the Trustees, around December 1733, *Egmont Papers* 14200, pp. 51-52. See also Pat Tailfer et al., *A True and Historical Narrative of the Colony of Georgia, With Comments by The Earl of Egmont*, edited by Clarence L. Ver Steeg (Athens, Georgia: University of Georgia Press, 1960), p. 48 noting the use of slaves to help build Savannah. *A True and Historical Narrative* was written by the major proponents of the admission of slaves, and therefore is not generally a reliable source on the use of slaves. However, in this case, the Lord of Egmont, who wrote a sentence-by-sentence critique of the narrative, did not challenge their statement on the use of slaves in building Savannah. Id.
28. Paul S. Taylor, *Georgia Plan, 1732-1752* (Berkeley: Graduate School of Business Administration, University of California, 1972), pp. 130-31, citing passages from Samuel Urlsperger's *Der ausfuhrlichen Nachrichten von der Konlighlich-Gross Britannischen Colonie Salzburgischer Emigranten in America* (Halle, 1741-1752), vol. I, pp. 104, 105, 118, 120, 129, 136, 138, 140.
29. *CROG*, vol. 32, p. 63. See also ibid., pp. 70, 90, 98, 111, 121, 202, 245,

261, 281, 336, 348, as cited by Betty Wood, " 'The One Thing Needful': The Slavery Debate in Georgia, 1732-1750," Unpublished Ph.D. Dissertation, The University of Pennsylvania (1975), p. 10.

30. Oglethorpe to the Trustees, Savannah, 12 August 1733. *Egmont Papers*, 14200, pp. 37-49. See generally Wood, " 'The One Thing Needful': The Slavery Debate in Georgia, 1732-1750," pp. 58-60.

31. Coleman, *Colonial Georgia*, p. 138.

32. *CROG*, vol. 1, p. 70.

33. The military rationale was cited specifically in the preamble to the 1735 antislavery law *CROG*, Vol. 1, p. 50. All three goals were also sanctioned by the trustees themselves when their Secretary, Benjamin Martyn, wrote his officially approved document, "An Account Showing the Progress of the Colony of Georgia in American from its First Establishment" as a rebuttal to the opponents of the antislavery law. *CROG*, vol. 3, pp. 369-403; approved by the trustees, ibid., vol. 1, pp. 378-81.

For various discussions by secondary authorities confirming the importance of these motives in the passage of the antislavery law, see Scarborough, *Opposition to Slavery*, pp. 10-20; Flanders, *Plantation Slavery*, pp. 7-9, 15; Boorstin, *The Americans*, pp. 81-2; Potter, "The Rise of the Plantation System in Georgia" 16 *GHQ*, 114, 123-26 (1932); Jones, *History of Georgia*, pp. 110-12; Saye, *NVIGH*, pp. 70-72; Miller, "Failure of the Colony," pp. 6-8; Coleman, *Colonial Georgia*, pp. 111-12; H. A. Scomp, "Georgia—The Only Free Colony," *Magazine of American History* (October, 1889): 280-81.

34. "Journal of William Stevens," *CROG*, vol. 4, Supplement, p. 201, William Bacon Stevens, *History of Georgia* (New York: D. Appleton and Company, 1847), vol. 1, pp. 287-88.

35. "Journal of the Earl of Egmont," *CROG*, vol. 5, pp. 378-79.

36. *CROG*, vol. 1, pp. 50-52.

37. Ibid., p. 50.

38. "Charter of the Colony," ibid., p. 19. Another provision in the charter proclaimed that "all . . . persons which shall happen to be born within the said province, and every of their children and posterity, shall have and enjoy all liberties, franchises and immunities of free denizens and natural born subjects, within any of our dominions, to all intents and purposes, as if abiding and born within this our kingdom of Great Britain, or any other dominion." Ibid., p. 21.

39. "An Act for rendering the Colony of Georgia more Defencible by Prohibiting the Importation and use of Black Slaves or Negroes into the same," *CROG*, vol. 1, p. 50.

40. Id.

41. Ibid., p. 51.

42. Ibid., pp. 51-52.

43. Several authorities have concluded that no judicial opinions remain from pre-1776 Georgia. See Annual Address by Mr. Justice Joseph R. Lamar, "The Bench and Bar of Georgia During the Eighteenth Century," reprinted in *Report of the Thirtieth Annual Season of the Georgia Bar Association* (Macon, Ga.: The J. W. Burke Co., 1913), pp. 74, 75. Letters on file from Professors Kenneth Coleman, Harold E. Davis, Ruth Scarborough, and the Georgia Department of Archives and History.

44. Stephens was Secretary of Georgia for the Trustees from 1737 to 1750 and President of the colony from 1741 to 1751. While he did not serve as an official court reporter, Stephens did have an extensive knowledge of English law and even acted as an informal advisor to the courts. According to Kenneth Coleman, "from the very beginning, Stephens was more than a reporter to the Trustees. He soon began attending court and advising the bailiffs on English law and legal procedure, something that he knew much more about than they did. Being of a higher social and educational level than most Georgians, he was in a good position to influence the colonists." Coleman, *Colonial Georgia*, pp. 95-96.

45. Although Stephens served as Secretary of the Colony for the Trustees from 1737 to 1750, records of his Journal only have been discovered from 1737-1745. The 1737-1741 segment is included in *CROG*, vols. 4 and 4 Supplement. The 1741-1743 period is included in E. Merton Coulter, ed., *The Journal of William Stevens, 1741-1743* (Athens, Ga.: University of Georgia Press, 1958), and the 1743-45 period in E. Merton Coulter, ed., *The Journal of William Stevens 1743-1745* (Athens, Ga.: University of Georgia Press, 1959).

46. It is possible that the courts were acting at the explicit direction of the trustees, since 1735 law gave the common council of the trustees authority over the disposition of captured slaves. According to the 1735 law, "Black or Blacks Negro or Negroes so seized and taken shall be deemed and adjudged and are hereby declared to be the Sole property of and to belong only to the said Trustees and their Successors and shall and may be Exported Sold and disposed of in such manner as the said Common Council of the said Trustees or the Major part of them for that purpose present and Assembled." *CROG*, vol. 1, p. 51.

However, we can find no record of the council directing the judicial treatment of captured blacks. While the trustees did pass an ordinance appointing special constables to enforce the prohibition, but it did not specify the disposition of the captured blacks. "The Constables of Savannah Appointed to Seize Blacks or Negroes" *CROG*, vol. 32, pp. 416-18. But even if the courts were enforcing an order of the trustees, then the trustees were rejecting options which could have been more favorable to blacks.

47. *CROG*, vol. 4, pp. 523-24. See also "Journal of Earl of Egmont," *CROG*, Vol. 5, p. 481.

48. *CROG*, vol. 4, Supplement, pp. 161-62.

49. Town Court, cites Frederica, 30 March 1741. "Copy of the Proceedings Relating to a Negro Slave Condemned in the Town Court of Frederica, Pursuant to the Law against Negroes," *Egmont Papers*, 14205, pp. 275-76. Betty Wood in " 'The One Thing Needful': The Slavery Debate in Georgia 1732-1750." This case is evidence that "settlers generally received financial rewards for informing on their neighbors." Wood, pp. 303-5. She notes that the trustee ordinance appointing special constables to enforce the prohibition included a provision requiring "all persons to be aiding and assisting to the said constables for the time being of the said Town of Savannah." "The Constables of Savannah Appointed to Seize Blacks or Negroes," *CROG*, vol. 32, pp. 416-18.

For other cases in which the slavery prohibition was enforced, see Jones to Oglethorpe, Savannah, 18 March 1741, *Egmont Papers*, 14205, p. 274

(where a Negro servant belonging to Mr. Mallair was found at work in Savannah); "Journal of the Earl of Egmont," *CROG,* vol. 5, p. 481 (where a "Negro" "taken at work on Mr. Upton's land" was sold for thirteen pounds); and Coulter, *Journal of William Stevens,* vol. 2, p. 103 (where two slaves, presumably imported illegally, were imprisoned and vigorously pursued after their escape).

50. *CROG,* vol. 4, pp. 192-97; Coulter, vol. 1, pp. 170-71; Coulter, vol. 2, pp. 17, 93, 96, 102, 225, 245, 263.

51. Coulter, vol. 1, pp. 170-71; vol. 2, pp. 17, 96, 245, 263.

52. Coulter, vol. 2, pp. 17, 24-25. See also p. 103.

53. Coulter, vol. 2, pp. 17, 93, 96, 102, 225, 263.

54. Coulter, vol. 2, p. 263; See also *CROG,* vol. 4, pp. 191-92.

55. Coulter, vol. 2, p. 17; See also Coulter, vol. 2, p. 93; *CROG,* vol. 4, pp. 191-92; Coulter, vol. 1, pp. 170-71.

56. *CROG,* vol. 4, pp. 191-92. The general failure of the South Carolina courts to return indentured servants is discussed *infra,* pp. 238-241.

57. Coulter, vol. 2, p. 225. Curassoe, or Curaçao, is an island in the Caribbean off Venezuela.

58. Ibid.

59. Ibid.

60. Ibid. Stephens never specifically reveals what would happen to the black even if he could prove he had been free. However, the mere fact that the black bothered to assert his prior freedom suggests that he might not have been sold into slavery if he had prevailed, but probably would have been banished from the province.

61. *CROG,* vol. 4, p. 427. Emphasis added.

62. Ibid., pp. 344-45.

63. Ibid., p. 345.

64. Ibid.

65. *CROG,* vol. 4, Supplement, p. 271.

66. Id.

67. Id.

68. Ibid., p. 272. A November 4 entry reports the capture in Purysburg of those two blacks. Stephens adds:

> the Captors desiring to know what Reward they were to have, it was thought Reasonable to allow the same Rate as usually had been paid for Runaway Servants, which is 50 pounds currency for each, whereupon we sent a person proper to take care about it, and payment was to be made or their being delivered into custody here. Coulter, vol. 1, p. 5.

However on November 5, Stephens writes that the blacks had fallen "into the hands of our Carolina Neighbours," who were unwilling to return them.

> Some of them now refused to deliver them, alledging that their Master owed them money and therefore they would stop them to make payment. This needs no Remark from me, but may pass among many other Instances of what may be expected from those people. Id. See also Nov. 25 report, Ibid., p. 12.

69. Coulter, vol. 1, pp. 170-71.

70. Captain Hugh McCall, The History of Georgia Containing Brief Sketches of the Most Remarkable Events Up to the Present Day (1784) (Atlanta:

Cherokee Publishing Company, 1909), p. 143; Jones, *History of Georgia*, p. 420; John Hurd, *The Law of Freedom and Bondage in the United States* (Boston: Little, Brown, 1858), vol. 1, p. 149; Scarborough, *Opposition to Slavery*, p. 46; Coleman, *Colonial Georgia*, p. 139.

71. Coulter, vol. II, p. 40.

72. This quotation is from Stephens's October 23, 1743 summary of another letter from MacCay discussing MacCay's political predicament. Ibid., p. 30.

73. Ibid., p. 53.

74. Ibid., pp. 67-68. Manslaughter is the unlawful killing of another without malice. Conviction for manslaughter is not as serious as conviction for murder, in which there is a finding that the defendant possessed express or implied malice.

75. *CROG*, vol. 3, p. 431; Wood, " 'The One Thing Needful,' " pp. 306-8.

76. Wood, ibid.

77. Jones, *History of Georgia*, p. 421. See also McCall, *History of Georgia*, p. 44; Allen Candler, "The Beginnings of Slavery in Georgia," *Magazine of History*, vol. 13, pp. 344-45; *CROG*, vol. 25, p. 295; Jones, *History of Georgia*, pp. 419-22.

78. Scarborough, *Opposition to Slavery*, pp. 24-26.

79. Coleman, *Colonial Georgia*, p. 51.

80. "Journal of William Stephens," *CROG*, vol. 4, Supplement, p. 272; McCall, *History of Georgia*, p. 143; Jones, *History of Georgia*, p. 420.

81. C. C. Jones, Jr. and Salem Dutcher, *Memorial History, of Augusta Georgia* (Syracuse, 1870), p. 34, cited by Scarborough, *Opposition to Slavery*, p. 24. See also the malcontents' letter alluding to widespread presence of blacks around Augusta, *CROG*, vol. 11, p. 260. But see, H. B. Fant, "The Labor Policy of the Trustees for Establishing the Colony of Georgia in America," 16 *GHQ*. 1, 9-10 (Macon, 1932).

82. *CROG*, vol. 1, p. 495. The Trustees' Journal stated on Dec. 29, 1746:

It appearing by Mr. Stephens's Journal August 21st, 1746 that the Rev. Mr. Thomas Bosomworth had sent to South Carolina for six Negroes to be employ'd at his Plantation at the Forks at the Alatamaha River; And that Negroes have been creeping into the colony at Augusta and other remote places.

Order'd

That the Secretary do write to Mr. Stephens, and acquaint him that the Trustees are surprised, that He as President, and the Assistants have not taken any Step to punish and put a Stop to such a Violation of the Law against Negroes, nor propos'd any Means for the Trustees doing it, but have contented themselves with seeing, and complaining of it.

83. *CROG*, vol. 25, pp. 236-37, Scarborough suggests that the local officials permitted the illegal use of slaves so as to pressure the trustees into repealing the slave law.

the Savannah officials know that negroes were creeping into the colony. They made little effort to enforce an unpopular statute. They conceded, as far as possible from the Trustees the fact of the Negroes' presence in the colony. It seems that they waited for the introduction of Negroes to become an actuality and then plead the impossibility of ridding the province of them, and the terrible consequences likely to follow. When concealment was no longer possible, fearing the displeasure of the trustees, and attempting to underate themselves, they acknowledged that Negroes had been introduced many years before and were employed at Augusta in spite of the parliament and trustees. Scarborough, *Opposition to Slavery*, p. 50. See also Jones, *History of Georgia*, p. 421.

84. "Letter of Oglethorpe to the Trustees," May 23, 1736, *CROG*, vol. 21, pp. 161-62.

85. Allen Candler, "The Beginnings of Slavery in Georgia," p. 345.

86. See *supra*, pp. 232-235.

87. Coleman, *Colonial Georgia*, p. 139.

88. Jones, *History of Georgia*, p. 143; Scarborough, *Opposition to Slavery*, pp. 48-57; McCall, *History of Georgia*, pp. 143-44; Flanders, *Plantation Slavery*, p. 20; James Ford Rhodes, *History of the United States* (New York, 1892), vol. 1, p. 5. See also *CROG*, vol. 25, p. 285; Stephens, vol. 1, p. 311.

89. *CROG*, vol. 25, p. 295.

90. Boorstin, *The Americans*, p. 81.

91. "Charter for Establishing the Colony of Georgia," *CROG*, vol. 1, pp. 20-22.

92. See Fant, "Labor Policy of the Trustees," p. 4; Taylor, *Georgia Plan*, p. 89.

93. *CROG*, vol. 3, p. 411.

94. Id. This credit was later restricted with the adoption of various financial arrangements. See Taylor, *Georgia Plan*, pp. 91-98.

95. *CROG*, vol. 2, p. 23.

96. James McCain, *Georgia As a Proprietary Province* (Boston: Richard G. Badger, 1917), pp. 233-34.

97. Taylor, *Georgia Plan*, p. 96; *Diary of Viscount Percival, Afterward First Earl of Egmont*, vol. 2, p. 190; *CROG*, vol. 2, p. 206.

98. *CROG*, vol. 1, pp. 414-15; vol. 2, p. 408.

99. See Fant, "Labor Policy of the Trustees," p. 5; Taylor, *Georgia Plan*, p. 90; Coleman, *Colonial Georgia*, pp. 137-38; Davis, *The Fledgling Province*, p. 148.

100. Coleman, *Colonial Georgia*, p. 52.

101. Taylor, *Georgia Plan*, p. 92.

102. Fant, "Labor Policy of the Trustees," p. 6; *CROG*, vol. 2, p. 368.

103. Coleman, *Colonial Georgia*, p. 52.

104. The 20 percent estimate is made by Coleman: "The proportion of servants in the colony was small, no more than 20 per cent of the population in 1741, and tended to decline as the permanent population built up after the Spanish War." Coleman, *Colonial Georgia*, p. 138. Taylor concludes that "probably servants always numbered below one-tenth of all colonists." Taylor, *Georgia Plan*, p. 96. He cites as evidence for his estimate the trustees' pamphlets replying to the malcontents, "An Impartial Inquiry into the State and Utility of the Province of Georgia" (London, 1741), p. 169. and "A New and Accurate Account of the Province of South Carolina and Georgia," *Georgia Historical Society Collections*, vol. 1, p. 66. H. B. Fant states: "the early ratio of indentured servants to all others was about as one to six, [and] did not greatly vary throughout the period of Trust Control." Fant, "Labor Policy of the Trustees," p. 3.

105. See *infra*, pp. 239-241.

106. Taylor, *Georgia Plan*, p. 92. Fant, "Labor Policy of the Trustees," p. 15.

107. *CROG*, vol. 3, p. 430. The Georgia Salzburgers were German Lutheran immigrants who had fled Salzburg Austria because of religious persecution. They made up a closeknit self-sufficient community at Ebenezer, which was the only center of opposition to slavery in Georgia.
108. See Fant, "Labor Policy of the Trustees," p. 15.
109. The antislavery petitions repeatedly compared the cost of labor in Georgia to that in South Carolina.
110. Davis, *The Fledgling Province* (Chapel Hill: University of North Carolina Press, 1976), p. 126.
111. For numerous examples, see Taylor, *Georgia Plan,* pp. 93-96.
112. Coleman, *Colonial Georgia,* pp. 137-38.
113. Thomas Causton held various governmental offices in Georgia during the 1730s and in Oglethorpe's absence was in charge of the colony's affairs. He was dismissed in 1739 for irregularities in his operation of the trustees' public stores.
114. *CROG*, vol. 4, pp. 171-72. Stephens states in his Journal on December 4, 1738 that South Carolina is a place "where the Arms of those People are always open to receive such as leave this Colony, be the Cause what it will; for even runaway Servants too often find it such an Asylum, as their Masters cannot easily recover them from." *CROG*, vol. 4, pp. 238-39. On May 8, 1739 he notes that "Divers Servants [had] lately run away from their Masters, which there was Reason to believe were got the Length of Charles-Town, where they found Shelter, as Experience had too often shown." Ibid., vol. 4, p. 333.
115. *CROG*, vol. 26, pp. 80-82.
116. *CROG*, vol. 4, p. 192. This case is discussed *supra*, p. 228. In a February 24, 1793 entry, Stephens describes the return of South Carolina slaves to their master's creditors and then observes that "It is much to be wished that we could find some instance of the like readiness among those our Neighbors to Check the course of too many who fly hence (particularly servants from their masters) and find protection in South Carolina." Coulter, vol. 1, p. 175.
117. *CROG*, vol. 26, p. 82.
118. Ibid., pp. 82-83.
119. See *infra,* p. 259.
120. See *infra,* pp. 259-262.
121. The law was generally interpreted as prohibiting free blacks from Georgia. However, arguably, some discretion was left to the common council in the disposition of captured slaves, as long as they were not runaways from another colony. The law stated:

> all and every the Black or Blacks Negroe or Negroes which shall at any time then after be found in the said Province of Georgia or within any Part or Place thereof in the Custody house or Possession of whomsoever the same may be shall and may be Seized and taken by such person or persons as for that purpose shall be authorized and Impowered by the said Common Council of the said Trustees or the Major part of them who shall for that purpose be present and Assembled and the said Black or Blacks Negroe or Negroes so seized and taken shall be deemed and adjudged and are hereby declared to be the Sole property of and to belong

only to the said Trustees and their Successors and shall and may be Exported Sold and disposed of in such manner as the said Common Council of the said Trustees or the Major part of them for that purpose present and Assembled shall think most for the benefit and good of the said Colony. *CROG*, vol. 1, p. 51.

Thus, it is possible that under this provision might have permitted the common council to allow captured free blacks to remain in Georgia. Neither the common council nor the courts ever officially followed this policy, however.

122. "Journal of the Earl of Egmont," *CROG*, vol. 5, p. 378.

123. Ibid., pp. 378–79.

124. The attorney general was consulted about this interpretation of the 1735 law as it applied to free blacks, but, according to Fant, "the intention of the law to exclude all blacks was perhaps too generally recognized to admit of legal quibbles." Fant, "Labor Policy of the Trustees," p. 9. Egmont makes no further reference in his Journal to the proposed change.

125. Coleman, *Colonial Georgia*, p. 140.

126. *CROG*, vol. 3, p. 422.

127. Ibid., p. 423.

128. Boorstin, *The Americans*, p. 89.

129. *CROG*, vol. 3, p. 422. The trustees relaxed their stringent land regulations in the late 1730s and 1740s and finally abolished them in 1750. See *CROG*, vol. 2, p. 50.

130. Ibid., vol. 3, p. 425.

131. "Letter of the Trustees to the Magistrates of Savannah," *CROG*, vol. 3, pp. 431–32.

132. Patrick Tailfer, Hugh Anderson, David Douglas, et al., "A True and Historical Narrative of the Colony of Georgia in America . . ." (1741), reprinted in Clarence L. VerSteeg, ed., *A True and Historical Narrative of the Colony of Georgia With Comments by The Earl of Egmont* (Athens, Ga.: University of Georgia Press, 1960).

133. Ibid., pp. 157–61.

134. Ibid., p. 17.

135. Ibid., pp. 49–51.

136. Ibid., pp. 74–136.

137. Ibid., p. 126.

138. Tailfer, "Narrative," p. 17. Note also Egmont response. Id.

139. Ibid., pp. 39–40.

One of the demands they listed at the end of the narrative was freedom from trustee laws that were inconsistent with those of England: "The REAL causes of the ruin and desolation of the colony . . . are . . . the denying us the privilege of being judged by the laws of our mother country; and subjecting the lives and fortunes of all people in the colony, to one person or set of men, who assumed the privilege, under the name of a Court of Chancery, of acting according to their own will and fancy." Ibid., pp. 157–59.

140. There were various trustee responses to these early petitions. After the 1738 petition William Stephens, the secretary of the colony, wrote a justification of the trustee policies in *"A State of the Province of Georgia, Attested upon Oath in The Court of Savannah Nov. 10, 1740* (London: W. Meadows,

1742). Benjamin Martin wrote for the trustees *An Impartial Inquirey into the State and Utility of the Province of Georgia* (London: W. Meadows, 1741), asserting that the goals of the colony were inconsistent with fee simple ownership of land and the presence of slavery. Also in 1741 he authored for the trustees *An Account Showing the Progress of the Colony of Georgia in America from its First Establishment* (Annapolis: reprint of the 1741 edition, London, 1742) (*CROG*, vol. 3, pp. 369-403), which was a more direct attack on the positions taken in and the authors of "A True and Historical Narrative. . . ."

141. The older Stephens opposed his son's actions and, at least at this point, expressed firm opposition to the admission of slaves, though for less than commendable reasons. For example, he announced to the trustees in his June 1, 1742 Journal entry: "It has always been a fundamental rule with me, I have at all times, and on all Occasions, openly declared it, nay, I have farther declared (without any Political Reason assigned) that I have a natural Aversion to Negroes, and Slaves of any kind." Coulter, vol. 1, p. 88. See also *CROG*, vol. 23, pp. 442-44.

142. Scarborough, *Opposition to Slavery*, pp. 46-47, 56-57; *CROG*, vol. 5, p. 607. See generally, Betty Wood, "Thomas Stephens and the Introduction of Black Slavery in Georgia," 58 *Georgia Historical Quarterly* (1974): 24-40.

143. *CROG*, vol. 5, pp. 648-49; vol. 30, p. 456; Scarborough, *Opposition to Slavery*, pp. 52-53; Flanders, *Plantation Slavery*, p. 19.

144. *CROG*, vol. 23, pp. 442-47. Stephens also advised that if Augustine remained under Spanish control after the war, the English should take "due care" to obtain terms that would "effectually" prevent "any runaway Negroes from being receivd or entertaind by the Spaniards. . . ." Such an agreement would be especially important if hostilities between England and Spain recommenced. According to Stephens, the consequence "of the Negro's revolting to the Enemy, who by that time might probably be some thousands in Number" was so worrisome that it had to be left "to the consideration of those whose capacities reach far beyond mine." Ibid., p. 45.

145. See, for example, *CROG*, vol. 31, p. 124; ibid., pp. 506-7; *CROG*, vol. 33, pp. 361-62.

146. Wood, " 'The One Thing Needful,' " pp. 309-10.

147. Scarborough, *Opposition to Slavery*, p. 68.

148. "A Brief Account of the Causes that have Retarded the Progress of the Colony of Georgia in America," *Georgia Historical Collections*, vol. 2, Appendix 4, pp. 113-14.

149. Jones, *History of Georgia*, p. 422; Flanders, *Plantation Slavery*, pp. 16-21.

150. *CROG*, vol. 24, pp. 434-44; see also note 53 on alleged activities of Reverend Bosomworth.

151. *CROG*, vol. 3, p. 429.

152. Ibid., p. 430. The petition was signed by fifty-one residents, including the two ministers of the congregation at Ebenezer, John Martin Bolzius and Israel Christian Cronau.

153. Ibid., p. 427. See David Brion Davis, *The Problem of Slavery in Western Culture* (New York: Pelican Books, 1970), p. 169.

154. *CROG*, vol. 25, p. 289. To be sure, Balzius prefaced those remarks by reaffirming his moral opposition to slavery.

155. See *supra*, pp. 53-58, 169-173.
156. See *supra*, ch. 4.
157. Peter Wood, *Black Majority: Negroes in Colonial South Carolina from 1670 through the Stono Rebellion* (New York: W. W. Norton, 1974), p. 52.
158. See Boorstin, *The Americans*, p. 95.
159. References to the "legislative" history of the law may be found at note 6 *infra*.
160. "An Act for repealing an Act Instituted (An Act for rendering the Colony of Georgia more defensible by prohibiting the Importation and Use of Black Slaves or Negroes into the same) and for permitting the Importation and Use of them in the Colony under proper Restrictions and Regulations and for other Purposes therein mentioned," *CROG*, vol. 1, pp. 56-62.
161. *CROG*, vol. 25, pp. 347-50. See note 6.
162. See *infra*, pp. 105-109, 322-324, 338-341.
163. From Davis, *The Fledgling Province*.
164. *CROG*, vol. 1, p. 58.
165. Ibid., p. 57.
166. Ibid., p. 59.
167. Ibid., pp. 58-59.
168. Ibid., p. 59.
169. Ibid., pp. 59-60. Although the trustees had abandoned their vision of a non-slave Georgia, they clung to their mercantile goal for Georgia to be a silk-producing colony. Thus, the 1750 law required that for every four male blacks a planter should own one female black

> well instructed in the Art of winding or reeling of Silk from the Silk Balls or cocoons and shall at the proper Season in every Year send such their Female Negroes or Blacks to Savannah in order to learn the said Art or to such other Place or Places within the said Province as the President and Magistrates thereof shall from time to time appoint for that purpose . . . Ibid., p. 60.

Moreover,

> every Planter within the said Province shall plant five hundred Mulberry Trees on every five hundred Acres of Land which they shall hold within the said Province and so in proportion to a lesser Number of Acres of Land and shall well and sufficiently fence in such Mulberry Trees so as to defend and protect them against Cattle and shall from time to time keep up the same Number and cultivate them according to the best of their Skill and Judgment Or in Default thereof shall forfeit the Sum of Ten pounds Sterling Money of Great Britain to be recovered and applied in such manner as is herein after mentioned . . . Ibid., pp. 60-61.

170. Ibid., p. 58.
171. Ibid., p. 59.
172. Saye, *NVIGH*, p. 73.
173. John Corry, "Racial Elements in Colonial Georgia," 20 *GHQ* 30, 40 (1936).
174. Coleman, *Colonial Georgia*, p. 229.
175. Corry, "Racial Elements," p. 40.
176. This was one year before their authority would have ceased under their twenty-one-year grant from the Georgia charter.

177. Saye, *NVIGH*, pp. 109-12.
178. Ibid., p. 123. See generally pp. 106-33. The trustees had established a representative assembly in Georgia at the very end of their rule. Ibid., pp. 98-99.
179. Ibid., pp. 102-43.
180. The 1755 law was patterned after the 1740 South Carolina law, which is discussed *infra*, pp. 193-198.
181. *CROG*, vol. 18, pp. 102-3. ALA adding to Fn.
182. Ibid., p. 103.
183. Ibid., p. 104.
184. Id. However, "if Judgment shall be given for the plaintiff a Special Entry shall be made declaring that the Ward of the Plaintiff is free and the Jury shall assess Damages which the Plaintiffs Ward hath sustained and the court shall give Judgment and award Execution Against the Defendant for such Damages with full Costs of Suit. . . ." Ibid., pp. 103-4.
185. Davis, *The Fledgling Province*, p. 128.
186. *CROG*, vol. 1, p. 57.
187. *CROG*, vol. 18, p. 137.
188. Benefit of clergy originally meant the exemption of clergymen from the secular courts. Afterward it came to mean an exemption from the punishment of death and was extended to "clerks" or those who could read. The privilege greatly mitigated the criminal law, but led to such abuses that Parliament began to enact that certain felonies should be without benefit of clergy. See Guild, *Black Laws of Virginia*, p. 154, n. 2.
189. *CROG*, vol. 18, p. 132.

> And in case any shall not be able to make the Satisfaction hereby required every such person shall be sent to any Frontier Garrison of this province or committed to the Goal at Savannah and there to remain at the public Expence for the Space of Seven years and to serve or to be kept to hard Labour and the pay usually allow'd by the public to the Soldiers of such Garrison or the profits of the Labour of the Offender shall be paid to the owner of the Slave murdered. Ibid., p. 132.

190. Ibid., p. 132. However, if there were no reliable white witnesses, this requirement might be waived and the burden of proof shifted to the defendant charged with murdering the slave. Ibid., p. 134.
191. Ibid., p. 132.
192. Ibid., pp. 105-6. A white person could "moderately correct" any slave who refused to be searched while outside his master's property. Id.
193. Ibid., pp. 137-38.
194. Ibid., p. 138.
195. Ibid., p. 140.
196. Ibid., pp. 137-38.

> Whereas from the Neighbourhood of Augustine and the encouragement there given to Runaway Slaves it is much to be feared that many Negroes will be tempted to desert from their Masters and fly there in hopes of being received and Protected which if not prevented may be attended with Consequences fatal to many of the Inhabitants of this Colony. Be it therefore Enacted by the Authority aforesaid that from and after the passing of this Act

any White person or persons free Indian or Indians or any other free person who shall take and Secure any runaway Slave on the Southside of the Altamaha River provided such Slaves be twenty Miles from the plantation he belongs to and shall from thence bring such Slave to the highest Justice of the peace and before him make Oath or otherwise prove that the said Slave was taken as aforesaid the said Justice of the peace give him or them a Certificate of the same by which he or they shall be intituled to a Reward of Five pounds Sterling for every gown Man Slave brought a Live and Three pounds Sterling for every Woman Boy or Girl above the Age of Twelve years brought a Live and for everyone under the Age of Twelve years brought a live the Sum or Two pounds Sterling and for every Scalp with Two Ears of a grown Man Slave the sum of One Pound Sterling—And for every grown Man Slave taken on the South Side of St. Johns River and brought a live as aforesaid the sum of Fifteen pounds Sterling, for a Woman Boy or Girl above the age of Twelve years brought alive the Sum of Ten pounds Sterling and for every Slave under the Age of Twelve Years the Sum of five pounds Sterling and for every Scalp with with Two Ears of a grown man Slave the Sum of Thirty Shillings Sterling the Several Sums above mentioned (excepting for the Scalps which shall be paid for by the Public) shall be paid by the Master or Owner of such Runaway upon delivery of the Slave but if the Master of such Slave cannot be readily found then the person in whose Custody the Slave is shall deliver him or her into the hands of the provost Marshal at Savannah who is hereby empowered to give such person an Order upon the Public Treasurer for the Reward which it shall appear by the Certificate he is intituled to for taking such Slave . . .

For one instance in which Indians were reimbursed for capturing runaway slaves, see *CROG*, vol. 10, pp. 585-86.

197. *CROG*, vol. 9, p. 55.
198. *CROG*, vol. 18, pp. 132-33.
199. Id. Another provision implicitly gave a master the right to brand his slaves. Ibid., p. 120.
200. Ibid., pp. 106-7.
201. Ibid., p. 134.
202. *CROG*, vol. 18, p. 113. A slave's conviction under this provision resulted in a mandatory death sentence. Ibid., p. 114.
203. Ibid., p. 113. The slave must have "actually prepared Provision Arms Ammunition Horse or Horses or any Boat Canon or other Vessel or done any other Overt Act whereby such their Intention shall be manifested."
204. Ibid., pp. 119-20. However, if "such Striking wounding Maiming or Bruising be not done by the Command and in the Defence of the person or property of the Owner or other person having the Care or Government of Such Slave in which case the Slave Shall be wholly excus'd and the Owner or other person having the care or government of such Slave shall be answerable as far as by Law he ought." Ibid., pp. 119-20.
205. Ibid., p. 119.
206. Ibid., p. 140.
207. Indians "in amity" with the government were excepted. Ibid., pp. 112-13.
208. Ibid., p. 112.
209. Ibid., p. 113. Another provision stated that any person who "shall actually

Steal a Slave or deface his her or their Mark shall be Guilty of felony and shall be Excluded the Benefit of Clergy." Ibid., p. 114.

210. Ibid., p. 113.
211. Ibid., pp. 112-13.
212. The governor and his council refused to grant mercy to slaves convicted of the capital crimes of committing robbery (*CROG*, vol. 10, pp. 245-46, 1767); murdering a free Negro (*CROG*, vol. 10, p. 631, 1768); and "breaking a Shop and Stealing Sundry goods thereout" (*CROG*, vol. 11, p. 305, 1777). In 1772 the governor and his council discussed the case of a South Carolina slave accused of murdering an Indian. The Board "were of Opinion that his honor should . . . assure [the leaders of the Lower Creeks tribe] that if it can be provd the Negro Fellow killed the Indian he shall suffer death for the Crime." *CROG*, vol. 12, p. 339, 1772. See also *CROG*, vol. 9, p. 55, 1763, discussed *supra*, (overseer murdered by slave); *CROG*, vol. 9, p. 438, 1765, discussed *infra*, (white man and Indian allegedly murdered by 5 slaves); *CROG*, vol. 12, p. 309, 1772 (slave convicted of "Felony for breaking open a Store of Rice and Conveying Several barrels of rice therefrom").
213. Davis, *The Fledgling Province*, pp. 128-30.
214. *CROG*, vol. 9, p. 438.
215. *CROG*, vol. 18, p. 108.
216. Ibid., p. 110.
217. Ibid., pp. 109-10.
218. Ibid., p. 111.
219. Ibid., pp. 116-17.
220. Ibid., p. 105.
221. Ibid., p. 135. Such slaves "shall be punished with Whipping on the Bare back not Exceeding Twenty Lashes." Ibid., p. 105.
222. Ibid., pp. 125, 126, 130. See also p. 128. In such cases, the profits from their commerce accrued to the master.
223. Ibid., pp. 117-18.
224. Ibid., p. 128.
225. Id.
226. Ibid., p. 135. See *CROG*, vol. 12, pp. 213-14 for a "presentment of the Grand Jury" of Savannah reporting
    That Slaves are permitted to Rent houses in the lands and Invirons of the town of Savannah in said houses meetings of Slaves are very frequent, Spirits and other liquors are sold, and Stolen goods often Concealed by Information of David Tolear and Adam Irick. Ibid., p. 214.
227. *CROG*, vol. 18, p. 136.
228. Ibid., pp. 132-33.
229. Ibid., p. 117.
230. Ibid., p. 136.
231. Ibid., p. 133.
232. Davis, *The Fledgling Province*, p. 128.
233. See Flanders, *Plantation Slavery*, p. 34; Scarborough, *Opposition to Slavery*, pp. 124-43. David writes, "The number of free blacks in Georgia was not large. In the 1760's the province anticipated taxes from twenty, but that estimate is only approximate." Davis, *The Fledgling Province*, p. 41.

234. "An Act for Regulating the Militia of this province and for the Security and better Defence of the same," *CROG*, vol. 18, pp. 7-48.
235. Ibid., p. 25.
236. Id.
237. Ibid., p. 39.
238. Ibid., p. 40.
239. Id.
240. Ibid., pp. 40-41.
241. Ibid., pp. 18-19.
242. See ibid., p. 41, for one explanation in the law itself for the special protection of slave masters.
243. Ibid., pp. 42-43.
244. Ibid., p. 44.
245. Ibid., p. 43. Technically, there was a different standard of proof for the valorous conduct of slaves and freemen. Proof of valorous conduct for a slave/white servant had to be provided "either by a Certificate of a field officer or Captain of any Company under his hand who shall be informed thereof by the Oaths of this credible white persons." Id. The valorous conduct of poor freemen/white servants only needed to be validated by "a certificate thereof, from a majority of field officers of the regiment of troop, to which such person belongs under their hands and seals." Ibid., p. 47.
246. *CROG*, vol. 18, p. 213. See also *CROG*, vol. 12, pp. 146-47.
247. *CROG*, vol. 18, p. 225.
248. Ibid., p. 225.
249. Ibid., p. 232.
250. Id.
251. Ibid., p. 233. For an example of the operation of the patrols, See *CROG*, vol. 19, part 1, pp. 185, 501, 502, in which payments were made to members of the patrols for their expenses in capturing escaped slaves. See also *CROG*, vol. 12, pp. 146-47, 325-26, in which members of the militia were ordered to search for encampments of blacks.
252. Technically, the 1765 law was never officially approved by the governor, though it served as the Georgia slave code until the passage of the 1770 law.
253. *CROG*, vol. 18, pp. 661, 662-63; 669-70; *CROG*, vol. 19, part 1, pp. 221-23, 228-29.
254. *CROG*, vol. 18, p. 662; *CROG*, vol. 19, part 1, p. 222.
255. *CROG*, vol. 19, part 1, p. 220.
256. Any slave, free black, mulatto, or Indian (not in amity with the government) "shall . . . thereof suffer death" if "he shall be guilty of homicide of any sort upon any white person," except if the act was committed by "misadventure, or in defense of his or her owner or other person under whose care and government such slave shall be." The sentence of death would also be imposed if he shall "delude or entice any slave or slaves to run away" so that the owner was or would have been "deprived" of the slaves; or "shall raise or attempt to raise any insurrection." *CROG*, vol. 19, part 1, p. 220.
257. Compare *CROG*, vol. 18, p. 137 (1755) with *CROG*, vol. 18, pp. 685-86 (1765) and *CROG*, vol. 19, part 1, pp. 245-46 (1770).
258. *CROG*, vol. 18, p. 682; *CROG*, vol. 19, part 1, p. 244.
     all Persons male and Female of what Nation or Colour soever being born

of free parents and now are or hereafter may come into this Province and give good Testimony of their humble duty and loyalty to his Majesty and their Obendience to the Laws and their Affection to the Inhabitants of this Province may be intituled to an Act of Assembly for Naturalizing them, and each of them, whereby they, their Wives, and Children may have, Use and enjoy, all the Rights, Priviledges, Powers and Immunities whatsoever which any person born of British parents within this Province, may, can, might, could or of Right ought to have, Use or enjoy except to vote for or be Elected a Member to serve in the general Assembly of this Province and from thenceforth be adjudged, reputed and taken to be in every Condition, Respect and Degree as free to all Intents, Purposes and Constructions as if they had been and were born of British Parents within this Province, anything herein contained to the contrary Notwithstanding.

259. *CROG*, vol. 18, p. 659.
260. See Winthrop Jordan, *White Over Black* (New York: W. W. Norton, 1968), pp. 169-71.
261. *CROG*, vol. 1, p. 61.
262. *CROG*, vol. 18, p. 66.
263. Ibid., pp. 164, 241.
264. Ibid., p. 253. Technically, this 1758 law is a reenactment of an earlier, evidently unsuccessful, 1758 tax which levied the same tax. Ibid., pp. 252-53.
265. Ibid., p. 338.
266. Ibid., p. 394. See also ibid., pp. 420-26.
267. Later, when free blacks were taxed separately under a different provision of the 1768 law, this tax became a tax on "all Negroes *or* other slaves" (italics added). See *CROG*, vol. 19, pt. 1, p. 31.
268. *CROG*, vol. 18, p. 659.
269. *CROG*, vol. 19, pt. 1, p. 31.
270. Ibid., p. 35. The discrimination in the level of taxation as well as the special burden on mulattoes held subject to the tax was continued in tax laws in 1768. (*CROG*, vol. 19, part 1, pp. 101, 105-6), 1770 (ibid., pp. 162-63, 167), and 1773 (ibid., pp. 451, 459. See also ibid., p. 148).
271. *CROG*, vol. 1, p. 61. Georgia President William Stevens and his assistants wrote to the trustees in 1750 that:

> as this is an Infant Colony its presumed if their Honors will reduce it to Fifteen Shillings Sterling at least for a few Years.) Importers will be encouraged to bring their Negroes here and thereby take of our produce and it may likewise induce persons to come and settle among us. The annual Tax (per) Head in the American British Colony is various as it is rated according to their public demands and tho' the Inhabitants of the Neighbouring Colony during the late War have paid from fourteen to eighteen Shillings their Currency (per) head Yet its supposed that this Tax the ensuing Year will be reduced to seven Shillings and six pence (per) head which is something less than Thirteen pence Sterling the usual Tax in times of Peace. *CROG*, vol. 25, pp. 436-37.

> It should be noted that under the 1750 law, owners who had illegally imported slaves into Georgia before the passage of the law paid the same tax on their domestic slaves as those who subsequently imported slaves after slavery was legal.

272. *CROG*, vol. 18, pp. 277-82. See also *CROG*, vol. 25, pp. 430-37, 432-33.
273. Ibid., pp. 279, 280, 281, 282. One of the major exceptions to this policy was the use of slaves for the building of forts and roads in Georgia. Numerous laws drafted slaves for projects. See *CROG*, vol. 18, pp. 87-101; 202-11; 408-17; 433-34; 472-79; 639-48; 717-42; *CROG*, vol. 19, pp. 54-59; 253-90.
274. *CROG*, vol. 18, p. 279.
275. *CROG*, vol. 19, part 2, pp. 23-30.
276. *CROG*, vol. 18, pp. 328-32.
277. *CROG*, vol. 18, pp. 465-66.
278. *CROG*, vol. 18, p. 323.
279. *CROG*, vol. 19, part 1, pp. 351-52. See also *CROG*, vol. 18, pp. 283-84, 288.
280. *CROG*, vol. 18, pp. 358-66; amended, ibid., pp. 799-802.
281. Copy to come
282. See A. Leon Higginbotham, Jr., unpub. ms., "Slavery and the Constitution," pp. 16, 33, 41, 42-46 (March 3, 1976 draft).

PENNSYLVANIA

1. Reprinted in Henry Steele Commager, ed., *Documents of American History*, 8th ed. (New York: Appleton-Century-Crofts, Meredith Corporation, 1968), pp. 37-38.
2. There was no census of the colonies during this period, but the 1790 census, the first in the United States, does suggest the difference between Pennsylvania and other colonies when their geographical location is taken into account. In 1790, blacks (both free and enslaved) made up 2.4 percent of the Pennsylvania population. In the New England states, the black population was less than 1.7 percent of the total population:

Percentage Negro in the Total Population, 1790

Maine	0.6	
New Hampshire	0.6	
Vermont	0.3	
Massachusetts	1.4	(no slave population)
Rhode Island	6.3	
Connecticut	2.3	

In the Middle Atlantic states the black population was 5.3 percent of the total population.

Percentage Negro in the Total Population, 1790

New York	7.6
New Jersey	7.7
Pennsylvania	2.4

In the South Atlantic states the black population was 36.4 percent of the total population.

Percentage Negro in the Total Population, 1790

Delaware	21.6
Maryland	34.7

North Carolina	26.8
Virginia	40.9
South Carolina	43.7
Georgia	35.9

From *Negro Population in the United States,* 1790-1918 (New York: Arno Press and the New York Times, 1968), p. 51. See Edward Turner, *The Negro in Pennsylvania* (Washington, D.C.: The American Historical Association, 1911), pp. 13-16, 67-68.

3. Technically, a 1652 act passed in Providence and Warwick, before Rhode Island came under one jurisdiction by a 1663 charter, banned lifetime servitude in the colony. It prohibited any "blacke mankind or white" from being forced by "covenant bond, or otherwise," to serve longer than ten years, except if he were "taken in" when under the age of fourteen, in which case he could not be forced to serve beyond age twenty-four. *Colonial Records of Rhode Island,* vol. 1, p. 243. However, Helen Catterall agrees that this prohibition was not enforced in the 18th century, and later 18th century statutory enactments regulating slavery in Rhode Island gave legal sanction to the slavery. See Helen Catterall, *Judicial Cases Concerning American Slavery* (New York: Negro University Press, 1968), vol. 4, p. 448.

4. John Hope Franklin, *From Slavery to Freedom,* 4th ed. (New York: Alfred A. Knopf, 1974), p. 64.

5. Samuel W. Pennypacker, "The Settlement of Germantown," in *Pennsylvania Magazine,* vol. IV, pp. 30-31.

6. Turner, *The Negro in Pennsylvania,* p. 22.

7. Breviate Dutch Records, no. 2, vol. 5, found in 2 *Pennsylvania Archives,* vol. 16, p. 234.

8. See E. B. O'Callaghan, ed., *Voyages of the Slavers St. John and Arms of Amsterdam . . . ,* p. 100, and Sprinchorn, *Kolonien Nya Sverlges Historia,* p. 217, as cited by Turner, *The Negro in Pennsylvania,* p. 17, n. 2.

9. C. T. Odhoner, "The Founding of New Sweden, 1637-1642," trans. G. B. Keen, in *Pennsylvania Magazine of History and Biography,* vol. 3, p. 277.

10. See section on Virginia, *supra,* pp. 20, 408 n. 5.

11. Gail McKnight Beckman, ed., *The Statutes at Large of Pennsylvania in the Time of William Penn,* 1680-1700 (New York: Vantage Press, 1976), vol. 1, pp. 71-110. See also pp. 27-29 and discussion in section on New York, *supra,* pp. 114-115.

12. Sydney George Fisher, *The Making of Pennsylvania* (Philadelphia: J. B. Lippincott, 1896), p. 31.

13. *The Record of the Court at Upland in Pennsylvania, 1676 to 1681* (Philadelphia: Joseph M. Mitchell Co., 1959), pp. 39-43, Sept. 25, 1676; *Record of the Courts of Chester County, Pennsylvania,* 1681-1697. (Philadelphia: The Colonial Society of Pennsylvania, 1910).

14. *Statutes at Large,* vol. 1, p. 78. Emphasis added.

15. *Colonial Laws of Massachusetts* (reprinted 1660 edition), Section 91, 125, later affirmed in *Codification of Laws of 1649-1672, General Laws and Liberties for the Massachusetts Colony.* See discussion in section on Massachusetts, *supra,* p. 62, 64-65.

16. Richard A. Wright, Jr., *The Negro in Pennsylvania: A Study in Economic History* (New York: Arno Press and the New York Times, 1969), p. 6.

17. *The Record of the Court at Upland, in Pennsylvania 1676 to 1681,* Nov. 13, 1677, p. 79.

18. Ms Minute Book, Common Pleas and Quarter Sessions, Bucks County, 1684-1730, pp. 56-57 as cited by Turner, *The Negro in Pennsylvania,* p. 18. See also the 1694 Will of Thomas Lloyd, M.S. Phila. Wills, Book A, p. 26, evidently bequeathing his slaves and their children.

> "I do hereby give . . . pow^r . . . to my s^d Exers . . . eith^r to lett or hire out my five negroes . . . and pay my s^d wife the one half of their wages Yearly during her life or Oth^{r}wise give her such Compensacon for her int^{r}est therein as shee and my s^d Exers shall agree upon and my will is that the other half of their s^d wages shall be equally Devided between my aforsd Children, and after my sd wife decease my will also is That the sd negroes Or such of them and their Offsprings as are then alive shall in kind or value be equally Devided between my s^d Children"

In addition note M.S. Philadelphia Reed Book, E,1, Vol. V, pp. 150-51 where a "Negro man named Jack" was sold by Patrick Robinson Countie Clark to Joseph Browne for 14 pounds for "himselfe, . . . heirs . . . and assigns" "forever."

> "Know all men by these presents That I Patrick Robinson Countie Clark of Philadelphia for and in Consideration of the Sum of fourtie pounds Current Money of Pennsilvania . . . have bargained Sold and delivered . . . unto . . . Joseph Browne for himselfe, . . . heirs exers admrs and assigns One Negro man Named Jack, To have and to hold the Said Negro man named Jack unto the said Joseph Browne for himself . . . for ever. And I . . . the said Negro man unto him . . . shall and will warrant and for ever defend by these presents." MS Phila. Deed Book E.

as cited by Turner, p. 19. For further historical evidence on the use of blacks during this period, see "Ik hebbe geen vaste Dienstbode, als een Neger die ik gekocht heb. *Missive van Cornelis Bom, Geschreven uit de Stadt Philadelphia,* etc. (Oct. 12, 1684). "Man hat hier auch Zwartzen oder Mohren zu Schlaver in der Arbeit." Letter, probably of Hermans Op den Graeff, Germantown, Feb. 12, 1684, in Sachse, *Letters relating to the Settlement of Germantown,* 25. *Cf.* also MS. in American Philosophical Society's collection, quoted in *Pa. Mag.,* VII, 106: "Lacey Cocke hath a negro . . . , "Pattrick Robbinson-Robert neverbeegood his hegor sarvant" . . . "The Defendts negros" are mentioned in a suit for damages in 1687. See Ms. Court Records of Penna. and Chester Co., 1681-1688, p. 72.

as cited by Turner, *The Negro in Pennsylvania,* p. 2, n. 7.

19. W. E. B. DuBois, *The Philadelphia Negro: A Social Study* (New York: Schocken Books, 1967), p. 11.

20. William Penn's Domestic Letters, p. 17, as cited by Turner, *The Negro in Pennsylvania,* p. 19.

21. After discussing the political opposition to slavery in 17th century Pennsylvania, Turner (p. 22) writes:

> "Accordingly at first there may have been some negroes who were held as servants for a term of years, and who were discharged when they had served their time. There is no certain proof that this was so, and the prob-

abilities are rather against it, but the contientious scruples of some of the early settlers at least make it possible."
For evidence of black slaves in the colony, see note 16.

22. See section on Virginia, *supra*, pp. 21-24.
23. *Records of the Courts of Quarter Sessions and Common Pleas of Bucks County, Pennsylvania 1684-1700* (Meadville, Pa.: The Colonial Society of Pennsylvania, 1943), pp. 177-78.
24. M.S. Ancient Records of Sussex County, 1681-1709, 7th mo. 1687.
25. *Record of the Court of Chester County, 1681-1697*, pp. 112-13.
26. The Record of the Court at Upland in Pennsylvania, 1676 to 1681, pp. 51-52.
27. See Section on Virginia, *supra*, pp. 40-47. Unfortunately, like most other opinions from the seventeenth century, this Pennsylvania report does not include a verbatim transcript of the proceedings, and its summarized, though official, published report is ambiguous by failing to reveal all of the underlying facts, the complete disposition, and its full rationale. This ambiguity may mask discriminatory treatment of the mulatto Anna, for there is no discussion of how or whether Anna was punished, or why she did not receive custody of the child. The pardon of Duckett may have been because Anna was a mulatto, rather than a black; or because the offense of interracial sex was committed by a white man, rather than a black man. The humiliation referred to by the court may have even been the humiliation associated with *interracial* sex, not premarital sex.
28. *Court of Quarter Sessions and Common Pleas for Bucks County, 1700-1730*, pp. 373, 376, 393.
29. M.S. Chester County Courts, 1697-1710, p. 24, as cited by Turner, *The Negro in Pennsylvania*, p. 29. Emphasis added.
30. *Records of the Courts of Quarter Sessions and Common Pleas of Bucks County, Pennsylvania, 1684-1700*, pp. 198, 202-3, 205-6, 257-58, 259.
31. The report describes George only as a runaway from Virginia, but it is probable that a black runaway from Virginia at this time was a slave.
32. The defendant George was forced under its decision to serve fifteen years' servitude and receive forty-one stripes on his bare back for stealing a total of six pounds, eleven shillings worth of goods. In a comparable 1699 case involving two runaway white servants, the defendants who "feloniously" took "two of Theire Said masters horses" worth twelve pounds each, received only seven lashes on their bare back and *two* years' additional servitude. *Records of the Courts of Quarter Sessions and Common Pleas of Bucks County, Pennsylvania 1684-1700*. In another case, Peter Steward, the white servant of John Wickham, was found guilty of a presentment against Wickham valued at eighteen pounds. Steward was first given the opportunity to avoid punishment by paying twenty-five pounds and twelve shillings to the attorney general. If he was unable to raise this reimbursement, he only had to "remain a servant [to] ye said Wickham or his assignes for ye full term of 9 years ensuing from this instant." *Record of the Courts of Chester County, Pennsylvania 1681-1697*, p. 137. Emphasis added.
33. *Colonial Records of Pennsylvania (CROP)*, (Philadelphia, 1838-1853), vol. 4, pp. 289, 296.
34. Ibid., p. 289. Emphasis added.

35. Ibid., p. 296.

36. Samuel W. Pennypacker, *Pennsylvania Colonial Cases* (Philadelphia: Rees Welsh and Company, 1892), pp. 54-55. See also *CROP*, vol. 1, pp. 380-81.

37. See note 30.

38. See the chapter on Virginia, discussed *supra*, pp. 34-40; and the chapter on South Carolina, discussed *supra*, pp. 169-201.

39. Turner, *The Negro in Pennsylvania*, p. 22.

40. "The Great Law," chapters 57, 58, *Statutes at Large*, vol. 1, p. 134.

41. "Laws made At An Assembly Held Att Philadelphia in the Province of Pennsylvania the 10th Day of 1st Month March 1683," chapter 134, *Statutes at Large*, vol. 1, p. 156; See also chapter 135, ibid., p. 156.

42. Ibid., chapter 139, p. 157; see also "The law About the Custom of the Country of Servants," May 31st, 1693, *Statutes at Large*, vol. 1, p. 202.

43. See, for example, *Record of the Court of Chester County, Pennsylvania, 1681-1697*, pp. 38, 41, 42, 43, 53, 54 (abuse of servants); *Record of the Courts of Quarter Sessions and Common Pleas of Bucks County, Pennsylvania 1684-1700*, p. 273 (selling servant out of the Province); *Pennsylvania Colonial Cases*, p. 86 (masters ordered to pay for care of ill servant), 110 (servant sued master for freedom and pay "according to the law of the province.").

44. *Pennsylvania Colonial Cases*, pp. 96-98.

45. "Laws Made att an Assembly Held Att Philadelphia in the Province of Pennsylvania the 10th Day of 1st Month March 1683," chapter 138, *Statutes at Large*, vol. 1, p. 157.

46. Ibid., chapter 134, p. 156.

47. Ibid., chapters 134, 137, pp. 156-57.

48. Ibid., p. 157.

49. "An Act for the better Regulation of Servants in this Province and Territories," *Pennsylvania Laws*, vol. 1, p. 13.

50. For a similar, though much earlier legislative development in Virginia, see section on Virginia, *supra*, pp. 34-35.

51. "An Act for the Trial of Negroes," *Statutes at Large*, vol. 2, pp. 77-79. There were some changes made in the law when it was passed again with modifications in 1705-1706. "An Act for the Trial of Negroes," *Statutes at Large*, vol. 2, pp. 233-36. The main difference was that under the 1705-1706 act, a black convicted of attempted rape was not castrated but "whipped with thirty-nine lashes, and branded on the forehead with the letter R or T, and exported out of this province by the master or owner within six months after conviction, never to return into the same, upon paine of death. . . ." Blacks convicted of stealing goods valued *over* five pounds also received this whipping and deportation under the 1705-1706 law, though under the 1700 law they could only have been whipped.

52. *CROP*, vol. 1, p. 61; vol. 2, pp. 405-6.

53. *Statutes at Large*, vol. 2, pp. 77-78.

54. Turner, *The Negro in Pennsylvania*, p. 26.

55. "An Act for the Gradual Abolition of Slavery," *Pennsylvania Laws*, vol. 1, p. 841. This statute is discussed *infra*, pp. 299-303.

56. Id.

57. *Laws of Assembly*, 1847, p. 208.

58. The 1705-1706 act on the trial of Negroes amended this provision to punish blacks convicted of attempted rape by whipping, branding, and deportation out of the province. See note 50.
According to Wright, *Negro in Pa.* (p. 11) a white man convicted of rape was "publicly whipped, not exceeding thirty-one lashes and given seven years imprisonment."

59. Turner, *The Negro in Pennsylvania,* p. 111, n. 7.

60. "An Act for the Better Regulating of Negroes," *Statutes at Large,* vol. 4, pp. 59-64.

61. Ibid., p. 59.

62. Ibid., p. 60.

63. Turner, *The Negro in Pennsylvania,* pp. 8-9.

64. *Statutes at Large,* vol. 4, p. 61.

65. Archmead, *History of Delaware County,* p. 203. M.S. Ancient Records of Sussex County, 1681-1709, p. 116.

66. *CROP,* vol. 2, pp. 129, 121. See also M.S. Records of Christ Church, p. 46.

67. *Statutes at Large,* vol. 4, p. 61.

68. Turner, *The Negro in Pennsylvania,* pp. 54-63.

69. Ibid., p. 56. See also Kalm, *Travels I,* p. 394 (1748).

70. Another example in the 1725-1726 law of this type of change is the prohibition against masters letting their slaves "rambling about under pretence of getting work, give liberty to their negroes to seek their own employ and so to work at their own will." *Statutes at Large,* vol. 4, p. 64.

71. Ibid., p. 62.

72. Id.

73. Wright, *Negro in Pa.,* p. 11.

74. *Statutes at Large,* vol. 4, pp. 62-63.

75. Turner, *The Negro in Pennsylvania,* p. 29.

76. Ibid., p. 30.

77. Ibid., pp. 30-31.

78. Ibid., p. 31.

79. Ibid.

80. Ibid.

81. Ibid. Cf. *What is Sauce for A Goose is Also Sauce for a Gander, etc.* (1764), p. 6, and *A Humble Attempt at Scurrility, etc.* (1765), p. 40, as quoted in Turner, p. 31, n. 43.

82. *Statutes at Large,* vol. 4, pp. 62-63.

83. Ibid., p. 62.

84. *Statutes at Large,* vol. 2, p. 56.

85. *Statutes at Large,* vol. 4, p. 62.

86. Ibid., p. 64.

87. Ibid., pp. 63-64.

88. "An Act for Preventing Accidents that May Happen By Fire," *Statutes at Large,* vol. 3, p. 254; "An Act to Prevent the Damages Which May Happen by Firing of Woods," *Statutes at Large,* vol. 4, p. 282; "An Act For The More Effectual Preventing Accidents Which May Happen By Fire And For Suppressing Idleness, Drunkenness and other Debaucheries," *Statutes at Large,* vol. 5, pp. 109, 126. See also *Statutes at Large,* vol. 5, p. 241; *Statutes at Large,* vol. 6, p. 49; *Statutes at Large,* vol. 7, pp. 359-60.

89. See, for example, *Statutes at Large,* vol. 4, p. 282; vol. 6, p. 49; vol. 8, pp. 113-14; vol. 7, pp. 359-60.
90. We cannot make definitive interpretations of the wordings of many of these statutes, especially the earlier ones, for they refer to "negro or Indian slaves," Negro may be used as a noun or an adjective. The ambiguous statutes are *Statutes at Large:* vol. 3, p. 254; vol. 5, p. 109. Later statutes are clearer in their application only to black slaves. See *Statutes at Large,* vol. 5, pp. 126, 241; vol. 6, p. 49; vol. 7, pp. 359-60.
91. Turner, *The Negro in Pennsylvania,* p. 27. Emphasis added.
92. Copies of *Special Court for the Trial of Negroes in Chester County, 1762-1772,* as compiled by Gilbert Cope in the folder of the Historical Society of Chester County.
93. Cope, King v. Johnson.
94. Cope, King v. Sam and Cambridge; King v. Phobe; King v. Philip; King v. Prime.
95. Cope, King v. Martin; King v. Dick.
96. Cope.
97. Turner alleges that the law for the special courts for the trial of Negroes was "not universally applied at first. In 1703 a negro was tried for fornication before the Court of Quarter Sessions." M.S. Minutes Court of Quarter Sessions Bucks County, 1684-1739, p. 378. Turner, *The Negro in Pennsylvania,* p. 27, n. 29.
98. Cope.
99. Cope, King v. Phobe.
100. Cope, King v. Prime.
101. Cope, King v. Johnson.
102. Cope, King v. Martin.
103. Cope, King v. Dick.
104. Id.
105. Cope, King v. Sam and Cambridge.
106. *CROP,* vol. 2, pp. 421-22.
107. *CROP,* vol. 4, pp. 243-44.
108. Ibid., p. 244. Emphasis added.
109. Ibid., p. 259.
110. John F. Watson, *Annals of Philadelphia and Pennsylvania in the Olden Time* (Philadelphia: Edwin S. Stuart, 1884), p. 262.
111. Turner, *The Negro in Pennsylvania,* pp. 13, 68-69.
112. Edmundson's *Journal,* p. 61.
113. Peter M. Bergmen, *The Chronological History of The Negro in America* (New York: Harper and Row, 1969), p. 22.
114. Turner, *The Negro in Pennsylvania,* p. 66.
115. Ibid., p. 58.
116. See resolution of the 1693, 1696, 1712, 1713 Quaker Meetings. Turner, p. 66.
117. Bergman, *The Chronological History,* p. 22.
118. Turner, *The Negro in Pennsylvania,* p. 67.
119. *Statutes at Large,* vol. 2, p. 107.
120. Ibid., p. 283.
121. Ibid., pp. 543-44.

122. M.S. Board of Trade Papers, Proprietor IX, Q, pp. 39, 42.
123. Turner, *The Negro in Pennsylvania*, p. 5.
124. *Statutes at Large*, vol. 6, pp. 104-10.
125. Ibid., vol. 7, pp. 156, 159.
126. Ibid., vol. 8, pp. 330-32.
127. Turner, pp. 8-9. See also, p. 67. The motive of restriction refers to any goal—whether morally or racially based—to limit the number of blacks, rather than to raise revenue.
128. Turner, p. 63.
129. M.S. Yearly M.M., pp. 23-29 4th mo., 1758, as cited by Turner, pp. 73-74.
130. *Pennsylvania Laws*, vol. 1, p. 838. See note 3 on the experience in Rhode Island.
131. Ibid., pp. 839-40, section 4.
132. Jordan, *White Over Black*, p. 345.
133. *Pennsylvania Laws*, vol. 1, p. 840, section 5.
134. Id.
135. Ibid., p. 841, section 7.
136. Ibid., section 10.
137. Id.
138. Catterall, *Judicial Cases*, vol. 4, p. 245.
139. Robinson, *Slavery in the Structure of American Politics* (New York: Harcourt, Brace, Jovanovich, 1971), p. 30.
140. Catterall, *Judicial Cases*, vol. 4, p. 247.
141. Turner, p. 81.
142. Catterall, *Judicial Cases*, vol. 4, pp. 246-47; cf. Wilson v. Belinda, 3 S & R 396 at 400 (1817).
143. For a contrary presumption favoring slavery, see the Virginia case of Butterwood Nan (Hudgins v. Wright, Hen. & M., Va. 134 (1806) and also pp. 59-60. Cf. Prigg v. Pennsylvania, 41 U.S. (16 Pet.) 1849, particularly Justice McLean's opinion.
144. 10 Pa. Stat. at L. 67 (March 1, 1780).
145. Robinson, *Slavery in Politics*, p. 30.
146. Ibid., p. 31. The black population of Pennsylvania in 1790 was 6537 free Negroes and 3737 slaves; thus, a total of 10,274 blacks as compared with 424,099 whites. Turner, p. 253.
147. Robinson, *Slavery in Politics*, p. 31.
148. See unpublished monographs of Jennifer Johnson, University of Pennsylvania Law School, and Geraldine Segal, University of Pennsylvania, Department of Sociology.
149. Louis Filler, *The Crusade Against Slavery* (New York: Harper and Brothers, 1960), p. 23. See generally, *The Antislavery Argument*, by Pease and Pease (Indianapolis: Bobbs Merrill, 1965), pp. xxviii to l.
150. *Statutes at Large*, vol. 10, p. 462, section 2.
151. *Statutes at Large*, vol. 13, p. 52.
152. Ibid., section 1.
153. Commonwealth v. Chambre, 4 Dallas 143 (1794).
154. *Statutes at Large*, vol. 13, p. 52.
155. Ibid., p. 53.
156. Ibid., p. 56.

157. See *supra*, pp. 91-98.
158. For Georgia, see 1755 law "An Act for the Better Ordering and Governing Negroes and Other Slaves in this Province," discussed *supra*. For South Carolina, see 1740 law, discussed *supra*, p. 195.
159. Ibid.
160. Kalm, *Travels*, vol. 1, pp. 391, 392.
161. Turner, pp. 14-16.
162. Pennypacker, pp. 54-55.
163. *Statutes at Large*, vol. 2, p. 79.
164. *Statutes at Large*, vol. 4, p. 63.
165. Ibid., p. 64.
166. See section on Georgia, "Laws on the Hiring of Slaves," *supra*, p. 258.
167. Benjamin Quarles, *The Negro in the Making of America*, rev. ed. (New York: Collier Macmillan, 1969); Gunnar Myrdal, *An American Dilemma, The Negro Problem in a Modern Democracy* (New York: Harpers, 1944); Charles S. Magnum, Jr. *The Legal Status of the Negro* (Chapel Hill: University of North Carolina Press, 1940).
168. For New Jersey, see N.J. Statutes 29 sess I, p. 460; New York, see *supra*, p. 143, see also, Connecticut Acts in Laws (1796), p. 399, and Public Statutes (1808), p. 626.
169. Douglass, *Life and Times*, p. 608 (1884).

THE SETTING

1. As to the Rhode Island experience with slavery, see note 3, Pennsylvania.
2. One important example of this rarely exercised activism in favor of anti-slavery tenets was the Quock Walker decision, issued by Chief Justice Cushing for the Massachusetts Supreme Court in 1781. Quock (or Quork) Walker v. Jennison (the case is also known as Jennison v. Caldwell), Proc. Mass. Hist. Soc. (1873-1875), 296 (1781). See also Commonwealth v. Jennison, Proc. Mass. Hist. Soc. (1873-1875), 293 (1783) discussed at pp. 91-96 *supra*.
3. King's Bench: 12 George III A.D. (1771-1772) Lofft, 20 Howell's State Trials 1 (hereinafter How. St. Tr.).
4. Reginald Coupland, The British Anti-Slavery Movement (London, 1933), pp. 55-56.
5. Wylie Sypher, *Guinea's Captive Kings: British Anti-Slavery Literature of the 18th Century* (Chapel Hill: University of North Carolina Press, 1942), p. 63.
6. David Brion Davis, *The Problem of Slavery in the Age of Revolution 1770-1823* (Ithaca, N.Y.: Cornell University Press, 1975), p. 470.
7. The slaves from that expedition were sold to Spaniards.
8. Eric Williams, *Capitalism and Slavery*, 4th ed. (New York: Penguin Books, 1966), pp. 30-32.
9. The term "triangular trade" refers to the circular exchange established in the seventeenth and eighteenth centuries whereby England, and to some extent the North American colonies, supplied the exports and the ships; Africa provided the slaves; and the plantations produced the raw materials. A ship from England to Africa carried manufactured goods to exchange for slaves, who were traded in the colonies for raw materials. See ibid., pp. 51-84.

10. Ibid., pp. 123-24.

11. Thomas Clarkson, *An Essay on the Impolicy of the African Slave Trade* (Philadelphia: Bailey, 1788), p. 34, as quoted in Williams, *Capitalism and Slavery,* p. 120.

12. Quoted in Williams, *Capitalism and Slavery,* pp. 40-41. See also Elizabeth Donnan, ed., *Documents Illustrative of the History of the Slave Trade to America,* vol. 2 (Washington, D.C.: Carnegie Institution of Washington, 1930-1935), p. 45.

13. For example, the 1773 attempt by the Jamaican assembly to reduce the fear of slave rebellion by imposing a duty on each imported slave was condemned by the merchants of Liverpool, London, and Bristol and the Board of Trade; the colonial governor was reprimanded for failure to check efforts aimed at disrupting so beneficial a trade. Williams, *Capitalism and Slavery,* p. 41, citing Hof. C. Sess. Pop. Accounts and Papers 1795-1796 A&P 42, Series #100 Document 848, 1-21.

14. "Williamson's Liverpool Memorandum Book" (1753), cited by Gomer Williams, *History of the Liverpool Privateers and Letters of Marque* (London: Heinemann, 1897), pp. 472-73.

15. Williams, *Capitalism and Slavery,* p. 34.

16. J. Wallace, *A General & Descriptive History of the Ancient and Present State of the Town of Liverpool . . . together with a Circumstantial Account of the True Causes of its Extensive African Trade* (Liverpool, 1795), pp. 229-30, cited by Williams, *Capitalism and Slavery,* p. 34.

17. Williams, *History of the Liverpool Privateers,* p. 473.

18. Williams, *Capitalism and Slavery,* pp. 47-48.

19. Ibid., p. 45.

20. Williams, *History of the Liverpool Privateers,* p. 475.

21. Ibid., p. 476.

22. T. F. Martin, "Pleadings Rules at Common Law," 25 Law Q. Rev. 284 (1909); John A. Inglis, "Eighteenth Century Pleading," 19 Jurid. Rev. 42 (1907); A. Reppy, "Development of the Common Law Forms of Action," 22 Brooklyn L. Rev. 179 (1956).

23. 2 Rushworth 468 (1569).

24. Id.

25. 2 Salkeld 666 (no date officially reported, but probably 1706). See Helen Catterall, ed., *Judicial Cases Concerning American Slavery and the Negro,* vol. 1 (Washington, D.C.: Negro University Press, 1926), p. 37.

26. 2 Levinz 201, Trin. (1677), also reported with variation in 3 Keble 785.

27. A *trover* is an action to recover for wrongful interference with or detention of the goods of another, 3 Steph. Comm. 425; and also a common law remedy to recover the value of personal chattels wrongfully converted by another, 1 Burr 3.

It should be noted that in Levinz the action was recorded as being for 200 blacks. Keble and the original records list the number involved to be 10. See Keble 785 and Note to Somersett v. Stuart, 20 How. St. Tr. 1 at 51.

28. 2 Levinz 201, Trin. (1677).

29. 3 Keble 785 (1677).

30. 2 Levinz 201, Trin. (1677).

31. See Davis, *The Problem of Slavery,* pp. 469-522.

32. Ibid., pp. 482-88.
33. *Black's Law Dictionary,* 4th ed., p. 1741.
34. Winthrop Jordan, *White Over Black* (Chapel Hill: University of North Carolina Press, 1968), p. 49.
35. See argument by Francis Hargrave in Sommersett, 20 How. St. Tr. 1 at 37-48, discussed *infra,* in section on "Hargrave's Arguments in Behalf of Sommersett."
36. Argument by Hargrave, 20 How. St. Tr. 1 at 37, 40.
37. Jordan, *White Over Black,* p. 49.
38. 1 Vernon 453 (1687).
39. 1 Ld. Raym. 147 (1694).
40. Id.
41. See chapters on Virginia and Massachusetts.
42. 3 Ld. Raym. 129 (1696, 1697).
43. Id., p. 133.
44. Carthew 397 (1696, 1697).
45. 2 Salkeld 666.
46. Id.
47. The final disposition of the case was not recorded.
48. 2 Salkeld 666, Pasch 2 Ld. Raym. 1274 (1706).
49. 2 Ld. Raym. 1274 (1706).
50. 33 Dict. of Dec. 14547 (1729).
51. Thomas Clarkson, *History of the Rise, Progress, & Accomplishment of the Abolition of the African Slave Trade By the British Parliament* (Philadelphia: James P. Parke, 1808), pp. 54-65, quoted by Harold W. Horowitz and Kenneth L. Karst, eds., *Law, Lawyers and Social Change* (New York: Bobbs Merrill Co., 1969), pp. 6-10.
52. Ambler 75 (1749).
53. Id., p. 76.
54. 2 Salkeld 666, Pasch. (1706).
55. Ambler 77 (1749).
56. 2 Eden 125 (1762).
57. Id., p. 126.
58. The abolitionist movement, of course, was critical to Sommersett's victory, but the subtlety and limitations of its beliefs are often not appreciated. For example, much of the antislavery literature of the eighteenth century tended to characterize the slave as the "noble negro," a prince unjustly enslaved, an individual who was superior to all, even his master; yet, as Professor Sypher suggests, this literature implied that the average, ordinary black could be justly enslaved. Sypher, *Guinea's Captive Kings,* pp. 157-58, 162-63, 186-88, 217-19.
59. Davis, *The Problem of Slavery,* p. 391.
60. Ibid., p. 392. See also Prince Hoare, *Memoirs of Granville Sharp Esq. Composed From His Own Manuscripts* (London: H. Colburn, 1820), pp. 32-37, 38-40.
61. William Blackstone, *Commentaries on the Laws of England,* vol. 1 (Oxford, 1765), p. 123; vol. 3 (1768-1769), as quoted in Davis, *The Problem of Slavery,* p. 485. Emphasis added.
62. Blackstone, *Commentaries,* 1st ed., vol. 1, pp. 412-13. Blackstone expressed

these views in letters dated February 20 and May 25, 1767. See Davis, *The Problem of Slavery*, p. 486, n. 29.

63. (London: Benjamin White and Robert Horsefield, 1769), pp. 10-41.
64. Davis, *The Problem of Slavery*, p. 375.
65. Noted in Horowitz and Karst, *Law, Lawyers and Social Change*, pp. 9-10. See also Edward Lascelles, *Granville Sharp and the Freedom of Slaves in England* (London: Oxford University Press, 1928), p. 29.
66. Hoare, *Memoirs of Granville Sharp*, pp. 78-92.

THE CASE OF JAMES SOMMERSETT: A NEGRO

1. 20 How. St. Tr. 1 at 3.
2. Id., pp. 19-20, 22.
3. Id., p. 23.
4. 20 How. St. Tr. 48. Both sides debated what type of relationships established abroad should be enforced automatically by English courts. As counsel for Sommersett, Hargrave argued on pragmatic grounds that the common law's abhorrence for slavery prevented the importation of foreign bondage: "To prevent the revival of domestic slavery effectually, its introduction must be resisted universally, without regard to the place of its commencement; and therefore in the instance of slavery, the *lex loci* must yield to the municipal law." Id., p. 60. Hargrave's co-counsel, Mr. Davy, buttressed this position when he suggested that English courts should not enforce unnatural relations, which he defined as immoral obligations. Slavery was clearly such an immoral obligation. Id., pp. 77-79.

  This distinction between natural and unnatural relations was echoed in the presentation by another of Sommersett's lawyers, Mr. Alleyne. Alleyne's argument has not been included in the main text because, for the most part, his ideas are already summarized in the other sections. Alleyne identified slavery as a "municipal relation," not a "natural" relation. Slavery was "therefore confined to certain places, and necessarily dropt by passage into a country where such municipal regulations do not subsist." Id., p. 68.

  In response, Mr. Dunning, counsel for Stuart, maintained that all natural relations should be enforced if the *relation* was recognized in England; the particular method by which that relation commenced abroad did not need to be legal in England for the relationship to be sanctioned domestically. Moreover, he accepted a broad definition of "natural relation" which included slavery. Id., pp. 73-76. Thus, if the slave relation merely found precedent in the English law of villenage, slavery should be protected even though its means of commencement was not legal in England.
5. Id., p. 24.
6. Discussion by Mr. Dunning, id., p. 74.
7. Id., p. 24.
8. Id., pp. 26-27.
9. Thomas Jefferson shared Hargrave's perceptions of the malevolent consequences of slavery upon white masters. He wrote: "There must doubtless be an unhappy influence on the manners of our people produced by the existence of slavery among us. The whole commerce between master and slave is

a perpetual exercise of the most boisterous passions, the most unremitting despotism on the one part, and degrading submissions on the other. Our children see this, and learn to imitate it; for man is an imitative animal. This quality is the germ of all education in him. From his cradle to his grave he is learning to do what he sees others do. If a parent could find no motive either in his philanthropy or his self-love, for restraining the intemperance of passion towards his slave, it should always be a sufficient one that his child is present. But generally it is not sufficient. The parent storms, the child looks on, catches the lineaments of wrath, puts on the same airs in the circle of smaller slaves, gives a loose to the worst of passions, and thus nursed, educated, and daily exercised in tyranny, cannot but be stamped by it with odious peculiarities. The man must be a prodigy who can retain his manners and morals undepraved by such circumstances. And with what execration should the statesman be loaded, who, permitting one half the citizens thus to trample on the rights of the other, transforms those into despots, and these into enemies, destroys the morals of the one part, and the *amor patriae* of the other. For if a slave can have a country in this world, it must be any other in preference to that in which he is born to live and labor for another; in which he must lock up the faculties of his nature, contribute as far as depends on his individual endeavors to the evanishment of the human race, or entail his own miserable condition on the endless generations proceeding from him. With the morals of the people, their industry also is destroyed. For in a warm climate, no man will labor for himself who can make another labor for him. This is so true, that of the proprietors of slaves a very small proportion indeed are ever seen to labor. And can the liberties of a nation be thought secure when we have removed their only firm basis, a conviction in the minds of the people that these liberties are of the gift of God? That they are not to be violated but with his wrath? Indeed I tremble for my country when I reflect that God is just; that his justice cannot sleep forever; that considering numbers, nature and natural means only, a revolution of the wheel of fortune, an exchange of situation is among possible events; that it may become probable by supernatural interference! The Almighty has no attribute which can take side with us in such a contest. But it is impossible to be temperate and to pursue this subject through the various considerations of policy, of morals, of history natural and civil. We must be contented to hope they will force their way into every one's mind. I think a change already perceptible, since the origin of the present revolution. The spirit of the master is abating, that of the slave rising from the dust, his condition mollifying the way I hope preparing, under the auspices of heaven, for a total emancipation, and that this is disposed, in the order of events, to be with the consent of the masters, rather than by their extirpation." Thomas Jefferson, *Notes on the State of Virginia* (New York: Harpers, 1964), pp. 155-56.

10. 20 How. St. Tr. 1 at 30. Hargrave was referring approvingly to John Locke's argument against slavery.
11. Id., p. 33.
12. David Brion Davis, *The Problem of Slavery in the Age of Revolution 1770-1823* (Ithaca, N.Y.: Cornell University Press, 1975), p. 483.
13. 20 How. St. Tr. 1 at 36.
14. Id., p. 40.

15. Id., pp. 41-47.
16. Id., p. 41.
17. Id., p. 48.
18. Davis, *The Problem of Slavery*, p. 483.
19. 20 How. St. Tr. 1 at 48.
20. At the core of Hargrave's argument against slavery by contract lay a distinction between ordinary wage contracts and the more pernicious type of slave "contracts" being challenged by Sommersett. Hargrave argued that although the courts might enforce a contract to serve for life, this was the *"ne plus ultra* of servitude by contract in England." The courts, he said, "will not allow the servant to invest the master with the arbitrary power of correcting, imprisoning or allienating him; it will not permit him to renounce the capacity of acquiring and enjoying property, or to transmit a contract of service to his issue. In other words, it will not permit the servant to incorporate into his contract the ingredients of slavery." Id., p. 50. Thus, Hargrave distinguished those legal protections applied to wage contracts from the absolute subjugation of black slaves. The plight of white workers did not provide judicial precedent for slavery.

    Mr. Alleyne developed this distinction between regular contracts and slave contracts by pointing to the impossibility of any adequate consideration for a slave's "agreement" to enter into bondage. He observed that "in all contracts there must be power on one side to give, on the other to receive; and a competent consideration. Now, what power can there be in any man to dispose of all the rights vested by nature and society in him and his descendants? He cannot consent to part with them, without ceasing to be a man; for they immediately flow from, and are essential to, his condition as such. . . . With respect to consideration, what shall be adequate?" Id., p. 68.

    Hargrave's distinction probably improved the likelihood of judicial acceptance of their legal position in the trial. Slavery did not find precedent in judicial treatment of poor whites and, conversely, the abolition of slavery did not threaten those laws regulating whites; frequently no substantive differences existed between the paltry wages some white workers received and the minimal sustenance provided for slaves. See Davis, *The Problem of Slavery*, pp. 489-501. Indeed, John Dunning, counsel for Stuart, noted this possible inconsistency between abolitionists' arguments for slaves and those for white workers when he observed that many "idle or desolate persons of various ranks and denominations" were forced by the courts to work and live much like a slave. 20 How. St. Tr. 1 at 75-76.
21. 20 How. St. Tr. 1 at 50.
22. 20 How. St. Tr. 1 at 48.
23. See note 70.
24. See Pearne v. Lisle, Ambler 75 (1749), discussed *supra*, pp. 327-329.
25. 20 How. St. Tr. 1 at 50.
26. The English courts have generally been more deferential to the legislative branch than their American counterparts. See Brian Abel Smith and Robert Stevens, *Lawyers and the Courts: A Sociological Study of the English Legal System 1850-1965* (London: Heinemann, 1967), pp. 8-9, cited by Davis, *The Problem of Slavery*, pp. 470-71.
27. Id., pp. 59-60.

28. Id., p. 60. Hargrave rejected the suggestion that the importation of foreign slaves only touched the interests of foreign countries: "Our law prohibits the commencement of domestic slavery in England; because it disapproves of slavery, and considers it operation as dangerous and destructive to the whole community. But would not this prohibition be wholly ineffectual, if slavery could be introduced from a foreign country? In the course of time, though perhaps in a progress less rapid, would not domestic slavery become as general, and be as completely revived in England by introduction from our colonies and from foreign countries, as if it was permitted to revive by commencement here; and would not the same inconveniences follow?" Id.

29. Id., p. 64.

30. Id.

31. Dunning and Wallace, counselors for Stuart, each compared the deportation of Sommersett to the enforcement of a normal service contract. See id., pp. 74-76 (Dunning), p. 70 (Wallace). The sanctioning of slavery as a contract for services had found some legal support in Chamberlaine v. Harvey, 1 Ld. Raym. 146 (1696, 1697). Although the court in that case prevented the defendant's reenslavement, it added that no trespass would lie for the taking away a man generally, but that there might be a special action of trespass for taking a servant, *er quod servitium amisit.* id. Dunning relied on this precedent during his presentation when he stressed:

> "[M]y argument does not require trover should lie, as for recovering of property, nor trespass [because] there is a form of action, the writ Per Quod Servitium Amisit, for loss of service, which the court would have recognized [in *Chamberlaine*]; if they allowed [in *Chamberlaine*] the means of suing a right, they allowed the right. The opinion cited, to prove the negroes free on coming hither, only declares them not saleable. . . ." Id., p. 76.

32. Noted in Horowitz and Karst, *Law, Lawyers and Social Change,* pp. 9-10.

33. William Holdsworth as quoted in Davis, *The Problem of Slavery,* p. 493.

34. Humphry W. Woolrych, *Lives of Eminent Sergeants-At-Law of the English Bar* (London: W. H. Allen & Co., 1869) p. 617, cited in Horowitz and Karst, *Law, Lawyers and Social Change,* p. 20.

35. The American Bar Association's *Canon of Ethics,* however, is similar to Sharp's view. "No lawyer is obliged to act either as advisor or advocate for every person who may wish to become his client." Horowitz and Karst, *Law, Lawyers and Social Change,* p. 21. See also H. Drinker, *Legal Ethics* (1953), pp. 23-30; Rostow, "The Lawyer and His Client," 48 A.B.A.J. 25, 29 (1962).

36. 20 How. St. Tr. 1 at 71.

37. See note 97, *supra.*

38. 20 How. St. Tr. 1 at 72.

39. Of course, Hargrave had given reasons why Sommersett's enslavement could not be justified as criminal punishment, even if it could have been proved that a criminal conviction was the basis of his enslavement. Unlike slavery resulting from a criminal conviction, racial enslavement (such as Sommersett's) required personal or family service: as distinguished from work owed to the state, and never extended to the offender's issue. Id., pp. 30-31.

40. Id., p. 73.

41. Id.

42. Id.
43. Id., pp. 74-75.
44. Id., p. 77.
45. 20 How. St. Tr. 1 at 78.
46. See note 70.
47. 20 How. St. Tr. 1 at 78.
48. Id., p. 79.
49. See pp. 327-329 *supra*.
50. William Holdsworth, *Some Makers of English Law* (Cambridge: Cambridge University Press, 1938), pp. 161-62.
51. While there appears to be no official citation, this case is reported in C. H. S. Fifoot, *Lord Mansfield* (Oxford: Clarendon Press, 1936), p. 41.
52. See discussion in F. Birkenhead, *Fourteen English Judges* (London: Cassell and Co., 1926), p. 180.
53. 1 William and Mary 51 C. 18.
54. *Parliament History*, vol. 16, p. 316, as cited by J. Holliday, *The Life of William, late Earl of Mansfield* (London: printed for P. Elmsley, 1797), pp. 260-61.
55. 1 Cow 382 (1776).
56. Id., pp. 384, 388.
57. Lord Campbell, *The Lives of the Chief Justices of England,* vol. 3 (Boston: Estes & Lauriat, 1873), p. 365.
58. 20 How. St. Tr. 1 at 79.
59. Id.
60. Id., p. 80.
61. Id., pp. 81-82.
62. Id., p. 79.
63. Id., p. 82; for an excellent analysis of Sommersett see; William M. Wiecek, *Somerset: Lord Mansfield and the Legitimacy of Slavery in the Anglo-American World,* 42 University of Chicago Law Review 86 (1974).

THE LEGACY OF SOMMERSETT

1. I Term R. 130 n. (1785).
2. 33 Dict. of Dec. 14545 (1778).
3. Id., p. 14549.
4. 4 Douglass K.B. 300 (1785).
5. Id., pp. 301-2.
6. III Bos. and Pul. 69 (1802).
7. 2 Hagg. Adm. 94 (1827).
8. 3 Bos. and Pul. 73-74 (1802).
9. 2 Hagg. Adm. at 105.
10. Id., pp. 126-28.
11. Helen Catterall, ed., *Judicial Cases Concerning American Slavery and the Negro,* vol. 1 (Washington, D.C.: Negro University Press, 1926), p. 37.
12. W. W. Story, ed., *Life of Justice Story* I (Boston, 1851), pp. 552 *et seq.;* Catterall, *Judicial Cases* I, pp. 36-37.
13. David Brion Davis, *The Problem of Slavery in the Age of Revolution 1770-1823* (Ithaca, N.Y.: Cornell University Press, 1975), pp. 500-501.

14. Reginald Coupland, *The Empire in These Days* (London, 1935), p. 264; Reginald Wilberforce, *Life of Wilberforce*, vol. 3 (New York: Randolph, 1889), p. 295; Eric Williams, *Capitalism and Slavery*, 4th ed. (New York: Penguin Books, 1966), p. 178.

15. Sir G. Stephen, *Anti-Slavery Recollections* (London, 1854), pp. 77, 79.

16. *Hansard, Parliamentary Debates* IX, pp. 143-44 (March 17, 1807); *Hansard, New Series* XIX 1469, quoted by Lord Seaford June 23, 1828 as cited by Williams, *Capitalism and Slavery*, p. 182.

17. Williams, *Capitalism and Slavery*, p. 178; Davis, *The Problem of Slavery*, p. 446.

18. *Hansard* VIII, pp. 238-39 (December 30, 1806); Williams, *Capitalism and Slavery*, p. 149.

19. *House of Commons Sess. Papers Report on the Commercial State of the West India Colonies*, 1307, 4-6; *Hansard* IX, p. 98. Hibbert, March 12, 1807; Williams, *Capitalism and Slavery*, p. 149.

20. Williams, *Capitalism and Slavery*, p. 150.

21. Quotation of Buxton, *Hansard, New Series* IX, pp. 265, 266 (May 15, 1823); Williams, *Capitalism and Slavery*, p. 182.

22. Williams, *Capitalism and Slavery*, pp. 197-98.

23. Ibid., p. 205.

24. Acts III and IV William IV. Cf. Catterall, *Judicial Cases I*, p. 8.

25. W. E. P. Ward, *The Royal Navy and the Slavers: The Suppression of the Atlantic Slave Trade* (New York: Schocken, 1969), p. 124.

26. 3 Knapp 155 (1835).

THE DECLARATION OF INDEPENDENCE

1. The term "self-evident lie" was used by Abraham Lincoln in a letter to Hon. George Robertson in 1855 in John G. Nicolay and John Hay, *Abraham Lincoln A. History*, vol. 1 (New York: The Century Co., 1890), pp. 390-91. Originally, Senator John Pettit of Indiana in his "forcible declaration . . . upon the floor of the United States Senate . . . [called] The Declaration of Independence . . . a "self-evident lie. . . ." See Roy P. Basler, ed., *The Collected Works of Abraham Lincoln* (New Brunswick, N.J.: Rutgers University Press, 1953), vol. 3, pp. 301-2, vol. 2, pp. 275, 283.

2. See generally Benjamin Quarles, *The Negro in the American Revolution* (New York: The Norton Library, W. W. Norton and Company, Inc., 1973).

3. "The Meaning of the Fourth of July to the Negro, 1852," in Philip S. Foner, ed., *The Life and Writings of Frederick Douglass* (New York: International Publishers, 1950), vol. 2, p. 189.

4. Francis Berkeley, *Dunmore's Proclamation of Emancipation* (The Tracy W. McGregor Library, University of Virginia, 1941); Sidney Kaplan, *The Black Presence in the Era of the American Revolution 1770-1800* (Washington: New York Graphic Society Ltd. in association with the Smithsonian Institution Press, 1973), p. 62; Quarles, *The Negro in the American Revolution*, ch. 2.

5. Quarles, *The Negro in the American Revolution*, p. vii.

6. See William C. Nell, *The Colored Patriots of the American Revolution* . . .

with an introduction by Harriet Beecher Stowe (New York: Arno Press and the New York Times, 1968), p. 5.

7. See Quarles, *The Negro in the American Revolution*, pp. vii-x; 71-75, 80-93. See also Kaplan, *The Black Presence in the Era of the American Revolution*, pp. 15-21, 32, 41, 55.

8. See Kaplan, *The Black Presence in the Era of the American Revolution*, pp. 27-38.

9. As quoted in Carl Becker, *The Declaration of Independence, A Study in the History of Political Ideas* (New York: Alfred A. Knopf, 1942), p. 30.

10. As quoted in Catherine Drinker Bowen, *John Adams and the American Revolution* (Boston: Little, Brown, 1950), p. xiv; see also Charles Francis Adams, *The Works of John Adams* (Boston: Little, Brown, 1856), vol. x, pp. 182, 282.

11. Becker, *The Declaration of Independence*, p. 81.

12. Ibid., p. 80.

13. Donald L. Robinson, *Slavery in the Structure of American Politics 1765-1820* (New York: Harcourt Brace Jovanovich, Inc., 1971), p. 70.

14. Stephen Hopkins, "The Rights of Colonies Examined," Providence, 1765, in Bernard Bailyn, ed., *Pamphlets of the American Revolution 1750-1776* (Cambridge, Mass.: The Belknap Press of Harvard University Press, 1965), vol. 1, p. 521.

15. Robinson, *Slavery in the Structure of American Politics*, pp. 57-58, 462 n. 13; see also Lorenzo J. Greene, *The Negro in Colonial New England, 1620-1776* (New York: Columbia University Press, 1942), pp. 24-25; Bernhard Knollenberg, *Origin of The American Revolution* (New York: Macmillan Co., 1960), pp. 146-47; James Pope-Hennessy, *Sins of the Fathers* (New York: Alfred A. Knopf, 1968), ch. 2; Clinton L. Rossiter, *Seedtime of the Republic* (New York: Harcourt, Brace and Co., 1953), pp. 66-67, 80-81; and Eric Williams, *Capitalism and Slavery* (Chapel Hill: University of North Carolina Press, 1944), ch. 3. See an interesting section of the play *1776* by Peter Stone and Sherman Edwards, *1776* (New York: Viking Press, 1969), pp. 118-21, which is devoted to the debate in Congress concerning the slavery proviso originally inserted by Jefferson. John Adams complained that Rutledge and the South were so economy-oriented, "There's more to this than a filthy purse-string, Rutledge. It's an offense against man and God." To which Rutledge replied: "Is it really . . . ? Then what's that I smell floatin' down from the North— Could it be the aroma of hy-procisy? For who holds the other end of that filthy purse-string, Mr. Adams. Our Northern brethren are feeling a bit tender toward our slaves. They don't keep slaves, no-o, but they're willin' to be considerable carriers of slaves—to others. They are willin', for the shillin'—"

16. John Hope Franklin, *From Slavery to Freedom*, 4th ed. (New York: Alfred A. Knopf, 1974), p. 86.

17. As quoted in B. J. Lossing, *Biographical Sketches of Signers of the Declaration of Independence* (New York: George F. Cooledge & Brothers, 1848), p. 245.

18. Winthrop D. Jordan, *White Over Black* (Chapel Hill: University of North Carolina Press, 1968), p. 289; see Carl Becker, *The Declaration of Independence*, ch. 2; J. W. Gough, ed., *The Second Treatise of Government by*

John Locke (New York: The Macmillan Company, 1956); and Peter Laslett, ed., *John Locke: Two Treatises of Government* (Cambridge: Cambridge University Press, 1963).

19. Lillian B. Miller, *"The Dye is Now Cast": The Road to American Independence, 1774-1776* (Washington: Smithsonian Institution Press, 1975), p. 3.

20. Ibid.

21. Ibid.

22. Ibid. (pre-title page)

23. See Bailyn, *Pamphlets,* vol. 1, p. 507.

24. As quoted in Bernard Bailyn, *The Ideological Origins of the American Revolution* (Cambridge, Mass.: The Belknap Press of Harvard University Press, 1971), pp. 232-33.

25. Ibid., p. 233.

26. John Adams in "Novanglus," in Charles Francis Adams, *The Works of John Adams* (Boston: Charles C. Little and James Brown, 1851), vol. 4, p. 28.

27. See Henry Steele Commager, ed., *Documents of American History,* 8th ed. (New York: Appleton-Century-Crofts, Meredith Corporation, 1968), p. 92; see also C. J. Stille, *Life and Times of John Dickinson,* vol. 1, p. 353 ff, and Appendix IV concerning the authorship of the Declaration; C. H. Van Tyne, *The War of Independence: American Phase.* (Cambridge: The Riverside Press, 1929), p. 295.

28. See "Taxation No Tyranny," in *The Works of Samuel Johnson* (Oxford: Talboys and Wheeler, 1825), vol. 6, p. 262.

29. As quoted in Lillian B. Miller, *"The Dye is Now Cast,"* p. 163.

30. See James Otis, "The Rights of the British Colonies Asserted and Proved," in Bailyn, *Pamphlets,* vol. 1, p. 408.

31. Ibid., p. 439.

32. Ibid.

33. *The Journal of Negro History,* reprint (Washington, D.C. United Publishing Corporation, 1969), vol. 2, p. 84. Benezet himself noted that the date of the letter was "about the year 1758." See generally Anthony Benezet and John Wesley, *Views of American Slavery* (New York: Arno Press & The New York Times, 1969). See Wilson Armistead, *Anthony Benezet* (London: A. W. Bennett, 1859), p. 29.

34. George S. Brookes, *Friend Anthony Benezet* (Philadelphia: University of Pennsylvania Press, 1937), pp. 443-444. See generally Armistead, *Anthony Benezet,* pp. 79-80.

35. Brookes, *Friend Anthony Benezet,* p. 443.

36. "A Forensic Dispute on The Legality of Enslaving the Africans, held at the public Commencement in Cambridge, New-England, July 21st, 1773. By two candidates for the Bachelors Degree" (Boston: John Boyle, 1773).

37. Ibid., pp. 4-6. Old English spelling has been corrected to current usage.

38. Samuel Hopkins, "A Dialogue Concerning the Slavery of the Africans, showing it to be the duty and interest of the American colonies to emancipate all the African slaves, with an Address to the owners of Such Slaves," in Samuel Hopkins, *Timely Articles on Slavery* (Miami, Fla.: Mnemosyne Publishing Inc., 1969).

39. As quoted in Kaplan, *The Black Presence in the Era of the American Revolution,* pp. 13-14.

40. For purposes of convenience, we have referred to the draft mentioning the international slave trade as July 2, because that appears to be the day when it was considered and discarded. It was first written in June by Jefferson. See Julian Boyd, ed., *The Papers of Thomas Jefferson* (Princeton, N.J.: Princeton University Press, 1950), vol. 1, pp. 413-17, 426, 427 n. See generally Carl Becker, *The Declaration of Independence,* ch. 4, p. 141; Julian P. Boyd, *The Declaration of Independence: The Evolution of the Text* (Princeton, 1945), pp. 18-22; John Hazelton, *The Declaration of Independence: Its History* (New York: Dodd, Mead, 1906), pp. 306-42.

41. See Becker, *The Declaration of Independence,* p. 135; Boyd, *The Papers of Thomas Jefferson,* vol. 1, p. 414.

42. See Becker, *The Declaration of Independence,* p. 151; Boyd, id. It is not exactly certain when Jefferson first finished his first draft and submitted it to Benjamin Franklin. See Becker, pp. 137-41, 151; Boyd, pp. 413-17, 427 n; Boyd, *The Declaration of Independence,* pp. 28-38; and Hazelton, *The Declaration of Independence,* pp. 306-42.

43. Becker, *The Declaration of Independence,* p. 135; Boyd, *The Papers of Thomas Jefferson,* vol. 1, p. 414.

44. Adams disagreed that Jefferson was given this responsibility, but instead asserted that he and Jefferson were appointed as a subcommittee to draw up the draft "in form." Becker, *The Declaration of Independence,* p. 135.

45. See Boyd, *The Papers of Thomas Jefferson,* vol. 1, pp. 317-18, 426; see also Becker, pp. 147, 166-67, 180-81. As to Jefferson's "phillipic against slavery" John Adams later said:

> I was delighted with its high tone and the flights of oratory with which it abounded, especially that concerning negro slavery, which, though I knew his Southern brethren would never suffer to pass in Congress, I certainly never would oppose . . . Congress cut off about a quarter of it, as I expected they would; but they obliterated some of the best of it, and left all that was exceptionable, if anything in it was. I have long wondered that the original draught has not been published. I suppose the reason is, the vehement philipic against negro slavery.

See Charles Francis Adams, ed., *The Works of John Adams* (Boston: Charles C. Little, and James Brown, 1850), vol. 2, p. 514.

46. See Higginbotham, *Slavery and the Constitution,* unpublished monograph, debates on the international slave trade at the Constitutional Convention, p. 33 and generally pp. 28-47.

47. See p. 372 *supra.*

48. See also Boyd, *Papers,* vol. 1, p. 318.

49. See Winthrop Jordan, *White Over Black,* Ch. 12, p. 430.

50. Boyd, *Papers,* pp. 314-15.

51. As quoted in Hazelton, *The Declaration of Independence,* p. 209.

52. The complete advertisement read as follows:

[7 September 1769]

Run away from the subscriber in *Albemarle,* a Mulatto slave called Sandy, about 35 years of age, his stature is rather low, inclining to corpulence, and his complexion light; he is a shoemaker by trade, in which he uses his left hand principally, can do coarse carpenters work, and is something of a horse jockey; he is greatly addicted to drink, and when drunk is insolent and disorderly, in his conversation he swears much, and his behaviour is artful and knavish. He took with him a white horse, much scarred with traces, of which it is expected he will endeavour to dispose; he also carried his shoemakers tools, and will probably endeavour to get employment that way. Whoever conveys the said slave to me in *Albemarle,* shall have 40 s. reward, if taken up within the county, 4 l. if elsewhere within the colony, and 10 l. if in any other colony, from

THOMAS JEFFERSON

Printed from *Virginia Gazette* (Purdie & Dixon), 14 Sept. 1769. (The Advertisement first appeared in the preceding issue, 7 Sept., but the text is not available there because of mutilation). Thomas Jefferson's comments on the deletion of the July 2nd condemnation of the international slave trade was:

What a stupendous, what an incomprehensible machine is man! He can endure toil, famine, stripes, imprisonment and death itself in vindication of his own liberty—and the next moment be deaf to all those motives whose power supported him through his trial, and inflict on his fellow men a bondage . . . which he rose in rebellion to oppose! . . . Nothing is more certainly written in the book of fate than that these people are to be free!

As quoted in Cornel Lengyel, *Four Days in July* (New York: Doubleday, 1958), p. 248.

53. Thomas Jefferson, *Notes on the State of Virginia* (New York: Harper and Row. 1964), p. 156; In two paragraphs John Hope Franklin captured the essence of Jefferson and his enigma on slavery:

As a large slaveholder, Jefferson knew well the interests of those who held men in bondage. As a man of the Enlightenment, he had a deep appreciation of the meaning of freedom as a state of existence that could scarcely be determined on the basis of class or race. As a very sensitive human being, he knew the warmth and depth of a personal relationship that could indeed transcend race, as his personal servant, Isaac, has told us. That he had serious reservations about slavery was attested by his early, futile efforts, in 1769, to change the Virginia law of manumission to facilitate the master's emancipation of a slave. How deeply he regretted his failure we do not know.

For although Jefferson insisted he was strongly anti-slavery, his antipathy toward the institution never took him to the point of freeing his own slaves or of using his enormous prestige to oppose slavery unequivocally in word or deed. His status as a large slaveholder and his constant preoccupation with financial matters led him, on occasion, to sell his slaves to pay off his debts and blurred the distinction between him and his fellow slaveholders who generally regarded capital in slaves as more important than Revolutionary ideology.

John Hope Franklin, *Racial Equality in America* (Chicago: The University of Chicago Press, 1976), pp. 12-13, 14-15.

54. Benjamin N. Cardozo, *The Nature of the Judicial Process* (New Haven: Yale University Press, 1932), p. 51.

55. Louis H. Pollak, *The Constitution and the Supreme Court: A Documentary History* (New York: World Publishing Company, Meridian Books, 1968), vol. 1, pp. 16-17.

56. See Charles A. Miller, "Constitutional Law and the Rhetoric of Race," in Donald Fleming and Bernard Bailyn, ed., *Perspectives in American History* (Cambridge, Mass.: Charles Warren Center for Studies in American History, 1971), vol. 5, p. 148. The term "moral overstrain" appears in Gunnar Myrdal, *An American Dilemma* (New York: Harper & Row, 1944), p. 21. He states: "The conflict in the American concept of law and order is only one side of the 'moral overstrain' of the nation. American believes in and aspires to something much higher than its plane of actual life. The subordinate position of Negroes is perhaps the most glaring conflict in the American conscience and the greatest unsolved task for American democracy." Id. "The Negro problem in America would be of a different nature, and, indeed, would be simpler to handle scientifically, if the moral conflict raged only between valuations held by different persons and groups of persons. The essence of the moral situation is, however, that the conflicting valuations are also held by the same person. *The moral struggle goes on within people and not only between them. As people's valuations are conflicting, behavior normally becomes a moral compromise. There are no homogeneous 'attitudes' behind human behavior but a mesh of struggling inclinations, interests, and ideals, some held conscious and some suppressed for long intervals but all active in bending behavior in their direction.*" Ibid., pp. XLVII-XLVIII.

57. William Lloyd Garrison, *Selections from the Writings and Speeches of William Lloyd Garrison* (New York: The New American Library, 1969), pp. 62-63.

58. As quoted in Jordan, *White Over Black,* p. 290.

59. Ibid.

60. Frederick Douglass, "The Meaning of the Fourth of July to the Negro, 1852," in Philip E. Foner, ed., *The Life and Writings of Frederick Douglass* (New York: International Publishers, 1950), vol. 2, p. 192.

61. See Truman Nelson, ed., *Documents of Upheaval* (New York: American Century Series, Hill and Wang, 1969), p. 6.

62. See David Walker, *Walker's Appeal in Four Articles* (New York: Arno Press and the New York Times, 1969), pp. 27, 76.

63. See Carter G. Woodson, ed., *The Mind of the Negro as Reflected in Letters Written During the Crisis 1800-1860* (New York: Negro Universities Press, repr. 1969), p. 226.

64. The Amistad Case, 40 U.S. (15 Pet.) 518 (1841); see *Argument of John Quincy Adams, Before The Supreme Court of the United States, Appellants, v. Cingue, and Others, Africans, Captured in the Schooner Amistad, by Lieut. Gedney* reprint (New York: Negro Universities Press, 1969), p. 89.

65. See Roy P. Basler, ed., *The Collected Works of Abraham Lincoln* (New Brunswick, N.J.: Rutgers University Press, 1953), vol. 2, p. 406; As to Taney see p. 406 n. 11.

66. Charles Sumner to The American Antislavery Society at its Final Meeting, April 8, 1870, in *The Works of Charles Sumner* (Boston: Lee and Shepard, 1880), vol. 13, pp. 375-76.

67. Philip S. Foner, ed., *The Voice of Black America: Major Speeches by Negroes*

in the United States, 1797-1971 (New York: Simon and Schuster, 1972), p. 974.
68. "The Crisis in American Justice," New York (NAACP Legal Defense and Educational Fund), 1970. Address delivered May 15, 1970; unpaged.
69. 42 U.S.C. § 2000a; Pub. L. 88-352, Title II, § 201, July 2, 1964, 78 Stat. 243.
70. 42 U.S.C. § 2000e-2, (a)(1); Pub. L. 88-352, Title VII, § 703, July 2, 1964, 78 Stat. 255, as amended March 24, 1972, Pub. L. 92-261, 86 Stat. 103.

APPENDIX

1. Abbott E. Smith, *Colonists in Bondage* (Chapel Hill: University of North Carolina Press, 1947), p. 18.
2. Eric Williams, *Capitalism and Slavery* (Chapel Hill: University of North Carolina Press, 1944), p. 14.
3. Ibid., p. 15.
4. Smith, *Colonists,* ch. 1.

INDEX

Abercorn, Georgia, 223
Abolition Committee, England, 364
Abolition movement: in Massachusetts, 82–88; and *Quock Walker* case, 91–95; and Justice Cushing, 95–96; and the Quakers, 130–131; and New York statutes, 135–140, 143–147; in Georgia, 217; in Pennsylvania, 267–269, 292–305; in England, 313–314, 319, 320–321, 329–332, 363–368; and *Sommersett* case, 336, 367–368; and British Act of 1833, 367; and the Revolutionary War, 372–373; and antislave movement, 377–380; and Declaration of Independence, 381–389
Act About the Casuall Killing of Slaves (1669), Virginia, 36
Act for Explaining and Rendring more Effectual an Act of the Generall Assembly of this Colony . . . , New York, 119
Act for Preventing the Conspiracy of Slaves, New York, 123
Act for Preventing Suppressing and Punishing the Conspiracy and Insurrection of Negroes and other Slaves, New York, 119
Act for Regulating of Slaves, New York basic slave code, 116, 119
Act for Raising the Sum of Five Thousand Pounds, South Carolina (1708), 161
Act for the Abolition of Slavery Throughout the British Colonies (1833), 367

Act for the Better Governing and Regulating White Servants, South Carolina (1717), 154n, 158–159
Act for the Better Ordering and Governing Negroes and Other Slaves in this Province (1755), Georgia, 252
Act for the Better Regulation of Servants in this Province and Territories, Pennsylvania (1700), 280
Act for the Better Regulation of Negroes (1725–1726), Pennsylvania, 282–288
Act for the Gradual Abolition of Slavery (1780), Pennsylvania, 268, 281–282, 299–303; status of children born after passage, 299, 304–305; registration of slaves (Section 5), 299–300; equalization of judicial process (Section 7), 299; exemptions, 299–300; penalties for noncompliance, 300; preamble, 300–303; registration dates extended for Westmoreland and Washington counties (1782), 303–304; impact of softened by Act of 1788, 304–305; status of visitors' slaves (Section 10, Act of 1788), 304; compared with codes of other colonies, 305–310
Act for the rendering the Colony of Georgia more Defencible by Prohibiting the Importation and use of Black Slaves or Negroes into the same, Georgia, 225
Act Inhibiting the Trading With Servants or Slaves, South Carolina (1686), 157

481

Act to Incourage the Baptizing of Negro, Indian and Mulatto Slaves, New York, 128

Act to Prevent the Runing away of Slaves . . . , New York, 119, 121

Act LX (1642), dealing with trading with servants, Virginia, 33

Act VI (1654), concerning Irish servants, Virginia, 33

Act CXIII (1657), established colonial militia to track runaways, Virginia, 33

Act XVI (1659), concerning duties for importing of slaves, Virginia, 34

Act XXII (1660), concerning alliance of underlings, Virginia, 34

Act XII (1662), dealing with interracial sex, Virginia, 43

Act III (1667), concerning baptism, Virginia, 36–37

Act IV (1671), regarding property status of slaves, Virginia, 51

Act X (1680), restricting rights of blacks, Virginia, 39–40

Act III (1682), restricting mobility of slaves, Virginia, 40

Act XVI (1691), concerning interracial sex, Virginia, 44–45, 48

Act of 1705, dealing with interracial relationships, Virginia, 45–47

Act of 1792, minimizing economic actions of blacks, Virginia, 47

Act of April 9, 1813, attempting to expand options for emancipation while maintaining vestiges of slavery, New York, 145–146

Adams, Abigail, 88, 380

Adams, John, 5, 88, 90, 97, 380; quoted, 373, 375; and Committee of Five, 381

Adams, John Quincy, 387

Adultery, 110, 285

Adventurers, Georgia emigrants, 237. See also Company of Royal Adventurers

Africa, 63, 102, 111, 143, 163, 168; non-Christian slaves from, 37; and international slave trade, 62–63, 164, 356; economic difficulties involved in purchase of slaves from, 164–165; and South Carolina rice economy, 165–

166; and South Carolina revenue-raising efforts (1703), 191; and Georgia, 251; British desire to normalize trade relations with, 366; and New England rum trade, 374. See also Slave trade, international

Albermarle settlement (later North Carolina), 153

Alcohol, see Liquor

Alexander, John, 294

Allan, Mrs. of Antigua, 360

Allen, James, Esq., 80

Alleyne, Mr., 334, 346, 469 n4

Alliances (of underlings), 192; white fear of, 9, 26–30, 76–80; Virginia response to, 26–31; black-white, 34–35; South Carolina response, 158. See also Revolt, slave

Altamaha River, Georgia, 254

Alvanely, Lord, Chief Justice, King's Bench, 360

American Antislavery Society, 387–388

American Revolution, see Revolutionary War

Amputation: punishment for runaways, South Carolina, 177; in Georgia slave code, 255, 258

Anderson, Hugh, 243

Andrada, Salvador d', 109

Andrews, Charles M., 153

Androws, William, 66–67

Angola, 101, 111

Annulment, and interracial sex, 46

Anthony, black in service to Pennsylvania Governor Prince, 270

Anthony Portugis, 106

Antigua, 327, 360; slave revolt, 367

Antislavery law (1735), Georgia, 222–236; banning importation of blacks and use of as slaves, 216–217; ambiguous thinking of Trustees, 222–225; banning of free blacks, 224–226; provisions of, 225–227; penalties imposed by, 226–227; enforcement failures of, 227–230; and burden of proof, 229–230; judicial disregard of, 230–236; increasing public hostility toward, 235–236; prohibition against slavery enforced outside Augusta area, 236; political opposition to,

241–247; violations of (mid-1740s), 245, 248; limited support for, 246; lack of humanitarian motive in, 248–249. *See also* Georgia

Antislavery petition, Mennonites, Pennsylvania, 267, 269, 271, 293

Antislavery resolution, New York (1777), 136

Antislave trade bill, New York (1785), 140, 141; and 1788 statute, 141

Antislave trade patrols, British, 366

Antonio, Spanish mulatto, 38, 63

Apothecary, occupation restricted for blacks, South Carolina, 198

Appeal, blacks' right of, South Carolina, 180

Appeals Court of Georgia, *see* Georgia Court of Appeals

Apprenticeship, slave, restriction on in Georgia law (1750), 251

Arawak Indians, 409 n28

Arms and ammunition, restrictions on slaves' rights to, 58; in Virginia, 32, 39, 40, 56, 58; in Massachusetts, 76; in New Netherlands, 108; in New York, 117, 131–132; in South Carolina, 173, 183n, 184; ticket (license) requirement, South Carolina, 184; ticket requirement, Georgia, 258, 260; in Pennsylvania, 282, 307

Arson, penalties for, 75–76, 112, 131–135; in South Carolina Act of 1712, 181, 182; in Georgia slave codes, 263

Articles for the Better Regulating Indians, Negroes, and Molattos Within this Town . . . , Boston, 76

Articles of Capitulation, ceded New Netherlands to English control, 114

Assault, slave on white: South Carolina slave code, 171, 186–187, 195, 306; Georgia (1755) slave code, 256, 306

Assault, white on slave, Georgia: law of 1750, 249–250; 1755 slave code, 254, 255–256; 1770 slave code, 263

Assembly, slaves' right to: Virginia, 40; New York, 117, 119, 423 n53; Pennsylvania, 282, 307

Assiento, 63

Assumpsit, 325

Aubert, Vilhelm, 13–14

Auctions, slave, 319, 320

Attacks, *see* Assaults

Augusta, Georgia, use of slaves in, 232–233, 235–236

Augustine, 192n, 197, 245

Bacon, Reverend Thomas, 37

Bacon's Rebellion (1675, 1676), 31

Bailee, Theodore, 243, 257

Baldwin, Mercy, 297

Ballagh, J. C., his *A History of Slavery in Virginia,* 21

Balzius, John Martin (Johann), 223, 239–240, 245, 247

Banishment, as penalty: for interracial marriage, Virginia, 45–46; for crime, Massachusetts, 67–70, 77

Baptism, 21, 26; and black man's bondage, Virginia, 36–37; and manumission, New York, 127–128, 141; New York statute(1706), 128; and slavery in South Carolina, 200–201; and English Common law, 324–325, 327, 328, 352

Barbados, 152–153, 164, 165, 168, 193, 215, 295, 324, 329; and freehold concept, South Carolina, 170; and English slave trade, 365; slave revolt in (1816), 366

Barnard, Thomas, 289

Barnes, John, 72–73

Barton, Marmaduke, 67

Battery, 8–9. *See also* Assault

Beating, of slaves, 36; in South Carolina slave code (1712), 171; in Georgia, 223, 232, 255, 262; in Pennsylvania, 306

Belknap, Jeremy, 91, 97

Benefit of clergy, 453 n188

Benezet, Anthony, 378, 379

Bernard, Sir Francis, 83

Bible, New York statute requiring masters to teach children of slaves, 143

Big Manuel, 106

Billing, Joseph, 84

Birnie, C. W., 201

Black Natt, 203

Blacks: population, 9, 26–31, 82–83, 116, 458 n2; white fears of alliance of underlings, 9, 26–30, 76–80; per-

Blacks (*Cont.*)
ceived as inferior, 23–24, 28, 30–31,
38–40, 109, 150, 309–310; in New
England colonies, 71, 81, 113–114; as
prisoners of war, 88; in New Netherlands, 113–114; in New York, 115,
116, 136, 142; in Revolutionary War,
136–138; in South Carolina, 152, 154,
159, 160, 163, 166, 169, 190–192,
215, 222, 224, 248; in Georgia, 223–
225, 251, 259, 448 n104; in Pennsylvania, 268, 272, 277, 283, 302; in England, 314, 318–319; in British colonies, 365–366. *See also* Free blacks;
Slaves
Blackstone, William, 329–330; *Commentaries,* 329
Board of Commissioners, Georgia, and
laws on hiring blacks, 265
Board of Trade, England, 317; and
Georgia, 251; and Pennsylvania,
295–298
Board of Trustees, Georgia, 218–220,
227, 236, 266, 440 n12, 441 n13, 442
n14; political independence of, 219;
and land grants, 219, 223, 242–243;
ambivalence regarding slavery, 223–
225; prohibition against free blacks,
224–225, 240; and disposition of captured slaves, 226–227; and proslavery
petitions, 234–235, 241–243; and indentured servants, 237–238; and political opposition to antislavery law,
241–247; power over selection of
magistrates and justices, 243; appointment of committee to study introduction of Negroes, 244–245; limited support for slavery prohibition, 246; and
1750 slavery law, 248–251; relinquish
control to Crown of England, 251.
See also Georgia
Body of Liberties, Massachusetts
(1641), 62, 64–65; protection of
basic rights of slaves, 62, 72, 73; prohibition on bond slavery, villenage,
or captivity, 68, 126, 270–271. *See
also* Massachusetts
Bolzius, John Martin (Johann), *see*
Balzius, John Martin (Johann)
Bonaparte, Napoleon, 365

Bonavista, Cape de Verde Islands, 275–
276
Bond, Samuel, 297
Bond slavery: and Massachusetts Body
of Liberties, 68, 126, 270–271; and
Duke of York Laws (New York),
126, 270
Bonn, Cornelius, 271
Bonny, Hannah, 74
Boorstin, Daniel, 242
Boston, Massachusetts, 374; General
Council, 65; restrictions on blacks in,
78–80; black population (1750s), 81
Bounty, 308; on imported white serv-
ants, South Carolina, 159–160; Geor-
gia, 254–255, 435 n291
Boycott, by antislavers in New York,
142
Branding of slaves, South Carolina, 177;
as punishment for felonies, 182; in-
centives for compliance with court
orders, 186; as punishment for as-
sault, 186–187
Branding of whites, South Carolina, 188
Brazil, 111, 365
Bright, Lydia, 46
British Empire, 314. *See also* England
British Guiana, 366; slave uprisings in,
366–367
Bromfield, Edward, 80
Brown case, 41
Bruce, Philip A., 21
Bucks County, Pennsylvania, 272, 274
Buggery, 281, 282
Bull, Lieutenant Governor, South Caro-
lina, 192n
Burden of proof: in Georgia antislavery
law (1735), 229–230; in Georgia
slave law (1755), 252, 255–256,
(1770) 263; in Pennsylvania aboli-
tion statute (1780), 300, 308; and
English villenage system, 339; in
Sommersett case, 345–346
Burgess, Gervase, 290
Burglary, penalties for: South Carolina
(Act of 1712), 181, 182; in Pennsyl-
vania, 281, 282, 290
Burial, 39, 78, 417 n69
Burr, Aaron, 139
Burton, Mary, 134–135

Butler, Edward, 68
Butt, Benjamin, Jr., 46
Butts case, England, 21, 126–127, 321–322, 324, 325, 327

Cade, Elizabeth, 333
Caldwell, John, 91, 92
Caldwell, Seth, 91, 92
Cambridge, Massachusetts, 82
Cameron, Dougall, 297
Canada, 114, 119, 122
Capital cases, Georgia law (1755), 257–258
Capital offense: South Carolina, 182, 185; Georgia, 255–258, 262–263; Pennsylvania, 282
Capitation tax, South Carolina, 204. *See also* Head tax
Captivity: and Massachusetts Body of Liberties, 68; and Duke of York Laws, New York, 126
Capture, of runaways, *see* Runaways
Cardozo, Benjamin N., 384
Carlton, General Sir Guy, 138
Carlton, Stephen, 26
Carolina (ship), 155
Castration, 58; in South Carolina slave code, 168, 177; in Georgia slave code, 258; in Pennsylvania law, 282
Catholics, 135; in South Carolina, 160, 201; in England, 349
Catterall, Helen, 22, 35
Cattle, 181; slave-owned, 56; in South Carolina, 173
Causton, Thomas, 238–239, 449 n113
Certificates, *see* Pass system
Ceylon, 367
Chamberlaine suit, England, 324–326
Chambre, Justice, 359
Charity colonists (unindentured servants), Georgia, 237
Charles II, 427 n12
Charleston Negro School, South Carolina, 200
Charlestown (later Charleston), South Carolina, 153, 166, 172, 192n, 238; free blacks in, 202–203; indentured servants, escaped from Georgia, in, 239

Chateaubriand, Vicomte François de, 373
Chattel slavery, 22, 25; in Virginia, 27, 50–52, 60; in Massachusetts, 78, 98; in New Netherlands, 106, 113; in New York, 121, 125; in South Carolina, 169–170, 194, 204, 209, 211–212, 438–439 n383; and English villenage system, 323; and English law, 325, 331, 336, 339–340; and British planters, 366. *See also* Property, slave as
Cheffaleer, black servant, 75
Chester County, Pennsylvania, 274; Historical Society, 288; court cases, 288–290
Cheston, Daniel, 275–276
Children, 143; sale of, 12; status of, 43–47, 127–128, 139, 141, 143, 158–159, 194, 204, 252, 299, 302, 304–305, 308; mulatto, Virginia, 45–47; illegitimate, 43–45, 74, 158–159, 273–274; and perpetual servitude, 71; manumission of, New York, 145; free black, 203, 309; bounty for, 254–255; Pennsylvania act of 1780, 299, 304–305
Chousop, "the Indian of Black Island," 66, 67, 415 n34
Christianity, 20–21, 23, 140; effect of conversion on Virginia slaves, 36–37; and rights of servants, 53; and New England Indians, 69; and Duke of York Laws, 126, 270; in New York slave codes, 126–128; and slavery in South Carolina, 199–201; and vote in South Carolina, 203; and Georgia Charter, 216; and Pennsylvania abolitionists, 295. *See also* Baptism; Religion
Citizenship rights, 300–302
Civil rights, for blacks, 3; in post-Revolutionary New York, 139, 143, 149
Civil Rights acts (1960s), 3, 388–389
Civil suits: South Carolina, 206; Pennsylvania, 282
Civil War, U.S., 7, 313, 372
Clark, Daniel, 247
Clark, Donald, 247
Clark, Ramsey, 4

Clarke, Alexander, 247
Clarke, Lieutenant Governor, New York, 118
Clarkson, Thomas, 317
Clinton, Sir Henry, 137
Clothing, slave's, 232; and South Carolina statute, 173–174, 196–197; in Georgia slave code, 259, 263
Coaley, John, 124
Cock, Lace, 273
Codman, John, 82
Coercive Acts, 374
Cohabitation, interracial, 285–286
Coin, South Carolina slaves prohibited from dealing in, 199
Coke, Sir Edward (Lord Coke), *Institutes of the Laws of England,* 322
Coleman, Kenneth, 220
Colleton, James, 429 n91
Colleton County, South Carolina, 203
Commercial law, England, 349, 353–354
Common Council of Trustees, Georgia, 440 n9
Common Whipper, office created by New York slave codes, 119
Company of Royal Adventurers, 316, 318; nobility in, 318
Congrees, Carolina settlement, 239
Connecticut, 310
Conspiracy, black, 27, 88; and manumission, Virginia, 48; and New York slave codes, 119, 122, 123, 124; and Massachusetts statutes, 73, 77. *See also* Alliances; Revolt, slave
Constable, restriction of black's serving as, Georgia, 265
Constitution, U.S., 5; black view, 6; legacy of racial tensions, 6–7; and the slave in taxation and representation issues, 145; Fifteenth Amendment, 148; passage of Thirteenth, Fourteenth, and Fifteenth Amendments, 313, 314; Fourteenth Amendment's "equal protection," 384
Constitutional Convention (1778): Massachusetts, 89–91; Georgia, 266
Continental Congress, 374, 379; Committee of Five, 381
Contracts, law of, 341–342, 343–344. *See also* Slave contracts

Convicts, imported into South Carolina, 154–155
Cooke, John, 213–214
Cookson, Richard, 27
Cooper, David, 385
Cooper, Sarah, 274
Coopers, restricted occupation in New York, 118
Corporal punishment, *see* Beating; Punishment
Coupland, Reginald, 314, 364
Court of Appeals, Virginia, 22
Court of Chancery, England, 362
Court of Chancery, Virginia, 22
Court of Chancery, South Carolina, 209–214; decisions regarding slaves as chattel property, 211–212; protection of white servants, 212–214
Court of King's Bench, 21, 360
Court of Quarter Sessions for the County of Philadelphia, 276
Courts, Negro, *see* Negro courts
Cowell, John, *The Interpreter* (1607), 322
Crawford, Alexander, 255
Creditor and estate rights: Virginia, 50–53, 60; New York, 125
Crime: enslavement as punishment of, 66–70, 98; in New York slave codes, 124; reporting of, South Carolina, 184–185, 186; equal penalties for blacks and whites in 1750 Georgia law, 250; and execution (1755 Georgia slave code), 252; in Pennslyvania, 269, 282, 287; and indenture, 393–394. *See also* Capital offense
Criminal offenses, South Carolina, 181–186; detection of, 183–184
Criminal slaves, and South Carolina slave codes, 179–190
Criminal statutes, South Carolina: for runaway slaves, 176–179; and magistrate's court, 179–181; act of 1712, 181–182; acts of 1722 and 1735, 182–183; compensation and incentives to enforce, 184–186; legislative recognition of class stratification in, 189–190; and economic injury, 195; slaves to implement judicial penalties against slaves, 197; slave testimony, 197

Cuba, 365

Cunliffe, Ellis, 318

Curaçao, 102, 229, 230

Curfew, for nonwhites: Massachusetts, 76, 77, 78–79; New York, 133, 149; Pennsylvania, 307

Cushing, William, 91, 93, 94–95, 96

Darien, Georgia, 245; antislavery petition, 246

Dartmouth, Massachusetts, 89

Davis, Benjamin, 12

Davis, Captain, Georgia slave master, 230; relationship with mulatto slave, 231; and firing of his white ship captain, 231–232

Davis, David Brion, *The Problem of Slavery in the Age of Revolution,* 363

Davis, Hugh, Virginia slave, 23

Davy, Mr. Serj., 334, 347–348, 469 n4

Death penalty: in New Netherlands, 112; in New York, 132; in South Carolina, 168, 172, 176, 177, 178, 179–180, 181–182; incentive for compliance with court order, South Carolina, 186; in Georgia slave code (1755), 256–257

Debasement: of blacks, 19, 20, 26, 29, 30, 58–59; of free blacks, Pennsylvania, 308–309

Declaration of Independence, 5, 7, 84, 367, 371–389; black view, 5–6; moral antecedents, 10; effect on eventual legal freedom for blacks, 373; deleted clause on slavery and international slave trade, 380–383; three stages in writing of, 381; impact of, 383–389

Declaration of Rights, Massachusetts Constitution (1780), 90, 95, 97, 99. *See also* Massachusetts

Declaration of the Causes and Necessities of Taking Up Arms (1775), 376–377

Deed Book of Pennsylvania counties, 293

Defendants, slaves as, in Georgia slave code (1755), 256. *See also* Testimony

Defense, military, 154, 215; and importation of white servants, South Carolina (1716 statute), 160; and 1708 act providing manumission of slaves, South Carolina, 175; by black slaves, South Carolina, 214, 215; in Georgia charter, 220, 221, 224; and indentured servants, Georgia, 237; and Georgia slave code (1755), 259–261

Delaware, 268, 270

Delaware River, 270

Desaussure, Judge, 209

Detection, in South Carolina acts, 183–184; of abuses on slave by master, 189–190

Deterrence: South Carolina, 184–186; Georgia, 258

Dickinson, John, 375, 376

Director and Council of New Netherlands, 106–107, 113; ordinance exempting Jews from military service, 109; ordinance in response to problem of runaway servants, 111. *See also* New Netherlands

Disabling, in Georgia slave code (1755), 255

Discrimination: in colonial Virginia, 20, 32–36; in New Netherlands, 109; in New York, 115–123; Pennsylvania, 273–274; and Declaration of Independence, 383; and Civil Rights acts (1960s), 389

Dismemberment, of blacks: prohibited in Virginia, 56–57, 58; in New York statutes, 119, 132, 146

Disobedience, 197. *See also* Obedience

Divorce, and interracial sexual relations, 46

Doctors, restricted occupation, South Carolina, 198–199

Dodge, Caleb, black slaves, 85–86

Douglass, David, 243

Douglass, Frederick, 5, 310, 371; on total submission of slave, 9; quoted, 385

Downing, Edward, 71

Duckett, Richard, 273, 274, 461 n27

Duke of York Laws: and New York, 114–115, 126, 270; prohibition against enslavement of Christians, 126, 270–271; and Pennsylvania, 270–271

Dunbar, Captain, 241

Dunmore, Lord, 372, 382

Dunning, John, 331, 334, 335–336, 469
n4; and *Lewis* case, 344; arguments
in *Sommersett* case, 344–347; legal
defense of slavery, 345–346; and
precedent of villenage, 346; Davy's
rebuttal to arguments of, 347–348

Dutch, 269; in Virginia, 20, 28, 29; in
New Netherlands, 100–114; treatment
of slaves, 103; social rather than legal
distinction between freedom and slavery, 103–105, 108; nondiscriminatory
attitude toward free blacks, 108–109;
and legislative process in New Netherlands, 109–114

Dutch West India Company, 100–102,
110; and half-free status of slaves,
106–108; nondiscriminatory attitude
toward blacks, 109

Duty, *see* Taxation

Dyson, Mr., 227

Dyssli, Samuel, 192

East India Company, 367

Ebenezer, Georgia, 223, 236, 246

Economic autonomy, black: in Virginia,
25; and New York slave codes, 117–
119, 122–123; and South Carolina
slave codes, 173–175

Economics, of slavery, 8, 15, 20, 136;
and sale of slaves, 11–13; and punishment of runaways, 28–29; and statutes concerning interracial sexual relations, 43–44, 46; and slaves as chattel, 50–52, 60, 78; and importation of
slaves, 82–83, 86; and abolition in
Massachusetts, 97–98; and institutionalization of slavery in New Netherlands, 100–105; and Duke of York
Laws, 115; and New York slave
codes, 120, 125, 149; and manumission in New York (1780s), 142; and
emancipation statute, New York, 147,
148; and South Carolina, 151–152,
164–165, 167–168, 177, 179, 215; and
Georgia charter, 219; and proslavery
movement, Georgia, 241–242, 266;
and Pennsylvania law, 281, 282, 283;
and Pennsylvania abolition statute
(1780), 302; England, 316–320; and

end of English involvement in slave
trade, 365–366

Education: integrated, 41–42; New
York Manumission Society schools,
142–143; of blacks, South Carolina,
198, 200–201; of Georgia slaves, 258–
259; of Pennsylvania slaves, 308. *See
also* Reading; Writing

Edwards, Christopher, 213

Egmont, Earl of, 240–241, 243

Elective office: unqualified male eligibility, Massachusetts, 90; restrictions
on blacks, New York, 139

Eliot, John, 65, 78, 97

Elizabeth.I, of England, 323

Emancipation, 284; in Virginia, 47–50,
74–75; in Massachusetts, 74–75, 90;
in New Netherlands, 106–108; in New
York, 122–123, 126–128, 136, 139–
147, 149–150; of Quaker-owned
slaves, South Carolina, 201; gradual,
in Pennsylvania (1780), 268, 281–
282, 299–305; in England, 352, 364,
366. *See also* Manumission

Emancipation Proclamation, 15, 384

Emmanuel, black slave, 27

Employment, 302. *See also* Occupation

Endicott, John, 38, 63

Enfranchisement, 139; in colonial Virginia, 20–22; *Butts* v. *Penny,* 21;
South Carolina, 203–204

England, 114, 164, 313–332; and slavery in the colonies, 88; and New
York legal process, 100; and Revolutionary War, 135, 317, 371–389
passim; abolition movement in, 313–
314, 319, 320–321, 329–332, 363–
368; and *Sommersett* case, 313–315,
333–355; black population in, 314;
vascillation of courts on legality of
slavery, 314, 320–332; and international slave trade, 314, 316–320; domestic economy, 317–318; *Cartwright*
case (1569), 321; "no man can be a
slave" dictum, 325–326, 328–329,
333; influence of abolitionists, 329–
332; Court of Chancery, 362

English Common law, 21, 177, 216,
218, 315–316; and Georgia, 251, 253;
and slavery case law, 320–329; tech-

nical matter of pleadings, 320; *in favorem liberatis,* 320, 333, 337, 339, 340, 341–342, 354; *trover,* 321, 322, 324, 326, 328, 467 n27; villenage system, 322–323, 331, 339–341, 344; and chattel slavery, 325, 331, 336, 341; and *Sommersett* case, 333–346; legal presumption against slavery by law of contracts, 341–344; and legality of colonial slavery, 342–344

Enslavement, 249; Massachusetts, 66–70; attitude of South Carolina colonists toward, 152; in Georgia, 229–230, 252, 264; in Pennsylvania, 269, 299; and English Common law, 320–322, 325–326, 328–329, 333, 336. *See also* Slavery

Equality, racial: in Massachusetts, 89; litigation by blacks to secure, 91–98; in New York, 139, 147; and Pennsylvania abolition statute (1780), 300–303; and Declaration of Independence, 384–389; and civil rights legislation (1960s), 388–389

Escape, slave, South Carolina act concerning, 187–188. *See also* Runaways

Essex Inferior Court of Common, Massachusetts, 85–86

Estate, and slave properties, 51–52; South Carolina Chancery Court decisions regarding, 210–212. *See also* Creditor and estate rights

Ethnic distinctions, in Virginia statutes, 33

Evans, William, Virginia slave-holder, 25

Evidentiary requirements: in South Carolina statutes, 180–181; in Georgia, 234, 254

Examination, of slave by white, South Carolina, 195

Execution, as punishment: Virginia, 36, 39, 55–57; and New York slave codes, 121, 122, 123, 125; and South Carolina slave codes, 171, 187, 195, 197; in Georgia antislavery law (1735), 230; in Georgia 1755 slave code, 252, 254, 256–257, 263; Pennsylvania, 274–275, 282, 283, 306. *See also* Death penalty

"Exhortation and Caution to Friends Concerning Buying or Keeping Negroes" (Keith), 1693 condemnation of slavery, 293–295

Exporting of slaves, and New York emancipation statute, 143–144

Family, black: destruction of, 12; in Dutch colony, 104; legitimized by New York legislation (1809), 144; in Pennsylvania, 268, 305, 309

Favorem liberatis, in English Common law, 320, 333, 337, 339, 340–342, 354

Federalists, 140

Felony: South Carolina, 182, 185–186; Pennsylvania code (1725–1726), 283; and indenture, 393–394

Fiat justitia, ruat coelumtet, 350, 352

First General Militia Act of 1785, Massachusetts, 88

Flogging, 125. *See also* Whipping

Florida, 197, 222

Foner, Philip S., 137

Food, 196–197, 232; black subsistence level inadequate for whites, South Carolina court decision, 210–211; in Georgia slave code, 259, 263

Foreign Slave Trade Bill (1807), England, 365

Fornication, 42–44, 74; in Pennsylvania law, 273, 285. *See also* Sex, interracial

Fort Orange, Jan, 106

Fox, George, Quaker leader, 293

France, 153, 222; colonists' fears of black alliance with, 192

Franchise, *see* Enfranchisement

Franklin, Benjamin, 5, 268, 314, 376; and his Negro paramours, 286; and Committee of Five, Continental Congress, 381; and Declaration of Independence, 383

Franklin, John Hope, 21, 268, 383. 478 n55

Frederica, Georgia, fort at, 236, 246

Free blacks, 449 n121; South Carolina, 201–207; numbers and origin, South Carolina, 201–203; legal status of, South Carolina, 203–207; enfranchisement, 203–204; as slave owners, 204; regulation of their lives, South

Free blacks (*Cont.*)
    Carolina, 205; reduced distinctions
    between slaves and, South Carolina,
    205; claims to freedom, 206–207; in
    Spanish-held areas, 222; banned from
    importation into Georgia, 224–225,
    226, 240–241, 246; in Georgia slave
    code (1755), 256, 450 n124; re-
    warded for serving in Georgia militia,
    260; and Georgia slave laws of 1765
    and 1770, 262–263, 264; and Georgia
    tax policy, 264; legal treatment in
    Pennsylvania, 269, 282; and Pennsyl-
    vania slave code of 1725–1726, 283,
    288; restrictions on their lives, Penn-
    sylvania statute of 1725–1726, 283–
    285; and Pennsylvania abolition stat-
    ute (1780), 299–303 *passim;* debase-
    ment of, Pennsylvania, 308–309; chil-
    dren of, 309
Freedom cases, *see* Freedom suits
Freedom certificates, Pennsylvania, 293,
    294
Freedom dues, for indentured servants,
    54, 55, 392
Freedom suits, 21; in Massachusetts, 74,
    84–85, 98–99; in South Carolina,
    194–195, 206–207; in Georgia, 252,
    253; in Pennsylvania, 284, 308; in
    villenage system, 339–340
Freehold: in South Carolina, 169–170,
    211; in Georgia, 237
Free Society of Traders, Pennsylvania,
    271
French, in Canada, 114, 119, 122. *See
    also* France
French and Indian War, 84
Fugitive slaves, 111; in Georgia, 218,
    233, 239. *See also* Runaways
Fundamental Constitution of 1669,
    South Carolina, 163; and religion of
    slaves, 200; hostility against lawyers,
    208

Gage, Governor Thomas, 86, 87–88
Gambling, nonwhite, restrictions on,
    Massachusetts, 78, 81
Garrison, William Lloyd, "The Libera-
    tor," 385

General Court of Assizes, New York,
    116–117
General Court of Virginia, 21, 22; early
    composition of, 22–23; ambiguities
    regarding legal position of black, 23–
    25
Gentlemen's Magazine, 319
George, runaway slave from Virginia,
    tried in Pennslyvania, 275
George III, of England, 59, 349, 372,
    374, 381
Georgia, 12–13, 15, 148, 216–266, 284,
    307, 308; law (1735) banning im-
    portation of blacks and use of blacks
    as slaves, 216–217, 222–236, 266;
    abolition movement, 217; repeal of
    antislavery law (1750), 217, 266;
    harshness of slave codes of 1755,
    1765, and 1770, 217, 259, 306; con-
    stitutional convention (1787), 218;
    charter (1732), 218–220; origins of
    antislavery law, 218–220; Board of
    Trustees, 218–219, 223–225, 226–227,
    234–235, 237–238, 241–248; popular
    proslavery views, 219, 266; goals of
    the charter, 220–222, 244; fear of
    slave revolt, 222, 225, 240, 247, 263;
    arrival of first English settlers (1733),
    223, 224; treatment of runaways, 223,
    226–230, 240, 254–255; protection of
    white interests, 224; provisions of
    antislavery law (1735), 225–227;
    slave viewed as property, 226, 308;
    judicial policy and 1735 law, 227–
    230; sale of slaves, 227–229, 236;
    judicial disregard of 1735 law, 230–
    235; fugitive slaves from South Caro-
    lina in, 233, 235, 239; magistrates'
    proslavery petitions to trustees (1738,
    1740), 234–235; slavery during anti-
    slavery period, 235–236; fugitive
    slaves in Augusta, 235; indentured
    servant system, 236–241, 245, 248,
    260; slave patrols, 240, 250, 261–262,
    307, 456 n245; political opposition to
    slavery, 241–248, 266; last colony to
    be settled, 247–248; economic com-
    petition from South Carolina, 248;
    emigration from, 248; 1750 slavery
    law, 248–251; black population in,

251, 259; 1755 slave code, 252–261; contrast between 1750 and 1755 slave laws, 252; protection of slave's life under 1755 code, 253–255; Governor's Council, 255; Court of Appeals, 255, 256; assaults on slaves (1755 code), 255–256; death penalty, 256–257; slaves as defendants (1755 code), 256–257; restrictions on slave's right to self-defense, 256; trial procedures for slaves (1755 code), 257–259; black testimony, 258; manumission, 259; militia law, 259–262; laws of 1765 and 1770, 262–263; tax policy, 264; laws concerning hiring of blacks, 264–265; compared to Pennsylvania, 306; and Declaration of Independence, 383

Georgia Court of Appeals, 255, 256
German, William, 228
Germantown Mennonites, Philadelphia, 10; antislavery petition, 267, 269, 271; opposition to slavery, 293, 377–378, 379
Gerret de Reus, Manuel de, 106
Gettysburg Address, 384
Gibson, Judge, 300
Glascow, Pennsylvania slave, 289
Glynn, Mr. Serj., 334
Goodell, William, 7
Gordon, Peter, First Bailiff of Savannah, 234
Gordon riots, England, 351
Governor's Council, Georgia, 255
Governor's Provincial Council, Pennsylvania, 290
Gracia, 106
Grand Council Journals, South Carolina, 214
Grapes, 221, 224
Graweere, John, 24–25, 26, 29
Great Britain, see England
Greene, Lorenzo, 71, 83
Gronau, Israel, 223
Guy, a Negro, 202

Habeas corpus, writ, 333, 352
Habeas Corpus Act of 1679, England, 330, 331

Haiti, 365
Half-freedom status, New Netherlands, 105–109, 113, 148, 248, 249
Hallet, William, Jr., 122
Hamilton, Alexander, 140
Hamilton, Margaret, 328–329
Hammon, Jupiter, his "Address," 140–141
Hancock, Durham, 257
Hancock, John, 96
Handlin, Mary, 21
Handlin, Oscar, 21
Hanging, 131, 134, 135, 289
Harboring of slaves, Pennslyvania, 286–287, 307. See also Runaways
Hardman, Mr., 358
Hardwicke, Lord (Sir Phillip Yorke), 327–328, 342, 348, 352
Hargrave, Francis, 334–336, 345, 346, 469 n4; arguments on behalf of Sommersett, 336–338; opening remarks, 337; critique of slavery, 337–338; analysis of legal precedents against slavery, 338–344; and issue of legality of colonial slavery, 341–342
Harvard University, Commencement of 1773, 379
Harvey, Joseph, 328–329
Hasell, Reverend Thomas, 202
Hawkins, Sir John, 316
Head-right system, South Carolina, 156, 159, 162, 165; statutory amendments reducing acreage, 165
Head tax, Georgia, 264. See also Capitation tax
"Heathenism," 424 n66; in Butts v. Penny, 322; in Gelly v. Cleve, 324. See also Baptism; Christianity
Hector, Pennsylvania slave, 294
Henley, Robert, 328
Henry, H. M., 180, 201
Henry, Patrick, 19, 374, 378–379
Henson, John, 273
Higginbotham, Archy, 49
Higginbotham, Daniel, 49
Highlander Scots, Darien, Georgia, 246. See also Lowlander Scots
Hill, Lancaster, 87
Hillsborough, Lord, Secretary of State for the colonies, 83

Hiring-out system, regulated by South
  Carolina act of 1722, 174
Hispaniola, 160, 409 n28
Hogs, black-owned, 79–80, 173
Holbrook, Felix, 86
Holdsworth, William, 344
Holland, 112, 339–340. See also Dutch
Holmes, Oliver Wendell, 14
Holt, Sir John, Chief Justice, King's
  Bench, 325–326, 328, 349
Homicide: capital crime, Georgia slave
  code (1755), 256; in Pennsylvania,
  289
Hope, the Indian, 69
Hopkins, Samuel, 379
Hopkins, Stephen, Governor of Rhode
  Island, 375
Horses, slave-owned, prohibited, South
  Carolina, 173
Horsmanden, Daniel, 135
House, Charlotte, 357
House of Burgesses, Virginia, 52
House of Commons, England, 365
House of Lords, England, 318; and
  abolition, 365
House of Representatives, Massachu-
  setts: and manumission of blacks, 75;
  and importation of slaves, 83; and
  liberty for slaves, 86; and sale of
  black prisoners of war, 88
Housing, 302
Howe, Captain, 357
Hubbard, Thomas, Esq., 79–80
Hughson, John, 134, 135
Hugo, Negro slave, Pennsylvania, 274
Humphrey, Hubert H., 4
Humphreys, David, 202
Hunter, Governor Robert, 123, 129
Hutchinson, Thomas, 83, 86

Illegitimacy, 43–45, 74; and indentured
  servants, 42–43; and New York legal
  recognition of slave marriages
  (1809), 144; South Carolina, 158–
  159; Pennsylvania, 273, 274
Immigrants: in South Carolina, 154–
  155; charity colonists, Georgia, 237
Immigration: of English poor, Georgia,
  220–221; and Oglethorpe, 224; of
  free blacks, Georgia, 224–225, 240;

of free mulattoes, Georgia, 263, 264;
  of free blacks, Pennsylvania, 303
Importation, of blacks: and Virginia
  law, 34, 37–38; and Massachusetts,
  82–83, 86; in New York, 114, 115,
  140, 146; into South Carolina, 151–
  152, 154, 159, 163–165, 190–192,
  215, 251; in Georgia, 216, 217, 218,
  224–225, 234, 242, 246, 247, 264;
  fines imposed for, in Georgia law
  (1735), 226; and Georgia slave law
  (1750), 249; taxation on in Pennsylvania, 268; in Pennsylvania law, 279,
  283; and Quakers, Pennsylvania, 293,
  295–298; and Sommersett case, 333–
  336, 337, 472 n28; continuance of
  after Revolutionary War, 382. See
  also Slave trade
Imprisonment, 120; as penalty for interracial marriage, 46; as penalty for
  striking white, 142; in South Carolina
  act of 1712, 179; in Georgia, 228,
  265; Pennsylvania, 276, 282, 288; in
  English villenage system, 339
Incarceration, of blacks, Georgia
  (1763), 265
Indenture, 394; statute governing extension of, Virginia, 54–55; limitation on
  length of service, South Carolina,
  155; Pennsylvania black and white
  compared, 278; and free black children, Pennsylvania, 309
Indentured servants, 8, 9, 164, 392–395;
  fear of alliance among Indians,
  blacks, and, 9, 26–31; in Virginia,
  20–22, 272; and early Virginia legal
  decisions, 23–26; Virginia statutes
  governing, 32, 35, 45, 50; legislative
  privileges accorded, 38, 54–55; and
  statutes governing status of unwed
  mothers, 42–43; rights of distinguished from rights of slaves, 53–55;
  legal rights accorded, 54–55; "freedom dues," 54, 55, 392; inferiority
  of, 55; as labor force in Massachusetts, 71; under Dutch in New Netherlands, 102–104, 115; and free
  blacks in New Netherlands, 108; and
  Duke of York Laws, New York, 115–
  116; elimination of distinctions be-

tween slaves and, New York, 116; and New York ban on manumission, 129; in New York emancipation statute, 143; imported in South Carolina labor force, 152, 154–160, 191; length of indenture protected in South Carolina, 155; fair treatment of legislated, South Carolina, 155–157; and headright system, 156, 159, 165; acts concerning bounty for importation of, South Carolina (1698, 1716), 159–160; South Carolina courts' protection of, 209, 212–214, 228–229; and Georgia antislavery law of 1735, 232; and labor supply, Georgia, 236–241, 245, 248; land grants to, Georgia, 237; population, Georgia, 238; in Georgia militia, 260; in Pennsylvania, 272, 275, 277–278; Pennsylvania law limiting indenture (1682), 279; defined, 392; contract of servitude, 392–393; colonial board (England) to regulate trade of, 394

Indian Hoken, 69–70

Indian Tom, 70

Indian Wars (1641–1643), 104

Indians: and white fears of alliance of underlings, 9, 26–30, 76–80, 192; special treatment of in Virginia, 31; ethnic distinctions in Virginia statutes, 33, 55; Virginia statutes dealing with master-slave relationship, 33; and Virginia acts regarding status of slaves' conversion to Christianity, 36–37; and interracial sexual relations, 42; enslavement of as punishment for crimes, Massachusetts, 66, 68–70; ambivalence toward, New England, 68, 74, 98; right to petition courts for freedom, Massachusetts, 74; restrictions on actions of, Massachusetts, 76–77, 79–80, 88; restrictions on importation of, Massachusetts, 82–83; regulations concerning, New Netherlands, 113; enslavement of prohibited, New York, 116; restrictions on, New York, 116–118, 122–123; in South Carolina, 152, 160–162, 164, 194–195, 204, 210; and North Carolina, 153; export condemned by South

Carolina statutes, 161–163; right to testify, South Carolina, 197; rewarded for aiding in capture of runaways, 198; in Georgia slave code (1775), 252, 253; in Georgia codes of 1765 and 1770, 262

Indicott, John, see Endicott, John

In Favorem Liberatis, see Favorem Liberatis

Inferior Court of Common Pleas, Massachusetts, 84–85

Inferiority, black, 10; white perception, Virginia, 23–24, 28, 30–31, 39; codified in Virginia law (1680 and 1682), 38–40; of indentured servant, 55; in New Netherlands, 109; New York perception of, 150; Pennslyvania, 309–310

Informants, black, South Carolina, 173, 175, 177

Inheritance: of slaves, 51; black's right to, 145; and free blacks, 204

Insurrections, slave, Georgia slave code (1755), 256. *See also* Revolt, slave

Intermarriage, *see* Marriage, interracial

International (transmarine) law, 361

Intimidation, *see* Deterrence

Ipswich, Massachusetts, 67

Irish: in Virginia, 33, 35; in South Carolina, 159, 160; in Georgia, 238

Jack Negro, 75

Jackson, Abraham, freed slave, 204

Jacobs, Elizabeth, 297

Jacobs, John, 296

Jail, *see* Imprisonment; Incarceration

Jamaica, 328, 329, 331, 333, 334, 344, 365, 366; slave revolt, 367

James, black slave, 84–85

James I, of England, 323

Jamestown, Virginia, 20–22, 31, 32

Jan Francisco, 106, 111

Jansen, Anthony, 104–105

Jay, John, 136, 140, 303, 376

Jay, William, 303

Jefferson, Thomas, 5, 19, 84, 376; view of inherent inferiority of blacks, 10; and status of women, 41; and natural rights doctrine, 374; and immorality of slavery, 380, 469 n9; condemna-

Jefferson, Thomas (*Cont.*)
  tion of international slave trade, 380;
  and Committee of Five, 381–383;
  fear of slave revolt, 382, advertise-
  ment for runaways, 383, 477 n52
Jeffrey, Judge, 394
Jennison, Nathaniel, 91–95, 420 n121
Jews, 109, 203
Jnoson, Francis, 272
Johnson, Mr., 376
Johnson, Abraham, Pennslyvania slave,
  289
Johnson, Lyndon B., 3
Johnson, Sir Nathaniel, 429 n91
Johnson, Robin, free Negro, 202, 204n
Johnson, Dr. Samuel, 377
Jones, Mr., Georgia magistrate, 227
Jones, Cadwallader, 296
Jones, Dinah, 290
Jones, Grace (Slave Grace), 360–363
Jones, Peggy, 46
Jones, Philip, 213
Jones, Richard, 46
Jordan, Winthrop D., 7–8; *White Over
  Black,* 134; on villenage system, 323–
  324
Jury duty, 340

Kalm, Peter, 306–307
Keith, George, Pennsylvania Quaker,
  293–295
Kennedy, Sam, 289
Kenny, James, 297
Kent, Captain, of Georgia, 232
Kenyon, David, 319
Keyser, Thomas, 64–65
Kidnapping, 62; in New York Act of
  April, 1813, 146; and indenture sys-
  tem, 394
Kieft, William, 106
Killing, of slaves: Virginia statutes le-
  galizing, 36, 39, 55, 56; and the eco-
  nomic value to master, 57; in South
  Carolina slave code, 171, 187, 195,
  197; Georgia, 240, 254, 263; Pennsyl-
  vania, 306–307. *See also* Death pen-
  alty; Execution
King, Martin Luther, Jr., assassination
  of, 3–4, 5; March on Washington
  (1963), "I have a dream" speech, 388

King's Privy Council, England, 362
Kinte, Kunta, 6
Klingsburg, Frank, 199, 201
Knight, Joseph, 356–357
Knight case (1778), Scotland, 356–357,
  358
Knowles, Captain, 333–334, 344

Labor, slave: value in colonial Virginia,
  34, 71; Virginia statutes enacted to
  protect existence of, 34–36; and Virginia statutes governing manumission
  and emancipation, 47–48; imported
  into New Netherlands (1626), 101;
  importance of to New Netherlands,
  102–103, 106, 108; lenient treatment
  under Dutch law, 112; and Duke of
  York Laws, New York, 115–116;
  racially restricted occupations, New
  York, 118; and increase of free laborers, New York (1780s), 142; dependence on, South Carolina, 151, 164; in
  South Carolina rice economy, 165–
  166; protection against misappropriation of, South Carolina, 176; and
  punishment of runaways, South Carolina, 177–178; scarcity of, Georgia,
  238–241, 243–244, 245–246; Pennsylvania, 298; and English courts,
  325; and indentured servant, 394–
  395. *See also* Economics, of slavery
Labor, white servant, 394–395; in South
  Carolina, 152–160, 165; in Georgia,
  237. *See also* Indentured servants
Laborers, Georgia law regulating hire
  of slaves as (1744), 265
La Garce, privateer, 112
Land, usurpation of Indian-owned, New
  England, 69
Land grants: white servants' eligibility,
  South Carolina, 156; for importers of
  black slaves, South Carolina, 165;
  Georgia, 219, 223, 242; to charity
  colonists, Georgia, 237; to Adven-
  turers, Georgia, 237
Land ownership: Georgia, 242–243; and
  villenage system, 340
La Roche, John, 240–241
Lawes Divine, Morall and Martiall, Vir-
  ginia, 31

Lawyers, scarcity of in South Carolina, 208
"Lease" slaves, from South Carolina, 233
Lechmere, Richard, 84
Leffette, Mr., Carolina justice of the peace, 238–239
Legal process, and racism, 3–16; interrelationship between color and race, 5–9; economic factors of, 8, 11, 12–13; and fear of revolt or rebellion, 8, 9; moral and religious issues, 9–10; slaves as property, 11–12; and establishment of tradition of enslavement of blacks, 14; in colonial Virginia, 20–26; as response to fears of an alliance of underlings, 26–31. See also specific colony
Le Jau, Reverend, 201
Lewis (Thomas) case (1771), England, 330–331, 344
Lex loci, 343
Liberate Probanda, 339–340
Liberty, black's right to, Massachusetts, 85–87, 93–95. See also Freedom suits
Life, protection of slave's, 253–255. See also Killing, of slaves
Lightfoot, Thomas, 297
Lightfoot, William, 296
Lincoln, Abraham, 474 n1; quoted, 371, 387
Lincoln, Levi, 91, 92–93
Lincoln's Inn Hall, 327
Liquor, 149, 287, 307, 417 n63
Litigation, brought by Massachusetts blacks, 91–98. See also Freedom suits
Little Anthony, 106
Little Manuel, 106
Littleton, Sir Thomas, Tenures (1268), 322
Liverpool, England, 317–318; slave auctions in, 319
Livingston, Robert R., 376, 381
Locke, John, 163, 374, 429 n86
Loitering, 269, 309
London, England, 319, 327
Long Island, 115
Lopotre, Mr., Georgia trustee, 240
Lowland Scots, Georgia, 241
Lucayos, island, 160

Lutherans, German, see Salzburgians, Georgia
Lynvilge, John Mackintosh, 247

McCrady, Edward, 160, 166, 192n; on economic value of South Carolina slave, 188; and Charleston Negro School, 201; and black voter, 203
M'Donald, Ranald, 247
Mackay, Captain, of Fort Augusta, 234
McLeod, John, 245
McManus, Edgar J., 108–109, 112, 129–130, 133–134, 140
Madagascar, 63
Madison, James, 5, 19
Mahoon, Dennis, 213–214
Maiming: one slave by another, South Carolina, 181–182; in Georgia slave code (1755), 255. See also Mutilation
Malcontents, Georgia, 242, 243; proslavery petition (1738), 241, 246; their pamphlet "A True and Historical Narrative of the Colony of Georgia in America" (1741), 243–244; basis of legal claims of, 244; petition to Crown and parliament (1741), 244
Male, in colonial culture, 41–47; and Georgia land titles, 242; and feudal villenage system, 323
Manley, Henry, 228
Manpower programs, 3
Mansfield, Lord, Chief Justice of the King's Bench, 11, 85, 329; and Sommersett case, 313, 315, 320–321, 328, 333–334, 336, 351–353; and Lewis case, 331–332; his independence and ability, 348–351; and commercial law of England, 349, 353–354; and religious tolerance, 349–350; and Wilkes judgment, 350–351, 352; positions on race and slavery unclear prior to Sommersett, 353; and categorization of slavery, 354–355; and international slave trade, 356–358, 363; and Jones v. Schmoll, 356; and King case, 357–358; criticism of, 368
Manslaughter, 234, 281
Mansteaking, in Massachusetts law, 64–65

Manumission, 26, 29, 320; Virginia statutes, 47–50, 74; Massachusetts, 95, 99; New Netherlands, 110; and conversion of slave to Christianity, 127, 128, 200; New York, 128–131; and the Quakers, 130–131; for slaves who joined the British armed forces (1779), 137; for slaves who served in Revolutionary Army, 138–139; and 1788 New York statute, 141–142; increase in New York (1780s), 142; encouraged by New York emancipation statute (1799), 143, 149; and inheritance of property, New York, 145; of children, New York, 145; and New York Act of April 9, 1813, 145–146; South Carolina statutes, 175–176, 200, 204; and South Carolina free blacks, 203; and free black ownership of slaves, 204, 207; Act of 1800, South Carolina, 207; in Georgia slave code (1755), 259; in Pennsylvania, 268, 284–285, 292–299, 308; in England, 321, 340, 344; in West Indies, 365–366
Marja, black servant, 75
Marlow, John, 333
Marriage, interracial, 14; and U.S. Supreme Court decision (1974), 41; Virginia statutes dealing with, 44–47; and banishment from Virginia colony, 45–46; in New Netherlands, 108; in New York, 139; in Georgia, 251; in Pennsylvania, 269, 286, 309
Marriages, between slaves: recognized by New York laws (1809), 144–145; and New York Act of April 9, 1813, 145. See also Family, black
Marshall, Humphrey, 289
Martyn, Benjamin, 235, 239
Maryland, 155
Marshall, Thurgood, 4; quoted, 3
Massachusetts, 15, 61–99, 148, 269; legal sanction of slavery (1641), 61–62, 66; and international slave trade, 62–65, 83–84; protection of basic rights of slaves, 62, 72, 73; General Court, 64–65; enslavement as punishment for crime, 66–70, 98; enslave-

ment of whites, 66–68; judicial inconsistency, 67, 73–74; right of blacks to petition for freedom, 74, 84–85, 98–99; fear of slave revolt, 75–80, 87; House of Representatives, 75, 83, 86, 88; legal restrictions on life of blacks, 76, 78–82; Province Laws, 77; duty on imported blacks, 78; slave codes, 80–82; attempts to minimize black population, 82–83; abolition movement, 82–88, 98–99, 306; Superior Court of Judicature, 84; Inferior Court of Common Pleas, 84–85; Suffolk Superior Court, 85; testimony of blacks, 85; blacks' rights to liberty, 85–87, 93–95; First General Militia Act (1785), precluding blacks from militia, 88; constitution of 1780, 89–99; Declaration of Rights (1781), 90, 95, 97, 99; Quock Walker cases, 91–98; Supreme Judicial Court, 93, 96, 99; compared to Pennsylvania, 306
Massachusetts Bay Court of Assistants, 72
Massachusetts General Court, 64–65
Massachusetts Historical Society, 91
Master class, slave-owners: rights of, 8–9, 57; security of, 9; duties owed to servants, 53–54; Virginia statute (1705) increasing control over slave, 55–57; New Netherlands, 102, 103–104, 108; and New York slave codes, 121–122, 123–124, 125; regulation of right to manumission, New York, 128–131; rights of during Revolutionary War, 138; obligations of, New York emancipation statute, 143; tensions and confrontations in relationship with slaves, New York, 149; legal obligation to white servants, South Carolina, 155–156, 212–214; fear of alliance of underlings, South Carolina, 158; and status and profitability motives, South Carolina, 164; restrictions and prohibitions on right to free slaves, South Carolina, 170–171; restrictions on economic autonomy of blacks, South Carolina, 173–174; South Carolina legislation re-

stricting rights of manumission, 175–176; penalties for failure to punish runaways, South Carolina, 177; protection of property interests of, South Carolina, 184–189, 195; legislative recognition of brutality of, South Carolina, 189–190; reimbursement for disabled or executed slaves, Georgia slave code (1755), 255, 257, 258–259, 283; reimbursed for slaves serving in Georgia militia, 259–261; reimbursed for execution of slave, Pennsylvania code (1725–1726), 283; protection of rights of, Pennsylvania, 288, 289–290

Master-slave system, 8; earliest Virginia statutes dealing with, 32–35; and interracial sexual relations, 40–47; and manumission and emancipation, 47–50; in New Netherlands, 102–105; undetermined by British during Revolutionary War, 136–137; and Pennsylvania abolition statute (1780), 300; in *Sommersett* case, 345–347, 348, 358

Mauritius, 366

Medlicott, Richard, 38, 63

Megapolenisis, Reverend Dom Johannes, 111

Memorialists, Georgia, 241; proslavery petition (1738), 241–242

Mennonites, *see* Germantown Mennonites, Philadelphia

Mercantile system, 361; protection of, and Georgia charter, 220, 221, 224, 452 n169; and English slave trade, 316, 317–318

Meredith, Dinah, 297

Meredith, Simon, 296

Mestizos: South Carolina, 194–195, 204; Georgia, 252, 253, 256, 262–263; and Georgia tax policy, 264

Michell, John, 74

Milhous, Robert, 297

Militia, 38; and tracking of runaways, Virginia, 33; nonwhites precluded from serving in, Massachusetts, 88; Negroes in, New Netherlands, 104, 108; exemption of Jews from serving in, New Netherlands, 109; blacks ac-

cepted in, Revolutionary War, 137; regulation of (1755 act), Georgia, 259–261; Pennsylvania, 307

Miller, Christopher, 27

Mincarry, the blackmore, 72

Ministers, as slave-owners, South Carolina, 199–200

Miscegenation, 41–47; judicial punishment prior to 1662, Virginia, 42. *See also* Sex, interracial

Missionaries, South Carolina, 200–201

Mitchell, Clarence, 4

Mobility, of slave: Virginia statutes restricting, 39–40, 56; and New York slave codes, 116–117; compared to white servants, South Carolina, 157–158; and pass system, South Carolina, 170–172, 215; in Georgia slave code (1755), 252, 258; in Pennsylvania slave code (1725–1726), 287

Moiety, 324

Molasses, 136, 374

Moore, John Mackintosh, 247

Morality, of slavery, 9–10, 98; and evolution of New Netherlands law, 109; and South Carolina, 154; and Georgia charter, 216, 217; and Georgia antislave petitions, 246–247; and Pennsylvania abolitionists, 267, 293, 298; in Hargrave's critique of slavery (*Sommersett* case) 337–338; and England's abolition of slavery, 364; and continuance of slavery (1776), 377–380

Morgan, Edmond S., 35–36

Morris, Gouverneur, 136

Mortality rates, black, South Carolina, 166

Morton, Joseph, 429 n91

Mothers: and status of offspring, 43–45, 127–128, 141; Virginia, 45–47; and New York emancipation statute, 143; and South Carolina statutes, 158–159, 194, 204; and South Carolina free blacks, 203; and Georgia slave codes, 252; and status of children born after passage of Pennsylvania abolition act (1780), 299, 302, 304–305, 308. *See also* Unwed mothers

Mulattoes, 38, 55; Virginia statutes governing status of children, 45–47; statutes governing manumission and emancipation, 48; restrictions on in Massachusetts, 76–80, 88; in New Netherlands, 104–105; in New York, 116, 118, 122–123; in South Carolina, 194–195, 204; in Georgia, 252, 253, 256, 262–263, 264; and 1770 Georgia law, 263; and Georgia tax policy, 264

Mulatto Hall, land tract, Pennsylvania, 286

Mulraynes, Mr., Georgia slave-owner, 229

Municipal law, 343

Murder: in Massachusetts law, 64–65; in New York law, 119, 123; in South Carolina law, 179, 180–182; in Georgia slavery law (1750), 249; in Georgia 1755 slave law, 252, 253–254; in Pennsylvania, 281, 306

Murray, John, Earl of Dunmore, see Dunmore, Lord

Murray, William, see Mansfield, Lord

Mutilation, 36, 132, 146; in South Carolina slave codes, 168, 171, 177, 182; incentives for compliance with court orders, South Carolina, 186; as punishment for assault, South Carolina, 186–187; in Georgia slavery law (1750), 249, 250. See also Maiming

National Commission on Civil Disorders, 11

Nativo Habendo, 339–340

Napoleon Bonaparte, See Bonaparte, Napoleon

Natural rights doctrines, 135, 316, 339, 374–375, 382

Negro Cambridge, Pennsylvania slave, 290

Negro courts, Pennsylvania, 281–282, 288–290; court of appeals for, 290; protection of rights of master, 290–291; lack of protection of Negro rights, 291–292

Negro Dick, Pennsylvania slave, 290

Negro Prime, Pennsylvania slave, 289

Negro Sam, Pennsylvania slave, 290

Nero, an Indian, 202

New Amsterdam, 109, 113. See also New York City

New England, 114; earliest recorded account of Negro slavery in, 61; black population in, 71, 81, 113–114; black slavery in, 71–77; indentured servants in, 71, 116; West Indian molasses trade, 374

N.E. Courant, Massachusetts newspaper, 76

New Jersey, 140, 148, 268, 310

New Netherlands, 100–114, 148; introduction of slavery in, 100–102, 113; slave-owning pattern, 102–103; compassion toward slaves in, 103–104, 113; rights and legal status of slaves in, 104–105, 108–114; half-freedom status for black slaves, 105–109, 113, 148; blacks' acquisition of total freedom, 106–108; discrimination against Jews, 109; ordinances and judicial rulings of, 109–114; statutes dealing with runaways, 111; importation of slaves authorized (1648), 111; death penalty, 112; black population (1660s), 113–114; Dutch cede control to British, 114. See also New York

New Orleans Bee, advertisements concerning sale of Negroes in, 12

Newport, Amon, slave, 84

Newport, Rhode Island, 374

New York, 15, 76, 114–150, 269, 310; Dutch surrender to British, 114; importation of slaves, 114, 115, 140, 146; statutory recognition of slavery, 114–116; and slave trade, 114–116, 136, 139–142, 149; black population, 115, 116, 136, 142, 268; Duke of York Laws, 115, 126, 270; Common Council, 116; development of slave codes, 116–123, 141–150, 248; General Court of Assizes, 116–117; statutes dealing with runaways, 116, 119, 121, 125, 131; fear of slave revolt, 116, 119, 122, 129, 131–135, 149; black testimony, 119–20, 124, 133, 139, 142, 146; punishment provisions, 119–121, 123–124, 125; restrictions

on black's right to self-defense, 120–121, 142, 146; reimbursement provisions, 121–122; preclusion of slaves' right to freedom, 122–123; General Assembly, 123; procedural rights for blacks and slaves, 123–124; denial of basic due process procedures for blacks, 124–125; relevance of religion, 126–128; manumission, 128–131, 138–139; legislative reaction to fear of slave revolt, 131–135; death penalty, 132; slave as witness, 133; abolition movement, 135–140, 143–147; and Revolutionary War, 135–138; antislavery resolution (1777), 136; post-Revolutionary War, 138–143; first constitution (1777), 139; emancipation efforts, 139–140, 149; antislave trade bill (1785), 140, 141; emancipation statute, 143–147, 149; post-emancipation slave trading, 143–144; legitimization of black family (1809), 144; attempts to strike balance between freedom and slavery (Act of April 9, 1813), 145–146; end of slavery in, 147; civil rights for freed blacks, 147, 148; white working class attitudes toward emancipation, 147
New York African Free School, 142–143
New York City, 115; growth of black slave population, 116; 1712 fires, 128–129, 131–133; fear of slave revolt, 129, 131–135, 149; difficulty of controling slaves in, 133–134; slave patrols, 133; 1740–1741 fires in, 134; British evacuation, 138
New York Common Council, 116
New York General Assembly, 123
New York Society for Promoting the Manumission of Slaves (New York Manumission Society), 140, 142
New York Weekly Journal, 124
New York Weekly Post-Boy, 136
Nimrod, a black man, 74
Nixon, Richard M., 5
Noel, Sir Martin, 324
North, free blacks in, 309–310
North Carolina, 153; judgments regarding submission and obedience of blacks, 8–9; isolation of from South Carolina, 153

Obedience, 8–9; Christianity as means to extort, 37; and South Carolina slave code (1750), 168, 193–198
O'Callaghan, E. B., 103
Occupations, and race: New York, 118; South Carolina, 198; Georgia, 251, 264–266; Pennsylvania, 287, 308
Oglethorpe, James, 216, 218, 219, 222, 223–224, 227, 236, 246; and emigration of English poor to Georgia, 221; as slave-owner, 224; and Carolina runaways in Georgia, 230; Irish convicts purchased by, 238; departure from Georgia, 245
O'Neall, Judge John Belton, 180
Onus probandi, see Burden of proof
Orion, William, 272
Otis, James, 7, 374, 378

Paine, Robert, 93
Parliament, British, 318, 320, 342, 353; and abolition of slave trade and slavery, 363–368
Partus sequitur ventrem doctrine, 159, 194
Pass system: Virginia, 39–40; South Carolina, 170–172, 215; Georgia, 258, 262; Pennsylvania, 273, 276–277, 280, 307
Paternity: Virginia statutes governing, 44–45; New York statutes governing, 128
Paulo Angola, 106
Pearne case, 327, 328
Penn, William, 269, 271; tacit recognition of slavery (1682), 271; and establishment of special Negro courts, 281, 288
Pennsylvania, 10, 15, 130, 148, 155, 216, 267–310; development of slavery in, 267, 269, 293; antislavery petition (1688), 267, 269, 271, 293; abolitionists, 267–268, 292–305; race relations, 268; black population in, 268, 283–284, 302; issue of interracial sex, 269, 273, 285–286; statutory recogni-

Pennsylvania (*Cont.*)
tion of slavery (pre-1700), 269–277; earliest blacks in (1639), 270; and Duke of York Laws, 270–271; court cases (pre-1700), 272; treatment of runaways, 272–273, 275, 280; procedural rights of blacks, 272–276; ticket system, 273, 276–277, 280, 307; first legal restrictions on blacks (1693), 276–277; comparative legal status of white servants and slaves, 277–280, 288; protection of white servants, 278–279; sale of blacks, 279, 290, 305; statutory restrictions on blacks, 280–288; statute of 1700, 280–281; Negro courts, 281–282, 288–292; slaves' right of assembly, 282, 307; statute of 1725–1726, 282–288; trial procedures, 282–283; slave as witness, 282; restrictions on free blacks, 283–285; economic value of slave to master, 283; manumission, 284–285; punishment for harboring or trading with slaves, 286–287; restrictions on mobility and occupations of slaves, 287, 308; gradual emancipation statute (1780), 287, 299–303, 306; judicial policy toward blacks, 288–292; Governor's Provincial Council, 290; abolition movement, 292–299; slave revolt, 298; black testimony, 299; status of children born after passage of 1780 act, 299; registration of slaves, 299; equalization of judicial process, 299; 1782 act, 303–304; 1788 act, 304–306; relative benignity of slave codes, 306–310; slave patrols, 307
Pennsylvania Society for Promoting Abolition of Slavery, 267
Perpetual servitude: New England, 68, 71–72, 98; and status of children, 71; and South Carolina slave code (1740), 194, 215; morality of and Georgia antislavery petitions, 246–247; and Georgia slave code (1755), 252; Pennsylvania blacks, 272, 278
Personal property, slave as, 50–51; and Massachusetts tax assessment statutes, 78. *See also* Chattel slavery; Property

Petition, right to, 25; Massachusetts, 73, 74, 85, 98–99
"Petition of Slaves in Boston" (1773), 86
Philadelphia: Constitutional Convention, 145; County Court of Quarter Sessions, 276
Philip, John, 21
Phobe, Pennslyvania slave, 289
Pickins, Sam, an Indian, 202
Pierce, Captain W., 413 n1
Pickney, General Charles Cotesworth, 151
Plantations, 8, 210; South Carolina, 191; size, and Georgia land grant restrictions, 242; legal number of slaves (1755 Georgia slave code), 252, 253, 263
Planter, 327; South Carolina, 164, 165; and British abolition movement, 364–366
Plymouth Colony, 61
Poisoning: in South Carolina statutes, 198, 205; in Georgia slave codes, 256, 262
Polhemius, Reverend, 113
Pollak, Louis, 384
Pomfret, William, 271
Poor: white Protestant, South Carolina, 192, 196; aiding of in Georgia charter, 220–221, 224; and military needs of Georgia, 224
Popanooie, Massachusetts Indian, 70, 415 n34
Pope, Captain, 230, 231–232
Population, black, 458–459 n2; correlation between growth and repression, 9, 116; expansion and heightening of white fears, 26–31; in New England colonies, 71, 81, 113–114; attempts to limit by prohibiting importation of slaves, 82–83; in New Netherlands, 113–114; in New York, 115, 116, 136, 142; in South Carolina, 152, 154, 159, 160, 163, 166, 169, 215, 222, 224, 248; efforts to restrict, South Carolina, 190–192; of free blacks, South Carolina, 201–202, 207; in Georgia, 251, 259, 448 n104; in Pennsylvania, 268, 283, 302; free

blacks limited in Pennsylvania statute (1725–1726), 284; in England, 314, 318–319; in British colonies, 365–366

Portugal, 63

Potts, Francis, 26

Prejudice: Virginia, 32–36, 38–39; and Massachusetts laws, 82; and New Netherlands, 109

Presidential commissions, 3–4

Prince, Governor, Pennsylvania, 270

Prisoners of war, 88, 429 n77

Privacy, slaves' lack of, and South Carolina slave codes, 183, 195

Privy Council of England, 218

Profit maximization, and South Carolina slave codes, 151–152, 163–165, 167–168. See also Economics of slavery

Property, slaves as, 9, 11–12, 98; and statutes regarding runaway slaves, 12–13; and manumission, 47; Virginia statute defining, 50–53, 308; and Quock Walker cases, Massachusetts, 91–98; under New York slave codes, 121, 125; South Carolina, 211–212, 308; in Georgia antislavery law (1735), 226, 308; in Pennsylvania (1700 statute), 288, 308; and Pennsylvania abolition statute (1780), 302; trover action in, 321, 322, 324, 326, 328, 467 n27; in English Common law, 324–326, 328, 330, 363. See also Chattel slavery

Property-ownership, 38; Virginia statutes restricting, 56; Massachusetts statutes restricting, 79–80; New Netherlands, 104, 105, 108, 113; New York statutes concerning, 145; by white servants, South Carolina, 156; and South Carolina slave codes, 170, 173–174, 194; and free blacks, South Carolina, 204; by villein, feudal England, 323, 339

Proprietors, South Carolina, 153, 161, 162, 163, 165, 208, 426 n12; disallow 1690 slave law, 169, 200; and vote, 203

Protection, slave, under 1755 Georgia slave code, 253–255

Protestants, limitation of slave baptisms, South Carolina, 201

Province Laws, Massachusetts, 77

Prudence, Pennsylvania black, 272

Public accommodations, nondiscrimination legislation concerning, 302

Public office, see Elective office

Public service, manumission as reward for, 48, 74

Public tranquility, 9

Punch, John, 28, 29

Punishment, black, 283; in Virginia, 24, 39–40, 42; enslavement as, Massachusetts, 66–70; in New Netherlands, 112; in New York, 119–121, 123–124, 125, 131–132, 135; compared to white servant, South Carolina, 157–158; of runaways, South Carolina, 176–177; for criminal conduct, South Carolina, 179, 181–183, 188–189, 197; for freedom suits, South Carolina, 195; Georgia, 251, 253, 258; in Pennsylvania, 272, 273, 274, 275, 282, 287; for restricting activities of "servants," Pennsylvania, 280; for harboring or trading with slaves, 286–287; and holding up Negro as example, 290–291. See also Criminal penalties

Puritans, ambivalent attitudes toward slavery, 61–65

Purysburgh, Georgia, 238, 449 n68

"Quaker freedoms," 130–131

Quakers, 67–68, 130–131, 146; in South Carolina, 201; in Pennsylvania, 216, 268–269, 271, 284, 293; opposition to slavery, 293–299; and ownership of slaves, 298–299; prevention of establishment of militia, Pennsylvania, 307; in England, 349–350

Quarles, Dr. Benjamin: The Negro in the Making of America, 116; The Negro in the American Revolution, 372

Quasby, Pennsylvania slave, 290

Quincy, Josiah, 375

Racism, and the legal process, 3–16; colonists' predisposition toward, 29;

Racism, and the legal process
(*Cont.*)
and Indians in Virginia, 31; and distinctions in Virginia statutes, 33, 37–
38; and regulations governing life of
Massachusetts blacks, 80–81; in New
Netherlands, 112–113; in New York,
118, 128; and Georgia antislavery
law (1735), 217, 249
Ramsay, William, 212, 364
Rape, 70, 73, 146, 232; in Georgia slave
codes, 263; in Pennsylvania statutes,
281, 282; Pennsylvania trials, 288,
289, 290, 462 n51
Reading, teaching of to Negroes: South
Carolina, 201; Georgia, 250, 258,
259. *See also* Education
Real estate: slave as, 50–52, 60; Negro-
owned, New Netherlands, 109. *See
also* Property, slave as
Rebellion, slave, *see* Revolt, slave
Redemption, indentured servant system,
394–395
Redemptioners, German, 394–395; in
South Carolina, 154
Reenslavement: of improperly freed
slaves, Virginia, 48; and New York
Manumission Society, 142; of manumitted slaves, South Carolina slave
code (1722), 175
Registration, Pennsylvania abolition law
(1780), 299–300; status of children,
299, 304–305; penalties for noncompliance, 300
Religion, 9–10; impact on colonial legal
system, 23–24; in Virginia, 24–26,
36–37; and New England Indians, 69;
and New York slave codes, 126–128;
and South Carolina, 199–201, 429
n84; and Pennsylvania abolitionists,
293, 303; and villenage system, 340;
freedom protected in England, 349;
and English abolition of slavery, 364
Representation, 145
*Representation of the Injustice and Dan-
gerous Tendency of Tolerating Slavery . . . in England* (White and
Horsefield), 330
Residency, Pennsylvania, 299–300, 304
Revenue: South Carolina efforts to
raise, 190–192; and free blacks, 205;
and the English, 317. *See also* Economics, of slavery; Taxation
Revolt, slave: white fear of, 8, 9, 35, 38,
71; in Virginia, 26–30, 34–35, 40, 76,
81, 382; in Massachusetts, 75–80, 87;
in New York, 116, 119, 122, 134; and
New York City, 129, 131–135, 149;
in South Carolina, 168, 173, 181, 190,
192–193, 199; and Stono Rebellion,
192–193; and Georgia, 222, 225, 240,
247, 263; Pennsylvania, 298; and abolition in England, 365; in Haiti, 365;
in West Indies, 366–367; in pre-Revolutionary colonies, 378
Revolutionary War, 19, 206, 317, 371–
389; British attempts to turn slavery
to political advantage, 87–88; black
prisoners of war, 88; and impetus
toward abolition, New York, 135–
138; blacks in, 137–138, 372; manumission for service in, 138–139; impact on freedom of blacks, 372; Sugar
Act of 1764, 373–374; and natural
rights doctrine, 374; First Continental
Congress, 374
Rhode Island, 313, 375, 459 n3
Rice: South Carolina crop, 151, 164,
215, 306; predominance in later colonial period, 165–166; and mortality
rate of blacks, 166; slaves prohibited
from dealing in, 199; Georgia crop,
246, 256
Rice, John, 79
Richardson, Ischarioth, 239
Richardson, Joseph, 289
Riots (1960s), 15; after assassination of
Reverend King, 3, 4. *See also* Revolt,
slave
Rivers, John, 213–214
Robbery: enslavement as punishment
for, Massachusetts, 66; penalties for,
Act of 1712, South Carolina, 181,
182. *See also* Burglary; Theft
Rolfe, John, 20
Roman Catholic Relief Act of 1778,
England, 351
Roman Catholics, *see* Catholics
Rowser, Richard, 213
Roxbury, Massachusetts, 75

Royal Adventurers, *see* Company of Royal Adventurers

Royal African Company, 63, 114, 163, 224; established (1672), 316

Ruffin, Justice Robert, 25, 412 n77

Rum, 374

Runaways, 12–13, 224, 306; Virginia statutes regarding, 27–28, 33–35; disparity in punishment for blacks and whites, 28–29; statutes dealing with in New Netherlands, 111; and New York slave codes, 116, 119, 121, 125, 131; in South Carolina slave code, 171, 176–179, 197–198; rewards for, South Carolina, 197–198, 431 n160; and free blacks, South Carolina, 205; treatment of, Georgia, 223, 226–230, 240; and Georgia antislavery law of 1735, 228–230; burden of proof in Georgia law, 229; indentured servants, Georgia, 236–240; and Georgia slave code of 1755, 254–255; in Pennsylvania, 272–273, 275, 280; requests for return of honored by Pennsylvania courts, 275; in England, 319

Rutledge, John, 376

Sabbath-breaking, Massachusetts law, 64–65

Safety, 8; and Georgia slave codes, 217. *See also* Defense

Saffin, John, 63

St. Georges parish, South Carolina, 202

Saint Helena Island, 367

Sale, of blacks, 11–13, 62, 88; in New York, 140, 141; in Georgia, 227–229, 236; in Pennsylvania, 279, 290; and Pennsylvania Act of 1788, 305; and English courts, 325

Salem, Massachusetts, 67, 134

Sallo, Pennsylvania slave, 294

Salzburgians, Georgia, 238, 449 n107; antislavery petition, 246–247; eventual support of admission of slaves, 247

Sanderling, James, 271

Santo Domingo, 374

Santomee, Peter, 106

Sargeant, Justice, 93, 96

Savannah, Georgia, 226, 230, 232, 234, 235, 240, 258; black slaves used in construction of, 223; slaves sold openly in, 236; "watch" in (1757), 261–262; laws on hiring of blacks in, 264–265. *See also* Georgia

Savannah Market House, 265

Savannah River, 197

Savory, Thomas, 67

Saye, Albert, 219

Sayle, Captain Nathaniel, 151

Sayle, William, 429 n91

Schepmoes, Willem, 104–105

Schools: established by New York Manumission Society, 142–143; South Carolina, 200. *See also* Education

Scotland, 356–357

Scotsmen: in Virginia, 28; in Georgia, 241, 246

Seizure, of blacks in Georgia, 226–229, 233, 445 n46; apportionment of profits from sale, 228

Self-defense, black: in Virginia law, 39, 56; in New York law, 120–121, 142, 146; in South Carolina law, 187, 195; in Georgia slave code (1755), 256

Self-protection, slaves' right to, New York, 120

Self-sufficiency, *see* Economic autonomy, black

Servant obligation, Virginia statute dealing with (1642), 32. *See also* Indentured servants

Servants, *see* Indentured servants

Service obligations, 343–347, 472 n31

Servitude, institutionalization of, colonial Virginia, 25–26. *See also* Perpetual servitude; Slavery, racial

Settlement: South Carolina, 154; Georgia, 243; and fear of slave revolt, 378

Sewall, Jonathan, 93

Sewall, Samuel, 61, 78, 83; "The Selling of Joseph," 61

Sex, interracial, 14; and white male domination, 40–47; Virginia statutes governing, 42–45; and annulment, 46; Massachusetts statutes governing, 81; South Carolina statute governing (1717), 158–159; Georgia, 251; Pennsylvania, 269, 273, 285–286, 309

Shaftesbury, Earl of, 163, 429 n86
Shanley, Edward, 328–329
Sharp, Granville, 329–331, 336, 339, 344
Sheppard, Lieutenant, 24, 25
Sherman, Roger, 381
Shipbuilding, in British economy, 318
Silk, 221, 224
Sill, Edmund, 319
Simcocke, John, 272–273
Simon Congo, 106
Skinner, Charles, Chief Justice, South Carolina, 208–209
Skirving, James, 211
Slave codes, 249, 250; Virginia, 19–20, 32–36, 38–40, 50–53, 58, 60, 76, 248; Massachusetts, 80–82; New Netherlands, 111–112; New York, 115–123, 141–150, 248; as reflection of colony's fears and apprehensions, 116, 154; South Carolina, 154, 155, 167–168, 170–190, 192, 193–201, 208, 215, 248, 250; Georgia, 216–218, 252–261, (1735 law) 216–217, 222–236, (1750 law) 248–251, (1755 law) 252–257; Pennsylvania, 280–288, 299–305, 306; and English Common law, 343, 362
Slave contract, 343–344, 363, 470 n20; in *Sommersett* case, 344–348; in *Williams* case, 359
Slave-owner, *see* Master class
Slave patrols: New York City, 133; Georgia, 240, 250, 261–262, 307, 456 n245; Pennsylvania, 307
Slavery: and plantation system, 8–9; economic aspects of, 8, 11–13, 15, 20; moral and religious issues of, 9–10, 12–13, 23; and statutes regarding runaways, 12–13; entrenchment in colonial America, 15–16; institutionalization in colonial Virginia, 19–60; defined as servitude by late seventeenth century, 25; and international slave trade, 34, 62–65; legal recognition of, Virginia, 34–36; racial foundation of, 37; attitudes toward in Massachusetts, 61–62; authorized by legislative enactment, Massachusetts (1641), 61–62; black, in New England, 71–77;

move toward abolition, Massachusetts, 82–88; "freedom cases," Massachusetts, 84–88; abolition efforts, Massachusetts, 88–98; in New Netherlands, 100–102, 222; ordinances and judicial rulings, New Netherlands, 109–114; statutory recognition, New York, 114–123; attempts to eliminate distinctions between indentured servitude and, New York, 116; pre-Revolutionary War opposition to, 135–136; post-Revolutionary War attempts to end, 138–143; system modified in New York, 143–147, 149; Barbadian heritage in South Carolina, 152; South Carolina's predisposition toward, 162–163, 215; entrenched by South Carolina rice economy, 165–166; legislative enforcement, South Carolina, 167–190, 193–198; definition of status, South Carolina, 169–170; limitation of liberties, South Carolina, 170–190; encouraged by religious organizations, South Carolina, 199–201; and South Carolina judicial system, 207–214; and Georgia charter, 216–218, 220, 222–223, 244, 245; outlawed in Georgia (1735 antislavery law), 216–217, 222–236; judicial disregard for illegality of (1735), 230–235; political opposition to, Georgia, 241–248; ambiguities in antislavery petitions, Georgia, 246–247; pressures to permit, Georgia, 248; condemned by Pennsylvania Mennonites (1688), 267; lack of statutory recognition (pre-1700), Pennsylvania, 268; development and solidification of, Pennsylvania, 269–277; English experience, 313–316; consistently upheld by colonial courts, 313; outlawed in British colonies (1833), 314; setting for, England, 315–320; vascillation of English courts regarding, 320–329; and feudal villenage system, 323–324; issue of legality in England, 334–335, 338; Hargrave's critique of, 337–338; legal precedents, England, 338–344, 346–348; Dunning's critique of, 344–347; categorized by Mansfield (*Sommersett* case), 354–355; and limited liberation (*Sommersett* case), 356–363; English abolition of, 363–368; and Declaration of Independence, 371–389

Slavery law, *see* Slave codes

Slaves: rights of, 8–9; Virginia, 20–26; as real property, 50–53; nonrights of, 54–57; as taxable property, 78; in New Netherlands, 102–114; in New York, 115–124; and South Carolina judicial system, 209–211; freehold vs. chattel status, 211–212; Georgia, 216, 230–235; Pennsylvania, 283; significance of term, 324

Slave trade, 62–63, 98, 164, 356; encouraged by Virginia statutes, 34; New England participation in, 62–65; and Massachusetts restrictions of importation of slaves, 83–84; and Dutch West India Company, 101–103; and the British, 114, 136; and Duke of York Laws, New York, 115; centered in New York City, 116; growth of opposition to, pre-Revolutionary War, 136; post-Revolution legislative attempts to end, New York, 139–142, 149; and New York emancipation statute (1799), 143; and South Carolina, 164, 185; and Oglethorpe of Georgia, 224; and Georgia 1750 slavery law, 249–250; British participation in outlawed (1807), 314; and English economy, 314, 316–320; and British abolitionists, 329; and *Sommersett* case, 342, 356–368; end of English involvement in, 363–368; and Foreign Slave Trade Bill (1807), 365; and Revolutionary War, 373–375; condemned by Revolutionary patriots, 378; condemned by Jefferson and the Committee of Five, 380–383

Slew, Jenny, of Ipswich, 84

Smith, John, of Plymouth, 72–73

Smith, Thomas, 273

Smith, William S., 64–65

Smuggling, of slaves, 236

Society for the Propagation of the Gospel in Foreign Parts (SPG), South Carolina, 199–201, 202

Society of Friends, 293, 295. *See also* Quakers

Solomon, Pennsylvania slave, 294

Sommersett, James, 11, 85, 315, 323, 333–355; Hargrave's arguments in behalf of, 336–338; in Dunning's arguments, 346

Sommersett case, 10–11, 85, 154, 313, 320–321, 322, 328, 329, 333–355; narrowness of focus, 314, 354; legal issues presented, 334–336; conflict as to which law would be honored (Virginia law or English Common law), 334–335; Hargrave's arguments, 336–338; and English Common law precedents, 338–344; Dunning's arguments, 344–347; Davy's rebuttal of Dunning, 347–348; and Lord Mansfield, 348–351; decision-making process, 351–353; Mansfield's preliminary opinion, 351–353; significance of case, 353–355, 367–368; legacy of, 356–368; compared to *Knight v. Wedderburn* (1778), 356–357; and *King v. Inhabitants of Thames Ditton*, 357–358; later cases testing applicability of decision, 358–363

Sothell, Seth, 429 n91

South Carolina, 12–13, 15, 96, 151–215, 269, 283, 307; contrasted with New Netherlands, 102–103; compared to New York, 148; importation of slaves, 151–152, 154, 159, 163–165, 190–192, 215, 251; economic necessity of slavery, 151–152, 163–165, 167–169, 191, 215; black population, 152, 154, 159, 160, 163, 166, 169, 215, 222, 224, 248; Barbadian influence, 152–153, 164, 165, 168, 169, 193, 215; and morality of slavery, 154; white servants in, 154–160; slave codes, 154, 155, 167–168, 170–190, 192–201, 208, 215, 248, 250; adjudicative fairness for white servant class, 155–158, 212–214; fear of alliance of underlings, 158; statute governing illicit sexual relations (1717), 158–159; legislative acts authorizing bounty for imported white servants (1698, 1716), 159–160; Indian slavery in,

South Carolina (*Cont.*)
160–162; statutes governing Indian export trade, 161–163; preference for black slaves, 162–163; constitutional provision for slavery (1669), 163; profitability of enslavement of blacks, 164–165, 215; slavery entrenched by rice economy, 165–166, 215; legislative enforcement of racial slavery, 167–190; Act of 1712 (first slave code), 167, 169, 170, 189, 200; Act of 1722, 167, 169, 173, 174, 175–176, 178, 181, 182, 183, 186, 189, 194; Act of 1735, 167, 169, 172, 173, 175, 178, 181, 183, 188, 189–190, 195; fear of slave revolt, 168, 173, 181, 190–192, 193, 199; slave code of 1740, 168–169, 170, 193–198, 199, 204–205, 212; death penalty, 168, 172, 176, 177, 179–180, 181–182; earliest slave law, disallowed (1690), 169–171, 176, 188–189, 200; freehold concept, 169–170; pass system, 171–172, 215; restrictions on economic autonomy of slaves, 173–175; restrictions on manumission, 175–176, 207; treatment of runaways, 176–179, 197–198; criminal justice system, 179–190; magistrates court, 179–181; testimony by blacks, 180–181, 197, 205, 206; criminal offenses and penalties, 181–183; detection of criminal offenses, 183–184; compensation and incentives to enforce criminal penalties, 184–186; statutes governing slave assaults, 186–187, 195–196; restrictions of right of self-defense for slave, 187, 195; legislative protection of slave, 187–190, 196; revenue-raising legislation (1703, 1706, 1716), 191–198; 1751 slave legislation, 198–201, 215; Christianity and slavery, 199–201; free blacks in, 201–207; statute of 1721, limiting right of suffrage, 203–204; slave as witness, 206; Act of 1800, 207; judicial system, 208–214; Court of Chancery, 209–214; general conditions of slaves, 210–211; slave as chattel property, 211–212, 308; court protection of white servants, 212–214, 228–229; and Georgia, 221–222, 223, 224; runaways, and Georgia courts, 228–230, 239; claims of South Carolinians to captured Georgia slaves, 233, 239; Georgians' "leasing" of South Carolina slaves, 233; flight to Georgia of indentured servants, 238; opposition to Georgia antislavery law (1735), 241; compared to Pennsylvania, 306–308; and Declaration of Independence, 382–383

South Carolina Gazette, 208–209

South Carolina Magistrates' Court, 179–181; Judge O'Neall's critique on abuses of, 180; Henry's example of flaws in, 180

Southeby, William, 295

Southwicke, Lawrence, 67–68

Spain, 20–21, 153, 160, 248; colonists' fears of black alliance with, 192, 241; and Florida, 222, 245

Spanish Augusta, *see* Augustine

Stapylton, Robert, 331

Statutes at Large of South Carolina, 153

Stearns, Attorney, 92

Steel, Captain John, 79

Steendam, Jacob, 102

Stephen, Sir G., 364

Stephens, Thomas, 244

Stephens, William, 244; his Journal, 227–235, 239, 445 n44–45; his sexual attitude toward blacks, 231; chastised by trustees for failing to enforce antislave prohibition, 235–236; complaints regarding European servants, 238; survey of public opinion regarding slavery (1742), 245

Stirling, William, 243

Stono Rebellion (1739), South Carolina, 192–193, 198, 199; casualties in, 193n

Strengwits, William, 104–105

Strong, Caleb, 92

Story, Joseph, 361–362

Stowe, Harriet Beecher, 372

Stowell, Lord, 360, 363; and language of *Sommersett* decision, 361–362

Strong, Jonathan, 329

Stuart, Charles, 315, 338, 345; and for-

cible return of his slave to Jamaica, 333–334; and Lord Mansfield, 352
Stuyvesant, Peter, 114
Submission, 8–9, 38; and South Carolina slave codes, 171, 193–198, 199
Suffrage, see Vote
Sugar, 365
Sugar Act (1764), 373–374, 375
Suicide, black, 131
Sullivan, Reverend Leon, 4
Sumner, Charles, 85, 387–388
Sumner, Increase, 93
Sumner, William, 61, 62
Superior Court of Judicature, Massachusetts, 84
Superior Court of Suffolk, Massachusetts, 85
Supreme Judicial Court, Massachusetts, 93, 96, 99
Sussex County, Pennsylvania, 272
Sutton, Massachusetts, 90
Swart Anna, 273, 274, 286, 461 n27
Sweat, Robert, 23–24
Swedes, 270

Tailfer, Dr. Patrick, 243
Talbot, Mr., Solicitor General, 327, 348, 352
Taney, Roger, 6, 387
Taxation, 83, 89, 90; and chattel status of Massachusetts slaves, 78; and half-freedom status in New Netherlands, 106; and issue of slaves as persons or property, Constitutional Convention, 145; on black imported slaves, South Carolina, 190–192; and freed slaves, South Carolina, 205; of domestic and imported slaves, Georgia, 264, 457 n271; on importation of slaves, Pennsylvania, 268, 283, 293, 295–298; and the English, 317
Test Act, England, 349
Testimony, by blacks, 413 n109; in Virginia, 21, 58; in Massachusetts, 85; in New Netherlands, 104, 112; in New York, 119–120, 124, 133, 139, 142, 146; in South Carolina statutes, 180–181, 197, 206; of free blacks, South Carolina, 205; in Georgia slave code

(1755), 258; in Pennsylvania, 299
Theft, in South Carolina statutes, 182; in response to hunger, 182–183; punishment reduced in later acts (1722, 1735), 183; of slaves by whites, 187–188
Thievery, 118; and Massachusetts statute prohibiting black ownership of hogs, 79–80; and South Carolina statutes concerning rights of white servants, 157–158; and South Carolina slave codes, 172; and Georgia slave code, 256; and Pennsylvania law, 275, 282, 288–289. See also Robbery, Burglary
Thompson, Captain, of Georgia, 227
Threat, social, moral, and legal acceptability of: Virginia, 35–36; Georgia, 223. See also Deterrence
Ticket, see Pass system
Tocqueville, Alexis de, 147
Toleration Act of 1689, England, 349
Tomkins, Anne, 294
Toney, Pennsylvania slave, 290
Torture, 112. See also Beating, Decapitation, Maiming, Mutilation, Punishment, Whipping
Trading, with blacks: prohibited by Virginia statutes, 33; prohibited by New York statutes, 117–118, 119, 142, 149; South Carolina act inhibiting (1686), 157; and South Carolina slave code (1712), 170, 172–173; and Georgia slave code (1755), 258; and Pennsylvania code (1725–1726), 286–287
Transmarine law, see International law
Transporting, of blacks, see Slave trade
Trespass, 324, 325
Trinidad, 366
Trial, 131; in Massachusetts, 73; in New York slave codes, 124–125, 142, 146; and South Carolina Magistrates' Court, 179–181; and Georgia slave code (1755), 257–259; Pennsylvania, 272, 280–282, 288–289, 462 n51; in Pennsylvania slave code of 1725–1726, 283
Triangular trade, 316, 466 n9
Trott, Nicholas, 208

Trover, 321, 322, 324, 326, 328, 347, 352; defined, 467 n27

"True and Historical Narrative of the Colony of Georgia in America, A" (1741), pamphlet, 243–244

Tucker, St. George, 59–60, 91, 97

Turner, Edward, 277–278, 286, 298, 300, 308; his *The Negro in Pennsylvania,* 269

Tuscarora Indians, 83

Twain, Mark, *Huckleberry Finn,* 7

Tybee Island, Georgia, 250

United State Senate, 85

United States Supreme Court, 136; and status of women, 41; and statutes governing interracial marriages, 41. *See also* Table of Cases

Unwed mothers, 42–43, 45. *See also* Mothers, Illegitimacy

Upland, Pennsylvania, Court of, 271

Upton, Thomas, 228

Vacuum domiculium codit occupanti, doctrine, 69

Vanga, A., 47

Vernod, Reverend Francis, 202

Vernon, James, 240

Vigilantes, 171–172

Villenage system, England, 108, 249, 326, 354; and Massachusetts Body of Liberties, 68; and Duke of York Laws (New York), 114, 126, 270; in *Butts v. Penny* (1677), 322, 324; defense in English slave cases, 322; decline of, 323–324; and *trover,* 328; declared illegal, 331, 352; and *Sommersett* case, 335, 336, 338–339, 342–347 *passim;* similarity to slavery, 339; legal bias in favor of liberty, 339–340; restrictions preventing any new slavery, 340; as permit for forms of involuntary servitude, 346; in Dunning's defense in *Sommersett,* 346–347

Villein, 323, 328, 339–340; legal bias in favor of liberty for, 339–340

Virginia, 15, 19–60, 110, 114, 148, 155, 158, 248, 250, 277, 283, 307; institutionalization of slavery, 19–20; ar-

rival of first "Negers," 20–21; General Court, 21–25; testimony of blacks, 21, 58; enfranchisement doctrine, 21–22, 321; Court of Chancery, 22; Court of Appeals, 22, 58, 59; earliest cases, 22–26; impact of religion on legal system, 23; blacks perceived as inferior, 23–24, 28, 30–31, 39; fear of slave revolt, 26–30, 34–35, 40, 76, 81, 382; special treatment of Indians, 31; codification of prejudice, 32–36, 269; first legal enactment referring to blacks (1639), 32; act (1639) excluding blacks from arms subsidy, 32; acts dealing with master-slave relationship, 32–36; act dealing with servant obligations (1642), 32; act dealing with trading with slaves, 33; acts dealing with runaway slaves, 33–35; first direct reference to blacks as slaves, 33–34; and slave trade, 34, 63, 382; recognition of value of slave labor, 34–36, 47–48, 71; acts concerning status of Christian slaves, 36–37; restriction on black's right to self-defense, 39, 56; acts restricting mobility of blacks, 39–40, 56; restrictions on blacks' rights of assembly, 40; issue of interracial sexual relations, 41–42, 43–45, 48, 159; General Assembly, 45–47, 50; statutes governing manumission and emancipation, 47–50; Constitution of 1850–1851, 49; statutes classifying blacks as real property, 50–53, 308; House of Burgesses, 52; rights of servants, 53–55; masters' obligations to slaves, 54, 55–57; Bill of Rights (June 12, 1776), 59–60; slavery patterns contrasted with New Netherlands, 102–103; South Carolina's isolation from, 153; geographic closeness to North Carolina, 153; and English law, 326; and *Sommersett* case, 334–335; and freedom for those who bore arms in Revolutionary War, 372; sporadic opposition to international slave trade, 382

Virginia Court of Appeals, 22, 58, 59

Virginia General Assembly: Act of

1705 (interracial sexual relations), 45–47; and classification of blacks as real property, 50
Virginia Company of London, 22–23
Vote, slave, 89–90, 302; in New York, 139, 148, 149, 150; South Carolina, 203–204; in villenage system, 340

Wages: to slave, 85, 104–105; to indentured servant, South Carolina, 156; in Georgia, 241; and *King* v. *Thames Ditton*, England, 357–358; and *Williams* v. *Brown* (1802), England, 358–359
Walker, David, 386
Walker, Quock, 91–98, 420 n121
Wallace, Mr., 334
Wallace, David, 165
Warden, Prince, 95
War of Independence, *see* Revolutionary War
Warren, Charles, 14
Warren, Chief Justice Earl, 388, 391
Warwick, Hannah, 29–30
Washington, George, 5, 19
Washington County, Pennsylvania, 303–304
Watkins, Thomas, 333
Weapons, *see* Arms and ammunition
Weaver, Robert C., 4
Wedderburn, Mr., 356–357
Wesley, John Charles, 245, 364
West Indies, 63, 77, 101, 102, 166, 314, 324, 325, 327, 356, 363; influence on South Carolina, 152; influence on South Carolina slave laws, 154; Indians exported from South Carolina to, 160–161; importation of black slaves from, 164, 251; and end to English involvement in slave trade, 365–366; British government attempts to introduce slave code reform, 366; molasses trade, 374
Westminister, Massachusetts, 89
Westmoreland, Earl of, 318
Westmoreland County, Pennsylvania, 303–304
Wheatley, Phyllis, 140
Whipping, 23, 24, 28; in Virginia statutes, 39, 53, 55, 56; in Massachusetts statutes, 73, 77; of South Carolina white servants, 157; in South Carolina slave codes, 171, 172, 176, 177, 182, 183, 186, 187; incentives for compliance with court orders, South Carolina, 186, 197; of whites involved in slave stealing, South Carolina, 188; of Georgia slaves and servants, 232; in Georgia slave code (1755), 255, 262; Pennsylvania law, 274, 275, 276–277, 280, 287–288. *See also* Beating
Whipple, John, of Ipswich, 84
Whitefield, Reverend George, 245
White House, Washington, D.C., 3–4
Whittington, William, 26
Wilberforce, William, 364
Wilkes, John, 350–351, 352; his poem, "Essay on Women," 350
Wilkins, Roy, 4
Willcocke, Peter, 27
William III, 349
Williams, Eric, 316, 319; quoted, 394
Williams, George W., 104
Williams, John, 27
Williams v. *Brown* (1802), England, 358–359
Williamson, Robert, 319
Williamson's *Advertiser,* Liverpool, 319
Wilson, Samuel, "An Account of the Province of Carolina," 162–163
Winthrop, James, 96–97
Winthrop, John, 61, 69, 71
Witness, slave as: New York, 133; South Carolina, 206; Pennsylvania, 282. *See also* Testimony
Women, 24, 40–41; and white male domination, 40–47; and derivation of child's status, 43–44, 45–47, 127–128, 139, 141, 143, 158–159, 194, 204, 252, 299, 302, 304–305, 308; and interracial sex, 43–45; exploitation of encouraged, Virginia, 47; Dutch slave owners' compassion toward, 104; in South Carolina statutes dealing with sexual behavior, 158–159. *See also* Mothers, Unwed mothers
Wood, Peter H., 153, 162, 163, 166, 178–179, 192n, 193, 202

Woodby, John, 79
Woodward, C. Vann, 7–8
Worcester County, Massachusetts, 90
Worcester County Court, Massachusetts,
    91
Work day, limitation on length, Georgia
    slave codes, 258–259, 263
Writing, teaching of to slave: South
Carolina, 198, 200; Georgia, 258,
    259. See also Education, Schools

Xenophobia, 82

Yeamans, Sir John, 429 n91
York, Duke of, 114
Yorke, Sir Phillip, see Hardwicke, Lord
Young, Whitney, 4

TABLE OF CASES

Amistad case, 40, U.S. (15 Pet.) 518 (1841), 387

Andro(w)s, 1 Mass. Recs. 246 (1638), Massachusetts, 66

Atcheson v. *Everitt,* 1 Cow 382 (1776), England, 349

Bonny case, 6 Plym. Col. Recs. 177 (1685), Massachusetts, 74

Brown v. *Board of Education,* 347 U.S. 483 (1954), 3, 41

Brown v. *Wright,* Records of the Court of Chancery, p. 178, South Carolina (1717), 210

Butts v. *Penny* 3 Keble 585 (1677), England, 21, 126–127, 321–322, 324, 325, 327

Caesar v. *Taylor,* Quincy Reports, 30, (1772), Massachusetts, 85

Cartwright case, 2 Rushworth 468 (1569), England, 321, 322, 329–330, 346

Chamberlin v. *Evans,* England, 349

Chamberlaine v. *Harvey,* 3 Ld. Raym. 129 (1696, 1697), England, 128, 324, 325, 326, 358

Chousop case, 1 Mass. 181 (1636), Massachusetts, 66–67

Commonwealth v. *Jennison,* Proc. Mass. Hist. Soc., 1873–1875, 293 (April, 1783), Massachusetts, 91

Compensation Commissioners Under the Act for the Abolition of Slavery, 3 Knapp 155 (1835), England, 367

Davis, McIlwaine 479 (September, 1630), Virginia, 23, 25, 26, 42

Emmanuel case, McIlwaine 467 (July, 1640), Virginia, 27

Franck Negro, 3 Mass. Bay Ct. of Assts. 194 (1669), Massachusetts, 73

Guardian of Sally v. *Beaty,* 1 Bay 260 (S. C. Super. Ct., 1792), South Carolina, 206

Gelly v. *Cleve,* 1 Ld. Raym. 129 (1696, 1697), England, 324

Graweere, McIlwaine 477 (March, 1641), Virginia, 24–26, 29

Groning v. *Devann,* 2 Bailey 192 (S. C. Ct. of App., 1831), South Carolina, 206

Hope, 1 Mass. Recs. 298 (1640), Massachusetts, 69

Hudgins v. *Wright,* Hen. and M. 1 Va., 134 (1806), Virginia, 59

Indian Hoken, 5 Plym. Col. Recs. 151–152 (1674), Massachusetts, 69–70

Indian Tom, 5 Mass. Recs. 25 (1674), Massachusetts, 70

Jack v. *Martin,* 14 Wendell 507, 528, 530 (Court of Corrections, December, 1835), New York, 147

Jansen case, Berthold Fernow, *Records of New Amsterdam,* Vol. 1, p. 204, New Netherlands, 104–105

Jennison v. *Caldwell,* Proc. Mass. Hist. Soc., 1873–1875, 296 (September, 1781), Massachusetts, 92

Jones v. *Schmoll,* 1 Term R. 130 n. (1785), England, 356

Kettletas v. *Fleet,* 1 Antou's Nisi Pruis Repts. 36 (New York, 1808), 130

511

Kineard v. *Beard* (1715), Records of the Chancery Court, p. 120, South Carolina, 210

King v. *Dick,* Cope, Chester County, Pennsylvania, 289

King v. *Inhabitants of Thames Ditton,* 4 Douglass K. B. 300 (1785), 357–358, 368

King v. *Martin,* Cope, Chester County, Pennsylvania, 289

King v. *Phobe,* Cope, Chester County, Pennsylvania, 289

Knight v. *Wedderburn,* 33 Dict. of Dec. 14545 (1778), Scotland, 356–357, 358

Laborne case, 4 Mass. Recs. (part 2) 153 (1665), Massachusetts, 68

Lechmere case, Records, 1769, Fol. p. 196, Massachusetts, 85

Lewis case (1771), England, 330–331, 344, 353

Loving v. *Virginia,* 388 U.S. I, 87 S. Ct. 1817 (1967), 41–42

Marja, 1 Mass. Bay Ct. of Assts., 198, 199 (1681), Massachusetts, 75

Mayrant v. *Williams,* Anne King Gregorie, Records of the Court of Chancery of South Carolina, 1671–1779 (Washington, D.C.: American Historical Association, 1950), 205–206

Murray v. *Nairne* (1717), Records of the Court of Chancery, p. 237, South Carolina, 210

Negro, 3 Plym. Col. Recs. 39 (1653), Massachusetts, 72

Negro James, The Acts and Resolves, Public and Private of the Province of Massachusetts Bay 1734–1741 (Boston, 1904), vol. 12, p. 413 (1737), Massachusetts, 74

Negro Sebastian, 5 Mass. Recs. 117 (1676), Massachusetts, 73–74

Noel v. *Robinson,* 1 Vernon 453 (1687), England, 324

Pataddes case, Berthold Fernow, *Records of New Amsterdam,* vol. 1, p. 204, New Netherlands, 105

Pearne v. *Lisle,* Ambler 75 (1749), England, 327, 328, 342

Popanooie case, 5 Plym. Col. Recs. 243–244 (1677), Massachusetts, 70

Punch, McIlwaine 466 (July, 1640), Virginia, 28–29

Ramsay's Executors (1736), Records of the Court of Chancery, p. 384, South Carolina, 212

Raper Administrator v. *Executors of Hill Defendants* (1753), Records of the Court of Chancery, p. 465, South Carolina, 211

Rex v. *Webb* (1767), England, 349

Schenkingh v. *Howes and Grange* (1704), Records of the Court of Chancery, p. 82, South Carolina, 212

Scott v. *Sandford,* 60 U.S. 393, 407 (1857), 6

Shanley v. *Harvey,* 2 Eden 125 (1762), England, 328

Skirving (1755), Records of the Court of Chancery, p. 465, South Carolina, 211

Slave Grace, 2 Hagg. Adm. 94 (1827), 358, 360–363

Smith v. *Brown and Cooper,* 2 Salkeld 666 (1706), England, 321, 325

Smith v. *Gould,* 2 Salkeld 666, Pasch 2 Ld. Raym. 1274 (1706), England, 325n, 326, 328

Smith v. *Keyser,* 2 Mass. Recs. 168 (1646), Massachusetts, 63–65

Snow v. *Callum,* 1 Des. 542 (S. C. Ch. Ct., 1797), South Carolina, 207

Sommersett v. *Stuart,* 20 How. St. Tr. 1 (1771–1772), England, 10–11, 85, 154, 313–314, 320, 333–355

Southwicke, 4 Mass. Recs. (part 1) 366 (1659), Massachusetts, 67–68

State v. *Mann,* North Carolina, 13 N.C. 263 (1829), 8

Sweat, McIlwaine 477 (October, 1640), Virginia, 23–24, 25

Tucker v. *Sweeney,* Rand, Sir G. 39 (April, 1730), Virginia, 53

Walker v. *Jennison,* Proc. Mass. Hist. Soc., 1873–1875, 296 (September, 1781), Massachusetts, 91–98, 99

Warwick, McIlwaine 513 (April, 1669), Virginia, 29–30

Williams v. *Brown,* III Bos. and Pul. 69 (1802), England, 358–359